# Natural Language Processing (NLP) and Machine Learning (ML)—Theory and Applications

# Natural Language Processing (NLP) and Machine Learning (ML)—Theory and Applications

Editors

**Florentina Hristea**
**Cornelia Caragea**

MDPI • Basel • Beijing • Wuhan • Barcelona • Belgrade • Manchester • Tokyo • Cluj • Tianjin

*Editors*

Florentina Hristea
University of Bucharest
Romania

Cornelia Caragea
University of Illinois at Chicago
USA

*Editorial Office*
MDPI
St. Alban-Anlage 66
4052 Basel, Switzerland

This is a reprint of articles from the Special Issue published online in the open access journal *Mathematics* (ISSN 2227-7390) (available at: https://www.mdpi.com/si/mathematics/Natural_Language_Processing_Machine_Learning).

For citation purposes, cite each article independently as indicated on the article page online and as indicated below:

LastName, A.A.; LastName, B.B.; LastName, C.C. Article Title. *Journal Name* **Year**, *Volume Number*, Page Range.

**ISBN 978-3-0365-5579-9 (Hbk)**
**ISBN 978-3-0365-5580-5 (PDF)**

# Contents

# About the Editors

**Florentina Hristea**

Florentina Hristea, Ph.D., is currently Full Professor in the Department of Computer Science at the University of Bucharest, Romania. Here, she received both her B.S. degree in mathematics and computer science and Ph.D. degree in mathematics, in 1984 and 1996, respectively. She received her habilitation in computer science from this same university, in 2017, with the habilitation thesis "Word Sense Disambiguation with Application in Information Retrieval". Her current field of research is artificial intelligence, with specialization in knowledge representation, natural language processing (NLP) and human language technologies (HLT), computational linguistics, as well as computational statistics and data analysis with applications in NLP. She has been Principal Investigator of several national and international interdisciplinary research development projects and is Expert Evaluator of the European Commission in the fields of NLP and HLT. Professor Hristea is author or co-author of 9 books, 2 chapters in books, and of various scientific papers, of which 32 are articles in peer reviewed scholarly journals. She is the author of an outlier detection algorithm which is named in her respect (Outlier Detection, Hristea Algorithm. Encyclopedia of Statistical Sciences, Second Edition, Vol. 9, N. Balakrishnan, Campbell B. Read, and Brani Vidakovic, Editors-in-Chief. Wiley, New York, p. 5885–5886, 2005) and is an elected member of ISI (International Statistical Institute). She is also a member of GWA (Global WordNet Association). Professor Hristea was a Fulbright Research Fellow at Princeton University, USA, an Invited Professor at the University of Toulouse, France, and has been a visiting scientist at Heidelberg Institute for Theoretical Studies, Germany; University of Toulouse Paul Sabatier III, France; Institut de Recherche en Informatique de Toulouse, France; and L' école Polytechnique "Polytech Montpellier", France.

**Cornelia Caragea**

Cornelia Caragea, Ph.D., is currently Full Professor in the Department of Computer Science at the University of Illinois at Chicago, USA, and Adjunct Associate Professor at Kansas State University, USA. She received her B.S. in computer science from University of Bucharest in 1997 and Ph.D. degree in computer science from Iowa State University, USA, in 2009. Her research interests are in natural language processing, artificial intelligence, deep learning, and information retrieval. From 2012 to 2017, she was Assistant Professor at University of North Texas; from 2017 to 2018, she was Associate Professor at Kansas State University, where she has been Adjunct Associate Professor since 2018. Professor Caragea has received more than USD 4.5M in NSF funding for her research initiatives, including ten NSF grants as the Principal Investigator. She is author or co-author of more than 125 international journals and 7 book chapters, tutorials, and other technical reports. Professor Caragea has been invited to give talks and presentations at more than 30 national and international conferences. She is a member of the Association for Computing Machinery and the Association for the Advancement of Artificial Intelligence.

**MDPI**

*Editorial*

# Preface to the Special Issue "Natural Language Processing (NLP) and Machine Learning (ML)—Theory and Applications"

**Florentina Hristea [1],\* and Cornelia Caragea [2],\***

[1] Department of Computer Science, Faculty of Mathematics and Computer Science, University of Bucharest, 010014 Bucharest, Romania

[2] Department of Computer Science, University of Illinois at Chicago, Chicago, IL 60607, USA

\* Correspondence: fhristea@fmi.unibuc.ro (F.H.); cornelia@uic.edu (C.C.)

**Citation:** Hristea, F.; Caragea, C. Preface to the Special Issue "Natural Language Processing (NLP) and Machine Learning (ML)—Theory and Applications". *Mathematics* **2022**, *10*, 2481. https://doi.org/10.3390/math10142481

Received: 12 July 2022
Accepted: 14 July 2022
Published: 16 July 2022

**Publisher's Note:** MDPI stays neutral with regard to jurisdictional claims in published maps and institutional affiliations.

Natural language processing (NLP) is one of the most important technologies in use today, especially due to the large and growing amount of online text, which needs to be understood in order to fully ascertain its enormous value. During the last decade, machine learning techniques have led to higher accuracies involving many types of NLP applications. Although numerous machine learning models have been developed for NLP applications, recently, deep learning approaches have achieved remarkable results across many NLP tasks. This Special Issue has focused on the use and exploration of current advances in machine learning and deep learning for a great variety of NLP topics, belonging to a broad spectrum of research areas that are concerned with computational approaches to natural language.

The paper authored by Mothe [1] concentrates on better understanding information retrieval system effectiveness when taking into account the system and the query, while the other existing dimensions (document collection, effectiveness measures) are left in the background. The paper reviews the literature of the field from this perspective and provides a clear negative answer to the basic but essential question: "Can we design a transparent model in terms of its performance on a query?" The review concludes there is "lack of full understanding of system effectiveness according to the context although it has been possible to adapt the query processing to some contexts successfully". It equally concludes that, so far, neither the system component analysis, nor the query features analysis has proven successful "in explaining when and why a particular system fails on a particular query". This leaves room for further analyses, which prove to be necessary.

The paper authored by Donaj and Maučec [2] reports the results of a systematic analysis of adding morphological information into neural machine translation (NMT) system training, with special reference to languages with complex morphology. Experiments are performed on corpora of different sizes for the English–Slovene language pair, and conclusions are drawn for a domain-specific translation system and for a general-domain translation system. The authors conclude that NMT systems can benefit from additional morphological information when one of the languages in the translation pair is morphologically complex, with benefits depending on the size of the training corpora, on the form in which morphological information is injected into the corpora, as well as on the translation direction. We hope the conclusions of this paper will stimulate further research in order to see if they could apply to other language pairs containing English and highly inflected languages.

The paper authored by Nisioi et al. [3] studies the degree to which translated texts preserve linguistic features of dialectal varieties. The paper provides the first translation-related result (to the best of our knowledge), showing that translated texts depend not only on the source language, but also on the dialectal varieties of the source language, with machine translation being impacted by them. These authors show that automatically distinguishing between the dialectal varieties is possible, with high accuracy, even after translation. Another benefit of this research is represented by the release of a dataset of augmented annotations to the Proceedings of the European Parliament that cover dialectal speaker information.

The paper authored by Banbhrani et al. [4] proposes a novel sentiment classification approach, leading to a robust sentiment classification model for recommending courses with Taylor-chimp Optimization Algorithm enabled Random Multimodal Deep Learning (Taylor ChOA-based RMDL). Extensive experiments are conducted using the E-Khool dataset and the Coursera course dataset, with empirical results demonstrating that the proposed Taylor ChOA-based RMDL model significantly outperforms state-of-the-art methods for course recommendation tasks.

The paper authored by Haynes et al. [5] proposes an innovative classification pipeline for the automatic classification of national health service (NHS) feedback. This pipeline switches between different text pre-processing, scoring, and classification techniques during execution and, as a result, attains a high level of accuracy in the classification of an entire range of datasets. The paper equally analyzes the limiting factors that can intervene in the classification process, impacting its accuracy, and identifies them as being: (i) the imbalanced category distribution, (ii) the use of repeated common terms across different categories, and (iii) the subjective nature of the manual classification. This research ultimately provides NHS with a tool which is proven can be used in place of manual classification.

The paper authored by Dascalu and Hristea [6] discusses automatic Hate Speech detection, which has become a very important topic for major social media platforms and an increasingly hot topic for the field of NLP. These authors comment that recent literature on Hate Speech detection lacks a benchmarking system that can evaluate how different approaches compare against each other. Their study intends to determine if sentiment analysis datasets, which by far outweigh Hate Speech ones in terms of data availability, can help train a Hate Speech detection problem for which multi-task learning is used. The aim is ultimately that of establishing a Dataset list with different features, available for testing and comparisons, since a standardization of the test Datasets used in Hate Speech detection is still lacking, making it difficult to compare the existing models. The secondary objective of the paper is to propose an intelligent baseline as part of this standardization, by testing multi-task learning, and to determine how it compares with single-task learning with modern transformer-based models in the case of the Hate Speech detection problem.

The paper authored by Savini and Caragea [7] deals with automatic sarcasm detection, the results of which are equally scattered across datasets and studies. This paper brings in strong baselines for sarcasm detection based on BERT pre-trained language models. The discussed BERT models are further improved by fine-tuning them on related intermediate tasks before fine-tuning them on the target task. The employed technique relies on the correlation between sarcasm and (implied negative) sentiment and emotions. A transfer learning framework that uses sentiment classification and emotion detection as individual intermediate tasks, to infuse knowledge into the target task of sarcasm detection, is designed and explored. One of the main conclusions of this research is that, if the dataset size for the target task—sarcasm detection—is small, then intermediate task transfer learning (with sentiment as the intermediate task) can significantly improve the performance.

The paper authored by Škorić et al. [8] explores the effectiveness of parallel stylometric document embeddings in solving the authorship attribution task, by testing a novel approach on literary texts in 7 different languages. The authors conclude that the combination of word, lemma, and PoS-based document representations can model the language to a greater extent than any of them alone, especially with respect to the authorship attribution task. Most of the presented composition methods outperform the baselines, with or without mBERT inputs, which, surprisingly enough, are found to have no significant positive impact on the results of these methods. Another benefit of this research is represented by the creation of the multilingual document representations dataset (28,204 10,000-token documents), 133 literary document embeddings for 7 European languages and multilingually trained weights grouped by document representation and language, all of which can be used in future research in stylometry and in NLP, with focus on the authorship attribution task.

The paper authored by Badache et al. [9] refers to unsupervised and supervised methods to estimate temporal-aware contradictions in online course reviews. It studies contradictory opinions in MOOC comments with respect to specific aspects (e.g., speaker, quiz, slide), by exploiting ratings, sentiment, and course sessions where comments were generated. The contradiction estimation is based on review ratings and on sentiment polarity in the comments around specific aspects, such as "lecturer", "presentation", etc. The reviews are time dependent, since users may stop interacting and the course contents may evolve. Thus, the reviews taken into account must be considered as grouped by course sessions. The contribution is threefold: (a) defining the notion of subjective contradiction around aspects, then estimating its intensity as a function of sentiment polarity, ratings and temporality; (b) developing a data set to evaluate the contradiction intensity measure, which was annotated based on a user study; (c) comparing the unsupervised method with supervised methods with automatic criteria selection. The data set is collected from coursera.org and is in English. The results prove that the standard deviation of the ratings, the standard deviation of the polarities, and the number of reviews represent suitable features for estimating the contradiction intensity and for predicting the intensity classes.

The paper authored by Fuad and Al-Yahya [10] aims to explore the effectiveness of cross-lingual transfer learning in building an end-to-end Arabic task-oriented dialogue system (DS), using the mT5 transformer model. The Arabic-TOD dataset was used in training and testing the model. In order to address the problem of the small Arabic dialogue dataset, the authors present cross-lingual transfer learning using three different approaches: mSeq2Seq, Cross-lingual Pre-training (CPT), and Mixed-Language Pre-training (MLT). The conclusion of this research is that cross-lingual transfer learning can improve the system performance of Arabic in the case of small datasets. It is also shown that results can be improved by increasing the training dataset size. This research and corresponding results can be used as a baseline for future study aiming to build robust end-to-end Arabic task-oriented DS that refer to complex real-life scenarios.

The paper authored by Ouyang and Fu [11] is concerned with improving machine reading comprehension (MRC) by using multi-task learning and self-training. In order to meet the complex requirements of real-life scenarios, these authors construct a multi-task fusion training reading comprehension model based on the BERT pre-training model. The proposed model is designed for three specific tasks only, which leaves an open window toward future study. It uses the BERT pre-training model to obtain contextual representations, which are then shared by three downstream sub-modules for span extraction, yes/no question answering, and unanswerable questions. Since the created model requires large amounts of labeled training data, self-training is additionally used to generate pseudo-labeled training data, in order to improve the model's accuracy and generalization performance. An improvement of existing results occurs, in terms of the F1 metric.

The paper authored by Curiac et al. [12] discusses the evaluation of research trends by taking into account research publication latency. To our knowledge, this is the first work that explicitly considers research publication latency as a parameter in the trend evaluation process. A new trend detection methodology, which mixes auto-ARIMA prediction with Mann–Kendall trend evaluations, is presented. Research publication latency is introduced as a new parameter that needs to be considered when evaluating research trends from journal paper metadata, mainly within rapidly evolving scientific fields. The performed simulations use paper metadata collected from IEEE Transactions on Computer-Aided Design of Integrated Circuits and System and provide convincing results.

The paper authored by Masala et al. [13] introduces a method for discovering semantic links embedded within chat conversations using string kernels, word embeddings, and neural networks. The identification of these semantic links has become increasingly necessary since the mixture of multiple and often concurrent discussion threads leads to topic mixtures and makes it difficult to follow multi-participant conversation logs. The authors come to very clear conclusions: "string kernels are very effective at utterance level, while state-of-the-art semantic similarity models under-perform when used for utterance similarity. Besides higher accuracy, string kernels are also a lot faster and, if used in conjunction with a neural network on top of them, achieve state of the art results with a small number of parameters".

The paper authored by Vanetik and Litvak [14] uses deep ensemble learning in order to extract definitions from generic and mathematical domains. The paper concentrates on automatic detection of one-sentence definitions in mathematical and general texts, for which this problem can be viewed as a binary classification of sentences into definitions and non-definitions. Since the general definition domain and the mathematical domain are quite different, it is commented that transfer cross-domain learning performs significantly worse than traditional single-domain learning. The superiority of the ensemble approach for both domains is empirically shown, together with the fact that BERT does not perform well on this task. Experiments performed on four datasets clearly show the superiority of ensemble voting over multiple state-of-the-art methods.

Finally, the paper authored by Burdick et al. [15] presents a systematic analysis of different curriculum learning strategies and different batching strategies. The three considered tasks are text classification, sentence and phrase similarity, and part-of-speech tagging, for which multiple datasets are used in the experiments. The paper takes into account different combinations of curriculum learning and batching strategies across the three mentioned downstream tasks. While a single strategy does not perform equally well on all tasks, it is shown that, overall, cumulative batching performs better than basic batching. We especially retain the general conclusion that "the observed batching variation is something that researchers should consider" more in the future.

We hereby note the large range of research topics that have been touched within this Special Issue, showing the diversity and the dynamic of a permanently evolving field, which is giving one of the most important technologies in use today, that of natural language processing (NLP). This Special Issue has provided a platform for researchers to present their novel work in the domain of NLP and its applications, with a focus on applications of machine learning and deep learning in this field. We hope that this will help to foster future research in NLP and all related fields.

As Guest Editors of this Special Issue we would like to express our gratitude to the 47 authors who contributed their articles. We are equally grateful to a great number of dedicated reviewers, whose valuable comments and suggestions helped improve the quality of the submitted papers, as well as to the MDPI editorial staff, who helped greatly during the entire process of creating this Special Issue.

**Funding:** This research received no external funding.

**Conflicts of Interest:** The authors declare no conflict of interest.

## References

1. Mothe, J. Analytics Methods to Understand Information Retrieval Effectiveness—A Survey. *Mathematics* **2022**, *10*, 2135. [CrossRef]
2. Donaj, G.; Sepesy Maučec, M. On the Use of Morpho-Syntactic Description Tags in Neural Machine Translation with Small and Large Training Corpora. *Mathematics* **2022**, *10*, 1608. [CrossRef]
3. Nisioi, S.; Uban, A.S.; Dinu, L.P. Identifying Source-Language Dialects in Translation. *Mathematics* **2022**, *10*, 1431. [CrossRef]
4. Banbhrani, S.K.; Xu, B.; Lin, H.; Sajnani, D.K. Taylor-ChOA: Taylor-Chimp Optimized Random Multimodal Deep Learning-Based Sentiment Classification Model for Course Recommendation. *Mathematics* **2022**, *10*, 1354. [CrossRef]
5. Haynes, C.; Palomino, M.A.; Stuart, L.; Viira, D.; Hannon, F.; Crossingham, G.; Tantam, K. Automatic Classification of National Health Service Feedback. *Mathematics* **2022**, *10*, 983. [CrossRef]
6. Dascălu, Ş.; Hristea, F. Towards a Benchmarking System for Comparing Automatic Hate Speech Detection with an Intelligent Baseline Proposal. *Mathematics* **2022**, *10*, 945. [CrossRef]
7. Savini, E.; Caragea, C. Intermediate-Task Transfer Learning with BERT for Sarcasm Detection. *Mathematics* **2022**, *10*, 844. [CrossRef]
8. Škorić, M.; Stanković, R.; Ikonić Nešić, M.; Byszuk, J.; Eder, M. Parallel Stylometric Document Embeddings with Deep Learning Based Language Models in Literary Authorship Attribution. *Mathematics* **2022**, *10*, 838. [CrossRef]

9. Badache, I.; Chifu, A.-G.; Fournier, S. Unsupervised and Supervised Methods to Estimate Temporal-Aware Contradictions in Online Course Reviews. *Mathematics* **2022**, *10*, 809. [CrossRef]
10. Fuad, A.; Al-Yahya, M. Cross-Lingual Transfer Learning for Arabic Task-Oriented Dialogue Systems Using Multilingual Transformer Model mT5. *Mathematics* **2022**, *10*, 746. [CrossRef]
11. Ouyang, J.; Fu, M. Improving Machine Reading Comprehension with Multi-Task Learning and Self-Training. *Mathematics* **2022**, *10*, 310. [CrossRef]
12. Curiac, C.-D.; Banias, O.; Micea, M. Evaluating Research Trends from Journal Paper Metadata, Considering the Research Publication Latency. *Mathematics* **2022**, *10*, 233. [CrossRef]
13. Masala, M.; Ruseti, S.; Rebedea, T.; Dascalu, M.; Gutu-Robu, G.; Trausan-Matu, S. Identifying the Structure of CSCL Conversations Using String Kernels. *Mathematics* **2021**, *9*, 3330. [CrossRef]
14. Vanetik, N.; Litvak, M. Definition Extraction from Generic and Mathematical Domains with Deep Ensemble Learning. *Mathematics* **2021**, *9*, 2502. [CrossRef]
15. Burdick, L.; Kummerfeld, J.K.; Mihalcea, R. To Batch or Not to Batch? Comparing Batching and Curriculum Learning Strategies across Tasks and Datasets. *Mathematics* **2021**, *9*, 2234. [CrossRef]

*Article*

# Analytics Methods to Understand Information Retrieval Effectiveness—A Survey

Josiane Mothe

INSPE, IRIT UMR5505 CNRS, Université Toulouse Jean-Jaurès, 118 Rte de Narbonne, F-31400 Toulouse, France; Josiane.Mothe@irit.fr; Tel.: +33-5-61556444

**Abstract:** Information retrieval aims to retrieve the documents that answer users' queries. A typical search process consists of different phases for which a variety of components have been defined in the literature; each one having a set of hyper-parameters to tune. Different studies focused on how and how much the components and their hyper-parameters affect the system performance in terms of effectiveness, others on the query factor. The aim of these studies is to better understand information retrieval system effectiveness. This paper reviews the literature of this domain. It depicts how data analytics has been used in IR to gain a better understanding of system effectiveness. This review concludes that we lack a full understanding of system effectiveness related to the context which the system is in, though it has been possible to adapt the query processing to some contexts successfully. This review also concludes that, even if it is possible to distinguish effective from non-effective systems for a query set, neither the system component analysis nor the query features analysis were successful in explaining when and why a particular system fails on a particular query.

**Keywords:** information systems; information retrieval; system effectiveness; search engine; IR system analysis; data analytics; query processing chain

**MSC:** 94A16; 68T20; 94A16

**Citation:** Mothe, J. Analytics Methods to Understand Information Retrieval Effectiveness—A Survey. *Mathematics* **2022**, *10*, 2135. https://doi.org/10.3390/math10122135

Academic Editors: Cornelia Caragea and Zhao Kang

Received: 31 January 2022
Accepted: 18 May 2022
Published: 19 June 2022
Corrected: 19 September 2022

**Publisher's Note:** MDPI stays neutral with regard to jurisdictional claims in published maps and institutional affiliations.

## 1. Introduction

Information retrieval (IR) aims to retrieve the documents that answer users' queries. It is a core functionality of many digital systems, such as web search engines and e-commerce recommender systems. The effectiveness of an IR system is not the same on all the queries it processes, this is the *query factor* of effectiveness variability.

In IR, documents are indexed to build document representations that will be used for the online query-document matching. The online process used to answer a user's query consists of different phases and aims to choose the documents to deliver to the user as well as their order. A typical online process consists of the following phases: query pre-processing, optional automatic query reformulation or expansion, search for documents matching the query, and retrieved document ordering (see Figure 1).

A variety of components have been defined in the literature for each phase. For example, the searching/matching, also called weighting model (it is called this because in this component each document will receive a score with regard to a given query), can be achieved by the Salton's Vector Space Model [1], the Roberston and Spark Jones' BM25 probabilistic model [2,3], the Ponte and Croft' Language Modelling [4], and others.

Defining an information search process chain implies we decide which component will be used in each phase. In addition to the wide choice of possible components, each one has a set of hyper-parameters that need to be set. For example, the number of terms to add to the query in the automatic query expansion phase is one of the parameters to be decided. A query processing chain $A$ will not result in the same retrieved documents, and, thus, not the same effectiveness, than a query processing chain $B$, even when considering the same query or queries, the same collection of documents, and the same effectiveness measure. This variability in effectiveness due to the system is also named as the system factor of variability in effectiveness.

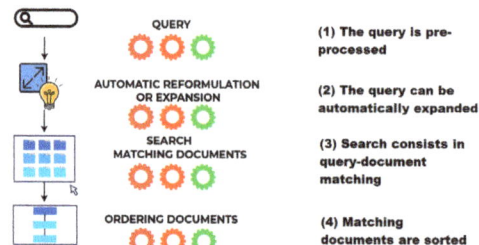

**Figure 1.** An online search process consists of four main phases to retrieve an ordered list of documents that answer the user's query. The component used at each phase has various hyper-parameters to tune.

Common practice in information retrieval is to tune the search process components' parameters once for all the forthcoming queries.

For example, Terrier, an open source search engine that implements state-of-the-art indexing and retrieval functionalities adapted to use on TREC-like collections [5], provides implementations of many weighting and query expansion models, along with default values of their hyper-parameters (http://terrier.org/docs/v4.0/configure_retrieval.html accessed on 15 May 2022). The optimal values of components hyper-parameters are obtained in an empiric way and different methods have been used for that, grid search is one of the most popular [6]. Optimal hyper-parameter values have been shown to be collection dependant.

Some studies have shown that the optimal hyper-parameters are not only collection dependent but query dependent as well. For example, considering the query expansion component, Ayter et al. reported that for the query 442 from the TREC7 reference collection, it is best to add 2 to 5 query terms to the initial query when expanding it, while for query 432, it is best to add 20 terms [7]. Note that evaluation forums distinguish between topics and queries. In evaluation frameworks, a topic consists of a title which is generally used as the query to submit to the search engine, a description of one or two sentences that explains the title, and a narrative that depicts what a relevant document is and what information will not be relevant. Because queries are usually formed from topic title, topic and query are often used interchangeably. The relationship between search components and system performance is worth studying in order to better understand the impact of the choice one makes when designing a query processing chain.

With regard to a better understanding of IR thanks to the system features, pioneer studies were based on the results from the participants at IR evaluation forums, such as TREC[5]. The strength of such evaluation campaigns is that a series of systems, each with different query processing chains, are using the same queries, the same document sets to search in, and the same evaluation measures. Because the results are obtained on the same basis, they are comparable and analyses are made possible [8–15]. The material which is used in such studies is the participants' results to shared tasks, that is to say from 30 to 100 systems (called *runs* in shared tasks). These studies suffer, however, from the lack of structured and easily exploitable descriptions of the query processing chains that the participants used. The components used in the indexing and query processing, as well as the values of their hyper-parameters, are described in papers and working notes both in verbose ways and with different levels of detail.

Further studies considered generated query processing chains [7,16,17]. Here, the data collections from shared tasks are also used, but rather than considering real participants' systems, a huge number of systems, from a few hundred to several thousands, are generated thanks to some tools [18,19]. The generated systems differ by the components used or their hyper-parameters. Such chains have the advantage of being deterministic in the sense that the components they used are fully described and known, and, thus, allowed deeper analyses. The effect of individual components or hyper-parameters can be studied.

Finally, some studies developed models that aim at predicting the performance of a given system on a query for a document collection [20–22]. The predictive models can help in understanding the system effectiveness. If they are transparent, it is possible to know what the most important features are, what deep learning approaches seldom do.

The challenge for IR we are considering in this paper is:

- Can we understand better the IR system effectiveness, that is to say successes and failures of systems, using data analytics methods?

The sub-objectives targeted here are:

- Did the literature allow conclusions to be drawn from the analysis of international evaluation campaigns and the analysis of the participants' results?
- Did data driven analysis, based on thorough examination of IR components and hyper-parameters, lead to different or better conclusions?
- Did we learn from query performance prediction?

The more long-term challenge is:

- Can system effectiveness understanding be used in a comprehensive way in IR to solve system failures and to design more effective systems? Can we design a transparent model in terms of its performance on a query?

This paper reviews the literature of this domain. It covers analyses on the system factor, that is to say the effects of components and hyper-parameters on the system effectiveness. It also covers the query factor through studies that analyse the variability due to the queries. Cross-effects are also mentioned. This paper does not cover the question of relevance, although it is in essence related to the effectiveness calculation. It does not cover query performance prediction either.

Rather, this paper question the understanding we have of information retrieval thanks to data analytic methods and provides an overview on which methods have been used in relation to which angle of effectiveness understanding the studies focused on.

The rest of this paper is organised as follows: Section 2 presents the related work. Section 3 presents the material and methods. Section 4 reports on the results of analyses conducted on participants obtained at evaluation campaigns. Section 5 covers the system factor and analyses of results obtained with systematically generated query processing chains. Section 6 is about the analyses on the query effect and cross effects. Section 7 discusses the reported work in terms of its potential impact for IR and concludes this paper.

## 2. Related Work

To the best of our knowledge, there is no survey published on this specific challenge. Related work mainly consists of surveys that study a particular IR component. Other related studies are of relevance in IR, query difficulty and query performance prediction, and fairness and transparency in IR.

### 2.1. Surveys on a Specific IR Component

Probably because of its long-standing history in IR and the large number of techniques that have been developed, several surveys focused on the **query expansion component**. Carpineto and Romano' survey [23] includes the different applications of query expansion, as well as the different techniques. They suggested a classification of QE approaches that Azad and Deepak [24] completed with a four-level taxonomy. To analyse the different methods, Carpineto and Romano did not use any data analytics, rather they used both a classification with various criteria and a comparison of method effectiveness. More precisely, the criteria they used are as follows: the data source used in the expansion (e.g., Wordnet, top ranked documents, . . . ), candidate feature extraction method, feature selection method, and the expanded query representation. With regard to effectiveness, they report mean average precision on TREC collections (sparse results). Mean average precision is the average of average precision on a query set. Average precision is one of the main evaluation measure in IR. It is the area under the precision–recall curve which, in practice, is replaced with an approximate based on precision at every position in the ranked sequence of documents, more at https://jonathan-hui.medium.com/map-mean-average-precision-for-object-detection-45c121a31173 accessed on 15 May 2022. The authors concluded that for query expansion, linguistics techniques are considered as less effective than statistic-based methods. In particular, local analysis seems to perform better than corpus based. The authors also mentioned that the methods seem to be complementary and that this should be exploited more. Their final conclusion is that the best choice depends on many factors among which the type of collection being queried, the availability and features of the external data, and the type of queries. The authors did not detail the link between these features and the choices of a query expansion mechanism.

Moral et al. [25] focuses on **stemming algorithms** applied in the indexing and query pre-processing and their effect. They considered mainly rule-based stemmers and classified the stemmers according to their features, such as their strength, the aggressiveness with which the stemmer clears the terminations of the terms, the number of rules and suffixes considered, their use of recoding phase, partial-matching, and constraint rules. They also compared the algorithms according to their conflation rate or index compression factor. The authors did not compare the algorithms in terms of effectiveness but rather refer to other papers for this aspect.

We can also mention the study by Kamphuis et al. in which they considered 8 variants of the **BM25 scoring function** [26]. The authors considered 3 TREC collections and used average precision at 30 documents. Precision at 30 documents is the precision, the proportion of relevant document within the retrieved document list where this list is considered up to the 30th retrieved document. They show that there is no significant effectiveness difference between the different implantation of BM25.

These analyses focus on a single component and do not analyse the results obtained strictly speaking but rather compare them using typical report means (mainly tables of effectiveness measures averaged over queries) as presented in Section 2.3.

### 2.2. Effectiveness and Relevance

System effectiveness is closely related to the notion of **relevance**.

Mizzaro [27] studied different kinds of relevance in IR, for which he defined several dimensions. He concluded that common practice to evaluate IR is to consider: (a) the surrogate, a representation of a document; (b) the query, the way the user expresses their perceive information need; and (c) the topic, that refers to the subject area the user is interested in. He also mentioned that this is the *lowest* level of relevance consideration in that it does not consider the real user's information need nor the perceived information need, nor the information the user creates or receives when reading a document. Ruthven [28] studied how various types of TREC data can be used to better understand relevance and found that factors, such as familiarity, interest, and strictness of relevance criteria, may affect the TREC relevance assessments.

Although relevance and the way relevance assessments are collected and considered can be a factor of IR system effectiveness, in this paper, we do not discuss the relevance point and consider effectiveness in its most common meaning in the IR field, as mentioned in [27].

### 2.3. Typical Evaluation Report in IR Literature

With regard to **hyper-parameters**, we should mention that it is a common practice nowadays in IR experimental evaluation (https://www.sigir.org/sigir2012/paper-guidelines.php accessed on 15 May 2022 is an example of paper guideline to write IR papers.) to analyse the hyper-parameters of the method one developed. Analysing the results is generally performed by comparing the results in terms of effectiveness in tables or graphs that show the effectiveness for different values of the hyper-parameters (see Figure 2 that represent typical reports on comparison of methods and hyper-parameters in IR papers). In these figures and tables, the parameter values change and either different effectiveness measures or different evaluation collections, or both are reported.

The purpose here is to emphasise that, even if extensive experimental evaluation is reported in IR papers, the reports are mainly under the form or tables and curves, which are low level data analysis representations that we do not discuss in the rest of this paper.

| Training Type | Encoder | L# | Batch Size | TREC-DL'19 | | | TREC-DL'20 | | | MSMARCO DEV | | |
|---|---|---|---|---|---|---|---|---|---|---|---|---|
| | | | | nDCG@10 | MRR@10 | R@1K | nDCG@10 | MRR@10 | R@1K | nDCG@10 | MRR@10 | R@1K |
| BM25 | – | – | – | .501 | .689 | .739 | .475 | .649 | .806 | .241 | .194 | .868 |
| ANCE | | | | .648 | – | – | – | – | – | – | .330 | .959 |
| LTRe | BERT-Base | 12 | 32 | .661 | – | – | – | – | – | – | .329 | .955 |
| ANCE + LTRe | | | | .675 | – | – | – | – | – | – | .341 | .962 |
| RocketQA | ERNIE-Base | 12 | 4,000 128 | – | – | – | – | – | – | – | **.364** .309 | – – |
| TCT | BERT-Base | 12 | 96 | .670 | – | .720 | – | – | – | – | .335 | .964 |
| TCT (ours) | DistilBERT | 6 | 32 | .680$^b$ | .857$^b$ | .745 | .631$^b$ | .773$^b$ | .792 | .372$^b$ | .315$^b$ | .951$^b$ |
| Margin-MSE | DistilBERT | 6 | 32 | .697 | .868 | .769 | – | – | – | .381 | .323 | .957 |
| Margin-MSE (ours) | | | | .687$^b$ | .851$^b$ | .767 | .654$^b$ | .812$^b$ | .801 | .385$^{bt}$ | .326$^b$ | .958$^{bt}$ |
| TAS-Balanced | DistilBERT | 6 | 32 | .712$^b$ | .892$^b$ | .845$^{btm}$ | .693$^{btm}$ | .843$^b$ | .865$^{btm}$ | .402$^{btm}$ | .340$^{btm}$ | .975$^{btm}$ |
| | | | 96 | .722$^{btm}$ | .895$^b$ | .842$^{tm}$ | .692$^{btm}$ | .841$^b$ | .864$^{btm}$ | .406$^{btm}$ | .343$^{btm}$ | .976$^{btm}$ |
| | | | 256 | .717$^{btm}$ | .883$^b$ | .843$^{tm}$ | .686$^{btm}$ | .843$^b$ | **.875**$^{btm}$ | **.410**$^{btm39}$ | .347$^{btm39}$ | **.978**$^{btm3}$ |

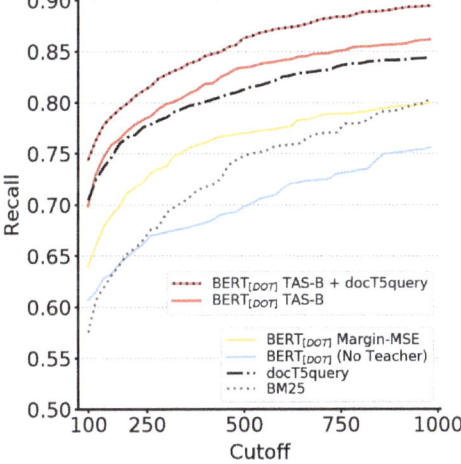

**Figure 2.** A common practice in IR literature is to analyse the effect of hyper-parameters on the overall system effectiveness and to present the results under the form of tables or graphs. The top part of this figure is a typical table that represents hyper-parameters or comparison of methods. Here, a deep learning-based model was used and comparisons are reported on the different training types, encoders, and batch sizes; using different effectiveness measures (nDCG@10, MRR@10, and R@1K), on different collections (here TREC DL'19, TREC-DL'20, and MSMARCO DEV). The best results are highlighted in bold font. the bottom part is a typical graph to compare different variants or hyper-parameters effect on effectiveness. Here, the lines represent different combination of hyper-parameters, effectiveness is measured in terms of recall (Y-axis) for different cut-off of the retrieved document list. Table and Figure adapted with permission from [29], Copyright 2021, Sebastian Hofstätter et al.

## 3. Materials and Methods

The analysis of effectiveness for better comprehensive understanding of IR relies on data analysis methods and analysable data that we describe in this section.

### 3.1. Data Analysis Methods

System effectiveness analyses rely on different statistical analysis methods, including, but not limited to, machine learning.

**Boxplot** is a graphical representation of a series of numerical values that shows their locality, spread, and skewness based on their quartiles. Whiskers extend the Q1–Q3 box, indicating variability outside the upper and lower quartiles. Beyond the whiskers, outliers that differ significantly from the rest of the dataset are plotted as individual points. Effectiveness under different conditions (different queries, different values of a component parameter) is a typical series that can be represented under the form of a boxplot.

**Correlation** is a family of analysis that measures the relationship between two variables, its strength and direction. Correlation calculation results in a value that ranges between −1 (strong negative correlation) and 1 (strong positive correlation); 0 indicating that the two variables are not correlated. The *p*-value indicates the confidence or risk of error in rejecting the hypothesis that the two variables are independent. The most familiar measure of correlation is the Pearson product-moment correlation coefficient which is a normalised form of the covariance. Covariance between two random variables measures their join distance to their expected values which can be the distance to the mean for numerical data. Pearson $\rho$ assumes linear relationship between the two variables. Spearman's correlation ($r$) considers the ranks rather than the values and measures how far from each other variable ranks are. $r$ is similar to Pearson on ranks. Spearman's assumes monotonic relationship between the two variables. Kendall correlation measures the correlation on ranks, that is the similarity of the orderings of data when ranked by each of the variable values. It is affected by whether the ranks between observations are the same or not without considering how far they are as opposed to $r$. It is thus considered as more appropriate for discrete variables. With regard to system effectiveness, correlation is used in query performance prediction to evaluate the accuracy of the prediction: the two analysed variables are the predictor (either a single predictor or a complex one) and the observed effectiveness.

**Analysis of variance (ANOVA)** encompasses different statistical models and estimation procedures used to highlight differences or dependencies between several statistical groups. It is used to analyse the difference between the means of more than two groups. In ANOVA, the observed variance in a particular variable is partitioned into components that are attributable to different sources of variation. A one-way ANOVA uses one independent variable, while a two-way ANOVA uses two independent variables. The General Linear Mixed Model [30] extends the General Linear Model [31] so that the linear predictor contains random effects in addition to the usual fixed effects.

**Factorial analysis** is used to describe variability among observed, correlated variables; it uses factors, here combinations of initial variables, to represent individuals or data in a space of a lower dimension. It uses singular value decomposition and is appropriate to visualise the link between elements (individuals) that are initially represented in a high dimensional space (variables). Two variants of factorial analysis are used in the context of IR system performance analysis. Factorial analysis is also the core model used in the Latent Semantic Indexing model [32] where documents are considered in the high dimensional space of words. It is also linked to the matrix factorisation principle used in recommender systems for example [33]. Principal Component Analysis (PCA) and Correspondence Analysis [34] which differ on the pre-treatment applied to the initial analysed matrix and on the distance used to find the links between variables and individuals. Although PCA reduces the dimensionality of the data by considering the most important dimensions as determined by the eigen values of the variance/covariance matrix using Euclidian distance, CA uses the $\chi^2$ distance on contingency matrices. Factorial analysis results on visual representations which can be manually interpreted. Among others, one interesting property of CA compared to PCA is that individuals and features can be observed all together in the same projected space. Factorial analyses are used in the context of IR effectiveness analysis.

**Clustering methods** is a family of methods that aims to group together similar objects or individuals. Under this group falls agglomerative clustering and k-means. In agglomerative clustering, each individual corresponds to a cluster; at each processing step, the two closest clusters are merged; the process ends when there is a single cluster. The minimum value of the error sum of squares is used as the ward criterion to choose the pair of clusters to merge [35]. The resulting dendogramme (tree-like structure) can be cut at any level to produce a partition of objects. Depending on its level, the cut will result in either numerous but homogeneously-composed clusters or few but heterogeneously-composed clusters. Another popular clustering method is k-means where a number of seeds, corresponding to the desired number of clusters, are chosen. Objects are associated to the closest seed. Objects can then be re-allocated to a different cluster if it is closer to the centroid of an other cluster. For system effectiveness analysis, clustering can be used to group queries, systems or even measures.

Although the previous methods are usually considered as descriptive ones, the two other groups of methods are predictive methods. That means they are used to predict either a class (e.g., for a qualitative variable) or a value (e.g., for a continuous variable).

**Regression methods** aim to approach the value of a dependent variable (the variable to be predicted) considering one or several independent variables (the variables or features that are used to predict). The regression is based on a function model with one or more parameters (e.g., linear function in the linear regression; polynomial, ... ). Logistic regression is for the case the variable to explain is binary (e.g., the individual belongs to a class or not). It is used, for example, in query performance prediction.

**Decision trees** show a family of non-parametric supervised learning methods that are used for classification and regression. The resulting model is able to predict the value of a target variable by learning simple decision rules inferred from the data features. CART [36] and random forests [37] are the most popular among these methods. They have been shown as very competitive methods. The extra advantage is that the model can combine both quantitative and qualitative variables. In addition, the obtained models are explainable. For system effectiveness analysis, the target variable is effectiveness measurement or class of query difficulty (easy, hard, medium, for example). The system hyperparameters or query features are used to infer the rules.

In this study, we do not consider **deep learning** methods as means to analyse and understand information retrieval effectiveness. Deep learning is more and more popular in IR but still these models lack interpretability. The artificial intelligence community is re-investigating the explainability and interpretability challenge of neural network based models [38]. For example, a recent review focused on explainable recommendation systems [39]. Still, model explanability is mainly based on model interpretability and prominent interpretable models are more conventional machine learning ones, such as regression models and decision tree models [39].

*3.2. Data and Data Structures for System Effectiveness Analysis*

There are different international challenges in IR where participants use the same data collections to answer shared tasks and, thus, that can be used to deeply analyse system effectiveness, its factors and parameters. In this paper, the studied papers focused on the pioneering TREC challenge. TREC considered many different languages, but when it began and nowadays it is mainly focused on English. TREC encompasses various tasks; the most popular and running from the largest number of years is ad hoc retrieval where the task is to retrieve the relevant documents, given a query. It was also the first and unique task introduced in TREC in 1992 [40]. This paper focuses on ad hoc retrieval.

System performance analyses (presented in Sections 4–6) share the same type of data structures, namely matrices.

In general, the participants' results consists in measurements across three dimensions (system, topic, measure). As a result of a challenge like TREC, we can thus build 3D matrices (see Figure 3) that report values for different systems, different topics, different effectiveness measures.

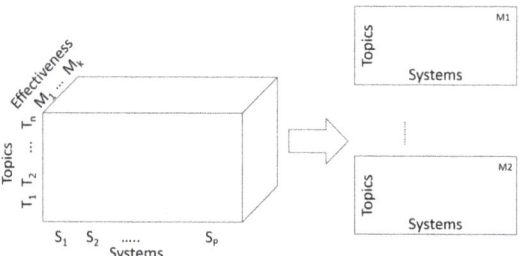

**Figure 3.** The 3D matrices obtained from participants' results to shared ad hoc information retrieval tasks that report effectiveness measurements for systems, topics, effectiveness measures can be transformed into 2D matrices that fit many data analysis methods.

Such a 3D matrix can be transformed into a 2D one for a given effectiveness measure where the two remaining dimensions are the systems and the topics. The resulting matrix can then be used as an input to many of the data analysis methods we presented in the previous sub-section where individuals are the systems represented according to the topics, or using the transposed matrix, individuals are topics represented according to the systems.

We can also have more information at our disposal on systems or on topics or on both. In that case, the data structures can be more complex. For example, if we consider a given effectiveness measure, systems can be represented by different features (e.g., the components that are used, their hyperparameters, ...). In the same way, topics can come with various features (e.g., linguistic or statistical features, ...) (see Figure 4).

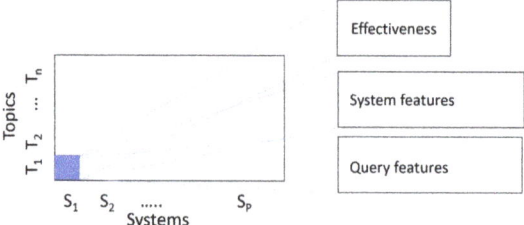

**Figure 4.** More complex data structures can be used that integrate features on topics, on systems or on both.

Finally, some studies consider aggregated values. For example, rather than considering each query individually, we can consider aggregated value across queries; this is commonly used to compare systems and methods at a upper level. On the other hand, it is possible not to consider each system individually but aggregate the results across systems (see Figure 5).

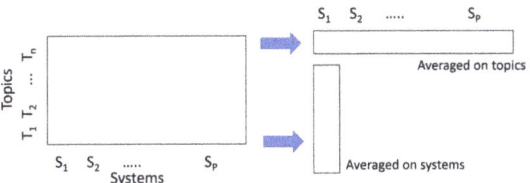

**Figure 5.** Aggregated values can be considered, either on the queries or systems.

## 4. System Performance Analysis Based on Their Participation to Evaluation Challenges

International evaluation forums such as TREC. TREC started in 1992 and supports research in the information retrieval and provides the framework for large-scale evaluation of information retrieval have provided shared collections consisting of queries, documents, and relevance judgements, but also consisting of participants' results. For a given collection, we have different systems that ran the queries over the same document set and are evaluated the same way. Indeed, each participant to TREC tracks receives a detailed report where their runs or systems are scored according to various effectiveness measures obtained by the open evaluation tool trec_eval described in https://github.com/topics/trec-eval accessed on 15 May 2022. This opened the opportunity to mine these results.

The first to analyse the results were the organisers. In the first TREC report, the results of the different participants were compared mainly through recall precision curves [41].

Additional analyses were made a few years later. One search engine (SMART system of Cornell University) which has been one of the most effective in TREC ad hoc task, was run in its versions used in each of the first seven TREC conferences on each of the first seven ad hoc test collections [42]. This longitudinal analysis of a system version shows that effectiveness increases over time, whatever the system variant used.

The reliable information access workshop was dedicated to the analysis of the participants' results. The organisers reported that a system can perform very well on a query A, very bad on a query B, while an other system will do the opposite [12]. At that time, it was not possible to understand the reasons of the variability in results; it was stated as being dependant on three factors: the query, the relationship between the query and the documents, and the system parameters; it was considered as a difficult problem to understand [14] and this difficulty remains.

Tague-Sutcliffe and Blustein [8] also reported such variability and showed that the variance due to queries was much greater than the one due to systems. This finding has encouraged the further study on the link between queries and system performance.

Banks et al. [9] considered a matrix in which rows and columns represent systems and topics/queries, and cells correspond to average precision (like the one presented in Figure 6). They also considered the retrieved document lists of each participant. Then, they applied six data analysis methods, trying to extract knowledge, relationships, clusters, ...from these data that would help to understand better the structure or derive general conclusions from the participants' results. Among them, the authors considered the analysis of variance to look for deviations and variability in retrieval performance that could be explained by the systems, topics, or both. They also tried to extract clusters of topics and systems. On document lists, they analysed the correlations on document orders and tried to extract the sub-patterns in the sequence of retrieved documents. The authors concluded "None of the work we have done using the six approaches discussed has provided the sort of insights we were seeking, and the prospects that additional work along these lines will yield significantly better results vary but are not generally promising." [9].

|       | APL985L | APL985LC | APL985SC | AntHoc01 | Brkly24 | Brkly25 |
|-------|---------|----------|----------|----------|---------|---------|
| T351  | 0.2257  | 0.2261   | 0.1655   | 0.2933   | 0.2987  | 0.3137  |
| T352  | 0.0229  | 0.0321   | 0.0594   | 0.0277   | 0.0379  | 0.0097  |
| T353  | 0.3271  | 0.3052   | 0.2852   | 0.2091   | 0.374   | 0.264   |
| T354  | 0.1119  | 0.1496   | 0.0908   | 0.0139   | 0.0192  | 0.1084  |
| T355  | 0.0973  | 0.0688   | 0.0327   | 0.1365   | 0.0987  | 0.183   |
| T356  | 0.052   | 0.0593   | 0.0462   | 0.0091   | 0.0128  | 0.0452  |
| T357  | 0.1358  | 0.1803   | 0.1391   | 0.0984   | 0.3284  | 0.3277  |
| T358  | 0.0994  | 0.0988   | 0.0489   | 0.1514   | 0.2078  | 0.3887  |
| T359  | 0.0378  | 0.0337   | 0.0146   | 0.0223   | 0.0319  | 0.0357  |
| T360  | 0.39    | 0.3825   | 0.4096   | 0.0404   | 0.3275  | 0.036   |

**Figure 6.** A 2D matrix representing the effectiveness of different systems (X axis) on different topics (Y axis). This matrix is an extract of the one representing the AP (effectiveness measure) for TREC 7 ad hoc participants on the topic set of that track.

Analyses were produced on web track overviews. On Web track 2009 [43], the organisers reported the plot representing the effectiveness of participants' system considering two evaluation measures, the mean subtopic recall and the mean precision (see Figure 7). This analysis showed that the two measures correlate, which means that a system A that is better than a system B on one of the two measures is also better when considering the second measure. When effective systems are effective, the measure that is used does not matter.

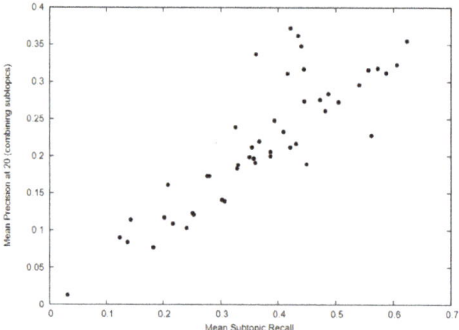

**Figure 7.** Effective systems are effective whatever the measure used. Web track 09 participants' results considering mean subtopic recall (X-axis) and mean precision (Y-axis); each dot is a participant systems. Figure reprinted with permission from [43], Copyright 2009, Charles Clarke et al.

In web track 2014 [44], the authors provided a different type of analysis with box plots that show the dispersion of the effectiveness measurements for each of the topics, across participants' systems (see Figure 8). This type of view informs on the impact of the system factor on the results. The smaller the box, the smaller the importance of the system factor is. Both some easy queries, for which the median effectiveness is high, and hard queries, for which the median effectiveness is low, have packed results (e.g., easy 285 topic in Figure 8 and hard 255 topic—not presented here). Both types have also dispersed results (e.g., easy 285 topic on Figure 8 and hard 269 topic—not presented here).

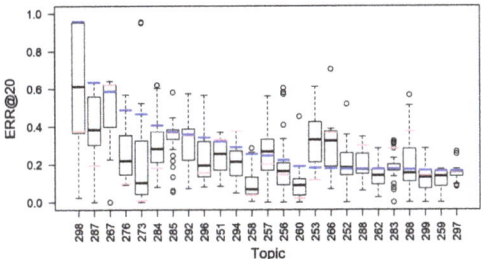

**Figure 8.** In the easiest topics according to the median effectiveness on the participants' results, there are both topics with very diverse system effectiveness results (e.g., 298) and very similar ones (e.g., topic 285)—Web track 2014—topics are ordered according to decreasing the err@20 of the best system. Figure reprinted with permission from [44], Copyright 2014, Kevyn Collins-Thompson et al.

On the same type of matrices than the ones Banks et al. used (see Figure 6), Dinçer et al. [10], Mothe et al. [11], and Bigot et al. [15] applied factorial analyses more successfully. These studies showed that topics and systems are indeed linked. Principal Component Analysis (PCA) and Correspondence Analysis were used.

On Figure 9 we can see PCA applied on a matrix that reports average precision for different queries (variables, matrix columns) by different systems (individuals, matrix rows) at TREC 12 Robust track. We can see on the left bottom part systems that behave similarly on the same queries (they fail on the same queries, succeed on the same queries) and that behave differently from the other systems. We can see another group of systems on the top left corner of the figure. Similar results where reported in [11] where PCA was applied on a matrix that studied recall at TREC Novelty track. In both studies, the results showed that there is not just two groups of systems, thus emphasising that systems behave differently on different queries but that some systems have similar profiles (behave similarly on the same queries).

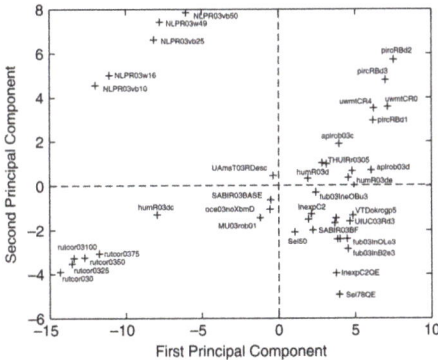

**Figure 9.** System failure and effectiveness depend on queries—not all systems succeed or fail on the same queries. The visualisation shows the two first principal components of a Principal Component Analysis, where the data of the system effectiveness is obtained for each topic by each participants' run. MAP measure of TREC 12 Robust Track participants' runs. Figure reprinted with permission from [10], Copyright 2007, John Wiley and Sons.

These results are complementary from Mizzaro and Roberston' findings which show that "easy" queries, the ones that on average systems can answer pretty well, are best to distinguish good systems from bad systems [13].

Kompaore et al. [45] showed that queries can be clustered in a more sophisticated way, based on their linguistic features. The authors extracted 13 linguistic features that they used to cluster queries—based on agglomerative clustering—and obtained three query clusters. Then, they ranked the TREC ad hoc task participants according to the result they obtained on mean average precision over the entire set of queries, and over each of the clusters. They showed that for each query cluster the best system is not the same (see Figure 10). For example, while ETHme1 was ranked first when considering the mean average precision on the entire set of queries and the query cluster 1, it is ranked the 10th on the query cluster 2. For that query cluster, the best performing system is uwgcx0, and it is LNaDesc1 for query cluster 3. This shows that there is also system profiles that can be extracted, considering topic difficulty levels.

Although these studies analysed TREC participants' systems, other studies have generated different combinations of search components and hyperparameters [15,16,18,45–47] and thus went a step further in understanding the factors of variability.

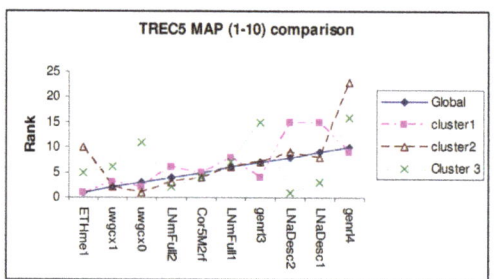

**Figure 10.** The first ranked system differs according to the query clusters. The rank of the system is on the Y-axis and the system is on X-axis. Blue diamonds correspond to the ranks of the systems when considering all the queries, pink squares when considering the query cluster 1, brown triangles are for query cluster 2, and green crosses for cluster 3. Systems on the X-axis are ordered according to decreasing effectiveness on average on the query set. Figure reprinted with permission from [45], Copyright 2007, Kompaore et al.

## 5. Analyses Based on Systems That Were Generated for the Study—The System Factor

The system factor is the factor that has been mentioned the first in shared tasks: systems do not perform identically. Thanks to the results the participants' system obtained in shared tasks, it has been possible to identify which techniques or systems work better in average over queries, but because the description of those systems was not enough, it has not been possible to study the important factors within the systems. This is what some studies aimed to analyse.

Two research groups deeply studied this specific point: the Information Management Systems Research Group of the University of Padua in Italy, starting from 2011 [48] and the Information System Research Group of the University of Toulouse in France, starting from 2011 [49]. Google Scholar was used to find what were the first pieces of work related to automatically generated IR chains in the objective to analyse the component effects. Although the two cited works did not obtain many citations, they mark the starting point of this new research track.

The analyses based on synthetic data are in line with the idea developed in 2010 in [46] for an evaluation framework where components would be run locally and where intermediate output would be upload so that component effects could be analysed deeper; evaluation as a service has further developed the same idea [50].

One of the first implementations of the automatic generation of a large series of query processing chains was the one in Louedec et al. [18]; in line with the ideas in [46,51] also implemented in [19]. It was made possible because of the valuable work that has been performed in Glasgow on Terrier [5] to implement IR components from the literature. Other platforms can also serve this purpose, such as Lemur/Indri (https://www.lemurproject.org/ accessed on 15 May 2022); https://sourceforge.net/p/lemur/wiki/

Indri%20Retrieval%20Model/ accessed on 15 May 2022 although more centred on language models or Cherche (https://github.com/raphaelsty/cherche accessed on 15 May 2022) for neural models.

Compared to using participants' systems, generated query processing chains gives the ability to know the exact components and hyper-parameters used and thus make deeper analysis possible.

One of the pioneer studies that analysed a huge number of automatically generated systems is Ayter et al. [7]. They used about 80,000 combinations of components in query processing chains with: 4 stemmers, 7 weighting models, 6 query processing, 7 query expansion models, and various numbers of query terms and documents to consider in query expansion. They used TREC 7 and 8 ad hoc collection (100 topics in total querying the same document collection) and average precision as the effectiveness measure. Among their findings, the authors concluded that the choice of the stemmer component had little to no influence, while the weighting model had an impact on the results (see Figure 11). Other findings were that dirichletLM is the weaker search model among the 7 studied, while BB2 is among the best; this when considering also all the other parameters. Their analyses also confirmed that systems behave differently and that the choice of the components at each phase of the retrieving process, as well as the component hyper-parameters, are an important part of system successes and failures.

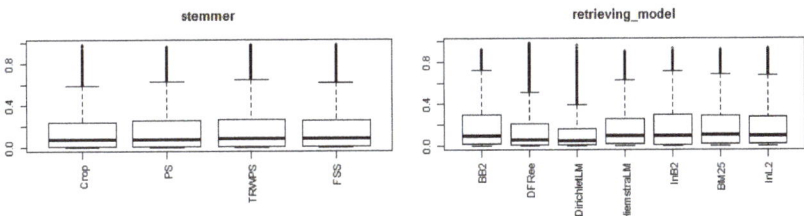

**Figure 11.** The choice of the weighting model has more impact than the stemmer used. Individual boxplots represent average precision on the TREC 7 and 8 topics when a given component is used in a query processing chain—80,000 query processing chains or component combinations were used. Figure reprinted with permission from [7], Copyright 2015, J.UCS.

Another important study is the one from Ferro and Silvello [16] followed up by [17] from the same authors. On TREC 8, they considered the cross effect of the component choice in the query processing chain. They considered three components: the stop list (5 variants), the stemmer (5 variants), and the weighting model (16 variants), for a total of 400 possible different combinations. As an effectiveness measure, they also used average precision. They show that variants of the stop word list used during indexing does not have a huge impact, but the system should use one (see Figure 12, subfigures A, B where the blue—no stopword—curve is systematically below the others and C where the starting point of the curve—no stopword—is lower than the rest of the curves). It also showed that, given a stopword list is used, the weighing model has the strongest impact among the three studied components (subfigures B and D, where waves show that the systems have different effectiveness).

Additionally, related to these studies, CLAIRE [52] is a system to explore IR results. When analysing TREC ad hoc and web tracks, the findings are consistent with previous analyses: dirichletLM is the weaker weighting model among the studied ones, IR weighting models suffer from the absence of a stop list and of stemmer. By such exploration, the authors were able to show which is the most promising combination of components for a system on a collection (e.g., jskls model equipped with a snowball stop list and a porter stemmer).

These data analytics studies allowed to understand the influence of the components and their possible cross-effect. They are using the results obtained on different collection; they do not aim to predict results.

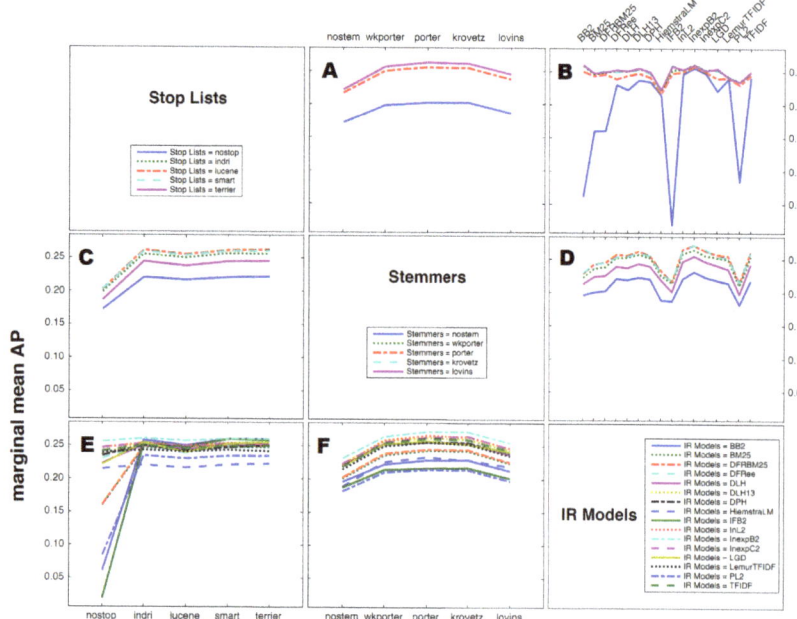

**Figure 12. Interaction between component choices.** The curves used in this representation are somehow misleading since the variables are not continuous but nevertheless can be understood, we thus kept the original Figures from [16]) where we added letters in each sub-figure for clarity. On the first row, the stop list effect is shown for different stemmers (**A**) and different weighting models (**B**). On the second row, the effect of stemmers is reported for different stop lists (**C**) and different weighting models (**D**). On the latest row, the weighting model effect is reported, for different stop lists (**E**) and different stemmers (**F**). Figure adapted with permission from [16], Copyright 2016, Nicola Ferro et al.

## 6. The Query Factor

### 6.1. Considering the Queries and Their Pre- and Post-Retrieval Features

The query is the main factor that explains variability in effectiveness [7,8,13,53]. The query factor, thus, attracted much research attention mainly under the query difficulty or query performance prediction research topics. Because this paper focuses on how data analytics can help IR effectiveness understanding, we do not survey query performance predictors but rather what we have learnt from the studies on the different types of query features used for effectiveness prediction.

The explanation of system effectiveness failure, which is strongly related to query difficulty in IR terminology, by the query it-self was studied considering different types of features:

- Linguistic features extracted from the query only [21,54–56];
- Other pre-retrieval features that use information on the document collection [57–61];
- Post retrieval features that consider the retrieved documents for that query [22,57,62–73].

Mothe and Tanguy [21] considered 16 linguistic query features. They observed the correlation of these features with average recall and precision obtained by TREC participant systems. Morphological, syntactical and semantic features were considered. Syntactic links span (distance between syntactically linked words) was shown as inversely correlated to precision while polysemy value, the number of semantic classes a given word belongs to in WordNet was shown to be inversely correlated to recall.

Molina [74] developed a resource where 258 features have been extracted from queries from Robust, WT10G and GOV2 collections. Among the features extracted from the query only, are aggregations (minimum, maximum, mean, quartiles, standard deviation, and total) over query terms on the number of synonyms, hyponyms, meronyms and sister terms from WordNet. The authors did not provide a deep analysis on how much each of these features correlate with the system performance.

Hauff et al. [60] surveyed 22 pre-retrieval features from the literature at that time, from which some use the query only to be computed. The authors categorised these features into four groups, depending on the underlying heuristic: specificity, ambiguity, term relatedness, and ranking sensitivity. Intuitively, the higher the term specificity the easier the query. Inversely, the higher the term ambiguity, the more difficult the query is. When analysed on three TREC collections, the authors found weak correlation between the system performance and features based on the query only. Among them, the features related to the term ambiguity where the most correlated to system performance, in line with [21]. Features that consider information on the documents were found more correlated to performance than the ones based on the query only.

The query effect was also studied in link with the document collection that is searched by considering information resulting from the document indexing. These query features are grounded on the same idea as term weighting is for indexation: terms are not equivalent and their frequency in documents matters. Inverse document frequency, based on the number of documents in which the term occurs has specifically been used, but other features were also developed [59,61,75].

Finally, the query effect was also studied considering post-retrieval features [57,62–67,69–73]. Post-retrieval predictors are categorised into clarity-based, score-based, and robustness-based approaches [22,68]. They imply that a first document retrieval is performed using the query before the features can be calculated. Post-retrieval features mainly used the document scores.

Considered individually, post-retrieval features have been consistently shown as better predictors than pre-retrieval ones. It appeared, however, that an individual feature, either pre- or post-retrieval, is not enough to predict whether the system is going to fail or not or to predict its effectiveness. That mean that none of these individual features "explained" the system performance.

Indeed, many studies have reported weak correlation values for individual features [60,71,76] with the actual system effectiveness. When considering a single feature, the correlation values differ from one collection to another and from one feature to another. Moreover, they are weak. For example, Hauff et al. [60] report 396 correlation values among which 13 only are over 0.5. Hashemi et al. [77] reported 216 correlation values including the ones obtained with a new neural network-based predictor, with a maximum value of 0.58, a median of 0.17. Chifu et al. [71] reported 312 values, none of which above 0.50. In the same way, Khodabakhsh and Bagheri report 952 correlation values, none of which are above 0.46 [73]. When correlation are low it is even likelier that there is either very weak or no correlation at all between the predicted value (here effectiveness) and the feature used to predict. Table 1 and Figure 13 illustrate this. For this illustration, we took $IDF_{Max}$ and $IDF_{AVG}$ which are considered as the best pre-retrieval features [60,69,78], as well as BM25, a post-retrieval feature. We can see that with a correlation of 0.29 for BM25 or 0.24 for IDF (see Table 1), there is no correlation between the two variables as depicted on the scatter plots (see Figure 13).

Papers on query performance prediction seldom plot the predicted and actual values which is however an appropriate mean to check whether the correlation exists or not. As a counter example of this, we should here recall that the Anscombe's quartet [79] effect on the Pearson correlation illustrates that even a Pearson correlation up to 0.816 can be obtained with no correlation between the two studied variables (see Figure 14).

Table 1. Correlation between query features and ndcg. WT10G TREC collection. * marks the usual <0.05 *p*-Value significance.

| Measure | Feature | | | |
| --- | --- | --- | --- | --- |
| | BM25_MAX | BM25_STD | IDF_MAX | IDF_AVG |
| Pearson $\rho$ | 0.294 * | 0.232 * | 0.095 | 0.127 |
| *p*-Value | 0.0034 | 0.0224 | 0.3531 | 0.2125 |
| Spearman *r* | 0.260 * | 0.348 * | 0.236 * | 0.196 |
| *p*-Value | 0.0100 | <0.001 | 0.0202 | 0.0544 |
| Kendall $\tau$ | 0.172 * | 0.230 * | 0.159 * | 0.136 * |
| *p*-Value | 0.0128 | <0.001 | 0.0215 | 0.0485 |

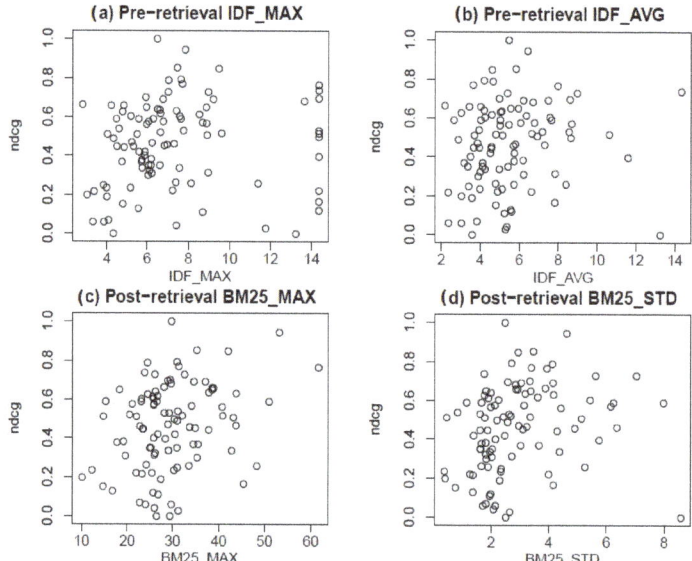

**Figure 13.** No correlation using pre- or post-predictors with the actual effectiveness—IDF preretrieval predictor and BM25 post-retrieval predictor (X-axis) and ndcg (Y-axis) values on WT10G TREC collection. Although the correlation values are up to 0.35, there is no correlation.

A single query feature cannot explain a single system effectiveness, but:

1. Combination of query features might;
2. It may explain that systems will fail in general.

Regarding (1), a series of studies have been produced to combine query features into models [78,80–82]. Grivolla et al. [80] grouped queries according to the predicted performance. They trained a model that combined various features, including linguistic, pre- and post- retrieval features, and used decision tree and SVM. The experiments they reported on TREC-8 participants' results showed that the model was not robust across systems: for some of them the prediction was accurate while it was not for some others. Raiber et al. combined various features in a Markov Random Fields model and reported a maximum correlation of 0.695 and a median of 0.32 [81]. Chifu et al. [71] combined Letor features using a linear model and reported a maximum correlation of 0.45. The only study we found that both reported positive results and plotted predicted vs actual effectiveness is Roy et al. [78]. They proposed a linear combination of a word embedding based pre-retrieval feature which measures the ambiguity of each query term, with the post-retrieval NQC feature (see Figure 15). However, the model performs well for easy queries only. However, we know from Mizzaro and Robertson [13] that easy queries do not help to distinguish effective systems from non-effective ones [13].

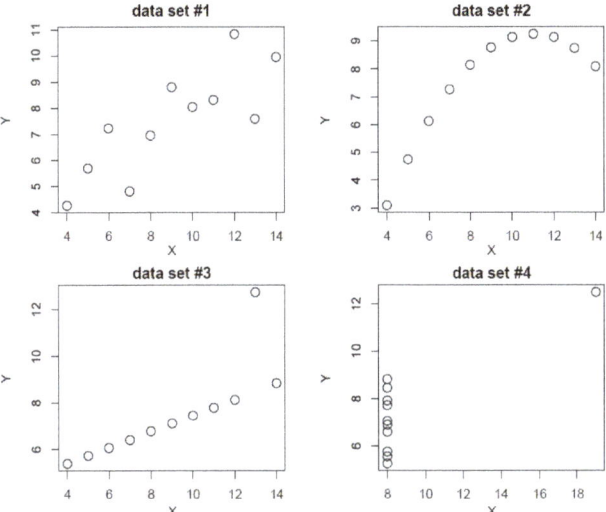

**Figure 14.** Pearson correlation value higher than 0.8 does not mean the two variables are correlated. The Anscombe's quartet presents four datasets that share the same mean, same number of values, same Pearson correlation value ($\rho = 0.816$) but for which this latter value does not always means the two variables X and Y are correlated. X and Y are not correlated on #4 despite high $\rho$ value. #2 X and Y are perfectly correlated but not in a linear way (Pearson cannot measure other than linear correlations) #1 and #3 illustrates two cases of linear correlation. Figures generated from the data in [79].

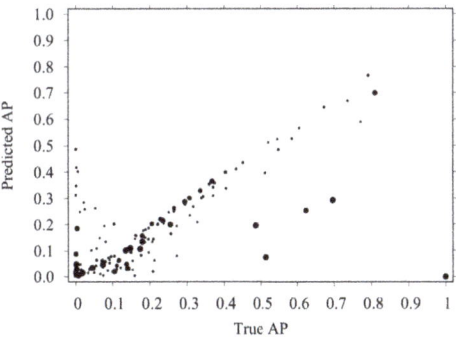

**Figure 15.** Predicted AP is correlated to actual AP for easy queries (the ones on the right part of the plot), although there are sparse. Figure reprinted with permission from Roy et al. [78], Copyright 2019, Elsevier.

With regard to (2), rather than considering individual system performance, Mizzaro et al. [82] focused on the average of average precision values over systems, this to detect the queries for which systems will fail in general. The authors showed that the correlation is more obvious between the predictor and the average system effectiveness than it was in other studies between the predictor and a single system (see Figure 16).

This call also for the need to try to understand the relationship between the query factor and the system factor.

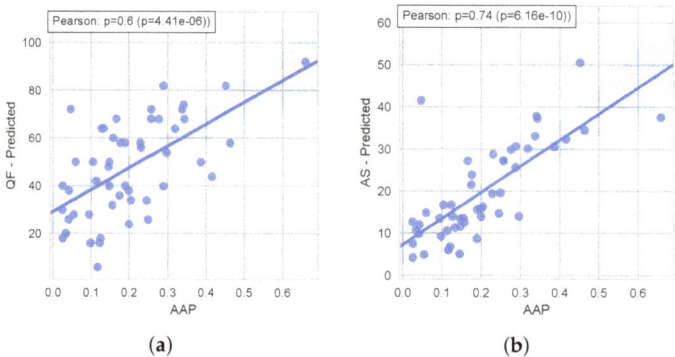

**Figure 16.** AS feature [83] is correlated to the average effectiveness of a set of systems. TREC7 Adhoc collection. Pearson correlation between AAP and (**a**) QF [66], (**b**) AS [83]. Dots correspond to actual and predicted AAP for individual topics; the cones represent the confidence intervals. Figure reprinted with permission from [82], Copyright 2018, Mizzaro et al.

*6.2. Relationship between the Query Factor and the System Factor*

In Section 5, we reported studies on system variabilities and the effect of the components used at each search phase on the results when averaged over query sets, not considering deeply the query effect.

Here, we consider studies that were conducted at a finer grain. These pieces of work tried to understand the very link between the level of query difficulty (or level of system effectiveness) and the system components or hyperparameters.

It was concretely used in Ayter et al. where 80,000 combinations of components and hyper-parameters were evaluated on the 100 queries of TREC 7 and 8 ad hoc track topics. The combinations differed on the stemmer used to index the documents (4 different stemmers were used), the topic tags used to build the query, the weighting model (7 different models), the query expansion model (6 different models) and the query expansion hyper-parameters which take different values as well. The authors showed that the most important parameters, the ones that influence the results the most, depend on the difficulty of the query, that is to say whether relevant documents will be easily found by the search engine or not [7] (see Figure 17).

In Figure 17a where the easy queries only are analysed, we can see that the most influential parameter is the query expansion model used because this is the one where the tree first split, here for the value c, which corresponds to the Info query expansion model. The retrieving or matching model is the second most influential parameter. For hard queries however, the most influential parameter is the topic part used for the query. In that research the authors either used the title only, or the other topic fields, narrative and descriptive, that provide more information on the users' need related to the topic. The leaves of the tree is whether the decision for a query is "easy" (good performance), "average" or "hard" (bad performance) when following a branch from the root to the leave. The main overall conclusion is that the influential parameters are not the same for easy and hard queries; giving the intuition that obtaining the best performance cannot be by applying the same process whatever the queries are. This was further analysed in [53], where more TREC collections were studied with the same conclusions.

These results are in favour of considering the system component parameters, not at a global level like search grid or other optimisation methods do in IR, but rather at a finer grain.

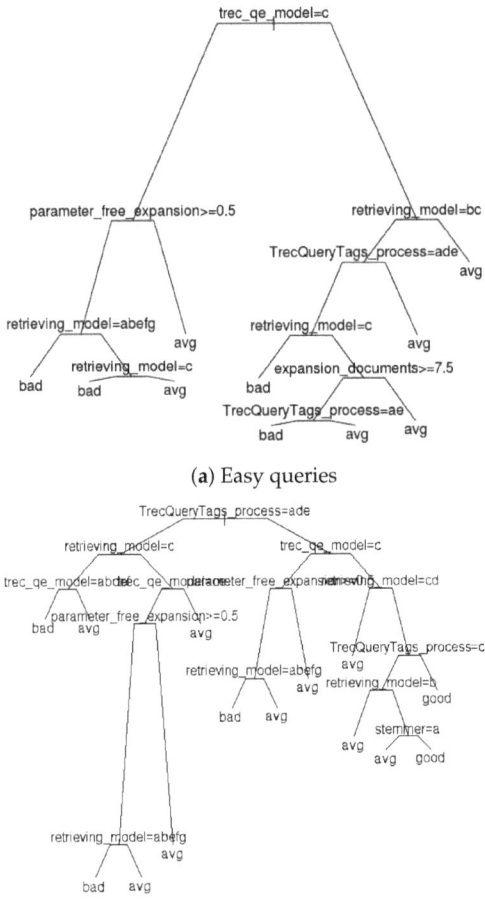

(a) Easy queries

(b) Difficult queries

**Figure 17.** The parameters that affect retrieval effectiveness the most depend on the query difficulty. On (**a**), for easy queries, the most important parameter for search effectiveness optimisation is the choice of the query expansion component; on (**b**), for hard queries, the most important parameter is the topic parts used for building the query, then the weighting component and in third the query expansion model. Figure reprinted with permission from [7], Copyright 2015, J.UCS.

## 7. Discussion and Conclusions

Understanding information retrieval effectiveness involves considering several dimensions. In this paper, we focused on the system and the query, while the document collection and the effectiveness measures were in the background.

From **evaluation forums and shared tasks**, although participants provide some detailed description of the systems they designed, the information is not enough structured or detailed to draw conclusions, except in broad strokes. The main conclusions from the analyses of shared tasks results are:

- C1: it is possible to distinguish between effective and non-effective systems on average over a query set;
- C2: effectiveness of systems has increased over years thanks to the effort put in the domain;

- C3: some queries are easy for all the systems while others are hard for all (see Figure 18, left-side part) but systems do not always fail or succeed on the same queries (see Figure 18, right side part). Some systems have a similar profile, they fail/success on the same queries.

However, it was not possible to understand system successes and failures.

Regarding C1, we also considered the participants' results from the first 7 years of TREC ad hoc for a total of 496 systems (or runs) and considered the 130 effectiveness measures from trec_eval that evaluate (system, query) pairs, such as in [84]. Correlation when considering pairs of measurements for a given topic and a given system are high, which means it is possible to distinguish between effective and non effective systems, it does not depend on the measure used (see Figure 19).

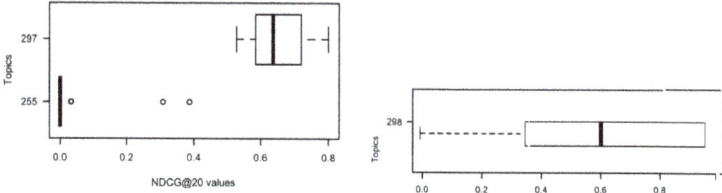

**Figure 18.** Some queries are easy for all the systems, some are hard for all, other depends on the system. On the TREC topic 297, all the analysed systems obtained at least 0.5 as NDCG@20, half of them obtained more than 0.65 and some obtained 0.8, which is high. For topic 255, all the systems failed but 3, only one obtained more than 0.3. The right part boxplot, as opposed to the left side ones, shows that for topic 298, the system effectiveness have a large span from 0 to almost 1.

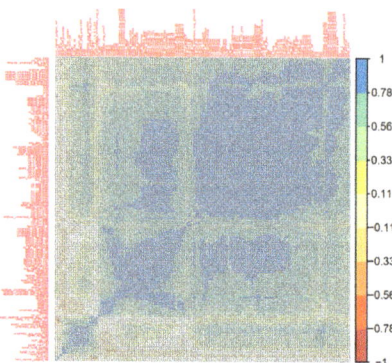

**Figure 19.** When considering a given system and a given query, the effectiveness measure used to compare the systems does not matter much: all are strongly correlated. Pearson correlation values between two effectiveness measurements on two measures for a given (system, query) pair. Correlations are represented using a divergent palette (a central colour, yellow, and 2 shades depending on whether the values go for negative—red—or positive values—blue).

Regarding C2, although it might be overgeneralisation of a single phenomenon, results from SMART system are convincing: the performances almost double when considering the results on the first participation to TREC ad hoc compared to the ones obtained 6 years later (see details Section 4).

Regarding C3, many studies agreed on this observation (see Figure 18). Moreover, systems with the same profiles belong generally to the same research group which means that they may be just small variants one from the other (e.g., different hyper-parameters but basically the same query processing chain, using the same components).

Different attempts to extract more information from official runs were not conclusive.

From **automatically generated query processing chains**, we have a deep knowledge on the systems, we know exactly what components are used with which hyper-parameters. From the analyses that used these data, we can conclude:

- C4: some components and hyper-parameters are more influential than others and informed choices can be made;
- C5: the choice of the most appropriate components depends on the query level of difficulty.

Regarding C4: for some components or their hyperparameters, their choice will have a huge impact on the system effectiveness, for some others, there is no or little impact on effectiveness. This means that if one wants to tune or decide on not all the parameters but a few they should start by the more influential ones. Moreover, we know what is the best decision on some components: a stoplist should be used, a stemmer should be used, but the choice of the stemmer does not matter much; considering the weighting models that are implemented in Terrier, dirichletLM should be avoid, BB2 is a much better option.

Regarding C5: the choice of the most appropriate query processing chain is in relation with the query level of difficulty. In other words, different queries need different processing chains. This means that if we want to increase system effectiveness in the future, we should not just tune the system on a per collection basis: grid searching or any other more sophisticated version of parameter optimisation is not enough. What we need rather is to adapt the processing chain to the query.

From **query analyses**, we can conclude:

- C6: a single query feature or a combination of features have not been proven to explain system effectiveness;
- C7: query features can explain somehow system effectiveness.

Despite their apparent contradiction, C6 and C7 are in fact complementary. Some query features or combination of them seems to be accurate to predict not individual systems but average system effectiveness; there is also some success on predicting easy queries. Systems are, however, more easily distinguishable based on the difficult queries, not the easy ones for which they are more homogeneous in their successes. Up to now, the accuracy of features or feature combinations has not demonstrated that they can explain system effectiveness; correlation values that are reported are seldom over 0.5 and more tricky studies do not report scatter plots.

Although we do not yet understand well the factors of system effectiveness, the studies show that not a single system, while effective in average on a query set, is able to answer all the queries well (mainly C5 in addition to C3 and C4). Advanced IR techniques can be grounded on this knowledge. Selective query expansions (SQE) for example, where a meta-system has two alternative component combinations which differ on using or omitting the automatic query reformulation phase, made use of the fact that some queries benefit from being expanded while other do not [85–87]. SQE has not been proven to be very effective, certainly due to both the limited number of configurations used at that time (two different query processing chains) and the relatively poor learning techniques used at that time. Selective query processing expand SQE concept, where the system decides which one, from a possibly large number of component combinations, should be used for each individual query [10,15,88]. Here, the results were more conclusive. For example, Bigot et al. [89] developed a model that learns the best query processing chain to use for a query based on subsets of documents. Although this makes the method applicable for repeated queries only, it can be an appropriate approach for real world web search engines. Deveaud et al. [90] learn to rank the query processing chain for each new query. They used 20,000 different query processing chains. However, this very large number of combinations makes it difficult to use in real world systems. Arslan and Dinçer [47] developed a meta-model that uses eight term-weighting models that could be chosen among for any new query. The meta-model has to be train, as well as the term-weighting models; this is performed by a grid search optimisation which limit the usability. Mothe and Ullah [91] present an approach to optimise the set of query processing chains that can be chosen among a selective query processing strategy. It is based on a risk-sensitive function that optimises the possible gain in considering a specific query processing chain. The authors show that 20 query processing chains is a good trade-off between the cost of maintaining different query processing chains and the gain on effectiveness. Still they do not explain the successes and failures.

Thus, to the question "Can we design a transparent model in terms of its performance on a query", I am tempted to answer: "No, at this stage of IR knowledge; further analyses are needed". I am convinced that data analytics methods can further been investigated to analyse the amount of data that have been generated by the community, both in shared tasks and in labs while tuning systems.

The robustness of the finding across collections would also worth investigating in the future.

**Funding:** This research received no external funding.

**Conflicts of Interest:** The author declares no conflict of interest.

## Abbreviations

The following abbreviations are used in this manuscript:

| | |
|---|---|
| AP | Average Precision |
| CA | Correspondence Analysis |
| CIKM | Conference on Information and Knowledge Management |
| CLEF | Conference and Labs of the Evaluation Forum |
| IR | Information Retrieval |
| MAP | Mean Average Precision |
| PCA | Principal Component Analysis |
| QE | Query Expansion |
| QPP | Query Performance Prediction |
| SIGIR | Conference of the Association for Computing Machinery Special Interest Group in Information Retrieval |
| SQE | Selective Query Expansion |
| TREC | Text Retrieval Conference |

## References

1. Salton, G.; Wong, A.; Yang, C.S. A vector space model for automatic indexing. *Commun. ACM* **1975**, *18*, 613–620. [CrossRef]
2. Robertson, S.E.; Jones, K.S. Relevance weighting of search terms. *J. Am. Soc. Inf. Sci.* **1976**, *27*, 129–146. [CrossRef]
3. Robertson, S.; Zaragoza, H. *The Probabilistic Relevance Framework: BM25 and Beyond*; Now Publishers Inc.: Delft, The Netherlands, 2009; pp. 333–389.
4. Ponte, J.M.; Croft, W.B. A Language Modeling Approach to Information Retrieval. In Proceedings of the 21st Annual International ACM SIGIR Conference on Research and Development in Information Retrieval, SIGIR '98, Melbourne, Australia, 24–28 August 1998; ACM: New York, NY, USA, 1998; pp. 275–281. [CrossRef]
5. Ounis, I.; Amati, G.; Plachouras, V.; He, B.; Macdonald, C.; Johnson, D. Terrier information retrieval platform. In *European Conference on Information Retrieval*; Springer: Berlin/Heidelberg, Germany, 2005; pp. 517–519.
6. Taylor, M.; Zaragoza, H.; Craswell, N.; Robertson, S.; Burges, C. Optimisation methods for ranking functions with multiple parameters. In Proceedings of the 15th ACM International Conference on Information and Knowledge Management, Arlington, VA, USA, 6–11 November 2006; pp. 585–593.
7. Ayter, J.; Chifu, A.; Déjean, S.; Desclaux, C.; Mothe, J. Statistical analysis to establish the importance of information retrieval parameters. *J. Univers. Comput. Sci.* **2015**, *21*, 1767–1789.
8. Tague-Sutcliffe, J.; Blustein, J. *A Statistical Analysis of the TREC-3 Data*; NIST Special Publication SP: Washington, DC, USA, 1995; p. 385.
9. Banks, D.; Over, P.; Zhang, N.F. Blind men and elephants: Six approaches to TREC data. *Inf. Retr.* **1999**, *1*, 7–34. [CrossRef]
10. Dinçer, B.T. Statistical principal components analysis for retrieval experiments. *J. Am. Soc. Inf. Sci. Technol.* **2007**, *58*, 560–574. [CrossRef]

11. Mothe, J.; Tanguy, L. Linguistic analysis of users' queries: Towards an adaptive information retrieval system. In Proceedings of the 2007 Third International IEEE Conference on Signal-Image Technologies and Internet-Based System, Shanghai, China, 16–18 December 2007; pp. 77–84.

12. Harman, D.; Buckley, C. The NRRC reliable information access (RIA) workshop. In Proceedings of the 27th Annual International ACM SIGIR Conference on Research and Development in Information Retrieval, Sheffield, UK, 25–29 July 2004; pp. 528–529.

13. Mizzaro, S.; Robertson, S. Hits hits trec: Exploring ir evaluation results with network analysis. In Proceedings of the 30th Annual International ACM SIGIR Conference on Research and Development in Information Retrieval, Amsterdam, The Netherlands, 23–27 July 2007; pp. 479–486.

14. Harman, D.; Buckley, C. Overview of the reliable information access workshop. *Inf. Retr.* **2009**, *12*, 615. [CrossRef]

15. Bigot, A.; Chrisment, C.; Dkaki, T.; Hubert, G.; Mothe, J. Fusing different information retrieval systems according to query-topics: A study based on correlation in information retrieval systems and TREC topics. *Inf. Retr.* **2011**, *14*, 617. [CrossRef]

16. Ferro, N.; Silvello, G. A general linear mixed models approach to study system component effects. In Proceedings of the 39th International ACM SIGIR conference on Research and Development in Information Retrieval, Pisa, Italy, 17–21 July 2016; pp. 25–34.

17. Ferro, N.; Silvello, G. Toward an anatomy of IR system component performances. *J. Assoc. Inf. Sci. Technol.* **2018**, *69*, 187–200. [CrossRef]

18. Louedec, J.; Mothe, J. A massive generation of ir runs: Demonstration paper. In Proceedings of the IEEE 7th International Conference on Research Challenges in Information Science (RCIS), Paris, France, 29–31 May 2013; pp. 1–2.

19. Wilhelm, T.; Kürsten, J.; Eibl, M. A tool for comparative ir evaluation on component level. In Proceedings of the 34th International ACM SIGIR Conference on Research and Development in Information Retrieval, Beijing, China, 24–28 July 2011; pp. 1291–1292.

20. Carmel, D.; Yom-Tov, E.; Darlow, A.; Pelleg, D. What makes a query difficult? In Proceedings of the 29th Annual International ACM SIGIR Conference on Research and Development in Information Retrieval, Seattle,WA, USA, 6–11 August 2006; pp. 390–397.

21. Mothe, J.; Tanguy, L. Linguistic features to predict query difficulty. In *ACM Conference on Research and Development in Information Retrieval, SIGIR, Predicting Query Difficulty-Methods and Applications Workshop*; ACM: New York, NY, USA, 2005; pp. 7–10.

22. Zamani, H.; Croft, W.B.; Culpepper, J.S. Neural query performance prediction using weak supervision from multiple signals. In Proceedings of the 41st International ACM SIGIR Conference on Research & Development in Information Retrieval, Ann Arbor, MI, USA, 8–12 July 2018; pp. 105–114.

23. Carpineto, C.; Romano, G. A survey of automatic query expansion in information retrieval. *ACM Comput. Surv. (CSUR)* **2012**, *44*, 1–50. [CrossRef]

24. Azad, H.K.; Deepak, A. Query expansion techniques for information retrieval: A survey. *Inf. Process. Manag.* **2019**, *56*, 1698–1735. [CrossRef]

25. Moral, C.; de Antonio, A.; Imbert, R.; Ramírez, J. A survey of stemming algorithms in information retrieval. *Inf. Res. Int. Electron. J.* **2014**, *19*, n1.

26. Kamphuis, C.; de Vries, A.P.; Boytsov, L.; Lin, J. Which BM25 Do You Mean? A Large-Scale Reproducibility Study of Scoring Variants. In *Advances in Information Retrieval*; Jose, J.M., Yilmaz, E., Magalhães, J., Castells, P., Ferro, N., Silva, M.J., Martins, F., Eds.; Springer International Publishing: Cham, Switzerland, 2020; pp. 28–34.

27. Mizzaro, S. How many relevances in information retrieval? *Interact. Comput.* **1998**, *10*, 303–320. [CrossRef]

28. Ruthven, I. Relevance behaviour in TREC. *J. Doc.* **2014**, *70*, 1098–1117. [CrossRef]

29. Hofstätter, S.; Lin, S.C.; Yang, J.H.; Lin, J.; Hanbury, A. Efficiently teaching an effective dense retriever with balanced topic aware sampling. In Proceedings of the 44th International ACM SIGIR Conference on Research and Development in Information Retrieval, Virtual Event, 11–15 July 2021; pp. 113–122.

30. Breslow, N.E.; Clayton, D.G. Approximate inference in generalized linear mixed models. *J. Am. Stat. Assoc.* **1993**, *88*, 9–25.

31. McCullagh, P.; Nelder, J.A. *Generalized Linear Models*, 2nd ed.; Chapman and Hall: London, UK, 1989.

32. Dumais, S.T. LSA and information retrieval: Getting back to basics. *Handb. Latent Semant. Anal.* **2007**, *293*, 322.

33. Sarwar, B.; Karypis, G.; Konstan, J.; Riedl, J. *Application of Dimensionality Reduction in Recommender System—A Case Study*; Technical Report; Department of Computer Science and Engineering, University of Minnesota: Minneapolis, MN, USA, 2000.

34. Benzécri, J.P. Statistical analysis as a tool to make patterns emerge from data. In *Methodologies of Pattern Recognition*; Elsevier: Amsterdam, The Netherlands, 1969; pp. 35–74.

35. Ward, J.H., Jr. Hierarchical grouping to optimize an objective function. *J. Am. Stat. Assoc.* **1963**, *58*, 236–244. [CrossRef]

36. Li, B.; Friedman, J.; Olshen, R.; Stone, C. Classification and regression trees (CART). *Biometrics* **1984**, *40*, 358–361.

37. Ho, T.K. Random decision forests. In Proceedings of the 3rd International Conference on Document Analysis and Recognition, Montreal, QC, Canada, 14–16 August 1995; Volume 1, pp. 278–282.

38. Gunning, D. *Explainable Artificial Intelligence*; Defense Advanced Research Projects Agency (DARPA): Arlington, VA, USA, 2017; p. 2.

39. Zhang, Y.; Chen, X. Explainable recommendation: A survey and new perspectives. *Found. Trends® Inf. Retr.* **2020**, *14*, 1–101. [CrossRef]

40. Harman, D. *Overview of the First Text Retrieval Conference (trec-1)*; NIST Special Publication SP: Washington, DC, USA, 1992; pp. 1–532.

41. Harman, D. Overview of the first TREC conference. In Proceedings of the 16th Annual International ACM SIGIR Conference on Research and Development in Information Retrieval, Pittsburgh, PA, USA, 27 June–1 July 1993; pp. 36–47.

42. Buckley, C.; Mitra, M.; Walz, J.A.; Cardie, C. *SMART high precision: TREC 7*; NIST Special Publication SP: Washington, DC, USA, 1999; pp. 285–298.
43. Clarke, C.L.; Craswell, N.; Soboroff, I. *Overview of the Trec 2009 Web Track*; Technical Report; University of Waterloo: Waterloo, ON, Canada, 2009.
44. Collins-Thompson, K.; Macdonald, C.; Bennett, P.; Diaz, F.; Voorhees, E.M. *TREC 2014 Web Track Overview*; Technical Report; University of Michigan: Ann Arbor, MI, USA, 2015.
45. Kompaore, D.; Mothe, J.; Baccini, A.; Dejean, S. Query clustering and IR system detection. Experiments on TREC data. In Proceedings of the ACM International Workshop for Ph. D. Students in Information and Knowledge Management (ACM PIKM 2007), Lisboa, Portugal, 5–10 November 2007.
46. Hanbury, A.; Müller, H. Automated component–level evaluation: Present and future. In *International Conference of the Cross-Language Evaluation Forum for European Languages*; Springer: Berlin/Heidelberg, Germany, 2010; pp. 124–135.
47. Arslan, A.; Dinçer, B.T. A selective approach to index term weighting for robust information retrieval based on the frequency distributions of query terms. *Inf. Retr. J.* **2019**, *22*, 543–569. [CrossRef]
48. Di Buccio, E.; Dussin, M.; Ferro, N.; Masiero, I.; Santucci, G.; Tino, G. Interactive Analysis and Exploration of Experimental Evaluation Results. In *European Workshop on Human-Computer Interaction and Information Retrieval EuroHCIR*; Citeseer: Nijmegen, The Netherlands, 2011; pp. 11–14.
49. Compaoré, J.; Déjean, S.; Gueye, A.M.; Mothe, J.; Randriamparany, J. Mining information retrieval results: Significant IR parameters. In Proceedings of the First International Conference on Advances in Information Mining and Management, Barcelona, Spain, 23–29 October 2011; Volume 74.
50. Hopfgartner, F.; Hanbury, A.; Müller, H.; Eggel, I.; Balog, K.; Brodt, T.; Cormack, G.V.; Lin, J.; Kalpathy-Cramer, J.; Kando, N.; et al. Evaluation-as-a-service for the computational sciences: Overview and outlook. *J. Data Inf. Qual. (JDIQ)* **2018**, *10*, 1–32. [CrossRef]
51. Kürsten, J.; Eibl, M. A large-scale system evaluation on component-level. In *European Conference on Information Retrieval*; Springer: Berlin/Heidelberg, Germany, 2011; pp. 679–682.
52. Angelini, M.; Fazzini, V.; Ferro, N.; Santucci, G.; Silvello, G. CLAIRE: A combinatorial visual analytics system for information retrieval evaluation. *Inf. Process. Manag.* **2018**, *54*, 1077–1100. [CrossRef]
53. Dejean, S.; Mothe, J.; Ullah, M.Z. Studying the variability of system setting effectiveness by data analytics and visualization. In *International Conference of the Cross-Language Evaluation Forum for European Languages*; Springer: Cham, Switzerland, 2019; pp. 62–74.
54. De Loupy, C.; Bellot, P. Evaluation of document retrieval systems and query difficulty. In Proceedings of the Second International Conference on Language Resources and Evaluation (LREC 2000) Workshop, Athens, Greece, 31 May–2 June 2000; pp. 32–39.
55. Banerjee, S.; Pedersen, T. Extended gloss overlaps as a measure of semantic relatedness. In Proceedings of the IJCAI 2003, Acapulco, Mexico, 9–15 August 2003; pp. 805–810.
56. Patwardhan, S.; Pedersen, T. Using WordNet-based context vectors to estimate the semantic relatedness of concepts. In Proceedings of the Workshop on Making Sense of Sense: Bringing Psycholinguistics and Computational Linguistics Together, Trento, Italy, 4 April 2006.
57. Cronen-Townsend, S.; Zhou, Y.; Croft, W.B. Predicting query performance. In Proceedings of the 25th Annual International ACM SIGIR Conference on Research and Development in Information Retrieval, Tampere, Finland, 11–15 August 2002; pp. 299–306.
58. Scholer, F.; Williams, H.E.; Turpin, A. Query association surrogates for web search. *J. Am. Soc. Inf. Sci. Technol.* **2004**, *55*, 637–650. [CrossRef]
59. He, B.; Ounis, I. Inferring query performance using pre-retrieval predictors. In *International Symposium on String Processing and Information Retrieval*; Springer: Berlin/Heidelberg, Germany, 2004; pp. 43–54.
60. Hauff, C.; Hiemstra, D.; de Jong, F. A survey of pre-retrieval query performance predictors. In Proceedings of the 17th ACM Conference on Information and Knowledge Management, Napa Valley, CA, USA, 26–30 October 2008; pp. 1419–1420.
61. Zhao, Y.; Scholer, F.; Tsegay, Y. Effective pre-retrieval query performance prediction using similarity and variability evidence. In *European Conference on Information Retrieval*; Springer: Berlin/Heidelberg, Germany, 2008; pp. 52–64.
62. Sehgal, A.K.; Srinivasan, P. Predicting performance for gene queries. In Proceedings of the ACM SIGIR 2005 Workshop on Predicting Query Difficulty-Methods and Applications. Available online: http://www.haifa.il.ibm.com/sigir05-qp (accessed on 15 May 2022).
63. Zhou, Y.; Croft, W.B. Ranking robustness: A novel framework to predict query performance. In Proceedings of the 15th ACM International Conference on Information and Knowledge Management, Arlington, VA, USA, 6–11 November 2006; pp. 567–574.
64. Vinay, V.; Cox, I.J.; Milic-Frayling, N.; Wood, K. On ranking the effectiveness of searches. In Proceedings of the 29th Annual International ACM SIGIR Conference on Research and Development in Information Retrieval, Seattle,WA, USA, 6–11 August 2006; pp. 398–404.
65. Aslam, J.A.; Pavlu, V. Query hardness estimation using Jensen-Shannon divergence among multiple scoring functions. In *European Conference on Information Retrieval*; Springer: Berlin/Heidelberg, Germany, 2007; pp. 198–209.
66. Zhou, Y.; Croft, W.B. Query performance prediction in web search environments. In Proceedings of the 30th Annual International ACM SIGIR Conference on Research and Development in Information Retrieval, Amsterdam, The Netherlands, 23–27 July 2007; pp. 543–550.

67. Shtok, A.; Kurland, O.; Carmel, D. Predicting query performance by query-drift estimation. In *Conference on the Theory of Information Retrieval*; Springer: Berlin/Heidelberg, Germany, 2009; pp. 305–312.

68. Carmel, D.; Yom-Tov, E. Estimating the query difficulty for information retrieval. *Synth. Lect. Inf. Concepts Retr. Serv.* **2010**, *2*, 1–89.

69. Cummins, R.; Jose, J.; O'Riordan, C. Improved query performance prediction using standard deviation. In Proceedings of the 34th International ACM SIGIR Conference on Research and Development in Information Retrieval, Beijing, China, 24–28 July 2011; pp. 1089–1090.

70. Roitman, H.; Erera, S.; Weiner, B. Robust standard deviation estimation for query performance prediction. In Proceedings of the ACM SIGIR International Conference on Theory of Information Retrieval, Amsterdam, The Netherlands, 1–4 October 2017; pp. 245–248.

71. Chifu, A.G.; Laporte, L.; Mothe, J.; Ullah, M.Z. Query performance prediction focused on summarized letor features. In Proceedings of the 41st International ACM SIGIR Conference on Research & Development in Information Retrieval, Ann Arbor, MI, USA, 8–12 July 2018; pp. 1177–1180.

72. Zhang, Z.; Chen, J.; Wu, S. Query performance prediction and classification for information search systems. In *Asia-Pacific Web (APWeb) and Web-Age Information Management (WAIM) Joint International Conference on Web and Big Data*; Springer: Cham, Switzerland, 2018; pp. 277–285.

73. Khodabakhsh, M.; Bagheri, E. Semantics-enabled query performance prediction for ad hoc table retrieval. *Inf. Process. Manag.* **2021**, *58*, 102399. [CrossRef]

74. Molina, S.; Mothe, J.; Roques, D.; Tanguy, L.; Ullah, M.Z. IRIT-QFR: IRIT query feature resource. In *International Conference of the Cross-Language Evaluation Forum for European Languages*; Springer: Cham, Switzerland, 2017; pp. 69–81.

75. Macdonald, C.; He, B.; Ounis, I. Predicting query performance in intranet search. In Proceedings of the SIGIR 2005 Query Prediction Workshop, Salvador, Brazil, 15–19 August 2005.

76. Faggioli, G.; Zendel, O.; Culpepper, J.S.; Ferro, N.; Scholer, F. sMARE: A new paradigm to evaluate and understand query performance prediction methods. *Inf. Retr. J.* **2022**, *25*, 94–122. [CrossRef]

77. Hashemi, H.; Zamani, H.; Croft, W.B. Performance Prediction for Non-Factoid Question Answering. In Proceedings of the 2019 ACM SIGIR International Conference on Theory of Information Retrieval, Paris, France, 21–25 July 2019; pp. 55–58.

78. Roy, D.; Ganguly, D.; Mitra, M.; Jones, G.J. Estimating Gaussian mixture models in the local neighbourhood of embedded word vectors for query performance prediction. *Inf. Process. Manag.* **2019**, *56*, 1026–1045. [CrossRef]

79. Anscombe, F. American Statistical Association, Taylor & Francis, Ltd. are collaborating with JSTOR to. *Am. Stat.* **1973**, *27*, 17–21.

80. Grivolla, J.; Jourlin, P.; de Mori, R. *Automatic Classification of Queries by Expected Retrieval Performance*; SIGIR: Salvador, Brazil, 2005.

81. Raiber, F.; Kurland, O. Query-performance prediction: Setting the expectations straight. In Proceedings of the 37th International ACM SIGIR Conference on Research & Development in Information Retrieval, Gold Coast, Australia, 6–11 July 2014; pp. 13–22.

82. Mizzaro, S.; Mothe, J.; Roitero, K.; Ullah, M.Z. Query performance prediction and effectiveness evaluation without relevance judgments: Two sides of the same coin. In Proceedings of the 41st International ACM SIGIR Conference on Research & Development in Information Retrieval, Ann Arbor, MI, USA, 8–12 July 2018; pp. 1233–1236.

83. Aslam, J.A.; Savell, R. On the Effectiveness of Evaluating Retrieval Systems in the Absence of Relevance Judgments. In Proceedings of the 26th ACM SIGIR, Toronto, ON, Canada, 28 July–1 August 2003; pp. 361–362.

84. Baccini, A.; Déjean, S.; Lafage, L.; Mothe, J. How many performance measures to evaluate information retrieval systems? *Knowl. Inf. Syst.* **2012**, *30*, 693–713. [CrossRef]

85. Amati, G.; Carpineto, C.; Romano, G. Query difficulty, robustness, and selective application of query expansion. In *European Conference on Information Retrieval*; Springer: Berlin/Heidelberg, Germany, 2004; pp. 127–137.

86. Cronen-Townsend, S.; Zhou, Y.; Croft, W.B. A framework for selective query expansion. In Proceedings of the Thirteenth ACM International Conference on Information and Knowledge Management, Washington, DC, USA, 8–13 November 2004; pp. 236–237.

87. Zhao, L.; Callan, J. Automatic term mismatch diagnosis for selective query expansion. In Proceedings of the 35th International ACM SIGIR Conference on Research and Development in Information Retrieval, Portland, OR, USA, 12–16 August 2012; pp. 515–524.

88. Deveaud, R.; Mothe, J.; Ullah, M.Z.; Nie, J.Y. Learning to Adaptively Rank Document Retrieval System Configurations. *ACM Trans. Inf. Syst. (TOIS)* **2018**, *37*, 3. [CrossRef]

89. Bigot, A.; Déjean, S.; Mothe, J. Learning to Choose the Best System Configuration in Information Retrieval: The Case of Repeated Queries. *J. Univers. Comput. Sci.* **2015**, *21*, 1726–1745.

90. Deveaud, R.; Mothe, J.; Nia, J.Y. Learning to Rank System Configurations. In Proceedings of the 25th ACM International on Conference on Information and Knowledge Management, CIKM '16, Indianapolis, IN, USA, 24–28 October 2016; ACM: New York, NY, USA, 2016; pp. 2001–2004.

91. Mothe, J.; Ullah, M.Z. Defining an Optimal Configuration Set for Selective Search Strategy-A Risk-Sensitive Approach. In Proceedings of the 30th ACM International Conference on Information & Knowledge Management, Online, 1–5 November 2021; pp. 1335–1345.

*Article*

# On the Use of Morpho-Syntactic Description Tags in Neural Machine Translation with Small and Large Training Corpora

Gregor Donaj * and Mirjam Sepesy Maučec

Faculty of Electrical Engineering and Computer Science, University of Maribor,
SI-2000 Maribor, Slovenia; mirjam.sepesy@um.si
* Correspondence: gregor.donaj@um.si; Tel.: +386-2-220-7205

**Abstract:** With the transition to neural architectures, machine translation achieves very good quality for several resource-rich languages. However, the results are still much worse for languages with complex morphology, especially if they are low-resource languages. This paper reports the results of a systematic analysis of adding morphological information into neural machine translation system training. Translation systems presented and compared in this research exploit morphological information from corpora in different formats. Some formats join semantic and grammatical information and others separate these two types of information. Semantic information is modeled using lemmas and grammatical information using Morpho-Syntactic Description (MSD) tags. Experiments were performed on corpora of different sizes for the English–Slovene language pair. The conclusions were drawn for a domain-specific translation system and for a translation system for the general domain. With MSD tags, we improved the performance by up to 1.40 and 1.68 BLEU points in the two translation directions. We found that systems with training corpora in different formats improve the performance differently depending on the translation direction and corpora size.

**Keywords:** neural machine translation; POS tags; MSD tags; inflected language; data sparsity; corpora size

**MSC:** 68T50

**Citation:** Donaj, G.; Sepesy Maučec, M. On the Use of Morpho-Syntactic Description Tags in Neural Machine Translation with Small and Large Training Corpora. *Mathematics* **2022**, *10*, 1608. https://doi.org/10.3390/math10091608

Academic Editors: Florentina Hristea and Cornelia Caragea

Received: 31 January 2022
Accepted: 6 May 2022
Published: 9 May 2022

**Publisher's Note:** MDPI stays neutral with regard to jurisdictional claims in published maps and institutional affiliations.

## 1. Introduction

In the last decade, research in machine translation has seen the transition from statistical models to neural net-based models for most mainstream languages and also some other languages. At the same time, researchers and developers got access to more and more parallel corpora, which are essential for training machine translation systems. However, many languages can still be considered low-resource languages.

Before the widespread use of neural machine translation (NMT), statistical machine translation (SMT) was the predominant approach. Additional linguistic information was added to deal with data sparsity or the morphological complexity of some languages. Often part-of-speech (POS) or morpho-syntactic description (MSD) tags were included in SMT systems in some way or the other. The tags can be included on the source side, the target side, or on both sides of the translation direction. This can be done either in the alignment or the training and translation phase.

Since the emergence of NMT, relatively few studies have explored the use of additional linguistic information for machine translation.

In this paper, we want to give an overview of the available studies and present experiments on using MSD tags for the translation between English and Slovene, a morphologically complex language. In order to provide a more comprehensive look at the usefulness of MSD tags, we perform several sets of experiments on a general domain corpus and a domain-specific corpus by using different training corpora sizes and methods to include MSD tags. In addition, we explore possibilities to reduce MSD tags, which can become rather complex in morphologically rich languages.

The rest of the paper is organized as follows. In Section 2 we present related work in machine translation and morphology. In Section 3 we present our experimental system, the used corpora, all corpora pre-processing steps, and the designed experiments. The results of the experiments are presented in Section 4 and discussed in Section 5. Our conclusions are presented in Section 6.

## 2. Related Work

### 2.1. Machine Translation

At first, machine translation was guided by rules. Corpus-based approaches followed. They were notably better and easier to use than the preceding rule-based technologies. Statistical machine translation (SMT) [1] is a corpus-based approach, where translations are generated on the basis of statistical models whose parameters are derived from the analysis of bilingual and monolingual text corpora. For a long time, SMT was the dominant approach with the best results. Migration from SMT to neural machine translation (NMT) started in 2013. In [2], a first attempt was made, where a class of probabilistic continuous translation models was defined that was purely based on continuous representations for words, phrases, and sentences and did not rely on alignments or phrasal translation units like in SMT. Their models obtain a perplexity with respect to gold translations that was more than 43% lower than that of the state-of-the-art SMT models. Using NMT was, in general, a significant step forward in machine translation quality. NMT is an approach to machine translation that uses an artificial neural network. Unlike SMT systems, which have separate knowledge models (i.e., language model, translation model, and reordering model), all parts of the NMT model are trained jointly in a large neural model. Since 2015, NMT systems have been shown to perform better than SMT systems for many language pairs [3,4]. For example, NMT generates outputs that lower the overall post-edit effort with respect to the best PBMT system by 26% for the German–English language pair [5]. NMT outperformed SMT in terms of automatic scores and human evaluation for German, Greek, and Russian [6]. In recent years NMT has also been applied to inflectional languages such as Slovene, Serbian, and Croatian. Experiments in [7] showed that on a reduced training dataset with around two million sentences, SMT outperformed the NMT neural models for those languages. In [8], NMT regularly outperformed SMT for the Slovene–English language pair. In the present paper, we will more systematically analyze NMT performance using training corpora of different sizes.

### 2.2. Neural Machine Translation

Neural machine translation is based on the recurrent neural network (RNN), which is a generalization of feedforward neural networks to sequences. Given a sentence in the source language as an input sequence of words $(x_1, \ldots, x_T)$, the RNN computes an output sequence of words $(y_i, \ldots, y_{T'})$ by using the equations:

$$h_t = \text{sigm}(W^{hx}x_t + W^{hh}h_{t-1})$$
$$y_t = W^{yh}h_t, \tag{1}$$

where $W^{hx}$, $W^{hh}$, and $W^{yh}$ are parameter matrices from the input layer to the hidden layer, from the hidden layer to itself, and from the hidden layer to the output layer; while $x_t$, $h_t$, and $y_t$ denote the input, hidden, and output layer vectors at word $t$ respectively.

The output sequence is a translation in the target language. The RNN presumes an alignment between the input and the output sequence, which is unknown. Furthermore, input and output sequences have different lengths. The solution is to map the input sequence to a fixed-sized vector using one RNN and then another RNN to map the vector to the target sequence. Another important phenomenon in natural languages is long-term dependencies which have been successfully modeled by using long short-term memory (LSTM) [9].

The goal of the LSTM is to estimate the conditional probability $p(y_1, \ldots, y_{T'} | x_1, \ldots, x_T)$, where $(x_1, \ldots, x_T)$ is an input sequence, and $(y_i, \ldots, y_{T'})$ is an output sequence, which can be of a different length than the input sequence. First, the LSTM obtains the fixed-dimensional representation $v$ of the input sequence $(x_1, \ldots, x_T)$ from the last hidden state. Then, the probability of $(y_i, \ldots, y'_T)$ is computed with another LSTM whose initial hidden state is $v$:

$$p(y_1, \ldots, y_{T'} | x_1, \ldots, x_T) = \prod_{t=1}^{T'} p(y_t | v, y_1, \ldots, y_{t-1}). \tag{2}$$

Here, $p(y_t | v, y_1, \ldots, y_{t-1})$ is represented with a softmax function over all words in the vocabulary.

Not all parts of the input sequence are relevant to producing an output word. The concept of attention was introduced to identify parts of the input sequence that are relevant [10]. The context vector $c_t$ captures relevant input information to help predict the current target word $y_t$. Given the target hidden state $h_t$ and the context vector $c_t$, a simple concatenation layer is used to combine the information from both vectors to produce a hidden attentional state:

$$\tilde{h}_t = \tanh(W_c[c_t, h_t]). \tag{3}$$

The attentional vector $\tilde{h}_t$ is then fed through the softmax layer:

$$p(y_t | v, y_1, \ldots, y_{t-1}) = \mathrm{softmax}(W_s \tilde{h}_t). \tag{4}$$

LSTM helps to deal with long sequences, but still, it fails to maintain the global information of the source sentence. Afterward, the transformer architecture was proposed, which handles the entire input sequence at once and does not iterate only word by word. The superior performance of transformer architecture was reported in [11].

### 2.3. Morphology of Inflected Language

Morphology is very important in machine translation as it directly affects the complexity and performance of a translation system. Among morphologically rich languages are inflected languages. In an inflected language, the lexical information for each word form may be augmented with information concerning the grammatical function, pronominal clitics, and inflectional affixes. As a result, the number of different word forms grows. Due to the high level of morphological variation, we may not find all morphological variants of a word even in very large corpora. When developing machine translation systems, we have to deal with data sparsity and high out-of-vocabulary rates.

The rich morphology in an inflected language permits a flexible word order because grammatical information is encoded within a word form. In English, grammatical information is expressed implicitly by word order and adjacency.

The complexity of the linguistic patterns found in inflected languages was shown to challenge machine translation in many ways. Translation results for inflected languages were much worse than for morphologically poor languages. Machine translation systems have been developed that take morphological information into account in one way or another. There is a big difference between translation from an inflected language and translation to an inflected language. If we are translating from an inflected language to English, the sparsity caused by the rich morphology of the source language is reduced in the translation process. However, if we are translating to an inflected language, the morphology of the target language needs to be generated in the translation process. Machine translation systems perform better in the former case. In this paper, we analyze these differences.

### 2.4. Morphological Information in SMT

Morphologically rich languages were extensively studied in the scope of phrase-based SMT. A factored translation model was proposed [1] as an extension of phrase-based SMT for incorporating any additional annotation to words, including morphological information, at decoding time. In factored models, a word is not a token but a vector of factors. Usually, factors in each word are the surface form of a word, lemma, POS tag, additional morphological information, etc. Factored models use more than one translation step and one generation step. Each translation step corresponds to one factor, e.g., lemma, POS factor, MSD feature vector, etc. Translation from the sequence of factors on the source side to the sequence of factors on the target side is trained. In the generation step, translated factors are combined into the final surface form of a word. Factored model training uses factors the same way as words in word-based models. In [1], gains of up to 2 BLEU points were reported for factored models over standard phrase-based models for the English–German language pair. Grammatical coherence was also improved.

In [12] a noisier channel is proposed, which extends the usual noisy channel metaphor by suggesting that an "English" source signal is first distorted into a morphologically neutral language. Then morphological processes represent a further distortion of the signal, which can be modeled independently. Noisier channel implementation uses the information extracted from surface word forms, lemmatized forms, and truncated forms. Truncated forms are generated using a length limit of six characters. This means that the maximum of the first six characters of each word is taken into account, and the rest is discarded. Hierarchical grammar rules are then induced for each type of information. Finally, all three grammars are combined, and a hierarchical phrase-based decoder is built. The authors reported a 10% relative improvement of the BLEU metric when translating into English from Czech, a language with considerable inflectional complexity.

In [13] the focus is on the three common morphological problems: gender, number, and the determiner clitic. The translation is performed in multiple steps, which differ from the steps used in factored translation. The decoding procedure is not changed. Only the training corpus is enriched with new features: lemmas, POS tags, and morphological features. Classic phrase-based SMT models are trained on this enriched corpus. They afterward use conditional random fields for morphological class prediction. They reported improvement of BLEU by 1 point on a medium-size training set (approximately 5 million words) for translation from English to Arabic.

In [14,15] the quality of SMT was improved by applying models that predict word forms from their stems using extensive morphological and syntactic information from both the source and target languages. Their inflection generation model was the maximum entropy Markov model, and it was trained independently of the SMT system. The authors reported a small BLEU improvement (<0.5) when translating from English to Russian and a larger BLEU improvement of 2 when translating English to Arabic. A similar approach was used in [16]. They trained a discriminative model to predict inflections of target words from rich source-side annotations. They also used their model to generate artificial word-level and phrase-level translations, that were added to the translation model. The authors reported BLEU improvement by 2 points when translating from English to Russian.

*2.5. Morphological Information in NMT*

In 2013, NMT emerged [2]. The NMT models did not achieve a good performance at the beginning because they were unable to handle the long-distance dependencies. With the introduction of long short-term memory [9] the results improved because, thanks to the gate mechanism, long-distance dependencies in a sentence were captured much better. Although translation results improved considerably, morphologically rich languages remain a challenge. The better translation capability of NMT models does not make linguistic features redundant. In some papers, they were incorporated to provide further performance improvements.

Factored representations of words were considered as input features [17]. The linguistic features improved results by 1.5 BLEU for Germain to English, 0.6 BLEU for English to German, and 1.0 BLEU for English to Romanian translation. The authors used 4.2 million sentence pairs for training the systems between English and German, and 0.6 million sentence pairs between English and Romanian. Using additional synthetic parallel data, they again achieved comparable improvements.

Lemma and morphological factors were also used as output features [18,19]. Results for English to French translation were improved by more than 1.0 BLEU using a training corpus with 2 million sentence pairs. They also used an approach that generates new words controlled by linguistic knowledge. They halved the number of unknown words in the output. Using factors in the output reduces the target side vocabulary and allows the model to generate word forms that were never seen in the training data [18]. A factored system can support a larger vocabulary because it can generate words from the lemma and factors vocabularies, which is advantageous when data is sparse.

The decoder learns considerably less morphology than the encoder in the NMT architecture. In [20], the authors found that the decoder needs assistance from the encoder and the attention mechanism to generate correct target morphology. Three ways to explicitly inject morphology in the decoder were explored: joint generation, joint-data learning, and multi-task learning. Multi-task learning outperformed the other two methods. A 0.2 BLEU improvement was reported for English to Czech translation. Authors argued that by having larger corpora, the improvement would be larger.

Unseen words can also be generated by using character-level NMT or sub-word units, determined by the byte-pair encoding (BPE) algorithm [21]. Character-level NMT outperformed NMT with BPE sub-words when processing unknown words, but it performed worse than BPE-based systems when translating long-range phenomena of morpho-syntactic agreement. Another possibility is to use morpheme-based segmentations [22]. A new architecture was proposed to enrich character-based NMT with morphological information in a morphology table as an external knowledge source [23]. Morphology tables increase the capacity of the model by increasing the number of network parameters. The proposed extension improved BLEU by 0.55 for English to Russian translation using 2.1 million sentence pairs in the training corpus.

The authors in [24] also investigate different factors on the target side. Their experiments include three representations varying in the quantity of grammatical information they contain. In the first representation, all the lexical and grammatical information was encoded in a single factor. In the second representation, only a well-chosen subset of morphological features was kept in the first factor, and the second factor corresponded to the POS tag. In the third representation, the first factor was a lemma, and the second was the POS tag. In some experiments, BPE splitting was also used. They reported that carefully selected morphological information improved the translation results by 0.56 BLEU for English to Czech translation and 0.89 BLEU for English to Latvian translation.

In [25], the authors focused on information about the subject's gender. For regular source language, words were annotated with grammatical gender information of the corresponding target language words. Information about gender improved the BLEU results by 0.4.

Most often, NMT systems rely only on large amounts of raw text data and do not use any additional knowledge source. Linguistically motivated systems can help to overcome data sparsity, generalize, and disambiguate, especially when the dataset is small.

*2.6. Aim and Research Contribution*

A literature review shows the potential of linguistic information for many highly inflected languages. However, we are not aware of any such research for the Slovene–English language pair in the scope of neural machine translation.

Some researchers noticed the correlation between the training corpus size and the improvement brought by linguistic features. Others may compare only a few different formats of adding linguistic features. However, they did not go into detail or perform a systematic comparison.

This paper aims to provide a more extensive analysis of the use of MSD tags in NMT between English and highly inflected Slovene language. The idea of our approach is to focus on data preparation rather than on NMT architecture. We used the same NMT architecture through all experiments. We only modify the data used for training the NMT systems, similarly to some systems presented in [20]. The advantage of our approach is that it can be easily transferred to other language pairs, as appropriate tools for lemmatization and MSD tagging are already available for several morphologically complex languages.

The literature review also shows that often changes in the architecture of the models are required, or that special translation tools are used, which enable a factored representation of the input tokens. However, the most widely used NMT tools do not enable such a representation. Thus, our approach can be more easily included in practical applications, such as the use of the OPUS-MT plugin for translation tools, which uses Marian NMT [26].

The main contributions of this paper are: (1) a review of literature on using morphological information in SMT and NMT; (2) an empirical comparison of the influence of different types of morphologically tagged corpora on translation results in both translation directions separately; (3) a comparison of the effect of morphologically pre-processed training corpora with regard to the training corpus size; (4) a comparison of results obtained on domain-specific corpus and general corpus.

## 3. Methods

### 3.1. Corpora

In our experiments, we used the freely available Europarl and ParaCrawls corpora for the English–Slovene language pair. Both can be downloaded at the OPUS collection website (https://opus.nlpl.eu/, accessed on 28 January 2022).

Europarl is extracted from the proceedings of the European Parliament and is considered a domain-specific corpus. It consists of approximately 600,000 aligned parallel segments of text. ParaCrawl was built by Web Crawling and automatic alignment. We consider it to be a more general domain corpus. It consists of approximately 3.7 million aligned segments of text. Both corpora are available for several language pairs. The above sizes refer to the English–Slovene language pair. Experiments were performed in the same way separately on both corpora. Therefore, all processing steps apply the same way for both corpora.

We divided the corpora into three parts by using 2000 randomly selected segment pairs as the development set, another 2000 randomly selected segment pairs as the evaluation set and the remaining segments as the training set. For some later experiments, we further divided the training set into ten equally sized parts.

### 3.2. Standard Pre-Processing

We performed the standard corpus pre-processing steps for machine translation training: cleanup, punctuation normalization, tokenization, and truecasing. During these steps, some segments were excluded due to their excessive length. The final sizes of all datasets are shown in Table 1.

**Table 1.** Number of segments (sentences) in each dataset.

| Dataset Part | Europarl | ParaCrawl |
|---|---|---|
| Training | 618,516 | 3,714,473 |
| Development | 1993 | 1987 |
| Evaluation | 1991 | 1990 |
| Total | 622,500 | 3,718,450 |

Punctuation normalization mainly ensures the correct placing of spaces around punctuation symbols and replaces some UTF-8 punctuation symbols with their ASCII counterparts. The most significant effect from the pre-processing steps can be seen between the normalized text (which after post-processing is also called de-truecased and de-tokenized text) and the tokenized and truecased text. A couple of examples from the ParaCrawl corpus are presented in Table 2. From them, we see that tokenization separates punctuation symbols into separate tokens by inserting spaces around them. Note, that in the second example, the point (".") is not tokenized, as it is used as a decimal symbol. Truecasing then converts all words to their lowercase forms, unless they are proper names.

De-truecasing and de-tokenization is the reverse process, i.e., rejoining punctuation symbols and capitalizing the first word in a segment (sentence). These steps are done in the post-processing stage in order to obtain a translation in the normalized form according to the grammar of the target language.

**Table 2.** Comparison between normalized segments (NM), and tokenized and truecased segments (TC).

| Form | Segment |
|------|---------|
| NM | After the fourth hour, Moda plays a major role. |
| TC | After the fourth hour, Moda plays a major role . |
| NM | User manual PDF file, 2.6 MB, published 19 October 2018 |
| TC | User manual PDF file, 2.6 MB, published 19 October 2018 |

*3.3. MSD Tagging and Lemmatization*

Part-of-speech (POS) tagging is the process of assigning POS tags to each word in a text. In morphologically rich languages, these tags are often referred to as morpho-syntactic description (MSD) tags. POS tags for English usually convey the part of speech of a word, and for some words type, degree (comparative, superlative), and number (singular or plural). MSD tags in Slovene, however, convey much more information: POS, type, number, case, gender, person, degree, etc. Consequently, MSD tags in Slovene are more complex and numerous.

For simplicity, we will refer to the tags in both languages as MSD tags.

Lemmatization is the process of assigning a lemma (the word's canonical form) to each word in a text. For example, the lemma "be" is the lemma for: am, are, is, was, were, etc. In English, words have a relatively small number of different surface word forms, mainly varying by number and tense. In Slovene, on the other hand, the main parts of speech (nouns, adjectives, and verbs) and pronouns vary by case, gender, number, person, and tense. This results in a higher number of different surface word forms.

We tagged and lemmatized all datasets using a statistical tagger and lemmatizer. For English, the tagger was trained on the Penn treebank using a modified Penn treebank tagset (https://www.sketchengine.eu/modified-penn-treebank-tagset, accessed on 28 January 2022), and for Slovene, the tagger was trained on the ssj500k training corpus [27] using the tagset defined in the JOS project [28]. Since the tagger was developed to work on standard text input, it has its own tokenizer built in. Therefore, we used the normalized text as the input for the tagger.

Table 3 shows the same sentence in English and Slovene in three forms: surface word forms, lemmatized text, and MSD tags. The complexity of the Slovene MSD tags can already be seen by their length, as each letter in the tag corresponds to one attribute of the given word.

**Table 3.** Example of a MSD tagged and lemmatized sentence in English (EN) and Slovene (SL).

| Language | Form | Text | | |
|----------|------|------|------|------|
| EN | Words | You | went | away |
| | Lemmas | you | go | away |
| | MSD Tags | PP | VVD | RB |
| SL | Words | Ti | si | odšel |
| | Lemmas | ti | biti | oditi |
| | MSD Tags | Zod-ei | Gp-sde-n | Ggdd-em |

The English tagset defines 58 different MSD tags for words and punctuations, all of which appear in the used corpora. The Slovene tagset defines 1902 different MSD tags.

However, only 1263 of them appear in the Europarl training corpus, and 1348 of them appear in the ParaCrawl training corpus.

### 3.4. Corpora Formats and Translation Combinations

The surface word-form corpora serve us as the basic format. We then used the tagged and lemmatized corpora to build corpora in five additional formats for each dataset by using different methods for constructing the final segments. The formats are as follows.

1. W: Surface word forms after tokenization and truecasing.
2. W+M: Words and MSD tags were written alternately as separate tokens.
3. WM: Words and MSD tags were written concatenated as one token.
4. L+M: Lemmas and MSD tags were written alternately as separate tokens
5. LM: Lemmas and MSD tags were written concatenated as one token.
6. WW-MM: Words were written consecutively, followed by a special tag, and then MSD tags were written consecutively.

We used the second format (W+M) as the most straightforward format to add morphological information. We then also wanted to explore the difference if the MSD tag is a separate token in the training and translation processes or not. However, from a combination of the lemma and the MSD tag of a word, we can replicate the surface word form. Additionally, in inflected languages, different lemmas can give the same surface form, e.g., there are some such pairs of adjectives and adverbs. Thus, the combination of a lemma and MSD tag can give the same amount of information as the combination of a word and MSD tag. Lastly, we explored the possibility of writing the MSD tags as an almost separate string and the end of the sentence, similar to one of the systems in [20].

Table 4 shows an example segment from the English Europarl corpus in all six formats. Surface word forms were unchanged, while lemmas and MSD tags were tagged with "LEM:" and "MSD:", respectively. Concatenation in the formats WM and LM were done with a hyphen. Surface word forms and MSD tags in the format WW-MM were divided with the tag "<MSD>".

**Table 4.** An example segment in the different formats of the corpora.

| Format | Segment |
|--------|---------|
| W | let us be honest . |
| W+M | let MSD:VV us MSD:PP be MSD:VB honest MSD:JJ . MSD:. |
| WM | let-MSD:VV us-MSD:PP be-MSD:VB honest-MSD:JJ .-MSD:. |
| L+M | LEM:let MSD:VV LEM:us MSD:PP LEM:be MSD:VB LEM:honest MSD:JJ LEM:. MSD:SENT |
| LM | LEM:let-MSD:VV LEM:us-MSD:PP LEM:be-MSD:VB LEM:honest-MSD:JJ LEM:.-MSD:SENT |
| WW-MM | let us be honest . <MSD> MSD:VV MSD:PP MSD:VB MSD:JJ MSD:. |

We build word-based vocabularies from both training corpora, containing 60,000 words on each translation side for the experiments with the Europarl corpus and 200,000 words on each side in the experiments with the ParaCrawl corpus.

The reason for the different sizes lies in the different text coverages given a particular vocabulary size. Table 5 shows the out-of-vocabulary (OOV) rates on the evaluation set in both corpora. We see that those rates are far lower in the domain-specific corpus Europarl. The remaining OOV rate at the larger vocabularies is due to words that do not appear in the training set at all. On the other hand, the OOV rates are higher in the general-domain corpus ParaCrawl, where a more diverse vocabulary is to be expected. Therefore, a more extensive vocabulary is needed to obtain reasonable results. From the data, we also see that OOV rates are significantly greater in Slovene, which is due to the high number of word forms.

**Table 5.** Out-of-vocabulary rates on both corpora for differently sized vocabularies.

| Vocabulary Size | ParaCrawl OOV Rate (%) | | Europarl OOV Rate (%) | |
|---|---|---|---|---|
| | Slovene | English | Slovene | English |
| 60k | 6.66 | 2.57 | 1.05 | 0.16 |
| 100k | 4.44 | 1.77 | 0.55 | 0.14 |
| 200k | 2.53 | 1.09 | 0.34 | 0.14 |
| 300k | 1.82 | 0.85 | 0.34 | 0.14 |

For the systems that use MSD tags as separate tokens (W+M, WW-MM), the vocabulary was simply extended with the MSD tags. In the system which uses the words and MSD tags concatenated to one token (WM), the vocabulary was extended so far that it includes all words in the original vocabulary in combination with all possible corresponding MSD tags that appear in the training set. Some word forms can have different grammatical categories. For example, feminine gender words ending in "-e" typically can have four different tags given their case and number: (1) singular and dative, (2) singular and locative, (3) dual and nominative, and (4) dual and accusative. This is similarly true for most words (primarily other nouns, adjectives, and verbs). Hence, the size of the vocabulary increases substantially for concatenated combinations.

In the systems using lemmas instead of words, the vocabularies are similarly built. The final sizes of all used vocabularies are presented in Table 6.

**Table 6.** Final vocabulary sizes on all tagged formats of the corpora.

| Corpora Format | Europarl Vocabulary Size | | ParaCrawl Vocabulary Size | |
|---|---|---|---|---|
| | Slovene | English | Slovene | English |
| Baseline | 60,000 | 60,000 | 200,000 | 200,000 |
| W+M | 61,263 | 60,058 | 201,348 | 200,058 |
| WM | 140,738 | 73,332 | 500,000 | 242,589 |
| L+M | 57,518 | 50,200 | 201,373 | 200,058 |
| LM | 211,499 | 71,943 | 500,000 | 313,135 |
| WW-MM | 61,264 | 60,059 | 201,349 | 200,059 |

Often BPE or other data-driven methods for splitting words into subword units are used to improve the results of NMT. However, since those methods are not linguistically informed, they can produce erroneous surface forms by concatenating incompatible subword units. Also, the generation of MSD tags is based on full word forms and cannot be performed on subword units. For this reason, we decided to avoid using data-driven segmentation in our paper.

*3.5. Training and Evaluation*

Having six formats of the corpora with the accompanying vocabularies on each translation side, we were able to build 36 translation systems for all possible combinations of any format on the source side and any format on the target side. The system, which contains only the surface word forms on both the source and target side, is the baseline system. The other 35 systems will be evaluated and compared to it.

The system was a neural net-based translation system, using a recurrent neural network-based encode–decoder architecture with 512 dimensions for the encoding vector and 1024 as the dimension for the hidden RNN states. The models were trained on all the possible training data format combinations. The training duration was limited to 20 epochs, and the development set was used for verification during the training process. Finally, the model update which gave the best results on the development set was kept. The model hyperparameters and other options for the training tools were kept at their default values for all experiments. The only exception was the maximal allowed sentence length which had to be doubled in all experiments that used MSD tags as separate tokens.

We used BLEU for the validation during training and the final evaluation of the models. BLEU is a widely used metric to evaluate the performance of machine translation systems, and it is defined by

$$BLEU = \min\left\{1, \frac{len_o}{len_r}\right\} \cdot \left(\prod_{i=1}^{4} prec_i\right)^{\frac{1}{4}}, \qquad (5)$$

where $len_o$ is the length of the evaluated translation, $len_r$ is the length of the reference translation, and $prec_i$ is the ratio between the number matched $n$-grams and the number of total $n$-grams of order $i$ between the reference translation and the evaluated translation.

The machine translation output was post-processed: de-truecased and de-tokenized during validation and final evaluation. Post-processing also included removing MSD tags, the special tag in format WW-MM. In the two systems that generated the lemma and MSD tag on the target side, we also had to employ a model that would determine the correct worm form.

Additionally, we performed statistical significance tests on all results compared to the baseline results. We used the paired bootstrap resampling test [29], a widely used test in machine translation with a $p$-value threshold value of 0.05 [12,13,17,23,25].

### 3.6. MSD Tag Reduction

Due to the high number of different MSD tags in Slovene, we also designed experiments using reduced MSD tags, that retain only the most important information. This was done only on the Slovene part of the corpora.

To construct the rules for MSD reduction, we used grammatical knowledge. For the main parts of speech, information was retained based on which the correct word form can be determined. These are the case, number, gender, and person. MSD tags for the minor parts of speech were reduced to the mere POS tag and sometimes the type. Table 7 shows a segment with full and reduced MSD tags.

**Table 7.** An example segment tagged with full and reduced MSD tags.

| Form | Segment | | | | | | |
|------|---------|---|---|---|---|---|---|
| Words | Gospod | predsednik | , | hvala | za | besedo | . |
| Full MSD tags | Ncmsn | Ncmsn | , | Ncfsn | Sa | Ncfsa | . |
| Reduced MSD tags | Nmsn | Nmsn | , | Nfsn | Sa | Nfsa | . |

The reduction of the MSD tag complexity resulted in a decreased number of different tags. In the Europarl training corpus, the number was reduced from 1263 to 418, and in the ParaCrawl training corpus from 1348 to 428.

### 3.7. Tools

In the pre-processing and post-processing steps, we used several scripts, which are part of the MOSES statistical machine translation toolkit [30]. Those steps are cleanup, tokenization, truecasing, de-truecasing, and de-tokenization. We used the SacreBLEU [31] evaluation tool for scoring and statistical tests.

MSD tagging and lemmatization were performed using TreeTagger [32] and the accompanying pre-trained models for Slovene and English.

Translation model training and translation were performed using Marian NMT [33] on NVIDIA A100 graphical processing units.

## 4. Results

### 4.1. Translation Systems

Table 8 shows translation results from English to Slovene for all combinations of corpora formats, and Table 9 shows the results for the same experiments from Slovene to

English on the Europarl corpus. In both cases, the result in the first line and first column is the baseline result (surface word form).

Below all results, we show $p$-values for the paired bootstrap resampling test between the given result and the baseline result.

**Table 8.** BLEU scores and $p$-values for the translations from English to Slovene for different systems on the Europarl corpus.

| Source Form | Target Form | | | | | |
|---|---|---|---|---|---|---|
| | **W** | **W+M** | **WM** | **L+M** | **LM** | **WW-MM** |
| W | 35.97 | 37.17 | 36.77 | 36.96 | 34.78 | 36.78 |
| | | $p < 0.001$ | $p = 0.003$ | $p = 0.002$ | $p = 0.001$ | $p = 0.004$ |
| W+M | 37.12 | 37.37 | 37.18 | 36.88 | 35.90 | 37.28 |
| | $p < 0.001$ | $p < 0.001$ | $p < 0.001$ | $p = 0.003$ | $p = 0.319$ | $p < 0.001$ |
| WM | 36.48 | 37.21 | 36.14 | 36.16 | 35.15 | 36.67 |
| | $p = 0.037$ | $p < 0.001$ | $p = 0.195$ | $p = 0.188$ | $p = 0.008$ | $p = 0.012$ |
| L+M | 37.24 | 36.57 | 36.73 | 36.31 | 34.92 | 36.66 |
| | $p < 0.001$ | $p = 0.033$ | $p = 0.011$ | $p = 0.117$ | $p = 0.001$ | $p = 0.011$ |
| LM | 35.90 | 36.20 | 35.77 | 35.52 | 33.64 | 36.01 |
| | $p = 0.305$ | $p = 0.158$ | $p = 0.202$ | $p = 0.071$ | $p < 0.001$ | $p = 0.342$ |
| WW-MM | 23.83 | 27.84 | 25.03 | 36.71 | 23.91 | 28.51 |
| | $p < 0.001$ | $p < 0.001$ | $p < 0.001$ | $p = 0.014$ | $p < 0.001$ | $p < 0.001$ |

**Table 9.** BLEU scores and $p$-values for the translations from Slovene to English for different systems on the Europarl corpus.

| Source Form | Target Form | | | | | |
|---|---|---|---|---|---|---|
| | **W** | **W+M** | **WM** | **L+M** | **LM** | **WW-MM** |
| W | 40.35 | 40.48 | 40.33 | 39.14 | 39.10 | 40.35 |
| | | $p = 0.222$ | $p = 0.366$ | $p < 0.001$ | $p < 0.001$ | $p = 0.421$ |
| W+M | 41.16 | 40.55 | 40.97 | 40.12 | 39.46 | 40.54 |
| | $p = 0.002$ | $p = 0.177$ | $p = 0.012$ | $p = 0.146$ | $p = 0.001$ | $p = 0.167$ |
| WM | 40.19 | 39.95 | 40.15 | 38.86 | 38.76 | 39.60 |
| | $p = 0.193$ | $p = 0.069$ | $p = 0.153$ | $p < 0.001$ | $p < 0.001$ | $p = 0.003$ |
| L+M | 42.03 | 41.80 | 41.53 | 40.40 | 40.27 | 41.01 |
| | $p < 0.001$ | $p < 0.001$ | $p < 0.001$ | $p = 0.347$ | $p = 0.288$ | $p = 0.006$ |
| LM | 39.66 | 39.87 | 39.70 | 38.79 | 38.50 | 39.83 |
| | $p = 0.004$ | $p = 0.040$ | $p = 0.007$ | $p < 0.001$ | $p < 0.001$ | $p = 0.029$ |
| WW-MM | 35.03 | 39.73 | 39.80 | 38.93 | 38.39 | 39.59 |
| | $p < 0.001$ | $p = 0.012$ | $p = 0.022$ | $p < 0.001$ | $p < 0.001$ | $p = 0.002$ |

When comparing baseline results with other models, we see that some combinations give better results and others give worse results than the baseline model.

In the direction from English to Slovene, the best results are achieved when using words and MSD tags as separate tokens on both translation sides. On the other hand, in the direction from Slovene to English, the best results are achieved with lemmas and MSD tags as separate tokens on the source side, and only the surface words form on the target side. We will refer to these two systems as the improved systems for their respective translation direction.

Tables 10 and 11 show the same results as the previous two tables, albeit on the ParaCrawl corpus. The results show that the best results are obtained with the same combination of formats as on the Europarl corpus.

**Table 10.** BLEU scores and $p$-values for the translations from English to Slovene for different systems on the ParaCrawl corpus.

| Source Form | Target Form | | | | | |
|---|---|---|---|---|---|---|
| | **W** | **W+M** | **WM** | **L+M** | **LM** | **WW-MM** |
| W | 44.09 | 44.51 $p = 0.103$ | 44.19 $p = 0.306$ | 41.78 $p < 0.001$ | 41.79 $p < 0.001$ | 44.65 $p = 0.059$ |
| W+M | 44.41 $p = 0.149$ | 44.80 $p = 0.025$ | 39.35 $p < 0.001$ | 42.00 $p < 0.001$ | 41.50 $p < 0.001$ | 44.65 $p = 0.053$ |
| WM | 44.01 $p = 0.315$ | 43.96 $p = 0.255$ | 44.64 $p = 0.071$ | 41.82 $p < 0.001$ | 41.88 $p < 0.001$ | 44.28 $p = 0.213$ |
| L+M | 42.95 $p = 0.001$ | 41.89 $p < 0.001$ | 42.50 $p < 0.001$ | 39.52 $p < 0.001$ | 39.75 $p < 0.001$ | 42.58 $p < 0.001$ |
| LM | 42.41 $p < 0.001$ | 41.91 $p < 0.001$ | 42.63 $p < 0.001$ | 40.41 $p < 0.001$ | 40.04 $p < 0.001$ | 42.34 $p < 0.001$ |
| WW-MM | 44.35 $p = 0.167$ | 43.50 $p = 0.052$ | 44.29 $p = 0.227$ | 41.83 $p < 0.001$ | 41.06 $p < 0.001$ | 44.15 $p = 0.354$ |

**Table 11.** BLEU scores and $p$-values for the translations from Slovene to English for different systems on the ParaCrawl corpus.

| Source Form | Target Form | | | | | |
|---|---|---|---|---|---|---|
| | **W** | **W+M** | **WM** | **L+M** | **LM** | **WW-MM** |
| W | 47.89 | 47.45 $p = 0.088$ | 47.34 $p = 0.045$ | 43.63 $p < 0.001$ | 42.88 $p < 0.001$ | 47.67 $p = 0.179$ |
| W+M | 47.84 $p = 0.340$ | 48.02 $p = 0.259$ | 47.44 $p = 0.087$ | 43.73 $p < 0.001$ | 42.70 $p < 0.001$ | 47.53 $p = 0.124$ |
| WM | 47.81 $p = 0.314$ | 47.67 $p = 0.187$ | 46.88 $p = 0.005$ | 43.12 $p < 0.001$ | 43.23 $p < 0.001$ | 47.57 $p = 0.136$ |
| L+M | 48.19 $p = 0.153$ | 48.06 $p = 0.221$ | 48.00 $p = 0.285$ | 43.98 $p < 0.001$ | 43.11 $p < 0.001$ | 47.60 $p = 0.181$ |
| LM | 46.79 $p = 0.002$ | 47.06 $p = 0.016$ | 46.84 $p = 0.003$ | 42.82 $p < 0.001$ | 43.23 $p < 0.001$ | 46.87 $p = 0.002$ |
| WW-MM | 47.53 $p = 0.127$ | 47.53 $p = 0.126$ | 41.99 $p < 0.001$ | 42.74 $p < 0.001$ | 42.76 $p < 0.001$ | 47.46 $p = 0.085$ |

### 4.2. Training Corpora Size

For the second set of experiments, we selected three combinations: the baseline system, the system that performed best in the given translation direction with full MSD tags, and the same two systems with reduced MSD tags. We explored the effect of the training corpora size by repeating the experiments with these three systems on smaller corpora from 10% of the full training corpora size to 100% of the size in increments of 10% for the experiments with the Europarl corpus. We then repeated the same set of experiments on the ParaCrawl corpus, albeit with training corpora sizes from 5% of the full training corpora size to 100%. The results are presented in Figures 1–4. For better readability, the x-axis is on a logarithmic scale.

We again used the paired bootstrap resampling test between the baseline results and the results with the full MSD tags and all corpora sizes. For the results on the Europarl corpus in Figures 1 and 2, we found that all differences are statistically significant at a threshold value of 0.05. The differences in Figure 3 are statistically significant, up to 30% of the full training corpora size, and in Figure 4, up to 70% of the full training corpora size.

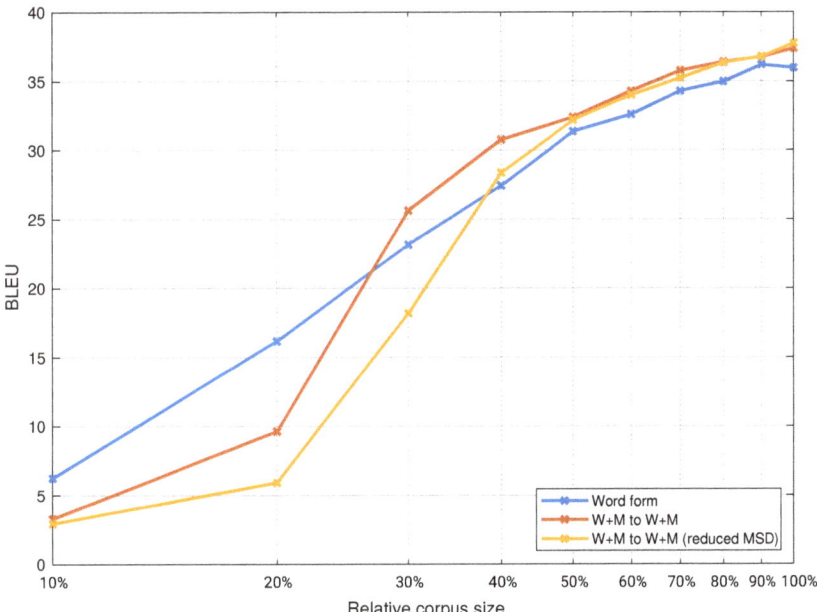

**Figure 1.** Translation results for the selected translation systems from English to Slovene using Europarl with respect to relative training corpora size.

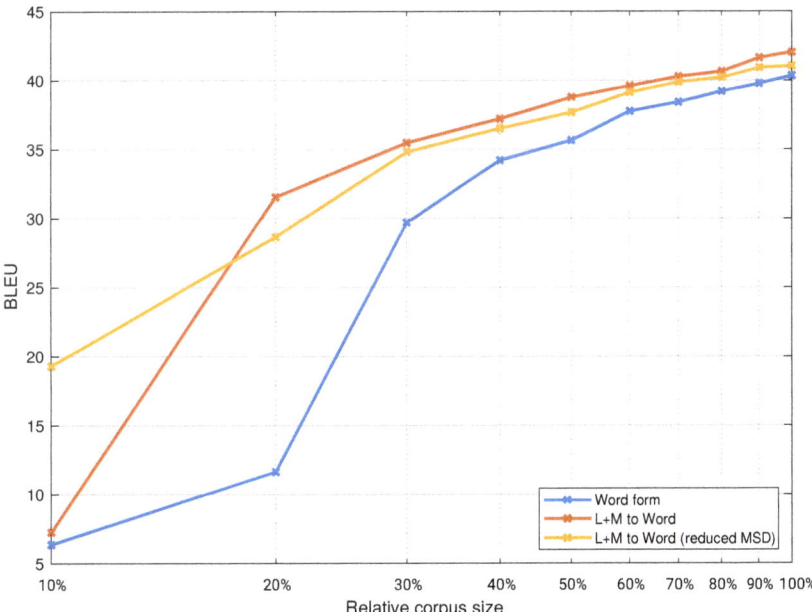

**Figure 2.** Translation results for the selected translation systems from Slovene to English using Europarl with respect to relative training corpora size.

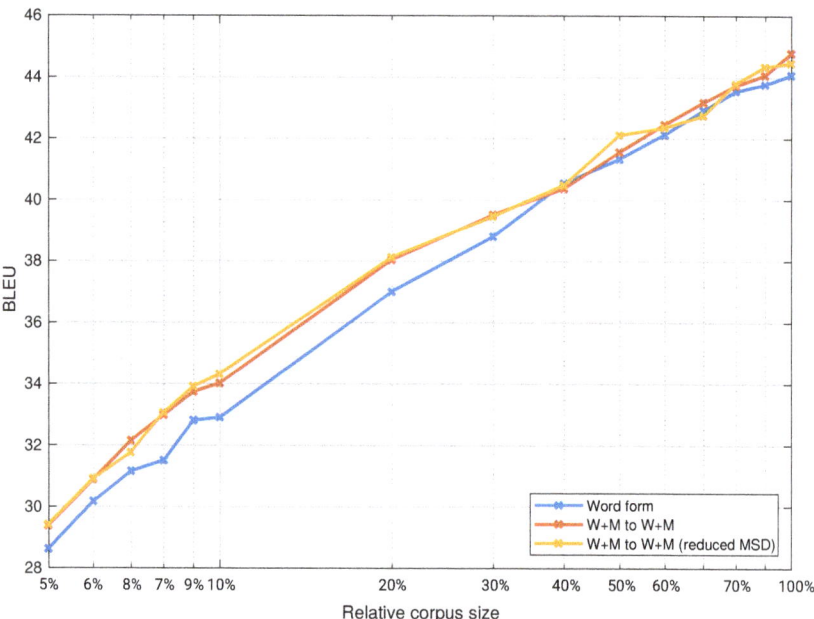

**Figure 3.** Translation results for the selected translation systems from English to Slovene using ParaCrawl with respect to relative training corpora size.

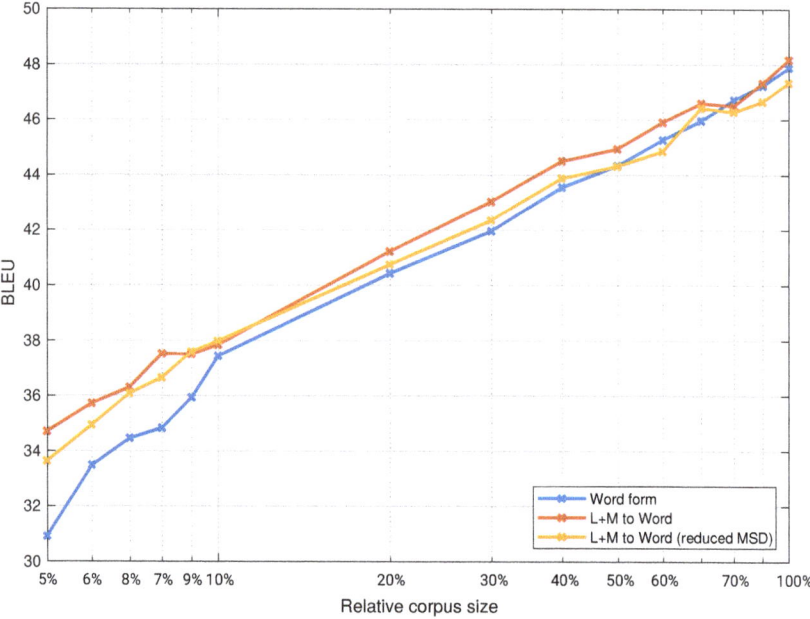

**Figure 4.** Translation results for the selected translation systems from Slovene to English using ParaCrawl with respect to relative training corpora size.

*4.3. Transformer Models*

The above-presented results were obtained using LSTM models. The transformer architecture is often found to give better results in NMT. However, our findings were that the results using transformers were slightly worse. When using transformers to translate from English to Slovene, the baseline systems gave a BLEU score of 30.90, and the improved system (W+M to W+M) gave a score of 32.64. When translating from Slovene to English, the baseline systems gave a BLEU score of 34.97, and the improved system (L+M to Words) gave a score of 36.21. Overall, the results were approximately 5 points below the results of the LSTM models. However, we can observe similar improvements and trends as with the LSTM models. Thus, the choice of model architecture does not impact our conclusions. Finally, we decided to use the better-performing models.

*4.4. Qualitative Analysis*

A comparison between the baseline translations and the translations from the improved systems can give us more insight into the different performances of the two systems. Examples from the translation from Slovene to English can be seen in Figure 5.

```
1   Source text : Ne sme se ga uporabiti kot nadomestilo za

    Reference  : It should not be used as a substitute   for
    Baseline   : It must  not be used as a substitute   for
    L+M to W   : It should not be used as    compensation

2   Source text : ... je na tem področju več možnosti.

    Reference  : There are several potential avenues ...
    Baseline   : There are several options         ...
    L+M to W   : There are several possibilities   ...

3   Source text : Vendar pa danes ni bilo zabavno.

    Reference  : Today,    however, it was not amusing.
    Baseline   : However, today    it was not fun.
    L+M to W   : Today,    however, it was not fun.

4   Source text : Kot je v svojem odličnem govoru dejala gospa Essayah ....

    Reference  : Just as Mrs Essayah       said in her excellent speech ...
    Baseline   :         As Mrs McClarkin has said in his excellent speech
    L+M to W   :         As Mrs Essayah       said in her excellent speech

5   Source text : Če bi ona in njeni prijatelji ...

    Reference  : If, however, she and her friends from ...
    Baseline   : If           she and her friends from ...
    L+M to W   : If           he  and his friends from ...
```

**Figure 5.** Selected translation examples from Slovene to English with the source text, reference translation, baseline system translation and improved system translation using lemmas and MSD tags (L+M to W).

In many cases, the difference consists of some words in one translation being replaced with synonyms or words with only slightly different meanings. Such are the first and second examples in Figure 5. In the first example, the first marked difference gives a better score to the improved system, while the second difference gives a better score to the baseline system. Other examples we found are this–that, final–last, manage–deal with, firstly–first of all. Similar differences can be seen in the translation from English to Slovene.

In the second example, we see that both systems generated different translations than what is in the reference translation.

In the third example, we see a restructuring of the sentence that results in a better score with the improved system, although both systems give a correct translation.

Examples that refer specifically to morphology in English translation are mostly found in prepositions. This can be seen in the last two examples. In the fourth example, the improved system produces a better translation, and in the fifth example, the baseline system produces a better translation.

With regard to morphology, a more interesting comparison can be done when translating from English to Slovene. Figure 6 shows four examples to illustrate some differences between the baseline and the improved system.

```
1  Source text : ... important incidents are a lot for one man.

   Reference   : ... pomembni pripetljaji so veliko za enega človeka.
   Baseline    : ... pomembni incidenti  so         za en     človek veliko.
   W+M to W+M  : ... pomembni incidenti  so veliko za enega človeka.

2  Source text : I was very surprised by this judgment ...

   Reference   : To       me je zelo presenetilo ...
   Baseline    : To sodbo me je zelo presenetilo ...
   W+M to W+M  : Ta sodba me je zelo presenetila ...

3  Source text : I could not agree more ...

   Reference   : S tem se povsem       strinjam ...
   Baseline    :        Se ne bi mogla bolj strinjati ...
   W+M to W+M  : S tem se ne bi mogel bolj strinjati ...

4  Source text : The US is one of our international partners ...

   Reference   : ZDA so ena od    naših mednarodnih ...
   Baseline    : ZDA je ena izmed naših mednarodnih ...
   W+M to W+M  : ZDA so ena izmed naših mednarodnih ...
```

**Figure 6.** Selected translation examples from English to Slovene with the source text, reference translation, baseline system translation and improved system translation using words and MSD tags (W+M to W+M).

In the first example, we have a sentence that ends with "a lot for one man". We can see that the improved system produces a translation that is identical (in the last part of the sentence) to the reference translation. The baseline system, on the other hand, places the word "veliko" (engl: much) at the end of the sentence, which is still grammatically correct. However, the baseline system translates "one man" to "en človek", which wrongly is the nominative case instead of the correct accusative case "enega človeka".

In the second example, we have a sentence with a reference translation that does not include the word for judgment but instead refers only to "this". Both translation systems added the phrase for "this judgment". However, it was added in different cases. The baseline system produced "To sodbo", which can be the accusative or instrumental case (the last of the six cases in Slovene grammar), both of which are grammatically incorrect. The improved system produced the correct nominative form "Ta sodba". There is another difference in the translations—the word "presenetilo" (engl: to surprise) is in the incorrect neutral gender form in the baseline system and in the correct feminine gender form in the improved system.

The third example is interesting from a different angle. The reference translation literally translates to "I agree completely", while both systems translate the phrase "I could not agree more", and the improved system also adds "S tem" (engl: with this). Interestingly, the word "could" is in the baseline system translated to the feminine form "mogla", and in the improved system to the masculine form "mogel". Both translations are grammatically correct, and since the source text is gender neutral, both translations can be considered correct. The reference translation is also gender neutral.

In the fourth example, we have the abbreviation "ZDA" (engl: USA), which is in Slovene used in the plural form. The baseline system produced the singular verb "je" (engl: is), while the improved system gave the correct plural form "so" (engl: are). This example clearly shows the usefulness of MSD tags, as they more often lead to grammatically correct translations. We speculate that this particular translation is improved since the MSD tag for "ZDA" included the information that it is a noun in female form. The baseline translation, on the other hand, may be wrong because "US" is in the source text (and in English in general) treated as a singular noun. Hence the English singular form "is" was translated to the Slovene singular form.

## 5. Discussion

The results obtained in experiments indicate the role of MSD tags in translation between English and Slovene. The first set of experiments, when translating from English to Slovene, showed that the best performance was achieved with models using words and MSD tags on both sides (W+M to W+M). To generate correct Slovene word forms, morphological information is needed. In Table 8, we see that the improvement on the Europarl corpus is 1.40 BLEU points. Examining Figures 1 and 3, we can see these models start outperforming the baseline models when using 30% of the Europarl training corpora (187,000 segments). They also outperformed the baseline models on the ParaCrawl corpus from the smallest tested size, 5% (186,000 segments), and up to 30% of the full size (1.1 million segments). The results on those corpora sizes are also statistically significant. At larger corpora sizes, these models at some data points also outperform the baseline models. However, the results are no longer statistically significant.

In the first set of experiments, for the translation from Slovene to English, we found the best performance with the models that use lemmas and MSD tags on the source side and words on the target side (L+M to W). To separate the meaning (i.e., lemma) and the morphology (i.e., MSD) on the Slovene side is beneficial, as almost no morphological information is needed to generate the correct English translations. Many different Slovene words are having the same lemma translate to the same English word. Using lemmas and MSD tags instead of words also reduce the data sparsity to a great extent. In Table 9, we see that the improvement on the Europarl corpus is 1.68 BLEU points. Examining Figures 2 and 4, we can see these models outperformed the baseline models at all data points on the Europarl corpus and on the ParaCrawl corpus up to 70% of its full size (2.6 million segments). These results are statistically significant, while the results from 80% of the ParaCrawl corpus upwards are not.

We can also examine the results in Tables 8–11 for format combinations other than the best. We see that models using lemmas on the target side generally perform the worst, regardless of the source side. Additionally, such models require the conversion from lemmas and MSD tags to surface word forms in the post-processing steps, making them more difficult to use. However, when lemmas are used as separate tokens with MSD tags on the source side, the models perform better than the baseline model, except on the ParaCrawl corpus when translating from English to Slovene.

We can also compare results where the MSD tags are separate tokens with the results where they are concatenated either to words or to lemmas. With a few exceptions, combinations with separate tokens perform better. We assume that this is due to the vocabulary sizes. When MSD tags are concatenated with words or lemmas, the vocabulary size increases significantly. Consequently, the model might need to learn more parameters to attain a comparable performance. However, this would mean that the models are no longer comparable and thus not suited for our research.

Next, we can compare results from models that use full MSD tags and their counterparts with reduced MSD tags. The differences are mostly small. However, we can see that in most cases, models with full MSD tags outperform models with reduced MSD tags. The most noticeable exception is in Figure 2 at 10% of the training corpora size. We speculate that this result is due to data sparsity with the very small training corpora size

(60,000 segments). Such corpora sizes might still be found for very specific domains. These results indicate that MSD reduction does not result in significant further improvements in translation performance, or might even lower the performance. Still, a reduction in the complexity of MSD tags to the most important features could have benefits, as such a tagging might be more precise and faster. This would be of importance in practical translation systems, where speed is important.

Our approach to this research consisted of data preparation rather than a modification of the translation architecture and available tools. This has the advantage that the approach can easily be transferred to other language pairs, as appropriate tools for lemmatization and MSD tagging are already available for several morphologically complex languages.

Several examples show that differences between translation systems often consist of producing synonyms or sentences with a different structure. Systems can generate grammatically correct and meaningful translations but receive worse scores with an automatic evaluation metric such as BLEU, as it compares them against gold standard translation. One method to alleviate this problem is the use of manual evaluation. The drawback here is cost and time. This further emphasizes the need for evaluation sets with several possible reference translations for each sentence on the source side.

It is more difficult to draw a conclusion when comparing the results in Figure 1 with the results in Figure 3, i.e., the same translation direction in different domains. All results show a dependency on corpora size, but the size of the Europarl training corpus is about 17% of the size of the ParaCrawl training corpus. We selected the first data point for the ParaCrawl corpus to be 5% of the full size, which is fairly similar to 30% of the Europarl corpus. In both figures, we can see a similar trend in the result up to the full size of the Europarl corpus, which is approximately 17% of the ParaCrawl corpus. Comparing those results in Figures 1 and 3 we can see that the improved system (W+M) outperforms the baseline system by approximate the same amount. The same can be seen in the other translation direction from Figures 2 and 4. Since we compare different domains with different test sets, it is not reasonable to compare exact numbers. From our results, we can only conclude that we found no strong indications for a difference in the inclusion of linguistic knowledge between the domain-specific system and the general domain system.

## 6. Conclusions

In this research, we presented a systematic comparison of translation systems trained on corpora in a variety of formats and of different sizes. Such a systematic approach for empirical evaluation of a large number of NMT systems has only recently become possible due to the availability of high-performance computing systems. Such systems employ a large number of graphical processing units, which are needed for training NMT systems.

In this research, we were able to show that NMT systems can benefit from additional morphological information if one of the languages in the translation pair is morphologically complex. We were also able to show that those benefits depend on the form in which morphological information is added to the corpora and the translation direction.

We were able to show which combination of corpora formats gives the best results when translating to or from a morphologically complex language. Those conclusions may apply to other language pairs of English and inflected languages. However, for translation pairs consisting of two complex languages, the experiments would have to be repeated to determine the best format on the source and the target side.

Mainly, we were able to confirm that the benefits heavily depend on the size of the training corpora. In the paper, we present empirical evidence for corpora of different sizes. Thus, we were able to give specific corpora sizes, at which the improvements cease to be statistically significant. On the other hand, we found that the same systems that outperform the baseline system on the small domain-specific corpus also outperform the baseline system on the larger general-domain corpus.

Hence, we would argue that the inclusion of morphological information into NMT is mostly beneficial for specific domains or, in general, for language pairs with a small amount of parallel data. However, even when a larger amount of training data is available, translation performance can still be improved.

Our qualitative analysis also showed that not all differences between the systems are recognized as improvements. Further work may include testing such systems with evaluation sets that have several reference translations or include a manual evaluation.

The presented approach for reducing the complexity of MSD tags was based on grammatical knowledge, and it brought only slightly improved translation accuracy. We would argue, however, that the tagging speed in practical applications would benefit from simpler tags. Here, further work may consist of testing data-driven approaches to reduce their complexity, retain translation performance, and increase the tagging speed.

One of the challenges of machine translation is the vocabulary sizes, especially in highly inflected languages. There are methods to alleviate this problem by using word splitting. Future work in this area might include combining the presented addition of linguistic knowledge with data-driven and knowledge-driven approaches for word splitting, e.g., BPE and stem-ending splitting.

**Author Contributions:** Conceptualization, G.D.; methodology, G.D. and M.S.M.; software, G.D.; formal analysis, G.D. and M.S.M.; writing, G.D. and M.S.M.; visualization, G.D. All authors have read and agreed to the published version of the manuscript.

**Funding:** This work was supported by the Slovenian Research Agency (research core funding No.P2-0069-Advanced Methods of Interaction in Telecommunications).

**Institutional Review Board Statement:** Not applicable.

**Informed Consent Statement:** Not applicable.

**Data Availability Statement:** Publicly available datasets were analyzed in this study. The data can be found here: https://opus.nlpl.eu/Europarl.php (accessed on 22 January 2021) and https://opus.nlpl.eu/ParaCrawl.php (accessed on 22 January 2021).

**Acknowledgments:** The authors thank the HPC RIVR (www.hpc-rivr.si, accessed on 31 January 2022) consortium for the use of the HPC system VEGA on the Institute of Information Science (IZUM). They also want to thank the authors of the Europarl and ParaCrawl parallel corpora.

**Conflicts of Interest:** The authors declare no conflict of interest.

## References

1. Koehn, P.; Hoang, H. Factored translation models. In Proceedings of the 2007 Joint Conference on Empirical Methods in Natural Language Processing and Computational Natural Language Learning (EMNLP-CoNLL), Prague, Czech Republic, 28–30 June 2007; pp. 868–876.
2. Kalchbrenner, N.; Blunsom, P. Recurrent continuous translation models. In Proceedings of the 2013 Conference on Empirical Methods in Natural Language Processing, Seattle, WA, USA, 18–21 October 2013; pp. 1700–1709.
3. Cettolo, M.; Jan, N.; Sebastian, S.; Bentivogli, L.; Cattoni, R.; Federico, M. The IWSLT 2015 evaluation campaign. In Proceedings of the 12th International Workshop on Spoken Language Translation, Da Nang, Vietnam, 3–4 December 2015; pp. 2–14.
4. Junczys-Dowmunt, M.; Dwojak, T.; Hoang, H. Is Neural Machine Translation Ready for Deployment? A Case Study on 30 Translation Directions. In Proceedings of the 9th International Workshop on Spoken Language Translation (IWSLT), Hong Kong, China, 6–7 December 2016.
5. Bentivogli, L.; Bisazza, A.; Cettolo, M.; Federico, M. Neural versus Phrase-Based Machine Translation Quality: A Case Study. In Proceedings of the 2016 Conference on Empirical Methods in Natural Language Processing, Austin, TX, USA, 1–5 November 2016; pp. 257–267. [CrossRef]
6. Castilho, S.; Moorkens, J.; Gaspari, F.; Calixto, I.; Tinsley, J.; Way, A. Is neural machine translation the new state of the art? *Prague Bull. Math. Linguist.* **2017**, *108*, 109–120. [CrossRef]
7. Arčan, M. A Comparison of Statistical and Neural Machine Translation for Slovene, Serbian and Croatian. In Proceedings of the Conference on Language Technologies & Digital Humanities 2018, Ljubljana, Slovenia, 20–21 September 2018; pp. 3–10.
8. Vintar, Š. Terminology Translation Accuracy in Phrase-Based versus Neural MT: An Evaluation for the English-Slovene Language Pair. In Proceedings of the Eleventh International Conference on Language Resources and Evaluation (LREC 2018), Miyazaki, Japan, 7–12 May 2018; Du, J., Arcan, M., Liu, Q., Isahara, H., Eds.; European Language Resources Association (ELRA): Paris, France, 2018.

9.  Sutskever, I.; Vinyals, O.; Le, Q.V. Sequence to Sequence Learning with Neural Networks. In Proceedings of the 27th International Conference on Neural Information Processing Systems, NIPS'14, Montreal, QC, Canada, 8–13 December 2014; MIT Press: Cambridge, MA, USA, 2014; Volume 2, pp. 3104–3112.

10. Luong, T.; Pham, H.; Manning, C.D. Effective Approaches to Attention-based Neural Machine Translation. In Proceedings of the 2015 Conference on Empirical Methods in Natural Language Processing; Association for Computational Linguistics, Lisbon, Portugal, 17–21 September 2015; pp. 1412–1421. [CrossRef]

11. Vaswani, A.; Shazeer, N.; Parmar, N.; Uszkoreit, J.; Jones, L.; Gomez, A.N.; Kaiser, Ł.; Polosukhin, I. Attention is all you need. In Proceedings of the Advances in Neural Information Processing Systems, Long Beach, CA, USA, 4–9 December 2017; pp. 5998–6008.

12. Dyer, C. The "noisier channel": Translation from morphologically complex languages. In Proceedings of the Second Workshop on Statistical Machine Translation, Prague, Czech Republic, 23 June 2007; pp. 207–211.

13. El Kholy, A.; Habash, N. Translate, predict or generate: Modeling rich morphology in statistical machine translation. In Proceedings of the 16th Annual Conference of the European Association for Machine Translation, Trento, Italy, 28–30 May 2012; pp. 27–34.

14. Minkov, E.; Toutanova, K.; Suzuki, H. Generating complex morphology for machine translation. In Proceedings of the 45th Annual Meeting of the Association of Computational Linguistics, Prague, Czech Republic, 23–30 June 2007; pp. 128–135.

15. Toutanova, K.; Suzuki, H.; Ruopp, A. Applying morphology generation models to machine translation. In Proceedings of the ACL-08: HLT, Columbus, OH, USA, 12–14 June 2008; pp. 514–522.

16. Chahuneau, V.; Schlinger, E.; Smith, N.A.; Dyer, C. Translating into morphologically rich languages with synthetic phrases. In Proceedings of the 2013 Conference on Empirical Methods in Natural Language Processing, Seattle, WA, USA, 18–21 October 2013; pp. 1677–1687.

17. Sennrich, R.; Haddow, B. Linguistic Input Features Improve Neural Machine Translation. In Proceedings of the First Conference on Machine Translation, Berlin, Germany, 11–12 August 2016; Research Papers; Association for Computational Linguistics: Berlin, Germany, 2016; Volume 1, pp. 83–91. [CrossRef]

18. García-Martínez, M.; Barrault, L.; Bougares, F. Factored Neural Machine Translation Architectures. In Proceedings of the 13th International Conference on Spoken Language Translation; International Workshop on Spoken Language Translation, Seattle, WA, USA, 8–9 December 2016.

19. Garcia-Martinez, M.; Barrault, L.; Bougares, F. Neural machine translation by generating multiple linguistic factors. In Proceedings of the International Conference on Statistical Language and Speech Processing, Le Mans, France, 23–25 October 2017; pp. 21–31.

20. Dalvi, F.; Durrani, N.; Sajjad, H.; Belinkov, Y.; Vogel, S. Understanding and improving morphological learning in the neural machine translation decoder. In Proceedings of the Eighth International Joint Conference on Natural Language Processing (Volume 1: Long Papers), Taipei, Taiwan, 27 November–1 December 2017; pp. 142–151.

21. Sennrich, R.; Haddow, B.; Birch, A. Neural Machine Translation of Rare Words with Subword Units. In Proceedings of the 54th Annual Meeting of the Association for Computational Linguistics (Volume 1: Long Papers), Berlin, Germany, 7–12 August 2016; Association for Computational Linguistics: Berlin, Germany, 2016; pp. 1715–1725. [CrossRef]

22. Passban, P. Machine Translation of Morphologically Rich Languages Using Deep Neural Networks. Ph.D. Thesis, Dublin City University, Dublin, Ireland, 2018.

23. Passban, P.; Liu, Q.; Way, A. Improving Character-Based Decoding Using Target-Side Morphological Information for Neural Machine Translation. In Proceedings of the 2018 Conference of the North American Chapter of the Association for Computational Linguistics: Human Language Technologies, Volume 1 (Long Papers), New Orleans, LA, USA, 1–6 June 2018; Association for Computational Linguistics: New Orleans, LA, USA, 2018; pp. 58–68. [CrossRef]

24. Burlot, F.; Garcia-Martinez, M.; Barrault, L.; Bougares, F.; Yvon, F. Word representations in factored neural machine translation. In Proceedings of the Second Conference on Machine Translation, Copenhagen, Denmark, 7–8 September 2017; pp. 20–31.

25. Stafanovičs, A.; Bergmanis, T.; Pinnis, M. Mitigating gender bias in machine translation with target gender annotations. *arXiv* **2020**, arXiv:2010.06203.

26. Tiedemann, J.; Thottingal, S. OPUS-MT—Building open translation services for the World. In Proceedings of the 22nd Annual Conferenec of the European Association for Machine Translation (EAMT), Lisbon, Portugal, 3–5 November 2020.

27. Krek, S.; Dobrovoljc, K.; Erjavec, T.; Može, S.; Ledinek, N.; Holz, N.; Zupan, K.; Gantar, P.; Kuzman, T.; Čibej, J.; et al. Training Corpus ssj500k 2.3, 2021. Slovenian Language Resource Repository CLARIN.SI. Available online: http://hdl.handle.net/11356/1434 (accessed on 22 January 2021).

28. Erjavec, T.; Fišer, D.; Krek, S.; Ledinek, N. The JOS Linguistically Tagged Corpus of Slovene. In Proceedings of the Seventh International Conference on Language Resources and Evaluation (LREC'10), Valletta, Malta, 17–23 May 2010; Choukri, K., Maegaard, B., Mariani, J., Odijk, J., Piperidis, S., Rosner, M., Tapias, D., Eds.; European Language Resources Association (ELRA): Valletta, Malta, 2010.

29. Koehn, P. Statistical Significance Tests for Machine Translation Evaluation. In Proceedings of the 2004 Conference on Empirical Methods in Natural Language Processing, Barcelona, Spain, 25–26 July 2004; Association for Computational Linguistics: Barcelona, Spain, 2004; pp. 388–395.

30. Koehn, P.; Hoang, H.; Birch, A.; Callison-Burch, C.; Federico, M.; Bertoldi, N.; Cowan, B.; Shen, W.; Moran, C.; Zens, R.; et al. Moses: Open Source Toolkit for Statistical Machine Translation. In Proceedings of the 45th Annual Meeting of the Association for Computational Linguistics Companion Volume Proceedings of the Demo and Poster Sessions, Prague, Czech Republic, 25–27 June 2007; Association for Computational Linguistics: Prague, Czech Republic, 2007; pp. 177–180.

31. Post, M. A Call for Clarity in Reporting BLEU Scores. In Proceedings of the Third Conference on Machine Translation: Research Papers, Brussels, Belgium, 31 October–1 November 2018; Association for Computational Linguistics: Brussels, Belgium, 2018; pp. 186–191. [CrossRef]

32. Schmid, H. Probabilistic Part-of-Speech Tagging Using Decision Trees. In Proceedings of the International Conference on New Methods in Language Processing, Yokohama, Japan, 18–22 September 1994.

33. Junczys-Dowmunt, M.; Grundkiewicz, R.; Dwojak, T.; Hoang, H.; Heafield, K.; Neckermann, T.; Seide, F.; Germann, U.; Fikri Aji, A.; Bogoychev, N.; et al. Marian: Fast Neural Machine Translation in C++. In Proceedings of the ACL 2018, System Demonstrations, Melbourne, Australia, 15–20 July 2018; Association for Computational Linguistics: Melbourne, Australia, 2018; pp. 116–121.

MDPI

*Article*

# Identifying Source-Language Dialects in Translation

Sergiu Nisioi *,†, Ana Sabina Uban *,† and Liviu P. Dinu

Human Language Technologies Center, Faculty of Mathematics and Computer Science, University of Bucharest, Academiei 14, 010014 Bucharest, Romania; ldinu@fmi.unibuc.ro
* Correspondence: sergiu.nisioi@unibuc.ro (S.N.); ana-sabina.uban@unibuc.ro (A.S.U.)
† These authors contributed equally to this work.

**Abstract:** In this paper, we aim to explore the degree to which translated texts preserve linguistic features of dialectal varieties. We release a dataset of augmented annotations to the Proceedings of the European Parliament that cover dialectal speaker information, and we analyze different classes of written English covering native varieties from the British Isles. Our analyses aim to discuss the discriminatory features between the different classes and to reveal words whose usage differs between varieties of the same language. We perform classification experiments and show that automatically distinguishing between the dialectal varieties is possible with high accuracy, even after translation, and propose a new explainability method based on embedding alignments in order to reveal specific differences between dialects at the level of the vocabulary.

**Keywords:** translationese identification; dialectal varieties; machine translation; feature analysis

**Citation:** Nisioi, S.; Uban, A.S.; Dinu, L.P. Identifying Source-Language Dialects in Translation. *Mathematics* **2022**, *10*, 1431. https://doi.org/10.3390/math10091431

Academic Editors: Florentina Hristea, Cornelia Caragea and Jakub Nalepa

Received: 31 December 2021
Accepted: 24 March 2022
Published: 24 April 2022

**Publisher's Note:** MDPI stays neutral with regard to jurisdictional claims in published maps and institutional affiliations.

## 1. Introduction

Computational approaches in Translation studies enforced the idea that translated texts (regarding translations, we will use the abbreviation SL to define source language and TL for target language) have specific linguistic characteristics that make them structurally different from other types of language production that take place directly in the target language. Translations are considered a sub-language (*translationese*) of the target language [1–3] and studies [4–9] imply that translated texts have similar characteristics irrespective of the target language of translation (*translation universals*). Universals emerge from psycholinguistic phenomena such as *simplification*— "the tendency to make do with less words" in the target language [10,11], *standardization*—the tendency for translators to choose more "habitual options offered by a target repertoire" instead of reconstructing the original textual relations [5], or *explicitation* —the tendency to produce more redundant constructs in the target language in order to explain the source language structures [12,13].

In addition, translated texts also exhibit patterns of *language transfer* or *interference* [14]—a phenomenon inspired by second-language acquisition, indicating certain source-language structures that get transferred into the target text. Using text mining and statistical analysis, researchers were able to identify such features [3,15,16] up to the point of reconstructing phylogenetic trees from translated texts [17,18].

Investigations with respect to translationese identification have strong potential for improving machine translation, as [19,20] pointed out for statistical machine translation, and more recently [21] showed that the effect of translationese can impact the system rankings of submissions made to the yearly shared tasks organized by The Conference of Machine Translation [22]. Ref. [23] show that a transformer-based neural machine translation (NMT) system can obtain better fluency and adequacy scores in terms of human evaluation, when the model accounts for the impact of translationese.

While the majority of translation research has been focused on how different source languages impact translations, to our knowledge, little research has addressed the properties of the source language that stem from dialectal or non-native varieties, how and to what degree they are preserved in translated texts.

In our work, we intend to bring this research question forward and investigate whether dialectal varieties produce different types of translationese and whether this hypothesis holds for machine-translated texts. We construct a selection of dialectal varieties based on the Proceedings of the European Parliament, covering utterances of speakers from the British Isles and equivalent sentence-aligned translations into French. Our results imply that *interference* in translated texts does not depend solely on the source language (SL), rather, different language varieties of the same SL can affect the final translated text. Translations exhibit different characteristics depending on whether the original text was produced by speakers of different regional varieties of the same language.

To our knowledge, this is the first result of its kind extracted from a stylistically uniform multi-author corpus using principles of statistical learning and our contribution can be summarized as follows:

1. We build and release an augmented version of the EuroParl [24] corpus that contains information about speakers' language and place of birth.

2. We investigate whether the dialectal information extracted is machine-learnable, considering that the texts in the European Parliament go through a thorough process of editing before being published,

3. Using sentence-aligned equivalent documents in French, we analyze to what degree dialectal features of the SL are preserved in the translated texts. Additionally, we employ a transformer architecture to generate English to French translations [25] and investigate whether dialectal varieties impact the machine-translated texts.

4. For each dialectal variety we fine-tune monolingual embeddings and align them to extract words whose usage differs between varieties of the same language. We analyze and interpret the classification results given the sets of aligned word pairs between different classes of speakers.

We perform a series of experiments in order to achieve our research goals. In order to observe the differences between our classes and to gain additional insights based on the obtained classification performance we compare several different solutions: we use a variety of linguistic features as well as several model architectures, including logistic regression log-entropy-based methods and neural networks. For the second stage of our experiments, we choose state-of-the-art methods used in lexical replacement tasks (including lexical semantic change detection [26], and bilingual lexicon induction [27]), based on non-contextual word embeddings and vector space alignment algorithms, in order to produce a shared embedding space which allows us to more closely compare word usage across the different varieties. We publicly share our code and detailed results (https://github.com/senisioi/dialectal_varieties, accessed on 30 November 2021), as well as the produced dataset.

## 2. A Corpus of Translated Dialectal Varieties

Our corpus is extracted from the collection of the proceedings of the European Parliament, which contains edited transcriptions of member's speeches together with their equivalent translations (The standard work-flow in EuroParl is to transcribe and edit the speech, and then to send the texts for translation [28]) made by native speakers into French. The core is based on a combination between multilingual sentence-aligned language annotated corpus released by [29,30]. To further extract the dialectal varieties, we had to re-crawl the EuroParl website, match each session to the existing corpus, and to disambiguate and match the utterances with the correct speaker (There is no convention on how the speaker names are written on the EeuroParl website, so we had to disambiguate them using a semi-manual process). We could only do this process for sessions after 1999 that are crawl-able on the current website. After matching each utterance to the correct speaker, we crawled the speaker place of birth from their personal page and traced it using geotagging to the actual state, country or region. At the same time, we annotated the equivalent French translations with the metadata extracted for the source language. We are aware, however, that the place of birth does not necessarily imply dialectal information. The same can be said about the representative country where there could be multiple official languages. We ignore speakers for whom the location is missing or who were invited as guests in the Parliament (e.g., speeches by the 14th Dalai Lama). We also acknowledge that speakers sometimes employ external teams to write their official speeches and that EuroParl transcriptions are strongly edited before being published in their final form.

Statistics regarding the corpus are rendered in Table 1 where we notice the group of speakers from Wales and the ones with Unknown source are underrepresented with a small amount of data, therefore we decide to ignore these categories from our experiments.

**Table 1.** Extracted statistics: mean and standard deviation sentence length, and type-token ratio (TTR). Both TTR and average sentence length are statistically significant under a permutation test, with $p$-value $< 0.01$ for original English documents from Scotland, pair-wise for: England vs. Scotland and Ireland vs. Scotland.

| Regional Variety | Sentences | English Originals | | | French Translations | | |
|---|---|---|---|---|---|---|---|
| | | Mean | std | TTR | Mean | std | TTR |
| Scotland | 15,646 | 26.02 | 13.59 | 3.87 | 29.99 | 16.14 | 4.27 |
| England | 60,179 | 26.40 | 13.82 | 1.76 | 30.01 | 16.07 | 1.95 |
| Ireland | 31,443 | 26.09 | 13.06 | 2.44 | 29.72 | 15.26 | 2.73 |
| Wales | 2466 | 25.76 | 12.30 | 8.92 | 29.33 | 14.71 | 10.04 |
| Unknown | 6607 | 25.84 | 13.19 | 5.79 | 29.19 | 15.26 | 6.59 |

We render the sentence length mean and standard deviation, and the overall type/token ratio to highlight shallow information with respect to the lexical variety of texts. At a first glance, original English texts appear to have shorter sentences and smaller type-token ratios (smaller lexical variety) compared to their French counterparts. Rich lexical variety in translated texts has been previously linked [31,32] to the *explicitation* phenomenon.

In addition, we construct a machine translated corpus of French sentences using a transformer-based [33] neural machine translation trained in a distributed fashion using the *fairseq-py* library (https://github.com/pytorch/fairseq, accessed on 30 November 2021). Ref. [25] report state-of-the art results on English-to-French translation for the WMT'14 dataset [34]. We acknowledge that the parallel data used for training the transformer contains also the EuroParl v7 (http://statmt.org/europarl/, accessed on 30 November 2021) [24] among Common Crawl, French-English $10^9$, News Commentary, and the United Nations Parallel Corpora. It is likely that the model has already "seen" similar data during its training which could probably lead to more fluent automatic translations. In our work we aim to see whether the dialectal information influences the machine-translated generated output.

### 3. Experimental Setup

In our experiments, we use statistical learning tools to observe the structural differences between our classes. Our aim is to minimize any type of classification bias that could appear because unbalanced classes, topic, parliamentary sessions, and specific user utterances, with the purpose of exposing grammatical structures that shape the dialectal varieties. To minimize the effect of uniform parliamentary sessions, we shuffle all the sentences for each dialectal variety. The data are split into equally-sized documents of approximately 2000 tokens to ensure the features are well represented in each document, following previous work on translationese identification [3,15,35,36]. Splitting is done by preserving the sentence boundary, each document consisting of approximately 66 sentences. Larger classes are downsampled multiple times and evaluation scores are reported as an average across all samples of equally-sized classes. To compare the classification of the same documents across different languages, we construct a test set of 40 sentence-aligned chunks. When not mentioned otherwise, we report the average 10-fold cross-validation scores across multiple down-samplings. We illustrate the stages performed from data collection to pre-processing and classification in Figure 1.

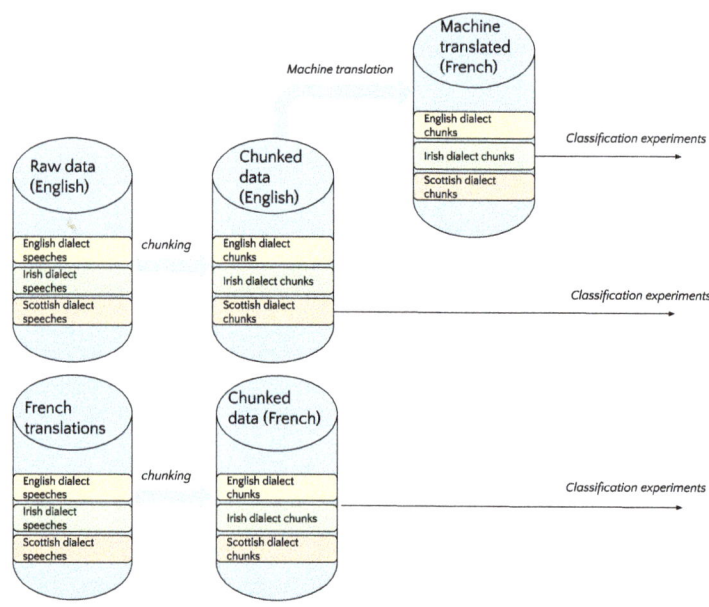

**Figure 1.** Data collection and pre-processing.

We adopt the log-entropy weighting scheme to vectorize documents, since log-entropy has been extensively used in information retrieval [37] and its purpose is to reduce the importance of high frequency features, and increase the weight for the ones that are good discriminants between documents. From our observations, this type of weighing scheme achieved the best results and it has been previously used to improve classification scores for medium-sized documents [38].

We compute the entropy for a feature $i$ by the following formula:

$$g_i = 1 + \sum_{j=1}^{\mathcal{N}} \frac{p_{ij} \log 1 + p_{ij}}{\log \mathcal{N}} \tag{1}$$

where $\mathcal{N}$ is the number of documents in the corpus and $p_{ij}$ is defined by the normalized frequency of term $i$ in document $j$.

To normalize the $p_{ij}$ values, we divide by the global frequency in the corpus:

$$p_{ij} = \text{tf}_{ij} / (\sum_{j=1}^{\mathcal{N}} \text{tf}_{ij})$$

The final weight of a feature is computed by multiplying the entropy with the log weight:

$$logent_{ij} = g_i \log(\text{tf}_{ij} + 1) \tag{2}$$

We apply this feature weighting in combination with a logistic regression classifier with liblinear optimizer [39] and $l_2$ penalty. Similar models based on BoW representations have been successfully used in tasks with small amounts of data for detecting the dialectal or native language variety of a speaker [40,41].

*Features*

**Function words (FW)** consist of conjunctions, preposition, adverbs, determiners, auxiliary and modal verbs, pronouns, qualifiers, and question words. Some function words are also part of the *closed class* because languages rarely introduce changes (historically) in this vocabulary subset [42,43]. They posses primarily a grammatical meaning and their frequency in a document reflects syntactical constructions that are particular to style. This word category has a long history of usage, being the primary features of analysis for the identification of authorship, translationese, or dialectal varieties [15,36,44,45] since they tend to be less biased by the topics or content covered in the texts. Ref. [46] argue that different brain functions are used to process the closed class and the open class of words.

**Pronouns** are a subclass of function words that have been previously tied to *explicitation* [12,47–49], translators showing an increased usage of personal pronouns. In our experiments, we observed that these features play a more important role in distinguishing human- and machine- translated dialectal varieties than original English texts.

**Part of Speech n-grams** are useful for capturing shallow syntactic constructs. We extract PoS bigrams and trigrams from our texts using the latest version of spaCy 3.2 [50] transformer models for English based on RoBERTa [51] and the French model based on CamemBERT [52] (Transformer-based models latest release https://spacy.io/usage/v3-2 accessed on 30 November 2021). We insert an additional token in the PoS list (SNTSEP) that indicates whether the next token is sentence end, in this way we hope to cover syntactic constructions that are typical to start/end the sentences. Unlike the previous features and due to the sheer size of possible combinations, PoS tag n-grams have a tendency to be sparsely represented in documents. This may lead to accurate classifications without exposing an underlying linguistic difference between the classes. To alleviate this, we have capped the total number of n-grams to 2000 and further conducted experiments with a list of 100 PoS n-grams curated using a Recursive Feature Elimination method [53] for both English and French corpora.

**Word n-grams** including function and content words. For each text replace all the entities discovered by spaCy with the corresponding entity type, including proper nouns that could potentially cover places, locations, nationality, and countries, but also numeric entities such as percentages and dates which could bias the classification. Using this feature set, we hope to understand how much the semantics of the texts, the usages and choices of content words, and potentially the topics addressed by different speakers contribute to separating between language varieties. This feature set is biased by the topics that are repeatedly addressed by different groups, given their regional interests in Scotland, Ireland or England. Furthermore, the feature set can potentially introduce sparsity and in order to alleviate this, we enforce a strict limit and cap the total number of allowed n-grams to the most frequent 300. We experimented with smaller numbers of word n-grams (100, 200) and observed that the majority of features were comprised of function word combinations and expressions such as: "I would like", "member states", "SNTSEP However", "we should", "the commissioner", "mr president I". We also experimented with larger numbers of n-grams: 400, 500 which easily achieved perfect accuracy due to the topic information embedded in the higher dimension.

**Convolutional Neural Networks (CNN)** are able to extract relevant semantic contexts from texts by learning filters over sequences of representations. We apply convolutions over word sequences (including all words in the text) using one 1-dimensional convolutional layer of 10 filters, with filter size 3, followed by a max pooling and an output layer.

## 4. Results

Table 2 contains the full set of classification results that compare the logistic regression log-entropy-based method with different features and the convolutional neural networks' results.

**Content-dependent methods** based on word n-grams and convolutional networks stand out as having the largest scores (above 0.9 for English and French) even though proper nouns and entities have been removed beforehand. This is an indicator that speakers belonging to these regions are classified based on different specific topics addressed in the European Parliament. Translated dialects appear to be easier to separate with word n-grams. Manually analysing the entity tagging and removing process for French, we could observe that markers of location (*irlandais, britannique*) were not completely removed from the texts. Content words as features for text classification are less relevant than content-independent features to test linguistic hypotheses. We can also observe here that CNNs obtain slightly lower scores for this task, possibly due to the small size of the dataset and the 2000-word length of the input classification documents.

**Table 2.** Average $F_1$ scores for distinguishing dialectal varieties and their translations into French. Values in bold indicate the best accuracy obtained using topic-independent features. The feature set *100 PoS En* are the most representative n-grams for classifying original English documents and similarly *100 PoS Fr*, for the human-translated French documents. Word n-grams (limited to a maximum of 300 most frequent) and convolutional neural networks (CNN) are covering content words and are biased by topic, therefore we do not highlight the classification scores of the two methods.

|  | Feature | En vs. Ir | En vs. Sc | Sc vs. Ir | 3-Way |
|---|---|---|---|---|---|
| French translations | function words | 0.84 | **0.87** | 0.78 | 0.71 |
|  | pronouns | 0.82 | 0.80 | 0.72 | 0.66 |
|  | PoS n-grams | **0.91** | 0.87 | **0.81** | **0.76** |
|  | 100 PoS En | 0.8 | 0.76 | 0.71 | 0.59 |
|  | 100 PoS Fr | 0.78 | 0.76 | 0.62 | 0.59 |
|  | Word n-grams | 0.95 | 0.89 | 0.89 | 0.84 |
|  | CNN | 0.95 | 0.8 | 0.95 | 0.84 |
| French machine transl. | function words | 0.88 | 0.84 | 0.81 | 0.72 |
|  | pronouns | 0.85 | 0.85 | 0.74 | 0.71 |
|  | PoS n-grams | **0.96** | **0.92** | **0.87** | **0.85** |
|  | 100 PoS En | 0.78 | 0.79 | 0.72 | 0.62 |
|  | 100 PoS Fr | 0.83 | 0.73 | 0.77 | 0.66 |
|  | Word n-grams | 0.96 | 0.91 | 0.87 | 0.85 |
|  | CNN | 0.94 | 0.9 | 0.91 | 0.89 |
| English originals | function words | 0.9 | **0.91** | 0.85 | 0.8 |
|  | pronouns | 0.63 | 0.76 | 0.69 | 0.57 |
|  | PoS n-grams | **0.91** | 0.87 | **0.91** | **0.83** |
|  | 100 PoS En | 0.88 | 0.85 | 0.86 | 0.78 |
|  | 100 PoS Fr | 0.82 | 0.71 | 0.77 | 0.64 |
|  | Word n-grams | 0.91 | 0.89 | 0.92 | 0.83 |
|  | CNN | 0.94 | 0.91 | 0.93 | 0.95 |

The magnitude of logistic regression coefficients can give an estimate of feature importance for classification corresponding to each class. A manual inspection (The supplementary material contains the full set of features ordered by importance.) of the most important classification features from Table 3 shows that certain debates have (key)words acting as good discriminators between our classes. The topics hint towards political tensions with respect to Northern Ireland, fishing rights, and state-policies in the region.

**Table 3.** The top most relevant word n-grams in binary text classification scenarios.

| Experiment | Function Words with High Discriminatory Value |
|---|---|
| En-Ir (en) | energy, regard, must, sure, research, policy, nuclear, food, s, recent, children, peace, farmers |
| En-Sc (en) | fisheries, we have, in writing, i voted, your, aid, human rights, want, research, policy |
| Ir-Sc (en) | he, fisheries, s, regard, people, want to, treaty, sure, report, peace, want, hope |
| En-Ir (fr) | nord, regions, secteur, amendement, trois, de l, son, enfants, traite, industrie, donc, nous |
| En-Sc (fr) | ai vote, regions, ecrit, votre, vote, processus, tres, secteur, mesures, mais, est un, reforme |
| Ir-Sc (fr) | ecrit, vote, traite, ont, de m, programme, ait, deja, du nord, rapport, certains, assemblee |

From the total most frequent words in the corpus, several function words appear to have a high importance for English: *regard, must, we, to, s, you, he, sure*; and French: *de l, son, donc, nous, votre, tres, mais, ont, de m, deja*. Table 3 contains several words marked as important in separating different classes, where we can observe that dialectal varieties are potentially influenced by function word and more specifically pronoun usage.

**Topic-independent features** that include function words, pronouns, and PoS n-grams yield relatively high scores for original English texts, indicating that *the place of birth is a valid indicator of dialectal information* for our particular dataset. The translations show significantly lower scores, but still above 0.8 for 3-way classification on both human and machine -translated versions. These features are an indicator of the grammatical structures that transfer from source to target language and we highlight in boldface the highest scores for each. PoS n-grams tend to achieve the highest classification scores among all experiments, when taking into account the sparse high dimensionality of each classification example. When restricting the overall set to the 100 most frequently occurring PoS n-grams, unsurprisingly, the overall scores drop by 10%. While taking into account this drop, we can still observe a fair degree of pair-wise separation between the classes. Furthermore, the curated list of PoS n-grams is language independent and we used the list extracted from the French corpus to classify the annotated documents in English and vice-versa. Original English can be separated with an $F_1$ score ranging from 0.71 to 0.82 when using PoS n-gram features extracted from the French data. A similar phenomenon occurs for translated French documents can be separated with an $F_1$ score ranging from 0.71 to 0.8 using PoS n-grams extracted from the English data. This is a clear indicator that shallow syntactic constructs that are specific to each class are transferred during translation into the resulting documents.

With respect to machine-translated texts, it appears that all the classification experiments achieve slightly higher scores than the equivalent human-translated data. Since machine-generated translations are more rudimentary, it could very well be that the original dialectal patterns are simply amplified or mistranslated into the target language, thus generating the proper conditions to achieve statistical separation between the classes.

**Pronouns** show the opposite result on both machine and human translation outputs. Original English dialectal varieties are weakly classifiable using pronouns - England vs. Scotland achieving at best a 0.74 score. Pronouns appear to be better markers of separation in translated texts, these words being markers of *explicitation*, as previous research hypothesised [12,47,48]. The results show that pronoun distribution in translation accentuates original patterns of the texts, mainly due to explicitaion, a phenomenon that appears to be mimicked by machine-translation systems trained on human translations. For example, the most important pronouns in English classification are: *we, this, anyone, anybody, several, everyone, what*. For French we observe several different personal pronouns of high importance: human translations: *nous, l, j, les, la, m, je*; and machine translation: *nous, j, la, en, l, qui, m, quoi que, celles*.

## 5. Classification Analysis

Given the high accuracy obtained on both English and French version of the corpora using PoS n-grams, we render in Table 4 the average confusion matrices across all cross-validation epochs for these results. On the English side of the table, the largest confusion is between speakers from England and Scotland, while on the French translations, the confusions are more uniformly distributed. From this result, it becomes clear that translations preserve certain syntactic aspects of the source-language dialect, although the differences between the classes are slightly lost in the process.

We have also constructed a comparable train/test split designed with the same documents in both English and French classification scenarios. The first four rows of Table 5 render the percentage of documents from the test set classified with the same label in both English and French human-translated versions. The process is similar to computing an accuracy score of the French classifications given the English equivalent as the gold standard. The result gives us an estimation of the number of test documents that have the same distinguishing pattern w.r.t a feature type. From Table 5 we confirm the fact that pronouns have different roles in translated texts—showing little overlap between the predictions on the French test set vs. the English equivalent. Function words and PoS n-grams have slightly higher overlap percentages, again, proving that certain grammatical patterns transfer from the dialectal variaties onto the French translation. Word n-grams and CNNs share the highest prediction similarities between the two test sets. We believe this is to a lesser degree due to source-language transfer, rather it corroborates that topics addressed in the debates determine similar classification patterns across languages.

**Table 4.** Comparison of average confusion matrices for original English and French classification experiments using PoS n-grams feautures.

|    |    | En | Ir | Sc |
|----|----|-----|-----|-----|
|    | En | 80 | 10 | 10 |
| Fr | Ir | 7.5 | 80 | 12.5 |
|    | Sc | 5 | 5 | 90 |
|    | En | 85 | 5 | 10 |
| En | Ir | 4.5 | 91 | 4.5 |
|    | Sc | 0 | 5 | 95 |

**Table 5.** The percentage of documents from the test set classified with the same label in both English and French translated versions. The last row compares the 3-way classification similarities between dialectal classification of documents from human and machine translated output.

|  | Function Wds. | Pronouns | PoS n-Grams | wd. n-Grams | CNN |
|----|----|----|----|----|----|
| 3-way | 64.2% | 44.2% | 75% | 82.5% | 79% |
| England vs. Ireland | 81.3% | 58.8% | 88.75% | 95% | 90% |
| England vs. Scotland | 80% | 65% | 87.5% | 91% | 88.2% |
| Ireland vs. Scotland | 73.8% | 65% | 76.3% | 91% | 87.5% |
| 3-way Human vs. MT | 67% | 70% | 78% | 84% | 85% |

For French human vs. machine translation, we present only the 3-way classification similarities (last row in Table 5), since the pair-wise versions have similar values. In this case we observe the divergence between human- and machine- generated translations in terms of different features. The output produced by the transformer-based NMT system does not resemble typical human language in terms of function words distribution, as seen in the low amount of classification overlap (67%). However, the machine appears to do better at imitating *translationese explicitaion*, given the higher importance of pronouns in classification (0.71 $F_1$ score and 70% overlap between human and machine translation classifications). Similarly, the ability of PoS n-grams to distinguish English varieties with a 0.83 $F_1$ score and with 78% similarity to classification human translation, indicates that dialectal syntactic structures are reasonably preserved in both human- and machine- translation. Content-wise, both CNNs and word n-grams lead to similar classification patterns on the test set (84% overlap and 0.95 avg. $F_1$ score). Overall, the dialectal markers yield prediction correlations between machine- and human- generated translations.

## 6. Words in Context

Using weights learned by a linear model to infer feature importance can be useful for interpreting the behavior of the classifier and explain some of the underlying linguistic mechanisms that distinguish between the classes considered, in our case - language varieties. Nevertheless, this method has its limits: based on feature importance in our classifier we are essentially only able to find differences between the word distributions of two corpora, in terms of frequencies. In order to gain more insight into the phenomena behind the aspects of language that make different varieties of English distinguishable with such high accuracy, we propose a novel method for feature analysis based aligned word embedding spaces in order to identify word pairs which are used differently in two corpora to be compared.

Aligned embedding spaces have previously been exploited in various tasks in computational linguistics, from bilingual lexicon induction [27], to tracking word sense evolution [54], and identifying lexical replacements [55,56]. We also propose using word embedding spaces for finding lexical replacements, this time across dialectal varieties. By training word embeddings on two different corpora, and comparing their structural differences, we can go beyond word frequency distribution, and look into the specific lexical differences that distinguish word usage between texts in the two classes. If the feature weight method could tell us, for example, that English speakers use *maybe* more than the Irish do, the embedding alignment based method should be able to show exactly how that word is used differently, what word Irish speakers use instead in their speech, in the form of a word analogy: where English speakers say *maybe*, Irish speakers say $X$.

*Word Embedding Alignment*

The algorithm for identifying pairs of words which are used differently in the two corpora (in our case, corresponding to different dialectal varieties) consists of the following steps:

**Separately train word embeddings** for each of the two corpora. We train word2vec on each of our datasets, using standard hyperparameters and embedding dimension 100. We use Wikipedia pre-trained embeddings to initialize the weights which we further fine-tune on our data.

**Obtain a shared embedding space**, common to the two corpora. Vectors in two separately trained embedding spaces are not directly comparable, so an alignment algorithm is necessary to obtain a shared embedding space. To align the embedding spaces, a linear transformation is applied to one of the spaces, such that the distance between a few seed word pairs is minimized (which are assumed to have the same meaning in both spaces/corpora). We use a linear regression method, and a random sample of the first 60% most frequent words from our vocabulary as seed—minimizing their pairwise distance will constitute the objective of training the linear regression model to obtain a transformation matrix.

**Identify misaligned word pairs**, where the nearest neighbor (based on cosine distance) of a word in the first corpus is not the same word in the second corpus, and extract the actual nearest neighbor. The resulted misaligned word pairs constitute words which are used differently in the two corpora. We also define a score of the misalignment, measuring strength of the difference in usage in different corpora for a word pair. The higher this score, the most significant the usage difference between the two corpora. Scores can range from 0 to 1, where scores of zero would be assigned to word pairs that show an identical usage pattern across the two corpora. Details on how this score is computed are described in Algorithm 1.

---

**Algorithm 1** Detection of misaligned word pairs between two corpora.

---

1: Given a word $w_1$ and its corresponding embedding $emb(w_1, C_1)$ in the embedding space of corpus $C_1$:

2: Find the word $w_2$ with embedding representation $emb(w_2, C_2)$ in the embedding space of corpus $C_2$ such that for any $w_i$ in $C_2$, $dist(emb(w_1, C_1), emb(w_2, C_2)) < dist(emb(w_1, C_1), emb(w_i, C_2))$

3: Extract $(w_1, w_2)$ as pair with unmatched usage, with the property that $w_1 \neq w_2$

4: $Score(w_1) = dist(emb(w_1, C_1), emb(w_1, C_2)) - dist(emb(w_1, C_1), emb(w_2, C_2))$

---

For each pair of dialects, we train embeddings, perform embedding space alignments and extract nearest neighbors for misaligned word pairs. Table 6 shows some descriptive statistics of the distribution of misalignment scores for all misaligned words in each corpus pair. A higher average misalignment score should point to a bigger difference in patterns of word usage between two corpora. The ranking of dialectal "similarities" inferred in this way is still maintained after translation into French, although, differences in language usage seem to be reduced after translation.

In Figure 2 we plot the distribution of misalignment scores for all words (including non-misaligned ones) and all dialect pairs, along with French translations. The distribution is skewed, with most words having a score in the vicinity of 0, showing similar usage patterns in the two corpora.

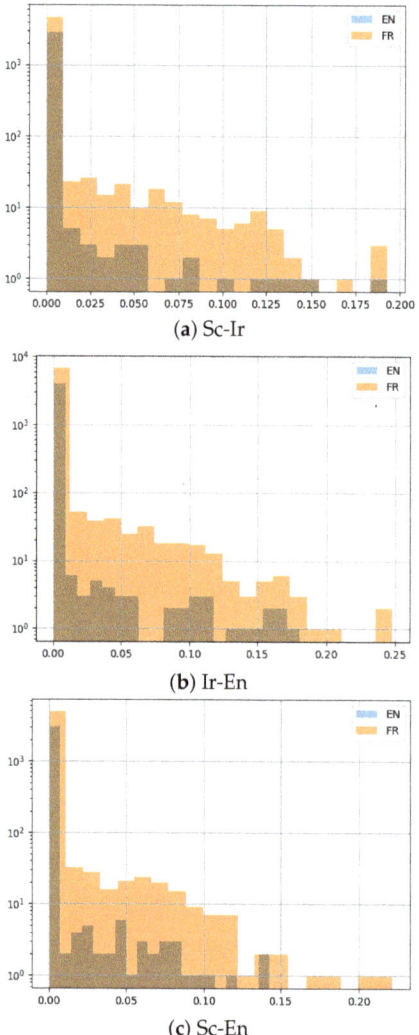

(a) Sc-Ir

(b) Ir-En

(c) Sc-En

**Figure 2.** Distribution of misalignment scores across dialect pairs for English and French data sets.

**Table 6.** Average and standard deviation of misalignment scores for all corpus pairs, in original and translated versions.

| Varieties | English | | French | |
| --- | --- | --- | --- | --- |
| | Mean | Std | Mean | Std |
| En-Sc | 0.049 | 0.040 | 0.048 | 0.040 |
| En-Ir | 0.063 | 0.053 | 0.058 | 0.048 |
| Ir-Sc | 0.053 | 0.048 | 0.050 | 0.040 |

We take a closer look at some examples of misaligned words (The full set of aligned words is available in the supplementary material along with their corresponding similarity scores.) that are used differently across corpora in Table 7. The method unveils word pairs that capture differences in topic content between the two corpora, further corroborating that topic contributes to distinguishing between texts written by speakers of different English varieties. Such an example is the pair *Scotland/England*, which captures mentions of proper nouns: in contexts where Scottish speakers say *Scotland*, the English say *England*. The same occurs in the case of *irlandais* and *écossais* for the French translations of Irish and Scottish texts.

More interestingly, the method helps capture an underlying stylistic dimension of content word usage as well, by identifying misaligned pairs of words with the same meaning (synonyms). Content-independent features are traditionally employed in stylistic analyses in order to remove bias from topic. Our analysis shows content words can encapsulate a stylistic dimension as well, and should not be ignored when considering aspects of the language independent from topic.

**Table 7.** Examples of unmatched embeddings.

| Corpora | Word | Nearest Neighbor |
| --- | --- | --- |
| En-Sc | England<br>reply<br>but<br>extremely | Scotland<br>answer<br>however<br>very |
| En-Sc (fr) | aspiration<br>reccomandation | ambition<br>proposition |
| Ir-Sc | plan<br>she | program<br>he |
| Ir-Sc (fr) | plan<br>irlandais | programme<br>écossais |
| Ir-En | absolutely<br>keep | perfectly<br>hold |
| Ir-En (fr) | absolument<br>comprendre | vraiment<br>croire |

To express the same concept, the Irish tend to use plan where the Scottish say program, and the same pattern can be observed in the translated versions of the texts: the French words plan and programme are nearest neighbors. The same is true for the Irish absolutely versus and the English perfectly, translated as absolument and vraiment in French. In addition, several example pairs may still yield an unwanted nearest neighbor, as it is the case for unless vs. if, indeed vs. nevertheless. These examples show that a certain threshold must be enforced in order to filter them out. A few examples of function words also stand out, such as very and extremely that distinguishes Scottish from English speakers. This last pair is also consistent with the feature importance analysis from our logistic regression results.

## 7. Conclusions

We construct an augmented version of the English-French parallel EuroParl corpus that contains additional speaker information pointing to native regional dialects from the British Isles (We will open-source the data and code for reproducing the experiments). The corpus has several properties useful for the joint investigation of dialectal and translated varieties: it is stylistically uniform, the speeches are transcribed and normalized by the same editing process, there are multiple professional translators and speakers, and the translators always translate into their mother tongue.

Our experimental setup brings forward the first translation-related result (to the best of our knowledge) showing that translated texts depend not only on the source language, but also on the dialectal varieties of the source language. In addition, we show that machine translation is impacted by the dialectal varieties, since the output of a state-of-the-art transformer-based system preserves (or exacerbates, see Table 2) syntactic and topic-independent information specific to these language varieties. W.r.t pronouns, we show that these are discriminating markers for dialectal varieties in both human- and machine-translations (as a source of explicitation), being less effective on original English texts.

We provide a computational framework to understand the lexical choices made by speakers from different groups and we release the pairs of extracted content words in the supplementary material. The embeddings-based method offers promising insights into the word choices and usages in different contexts and we are currently working on filtering aligned pairs and adapting it to phrases.

**Author Contributions:** Investigation, S.N. and A.S.U.; Methodology, S.N. and A.S.U.; Supervision, L.P.D. All authors have read and agreed to the published version of the manuscript.

**Funding:** This research was partially funded by two grants of the Ministry of Research, Innovation and Digitization, Unitatea Executiva pentru Finantarea Invatamantului Superior, a Cercetarii, Dezvoltarii si Inovarii-CNCS/CCCDI—UEFISCDI, CoToHiLi project, project number 108, within PNCDI III, and CCCDI—UEFISCDI, INTEREST project, project number 411PED/2020, code PN-III-P2-2.1-PED-2019-2271, within PNCDI III.

**Institutional Review Board Statement:** Not applicable.

**Informed Consent Statement:** Not applicable.

**Data Availability Statement:** Not applicable.

**Conflicts of Interest:** The authors declare no conflict of interest.

**Ethical Considerations:** The data we release with this paper, including speaker information, is publicly available in an electronic format on the European Parliament Website at https://www.europarl.europa.eu/ (accessed on 30 November 2021).

## References

1. Toury, G. *Search of a Theory of Translation*; The Porter Institute for Poetics and Semiotics; Tel Aviv University: Tel Aviv, Israel, 1980.
2. Gellerstam, M. Translationese in Swedish novels translated from English. In *Translation Studies in Scandinavia*; Wollin, L., Lindquist, H., Eds.; CWK Gleerup: Lund, Sweden, 1986; pp. 88–95.
3. Baroni, M.; Bernardini, S. A New Approach to the Study of Translationese: Machine-learning the Difference between Original and Translated Text. *Lit. Linguist. Comput.* **2006**, *21*, 259–274. [CrossRef]
4. Baker, M. Corpus Linguistics and Translation Studies: Implications and Applications. In *Text and Technology: In Honour of John Sinclair*; Baker, M., Francis, G., Tognini-Bonelli, E., Eds.; John Benjamins: Amsterdam, The Netherlands, 1993; pp. 233–252.
5. Toury, G. *Descriptive Translation Studies and beyond*; John Benjamins: Amsterdam, PA, USA, 1995.
6. Mauranen, A.; Kujamäki, P. (Eds.) *Translation Universals: Do They Exist?* John Benjamins: Amsterdam, The Netherlands, 2004.
7. Laviosa, S. Universals. In *Routledge Encyclopedia of Translation Studies*, 2nd ed.; Baker, M., Saldanha, G., Eds.; Routledge: New York, NY, USA, 2008; pp. 288–292.
8. Xiao, R.; Dai, G. Lexical and grammatical properties of Translational Chinese: Translation universal hypotheses reevaluated from the Chinese perspective. *Corpus Linguist. Linguist. Theory* **2014**, *10*, 11–55. [CrossRef]
9. Bernardini, S.; Ferraresi, A.; Miličević, M. From EPIC to EPTIC—Exploring simplification in interpreting and translation from an intermodal perspective. *Target. Int. J. Transl. Stud.* **2016**, *28*, 61–86. [CrossRef]

10. Blum-Kulka, S.; Levenston, E.A. Universals of lexical simplification. In *Strategies in Interlanguage Communication*; Faerch, C., Kasper, G., Eds.; Longman: London, UK, 1983; pp. 119–139.

11. Vanderauwera, R. *Dutch Novels Translated into English: The Transformation of a "Minority" Literature*; Rodopi: Amsterdam, The Netherlands, 1985.

12. Blum-Kulka, S. Shifts of Cohesion and Coherence in Translation. In *Interlingual and Intercultural Communication Discourse and Cognition in Translation and Second Language Acquisition Studies*; House, J., Blum-Kulka, S., Eds.; Gunter Narr Verlag: Tübingen, Germany, 1986; Volume 35, pp. 17–35.

13. Øverås, L. In Search of the Third Code: An Investigation of Norms in Literary Translation. *Meta* **1998**, *43*, 557–570. [CrossRef]

14. Toury, G. Interlanguage and its Manifestations in Translation. *Meta* **1979**, *24*, 223–231. [CrossRef]

15. Koppel, M.; Ordan, N. Translationese and Its Dialects. In Proceedings of the 49th Annual Meeting of the Association for Computational Linguistics: Human Language Technologies, Stroudsburg, PA, USA, 19–24 June 2011; Association for Computational Linguistics: Portland, OR, USA, 2011; pp. 1318–1326.

16. Rabinovich, E.; Wintner, S. Unsupervised Identification of Translationese. *Trans. Assoc. Comput. Linguist.* **2015**, *3*, 419–432. [CrossRef]

17. Rabinovich, E.; Ordan, N.; Wintner, S. Found in Translation: Reconstructing Phylogenetic Language Trees from Translations. *arXiv* **2017**, arXiv:1704.07146.

18. Chowdhury, K.D.; Espa na-Bonet, C.; van Genabith, J. Understanding Translationese in Multi-view Embedding Spaces. In Proceedings of the 28th International Conference on Computational Linguistics, Barcelona, Spain, 8–13 December 2020; pp. 6056–6062.

19. Kurokawa, D.; Goutte, C.; Isabelle, P. Automatic Detection of Translated Text and its Impact on Machine Translation. In Proceedings of the MT-Summit XII, Ottawa, ON, Canada, 26–30 August 2009; pp. 81–88.

20. Lembersky, G.; Ordan, N.; Wintner, S. Improving Statistical Machine Translation by Adapting Translation Models to Translationese. *Comput. Linguist.* **2013**, *39*, 999–1023. [CrossRef]

21. Zhang, M.; Toral, A. The Effect of Translationese in Machine Translation Test Sets. *arXiv* **2019**, arXiv:1906.08069.

22. Ondrej, B.; Chatterjee, R.; Christian, F.; Yvette, G.; Barry, H.; Matthias, H.; Philipp, K.; Qun, L.; Varvara, L.; Christof, M.; et al. Findings of the 2017 conference on machine translation (wmt17). In Proceedings of the Second Conference on Machine Translation, Copenhagen, Denmark, 7–8 September 2017; The Association for Computational Linguistics: Stroudsburg, PA, USA, 2017; pp. 169–214.

23. Graham, Y.; Haddow, B.; Koehn, P. Statistical Power and Translationese in Machine Translation Evaluation. In Proceedings of the 2020 Conference on Empirical Methods in Natural Language Processing (EMNLP), Online, 16–20 November 2020; pp. 72–81.

24. Koehn, P. Europarl: A Parallel Corpus for Statistical Machine Translation. In Proceedings of the Tenth Machine Translation Summit, AAMT, Phuket, Thailand, 13–15 September 2005; pp. 79–86.

25. Ott, M.; Edunov, S.; Grangier, D.; Auli, M. Scaling Neural Machine Translation. In Proceedings of the Third Conference on Machine Translation: Research Papers, Belgium, Brussels, 31 October–1 November 2018; pp. 1–9.

26. Schlechtweg, D.; McGillivray, B.; Hengchen, S.; Dubossarsky, H.; Tahmasebi, N. SemEval-2020 task 1: Unsupervised lexical semantic change detection. *arXiv* **2020**, arXiv:2007.11464.

27. Zou, W.Y.; Socher, R.; Cer, D.; Manning, C.D. Bilingual word embeddings for phrase-based machine translation. In Proceedings of the 2013 Conference on Empirical Methods in Natural Language Processing, Seattle, WA, USA, 18–21 October 2013; pp. 1393–1398.

28. Pym, A.; Grin, F.; Sfreddo, C.; Chan, A.L. *The Status of the Translation Profession in the European Union*; Anthem Press: London, UK, 2013.

29. Rabinovich, E.; Wintner, S.; Lewinsohn, O.L. A Parallel Corpus of Translationese. In Proceedings of the International Conference on Intelligent Text Processing and Computational Linguistics, Konya, Turkey, 3–9 April 2016.

30. Nisioi, S.; Rabinovich, E.; Dinu, L.P.; Wintner, S. A Corpus of Native, Non-native and Translated Texts. In Proceedings of the Tenth International Conference on Language Resources and Evaluation (LREC'16), Portorož, Slovenia, 23–28 May 2016.

31. Olohan, M.; Baker, M. Reporting That in Translated English: Evidence for Subconscious Processes of Explicitation? *Across Lang. Cult.* **2000**, *1*, 141–158. [CrossRef]

32. Zufferey, S.; Cartoni, B. A multifactorial analysis of explicitation in translation. *Target* **2014**, *26*, 361–384. [CrossRef]

33. Vaswani, A.; Shazeer, N.; Parmar, N.; Uszkoreit, J.; Jones, L.; Gomez, A.N.; Kaiser, Ł.; Polosukhin, I. Attention is all you need. *Adv. Neural Inf. Process. Syst.* **2017**, *30*, 5998–6008.

34. Bojar, O.; Buck, C.; Federmann, C.; Haddow, B.; Koehn, P.; Leveling, J.; Monz, C.; Pecina, P.; Post, M.; Saint-Amand, H.; et al. Findings of the 2014 Workshop on Statistical Machine Translation. In Proceedings of the Ninth Workshop on Statistical Machine Translation, Baltimore, MD, USA, 26–27 June 2014; Association for Computational Linguistics: Baltimore, MA, USA, 2014; pp. 12–58.

35. Ilisei, I.; Inkpen, D.; Pastor, G.C.; Mitkov, R. Identification of Translationese: A Machine Learning Approach. In Proceedings of the CICLing-2010: 11th International Conference on Computational Linguistics and Intelligent Text Processing, Iaşi, Romania, 21–27 March 2010; Gelbukh, A.F., Ed.; Springer: Berlin/Heidelberg, Germany, 2010; Volume 6008, pp. 503–511.

36. Rabinovich, E.; Nisioi, S.; Ordan, N.; Wintner, S. On the Similarities Between Native, Non-native and Translated Texts. *arXiv* **2016**, arXiv:1609.03204.

37. Dumais, S. Improving the retrieval of information from external sources. *Behav. Res. Methods Instruments Comput.* **1991**, *23*, 229–236. [CrossRef]

38. Jarvis, S.; Bestgen, Y.; Pepper, S. Maximizing Classification Accuracy in Native Language Identification. In Proceedings of the Eighth Workshop on Innovative Use of NLP for Building Educational Applications, Atlanta, GA, USA, 13 June 2013; Association for Computational Linguistics: Atlanta, Georgia, 2013; pp. 111–118.
39. Fan, R.E.; Chang, K.W.; Hsieh, C.J.; Wang, X.R.; Lin, C.J. LIBLINEAR: A Library for Large Linear Classification. *J. Mach. Learn. Res.* **2008**, *9*, 1871–1874.
40. Malmasi, S.; Evanini, K.; Cahill, A.; Tetreault, J.R.; Pugh, R.A.; Hamill, C.; Napolitano, D.; Qian, Y. A Report on the 2017 Native Language Identification Shared Task. In Proceedings of the 12th Workshop on Innovative Use of NLP for Building Educational Applications, Copenhagen, Denmark, 8 September 2017; pp. 62–75.
41. Zampieri, M.; Malmasi, S.; Scherrer, Y.; Samardžić, T.; Tyers, F.; Silfverberg, M.; Klyueva, N.; Pan, T.L.; Huang, C.R.; Ionescu, R.T.; et al. A Report on the Third VarDial Evaluation Campaign. In Proceedings of the Sixth Workshop on NLP for Similar Languages, Varieties and Dialects, Minneapolis, MN, USA, 7 June 2019; Association for Computational Linguistics: Ann Arbor, MI, USA, 2019; pp. 1–16.
42. Koppel, M.; Akiva, N.; Dagan, I. Feature instability as a criterion for selecting potential style markers. *J. Am. Soc. Inf. Sci. Technol.* **2006**, *57*, 1519–1525. [CrossRef]
43. Dediu, D.; Cysouw, M. Some structural aspects of language are more stable than others: A comparison of seven methods. *PLoS ONE* **2013**, *8*, e55009.
44. Mosteller, F.; Wallace, D.L. Inference in an authorship problem: A comparative study of discrimination methods applied to the authorship of the disputed Federalist Papers. *J. Am. Stat. Assoc.* **1963**, *58*, 275–309.
45. Nisioi, S. Feature Analysis for Native Language Identification. In Proceedings of the 16th International Conference on Computational Linguistics and Intelligent Text Processing (CICLing 2015), Cairo, Egypt, 14–20 April 2015; Gelbukh, A.F., Ed.; Springer: Berlin/Heidelberg, Germany, 2015.
46. Münte, T.F.; Wieringa, B.M.; Weyerts, H.; Szentkuti, A.; Matzke, M.; Johannes, S. Differences in brain potentials to open and closed class words: Class and frequency effects. *Neuropsychologia* **2001**, *39*, 91–102. [CrossRef]
47. Olohan, M. Leave it out! Using a Comparable Corpus to Investigate Aspects of Explicitation in Translation. *Cadernos de Tradução* **2002**, *1*, 153–169.
48. Zhang, X.; Kruger, H.K.; Fang, J. Explicitation in children's literature translated from English to Chinese: A corpus-based study of personal pronouns. *Perspectives* **2020**, *28*, 717–736. [CrossRef]
49. Volansky, V.; Ordan, N.; Wintner, S. On the Features of Translationese. *Digit. Scholarsh. Humanit.* **2015**, *30*, 98–118. [CrossRef]
50. Honnibal, M.; Montani, I.; Van Landeghem, S.; Boyd, A. spaCy: Industrial-Strength Natural Language Processing in Python. 2020. Available online: https://spacy.io/ (accessed on 30 November 2021).
51. Liu, Y.; Ott, M.; Goyal, N.; Du, J.; Joshi, M.; Chen, D.; Levy, O.; Lewis, M.; Zettlemoyer, L.; Stoyanov, V. Roberta: A robustly optimized bert pretraining approach. *arXiv* **2019**, arXiv:1907.11692.
52. Martin, L.; Muller, B.; Ortiz Suárez, P.J.; Dupont, Y.; Romary, L.; de la Clergerie, É.; Seddah, D.; Sagot, B. CamemBERT: A Tasty French Language Model. In Proceedings of the 58th Annual Meeting of the Association for Computational Linguistics, Online, 5–10 July 2020; pp. 7203–7219.
53. Guyon, I.; Weston, J.; Barnhill, S.; Vapnik, V. Gene selection for cancer classification using support vector machines. *Mach. Learn.* **2002**, *46*, 389–422. [CrossRef]
54. Hamilton, W.L.; Leskovec, J.; Jurafsky, D. Diachronic word embeddings reveal statistical laws of semantic change. *arXiv* **2016**, arXiv:1605.09096.
55. Szymanski, T. Temporal word analogies: Identifying lexical replacement with diachronic word embeddings. In Proceedings of the 55th Annual Meeting of the Association for Computational Linguistics (Volume 2: Short Papers), Vancouver, BC, Canada, 30 July–4 August 2017; pp. 448–453.
56. Uban, A.; Ciobanu, A.M.; Dinu, L.P. Studying Laws of Semantic Divergence across Languages using Cognate Sets. In Proceedings of the 1st International Workshop on Computational Approaches to Historical Language Change, Florence, Italy, 2 August 2019; Association for Computational Linguistics: Florence, Italy, 2019; pp. 161–166.

MDPI

*Article*

# Taylor-ChOA: Taylor-Chimp Optimized Random Multimodal Deep Learning-Based Sentiment Classification Model for Course Recommendation

**Santosh Kumar Banbhrani** [1,*], **Bo Xu** [1], **Hongfei Lin** [1] and **Dileep Kumar Sajnani** [2]

[1] School of Computer Science and Technology, Dalian University of Technology, Ganjingzi District, Dalian 116024, China; xubo@dlut.edu.cn (B.X.); hflin@dlut.edu.cn (H.L.)
[2] School of Computer Science and Engineering, Southeast University, Nanjing 210096, China; sajnani.dileep@gmail.com
\* Correspondence: banbhrani@gmail.com

**Abstract:** Course recommendation is a key for achievement in a student's academic path. However, it is challenging to appropriately select course content among numerous online education resources, due to the differences in users' knowledge structures. Therefore, this paper develops a novel sentiment classification approach for recommending the courses using Taylor-chimp Optimization Algorithm enabled Random Multimodal Deep Learning (Taylor ChOA-based RMDL). Here, the proposed Taylor ChOA is newly devised by the combination of the Taylor concept and Chimp Optimization Algorithm (ChOA). Initially, course review is done to find the optimal course, and thereafter feature extraction is performed for extracting the various significant features needed for further processing. Finally, sentiment classification is done using RMDL, which is trained by the proposed optimization algorithm, named ChOA. Thus, the positively reviewed courses are obtained from the classified sentiments for improving the course recommendation procedure. Extensive experiments are conducted using the E-Khool dataset and Coursera course dataset. Empirical results demonstrate that Taylor ChOA-based RMDL model significantly outperforms state-of-the-art methods for course recommendation tasks.

**Keywords:** chimp optimization algorithm; course recommendation; E-learning; long short-term memory; random multimodal deep learning; sentiment classification

**MSC:** 68T50

**Citation:** Banbhrani, S.K.; Xu, B.; Lin, H.; Sajnani, D.K. Taylor-ChOA: Taylor-Chimp Optimized Random Multimodal Deep Learning-Based Sentiment Classification Model for Course Recommendation. *Mathematics* **2022**, *10*, 1354. https://doi.org/10.3390/math10091354

Academic Editors: Florentina Hristea and Cornelia Caragea

Received: 26 December 2021
Accepted: 11 April 2022
Published: 19 April 2022

**Publisher's Note:** MDPI stays neutral with regard to jurisdictional claims in published maps and institutional affiliations.

## 1. Introduction

E-learning, termed as learning experiences or instructional content-enabled or delivered by electronic technology, particularly standalone computers and computer networks, is one of the foremost modernization that is gradually diffusing into community settings. In addition, web-driven intelligent E-learning environments (WILE) have gained significant attraction across the world, as they bear the power to enhance the superiority of E-learning services and applications. WILE can resolve the major limitation of E-learning methodologies by promoting adapted learning experiences, personalized to the specific individuality of every learner [1]. A course review process should find the quality of individual courses and establish areas in each course and potentially more global areas for development. This process should concentrate on foundation aspects of learning, teaching, and assessment, namely the presence of suitable learning objectives; degree of learning-centered activities; assessment techniques consistent with course objectives; and learning goals. Moreover, the course review process should also inspect consistency in coordination and suitable course contents and policies [2]. Furthermore, sentiment analysis should be conducted to quantify the user emotions involved in the review data [3], and the sentiment assessment should evaluate the words utilized in reviews, which permits visitors to find whether past visitors had an overall bad or good understanding of the listing [4,5].

In E-learning, a course recommendation system recommends the optimal courses in which the students are participating [6,7]. Numerous studies have shown that users face difficulties when choosing a course on an online educational website [8] because of the massive quantity of data. The course selection process is time-consuming and challenging. The important information offered by a course recommendation system can include relevant resource information, such as users' interests and job opportunities. Hence, the course recommendation systems on online education websites must exploit a variety of resources to match the objectives, knowledge structure, and interests of individual users [9]. In addition, selecting a proper course of study is very significant, as the users' futures are dependent on these decisions. The course recommendation system is necessary to assist the student in selecting appropriate courses. It can give a solution to help the student receive the appropriate target outcomes. On the other hand, the process of selecting a personalized course can be highly challenging and intricate for the user [10]. Recently, the recommendation system has become popular in both industry and academia as it reduces the information overloading problem. In numerous applications, the recommendation systems make an effort to evaluate the targeted ratings of the user on unrated items and thereafter recommend the items with high predicted ratings in order to minimize the user attempts and accordingly improve user contentment. Furthermore, data sparsity is the most commonly known issue in recommendation systems in which users have ratings on a lesser number of items, which makes it more difficult to learn efficient recommendation models [11].

Review data can consider the preferences of the user on every rated product and its particular data and can be considered as a carrier of significant information, which will control the character of other prospective users [12]. Review text is considered to be more vital for effective item representation and user learning for recommendation systems. Earlier research work have revealed that incorporating user reviews into the optimization of recommendation systems can extensively enhance the rating performance by reducing data sparsity issues [13,14]. Currently, deep learning methods have gained attraction from various domains due to their significant performance when compared with different traditional approaches [15]. Motivated by the successful exploitation of deep neural networks on the natural language processing (NLP) process, recent work has been committed to modeling user reviews using deep learning methods. Moreover, the most widely used techniques concatenate item reviews and users reviews initially and then accomplish neural network-enabled techniques, such as convolutional neural networks (CNNs) [16], long short-term memory (LSTM), and gated recurrent units (GRUs) [17] for extracting the vector form of the concatenated reviews. Nevertheless, not all the reviews are valuable for the given recommendation task. To emphasize the key knowledge in the comments, a few models exploited attention mechanisms for capturing key information [18,19].

The objective of this research is to design a method, named TaylorChOA-based RMDL, for course recommendation in the E-Khool platform using sentiment analysis for finding positively reviewed courses. The proposed method involves various phases, such as matrix construction, course grouping, course matching, sentiment classification, and course recommendation. Here, the input review data are fed to the matrix construction phase to transform the review data into matrix form. After constructing the matrix, the courses are grouped using deep embedded clustering (DEC) and then the course matching is done using the RC coefficient. After course matching, relevant scholar retrieval and matching are done using the Bhattacharya coefficient to select the best course. In the sentiment classification phase, the significant features, like SentiWordNet-based statistical features, classification-specific features, such as all-caps, numerical words, punctuation marks, elongated words, and time frequency-inverse document frequency (TF-IDF) features are effectively extracted and then sentimental classification is performed using RMDL, which is trained by the proposed TaylorChOA method. The developed TaylorChOA is designed by the incorporation of the Taylor concept and ChOA.

An effective sentiment analysis-based course recommendation method is developed for recommending the positively reviewed courses to the scholars. The courses are grouped by using DEC and then utilized for the matching process, which is carried out using the RV coefficient. The Bhattacharya coefficient is employed for the relevant scholar retrieval and matching process to select the best course. Moreover, the RMDL is used for classifying the sentiments by determining the positively and negatively reviewed courses. The training practice of the RMDL is effectively done using the developed Taylor ChOA, which is the hybridization of the Taylor concept and ChOA.

The major contribution of the paper is a novel sentiment classification approach that is proposed for recommending the courses using Taylor ChOA-based RMDL. Here, the proposed Taylor ChOA is devised by the combination of the Taylor concept and ChOA.

The remainder of the paper is organized as follows. Section 2 describes the review of different course recommendation methods. In Section 3, we briefly introduce the architecture of the proposed framework. Systems implementation and evaluation are described in Section 4. Results and discussion are summarized in Section 5. Finally, Section 6 concludes the overall work and discusses future research studies.

## 2. Related Work

### (a) Hierarchical Approach:

Chao Yang et al. [12] introduced a hierarchical attention network oriented towards crowd intelligence (HANCI) for addressing rating prediction problems. This method extracted more exact user choices and item latent features. Although valuable reviews and significant words provided a positive degree of explanation for the recommendation, this model failed to analyze the recommendation performance by explaining the method at the feature level. Hansi Zeng and Qingyao Ai [14] developed a hierarchical self-attentive convolution network (HSACN) for modeling reviews in recommendation systems. This model attained superior performance by extracting efficient item and user representations from reviews. However, this method suffers from computational complexity problems.

### (b) Deep Learing Approach:

Qinglong Li and Jaekyeong Kim [10] introduced a novel deep learning-enabled course recommender system (DÉCOR) for sustainable improvement in education. This method reduced the information overloading problems. In addition, it achieved superior performance in feature information extraction. However, this method does not consider larger datasets to train the domain recommendation systems. Aminu Da'u et al. [20] modeled a multi channel deep convolutional neural network (MCNN) for recommendation systems. The model was more effective in using review text and hence achieved significant improvements. However, this method suffers from data redundancy problems. Chao Wang et al. [21] devised a demand-aware collaborative Bayesian variational network (DCBVN) for course recommendation. This method offered accurate and explainable recommendations. This model was more robust against sparse and cold start problems. However, this method had higher time complexity.

### (c) Query-based Approach:

Muhammad Sajid Rafiq et al. [22] introduced a query optimization method for course recommendation. This model improved the categorization of action verbs to a more precise level. However, the accuracy of online query optimization and course recommendation was not improved using this technique.

### (d) Other Approaches:

Yi Bai et al. [19] devised a joint summarization and pre-trained recommendation (JSPTRec) for the recommendation based on reviews. This method learned improved semantic representations of reviews for items and users. However, the accuracy of rate prediction needed to be improved. Mohd Suffian Sulaiman et al. [23] designed a fuzzy logic approach for recommending the optimal courses for learners. This method significantly helped the students choose their course based on interest and skill. However, the sentiment analysis of user reviews was not considered for effective performance.

## 3. Proposed Method

The overall architecture of TaylorChOA-based RMDL method for sentiment analysis-based course recommendation, illustrated in Figure 1, contains several components. The detail of each component is presented next.

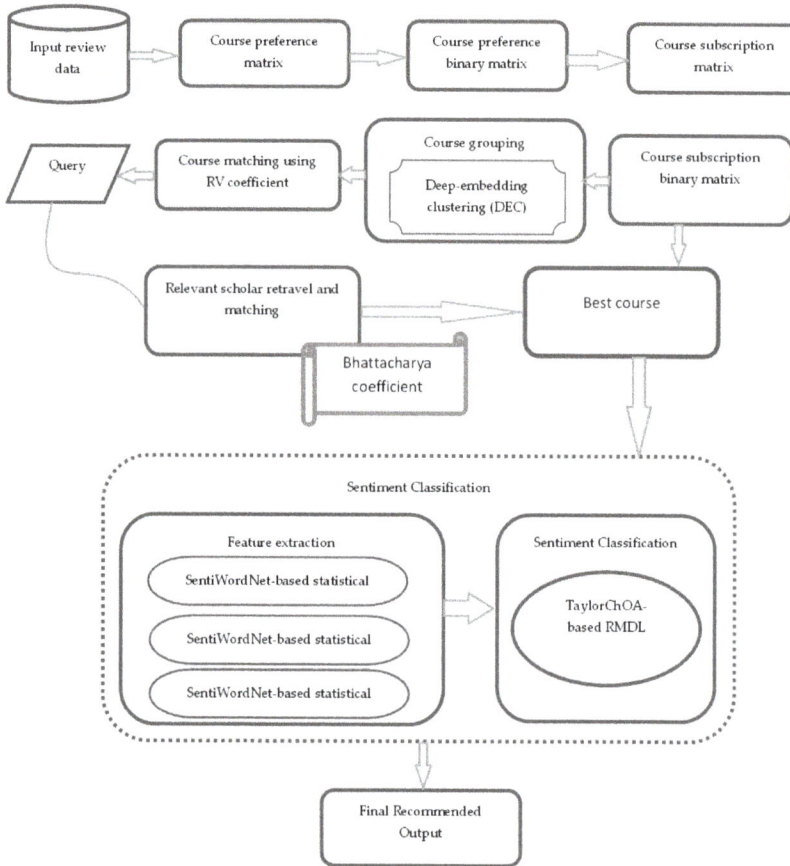

**Figure 1.** An illustration of TaylorChOA-based RMDL for sentiment analysis-based course recommendation.

Initially, the input review data are presented to the matrix construction phase to construct the matrix based on learners' preferences. Thereafter, the constructed matrix is presented to the course grouping phase so that similar courses are grouped in one group, whereas different courses are grouped in another group using DEC [24]. When the query arrives, course matching is performed using the RV coefficient to identify the best course groups from overall course groups. After finding the best course group, relevant scholar retrieval and matching are performed between the user query and best course group using the Bhattacharya coefficient to find the best course. Once course review is performed, sentimental classification is carried out by extracting the significant features, such as SentiWordNet-based statistical features, classification-specific features, and TF-IDF features. Finally, sentiment classification is done using RMDL [25] that is trained by the developed TaylorChOA, which is the integration of the Taylor concept [26] and ChOA [27]. Finally, the positively recommended reviews are provided to the users. Figure 1 portrays a schematic representation of the sentiment analysis-based course recommendation model using the proposed TaylorChOA-based RMDL.

### 3.1. Acquisition of Input Data

The input dataset consists of a set of scholars lists and course lists.

Let the scholar's list be given as

$$D_s = \{S_i\} 1 < i \leq n \tag{1}$$

where $n$ represents the total number of scholars, and $S_i$ denotes $i_{th}$ scholar. Each scholar learns a specific course. Let the course list be expressed as

$$D_c = \{C_j\} 1 < j \leq m \tag{2}$$

where $m$ signifies the overall courses.

### 3.2. Matrix Construction

The input data are transformed to matrix form to make the course recommendation process simpler and more effective.

*Course preference matrix*: The input data $D_s$ are acquired from the dataset and presented to the course preference matrix $U_i$. Each course has a specific ID that is denoted as service ID, and the Scholar ID who searched for the specific course is represented in the visitor preference matrix. The list of courses searched by scholars is given by

$$U_i = \left\{ C_1^i, C_2^i, \ldots, C_l^i, \ldots, C_k^i \right\} \tag{3}$$

where $C_1^i$ represents the $l_{th}$ course preferred by scholar $i$, $U_i$ indicates the course preferred by scholar $i$, and the total number of preferred courses is specified as $k$.

*Course preference binary matrix*: Once the course preference matrix $U_i$ is generated, the course preference binary matrix $B^{U_i}$ is performed based on the courses preferred, which is denoted as 0 and 1. For each course, the corresponding binary values of every course are given in the binary sequence. If a scholar preferred a course, then it is represented as 1, otherwise it is represented as 0. The course preference binary matrix is expressed as

$$B^{U_i} = \begin{cases} 1 & C_l^i \in C_j \\ 0 & \text{otherwise} \end{cases} \tag{4}$$

where $B^{U_i}$ represents the course preference binary matrix for the scholar $i$.

*Course subscription matrix*: The course subscription binary matrix $UL_j$ specifies the scholar who searches for a particular course. Thus, the courses searched by scholar are given as

$$UL_j = \left\{ s_1^j, s_2^j, \ldots, s_p^j, \ldots, s_x^j \right\} \tag{5}$$

where, $s_p^j$ indicates the $j^{th}$ course searched by $p^{th}$ scholar, $x$ denotes the total number of scholars.

*Course subscription binary matrix*: After generating the course subscription matrix $UL_j$, the course subscription binary matrix $B^{UL_j}$ is constructed based on courses subscribed, which is represented either as 0 or 1. For each course, the corresponding binary values for the subscribed course are given in the binary sequence. If the scholar searched for a course, it is denoted as 1, otherwise it is denoted as 0. The course subscription binary matrix is given as

$$B^{UL_j} = \begin{cases} 1 & S_p^j \in S_i \\ 0 & \text{Otherwise} \end{cases} \tag{6}$$

### 3.3. Course Grouping Using DEC Algorithm

The course grouping is performed using the DEC algorithm [24] for finding the best course groups. The DEC algorithm simultaneously learns the cluster assignments and feature representations by deep neural networks. This algorithm optimizes the clustering objective by understanding the mapping features from the data space to a low-dimensional space. It comprises two different phases, namely parameter initialization and clustering optimization, in which the auxiliary target distribution is computed and the Kullback–Leibler (KL) divergence is minimized.

The optimization of parameter or clustering optimization is illustrated by assuming a primary estimate of $\theta$ and $\{\ell_j\}_j^k = 1$.

***Clustering with KL convergence***: By considering an initial estimate of cluster centroids $\{\ell_j\}_j^k = 1$ and non-linear mapping $f_\theta$, an unsupervised algorithm with two steps is devised for improving the process of clustering. In the initial phase, soft assignment is measured among the cluster centroids and embedded points. In the second phase, deep mapping $f_\theta$ is updated and the cluster centroids are refined based on the present high confidence assignments in terms of the auxiliary target distribution. This procedure is iteratively performed until the convergence condition is satisfied.

***Soft assignment***: Here, the student's t-distribution is used as a kernel for measuring the similarity among the centroid $\ell_j$ and embedded point $S_i$.

$$H_{ij} = \frac{\left(1 + \left\| s_i - \ell_j \right\|^2 / \alpha \right)^{\frac{\alpha+1}{2}}}{\sum \left(1 + \left\| s_i - \ell_{j'} \right\|^2 / \alpha \right)^{-\frac{\alpha+1}{2}}} \tag{7}$$

where $\ell_j = f_\theta(y_i) \in S$ corresponds to after the process of embedding, the degree of freedom is represented as $\alpha$, and $H_{ij}$ denotes the probability of sample $i$ to cluster $j$.

***KL divergence optimization***: KL divergence optimization is designed for refining the clusters iteratively by understanding their assignments with higher confidence using the auxiliary target function. It computes the loss of convergence $a_i$ among the auxiliary distribution and soft assignment $b_i$.

$$L = KL(P\|Q) = \sum_i \sum_j a_{ij} \log \frac{a_{ij}}{b_{ij}} \tag{8}$$

Furthermore, the computation is done by initially raising to the second power and thereafter normalizing the outcome by frequency per cluster.

$$a_{ij} = \frac{b_{ij}^2 / f_j}{\sum_{j'} b_{ij'}^2 / f_{j'}} \tag{9}$$

where $f_j = \sum_j b_{ij}$ represents the frequency of soft cluster. Hence, the DEC algorithm effectively improves low confidence prediction results.

The process of course grouping is done to group similar courses into their groups. The course grouping is performed among the scholars and courses. Let the course group obtained by deep embedded clustering be expressed as

$$G = \{G_1, G_2, \dots, G_n\} \tag{10}$$

where $n$ denotes the total number of groups. Thus, the output obtained by the course grouping in finding and grouping the course is denoted as $G$.

### 3.4. Course Matching Using RV Coefficient

The course matching is done using the RV coefficient where the user query is transformed to a binary query so that the matching operation is done to retrieve the best groups. The steps are elucidated below.

***User query***: When the user query arrives, the sequence of queries is given as

$$Q_z = \{q_1, q_2, \ldots, q_d, \ldots, q_r\} \tag{11}$$

where $q_d$ specifies the total number of courses in query $d$ and $r$ represents the total number of queries.

***Binary query sequence***: The sequence of queries is transformed to binary query sequence formulated as

$$B^{Q_=} = \begin{cases} 1; & q_d \in C_j \\ 0; & \text{Otherwise} \end{cases} \tag{12}$$

where $q_d$ denotes the number of courses in query $d$ and $B^{Q_z}$ represents the binary query sequence.

***Course matching using RV coefficient***: The course grouping is done using the RV coefficient by considering the course grouped sequence $G$ and binary query sequence $B^{Q_z}$. Moreover, the RV coefficient is defined as the multivariate rationalization of the squared Pearson correlation coefficient because the RV coefficient considers the values within the range of 0 and 1. It measures the proximity of two sets of points characterized in a matrix form. The RV coefficient equation is given as follows:

$$RV\left(B^{Q_z}, G\right) = \frac{\text{Cov}\left(B^{Q_z}, G\right)}{\sqrt{\text{Var}(B^{Q_z})\,\text{Var}(G)}} \tag{13}$$

where $RV$ indicates the RV coefficient between $(B^{Q_z}, G)$, $B^{Q_z}$ denotes the binary sequence, $G$ specifies the grouped course, $Cov$ represents the co-variance of $(B^{Q_z}, G)$, and $Var$ specifies the variance of $(B^{Q_z}, G)$.

### 3.5. Relevant Scholar Retrieval

After performing the course matching, the relevant scholar retrieval is performed for identifying the best course group in a binary form. The scholar ID is identified based on the best group binary value, and the best course is preferred for scholars. Here, the list of courses is examined in terms of the scholars who are in the best groups.

***Best course group***: The best course group $R_c$ for the relevant scholar retrieval is expressed as

$$R_C = \left\{r_1^i, r_2^i, \ldots, r_y^i, \ldots, r_w^i\right\} \tag{14}$$

where $w$ represents the total number of best courses, and $r_y^i$ denotes the best course retrieved by the scholar $i$.

***Binary best course group***: For each best course group, the corresponding binary values for the retrieved best course are given in a binary sequence. If the best course is retrieved by the scholar, it is indicated as 1, otherwise it is denoted as 0.

$$B^{R_C} = \begin{cases} 1; & r_y^i \in C_j \\ 0; & \text{Otherwise} \end{cases} \tag{15}$$

***Matching query and best course group using Bhattacharya coefficient***: Once the scholar retrieved the best course, the binary query sequence $B^{Q_z}$ and the best course group $B^{R_c}$ are compared using the Bhattacharya coefficient. The Bhattacharyya distance computes the similarity of two probability distributions, and the equation is expressed as

$$BC\left(B^{Q_=}, B^{R_C}\right) = \sum_{x \in X} \sqrt{P(B^{Q_E}) \cdot P(B^{R_C})} \tag{16}$$

where $BC$ indicates the Bhattacharya coefficient. Once the query and best group binary sequence are matched, the minimum value distance is chosen as the best course based on the Bhattacharya coefficient. The output of matching result is scholar preferred courses, and it is expressed as $C_b$, given as

$$C_b = \{C_1, C_2, \ldots, C_h\} \tag{17}$$

where $C_h$ signifies courses preferred by a scholar that are the best courses. The best course $C_b$ undergoes a sentimental classification process to verify whether the recommended course is good or bad. Algorithm 1 provides the Pseudo-code of course review framework.

---

**Algorithm 1** Pseudo-code of Course Review Framework.

**Input:** UserID: $D_s$, ItemID: $D_c$, Review: $R$, Query $Q_s$, Cluster size $C_s = 3$; Parameter $= U_i$ course preference matrix, $G$ best-clustered course group, $R_C$ relevant scholar retrieved, $n$ courses in optimal clustered group, $B^U$ course preference binary matrix, $n$ number of scholars, $m$ number of courses, $k$ is the total number of preferred course.

**Output:** Best course $C_b$

**Begin**

**Read Input** $(D_{(s)}, D_{(c)}, R)$; $B^{(U_{(i)})}, B^{(UL_{(j)})} = U_{(i)}(D_{(s)}, D_{(c)})$

$G = DEC(B^{(UL_{(j)})},$ clustersize $= 3)$ Find $G$

$G =$ course Matching phase $(Q_z, G)$

Compute $R_C =$ Relevant visitor phase $\left(n, B^{U^{(i)}}\right)$;

$C_b =$ Matched visitor phase $(Q_z, R_C)$ //Course preference matrix phase $B^{U_i} = (D_s, D_c)$

**if** scholar search the course; Print 1

**else** Print 0

$B^{UL_j} = (D_s, D_c)$

**if** ($m$ course is visited by the scholar) Print 1

**else** Print 0

$Q_z$ generation based on $B^{UL_j}$ //Course matching phase

$RV.grp = []$

**for** $j = 1$ to $G$ $Sum_{RV_{val}} = 0$

For $j = 1$ to $len(h)$

$Sum_{RV_{val}} + = RV$ coeff $(Q_z,$ h$)$

End **for**

$RV.grp.app$ end$(Sum_{RV_{val}})$

End **for**

$G = \max(RV \cdot grp)$ //Relevant scholar phase

$R_C = []$

**for** j $= 1$ to $len(h)$

$C =$ got scholars who viewed the courses

$R_C.append\left(B^{U_i}(C)\right)$

End **for**

Return $R_C$

//Matched scholar phase $C_b = []$

**for** j $= 1$ to len

$(R_C)$

$C_b.append$ (Bhattacharya $(Q_z, R_C))$

End **for**

Sort by $\min(C_b)$

Return $C_b$

---

*3.6. Sentiment Classification*

The best course $C_b$ is fed as an input to the sentiment classification phase to classify the sentiments in terms of the sentimental polarities of opinions. The classified sentiments may have either a positive score or a negative score.

*Acquisition of significant features for sentiment classification*: The significant features, such as SentiWordNet-based statistical features, classification-specific features, and TF-IDF features, are extracted from the best course $C_b$ for improving the course recommendation process. The extracted features are elucidated below.

*(a) SentiWordNet-based statistical features*: SentiWordNet [28] groups the words into multiple sets of synonyms, called synsets. Every synset is associated with a polarity score, such as positive or negative. The scores take a value between 0 and 1, and their summation provides a value of 1 for every synset. By considering the scores provided, it is feasible to decide whether the estimation is positive or negative. The words present in the SentiWordNet database are based on the parts of speech attained from WordNet, and it utilizes a program to apply the scores to every word. The weight tuning of positive and negative score values can be expressed as

$$|\varphi^m(p), \varphi^m(n)| = h(w_m) \tag{18}$$

where $\varphi^m(p)$ represents the positive score, $\varphi^m(n)$ denotes the negative score, and $h$ specifies the SentiWordNet function. However, the SentiWordNet feature is denoted as $F_n$. With the SentiWordNet score, statistical features, such as mean and variance, are computed using the expressions given below.

(i) Mean: The mean value is computed by taking the average of SentiWordNet score for every word from the review, given as

$$\mu = \frac{1}{|U(x_n)|} \times \sum_{n=1}^{|U(x_n)|} U(x_n) \tag{19}$$

where $n$ represents the overall words, $U(x_n)$ signifies the SentiWordNet score of each review, and $|U(x_n)|$ represents the overall scores obtained from the word.

(ii) Variance: The variance $\sigma$ is computed based on the value of the mean, given as

$$\sigma = \frac{\sum_{n=1}^{|U(x_n)|} |x_n - \mu|}{U(x_n)} \tag{20}$$

where $\mu$ signifies the mean value. Thus, the sentiwordNet-based feature considers the positive and negative scores of each word in the review, and from that, the statistical features, like mean and variance, are computed.

*(b) Classification-specific features*: The various classification specific features, such as capitalized words, numerical words, punctuation marks, and elongated words are explained below.

(i) All caps: The feature $f_1$ specifies the all-caps feature, which represents the overall capitalized words in a review, expressed as

$$f_1 = \sum_{m=1}^{b} w_{\bar{C}}^m \tag{21}$$

where $w_{\bar{C}}^m$ indicates the total number of words with upper case letters. It considers a value 0 or 1 concerning the state that relies on the absence or presence of capitalized words as formulated below:

$$w_{\bar{C}}^m = \begin{cases} 1; & \text{if capsword} \\ 0; & \text{otherwise} \end{cases} \tag{22}$$

Here, the feature $f_1$ is in the dimension of $[10,000 \times 1]$.

(ii) Number of numerical words: The number of text characters or numerical digits used to show numerals are represented as $f_2$ with the dimension $[10,000 \times 1]$.

(iii) Punctuation: The punctuation feature $f_3$ may be an apostrophe, dot, or exclamation mark present in a review:

$$f_3 = \sum_{m=1}^{b} S_p^m \tag{23}$$

where $S_p^m$ represents the overall punctuation present in the $m_{th}$ review. Here, $S_p$ is given a value of 1 for the punctuation that occurred in the review and 0 for other cases. Moreover, the feature $f_3$ has the dimension of $[10,000 \times 1]$.

(iv) Elongated words: The feature $f_4$ represents the elongated words that have a character repeated more than two times in a review and is given as

$$f_4 = \sum_{m=1}^{b} w_E^m \tag{24}$$

where $w_E^m$ specifies the overall hashtags present in the $m$th review. The term is given with a value of 0 for every elongated word in the review and 1 for the nonexistence of an elongated word. Furthermore, the elongated word feature $f_4$ holds the size of $[10,000 \times 1]$.

The classification specific features are signified as $F_2$ by considering the seven extracted features and is given as

$$F_2 = \{f_1, f_2, f_3, f_4\} \tag{25}$$

where $f_1$ denotes the all-caps feature, $f_2$ signifies the numerical word feature, $f_3$ specifies the punctuation feature, and $f_4$ indicates the elongated word feature.

(c) **TF-IDF**: TF-IDF [29] is used to create a composite weight for every term in each of the review data. TF measures how frequently a term occurs in review data, whereas IDF measures how significant a term is. The TF-IDF score is computed as

$$F_4 = C \left( \frac{\log(1 + \phi_1)}{\log(\phi_2)} \right) \tag{26}$$

where $C$ specifies the total number of review data, term frequency is denoted as $\phi_1$, $\phi_2$ represents the inverse document frequency, and $F_3$ implies the TF-IDF feature with dimension $[1 \times 50]$.

Furthermore, the features extracted are incorporated together to form a feature vector $F$ for reducing the complexity in classifying the sentiments, which is expressed as

$$F = \{F_1, F_2, F_3\} \tag{27}$$

where $F_1$ signifies the SentiWordNet-based statistical feature, $F_2$ represents the classification specific features, $F_3$ implies the TF-IDF features, and $F$ implies the feature vector with dimension $[10,000 \times 834]$.

*3.7. Sentiment Classification Using Proposed TaylorChOA-Based RMDL*

Here, the feature vector $F$ is employed for classifying the sentiments effectively. The classification of sentiments is carried out using the proposed TaylorChOA-based RMDL. The RMDL [25] is trained with the proposed TaylorChOA algorithm, which is developed by combining the Taylor concept [26] and ChOA [27]. Thus, effective course recommendation is achieved by offering suitable courses for the learners. The architecture and training procedure of RMDL are explained below.

(a) **Architecture of RMDL**: RMDL [25] is a robust method that comprises three basic deep learning models, namely deep neural networks (DNN), recurrent neural networks (RNN), and a convolutional neural network (CNN) model. The structure of RMDL is presented in Figure 2.

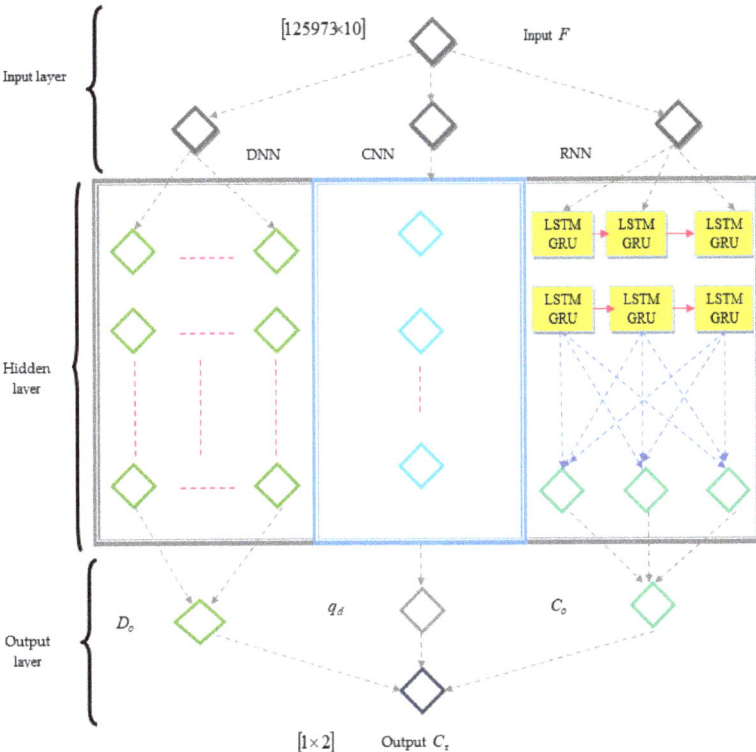

**Figure 2.** An illustration of random multimodel deep learning for sentiment analysis-based course recommendation.

(i) DNN: DNN architecture is designed with multi-classes where every learning model is generated at random. Here, the overall layer and its nodes are randomly assigned. Moreover, this model utilizes a standard back-propagation algorithm using activation functions. The output layer has a softmax function to perform the classification and is given as

$$f(x) = \frac{1}{1 + g^{-x}} \in (0, 1) \tag{28}$$

$$f(x) = \max(0, x) \tag{29}$$

The output of DNN is denoted as $D_o$.

(ii) RNN: RNN assigns additional weights to the sequence of data points. The information about the preceding nodes is considered in a very sophisticated manner to perform the effective semantic assessment of the dataset structure.

$$x_y = F_f(x_{y-1}, h_y, \theta) \tag{30}$$

$$x_y = U_{rec}\kappa(x_{y-1}) + U_{in}h_y + A \tag{31}$$

Here, $x_y$ signifies the state at the time $y$, and $h_y$ denotes the input at phase $y$. In addition, the recurrent matrix weight and input weight are represented as $U_{rec}$ and $U_{in}$, the bias is represented as $A$, and $\kappa$ indicates the element-wise operator.

***Long short-term memory (LSTM)***: LSTM is a class of RNN that is used to maintain long-term relevancy in an improved manner. This LSTM network effectively addresses the vanishing gradient issue. LSTM consists of a chain-like structure and utilizes multiple gates for handling huge amounts of data. The step-by-step procedure of LSTM cell is expressed as follows:

$$F_d = \Re(w_F[p_d, q_{d-1}] + H_F) \tag{32}$$

$$\widetilde{C}_d = \tan q(w_C[p_d, q_{d-1}] + H_C) \tag{33}$$

$$r_d = \Re(w_r[p_d, q_{d-1}] + H_r) \tag{34}$$

$$J_d = F_d * \widetilde{C}_d + r_d J_{d-1} \tag{35}$$

$$M_d = \Re(w_M[p_d, q_{d-1}] + H_M) \tag{36}$$

$$q_d = M_d \tan y(J_d) \tag{37}$$

where $F_d$ represents the input gate, $\widetilde{C}_d$ specifies the candidate memory cell, $r_d$ denotes the forget gate activation, and $J_d$ defines the new memory cell value. Here, $M_d$ and $q_d$ specify the output gate value.

**Gated recurrent unit (GRU)**: GRU is a gating strategy for RNN that consists of two gates. Here, GRU does not have internal memory, and the step by step procedure for GRU cells is given as

$$N_d = \Re_l(w_N p_d + V_N q_{d-1} + H_z) \tag{38}$$

where $n_d$ implies update gate vector of $d$, $p_d$ denotes the input vector, the various parameters are termed as $w$, $V$, and $H$, and $\Re_l$ represent the activation parameter.

$$\widetilde{S}_d = \Re_l(w_S p_d + V_S q_{d-1} + H_S) \tag{39}$$

$$q_d = N_d \circ q_{d-1} + (1 - N_d) \circ \Re_l(w_q p_d + V_q(S_d \circ q_{d-1}) + H_d) \tag{40}$$

Here, $q_d$ denotes the output vector, the reset gate vector is denoted as $S_d$, $N_d$ indicates the update gate vector of $d$, and the hyperbolic tangent parameter is signified as $\Re_l$.

(iii) CNN: CNN is the final deep learning method that contributes to RMDL and is mainly accomplished for the classification process. In CNN, the convolution of an image tensor is done with a group of kernels with dimension $p \times p$. These types of convolutional layers are known as feature maps, and they are stacked to offer numerous input filters. To decrease the computational complexity, a pooling function is employed for reducing the output dimension from one layer to the next. Finally, the feature maps are flattened into one column in such a way that the last layer is fully connected. The output of CNN is expressed as $C_0$.

For these deep learning structures, the total number of nodes and layers are randomly generated. The random creation process is given by

$$T(t_{d1}, t_{d2}, t_{d3,\ldots}, t_{dt}) = \left[ \frac{1}{2} + \frac{(\sum_{e=1}^{z} t_d) - \frac{1}{2}}{z} \right] \tag{41}$$

where $z$ denotes the overall random models, $t_{dz}$ specifies the output for a data point $i$ in $z$, and this equation is utilized for classifying the sentiments, $k \in \{0, 1\}$. The output space uses majority vote for final $\hat{t}_d$, and the equation is expressed as

$$\hat{t}_d = [\hat{t}_{d1} \ldots \hat{t}_{de} \ldots \hat{t}_{dt}]^N \tag{42}$$

where $\hat{t}_d$ specifies the classification label of review or data point of $E_d \in \{a_d, b_d\}$ for $e$, and $\hat{t}_d$ is represented as follows:

$$\hat{t}_{d,z} = \arg\max_k \left[ \text{softmax}\left(t_{d,z}^*\right) \right]^N \tag{43}$$

After training the RMDL model, the final classification is computed using a majority vote of DNN, CNN, and RNN models, which improve the accuracy and robustness of the results. The final result obtained from the RMDL is indicated as $C_\tau$.

**(b) Training of RMDL using the proposed TaylorChOA**: The training procedure of RMDL [25] is performed using the developed optimization method, known as TaylorChOA. The developed TaylorChOA is designed by the incorporation of the Taylor concept and ChOA. ChOA [27] is motivated by the characteristics of chimps for hunting prey. It is mainly accomplished for solving the problems based on convergence speed by learning through the high dimensional neural network. In addition, the independent groups have different mechanisms for updating the parameters to explore the chimp with diverse competence in search space. The dynamic strategies effectively balance the global and local search problems. The Taylor concept [26] exploits the preliminary dataset and the standard form of the system for validating the Taylor series expansion in terms of a specific degree. The incorporation of the Taylor series with the ChOA shows the effectiveness of the developed scheme and minimized the computational complexity. The algorithmic procedure of the proposed TaylorChOA algorithm is illustrated below.

(i) Initialization: Let us consider the chimp population as $Z_i (i = 1, 2, \ldots, m)$ in the solution space $N$, and the parameters are initialized as $n$, $u$, $v$, and $r$. Here, $n$ specifies the non-linear factor, $u$ implies the chaotic vector $v$, and $r$ denotes the vectors.

(ii) Calculate fitness measure: The fitness measure is accomplished for calculating the optimal solution using the error function and is expressed as

$$\zeta = \frac{1}{\ell} \sum_{\delta=1}^{\ell} [E_\tau - C_\tau]^2 \tag{44}$$

where $\zeta$ signifies fitness measure, $E_\tau$ specifies target output, $\ell$ indicates overall training samples, and the output of the RMDL model is denoted as $C_\tau$.

(iii) Driving and chasing the prey: The prey is chased during the exploitation and exploration phases. The mathematical expression used for driving and chasing the prey is expressed as

$$Z(s+1) = Z_{\text{prey}}(s) - x \cdot y \tag{45}$$

where $s$ represents the current iteration, $x$ signifies the coefficient vector, $Z_{\text{prey}}$ implies the vector of prey position, $y$ indicates driving the prey, and the position vector of chimp is specified as $Z$. Here, $y$ is expressed as

$$y = |r.Z_{\text{prey}}(s) - u.Z(s)| \tag{46}$$

Let us consider $Z_{\text{prey}}(s) > Z(s)$,

$$Z(s+1) = Z_{\text{prey}}(s) - x(r.Z_{\text{prey}}(s) - u.Z(s)) \tag{47}$$

$$Z(s+1) = Z_{\text{prey}}(s) - x.rZ_{\text{prey}}(s) + x.u.Z(s) \tag{48}$$

$$Z(s+1) = Z_{\text{prey}}(s)[1 - x.r] + x.u.Z(s) \tag{49}$$

By incorporating the Taylor concept [26] with the ChOA [27], the algorithmic performance is improved by minimizing the optimization problems. The standard equation of the Taylor concept [26] is expressed as

$$Z(s+1) = Z(s) + \frac{Z'(s)}{1!} + \frac{Z''(s)}{2!} \tag{50}$$

where

$$Z'(s) = \frac{Z(s) - Z(s-k)}{k} \tag{51}$$

$$Z''(s) = \frac{Z(s) - 2Z(s-k) + Z(s-2k)}{k^2} \tag{52}$$

Assume $s = 1$ and substitute $Z'(s), Z''(s)$ in Equation (50):

$$Z(s+1) = Z(s) + \frac{Z(s) - Z(s-1)}{1!} + \frac{Z(s) - 2Z(s-1) + Z(s-2)}{2!} \qquad (53)$$

$$Z(s+1) = Z(s)\left(1 + 1 + \frac{1}{2}\right) - Z(s-1) - \frac{2Z(s-1)}{2} + \frac{Z(s-2)}{2} \qquad (54)$$

By substituting Equation (56) in Equation (50), the equation becomes

$$Z(s+1) = \frac{5Z_{\text{mey}}(s)[1 - xs] + 4 \cdot x \cdot u \cdot Z(s-1) - x \cdot uZ(t-2)}{5 - 2x \cdot u} \qquad (55)$$

where the coefficient vector is denoted as $r$, the position of a chimp at iteration $s-1$ is specified as $Z(s-1)$, the position of a chimp at iteration $s-2$ is specified as $Z(s-2)$, $Z_{\text{prey}}$ indicates the vector of prey position, and $u$ implies the chaotic value. Moreover, $x = 2 \cdot v \cdot w_1 - v$, and $r = 2 \cdot w_2$ where the value of $v$ is reduced from 2.5 to 0 and $w_1, w_2$ denotes the random vector within the range $[0, 1]$.

(iv) Attacking strategy (exploitation phase): To mathematically formulate the attacking character of chimps, it is considered that the first attacker, driver, barrier, and chaser are informed regarding the position of potential prey. Thus, the four optimal solutions to update the position are given as

$$Z(s+1) = \frac{Z_1 + Z_2 + Z_3 + Z_4}{4} \qquad (56)$$

(v) Prey attacking: In this prey attacking phase, the chimps attack the prey and end the hunting operation once the prey starts moving. To mathematically formulate the attacking behavior, the value must be decreased.

(vi) Searching for prey (exploration phase): The exploration process is performed based on the position of the attacker, chaser, barrier, and driver chimps. Moreover, chimps deviate to search for the prey and aggregate to chase the prey.

(vii) Social incentive: To acquire social meeting and related social motivation in the final phase, the chimps release their hunting potential. To model this process, there is a 50% chance to prefer between the normal position update strategy and chaotic model for updating the position of chimps during the optimization. The equation is represented as

$$Z_{\text{chimp}}(s+1) = \begin{cases} Z_{\text{prey}}(s) - x \cdot y & \text{if } \omega < 0.5 \\ \text{Chaticvalue} & \text{if } \omega > 0.5 \end{cases} \qquad (57)$$

where, $\omega$ denotes the random number between $[0, 1]$.

(viii) Feasibility evaluation: The fitness value is calculated for each solution such that the best value of fitness is considered the best solution.

(ix) Termination: All the above-presented steps are iterated until the global optimal solution is achieved. Algorithm 2 provides the pseudo-code of the proposed TaylorChOA.

The developed TaylorChOA-based RMDL model achieved effective performance in recommending the positively reviewed courses to the scholars by classifying the positively and negatively reviewed courses.

---

**Algorithm 2** Pseudo-code of proposed TaylorChOA algorithm.

---

    **Input:** $Z_i$
    **Output:** $Z_{chimp}(s+1)$
Initialize population
Initialize the parameters, like $v, u, x$, and $r$
Determine the position of each chimp
**while** $(s < \aleph); \aleph-$ maximum iterations
**for** each chimp
Extract the group of chimps
Use the grouping mechanism to update $v, u$, and $r$
end **for**
**for** each search chimp
**if** $(\varpi < 0.5)$
**if** $(|x| < 1)$
Update position of search agent using Equation (56)
else **if** $(x > 1)$
Choose a random search agent
end **if**
else **if** $(\varpi > 0.5)$
Update position of search using the chaotic value
end **if**
end **for**
Update $v, u, x$, and $r$
$s = s + 1$
end **while**
Return the best solution

---

## 4. Systems Implementation and Evaluation

In this section, we first present the datasets, then details about the experimental setup, baseline benchmarks, and finally evaluation metrics are shown.

### 4.1. Description of Datasets

In order to evaluate our system, the E-Khool https://ekhool.com/ (accessed on 12 October 2021) and Coursera Course https://www.kaggle.com/siddharthm1698/coursera-course-dataset (accessed on 10 February 2022) datasets are adapted for sentiment classification based course recommendation.

The E-Khool dataset comprises 100,000 rows with 25 courses and 1000 learners. This dataset includes various attributes, such as learner ID, course ID, subscription date, ratings (1 to 5), and review.

The Coursera Course dataset was generated during a hackathon for project purposes. It contains 6 columns and 890 course data points. The columns are course-title, course-organization, course-certificate-type, course-rating, course-difficulty, and course-students-enrolled.

### 4.2. Experimental Setup

The method we proposed is implemented in Python programming language; our networks are trained on NVIDIA GTX 1080 in a 64-bit computer with Intel(R) Core(TM) i7-6700 CPU @3.4GHz, 16 GB RAM, and Ubuntu 16.04 operating system.

### 4.3. Evaluation Metrics

The performance of the developed TaylorChOA-based RMDL is analyzed by considering the evaluation measures, like precision, recall, and F1-score.

***Precision:*** This is the proportion of true positives to overall positives, and the precision measure is expressed as

$$\delta = \frac{A}{A+B} \tag{58}$$

where $\delta$ specifies the precision, $A$ denotes the true positives, and $B$ signifies the false positives.

***Recall:*** Recall is a measure that defines the proportion of true positives to the summing up of false negatives and true positives, and the equation is given as

$$\omega = \frac{A}{A+E} \tag{59}$$

where the recall measure is signified as $\omega$, and $E$ symbolizes the false negatives.

***F1-score:*** This is a statistical measure of the accuracy of a test or an individual based on the recall and precision, which is given as

$$F_m = 2 * \left( \frac{\delta * \omega}{\delta + \omega} \right) \tag{60}$$

where $F_m$ denotes the F1-score.

### 4.4. Baseline Methods

In order to evaluate the effectiveness of the proposed framework, our method was compared with several existing algorithms, such as:

- HSACN [14]: The method was formulated to learn item and user representations from reviews.
- MCNN [20]: Multichannel Deep Convolutional Neural Network for Recommender Systems.
- Query Optimization [22]: The Query Optimization method for course recommendation model designed to improve the categorization of action verbs to a more precise level.
- DCBVN [21]: Demand-aware Collaborative Bayesian Variational Network for course recommendation.
- Proposed TaylorChOA-based RMDL: Proposed TaylorChOA-based RMDL model is developed for recommending the finest courses.

### 5. Results and Discussion

The performance results of our proposed model are presented in this section. The results are compared with previously introduced methods, which were tested on the same datasets.

### 5.1. Results Based on E-Khool Dataset, with Respect to Number of Iterations (10 to 50)

5.1.1. Performance Analysis Based on Cluster Size = 3

Figure 3 presents the performance analysis of the developed technique with iterations by varying the queries with cluster size =3. Figure 3a presents the assessment based on precision. For the number of query 1, the precision value measured by the developed TaylorChOA-based RMDL with iteration 10 is 0.795, iteration 20 is 0.825, iteration 30 is 0.836, iteration 40 is 0.847, and iteration 50 is 0.854. Figure 3b portrays the analysis using recall.

By considering the number of query 2, the value of recall computed by the developed TaylorChOA-based RMDL with iteration 10 is 0.825, iteration 20 is 0.847, iteration 30 is 0.874, iteration 40 is 0.885, and iteration 50 is 0.895. The analysis using F1-score is depicted in Figure 3c. When the number of a query is 3, the value of F1-score computed by the developed TaylorChOA-based RMDL with iteration 10 is 0.830, iteration 20 is 0.854, iteration 30 is 0.886, iteration 40 is 0.900, and iteration 50 is 0.919.

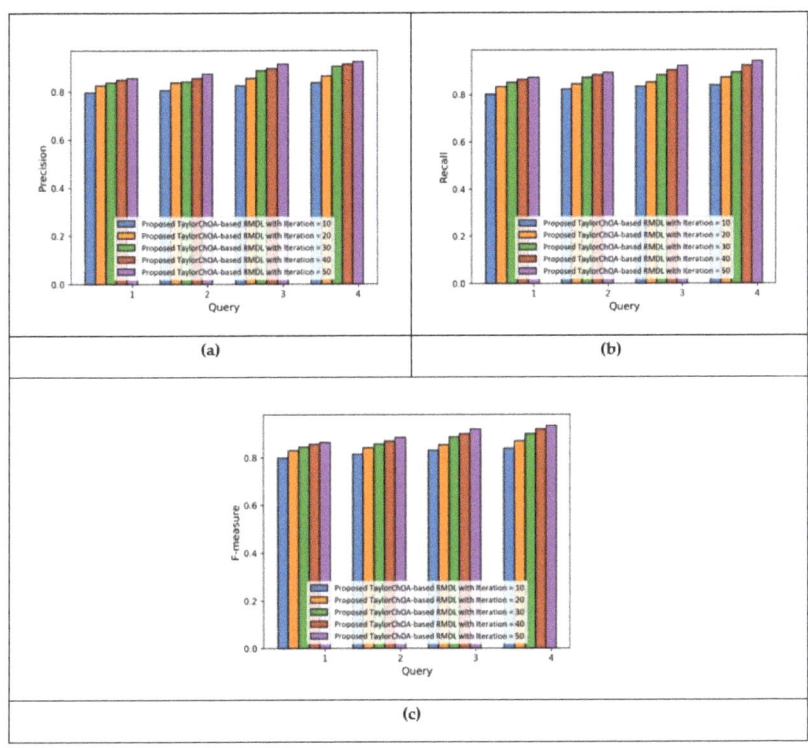

**Figure 3.** Performance analysis with cluster size = 3 using E-Khool dataset: (**a**) precision, (**b**) recall, and (**c**) F1-score.

5.1.2. Performance Analysis Based on Cluster Size = 4

Figure 4 shows the performance assessment of the developed technique with iterations by varying the queries. Figure 4a presents the analysis based on precision. For the number of query 1, the precision value measured by the developed TaylorChOA-based RMDL with iteration 10, iteration 20, iteration 30, iteration 40, and iteration 50 is 0.784, 0.804, 0.814, 0.825, and 0.836, respectively. Figure 4b portrays the analysis using recall. By considering the number of query 2, the value of recall computed by the developed TaylorChOA-based RMDL with iteration 10 is 0.835, iteration 20 is 0.854, iteration 30 is 0.865, iteration 40 is 0.885, and iteration 50 is 0.899.

The analysis in terms of F1-score is shown in Figure 4c. When the number of a query is 3, the value of F1-score computed by the developed TaylorChOA-based RMDL with iteration 10 is 0.841, iteration 20 is 0.865, iteration 30 is 0.881, iteration 40 is 0.897, and iteration 50 is 0.917.

**Comparison of existing methods and the proposed TaylorChOA-based RMDL using E-Khool dataset, in terms of precision, recall, and F1-score:**

The comparative assessment of the developed technique is performed by varying the queries with the cluster size = 3 and cluster size = 4 in terms of the evaluation metrics.

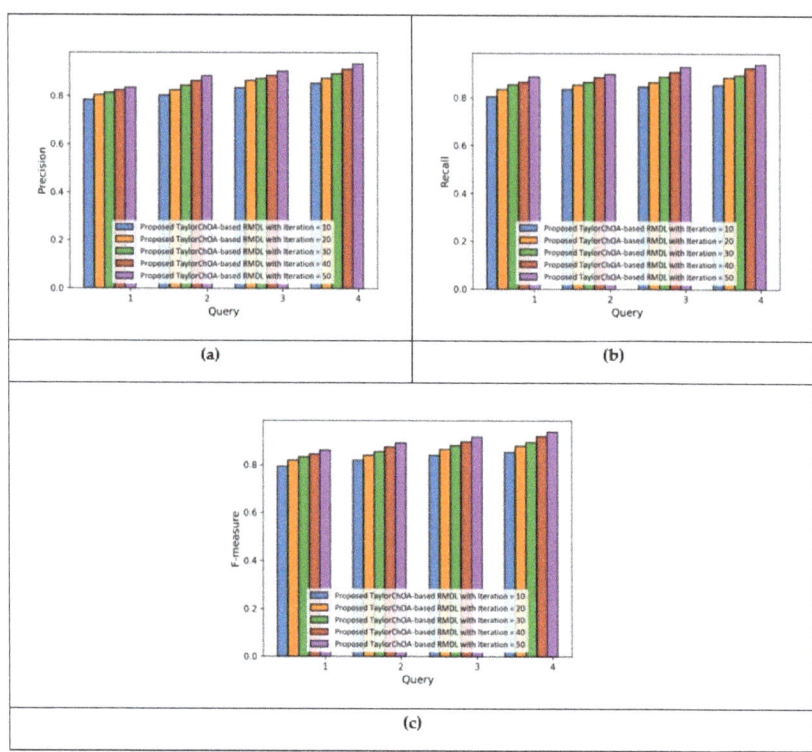

**Figure 4.** Performance analysis with cluster size = 4 using E-Khool dataset: (**a**) precision, (**b**) recall, and (**c**) F1-score.

5.1.3. Comparative Analysis Based on Cluster Size = 3 in terms of Precision, Recall, and F1-Score Using E-Khool Dataset

Figure 5 portrays the assessment with cluster size = 3 by varying the number of queries using the performance measures, such as precision, recall, and F1-score. Figure 5a) presents the analysis in terms of precision. When number of query is 1, the precision value measured by the developed TaylorChOA-based RMDL is 0.854, whereas the precision value measured by the existing methods, such as HSACN, MCNN, Query Optimization, and DCBVN is 0.575, 0.685, 0.736, and 0.832, respectively.

The analysis based on recall measure is portrayed in Figure 5b. By considering the number of query as 2, the developed TaylorChOA-based RMDL measured a recall value of 0.895, whereas the value of recall computed by the existing methods, such as HSACN, MCNN, Query Optimization, and DCBVN is 0.625, 0.754, 0.785, and 0.865, respectively. The assessment using F1-score is shown in Figure 5c. The F1-score value attained by the HSACN, MCNN, Query Optimization, DCBVN, and developed TaylorChOA-based RMDL is 0.634, 0.768, 0.815, 0.889, and 0.919, respectively, when considering the number of query as 3.

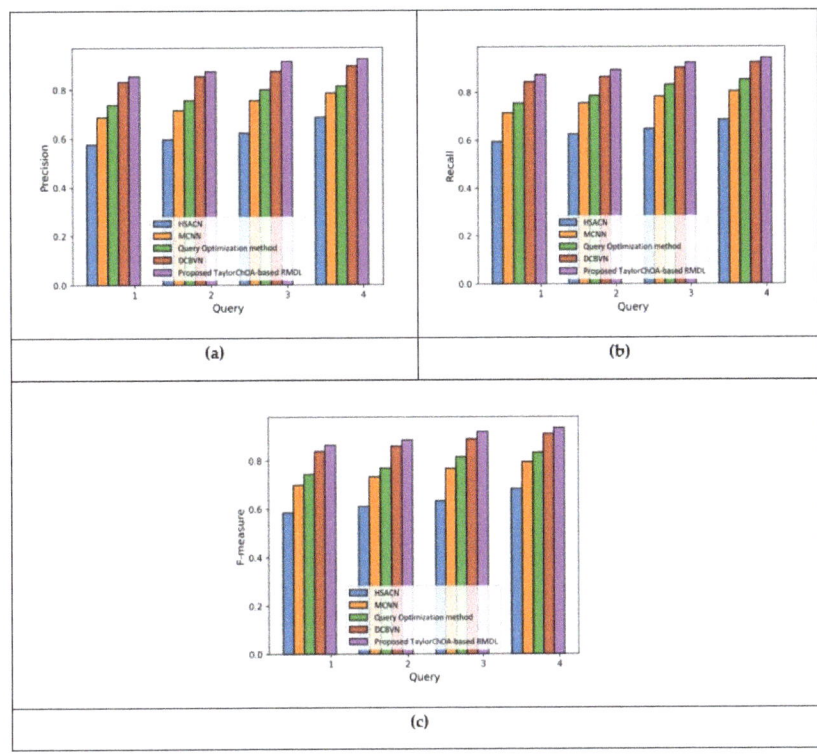

**Figure 5.** Comparative analysis with cluster size = 3 using K-Khool dataset: (**a**) precision, (**b**) recall, and (**c**) F1-score.

5.1.4. Comparative Analysis Based on Cluster Size = 4 in Terms of Precision, Recall, and F1-Score Using E-Khool Dataset

The analysis with cluster size = 4 using the evaluation metrics and varying the number of queries is portrayed in Figure 6. The analysis using precision is shown in Figure 6a. When considering the number of query as 1, the developed TaylorChOA-based RMDL computed a precision value of 0.836, whereas thepPrecision value achieved by the existing methods, such as HSACN, MCNN, Query Optimization, and DCBVN, is 0.584, 0.668, 0.725, and 0.812, respectively.

Figure 6b presents the assessment using recall. The recall values obtained by the HSACN, MCNN, Query Optimization, DCBVN, and developed TaylorChOA-based RMDL are 0.629, 0.765, 0.798, 0.874, and 0.899, respectively, for the number of query 2. The analysis in terms of recall measure is presented in Figure 6c. When the number of query is 3, the F1-score value of HSACN is 0.643, MCNN is 0.781, Query Optimization is 0.824, DCBVN is 0.899, and developed TaylorChOA-based RMDL is 0.917.

Table 1 presents a comparison of the results developed by the TaylorChOA-based RMDL technique with the existing techniques by considering the evaluation measures for the number of query 4. With cluster size = 3, the maximum precision of 0.925, maximum recall of 0.944, and maximum F1-score of 0.934 are computed by the developed TaylorChOA-based RMDL method.

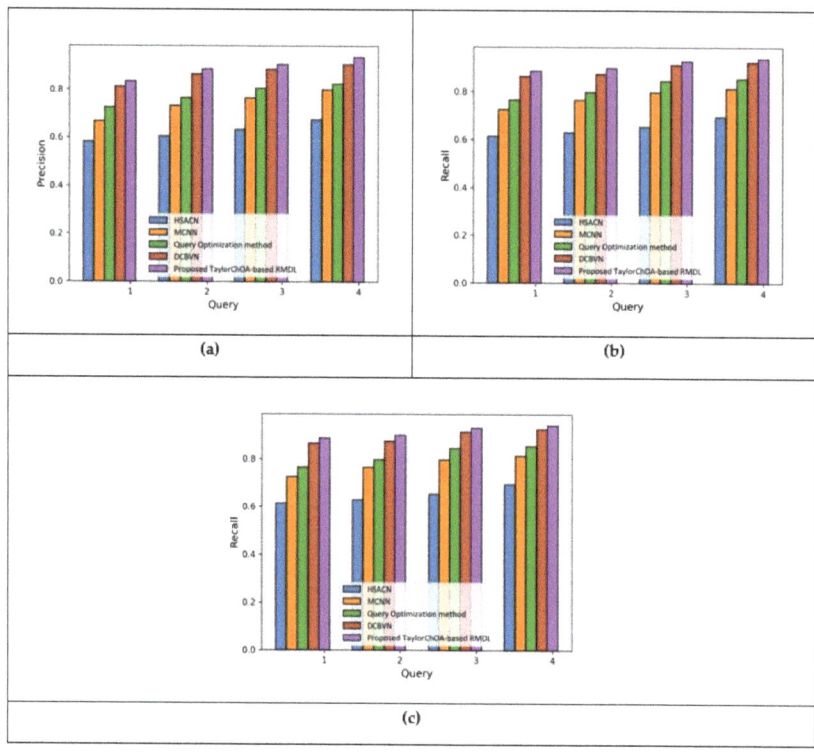

**Figure 6.** Comparative analysis with cluster size = 4 using E-Khool dataset: (**a**) precision, (**b**) recall, and (**c**) F1-score.

**Table 1.** Comparison of proposed TaylorChOA-based RMDL with existing methods using E-Khool dataset, in terms of precision, recall, and F1-score.

| Method | Metrics | HSACN | MCNN | Qu Opt. | DCBVN | Proposed Method |
|---|---|---|---|---|---|---|
| Cluster Size = 3 | Precision | 0.684 | 0.784 | 0.814 | 0.896 | **0.925** |
| | Recall | 0.685 | 0.805 | 0.854 | 0.925 | **0.944** |
| | F1-score | 0.684 | 0.794 | 0.833 | 0.910 | **0.934** |
| Cluster Size = 4 | Precision | 0.674 | 0.798 | 0.825 | 0.905 | **0.936** |
| | Recall | 0.695 | 0.814 | 0.854 | 0.925 | **0.941** |
| | F1-score | 0.685 | 0.806 | 0.839 | 0.915 | **0.938** |

Using cluster size = 4, the maximum precision of 0.936 is computed by the developed TaylorChOA-based RMDL, whereas the Precision value computed by the existing methods, such as HSACN, MCNN, Query Optimization, and DCBVN is 0.674, 0.798, 0.825, and 0.905, respectively. Likewise, the higher recall of 0.941 is computed by the developed TaylorChOA-based RMDL, whereas the precision value computed by the existing methods, such as HSACN, MCNN, Query Optimization, and DCBVN is 0.695, 0.814, 0.854, and 0.925, respectively. Moreover, the F1-score value obtained by the HSACN is 0.685, MCNN is 0.806, Query Optimization is 0.839, DCBVN is 0.915, and TaylorChOA-based RMDL is 0.938. Thus, the developed TaylorChOA-based RMDL outperformed various existing methods and achieved better performance with the maximum precision of 0.936, maximum recall of 0.944, and maximum F1-score of 0.938.

*5.2. Results Based on Coursera Course Dataset with Respect to the Number of Iterations (10 to 50)*

5.2.1. Performance Analysis Based on Cluster Size = 3

Figure 7 presents the performance analysis of the developed technique with iterations by varying the queries with cluster size = 3. Figure 7a presents the assessment based on precision.

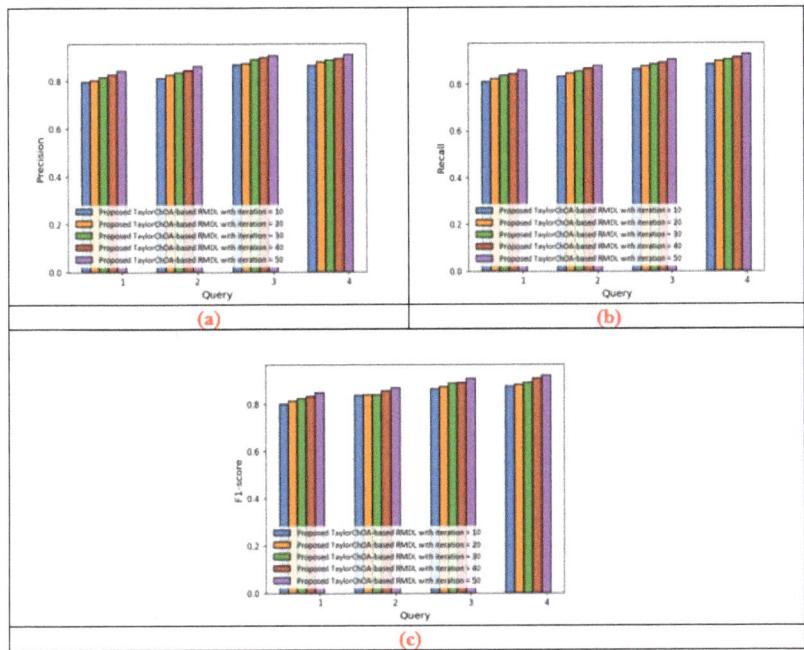

**Figure 7.** Performance analysis with cluster size = 3 using Coursera Course Dataset: (**a**) precision, (**b**) recall, and (**c**) F1-score.

For the number of query 1, the precision value measured by the developed TaylorChOA-based RMDL with iteration 10 is 0.795, iteration 20 is 0.825, iteration 30 is 0.836, iteration 40 is 0.847, and iteration 50 is 0.854. Figure 7b portrays the analysis using recall. By considering the number of query 2, the value of recall computed by the developed TaylorChOA-based RMDL with iteration 10 is 0.825, iteration 20 is 0.847, iteration 30 is 0.874, iteration 40 is 0.885, and iteration 50 is 0.895. The analysis using F1-score is depicted in Figure 7c. When the number of a query is 3, the value of F1-score computed by the developed TaylorChOA-based RMDL with iteration 10 is 0.863, iteration 20 is 0.871, iteration 30 is 0.886, iteration 40 is 0.890, and iteration 50 is 0.907.

5.2.2. Performance Analysis Based on Cluster Size = 4

Figure 8 presents the performance analysis of the developed technique with iterations by varying the queries with cluster size = 6.

Figure 8a presents the assessment based on precision. For the number of query 1, the precision value measured by the developed TaylorChOA-based RMDL with iteration 10 is 0.804, iteration 20 is 0.815, iteration 30 is 0.825, iteration 40 is 0.831, and iteration 50 is 0.848. Figure 8b portrays the analysis using recall. By considering the number of query 2, the value of recall computed by the developed TaylorChOA-based RMDL with iteration 10 is 0.843, iteration 20 is 0.854, iteration 30 is 0.865, iteration 40 is 0.871, and iteration 50 is 0.888. The analysis using F1-score is depicted in Figure 8c). When the number of a query is 3, the value of F1-score computed by the developed TaylorChOA-based RMDL with iteration 10 is 0.854, iteration 20 is 0.865, iteration 30 is 0.874, iteration 40 is 0.888, and iteration 50 is 0.898.

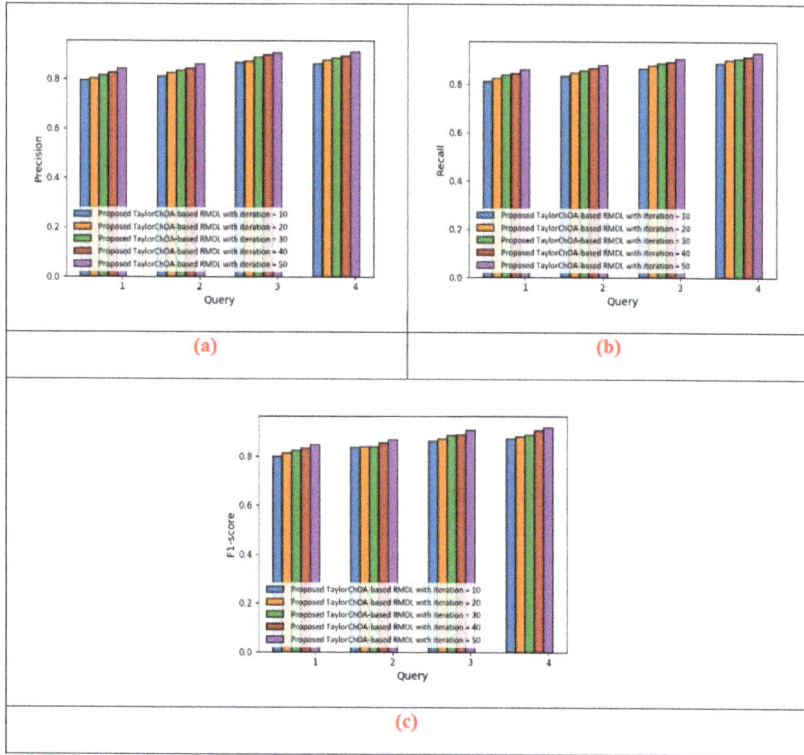

**Figure 8.** Performance analysis with cluster size =4 using Coursera Course Dataset: (**a**) precision, (**b**) recall, and (**c**) F1-score.

**Comparison of existing methods and the proposed TaylorChOA-based RMDL using Coursera Course Dataset, in terms of precision, recall, and F1-Score**

The comparative assessment of the developed technique is performed by varying the queries with the cluster size = 3 and cluster size = 4 in terms of the evaluation metrics.

5.2.3. Analysis Based on Cluster Size = 3 in Terms of Precision, Recall, and F1-Score

Figure 9 portrays the assessment with cluster size = 3 by varying the number of queries using the performance measures, such as precision, recall, and F1-score.

Figure 9a presents the analysis in terms of precision. When number of query is 1, the precision value measured by the developed TaylorChOA-based RMDL is 0.839, whereas the precision value measured by the existing methods, such as HSACN, MCNN, Query Optimization, and DCBVN is 0.556, 0.669, 0.716, and 0.816, respectively. The analysis based on recall measure is portrayed in Figure 9b. By considering the number of query as 2, the developed TaylorChOA-based RMDL measured a recall value of 0.878, whereas the value of recall computed by the existing methods, such as HSACN, MCNN, Query Optimization, and DCBVN is 0.606, 0.743, 0.769, and 0.849, respectively. The assessment using F1-score is shown in Figure 9c. The F1-score value attained by the HSACN, MCNN, Query Optimization, DCBVN, and developed TaylorChOA-based RMDL is 0.615, 0.756, 0.800, 0.870, and 0.907, respectively, when considering the number of query as 3.

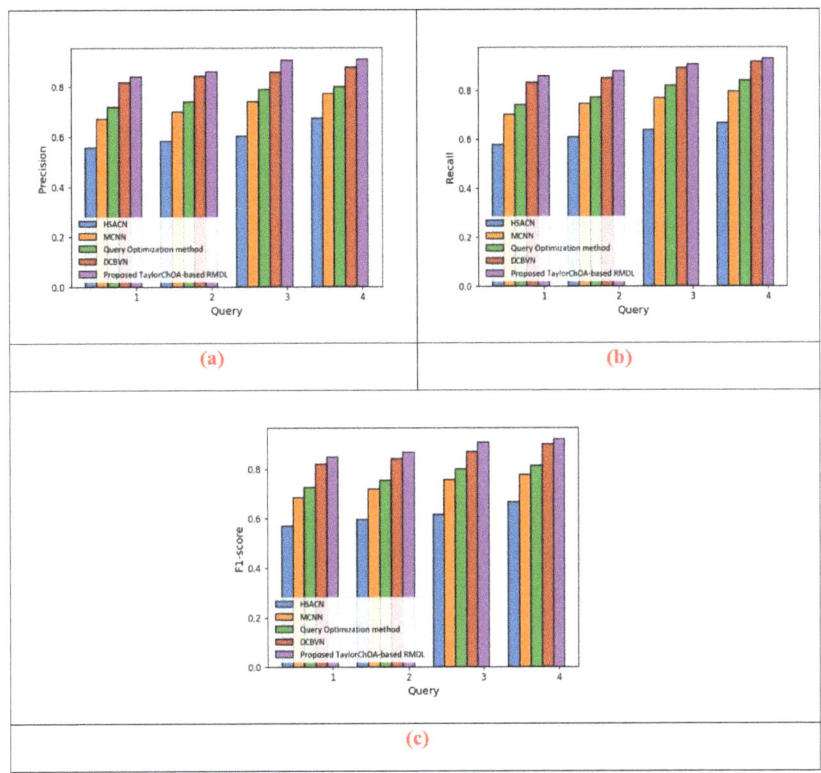

**Figure 9.** Comparative analysis with cluster size =3 using Coursera Course Dataset: (**a**) precision, (**b**) recall, and (**c**) F1-score.

5.2.4. Analysis Based on Cluster Size = 4 in Terms of Precision, Recall, and F1-Score

The analysis with cluster size = 4 using the evaluation metrics, by varying the number of queries is portrayed in Figure 10.

The analysis using precision is shown in Figure 10a. When considering the number of query as 1, the developed TaylorChOA-based RMDL computed a precision value of 0.836, whereas the precision value achieved by the existing methods, such as HSACN, MCNN, Query Optimization, and DCBVN is 0.584, 0.668, 0.725, and 0.812, respectively. Figure 10b presents the assessment using recall. The recall values obtained by the HSACN, MCNN, Query Optimization, DCBVN, and developed TaylorChOA-based RMDL are 0.629, 0.765, 0.798, 0.874, and 0.899, respectively, for the number of query 2. The analysis in terms of F-1 score is presented in Figure 10c. When the number of query is 3, the F1-score value of HSACN is 0.643, MCNN is 0.781, Query Optimization is 0.824, DCBVN is0.899, and developed TaylorChOA-based RMDL is 0.917.

Table 2 explains the comparative discussion of the developed Taylor ChOA-based RMDL technique in comparison with the existing techniques using the Coursera Course dataset for the number of query 4. With cluster size = 3, the maximum precision of 0.908, maximum recall of 0.928, and maximum F1-score of 0.919 are computed by the developed Taylor ChOA-based RMDL method. Using cluster size = 4, the maximum precision of 0.919 is computed by the developed Taylor ChOA-based RMDL, whereas the precision value computed by the existing methods, such as HSACN, MCNN, Query Optimization, and DCBVN is 0.667, 0.776, 0.813, and 0.899, respectively. Likewise, the higher recall of 0.926 is computed by the developed Taylor ChOA-based RMDL, and the F1-score value is 0.925.

From this table, it is clear that, the developed Taylor ChOA-based RMDL outperformed various existing methods.

Table 3 shows the computational time of proposed and existing methods for query = 1. The proposed system has the minimum computational time of 127.25 s and 133.84 s for E-Khool dataset, and Coursera Course dataset, respectively.

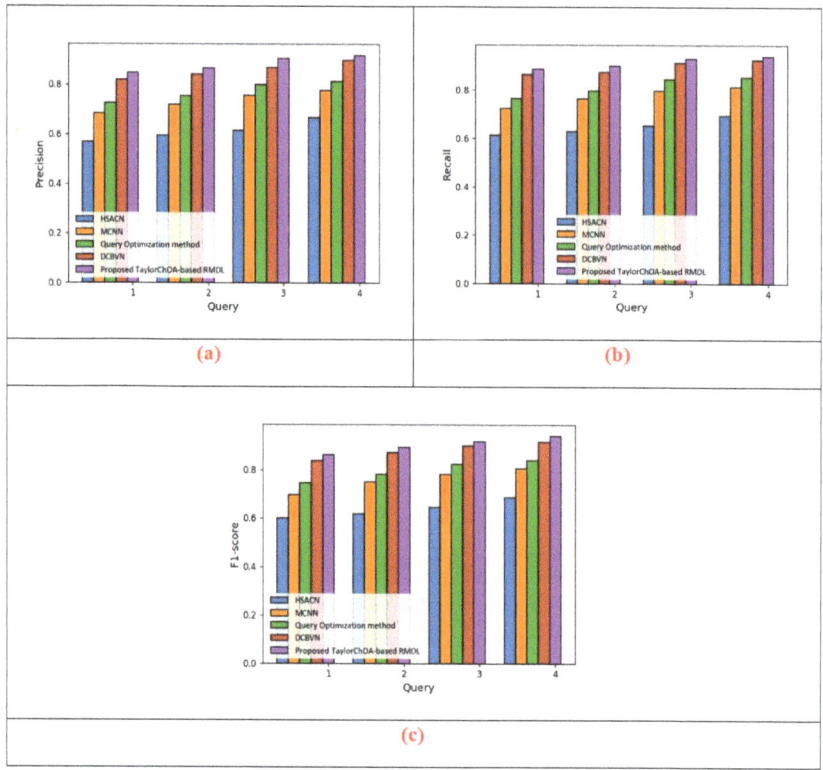

**Figure 10.** Comparative analysis with cluster size = 4 using Coursera Course Dataset: (**a**) precision, (**b**) recall, and (**c**) F1-score.

**Table 2.** Comparison of proposed TaylorChOA-based RMDL with existing methods using Coursera Course dataset, in terms of precision, recall, and F1-score.

| Method | Metrics | HSACN | MCNN | Qu Opt. | DCBVN | Proposed Method |
|---|---|---|---|---|---|---|
| | Precision | 0.672 | 0.772 | 0.798 | 0.877 | **0.908** |
| Cluster Size = 3 | Recall | 0.665 | 0.795 | 0.837 | 0.914 | **0.928** |
| | F1-score | 0.667 | 0.776 | 0.813 | 0.899 | **0.919** |
| | Precision | 0.667 | 0.776 | 0.813 | 0.899 | **0.919** |
| Cluster Size = 4 | Recall | 0.676 | 0.798 | 0.839 | 0.907 | **0.926** |
| | F1-score | 0.674 | 0.788 | 0.825 | 0.899 | **0.925** |

**Table 3.** Comparison of computational time, in terms of seconds.

| Dataset | Time | HSACN | MCNN | Qu Opt. | DCBVN | Proposed Method |
|---|---|---|---|---|---|---|
| E-Khool | Seconds | 182.41 | 180.41 | 162.25 | 145.36 | **127.25** |
| Coursera Course | Seconds | 192.45 | 187.52 | 170.54 | 153.25 | **133.84** |

## 6. Conclusions and Future Work

This research aims to resolve the problem of information overload in the online education field. Choosing a personalized course on an online education website may be extremely difficult and tedious. Hence, this research proposes a robust sentiment classification model to recommend the courses using the proposed TaylorChOA-based RMDL method. Here, a course review is performed by considering the review data for finding the best course. With the best course, various features, such as SentiWordNet-based statistical features, classification-specific features, and TF-IDF features, are effectively extracted from the review data. After the extraction of significant features, the RMDL model is used to classify the sentiments, and the training practice of RMDL is done using the developed optimization algorithm, known as Taylor ChOA. Thus, the course recommendation is done by offering positively recommended courses to the user. TaylorChOA is newly designed by the combination of the Taylor concept and the ChOA algorithm. Moreover, the developed technique attained better performance using precision, recall, and F1-score with the higher values of, 0.936, 0.944, and 0.938, respectively. However, the performance of the devised approach is not evaluated using more evaluation metrics. In the future, the developed work can be further extended by developing deep learning classifiers and evaluating the performance using more evaluation metrics.

**Author Contributions:** S.K.B. designed and wrote the paper; H.L. supervised the work; S.K.B. performed the experiments with advice from B.X.; and D.K.S. organized and proofread the paper. All authors have read and agreed to the published version of the manuscript.

**Funding:** This research received no external funding.

**Institutional Review Board Statement:** Not applicable.

**Informed Consent Statement:** Not applicable.

**Data Availability Statement:** The data used in the experiments are publicly available. Details have been given in Section 4.1.

**Conflicts of Interest:** The authors declare no conflict of interest.

## Abbreviations

The following abbreviations are used in this manuscript:

| | |
|---|---|
| ChOA | Chimp Optimization Algorithm |
| DCBVN | Demand-aware Collaborative Bayesian Variational Network |
| DÉCOR | Deep learning-enabled Course Recommender System |
| DNN | Deep Neural Networks |
| GRU | Gated Recurrent Unit |
| HANCI | Hierarchical Attention Network Oriented towards Crowd Intelligence |
| HSACN | Hierarchical Self-Attentive Convolution Network |
| LSTM | Long Short-Term Memory |
| MCNN | Multi-model Convolutional Neural Network |
| NLP | Natural Language Processing |
| RMDL | Random Multi-model Deep Learning |
| RNN | Recurrent Neural Network |

## References

1. Wen-Shung Tai, D.; Wu, H.-J.; Li, P.-H. Effective e-learning recommendation system based on self-organizing maps and association mining. *Electron. Libr.* **2008**, *26*, 329–344. [CrossRef]
2. Persky, A.M.; Joyner, P.U.; Cox, W.C. Development of a course review process. *Am. J. Pharm. Educ.* **2012**, *76*, 130. [CrossRef]
3. Guanchen, W.; Kim, M.; Jung, H. Personal customized recommendation system reflecting purchase criteria and product reviews sentiment analysis. *Int. J. Electr. Comput. Eng.* **2021**, *11*, 2399–2406. [CrossRef]
4. Gunawan, A.; Cheong, M.L.F.; Poh, J. An Essential Applied Statistical Analysis Course using RStudio with Project-Based Learning for Data Science. In Proceedings of the 2018 IEEE International Conference on Teaching, Assessment, and Learning for Engineering (TALE), Wollongong, Australia, 4–7 December 2018; pp. 581–588.

5.  Assami, S.; Daoudi, N.; Ajhoun, R. A Semantic Recommendation System for Learning Personalization in Massive Open Online Courses. *Int. J. Recent Contrib. Eng. Sci. IT* **2020**, *8*, 71–80. [CrossRef]
6.  Hua, Z.; Wang, Y.; Xu, X.; Zhang, B.; Liang, L. Predicting corporate financial distress based on integration of support vector machine and logistic regression. *Expert Syst. Appl.* **2007**, *33*, 434–440. [CrossRef]
7.  Aher, S.B.; Lobo, L. Best combination of machine learning algorithms for course recommendation system in e-learning. *Int. J. Comput. Appl.* **2012**, *41*. [CrossRef]
8.  Tarus, J.K.; Niu, Z.; Mustafa, G. Knowledge-based recommendation: A review of ontology-based recommender systems for e-learning. *Artif. Intell. Rev.* **2018**, *50*, 21–48. [CrossRef]
9.  Zhang, H.; Huang, T.; Lv, Z.; Liu, S.; Zhou, Z. MCRS: A course recommendation system for MOOCs. *Multimed. Tools Appl.* **2018**, *77*, 7051–7069. [CrossRef]
10. Li, Q.; Kim, J. A Deep Learning-Based Course Recommender System for Sustainable Development in Education. *Appl. Sci.* **2021**, *11*, 8993. [CrossRef]
11. Almahairi, A.; Kastner, K.; Cho, K.; Courville, A. Learning distributed representations from reviews for collaborative filtering. In Proceedings of the 9th ACM Conference on Recommender Systems, Vienna, Austria, 16–20 September 2015; pp. 147–154.
12. Yang, C.; Zhou, W.; Wang, Z.; Jiang, B.; Li, D.; Shen, H. Accurate and Explainable Recommendation via Hierarchical Attention Network Oriented Towards Crowd Intelligence. *Knowl.-Based Syst.* **2021**, *213*, 106687. [CrossRef]
13. Zheng, L.; Noroozi, V.; Yu, P.S. Joint deep modeling of users and items using reviews for recommendation. In Proceedings of the Tenth ACM International Conference on Web Search and Data Mining, Cambridge, UK, 6–10 February 2017; pp. 425–434.
14. Zeng, H.; Ai, Q. A Hierarchical Self-attentive Convolution Network for Review Modeling in Recommendation Systems. *arXiv* **2020**, arXiv:2011.13436.
15. Dong, X.; Ni, J.; Cheng, W.; Chen, Z.; Zong, B.; Song, D.; Liu, Y.; Chen, H.; De Melo, G. Asymmetrical hierarchical networks with attentive interactions for interpretable review-based recommendation. In Proceedings of the AAAI Conference on Artificial Intelligence, New York, NY, USA, 7–12 February 2020; Volume 34, pp. 7667–7674.
16. Wang, H.; Wu, F.; Liu, Z.; Xie, X. Fine-grained interest matching for neural news recommendation. In Proceedings of the 58th Annual Meeting of the Association for Computational Linguistics, Seattle, WA, USA, 5–10 July 2020; pp. 836–845.
17. Bansal, T.; Belanger, D.; McCallum, A. Ask the gru: Multi-task learning for deep text recommendations. In Proceedings of the 10th ACM Conference on Recommender Systems, Boston, MA, USA, 15–19 September 2016; pp. 107–114.
18. Tay, Y.; Luu, A.T.; Hui, S.C. Multi-pointer co-attention networks for recommendation. In Proceedings of the 24th ACM SIGKDD International Conference on Knowledge Discovery & Data Mining, London, UK, 19–23 August 2018; pp. 2309–2318.
19. Bai, Y.; Li, Y.; Wang, L. A Joint Summarization and Pre-Trained Model for Review-Based Recommendation. *Information* **2021**, *12*, 223. [CrossRef]
20. Da'u, A.; Salim, N.; Rabiu, I.; Osman, A. Recommendation system exploiting aspect-based opinion mining with deep learning method. *Inf. Sci.* **2020**, *512*, 1279–1292.
21. Wang, C.; Zhu, H.; Zhu, C.; Zhang, X.; Chen, E.; Xiong, H. Personalized Employee Training Course Recommendation with Career Development Awareness. In Proceedings of the Web Conference 2020, Taipei, Taiwan, 20–24 April 2020; pp. 1648–1659.
22. Rafiq, M.S.; Jianshe, X.; Arif, M.; Barra, P. Intelligent query optimization and course recommendation during online lectures in E-learning system. *J. Ambient. Intell. Humaniz. Comput.* **2021**, *12*, 10375–10394. [CrossRef]
23. Sulaiman, M.S.; Tamizi, A.A.; Shamsudin, M.R.; Azmi, A. Course recommendation system using fuzzy logic approach. *Indones. J. Electr. Eng. Comput. Sci.* **2020**, *17*, 365–371. [CrossRef]
24. Xie, J.; Girshick, R.; Farhadi, A. Unsupervised deep embedding for clustering analysis. In Proceedings of the International Conference on Machine Learning, New York, NY, USA, 19–24 June 2016; pp. 478–487.
25. Kowsari, K.; Heidarysafa, M.; Brown, D.E.; Meimandi, K.J.; Barnes, L.E. Rmdl: Random multimodel deep learning for classification. In Proceedings of the 2nd International Conference on Information System and Data Mining, Lakeland, FL, USA, 9–1 April 2018; pp. 19–28.
26. Mangai, S.A.; Sankar, B.R.; Alagarsamy, K. Taylor series prediction of time series data with error propagated by artificial neural network. *Int. J. Comput. Appl.* **2014**, *89*, 41–47.
27. Khishe, M.; Mosavi, M.R. Chimp optimization algorithm. *Expert Syst. Appl.* **2020**, *149*, 113338. [CrossRef]
28. Ohana, B.; Tierney, B. Sentiment classification of reviews using SentiWordNet. In Proceedings of the IT&T, Dublin, Ireland, 22–23 October 2009.
29. Christian, H.; Agus, M.P.; Suhartono, D. Single document automatic text summarization using term frequency-inverse document frequency (TF-IDF). *ComTech Comput. Math. Eng. Appl.* **2016**, *7*, 285–294. [CrossRef]

 *mathematics*

MDPI

*Article*

# Automatic Classification of National Health Service Feedback

**Christopher Haynes [1,\*], Marco A. Palomino [1,\*], Liz Stuart [1], David Viira [2], Frances Hannon [2], Gemma Crossingham [2] and Kate Tantam [2]**

[1]   School of Engineering, Computing and Mathematics, University of Plymouth, Plymouth PL4 8AA, UK; l.stuart@plymouth.ac.uk

[2]   Faculty of Health, University Hospitals Plymouth, Derriford Rd., Plymouth PL6 8DH, UK; dviira@nhs.net (D.V.); frances.hannon@nhs.net (F.H.); gemmacrossingham@nhs.net (G.C.); kate.tantam@nhs.net (K.T.)

\*   Correspondence: christopher.haynes@plymouth.ac.uk (C.H.); marco.palomino@plymouth.ac.uk (M.A.P.)

**Abstract:** Text datasets come in an abundance of shapes, sizes and styles. However, determining what factors limit classification accuracy remains a difficult task which is still the subject of intensive research. Using a challenging UK National Health Service (NHS) dataset, which contains many characteristics known to increase the complexity of classification, we propose an innovative classification pipeline. This pipeline switches between different text pre-processing, scoring and classification techniques during execution. Using this flexible pipeline, a high level of accuracy has been achieved in the classification of a range of datasets, attaining a micro-averaged F1 score of 93.30% on the Reuters-21578 "ApteMod" corpus. An evaluation of this flexible pipeline was carried out using a variety of complex datasets compared against an unsupervised clustering approach. The paper describes how classification accuracy is impacted by an unbalanced category distribution, the rare use of generic terms and the subjective nature of manual human classification.

**Keywords:** NLP; classification; clustering; text pre-processing; machine learning; National Health Service (NHS)

**MSC:** 68T50

**Citation:** Haynes, C.; Palomino, M.A.; Stuart, L.; Viira, D.; Hannon, F.; Crossingham, G.; Tantam, K. Automatic Classification of National Health Service Feedback. *Mathematics* **2022**, *10*, 983. https://doi.org/ 10.3390/math10060983

Academic Editors: Florentina Hristea, Cornelia Caragea and Victor Mitrana

Received: 9 February 2022
Accepted: 16 March 2022
Published: 18 March 2022

**Publisher's Note:** MDPI stays neutral with regard to jurisdictional claims in published maps and institutional affiliations.

## 1. Introduction

The quantity of digital documents generally available is ever-growing. Classification of these documents is widely accepted as being essential as this reduces the time spent on analysis. However, manual classification is both time consuming and prone to human error. Therefore, the demand for techniques to automatically classify and categorize documents continues to increase. Automatic classification supports the process of enabling researchers to carry out deeper analysis on text corpora. Practical applications of classification include library cataloguing and indexing [1], email spam detection and filtration [2] and sentiment analysis [3].

Since text documents and datasets exhibit such a wide variety of differences and combinations of features, it is impossible to adopt a standardized classification approach. One such feature is the length of the text available as input to the classification process. For example, a newspaper article is likely to contain significantly more text than a tweet, thus providing a larger vocabulary which will aid classification. Another important feature of text is the intended purpose of the text. The intended use of text can significantly affect the author's style and choice of vocabulary. Let us suppose you are required to determine Amazon product categories based on the descriptions of the products. Clearly, certain keywords are highly likely to appear on similar products, and those keywords are likely to have the same intended meaning wherever they are used. In contrast, consider the scenario where you are required to determine whether a tweet exhibited a positive or negative sentiment. In this case, the same keyword used in multiple tweets may have completely different meanings based on the context and tone of the author. The intended sentiment could vary considerably.

Of course, objectivity and subjectivity can also affect the accuracy of the classification process. If the same text, based on Amazon products and tweets, was used for manual classification, then there is likely to be more consensus on the category of a product description than on the sentiment of a tweet. This is due to the inherent objectivity of the categories. Aside from these examples, there are numerous other features of a dataset which can limit classification accuracy [4].

This paper describes the analysis of a complex UK National Health Service (NHS) patient feedback dataset which contains many of the elements known to restrict the accuracy of automatic classification. Throughout experimentation, several pre-processing and machine learning techniques are used to investigate the complexities in the NHS dataset and their effect on classification accuracy. Subsequently, an unsupervised clustering approach is applied to the NHS dataset to explore and identify underlying natural classifications in the data.

Section 2 describes existing work on automatic text classification and provides a theoretical background of the approaches used. Section 3 establishes our research problem statement and introduces the datasets used, incorporating both the NHS dataset and the benchmarking datasets used for evaluation. Section 4 details the pre-processing and classification pipeline, followed by the results of our experiments in Section 5. Finally, the findings and conclusions are discussed in Section 6.

## 2. Related Work and Theoretical Background

The field of automatic text classification incorporates many differing approaches which vary depending on the type of document and how it needs to be categorized.

The early work in this field focused on the manual extraction of features from text which were then applied to a classifier. This process of feature extraction has also been refined through feature weighting [5] and feature reduction [6] to extract a more detailed representation of input text. The structure of these features when used for classification can also take many forms with the most common approaches being the bag-of-words (BoW) model [7] or word-vector representations [8].

A range of different classification models have been used to produce high accuracy text classification with the most successful approaches being support vector machines (SVM) [9], naïve bayes classifiers [10] and more recently deep learning neural network architectures [11,12].

Although there is a broad variation in the specific processes used in automatic text classification, many of these processes can be summarized into four stages shown in Figure 1.

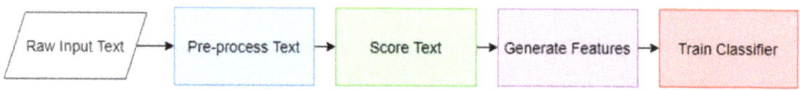

**Figure 1.** Procedural diagram of the processes used in automatic text classification approaches, where rhomboids represent data and rectangles represent processes.

The first stage of the pipeline, text pre-processing, primarily focuses on techniques to extract the most valuable information from raw text data [13]. Typically, this involves reducing the amount of superfluous text, minimizing duplication and tagging words based on their type or meaning. This is achieved by techniques such as:

- Tokenizing. This technique splits text into sentences and words to identify parts of speech (POS) such as nouns, verbs and adjectives. This creates options for selective text removal and further processing.
- Stop word removal. This technique removes commonly occurring words which are unlikely to give extra value or meaning to the text. Examples include the words "the",

"and", "for" and "of". There are many different open-source, stop word lists [14], which have been used in multiple applications with differing levels of success.

- Stemming or lemmatization. In this technique words are replaced with differing suffixes, whilst maintaining the same common stem. For example, the words "thanking", "thankful" and "thanks" would all be stemmed to the word "thank". Some of the most popular stemming algorithms, such as the Porter Stemmer algorithm [15], use a truncation approach, which although fast can often result in mistakes as it is aimed purely at the syntax of the word whilst ignoring the semantics. A slightly more robust, but slower, approach would be lemmatizing, which uses POS to infer context. Thus, it reduces words to a more meaningful root. For example, the words "am", "are" and "is" would all be lemmatized to the root verb "be".
- Further cleaning can also occur depending on the raw text data, such as removing URLs, specific unique characters or words identified by POS tagging.

The second stage of the pipeline, Word Scoring, involves transforming the text into a quantitative form. This can be to increase the weighting of words or phrases which are deemed more important to the meaning of a document. Different scoring measures can be applied. These include:

- Term Frequency Inverse Document Frequency (TF-IDF), a measure which scores a word within a document based on the inverse proportion in which it appears in the corpus [16]. Therefore, a word will be assigned a higher score if it is common in the scored document, but rare in all the other documents in the same corpus. The advantage of this measure is that it is quick to calculate. The disadvantage is that synonyms, plurals and misspelled words would all be treated as completely different words.
- TextRank is a graph-based text ranking metric, derived from Google's PageRank algorithm [17]. When used to identify keywords, each word in a document is deemed to be a vertex in an undirected graph, where an edge exists for each occurrence of a pair of words within a given sentence. Subsequently, each edge in this graph is deemed to be a "vote" for the vertex linked to it. Vertices with higher numbers of votes are deemed to be of higher importance, and the votes which they cast are weighted higher. By iterating through this process, the value for each vertex will converge to a score representing its importance. Note that, in contrast to the TF-IDF, which scores relative to a corpus, TextRank only evaluates the importance of a word within the given document.
- Rapid Automatic Keyword Extraction (RAKE) is an algorithm used to identify keywords and multi-word key-phrases [18]. RAKE was originally designed to work on individual documents focusing on the observation that most keyword-phrases contain multiple words, but very few stop words. Through the combination of a phrase delimiter, word delimiter and stop word list, RAKE identifies the most important keywords/key-phrases in a document and weights them accordingly.

The third stage of the pipeline is Feature Generation. It is essential to produce an input which can be used for the machine learning classifier. In general, these inputs need to be fixed length vectors containing normalized real numbers. The common approach is the BoW, which creates an $n$-length vector representing every unique word in a corpus. This vector can then be used as a template to generate a feature mask for each document. This resultant feature mask would also be an $n$-length vector. To produce the feature mask, each word in the document would be identified within the BoW vector. Subsequently, its corresponding index in the feature mask vector would be set, whilst all other positions in the vector would be reset to 0. For example, suppose there is a corpus of solely the following two sentences: "This is good" and "This is bad". Its corresponding BoW vocabulary would consist of four words {This, is, good, bad}. The first sentence would be represented by the vector {1, 1, 1, 0}, whilst the second sentence would be represented by the vector {1, 1, 0, 1}. In this example, the value used to *set* the feature vector is simply the binary representation (0 or 1) of whether the word exists in the given document. Alternatively, the values used to set the vector could also be any scoring metric, such as those discussed above. The BoW model is limited by the fact that it does not represent the ordering of words in their original document. BoW can also be memory intensive on large corpuses, since the feature mask of each document has to represent the vocabulary of the entire corpus. Therefore, for a vocabulary of size $n$ and a corpus of $m$ documents, a matrix of size $nm$ is required to represent all feature masks. Further, as the size of $n$ increases, each feature mask will also contain more 0 values, making the data increasingly sparse [19]. There are alternatives to the BoW model which attempt to resolve the issue of word ordering. The most common is the n-gram representation, where $n$ represents the number of words or characters in a given sequence [20]. The BoW model could be considered an n-gram representation where $n$ is set to 1, also known as a unigram. For example, given the sentence "This is an example", an n-gram of $n = 2$ (bigram) would be the set of ordered words {"This is", "is an", "an example"}. This enables sequences of words to be represented as features. In some text classification tasks, bigrams have proved to be more efficient than the BoW model [21]. However, it also follows that as $n$ increases, n-gram approaches, are increasingly affected by the size of the corpus and the corresponding memory required for processing [22].

Word embedding is an alternative to separating the preprocessing of text (second stage) from the scoring of text (third stage) of the generalized pipeline. It can be used to represent words in vector space, thus encompassing both sections [8]. A popular model for generating these vectors is word2vec [23], which consists of two similar techniques to perform these transformations (i) continuous BoW and (ii) continuous skip-n-gram. Both these processes manage sequences of words and support any length word encoding to a fixed length vector, whilst maintaining some of the original similarities between words [24]. Similar techniques can be used on word vectors to produce sentence vectors, and then on sentence vectors to produce document vectors. These vectors result in high-level representations of the document, with less sparse representation and a smaller memory footprint than n-gram and BoW models. They often outperform the n-gram and BoW models with classification tasks [25], but they do have a much greater computational complexity which increases processing time.

The fourth and final stage of the pipeline, Classification, uses the feature masks in training a classification model. There are many different viable classifiers available, some of the most widely used approaches in text classification are k-nearest-neighbor (KNN) [26], naïve bayes (NB) [27], neural networks (NN) [28] and support vector machines (SVM) [9]. Each of these classifiers have numerous variations, each with their own advantages and disadvantages. The specific variations used in our proposed pipeline will be discussed in further detail in Section 4.

### 3. Research Problem Statement and Input Data

*3.1. Research Problem Statement*

We plan to investigate how different dataset characteristics can affect the accuracy of automatic text classification. We propose to develop a novel, modular text classification pipeline, so that different combinations of text pre-processing, word scoring and classification techniques can be compared and contrasted. Our research will primarily focus on the complex NHS patient feedback dataset, but also consider other benchmark datasets which share some of the same dataset characteristics. Through experimentation on these datasets, with our novel pipeline, we aim to answer the following questions:

(R1) Can our automatic text classification pipeline reduce the workload of NHS staff by providing an acceptable accuracy compared to manual classification?

(R2) Can the same pipeline improve the automatic text classification accuracy on other benchmark datasets?

*3.2. Input Data*

This paper focuses on a challenging text classification dataset provided by University Hospitals Plymouth NHS Trust. This dataset is known as the "Learning from Excellence"

(LFE) dataset. It is composed of solely positive written feedback given to staff by patients and colleagues. These data were organized into 24 themes; categories where the same sentiment is expressed using slightly different terminology. Subsequently, each item of text (phrase, sentence) was manually classified into one or more theme. Each item may be associated with multiple themes which are ordered. The first theme can be considered the primary theme. As this paper focuses on single-label classification, only the primary themes will be used. Note that the full list of the themes and their descriptions is available in Appendix A, Table A1. The LFE dataset has several characteristics which intrinsically make its automatic classification a difficult task:

1. The dataset consists of 2307 items. Due to the text or theme being omitted, only 2224 items were deemed viable for classification. This is relatively small compared to most datasets used in text classification.
2. The length of each text item is short, the average item contained 49.7 words. The shortest text item is 2 words long and the longest text item is 270 words long.
3. The number of themes is large with respect to the size of the dataset. Even if the themes were evenly distributed, this would result in an average of less than 93 text items into each category.
4. The distribution of the themes is not balanced. For example, the largest theme "Supportive" is the primary theme for 439 items (19.74%). The smallest theme "Safe Care" is the primary theme for solely 1 item (0.04%). The number of items per category has a standard deviation of 111.23 items. The distribution for the remaining theme categories is also uneven, see Figure 2.
5. Since all the text is positive feedback, many of the text items share a similar vocabulary and tone regardless of the theme category to which they belong. For example, the phrase "Thank you" appears in 807 items (36.29%). However, only 61 items (2.74%) belong to the primary theme of "Thank You".
6. The themes are of a subjective nature, dependent on individual interpretation so they could be viewed in different ways. For example, the theme "Teamwork" is not objectively independent of the theme "Leadership". Thus, there may be some abstract overlap between these themes. Furthermore, there is no definitive measure to determine which theme is more important than another for a given text item, making the choice of the primary theme equally subjective.

Given the classification challenges posed by the LFE dataset, it was important to benchmark results. Thus, all experiments are compared to both well-known text classification datasets and other datasets which share one or more of the characteristics with the LFE dataset.

The first benchmark dataset was the "ApteMod" split of the Reuters-21578 dataset (Reuters). This consists of short articles from the Reuters financial newswire service published in 1987. This split solely contains documents which have been manually classified as belonging to at least one topic, making this dataset ideal for text classification. This dataset is already sub-divided into a training set and testing set. Since k-fold cross validation was used, the datasets were combined. Finally, since multiple themes were not assigned with any order of precedence, items which had been assigned to more than one topic were removed. Although this dataset does not share many of the classification challenges of the LFE dataset, it is widely used in text classification [29,30]. Thus, it provided indirect comparisons with other work in this field.

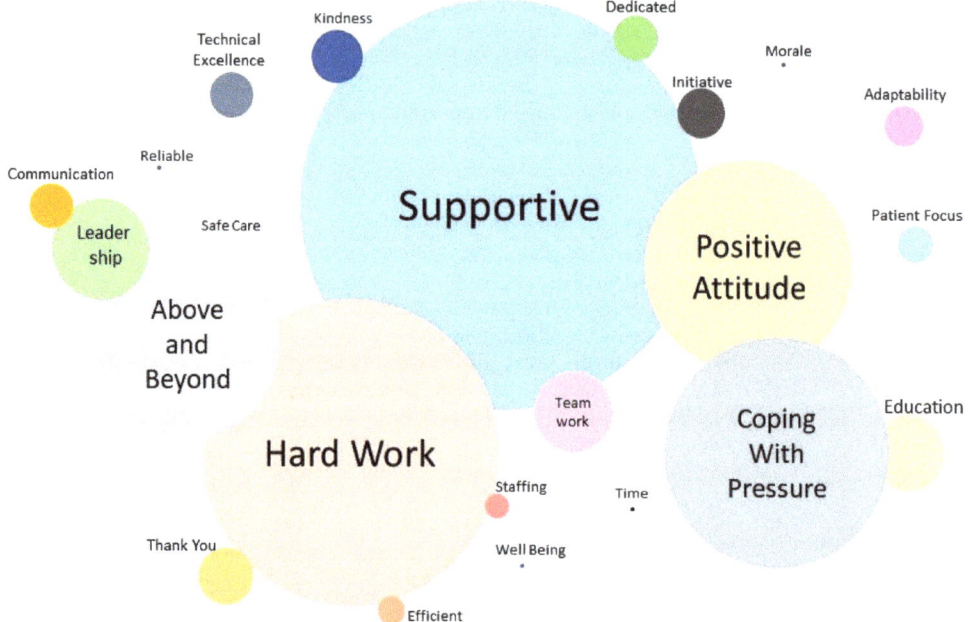

**Figure 2.** Chart of LFE theme category distributions, where the size of a bubble denotes the number of occurrences of each text item for a particular theme category. Note that the position of the bubbles is synthetic, solely used to portray that overlap occurs between themes.

Three other datasets were chosen since each share one of the characteristics of the LFE dataset.

- The "Amazon Hierarchical Reviews" dataset is a sample of reviews from different products on Amazon, along with the corresponding product categories. Amazon uses a hierarchical product category model, so that items can be categorized at different levels of granularity. Each item within this dataset is categorized in three levels. For example, at level 1 a product could be in the "toys/games" category. At level 2, it could be in the more specific "games" category. At level 3, it could be in the more specific "jigsaw puzzles" category. This dataset was selected as it provides a direct comparison of classification accuracy, when considering the relative dataset volume compared to the number of categories.
- The "Twitter COVID Sentiment" dataset is a curation of tweets from March and April 2020 which mentioned the words "coronavirus" or "COVID". This dataset was manually classified within one of the following five sentiments: extremely negative, negative, neutral, positive or extremely positive. The source dataset had been split into a training set and a testing set. As with the Reuters dataset, these two subsets were combined.
- The "Twitter Tweet Genre" dataset is a small selection of tweets which have been manually classified into one of the following four high level genres: sports, entertainment, medical and politics.

Each of these datasets share some of the complex characteristics of the LFE dataset described at the start of this section. Table 1 presents and compares these similarities. The full specification of all the datasets is available in Table 2.

**Table 1.** Comparison of the datasets based on the complexity of their classification characteristics. The numbered characteristics refer to the list at the start of this section.

| Dataset Name and Shared Characteristics | | Description |
|---|---|---|
| Reuters | 3 | There are 9160 documents, classified into one of 65 categories. Average of items per category of 140.90. |
| | 4 | The largest category "earn" contains 3923 documents (42.83%). The second largest category "acq" contains 2292 documents (25.02%). The smallest 9 categories only contain 1 document (0.0001%). The number of items per category has a standard deviation of 553.13. |
| Amazon Hierarchical Reviews | 2 | The average amount of words in a review is 76.5, with the shortest review [1] containing 1 word and the longest containing 1068 words. |
| | 3 | Based on level 3 categorizations, there are 39,999 documents, classified into one of 510 categories. Average of items per category of 78.4. |
| | 5 | Since all the text are reviews, there are common words in the vocabulary which have no relation to determining the product category. For example, "great" appears in 9762 reviews (24.41%). However, "great" bears no relation to the product category. |
| Twitter COVID Sentiment | 2 | The average number of words in a tweet is 27.8, with the shortest [2] containing 1 word and the longest containing 58 words. |
| | 6 | Sentiment analysis in general has a subjective nature to the classifications given [31]. This dataset also has some specific cases where two very similar tweets have been given opposing sentiments, an example can be found in Appendix C. |
| Twitter Tweet Genre | 1 | This dataset consists of only 1161 documents. |
| | 2 | The average amount of words in a tweet is 16 with the shortest [2] containing 1 word and the longest containing 27 words. |

[1] The shortest review in this dataset contains 0 words and only punctuation. However, this was discounted as it was removed during pre-processing and not used. [2] Some tweets in this dataset contain 0 words and only URLs, retweets or user handles. However, these were discounted as they were removed during pre-processing and not used.

**Table 2.** Full specification of datasets. All values presented in this table represent the raw datasets prior to removal of any invalid entries, pre-processing or text cleaning.

| Dataset Name | Items | Categories | Avg. Word Count | Avg. Character Count | Avg. Items per Category [1] |
|---|---|---|---|---|---|
| LFE | 2307 | 24 | 49.6 | 290.4 | 96 |
| Reuters | 9160 | 65 | 104.4 | 643.1 | 140 |
| Amazon Hierarchical Reviews | 39,999 | 6/64/510 [2] | 76.5 | 424.1 | 6666/624/78 [2] |
| Twitter COVID Sentiment | 44,955 | 5 | 27.8 | 176.4 | 8950 |
| Twitter Tweet Genre | 1161 | 4 | 16.0 | 101.9 | 290 |

[1] Assuming items were evenly distributed between categories, this is the minimum number of items assigned to each category. [2] Multiple values are presented for the Level 1, Level 2 and Level 3 hierarchy of categories, respectively.

Currently, the LFE dataset is manually classified by hospital staff, who have to read each text item and assign it to a theme. Therefore, we are the first to experiment with applying automatic text classification to this dataset. The Amazon Hierarchical Reviews, Twitter COVID Sentiment and Twitter Tweet Genre datasets were primarily selected for their similar characteristics to the LFE dataset. However, another advantage they provided was that they contained extremely current data having all been published in 2020 (April, September and January, respectively). Although these datasets were useful for our investigation into how dataset characteristics affect classification accuracy, it was difficult to draw direct comparisons with related work in this field due to the dataset originality. The Reuters dataset was selected because of its wide use in this field as a benchmark, allowing direct comparisons of our novel pipeline results to other well-documented work.

Some of the seminal work in automatic text classification on the Reuters dataset was by Joachims [32]. Through the novel use of support vector machines, a micro averaged precision-recall breakeven score of 86.4 was achieved across the 90 categories which contained at least one training and one testing example. After this, researchers have used many different configurations of the Reuters dataset for their analysis. Some have used the exact same subset but applied different feature selection methods [33], while other work has focused on only the top 10 largest categories [34,35]. Unfortunately, the wide range of feature selection and category variation limits reliable comparison. However, by selecting related work with either (i) similar pre-processing and feature section methods, or (ii) similar category variation, we aim to ensure our proposed pipeline is performing with comparable levels of accuracy.

## 4. Methodology

For this research, a software package was developed using the Python programming language (Version 3.7), making use of the NumPy (Version 1.19.5) [36] and Pandas (Version 1.2.3) [37] libraries for efficient data structures and file input and output. The core concept was to develop an intuitive data processing and classification pipeline based on flexibility, thus enabling the user to easily select different pre-processing and classification techniques each time the pipeline is executed. As discussed in Section 2, classification often uses a generalized flow of data through a document classification pipeline. The approach presented in this paper follows this model. Figure 3 shows an overview of the pipeline developed.

Since the LFE dataset contained a range of proper nouns which provided no benefit to the classification task, they were removed to optimize the time required for each experiment. The Stanford named entity recognition system (Stanford NER) [38] was used to tag any names, locations and organizations in the raw text. Subsequently, these were removed from the dataset. In total, 3126 proper nouns were removed. A manual scan was performed to confirm that most cases were covered. Some notable exceptions were the name "June" (which was most likely mistaken for the month) and the word "trust" when used in the phrase "NHS trust". Neither of these were successfully tagged by Stanford NER. The dataset used in this work is the final version with the names, locations and organizations removed.

To maintain similarity in the pre-processing approaches, the Stanford core NLP pipeline [39], provided through the Python Stanza toolkit (Version 1.2) [40], was used where possible. This provided the tools for tokenizing the text, and lemmatizing words. However, Stanford core NLP did not provide any stemming options, so an implementation of Porter Stemmer [41] from the Python natural language toolkit (NLTK) (Version 3.5) [42] was used. NLTK also provided the list of common English stop words for stop word removal. The remaining pre-processing techniques (removal of numeric characters, removal of single character words and punctuation removal) were all developed for this project. The final pre-processing component was used to specifically clean the text of the Twitter collections. This consisted of removing URLs, "#" symbols from Twitter hashtags, "@" symbols from user handles and retweet text ("RT"). This was the final part of the software developed for this project's source code.

A selection of four word scoring metrics is made available in the pipeline. RAKE [10] was used via an implementation available in the rake-nltk (Version 1.0.4) [43] Python module. A TextRank [9] implementation was designed and developed derived from an article and source code by Liang [44]. An implementation of TF-IDF and a term frequency model were also developed.

Within the stage of feature extraction, the BoW model was developed using standard Python collections. These were originally listed and subsequently converted to dictionaries to optimize the look-up speed when generating feature masks. Feature masks were represented in NumPy arrays to reduce memory overhead and execution time.

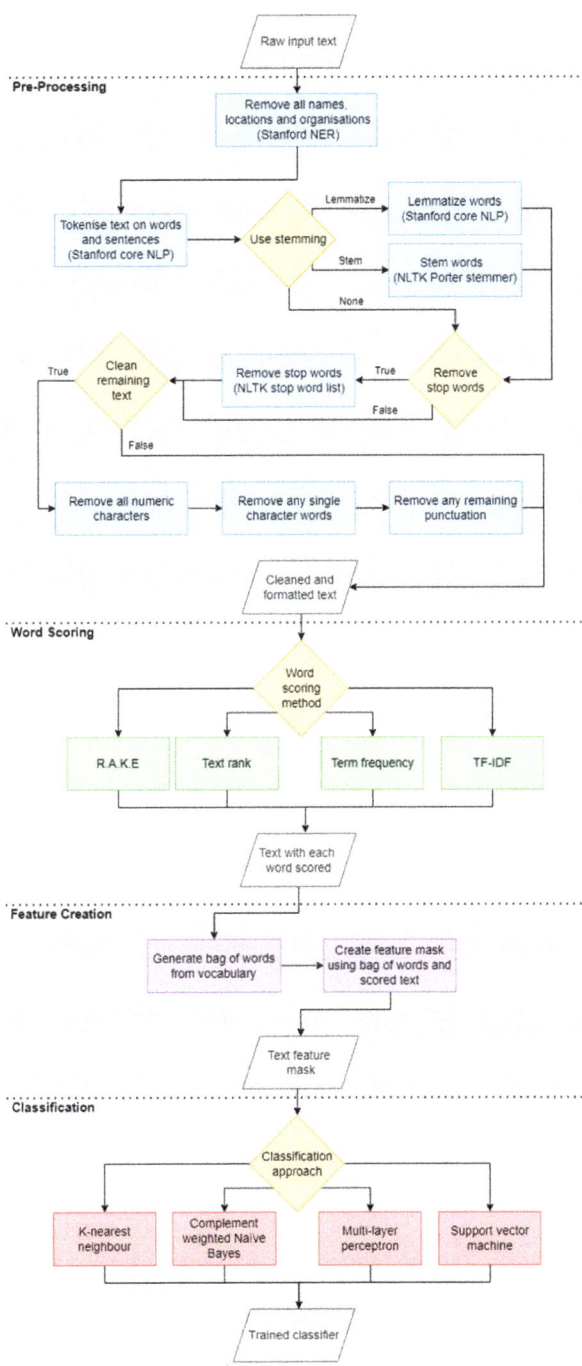

**Figure 3.** Representation of the text processing and classification pipeline, showing each stage described in Section 2. Rhomboids represent data, rectangles represent processes and diamonds represent decisions which can be made modified within the software parameters.

All classifiers used in this publication originate from the scikit-learn (Version 0.24.1) [45] machine learning library. This library was selected since (i) it provided tested classifier builds to be used, (ii) a range of statistical scoring methods and (iii) it is a popular library used in similar literature thereby enabling direct comparison with other work in this field. For this project a set of wrapper classes were designed for the scikit-learn classifiers. All classifier wrappers were developed upon an abstract base class to increase code reuse, speed up implementation of new classifiers and ensure a standardized set of method calls through overriding. The base class and all child classes are available in the "Classifiers" package within the source code. A link to the full source code can be found in the Supplementary Materials Section.

Within the final stage of Classification, four of the most common text classifiers are provided. These are k-nearest neighbor (KNN), compliment weighted naïve bayes (CNB), multi-layer perceptron (MLP) and support vector machine (SVM). Tuning the hyper parameters of each of these classifiers, for every dataset, would have produced too much variability in the results. Therefore, each classifier was tuned to the LFE dataset; the same hyper parameters were used on all datasets. When tuning was performed, only one variable was tuned at a time, the remainder of the pipeline remained constant, see Figure 4.

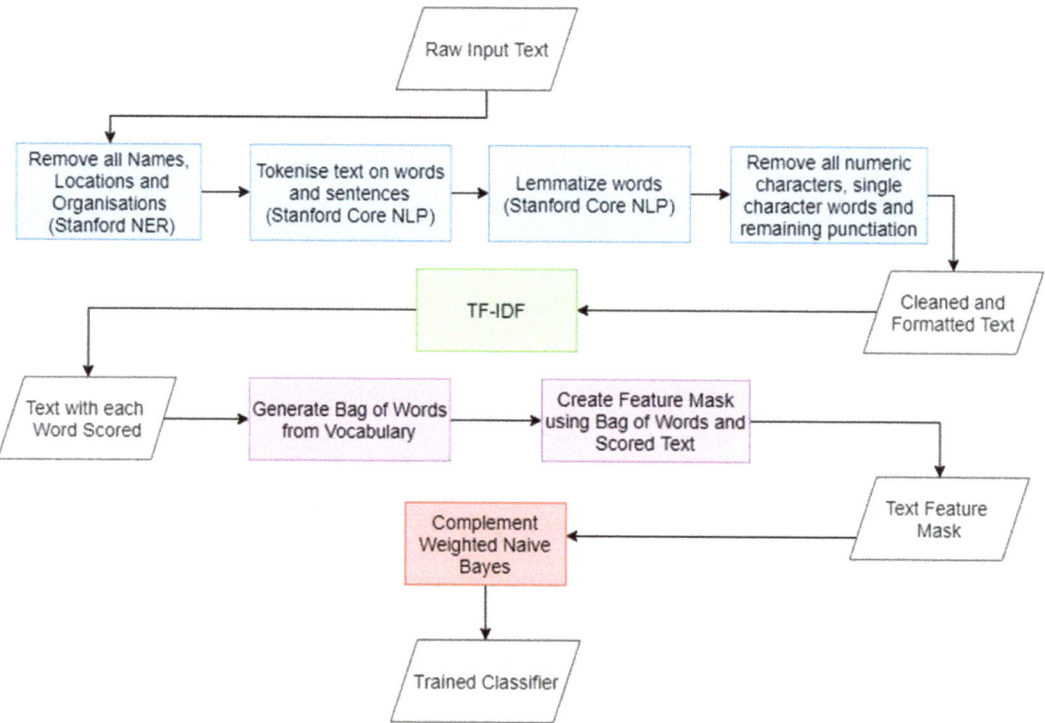

**Figure 4.** Representation of the processing pipeline used for hyper parameter tuning. From the text input all the way through the processes of tokenizing, lemmatizing, additional text cleaning, TF-IDF scoring, BoW modeling, creation of feature masks to the final stage of using the complement weighted naïve bayes classifier.

The first classifier, KNN, determines the category of an item based on the categories of the nearest neighbors in feature space. The core parameter to set is the value of $k$; the number of neighbors which should be considered when classifying a new item. To define $k$, a range of values were tested, and their accuracy was assessed based on their F1 score.

See the full results in Appendix C, Table A2. The value of $k$ was defined as 23. Work by Tan [46] suggested weighting neighbors based on their distance may improve results when working with unbalanced text corpuses. Thus, this parameter was also tuned. However, when this was applied to the LFE dataset, uniform weighting produced better results. The results of these tests are shown in Appendix C, Table A3.

The second classifier, Compliment weighted Naïve Bayes (CNB), is a specialized version of multinomial Naïve Bayes (MNB). This approach is reported to perform better on imbalanced text classification datasets, by improving some of the assumptions made in MNB. Specifically, it focuses on correcting the assumption that features are independent, and it attempts to improve the weight selection of the MNB decision boundary. This approach did not require any hyper parameter tuning, and the scikit-learn CNB was implemented as described by Rennie et al. [27].

The third classifier provided is based on the multi-layer perceptron (MLP). There are multiple modern text classification approaches which use deep learning variants of neural networks. Some notable examples are convolutional neural networks (CNN) [47] and recurrent neural networks (RNN) [11], both of which have been used extensively in this field. These approaches have a substantial computational overhead for feature creation. Therefore, deep learning would have been too unwieldly for some of the datasets used in this work. Furthermore, scikit-learn does not provide an implementation of CNN or RNN neural network architectures. Therefore, their use would require another library, reducing the quality of any comparisons made between classifiers. For these reasons, a more traditional, MLP architecture, with a single hidden layer, was used instead. The main parameter to tune for this model was the number of neurons used in the hidden layer. There is much discussion on how to optimize selection of this parameter, but the general rule of thumb is to select the floored mean between the number of input neurons and output neurons as defined below:

$$n_{hidden} = \lfloor \frac{n_{input} + n_{output}}{2} \rfloor$$

The remaining MLP hyper parameters are the default values from scikit-learn and a full list of these can be found in Appendix C, Table A4. The MLP was also set to stop training early if there was no change in the validation score, within a tolerance bound of $1 \times 10^{-4}$, over ten epochs.

For the fourth classifier, SVM, it has been reported that the selection of a linear kernel is more effective for text classification problems than non-linear kernels [48]. Four of the most commonly used kernels were tested and confirmed that this was also the case with the LFE dataset. Therefore, a linear kernel was selected for use in this classifier. The results of the tests are found in Appendix C, Table A5. To account for the class imbalance in the LFE dataset, each class is weighted proportionally in the SVM to reduce bias.

Aside from these supervised classification approaches, an unsupervised model was also developed using scikit-learn and the same classification wrapper class structure. The purpose of this was to examine whether any natural clusters form within the LFE dataset, to enable a wider range of comparisons. K-means [49] was selected as the unsupervised approach, where $k$ represents the number of groups the data should be clustered into. To tune this parameter, two metrics were recorded for a range of potential values of $k$: the j-squared error and the silhouette score [50]. A lower j-squared error represents a smaller average distance from any given data point to the centroid of its cluster, and a higher silhouette score represents an item exhibiting a greater similarity to its own cluster, compared to other clusters. Therefore, an optimal $k$ value should be minimizing j-squared error whilst maximizing silhouette score. However, j-squared error is likely to trend lower as more clusters are added, leading to diminishing returns for larger values of $k$. So, it is better suited to examining where the benefit starts to drop off, this is often referred to as finding the "elbow" in the graph.

Appendix C, Figure A1 shows the graph comparing the j-squared error and the average silhouette score for all clusters. From this analysis it was difficult to define the optimal value of $k$, since the j-squared error trended downwards almost linearly, and the average silhouette score was low for all values of $k$. Therefore, the LFE dataset was clustered using different small values of $k$, {2, 8, 13, 16, 20}, which performed better.

## 5. Results

This research evaluates how fundamental differences in database volume, category distribution and subjective manual classification affect the accuracy of automatic document classification. All experiments were performed on the same computer. It had the following hardware specification: Intel Core i5-8600K, 6 cores at 3.6 Ghz. RAM: 32 GB DDR4. GPU: Gigabyte Nvidia GeForce GTX 1060 6 GB VRAM. The Stanza toolkit for Stanford core NLP supported GPU parallelization, and all experiments exploited this feature. The scikit-learn library did not have any GPU enabled options, so all classification was processed by the CPU.

During experiments, each dataset was tested for the given variables. A fivefold cross validation was used, and the mean score for each validation is reported. If not otherwise stated, all other elements of the pipeline are identical to the constant processing pipeline, described in Section 4. The core metric used for evaluating accuracy was the F1 score, which combines both precision and accuracy into a single measure. This was recorded as both a micro average and a macro average.

Tables 3–5 contain the experimental results yielded by the evaluation of changes to the different sections of the proposed pipeline (pre-processing, word scoring and classification respectively). Based on the results from Tables 3–5, the optimum pipeline for each dataset was tested and the results can be found in Table 6.

**Table 3.** Evaluates the effect of different pre-processing techniques on the accuracy of classification. The same processing pipeline is maintained aside from pre-processing (TF-IDF, BoW, CNB).

| Dataset Name | Pre-Processing | F1 Score (Micro) | F1 Score (Macro) |
|---|---|---|---|
| LFE | None | 0.358 | 0.133 |
| | Stop Word Removal | 0.334 | 0.151 |
| | Word Lemmatizing | 0.351 | 0.136 |
| | Both | 0.323 | 0.153 |
| Reuters | None | 0.870 | 0.477 |
| | Stop Word Removal | 0.890 | 0.526 |
| | Word Lemmatizing | 0.858 | 0.446 |
| | Both | 0.886 | 0.505 |
| Amazon Hierarchical Reviews | None | 0.829 | 0.826 |
| | Stop Word Removal | 0.834 | 0.832 |
| | Word Lemmatizing | 0.827 | 0.825 |
| | Both | 0.837 | 0.833 |
| Twitter COVID Sentiment | None | 0.439 | 0.445 |
| | Stop Word Removal | 0.431 | 0.438 |
| | Word Lemmatizing | 0.434 | 0.438 |
| | Both | 0.427 | 0.434 |
| Twitter Tweet Genre | None | 0.800 | 0.801 |
| | Stop Word Removal | 0.786 | 0.787 |
| | Word Lemmatizing | 0.807 | 0.808 |
| | Both | 0.791 | 0.791 |

**Table 4.** Evaluates the effect of using different word scoring techniques on the accuracy of classification. The same processing pipeline is maintained aside from word scoring (stop words removal, words lemmatization, additional text cleaning, BoW, CNB).

| Dataset Name | Word Scoring Method | F1 Score (Micro) | F1 Score (Macro) |
|---|---|---|---|
| LFE | RAKE | 0.152 | 0.089 |
| | TextRank | 0.174 | 0.045 |
| | Term Frequency | 0.342 | 0.154 |
| | TF-IDF | 0.323 | 0.153 |
| Reuters | RAKE | 0.461 | 0.348 |
| | TextRank | 0.597 | 0.100 |
| | Term Frequency | 0.898 | 0.552 |
| | TF-IDF | 0.886 | 0.505 |
| Amazon Hierarchical Reviews | RAKE | 0.381 | 0.268 |
| | TextRank | 0.605 | 0.573 |
| | Term Frequency | 0.834 | 0.832 |
| | TF-IDF | 0.837 | 0.833 |
| Twitter COVID Sentiment | RAKE | 0.213 | 0.192 |
| | TextRank | 0.385 | 0.364 |
| | Term Frequency | 0.435 | 0.441 |
| | TF-IDF | 0.427 | 0.434 |
| Twitter Tweet Genre | RAKE | 0.427 | 0.422 |
| | TextRank | 0.658 | 0.608 |
| | Term Frequency | 0.826 | 0.827 |
| | TF-IDF | 0.791 | 0.791 |

**Table 5.** Evaluates the use of different classifiers. The processing pipeline is maintained aside from word scoring (stop words removed, words lemmatized, additional text cleaning, TF-IDF, BoW).

| Dataset Name | Classifier | F1 Score (Micro) | F1 Score (Macro) | Fit Time | Score Time |
|---|---|---|---|---|---|
| LFE | KNN | 0.224 | 0.053 | 0.039 | 0.0758 |
| | CNB | 0.323 | 0.153 | 0.050 | 0.0077 |
| | MLP | 0.329 | 0.099 | 49.029 | 0.0327 |
| | SVM | 0.241 | 0.102 | 12.865 | 2.2606 |
| Reuters | KNN | 0.624 | 0.297 | 9.618 | 132.67 |
| | CNB | 0.886 | 0.505 | 33.872 | 2.526 |
| | MLP | 0.928 | 0.656 | 46,840.85 | 31.941 |
| | SVM | 0.771 | 0.561 | 49,310.23 | 35.715 |
| Amazon Hierarchical Reviews | KNN | 0.652 | 0.624 | 10.831 | 145.69 |
| | CNB | 0.834 | 0.832 | 35.250 | 2.724 |
| | MLP | 0.841 | 0.839 | 50,840.12 | 35.769 |
| | SVM | 0.822 | 0.817 | 56,527.68 | 39.935 |
| Twitter COVID Sentiment | KNN | 0.313 | 0.302 | 7.787 | 149.136 |
| | CNB | 0.424 | 0.431 | 42.274 | 2.497 |
| | MLP | 0.387 | 0.384 | 48,257.21 | 30.676 |
| | SVM | 0.395 | 0.407 | 51,774.16 | 35.027 |
| Twitter Tweet Genre | KNN | 0.478 | 0.405 | 0.021 | 0.031 |
| | CNB | 0.791 | 0.791 | 0.026 | 0.004 |
| | MLP | 0.748 | 0.748 | 15.946 | 0.012 |
| | SVM | 0.761 | 0.765 | 2.095 | 0.605 |

**Table 6.** Optimum pipeline result for each dataset with F1 micro averaged score.

| Dataset Name | Pre-Processing | Word Scoring Method | Classifier | F1 Score (Micro) |
|---|---|---|---|---|
| LFE | None | Term Frequency | CNB | 0.358 |
| Reuters | Stop Word Removal | Term Frequency | MLP | 0.933 |
| Amazon Hierarchical Reviews | Both | TF-IDF | MLP | 0.841 |
| Twitter COVID Sentiment | None | Term Frequency | CNB | 0.440 |
| Twitter Tweet Genre | Word Lemmatizing | Term Frequency | CNB | 0.828 |

To benchmark the accuracy of our pipeline against other related work on automatic text classification, Table 7 presents our results on the Reuters corpus compared to the works mentioned in Section 3.2. As stated in this previous section, it should be noted that a direct comparison of these results is difficult due to the differences in document/category reduction, pre-processing approaches and feature selection. However, the results presented suggest that the approach outlined in this paper produces comparable accuracy to other state-of-the-art approaches.

**Table 7.** Comparison of the highest achieved micro-averaged score of our pipeline (shown in bold), compared to other published automatic text classification results on the "ApteMod" split of the Reuters-21578 corpus. Accuracy metrics are all F1 scores, except Joachims which is the precision-recall breakeven point.

| Automatic Text Classification Approach | Overall Accuracy (Micro-Averaged) |
|---|---|
| Joachims, T. SVM [32] | 0.864 |
| Banerjee, S. et al. SVC [33] | 0.870 |
| Ghiassi, M. et al. "DAN2" MLP [1] [34] | 0.910 |
| Zdrojewska A. et al. Feed-forward MLP with ADAM [35] | 0.924 |
| **Haynes, C. et al. Novel Pipeline MLP** | **0.933** |

[1] This score is not stated explicitly but was calculated as the average of the F1 testing scores provided in the referenced paper.

## 6. Discussion

### 6.1. Practical Implications

Based on the results of our experiments we will discuss the two research questions introduced in Section 3.1.

(R1) The NHS is likely to adopt our approach to automatically classify feedback. This means we have successfully reduced the workload of NHS staff by providing a tool which can be used in place of manual classification. Therefore, the answer to (R1) is positive. Although our proposed classification pipeline attained a lower micro-averaged F1 score on the LFE dataset compared to the benchmark datasets, given the limitations of the dataset, the NHS has found this better than the alternative of manually classifying future datasets.

(R2) The performance of the classification pipeline published in this paper is evaluated by comparing it against the results of the Reuters dataset with other published work. In this research, a micro-averaged F1 score of 93.30% was achieved. As shown in Table 7, that accuracy outperforms the seminal SVM approaches of Joachims [32], which achieved a micro-averaged breakeven point of 86.40%. Furthermore, the classification pipeline performed in-line with or surpassed more recent approaches [33–35]; demonstrating that this classification pipeline produces high accuracy results on other datasets. Therefore, the answer to (R2) is positive.

*6.2. Theoretical Implications*

Despite the classification pipeline performing very well, the LFE dataset attained a lower micro-averaged F1 score than the benchmark datasets. This discussion will outline the factors which may have caused this result. The four comparison datasets all outperformed the LFE dataset for almost all potential pipeline setups. This suggest that there is an underlying limiting factor, or factors, within the dataset itself. To break down this comparison, each of the characteristics (see Section 3) will be discussed.

1. *The dataset is relatively small.* The overall size of the items in the dataset may have resulted in an advantage to the Reuters and Amazon Hierarchical Reviews results, as it is widely accepted that a larger and more varied dataset will produce better classification results [51,52]. However, the much smaller Twitter Tweet Genre dataset, also achieved a high level of accuracy with a micro-averaged F1 score of 82.80%. Considering the LFE dataset had almost double the number of items, this characteristic alone is unlikely to be the sole cause of the low accuracy results.

2. *The length of each text item is short.* Both Twitter datasets attained vastly different results to the LFE dataset despite the fact they are similarly characterized as being short in length. These Twitter datasets also had considerably shorter average word counts than the LFE dataset and still outperformed it overall. In conclusion, the average length of each text item is unlikely to be a discriminatory characteristic.

3. *The number of text items per category is small.* The average distribution of items per category did not limit performance on the Reuters dataset. However, that could be attributed to the larger overall size, which would have provided more samples for each category in comparison to the LFE dataset.

4. *The distribution of categories is not balanced.* In terms of category distribution, all classification techniques for both the Reuters and LFE datasets suffered from the same issue, where the smallest categories were never applied when classifying the test dataset. Specifically, nine of the Reuters categories and five of the LFE categories never appeared in any of the test classifications. Although this did not impact the overall results of the Reuters classification, the percentage of small categories was much greater in the LFE dataset. In the LFE dataset, 25% of categories comprised less than 1% of the dataset compared with 13.8% in the Reuters dataset. These tiny categories are almost certainly a contributing factor to the lower accuracy of the LFE results.

5. *All the text is positive.* The use of common terms across all categories did not have a significantly negative impact on the classification accuracy of the Amazon Hierarchical Reviews dataset. However, the use of common terms did significantly impact the LFE results. This could be attributed to the fact that each Amazon review had an average word count of more than 50% the average LFE item, resulting in a diluting effect of the repeated common words. Due to the overall larger size of the Amazon Hierarchical Reviews dataset, it had a much larger vocabulary in comparison to the LFE dataset, which may explain why TF-IDF was the optimal scoring method for this dataset.

6. *The categories are subjectively defined.* The subjective nature of both the manual classification and the categories themselves are likely to have played a role in the lower scores for accuracy in both the LFE and the Twitter COVID Sentiment datasets. Although, if the accuracy alone is considered, it is not possible to determine a direct link.

Based on these comparisons, the limiting factors in the LFE classification results are most likely to be (i) the imbalanced category distribution, (ii) the use of repeated common terms across different categories and (iii) the subjective nature of the manual classification. To explore these factors, a manual analysis was performed on the K-means clustering result to see if these same factors were limiting when the LFE dataset was treated as an unsupervised clustering problem, rather than a supervised classification problem.

The first test was used to evaluate how evenly the text items are distributed for different values of $k$ (2, 8, 13, 16, 20 and 150). For any number of clusters, a similar trend emerged, where one cluster would account for between 51% and 98% of all the items. The remaining items were thinly spread between the remaining categories. Figures 5 and 6 depict how the data is unevenly distributed with $k$ values of 20 and 150, respectively. Therefore, there is no evidence of a natural separation for most of the text items in the LFE dataset. Thus, they are either sufficiently generic they get clustered into one large group or that they are overly similar leading to the formation of limited smaller clusters.

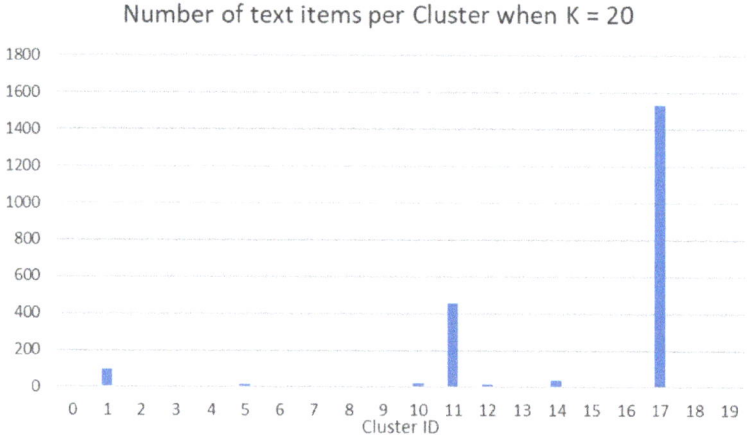

**Figure 5.** Distribution of LFE dataset when clustered using $k$-Means where $k = 20$.

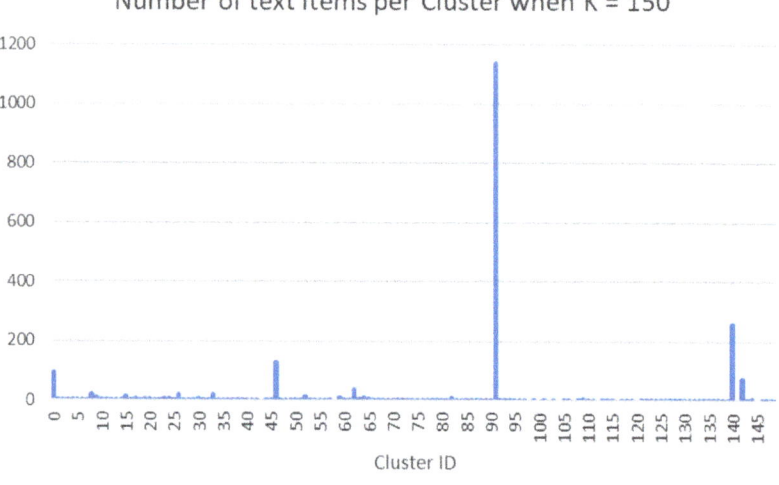

**Figure 6.** Distribution of LFE dataset when clustered using $k$-Means where $k = 150$.

To investigate this clustering and to evaluate other limiting dataset characteristics, a manual comparison of the text entries in the small and medium sized clusters was performed. When $k = 8$, a cluster emerged with only 29, out of the total 2307, items assigned to it. This cluster had a lot of similarities in its text items; almost always congratulating a member of staff on completing a course or gaining a qualification. Words such as "course", "success", "level", "pass" and "congratulations" appeared in this cluster in scales of magnitude higher than across the rest of the clusters. As the value of $k$ varied, this cluster appeared with a 96.6% overlap with a cluster in $k = 2$, and a 79.3% overlap with a cluster in $k = 13$.

Furthermore, when $k = 8$, there was an even smaller cluster identified which contained only 9, out of the total 2307, items. This tiny cluster came from sequential items in the dataset, which share almost exactly the same words. It appears that someone submitted multiple "excellence texts" for a range of different staff. They copied and pasted the same text framework, just changing the name, organization or slightly rewording the text. So, after using the NER, cleaning, lemmatization and removing the stop words, all these items are virtually identical. What is also interesting in this cluster is how the word "fantastic" appeared in every entry whereas it only appears in 5.98% of the whole corpus. This shows one of the downsides to TF-IDF in this case, as words which have no bearing on the classification are getting scored highly due to their rarity across the rest of the corpus. This also supports the argument that common terms, unrelated to the category, could be limiting the classification accuracy. A full breakdown of the occurrence of the most common words in each cluster when $k = 8$, shown in Table 8, shows a general theme can be manually identified for most of clusters.

**Table 8.** The percentage of times words appeared in each text item, in each cluster, when $k = 8$. Only the five largest clusters are shown, since the other three clusters only contained a single item each. Bold values represent statistically significantly values ($p < 0.5$) in a given cluster when compared to their occurrence in the entire dataset. The case (upper or lower) of the words was not considered.

| | Overall | Cluster ID 0 | Cluster ID 1 | Cluster ID 3 | Cluster ID 5 | Cluster ID 7 |
|---|---|---|---|---|---|---|
| Word/Size | 2307 | 9 | 1853 | 319 | 11 | 29 |
| Thank | 43.44% | **100.00%** | 39.50% | **70.22%** | 0.00% | 3.45% |
| Mentor | 1.66% | 0.00% | 0.81% | 6.27% | **18.18%** | 0.00% |
| Placement | 1.57% | 0.00% | 0.49% | 6.58% | **45.45%** | 0.00% |
| Support | 32.10% | 0.00% | 29.25% | **52.04%** | 36.36% | 3.45% |
| SAU | 0.90% | 0.00% | 0.27% | 4.70% | 0.00% | 0.00% |
| Work | 41.46% | **100.00%** | 43.82% | 26.33% | 9.09% | **55.17%** |
| Hard | 15.83% | 0.00% | 17.00% | 7.21% | 0.00% | **48.28%** |
| Help | 31.79% | 22.22% | 29.30% | **50.47%** | 0.00% | 3.45% |
| Team | 32.87% | 0.00% | 36.97% | 13.79% | 18.18% | 0.00% |
| Staff | 22.84% | 0.00% | 25.74% | 9.72% | 0.00% | 0.00% |
| Course | 2.52% | 0.00% | 1.35% | 2.19% | 0.00% | **86.21%** |
| Success | 3.33% | **100.00%** | 2.10% | 1.88% | 0.00% | **68.97%** |
| Level | 4.90% | 0.00% | 2.10% | 1.88% | 0.00% | **58.62%** |
| Pass | 5.94% | 0.00% | 6.58% | 1.25% | 0.00% | **20.69%** |
| Patient | 37.54% | 0.00% | 42.31% | 15.67% | 9.09% | 0.00% |
| Fantastic | 5.98% | **100.00%** | 5.45% | 3.45% | **81.82%** | 10.34% |
| Congratulation | 1.39% | 0.00% | 0.38% | 0.31% | 0.00% | 79.31% |
| Ward | 14.12% | 0.00% | 14.25% | 14.11% | 27.27% | 6.90% |

- **Placement.** Cluster ID 5 has a high prevalence of the words: "placement", "mentor", "support" and "team".
- **Course Pass.** Cluster ID 7 has a high prevalence of the words: "course", "success", "level", "pass", "hard" and "work".
- **General Support.** Cluster ID 3 has a high prevalence of the words: "thank", "support" and "help".

Consider how the large remaining cluster has a similar distribution of words when compared to the full dataset. This suggests that this large cluster is a 'catch-all' for all the items not specific enough to be classified elsewhere. This reinforces the conclusion that rarely used but generic terms in the LFE dataset are biasing the accuracy of classification.

This could also explain why the simple scoring metric of term count was optimal for the LFE data. The other single word scoring methods (Text Rank and TF-IDF) both give higher weight to words which are common in a given item, in comparison to the rest of the corpus. However, in this dataset the most commonly used words are actually those that most closely represent the categories:

- "Thank" appears in 43.44% of items.
- "Support" appears in 32.10% of items.
- "Work" appears in 41.46% of items, "Hard" appears in 15.83% of items.

When you consider there are categories specifically for "Thank you", "Supportive" and "Hard Work", it is clear these terms being underweighted could be another limiting factor of the LFE dataset. The limiting factor of subjective manual classification is evident in this same analysis. Although "Thank" appears in 43.44% of items, only 2.74% of the items have got a primary theme of "Thank you". A specific example of this can be seen in one of the text items, after it has been lemmatized and stop words have been removed. Consider the text *"ruin humor wrong sort quickly good day much always go help support thank"*. This seems quite generic and contains many keywords which might suggest "Supportive" or "Thank you" as the category. However, this text item was manually classified with a primary theme of "Positive Attitude" and a secondary theme of "Hard Work" despite it not having any of the common keywords associated with these themes.

Overall, the data suggest that the common limiting factors of classifying the LFE dataset are also present when it is clustered. Indeed, this means that there is an intrinsic limitation on the ability to classify this specific dataset.

### 6.3. Future Research

A number of open issues offer opportunities for future work. For example, it would be interesting to evaluate our pipeline with the latest iteration of the LFE dataset, as new entries are added every month. A larger dataset would hopefully provide more instances of different themes and reduce the imbalanced theme distribution.

An alternative option would be to see if the accuracy of our pipeline could be improved on the same dataset if the number of themes was reduced. For instance, some similar themes could be combined such as "Kindness" and "Positive Attitude", which have a high degree of overlap. Some of the more generic, larger themes could also be removed entirely, for example, "Supportive" and "Hard Work". Based on the discussion above, it would be expected that this would reduce the imbalanced theme distribution and increase the ratio of text items to themes.

A separate area of research would be improvements to novel pipeline software. Currently, it is a useful tool to test a range of different text pre-processing, word scoring and classification methods to determine which is the most suitable for a given dataset. However, it could be improved if this process was automated, so that the pipeline would test different combinations, rank them and automatically select the most efficient one. To achieve this, the novel pipeline would require a high level of optimization and structure reordering. However, this addition would make this tool more accessible to researchers outside the field, as it would require less inherent knowledge of the processes used.

**Supplementary Materials:** The full source code for the developed software tool can be downloaded from: https://github.com/ChristopherHaynes/LFEDocumentClassifier (accessed on 8 February 2022).

**Author Contributions:** Conceptualization, C.H. and M.A.P.; methodology, C.H. and M.A.P.; software, C.H.; validation, C.H.; formal analysis, C.H.; investigation, C.H. and M.A.P.; resources, D.V., F.H. and G.C.; data curation, D.V., F.H. and G.C. and C.H.; writing—original draft preparation, C.H.; writing—review and editing, C.H., M.A.P. and L.S.; visualization, C.H. and L.S.; supervision, M.A.P. and L.S.; project administration, L.S. and K.T. All authors have read and agreed to the published version of the manuscript.

**Funding:** This research received no external funding.

**Institutional Review Board Statement:** Not applicable.

**Informed Consent Statement:** Not applicable.

**Data Availability Statement:** "Reuters-21578 (ApteMod)": Used in our software package via Python NLTK platform, direct download available at http://kdd.ics.uci.edu/databases/reuters21578/reuters21578.html. Retrieved 25 April 2021 "Amazon Hierarchical Reviews": Yury Kashnitsky. *Hierarchical text classification.* (April 2020). Version 1. Retrieved 29 April 2021 from https://www.kaggle.com/kashnitsky/hierarchical-text-classification/version/1. "Twitter COVID Sentiment": Aman Miglani. *Coronavirus tweet NLP—Text Classification.* (September 2020). Version 1. Retrieved 27 April 2021 from https://www.kaggle.com/datatattle/covid-19-nlp-text-classification/version/1. "Twitter Tweet Genre": Pradeep. *Text (Tweet) Classification* (January 2020). Version 1. Retrieved 28 April 2021 from https://www.kaggle.com/pradeeptrical/text-tweet-classification/version/1.

**Acknowledgments:** The authors are grateful to the NHS Information Governance for allowing us to make use of the anonymized LFE dataset.

**Conflicts of Interest:** The authors declare no conflict of interest.

## Appendix A

**Table A1.** Full list of "Learning from Excellence" dataset themes.

| Theme | Description |
|---|---|
| Above and Beyond | Performing in excess of the expectations or demands. |
| Adaptability | Being able to adjust to new conditions. |
| Communication | Clearly conveying ideas and tasks to others. |
| Coping with Pressure | Adjusting to unusual demands or stressors. |
| Dedicated | Devoting oneself to a task or purpose. |
| Education | Achieving personal improvement through training/schooling. |
| Efficient | Working in a well-organized and competent way. |
| Hard Work | Working with a great deal of effort or endurance. |
| Initiative | Taking the opportunity to act before others do. |
| Innovative | Introducing new ideas; original and creative in thinking. |
| Kindness | Being friendly and considerate to colleagues and/or patients. |
| Leadership | Influencing others in a group by taking charge of a situation. |
| Morale | Providing confidence and enthusiasm to a group. |
| Patient Focus | Prioritizing patient care above other tasks. |
| Positive Attitude | Showing optimism about situations and interactions. |
| Reliable | Consistently good in quality or performance. |
| Safe Care | Taking all necessary steps to ensure safety protocols are met. |
| Staffing | Covering extra shifts when there is illness/absence. |
| Supportive | Providing encouragement or emotional help. |
| Teamwork | Collaboration with a group to perform well on a given task. |
| Technical Excellence | Producing successful results based on specialist expertise. |
| Time | Devoting additional time to colleagues and/or patients. |
| Thank You | Giving a direct compliment to a member of staff. |
| Well-Being | Making a colleague and/or patient, comfortable and happy. |

**Appendix B**

Examples of similar tweets from the Twitter COVID Sentiment dataset which have similar content, but were given opposing manual classifications:

- "My food stock is not the only one which is empty . . . PLEASE, don't panic, THERE WILL BE ENOUGH FOOD FOR EVERYONE if you do not take more than you need. Stay calm, stay safe.#COVID19france #COVID_19 #COVID19 #coronavirus #confinement #Confinementotal #ConfinementGeneral https://t.co/zrlG0Z520j\T1 \textquotedblright---Manually classified as "extremely negative".
- "Me, ready to go at supermarket during the #COVID19 outbreak. Not because I'm paranoid, but because my food stock is literally empty. The #coronavirus is a serious thing, but please, don't panic. It causes shortage . . . #CoronavirusFrance #restezchezvous #Stay-AtHome #confinement https://t.co/usmuaLq72n\T1\textquotedblright---Manually classified as "positive".

**Appendix C**

**Table A2.** KNN tuning: how the F1 score varied (micro and macro averaged) as the value of *k* was altered. Tests performed using the constant processing pipeline. Selected *k* value shown in bold.

| k | F1 Score (Micro) | F1 Score (Macro) |
|---|---|---|
| 9 | 0.205481 | 0.053783 |
| 11 | 0.215820 | 0.053813 |
| 13 | 0.223463 | 0.055129 |
| 15 | 0.223917 | 0.053341 |
| 17 | 0.227964 | 0.054558 |
| 19 | 0.232904 | 0.054457 |
| 21 | 0.230655 | 0.053048 |
| **23** | **0.242796** | **0.055268** |
| 25 | 0.241004 | 0.050718 |
| 27 | 0.238308 | 0.049159 |
| 29 | 0.230211 | 0.047173 |
| 31 | 0.232014 | 0.047116 |

**Table A3.** KNN tuning: F1 score (micro and macro averaged) using uniform weighting compared to distance weighting. Although the F1 macro average score is higher for distance weighing, micro averaging is less susceptible to fluctuations from class imbalance, therefore this was chosen as the deciding factor. Tests performed using the constant processing pipeline. Selected weighting method shown in bold.

| Weighting Method | F1 Score (Micro) | F1 Score (Macro) |
|---|---|---|
| **Uniform** | **0.242796** | **0.055268** |
| Distance | 0.236509 | 0.067957 |

**Table A4.** MLP hyper parameter list.

| Parameter | Type/Value |
|---|---|
| Activation function | Rectified linear unit function (RELU) |
| Weight optimization algorithm | Adam |
| Max epochs | 200 |
| Batch size | 64 |
| Alpha (regularization term) | 0.0001 |
| Beta (decay rate) | 0.9 |
| Epsilon (numerical stability) | $1 \times 10^{-8}$ |
| Early stopping tolerance | $1 \times 10^{-4}$ |
| Early stopping iteration range | 10 |

**Table A5.** SVM tuning: F1 score (micro and macro averaged) for different kernels. Although the F1 macro average score is higher for the linear kernel, micro averaging is less susceptible to fluctuations from class imbalance, therefore this was chosen as the deciding factor. Tests performed using the constant processing pipeline. Selected weighting method shown in bold.

| Kernel | F1 Score (Micro) | F1 Score (Macro) |
|---|---|---|
| RBF | 0.241 | 0.102515 |
| Polynomial (Degree 3) | 0.118252 | 0.026344 |
| Sigmoid | 0.369148 | 0.207289 |
| **Linear** | **0.375895** | **0.19138** |

**Figure A1.** K—Means Tuning Graph. Comparison of how the j-squared error and average silhouette score vary for differing numbers of clusters (*k*).

## References

1. Pong, J.Y.-H.; Kwok, R.C.-W.; Lau, R.Y.-K.; Hao, J.-X.; Wong, P.C.-C. A comparative study of two automatic document classification methods in a library setting. *J. Inf. Sci.* **2007**, *34*, 213–230. [CrossRef]
2. Androutsopoulos, I.; Koutsias, J.; Chandrinos, K.V.; Paliouras, G.; Spyropoulos, C.D. An evaluation of Naive Bayesian anti-spam filtering. In *Proceedings of the Workshop on Machine Learning in the New Information Age*; Potamias, G., Moustakis, V., van Someren, M., Eds.; Springer: Barcelona, Spain, 2000; pp. 9–17.
3. Connelly, A.; Kuri, V.; Palomino, M. Lack of consensus among sentiment analysis tools: A suitability study for SME firms. In Proceedings of the 8th Language and Technology Conference, Poznań, Poland, 17–19 November 2017; pp. 54–58.
4. Meyer, B.J.F. Prose Analysis: Purposes, Procedures, and Problems 1. In *Understanding Expository Text*; Understanding Expository Text; Routledge: Oxfordshire, England, UK, 2017; pp. 11–64.
5. Kim, S.-B.; Han, K.-S.; Rim, H.-C.; Myaeng, S.H. Some effective techniques for naive bayes text classification. *IEEE Trans. Knowl. Data Eng.* **2006**, *18*, 1457–1466.
6. Ge, L.; Moh, T.-S. Improving text classification with word embedding. In Proceedings of the 2017 IEEE International Conference on Big Data (Big Data), Boston, MA, USA, 11–14 December 2017; pp. 1796–1805.
7. Zhang, Y.; Jin, R.; Zhou, Z.-H. Understanding bag-of-words model: A statistical framework. *Int. J. Mach. Learn. Cybern.* **2010**, *1*, 43–52. [CrossRef]
8. Wang, S.; Zhou, W.; Jiang, C. A survey of word embeddings based on deep learning. *Computing* **2020**, *102*, 717–740. [CrossRef]

9.  Manevitz, L.M.; Yousef, M. One-class SVMs for document classification. *J. Mach. Learn. Res.* **2001**, *2*, 139–154.
10. Ting, S.L.; Ip, W.H.; Tsang, A.H.C. Is Naive Bayes a good classifier for document classification. *Int. J. Softw. Eng. Its* **2011**, *5*, 37–46.
11. Lai, S.; Xu, L.; Liu, K.; Zhao, J. Recurrent convolutional neural networks for text classification. In Proceedings of the Twenty-ninth AAAI Conference on Artificial Intelligence, Austin, TX, USA, 25–30 January 2015.
12. Conneau, A.; Schwenk, H.; Barrault, L.; Lecun, Y. Very deep convolutional networks for text classification. *Ki Künstliche Intell.* **2016**, *26*, 357–363.
13. Kannan, S.; Gurusamy, V.; Vijayarani, S.; Ilamathi, J.; Nithya, M. Preprocessing techniques for text mining. *Int. J. Comput. Sci. Commun. Netw.* **2014**, *5*, 7–16.
14. Nothman, J.; Qin, H.; Yurchak, R. Stop word lists in free open-source software packages. In Proceedings of the Workshop for NLP Open Source Software (NLP-OSS), Melbourne, Australia, 20 July 2018; pp. 7–12.
15. Jivani, A.G. A comparative study of stemming algorithms. *Int. J. Comp. Tech. Appl* **2011**, *2*, 1930–1938.
16. Ramos, J. Using tf-idf to determine word relevance in document queries. In Proceedings of the First Instructional Conference on Machine Learning, Citeseer, Banff, AB, Canada, 27 February–1 March 2011; Volume 242, pp. 29–48.
17. Mihalcea, R.; Tarau, P. Textrank: Bringing order into text. In Proceedings of the 2004 Conference on Empirical Methods in Natural Language Processing, Barcelona, Spain, 2 July 2004; pp. 404–411.
18. Rose, S.; Engel, D.; Cramer, N.; Cowley, W. Automatic keyword extraction from individual documents. *Text. Min. Appl. Theory* **2010**, *1*, 1–20.
19. Ljungberg, B.F. Dimensionality reduction for bag-of-words models: PCA vs. LSA. *Semanticscholar. Org.* **2019**. Available online: http://cs229.stanford.edu/proj2017/final-reports/5163902.pdf (accessed on 8 February 2022).
20. Cavnar, W.B.; Trenkle, J.M. N-gram-based text categorization. In Proceedings of the SDAIR-94, 3rd Annual Symposium on Document Analysis and Information Retrieval, Las Vegas, NV, USA, 1 June 1994; Volume 161175.
21. Ogada, K.; Mwangi, W.; Cheruiyot, W. N-gram based text categorization method for improved data mining. *J. Inf. Eng. Appl.* **2015**, *5*, 35–43.
22. Schonlau, M.; Guenther, N.; Sucholutsky, I. Text mining with n-gram variables. *Stata J.* **2017**, *17*, 866–881. [CrossRef]
23. Church, K.W. Word2Vec. *Nat. Lang. Eng.* **2016**, *23*, 155–162. [CrossRef]
24. Mikolov, T.; Chen, K.; Corrado, G.; Dean, J. Efficient Estimation of Word Representations in Vector Space. *arXiv* **2013**, arXiv:1301.3781.
25. Yang, Z.; Yang, D.; Dyer, C.; He, X.; Smola, A.; Hovy, E. Hierarchical attention networks for document classification. In Proceedings of the 2016 Conference of the North American Chapter of the Association for Computational Linguistics: Human Language Technologies, San Diego, CA, USA, 12–17 June 2016; pp. 1480–1489.
26. Han, E.-H.S.; Karypis, G.; Kumar, V. Text categorization using weight adjusted k-nearest neighbor classification. In Proceedings of the Pacific-Asia Conference on Knowledge Discovery and Data Mining, Hong Kong, China, 16–18 April 2001; pp. 53–65.
27. Rennie, J.D.; Shih, L.; Teevan, J.; Karger, D.R. Tackling the poor assumptions of naive bayes text classifiers. In Proceedings of the 20th International Conference on Machine Learning (ICML-03), Washington, DC, USA, 21–24 August 2003; pp. 616–623.
28. Wermter, S. Neural network agents for learning semantic text classification. *Inf. Retrieva* **2000**, *3*, 87–103. [CrossRef]
29. Yang, Y.; Liu, X. A re-examination of text categorization methods. In Proceedings of the 22nd Annual International ACM SIGIR Conference on Research and Development in Information Retrieval, Berkeley, CA, USA, 15–19 August 1999; pp. 42–49.
30. Frank, E.; Bouckaert, R.R. Naive Bayes for Text Classification with Unbalanced Classes. In *Lecture Notes in Computer Science*; Lecture Notes in Computer Science; Springer: Berlin/Heidelberg, Germany, 2006; pp. 503–510. [CrossRef]
31. Liu, B. Sentiment analysis and subjectivity. *Handb. Nat. Lang. Process.* **2010**, *2*, 627–666.
32. Joachims, T. Text categorization with support vector machines: Learning with many relevant features. In Proceedings of the European Conference on Machine Learning, Bilbao, Spain, 13–17 September 1998; pp. 137–142.
33. Banerjee, S.; Majumder, P.; Mitra, M. Re-evaluating the need for modelling term-dependence in text classification problems. *arXiv* **2017**, arXiv:1710.09085.
34. Ghiassi, M.; Olschimke, M.; Moon, B.; Arnaudo, P. Automated text classification using a dynamic artificial neural network model. *Expert Syst. Appl.* **2012**, *39*, 10967–10976. [CrossRef]
35. Zdrojewska, A.; Dutkiewicz, J.; Jędrzejek, C.; Olejnik, M. Comparison of the Novel Classification Methods on the Reuters-21578 Corpus. In Proceedings of the Multimedia and Network Information Systems: Proceedings of the 11th International Conference MISSI, Wrocław, Poland, 12–14 September 2018; Volume 833, p. 290.
36. Harris, C.R.; Millman, K.J.; van der Walt, S.J.; Gommers, R.; Virtanen, P.; Cournapeau, D.; Wieser, E.; Taylor, J.; Berg, S.; Smith, N.J. Array programming with NumPy. Version 1.19.5. *Nature* **2020**, *585*, 357–362. [CrossRef]
37. McKinney, W. Data structures for statistical computing in python. Version 1.2.3. In Proceedings of the 9th Python in Science Conference, Austin, TX, USA, 9–15 July 2010; Volume 445, pp. 51–56.
38. Finkel, J.R.; Grenager, T.; Manning, C.D. Incorporating non-local information into information extraction systems by gibbs sampling. In Proceedings of the 43rd Annual Meeting of the Association for Computational Linguistics (ACL'05), Stroudsburg, PA, USA, 25–30 June 2005; pp. 363–370.
39. Manning, C.D.; Surdeanu, M.; Bauer, J.; Finkel, J.R.; Bethard, S.; McClosky, D. The Stanford CoreNLP natural language processing toolkit. In Proceedings of the 52nd annual meeting of the association for computational linguistics: System demonstrations, Baltimore, MD, USA, 23–24 June 2014; pp. 55–60.

40. Qi, P.; Zhang, Y.; Zhang, Y.; Bolton, J.; Manning, C.D. Stanza: A Python Natural Language Processing Toolkit for Many Human Languages. Version 1.2. *arXiv* **2003**, arXiv:2003.07082.
41. Porter, M.F. An algorithm for suffix stripping. *Program* **1980**, *14*, 3. [CrossRef]
42. Bird, S.; Klein, E.; Loper, E. *Natural Language Processing with Python: Analyzing Text with the Natural Language Toolkit*; Version 3.5; O'Reilly Media, Inc.: Cambridge, UK, 2009.
43. Sharma, V.B. Rake-Nltk. Version 1.0.4 Software. Available online: https://pypi.org/project/rake-nltk/ (accessed on 18 March 2021).
44. Liang, X. Towards Data Science—Understand TextRank for Keyword Extraction by Python. Available online: https://towardsdatascience.com/textrank-for-keyword-extraction-by-python-c0bae21bcec0 (accessed on 15 April 2021).
45. Pedregosa, F.; Varoquaux, G.; Gramfort, A.; Michel, V.; Thirion, B.; Grisel, O.; Blondel, M.; Prettenhofer, P.; Weiss, R.; Dubourg, V. Scikit-learn: Machine learning in Python, Version 0.24.1. *J. Mach. Learn. Res.* **2011**, *12*, 2825–2830.
46. Tan, S. Neighbor-weighted k-nearest neighbor for unbalanced text corpus. *Expert Syst. Appl.* **2005**, *28*, 667–671. [CrossRef]
47. Kalchbrenner, N.; Grefenstette, E.; Blunsom, P. A convolutional neural network for modelling sentences. *arXiv* **2014**, arXiv:1404.2188.
48. Zhang, W.; Yoshida, T.; Tang, X. Text classification based on multi-word with support vector machine. *Knowl.-Based Syst.* **2008**, *21*, 879–886. [CrossRef]
49. MacQueen, J. Some methods for classification and analysis of multivariate observations. In Proceedings of the Fifth Berkeley Symposium on Mathematical Statistics and Probability, Oakland, CA, USA, 1 January 1967; Volume 1, pp. 281–297. Available online: https://projecteuclid.org/proceedings/berkeley-symposium-on-mathematical-statistics-andprobability/proceedings-of-the-fifth-berkeley-symposium-on-mathematical-statisticsand/Chapter/Some-methods-for-classification-and-analysis-of-multivariateobservations/bsmsp/1200512992 (accessed on 8 February 2022).
50. Rousseeuw, P.J. Silhouettes: A graphical aid to the interpretation and validation of cluster analysis. *J. Comput. Appl. Math.* **1987**, *20*, 53–65. [CrossRef]
51. Catal, C.; Diri, B. Investigating the effect of dataset size, metrics sets, and feature selection techniques on software fault prediction problem. *Inf. Sci.* **2009**, *179*, 1040–1058. [CrossRef]
52. Barbedo, J.G.A. Impact of dataset size and variety on the effectiveness of deep learning and transfer learning for plant disease classification. *Comput. Electron. Agric.* **2018**, *153*, 46–53. [CrossRef]

# Σ mathematics

MDPI

### Article

# Towards a Benchmarking System for Comparing Automatic Hate Speech Detection with an Intelligent Baseline Proposal

Ştefan Dascălu [†] and Florentina Hristea [*,†]

Department of Computer Science, University of Bucharest 14, Academiei Str., Sector 1, 010014 Bucharest, Romania; stefan.dascalu@s.unibuc.ro
* Correspondence: fhristea@fmi.unibuc.ro; Tel.: +40-722458143
† These authors contributed equally to this work.

**Abstract:** Hate Speech is a frequent problem occurring among Internet users. Recent regulations are being discussed by U.K. representatives ("Online Safety Bill") and by the European Commission, which plans on introducing Hate Speech as an "EU crime". The recent legislation having passed in order to combat this kind of speech places the burden of identification on the hosting websites and often within a tight time frame (24 h in France and Germany). These constraints make automatic Hate Speech detection a very important topic for major social media platforms. However, recent literature on Hate Speech detection lacks a benchmarking system that can evaluate how different approaches compare against each other regarding the prediction made concerning different types of text (short snippets such as those present on Twitter, as well as lengthier fragments). This paper intended to deal with this issue and to take a step forward towards the standardization of testing for this type of natural language processing (NLP) application. Furthermore, this paper explored different transformer and LSTM-based models in order to evaluate the performance of multi-task and transfer learning models used for Hate Speech detection. Some of the results obtained in this paper surpassed the existing ones. The paper concluded that transformer-based models have the best performance on all studied Datasets.

**Keywords:** BERT; transfer learning; multi-task learning; RoBERTa; LSTM; Hate Speech detection

**MSC:** 68T50

**Citation:** Dascălu, Ş.; Hristea, F. Towards a Benchmarking System for Comparing Automatic Hate Speech Detection with an Intelligent Baseline Proposal. *Mathematics* **2022**, *10*, 945. https://doi.org/10.3390/math10060945

Academic Editor: Marjan Mernik

Received: 29 January 2022
Accepted: 12 March 2022
Published: 16 March 2022

**Publisher's Note:** MDPI stays neutral with regard to jurisdictional claims in published maps and institutional affiliations.

## 1. Introduction

### 1.1. Hate Speech Definition

Hate Speech has multiple definitions, depending on the legal system of the involved country. In most European countries, the preferred interpretation is that of the European Council [1], which states that any provocation to violence or hatred that is targeted against a minority group (based on race, color, belief, or nationality) or a person that is part of that group is defined as Hate Speech. Likewise, the law classifies denying acts of genocide and war crimes when this action is likely to incite violence as part of the Hate Speech definition. Various definitions are more constraining, such as the U.K.'s definition, which removes the burden of demonstrating the incitement to violence. The United Kingdom forbids communication of hatred that is directed towards someone on the basis of that person's racial, nationality, or belief characteristics.

There are even opposing views, such as entities such as the U.S. Supreme Court, that do not recognize Hate Speech as a legal term because of the infringement upon free speech laws that take precedence and the fact that viewpoint-based discrimination cannot constrain free speech. This view is controversial, as the U.S. law recognizes hate bias toward minority groups [2] as an aggravating factor in committing a crime and classifies it as a hate crime.

In light of these facts concerning varying definitions, this article based its detections on the more constraining characterization of Hate Speech, which is the one applied in the U.K.

To further refine the presented term's discussion, many Datasets that are featured in this paper address the distinction between Hate Speech and Offensive Language by further splitting the two into distinct labels. This distinction is explained in the Venn diagram presented in Figure 1.

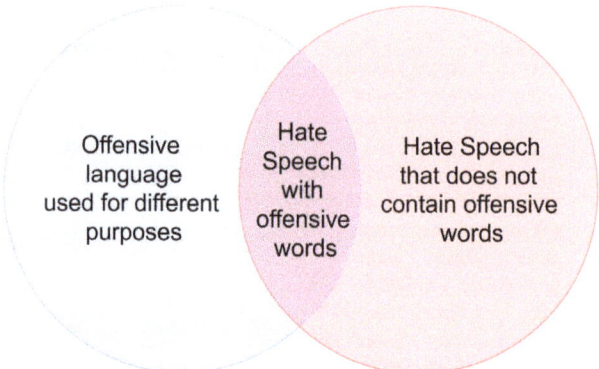

**Figure 1.** Venn diagram of positive labels used in the Datasets studied by this paper.

### 1.2. The Real-Life Context of This Study

Hate Speech is now the next term to be criminalized at the EU level [3]. This will constrain all EU member countries to adopt or to refine their legislation with respect to restricting this kind of speech. Inasmuch as the content host is responsible for removing banned content in major EU member states (the French Avia Law and the German Network Enforcement Act), a detection tool is required to flag Hate Speech. This requirement is stressed by the fact that in many countries, the law states that the removal of the illegal content must be performed within a narrow time frame such as one day from publication or from the first complaint.

Papers such as [4] state that Hate Speech found in various online mediums influences real-life violence and can lead to the radicalization of individuals. Moreover, the Facebook daily usage statistics from their third-quarter statement show an increase of 6% year over year [5] to 1.93 billion. Other platforms such as Twitter reported [6] a 13% increase in users over the last year. The pandemic is forcing more people to interact over social media platforms and to be exposed to their content, with this promoting the need for an automatic detector, as human-based Hate Speech detection cannot reasonably verify the entire content that is posted on a platform within a 24 h window.

Some studies [7] suggest that the current state of Hate Speech detectors presents a bias towards labeling minority-generated samples as hateful (the false positive rate for African American English speaking users is higher than that of other groups). From a moral standpoint, reducing the false positive rate of Hate Speech detection is important in order to protect the free speech of other platform users.

### 1.3. Objectives of This Work

One of the common problems in Hate Speech detection is that there are many different Datasets that are being used for testing, and there is no way of knowing how different models compare against each other. This is why establishing a Dataset list with different features on which to compare models is important.

The primary objective of this paper was reviewing popular Datasets and creating a testing pipeline with the aim to find which models currently produce state-of-the-art results and, thus, to standardize testing for Hate Speech detection. The secondary objective of

*Mathematics* **2022**, *10*, 945

this paper was to test multi-task learning and how it compares with single-task learning with modern transformer-based models for Hate Speech classification. Furthermore, a comparison between accuracies obtained by solely using a transformer embedding or combining it with pretrained word embeddings such as GloVe or ELMo can help boost performance. We also derived our own embeddings by using different transformers in order to average the contextual representation of each token (as in the case of the word-level ones derived in [8]) and then compared the results with the other models.

The article is organized into five sections, each introducing a new descriptive layer of this topic. The first (current) section explains how different countries treat Hate Speech and the importance of developing a capable detector for it. The section equally outlines the objectives of this paper. The second section refers to previous work in the domain of Hate Speech detection and to how our contribution complements this preexisting work. The third section defines the actual methods used to preprocess the data, as well as the models that were used in order to improve accuracy on the data classification objectives. The fourth section discusses the results obtained using the most relevant methods and how they compare to different results existing throughout the literature. The final section summarizes our work so far and offers a short description of what can be achieved using similar methods with respect to other types of NLP applications.

## 2. Related Work

Recent studies [9,10] pertaining to the analysis of Hate Speech reveal that keywords are not enough in order to classify its usage. The semantic analysis of the text is required in order to isolate other usages that do not have the intention or meaning required for the phrase to be classified as Hate Speech. The outlined [10] possible usages for Hate Speech words are:

- Homonymous, in which the word has multiple meanings and in the current sentence is used with a different meaning that does not constitute Hate Speech;
- Derogatory, this being the form that should be labeled as Hate Speech. This form is characterized by the expression of hate towards that community;
- Non-derogatory, non-appropriative, when the keywords are used to draw attention to the word itself or another related purpose;
- Appropriative, when it is used by a community member for an alternative purpose.

Figure 2 outlines examples of the presented ways of using Hate Speech key terms.

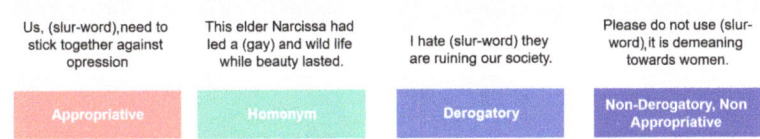

**Figure 2.** Usage types for Hate Speech key words.

In recent years, a tremendous amount of research [7,8,11] has gone into the classification of text snippets. Early methods relied on classic machine learning methods [12] such as SVMs, logistic regression, naive Bayes, decision trees, and random forests. Even earlier research [13] was focused on different ways of extracting textual features and text representations such as n-grams, lexicon, and character features. These laid a foundation for later research, which evolved with other related tasks, such as sentiment evaluation [14], culminating with the usage of transformer-based neural networks [15,16].

The topic of Hate Speech detection is a very active part of the NLP field [8,15–18]. Every modern advance in textual classification has been subsequently followed by an implementation in the field of Hate Speech detection [15,19–21].

One of the first modern articles was authored by Waseem and Hovey [19] and consisted of Twitter detection work. Their paper used character n-grams as features, and they used the labels racism, sexism, and normal. The method used by the authors is a logistic regression classifier and 10-fold cross-validation in order to make sure the performance of the model is not dependent on the way the test and training data are selected. The preprocessing solution employed by the authors was removing the stop-words, special Twitter-related words (marking retweets), user names, and punctuation. This type of solution is commonly used in approaches where sequential features of the text are not used.

Another article, which constitutes the base of modern Hate Speech detection, is [12]. The authors proposed [12] a three-label Dataset that identifies the need to classify offensive tweets in addition to the Hate Speech ones of the Waseem and Hovey Dataset [19]. Furthermore, the conclusion of the performed experiments was that Hate Speech can be very hard to distinguish from Offensive Language, and because there are far more examples of Offensive Language in the real world and the boundaries of Hate Speech and Offensive Speech intersect, almost 40% of the Hate Speech labeled tweets were misclassified by the best model proposed in [12]. The article used classic machine learning methods such as logistic regression, naive Bayes, SVMs, etc. It employed a model for dimensionality reduction, and as preprocessing steps, it used TF-IDF on bigram, unigram, and trigram features. Furthermore, stemming was first performed on the words using the Porter stemmer, and the word-based features were POS tagged. Sentiment analysis tools were used for feature engineering, computing the overall sentiment score of the tweet. It is important to specify that only 26% of the tagged Hate Speech tweets were labeled unanimously by all annotators, denoting the subjectivity involved in labeling these kinds of tweets.

Modern approaches are highlighted by the use of embeddings and neural networks capable of processing sequences of tokens. One such article is [17], in which the authors used ELMo embeddings for the detection of Hate Speech in tweets. Another technique that was present in this work was using one Dataset to improve performance on the primary Dataset (transfer learning).

The paper expressed this with a single-network architecture and separate task-specific MLP layers. In addition to these, the article compared the usage of LSTMs [22] and GRUs [23], noting that LSTMs are superior with respect to prediction accuracy. As preprocessing steps, the authors removed URLs and added one space between punctuation. This helps word embedding models such as GloVe, which would consider the combination of words and punctuation as a new word that it would not recognize. This article also introduced the concept of domain adaptation to Hate Speech detection. By using another Dataset to train the LSTM embeddings, the embeddings would be used to extract Hate-Speech-related features from the text, which would increase accuracy with subsequent Datasets.

One major downside of Hate Speech detection applications is given by the existing Datasets, which are very unbalanced (with respect to the number of Hate Speech labels), as well as by the small amount of samples that they contain. This means that the research in this field needs to make use of inventive methods in order to improve the accuracy. One such method is the joint modeling [21] approach, which makes use of complex architectures and similar Datasets, such as the sentiment analysis ones, in order to improve the performance of the model on the classification of Hate Speech detection. In [21], the use of LTSMs over other network architectures was also emphasized.

One of the more interesting models presented in [21] is parameter-based sharing. This method distinguishes itself by using embeddings that are learned from secondary tasks and are combined with the primary task embeddings based on a learnable parameter. This allows the model to adjust how the secondary task contributes to the primary one, based on the relatedness of the tasks.

As preprocessing, the tweets had their mentions and URLs converted to special tokens; they were lower-cased, and hashtags were mapped to words. The mapping of hashtags to words is important because the tweets were small (the most common tweet size was 33 characters), so for understanding a Tweet's meaning, we need to extract as much information from it as possible. Further improvement upon previous architectures within this model is the use of an additive attention layer.

As embeddings, GloVe and ELMo were used jointly, by concatenating the output of both models before passing it to the LSTM layer in order to make a task-specific embedding. This article [21] also compared the difference between transfer and multi-task learning, with both having some performance boost over simple single-task learning.

Finally, there are multiple recent papers that made use of the transformer architecture in order to achieve higher accuracies [8,15,16,18]. One such transformer-based method [8] that uses the Ethos [24] Dataset employs a fairly straight forward approach. It uses BERT to construct its own word embeddings. By taking every corpus word and the context in which it occurs and constructing an embedding, the authors proposed that averaging word embeddings will have an advantage over other word embedding techniques. Then, by using a bidirectional LSTM layer, the embeddings were transformed into task-specific ones in order to improve accuracy, after which a dense layer made the prediction. The accuracy improved overall when this method was used as opposed to simple BERT classification. Another article that made use of the transformer architecture was [15], introducing AngryBert. The model was composed of a multi-task learning architecture where BERT embeddings were used for learning on two Datasets at the same time, while LSTM layers were used to learn specific tasks by themselves. This is similar to the approach proposed in [21], but the main encoder used a transformer-based network instead of a GloVe + ELMo embedding LSTM network. The joining of embeddings was performed with a learnable parameter as in [21]. Another interesting trend is that of [18], where a data-centric approach was used. By fine-tuning BERT [25] on a secondary task that consisted of a 600,000-sentence-long Dataset, the model was able to generate a greater performance when trained on the primary Dataset.

Our approach complements those already used by proposing a method of encoding tokens that, while using the sub-word tokenizing architecture in order to handle new words, also makes use of the transformer performance, at the same time increasing the speed by running the transformer only to derive the embeddings. While RoBERTa-based transformer learning is still superior to using transformer-based token embeddings in terms of performance, if the training speed is of concern, then a viable alternative to the traditional multi-task learning methods and to the transformer-based paradigms is transformer-based token embeddings.

## 3. Materials and Methods

### 3.1. Datasets

This study wanted to determine if sentiment analysis Datasets, which by far outweigh Hate Speech ones in terms of data availability, can help in training for our Hate Speech detection problem. For this purpose, multi-task learning was used. Multi-task learning represents the method that leverages multiple learning tasks, trained at the same time, with the objective of exploiting the resemblances of the Datasets when training the parameters of the models. This method is used when the task is comprised of a very large Dataset for the secondary task and the primary (objective) task Dataset does not have sufficient data to produce an accurate result when trained by itself.

In order to conduct a comprehensive analysis of different methods used in Hate Speech detection and to study the effectiveness of each one of them, enough Datasets had to be gathered to test how these methods handle different sample types and labeling techniques.

Because there are different granularity levels for the labels, as well as the auxiliary data used by some models, in what follows, all the data collection processes that took place in the recreation of some of the more interesting state-of-the-art projects are explained. There are multiple types of Datasets already available, but the main concern of deciding which Datasets to use or how to construct a Dataset for the specific features of Hate Speech detection is choosing what features to leverage in this task and how those features can then be gathered in production environments. The main component of any Dataset should be the text itself, as this component allows us to examine the idea of the author of the sample at that particular time. Although it might be convoluted and new meanings of words appear all the time, the text feature is the easiest to retrieve from the perspective of a social platform owner as it is already in its database. This component is required for every employed Dataset and was constructed or harvested. If this was not possible, then the Dataset was discarded.

The Datasets chosen have different distributions of text length and different sources, which means that they were harvested from different social media platforms and use different labeling schemes. The most frequent labeling scheme observed is Amazon Mechanical Turk, but other crowdsourcing platforms [12,20,26] are used as well. Finally, other authors manually annotated their Dataset or sought professional help from members of different marginalized communities and gender studies students [10,19].

By selecting different types of Datasets, the comprehensive testing of methods and the discovery of how different approaches to feature extraction and text embedding affect performance can be facilitated.

Labels of different samples can be binary or multi-class, as a result of evaluating them with multiple techniques, such as the intended meaning of the slur (sexist, racist, etc.) or what kind of slur word is being used (classifying each token as being Hate Speech or not). However, in order to standardize the labels, we split the Datasets into two Dataset groups (3-label and 2-label Datasets if they do not contain offensive speech labels). This was performed by merging or computing labels.

Secondary components that could help us determine if a person is posting Hate Speech content are: comments given by other people to that person's post, user group names, user account creation timestamp (accounts participating in Hate Speech tend to be deleted so new accounts are created). Another secondary component that is recorded in some Datasets is user responses to the comment (not used for detection, but for generating responses to Hate Speech content). Some of these components were used, and the obtained accuracy was compared to the accuracy without them, in order to determine if there was an accuracy improvement over using text snippets only. Auxiliary Datasets, such as sentiment classification ones, can also be used (in multi-task learning). These Datasets do not have any constraints as they were only used to train the embedding vectors and, as such, to help the primary model's accuracy. During our experiments, in addition to the Datasets presented in Figure 3, the SemEval 18 [27] Task1 Dataset (sentiment classification Dataset) and OLID (Hate Speech detection Dataset) were used as auxiliary Datasets in the sections where multi-task machine learning was performed.

A problem that was found while evaluating possible Datasets to be used for testing was that there are so many Datasets in the domain of Hate Speech detection, that the approaches presented alongside them have not been benchmarked on the same data.

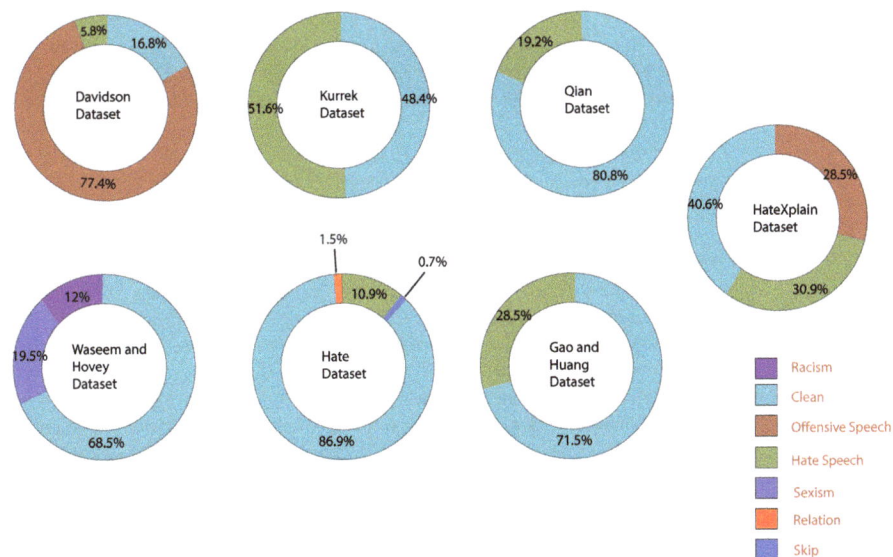

**Figure 3.** Dataset label distribution.

### 3.1.1. The HateXplain Dataset

This Dataset [11] contains already preprocessed tweets. It introduced the following token classes (<user>, <number>, <percent>, <censored>, etc.). In order to make sure this Dataset did not impact the pipeline, the tokens were implemented in the tokenizer so as to standardize every Dataset. Small problems were found with the human annotations: some of the annotators made mistakes such as when they considered more words than others for some sentences, for example the one at Index 17,891 (one annotator had 47 tokens, and another one had 48). The purpose of this Dataset was to use its attention annotations in order to harvest better scores in single-, multi-task, and transfer learning. Transfer learning is a method where the knowledge gathered while solving a secondary machine learning task is passed onto another similar task. One such example is attempting to predict sentiments that a text is supposed to convey and then taking that model and fine-tuning it in order to detect Hate-Speech-related texts. This technique is mostly used with the first layers of a deep neural network. The reason is that those layers are supposed to "understand" and to extract the features that are required by the later layers in order to make a decision.

### 3.1.2. The Waseem and Hovey Dataset

The raw data of this Dataset [19] contains 16,914 tweets, annotated with the labels racist, sexist, and neither. The Dataset [19] is available for download, but instead of Tweet text, its rows contain only tweet ids, and many of the tweets have been removed since its conception. However, some GitHub repositories might be used to combine the partial extraction attempts for obtaining over 90% of the original tweets. As for the original Dataset, the data are not balanced because the authors intended for it to represent a real-life scenario of Hate Speech detection. Furthermore, instead of basing their Hate Speech annotations solely on words that are commonly associated with Hate Speech, they labeled the tweets based on the significance of the tweet.

### 3.1.3. The Thomas Davidson Dataset

In [12], the problem of differentiating between Hate Speech and Offensive Language that does not constitute Hate Speech was addressed. The Dataset is made up of tweets gathered using crowd-sourced Hate-Speech-related words and phrases from the website

"Hatebase.org". The authors emphasized the difficulty of differentiating between tweets that contain offensive slurs that are not Hate Speech and Hate-Speech-containing tweets, as well as Hate Speech that does not contain offensive words. The authors constructed the labels by using CrowdFlower services. The agreement coefficient was 92%. During their examination of the Dataset, they found multiple mislabeled tweets. These had hateful slurs that were used in a harmless way, suggesting the bias towards misclassifying keyword-containing tweets. It is also important to remember that all labels were subjectively applied, and there is room for debate on the interpretation of some of the tweets being racist.

### 3.1.4. The Qian Reddit Dataset

This Dataset [20] focuses on the intervention part of Hate Speech detection. The data were annotated using the Amazon Mechanical Turk crowdsourcing platform; this consists of Hate Speech annotations and responses to the Hate Speech samples. The authors focused on two platforms (Reddit and Gab) as the main sources of their Datasets. For the Reddit Dataset, the authors collected data from multiple subreddits known for using Hate Speech and combined this heuristic with hate keywords, then rebuilt the context of each comment. The context was made up of all the comments around the hateful comment. For the Gab Dataset, the same methods were applied. Conversations of more than 20 comments were filtered out. The authors obtained less accuracy on the Reddit Dataset, and that is why the models featured in this paper were trained only on this part of the data. After looking through the data, there were a couple of extra preprocessing steps that needed to be implemented when using this Dataset. For example, in the data, there were some Unicode characters such as """, which is the Unicode variant of the apostrophe character. These need to be changed with their ASCII counterparts because of certain classic methods using the character as a separation of contractions.

### 3.1.5. The Kurrek Dataset

This Dataset [10] is comprised of the Pushshift Reddit corpus, which is filtered for bots and users with no history. In addition to the user filters, which are designed to help future users collect user metadata and use them in combination with the Dataset, the corpus was selected to contain comments with 3 known Hate-Speech-related keywords. The Dataset is labeled in accordance with the use of the slur (derogatory usage, appropriative usage, non-derogatory, non-appropriative usage, and homonymous usage).

### 3.1.6. The Gao and Huang Dataset

The data records featured in [28] were extracted from Fox news. The comments were taken from 10 discussion threads. The Dataset offers multiple metadata fields in addition to the sample text such as the nested nature of the comments and the original news article. The Dataset was annotated by two native English speakers.

### 3.1.7. Hate Speech Dataset from a White Supremacy Forum (the HATE Dataset)

The HATE Dataset, presented in [29], is interesting because instead of searching a platform by keywords, which have a high probability of being associated with Hate Speech, the authors used web-scraping on a white supremacist forum (Stormfront) in order to improve random sampling chances. In addition to this, the Dataset has a skipped class where information not pertaining to being labeled can be classified. Furthermore, for some tweets, the context was used to annotate. We removed the classes skipped and those that needed additional context before training the models.

### 3.2. Types of Embeddings Used in this Paper

In order to display the evolution of different types of embeddings and to compare the difference in the training/prediction time with the difference in performance, this paper aimed to use the following embeddings for the tokens:

- TF-IDF, which is the most basic type of encoding, being commonly used in combination with classic machine learning techniques or neural networks that cannot accept sequence-based features. For the purpose of this paper, the scikit-learn [30] implementation was used. This method of embedding words does not hold any of the information offered by the context in which the word is used or the way in which a word is written. Instead, the TF-IDF approach is used after the user has identified the words that he/she wants to keep track of in his/her data corpus (usually the most frequent ones after filtering stop words). Then, a formula is applied for each chosen word. The word count for that particular document is divided by the number of times the word occurs in the corpus:

$$\text{TFIDF}(\text{term}) = \text{COUNT}(\text{term}) * (\log_e(\text{DocNumber}/\text{TermDocFrequency}) + 1)$$

where DocNumber is the number of documents and TermDocFrequency is the number of documents in which the term occurs;

- Skipgram embedding takes tokens as the inputs, with the tokens being commonly given by the words in the text, while the tokenizer often separates words by the space character. The output of this technique is represented by a dictionary where the key is given by the word in question and the value held by the dictionary is an n-dimensional vector that hosts the hidden layer linear neurons weight values corresponding to that particular word. Skip-gram [31] is based on a shallow neural network model that features one hidden layer. This layer tries to predict neighboring words chosen at random within a window;

- CBOW is a similar technique to Skipgram, with one of the major differences being that the objective of the shallow network is to predict the target word from the context;

- GloVe embeddings, from the point of view of the user, work as a dictionary. Each word has a corresponding embedding. The downside of this form of word representation is that unknown tokens are represented with the same value regardless of their word composition or context. The embeddings are computed using a word co-occurrence count, which is more accurate than word2vec approaches because the whole corpus is taken into account as opposed to only the window from word2vec. One of the particularities of GloVe is choosing the padding and the unknown vectors. For the purpose of this empirical study, the padding was chosen to be a vector filled with 0s. For the unknown token, two approaches were compared. The first approach consisted of using the special token "<unknown>" that GloVe offers. The second approach involved averaging all the vectors and using the corresponding value as our unknown vector. Both of these variants offer the same result. Another particularity of using GloVe [32] embeddings is that, prior to training the model, we encoded each tokenized word as an index in the embedding dictionary. When training the input, the numeric tensors containing the indices of each sample were concatenated. The resulting matrix corresponded to our batch. Next, each of the indices was converted to its corresponding embedding. For the Twitter-trained GloVe, this embedding is made up of 200 elements. After the embedding layer, we had a sequence shaped as a tridimensional matrix with the column length corresponding to the sentence length, the row length corresponding to the batch size, and the element size equal to the embedding size (in our case, 200);

- ELMo, The Allennlp [33] framework, offers an interface to the model. The tokenized words (matrix of words corresponding to the batch) are passed to the batch_to_ids function, where each word is transformed into a vector. Suppose that one of the words was abc which in ASCII language corresponds to the vector [97, 98, 99]. When transformed by the tool, it will become [259, 98, 99, 100, 260, 261...padding continues]. From the output of the tokenizer, we can observe that 259 is a token used for the start and 260 is used to signal the ending. After the tokenization, the matrix is input to a neural network, which outputs an embedding vector for every word. This embedding approach is based on bidirectional LSTM networks [33];

- RoBERTa [34] embeddings are similar to BERT as model outputs. The embeddings resulting from the model are sequences of vectors that represent each sub-word. Besides the model difference from ELMo and GloVe, BERT and RoBERTa use different types of tokenizers. BERT uses WordPiece tokenization, which can use whole words when computing the indices to be sent to the model or sub-words. This method starts with the base vocabulary and keeps adding sub-words by the best likelihood until the vocabulary cap is reached. This is a middle ground between character-based ELMo embeddings and the word embeddings that GloVe uses. As opposed to the other types of tokenizers, RoBERTa uses a byte pair encoding. This means that in order to make the embeddings, all the characters are in the embedding dictionary at the start, and then, they are paired based on the level of appearance in the text, as opposed to WordPiece encoding, which chooses the new pair by the likelihood increase on the training data.

*3.3. Evaluation*

Hate Speech predictors focus on the macro F1 metric. This metric is especially important because the benign samples far outweigh the offensive ones. F1 is calculated as the harmonic mean of the recall and precision metrics. Furthermore, all metrics shown in this paper are macro, which means that the metrics are representative of all classes. The sampling procedure most used to evaluate classification models on a segmented Dataset is K-fold cross-validation. In the case of our tests, we chose 10-fold because it is the most popular for Hate Speech classification [8,19,21].

*3.4. Preprocessing*

In order to make use of all the Dataset features, we needed to preprocess it according to all the tokenizing module requirements, so as to form the word vectors and embeddings, as well as to perform the existing preprocessing steps that some of the Datasets in use already employ.

The first step is adhering to GloVe's special token creation rules. By following the token definitions in the paper, a script was created in order to create the tokens that were needed by GloVe. We used regex in order to create the tokens. The next preprocessing step was mandated by the HateXplain Dataset. The Dataset is already in a processed state. By searching for the pattern <Word>, a tokenizing program can be reverse engineered, at the end of which the embeddings are reconstructed (over 20 in the Dataset). Some of the words are censored, so in order to improve the accuracy of BERT, a translation dictionary can be created to accomplish this feat.

The final step was constructing two preprocessing pipelines, one for the HateXplain Dataset, in order to bring it to a standard format, and another preprocessing function was created for the other texts. Further modifications were needed for the other Datasets depending on how they were stored.

Because the study dealt with two different types of texts, the preprocessing should be different for each article. For the tweet Datasets/short-text Datasets, it is recommended that as much information as possible be kept, as these are normally very short. As such, the hashtags should be converted into text and emojis and other text emojis as well. For the longer texts, however, cleaner information had priority over harvesting the entire information, one such method difference being the deletion of emoticons instead of replacing them as in the tweet Datasets.

As such, the proposed pipeline for these kinds of models was, after preprocessing, composed of the following word embedding extraction methods:

- N-gram char level features;
- N-gram word features;
- POS of the word;
- TF (raw, log, and inverse frequencies)-IDF(no importance weight, inverse document frequency, redundancy);

- No lemmatization running words were directly taken as input—no lemmatization, but unlemmatizable words were deleted;
- GloVe
- ELMo;
- Transformers.

With the first types of models, multiple types of preprocessing were tested, in order to see which ones performed better than the others. One such example is represented by stemming and lemmatization. We tried different preprocessing steps in this first part of the Dataset, such as stemming or lemmatizing the words. Another preprocessing method that we tried was removing stop-words or using exclusively stop-words. We acknowledge that using our own encoding vector, as well as extracting word- or char-level features such as n-grams cannot be replicated on real-life data as easily as using already computed word embeddings such as GloVe or ELMo [33,35]. As such, we tried to only use open-source embedding methods on the classical machine learning algorithms.

All the classical machine learning models are formed of a sci-kit learn [30] pipeline with different parameters (depending on the model used). In order to tune the parameters, we used grid search and studied the different effects that different parameters had on the accuracy of the models. Furthermore, for the PyTorch [36] models, we additionally used ray tune from the PyTorch framework.

### 3.5. Optimizers

An optimizer is an algorithm that helps the neural network converge, by modifying its parameters, such as the weights and learning rate, or by employing a different learning rate for every network weight.

SGD [37] with momentum is one of the simpler optimizer algorithms. It uses a general learning rate as opposed to the Adam optimizer [38]. It follows the step size to minimize the function. Momentum is used to accelerate the gradient update and to escape local minima.

Adam [38] is a good choice over stochastic gradient descent because it has a learning rate for every parameter and not a global learning rate as classical gradient descent algorithms. The original Adam paper [38] claimed to combine the advantages of AdaGrad and RMSProp. The article claimed that the advantages of Adam were the rescaling invariance of the magnitudes of parameter updates to the rescaling of the gradient, the hyperparameter step size bounding the parameter step sizes, etc. The upper hand Adam has as an optimizer is generated by its step size choice update rule.

RMSProp is different from Adam as it does not have a bias correction term and can lead to divergence, as proven in [38]. Another difference is the way RMSProp uses momentum to generate the parameter updates.

AdaGrad [39] is suitable for sparse data because it adapts the learning rate to the frequency with which features occur in the data. It was used in [32] because of the sparsity of some words. AdaGrad is similar to Adam because it has a learning rate for every parameter. The main fault is adding the square gradients, which are positive. For big sets of data, this is detrimental as the learning rate becomes very small.

### 3.6. Models

In order to test the methods, we propose the pipeline in Figure 4.

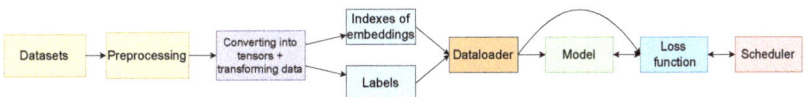

**Figure 4.** High-level architecture of the testing pipeline.

In order to streamline the process, the Datasets can be saved after preprocessing and then loaded up so as to not repeat this part of the experiment on subsequent tests. In addition to this, the model weights can be reset, as opposed to training the model again for the next folds, while performing the validation.

### 3.6.1. Classic Machine Learning

Our initial tests concentrated on classical machine learning models, and their results can be seen in Appendix A. The first models that were applied were from the family of SVM classifiers (Table A2). These classifiers work by establishing the biggest boundary between classes. The kernel function that differentiates between SVM methods helps shape the boundary and, as such, the decision-making capabilities of SVM classifiers. All the classic machine learning models are formed of a sci-kit learn pipeline with different parameters (depending on the model used).

In order to tune the parameters, we used grid search and studied the different effects that various parameters had on the accuracy of the models.

Other classifiers that were used during the first phase of the model preparation were decision tree classifiers (Table A3), which construct a tree-like structure. The goal was that of differentiating between classes based on boundaries set automatically by the algorithm. Furthermore, random forest (Table A4) and KNN classifiers (Table A1) were tested. Random forest classifiers work by combining multiple different decision tree classifiers, and KNN classifiers compare the similarity of the nearest neighbors and decide based on the labels of those neighbors.

The obtained results enabled us to conclude that, on this tier of classic machine learning classifiers, the SVM and random forest classifiers outperformed the rest of the models on the task of Hate Speech detection. The features were derived from the text using TF-IDF.

### 3.6.2. CNN, GRU, and RNN Models

The next class of tested models was represented by CNN-based models. These had better accuracy than obtained for the previous phase. As input for the network, GENSIM embeddings (either Cbow or skip-gram of dimension 200) trained on the Datasets were used. These were compared against GloVe embeddings in order to test which embeddings would be more appropriate for the task of Hate Speech detection. GloVe embeddings scored a higher accuracy overall, and because of this, they were used for the more advanced models.

There were multiple CNN approaches tested for this study. The first type has a bigger number of filters, essentially capturing more patterns from the texts, but fewer layers. Other CNN networks have a shorter filter size, but more layers so as to further refine the representations gathered from the text (Table A6). These approaches were used in order to establish if extracting more features from the text was more important than filtering and extracting more complex patterns.

Another tested model was described in [11] and is made up of convolutional neural networks combined with a GRU layer (Table A9). This model outperformed the other two. During the testing of this model, we also tested how skip-gram embeddings affect performance versus a more established embedding method.

Furthermore, several RNN setups have been tested, both bidirectional RNN (Table A7) and one-way interconnected RNN (Table A8) networks.

### 3.6.3. Preparing the Data for Recurrent Layers

In order to use recurrent networks, some precautions must be taken. For the LSTM, GRU, and RNN networks, the main methods for input encapsulation are as follows:

- Padding sequences of data to a fixed length represents the easiest way of preparing the input for recurrent layers. For this method to work, we needed to choose the correct length of the sentence. The length must be large enough so that we have a low probability of losing the meaning of the sequence (by not cutting out words that would be crucial to the understanding of the sentence). At the same time, this length must be small enough such that, when the input is grouped together, the batch fits on the GPU/TPU and the training/prediction time is reasonable.

In addition to the token length, one must consider the batch size. It is important to make sure that the GPU can handle the size of the model training/prediction data flow.

When testing on the tweet-based Datasets, the method chosen was to keep all input words and pad the shorter input samples to the same length. For tweet samples, this is easy as there is a limit to how many words a tweet can contain. As for our Datasets, the limit ranged from 70 to 90 tokens. Some words can be split by the sub-word tokenizer into two or more tokens, so based on what method of tokenization is chosen, the limit was either 70 or 90 tokens. However, handling inputs from Gab or Reddit, with sizes of over 330 words, required a different approach. For such Datasets, the Dataset length chart is plotted, and we considered the length that separates the smallest 95% of the samples, from the rest, as a cutoff point. The longer texts were then cut to that length, and all the shorter texts were padded to the same length;

- The second approach was packing the variable length sentences and unpacking them after the LSTM layer has finished. This approach is supported by PyTorch. It works by capturing LSTM inputs at the sequence when the true input ends.

These models performed poorly in comparison with the LSTM and transformer networks.

### 3.6.4. LSTM Based Networks

One of the more complex classification criteria for the models used in the experiments was whether they trained on one task or multiple tasks at the same time, with the goal of perfecting the training on one of them, called the primary task.

The single-task learning model was trained only on one Dataset. It can have one or multiple vector embedding inputs (GloVe (Table A5), GloVe + ELMo (Table A13), ELMo, BERT, BERT + GloVe, etc.). Parameters such as LSTM hidden sizes and dropouts were computed based on grid search on one Dataset and then reused in the testing on subsequent Datasets.

After the LSTM layers process the input, the output has to be reshaped and pooled in order to be used in future layers. If the input goes into other LSTM or time sequence computing layers, we kept the output as is, but if we intended to forward the output to the multilayer perceptron, we only took the last sequence embeddings. In order to achieve this, the matrix returned by the LSTM layer needed to be reshaped according to the following parameters: the number of layers, the number of directions, the batch size, and the hidden dimension of the LSTM layers. The last element of the output vector was used, and if the LSTM was bidirectional, both LSTM outputs needed to be concatenated. After each LSTM layer, there was a dropout layer that helped with overfitting.

The linear layer was composed of multilayer perceptrons, and its purpose was to reduce the pooled output of the BiLSTM to our label size. The last layer can be reset if we want to train multiple Datasets on the same model. The goal of this procedure is improving the accuracy of the model on the last Dataset (as in Figure 5).

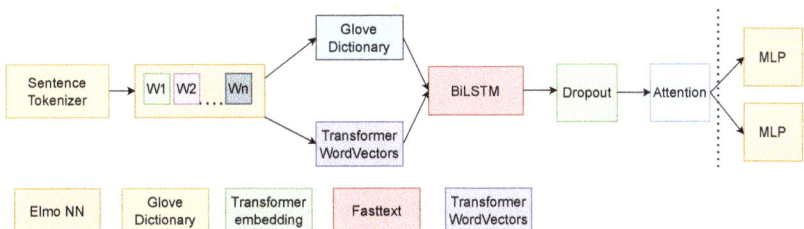

**Figure 5.** Transfer learning architecture.

### 3.6.5. Improving the LSTM Output

Other changes between models included, but were not limited to, the addition of an attention layer instead of the max pooling layer of the first model architecture.

The attention layer had the basic function to produce weights that helped a model focus on certain words in the sentence such that its accuracy was increased. Despite attention being used primarily in seq-to-seq translations, in order to relieve the encoder from condensing the data into a fixed-length sequence, it is also useful in classification scenarios, when we want to take advantage of the sequential nature of LSTMs. In our classification scenario, for each embedding dimension of a LSTM step, we had a weight that decided its importance. The weight was at the end multiplied with all the encoding vectors. We can replace the traditional max pooling approach or just use the output of the last layer and input it into the already described attention mechanism. The attention layer helps the model properly focus on the parts of the samples that help produce the right label.

### 3.6.6. Multi-Task Learning Models

Multi-task models require a different approach for training. First, the labels must be encoded such that there can be a distinction between our primary and alternate Datasets. In order to do this, a label value that was not in our Dataset was inserted (for example, 2 in binary classification, where there would be only 0 and 1 labels).

Every sample from the auxiliary Dataset was marked with the chosen label in the primary label column. Then, the secondary Dataset labels were placed in another column. For testing purposes, the fields that correspond to the unused label were filled with a random label that did not exist in our Datasets, such that, if there was an error and the separation of labels was not properly preformed, that error could propagate into the confusion matrix and be corrected. During training, both samples were dispatched to the embedding stage of samples and were then filtered in the order of the labels. The losses were computed separately and were afterwards multiplied by a factor (0.9 for our primary Dataset and 0.1 for our secondary Dataset). In the end, the weights were updated with backpropagation, and the model was trained. There were 3 types of multi-task learning models that were studied for the task under investigation. They were tested according to their description in [21].

The first tested multi-task model was "hard" multi-task learning (Table A11). This model has 3 separate BiLSTM structures. The first is composed of 2 layers and is used to process inputs from both the auxiliary and primary tasks. The second and third structures are task-specific, used to further enhance the representations given by the output of the first BiLSTM structure. There are two different loss calculation paths that intersect at the first BiLSTM structure. This means that, although task-specific representations would be trained separately, the first structure was jointly learned. This helped our primary task if sufficient data were not available, as well as in cases where these tasks were similar in nature.

Another variant, that is easier to train, was also designed and tested. This model does not contain the separate BiLSTM layers, but instead contains only one representation that is then separated into different dense layers (Table A12). The rationale was that the LSTM layers will interpret the sentences, and the output of the last layer will treat both tasks, which is why the BiLSTM-tested hidden dimensions would be larger than in previous models.

### 3.6.7. Learnable Parameter Multi-Task Learning Models

Another multi-task learning model is obtained by having a learnable parameter (Table A10, Figure 6), as depicted in [21]. For the implementation in PyTorch, a random tensor was made (containing 2 values, initialized with Xavier initialization), after which gradients were enabled on that tensor so that the backpropagation could change its value.

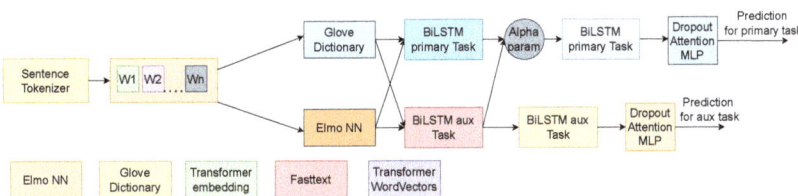

**Figure 6.** Multi-task architecture.

When the BiLSTM results were to be concatenated, SoftMax was applied on the parameter tensor, which normalizes the 2 values in the vector as a probability distribution (they are complementary, summing to 1). Then, each corresponding embedding is multiplied with its corresponding vector value. Other modifications were that the common BiLSTM layer no longer existed, so that each task built its own interpretation of the input sequence. As a sanity check, as the one in the previous example, a model was built that was trained in the same manner, but without connecting the BiLSTM of the auxiliary model to the Alpha parameter. If both models performed identically, this meant that there was no performance gain out of using a flexible parameter multi-task model.

### 3.6.8. Speed, Ease of Training, Sanity Checking, and Other Particularities

The GloVe model was the easiest to train, with 10 min per epoch on the largest Dataset (combined two-label Dataset). On the other side, there was the multi-task parameter model, which took 2 h and 30 min per epoch (both models were trained on a server V100 graphics card with 16 GB or VRAM). Because the majority of the multi-task models were bigger than the 12 GB of video RAM of the NVIDIA 3060, it is harder for a consumer GPU to train them, as the batch sizes have to be set low in order to not overflow the GPU memory. Furthermore, a compromise between performance and ease of training has to be made, and that could be using token embeddings derived from transformer models combined with the speed of single-task models.

In order to test if the design of multi-task architectures improved the performance of the model, a testing architecture was conceived by us. It follows the same paths as in the case of the above-presented hard multi-task models, except that it is missing the first BiLSTM structure (which learns the shared embedding). This impairs shared learning, but the process of training is exactly the same. When testing this model, if observing the same performance, we could conclude that there was no performance gain in hard multi-task learning.

As optimizers, two types were tested: Adam and SGD with momentum. In practice, Adam seemed to be a better fit for this task, especially the corrected method AdamW implemented in PyTorch. As loss functions, binary cross-entropy loss was used for the models, which requires binary classification, and categorical cross-entropy loss was used for models that require multiple class classification.

### 3.6.9. Transformer-Based Models

Our study used the BERT model in 3 architectural ways.

The first and most basic way in which we could employ BERT (presented in Figure 7) was by using the BertForSequenceClassification function in PyTorch. The model should be trained according to the original paper [25] that introduced it:

- Batch size should be 16 or 32;
- Learning rate for Adam optimizer should be $5 \times 10^{-5}$, $3 \times 10^{-5}$, or $2 \times 10;^{-5}$
- Number of epochs should be small. between 1 and 5.

The second possibility is using Bert's output layer as an input to a multilayer perceptron or any other non-sequential network. The training was performed by freezing the BERT layers and training the rest of the network, then unfreezing the BERT layers and adjusting the optimizer, learning rate, and batch size to the ones in the above guidelines, as well as retraining for a small number of epochs [11].

The final method in which BERT can be used is for embedding vector creation. By freezing the weights as in the previous model, we could use the sequential output of BERT as a word embedding vector. In some of the experiments, the coupling of transformer-based models together with GloVe embeddings was tested in multiple multi-task learning use cases, as well as in single-task use cases, as depicted in Figure 8. BERT was used in combination with GloVe in two ways: by using it as an embedding vector or as a sequential model. The training was identical to the above-described process.

While training the transformer-based models, one problem was the high cost of training, as well as the longer training time than for LSTM-based networks, and as such, a good method was stated by [8]. Instead of taking the word-level embeddings as in [8], we used the RoBERTa tokenizer to obtain token-level embeddings for multiple Datasets. Using those embeddings, we then trained a multi-task architecture based on bidirectional LSTM networks with an addition-based attention mechanism.

The pipeline began with the sentence, which was tokenized using the standard BERT/RoBERTa tokenizer (depending on the model used). Then, each sample was input into the model (standard model with no gradients computed to save the GPU), and after obtaining the embeddings from the models, we assigned them to each of the tokens that served as the input. We summed up all the different representations a token would have, within the Dataset, and in the end, we averaged the vectors for each token, by dividing the token vector by the number of times the token had occurred throughout the Dataset. In the end, we converted the embeddings to PyTorch embeddings, because it was much faster than using a Python dictionary.

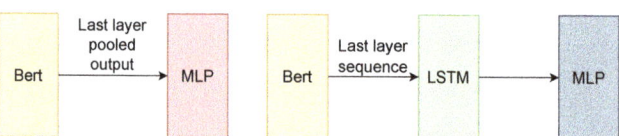

**Figure 7.** Simple BERT usages.

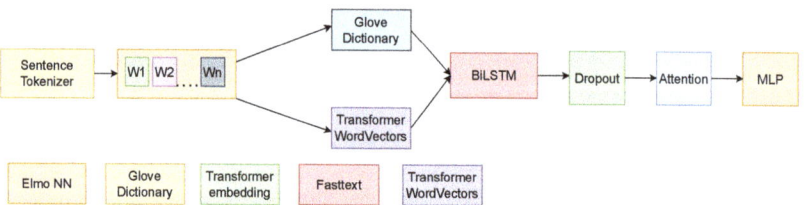

**Figure 8.** Single-task architecture.

For the next batch of models, we employed the multi-task architecture with word embeddings computed using the RoBERTa-based model. For this purpose, we took all the Datasets, as well as the auxiliary Datasets, and we created token vectors for all of them. The process of obtaining transformer token vectors is depicted in Figure 9.

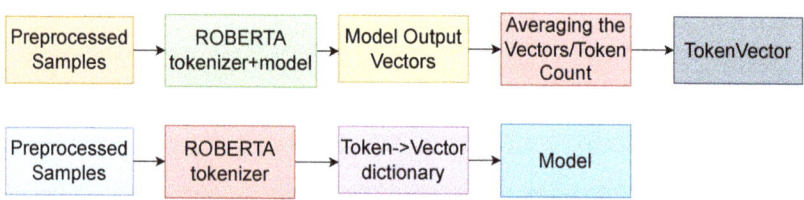

**Figure 9.** Transformer token vector usage.

### 3.6.10. BERT Token Embeddings for Single-Task Learning

The first experiments involving transformer-based token embeddings consisted of using the BERT-based token embeddings with an additional LSTM layer. By doing this, we obtained the approximate performance of the BERT model alone, but with a speed advantage given by using word embeddings.

### 3.6.11. RoBERTa Token Embeddings for Multi-Task Learning

Secondary experiments were composed of using multi-task experiments by combining the SemEval Dataset with all the different Datasets. As word embeddings, the RoBERTa-derived token embeddings were used. While testing, transformer-based architectures proved far superior to the GloVe and ELMo embeddings, and among the transformer models, RoBERTa had the highest accuracy on the Hate Speech Datasets. The three multi-task architectures outlined in [21] were adapted to use RoBERTa word embeddings instead of the standard ones.

### 3.6.12. Training Particularities

During the training, all the models converged. However, employing early stopping mechanisms and tuning the hyperparameters helped the models achieve better results. A problem was using larger text Datasets with multi-task learning. It would not be suitable for texts over 250 words, as the batch size would have to be considerably reduced, in order to facilitate the training. Another problem is not using the same type of text for the primary and auxiliary Datasets. If this constraint is not met, then the primary Dataset will have a hard time surpassing the single-task learning method accuracies.

## 4. Results

In this section, we outline the top-performing approaches that can contribute to an intelligent baseline proposal for Hate Speech detection. These top-performing approaches were selected from among the previously described models and were tested on each selected Dataset. The test results can be seen in Tables 1–5. These tests used only the textual features of the samples. The results were rounded to the nearest hundredth (so the approximation error was ±0.005).

The results obtained on the HateXplain Dataset using RoBERTa were marginally better than those obtained in [11] without the addition of metadata collected during training and on par with those trained with additional annotation features. The results from the hate supremacist forum could not be compared with the ones from [29] as the authors only used a subset of about 2000 samples from their own Dataset in order to balance the classes. The results obtained on the Qian Dataset were better (77.5 F1 → 88 F1 macro) than those obtained in the original article [20].

For the Gao and Huang Dataset [28], there was an improvement in the F1 accuracy from 0.6 obtained with an ensemble model (with additional textual features) to 0.71 obtained using the RoBERTa transformer model on the text samples alone. On the Davidson Tweet Dataset, our approach had a marginally lower weighted F1 score of 90 (when trained for macro F1) compared with [15], which had a score of 91. However, if the model was trained for weighted performance (without early stopping), the same F1 score was obtained. As for the Waseem Dataset, our results were better (81 F1 compared with 80 F1) than those obtained in [21], which used the same variant of the Dataset from [19]. The numerical results of all the performed experiments (see Tables 1–5 and A1–A13) point to the fact that using transformer models yielded better accuracies overall than using token embeddings.

**Table 1.** BERT token embeddings.

| Dataset | Accuracy | Precision Macro | Precision Weighted | Recall Macro | Recall Weighted | F1 Macro | F1 Weighted |
|---------|----------|-----------------|--------------------|--------------|------------------|----------|-------------|
| Xplain | 0.67 | 0.66 | 0.67 | 0.66 | 0.67 | 0.66 | 0.67 |
| Waseem | 0.84 | 0.81 | 0.84 | 0.78 | 0.84 | 0.79 | 0.84 |
| Kurrek | 0.86 | 0.86 | 0.87 | 0.86 | 0.86 | 0.86 | 0.86 |
| Gao–Huang | 0.75 | 0.69 | 0.74 | 0.68 | 0.75 | 0.68 | 0.74 |
| Hate | 0.91 | 0.78 | 0.9 | 0.74 | 0.91 | 0.74 | 0.9 |
| Davidson | 0.91 | 0.78 | 0.90 | 0.72 | 0.91 | 0.74 | 0.90 |
| Qian-Reddit | 0.91 | 0.89 | 0.91 | 0.88 | 0.91 | 0.88 | 0.91 |

**Table 2.** RoBERTa-based transformer model.

| Dataset | Accuracy | Precision Macro | Precision Weighted | Recall Macro | Recall Weighted | F1 Macro | F1 Weighted |
|---------|----------|-----------------|--------------------|--------------|------------------|----------|-------------|
| Xplain | 0.7 | 0.69 | 0.7 | 0.69 | 0.7 | 0.69 | 0.7 |
| Waseem | 0.86 | 0.81 | 0.86 | 0.82 | 0.86 | 0.81 | 0.86 |
| Kurrek | 0.89 | 0.89 | 0.89 | 0.89 | 0.89 | 0.89 | 0.89 |
| Gao–Huang | 0.77 | 0.73 | 0.77 | 0.71 | 0.77 | 0.71 | 0.77 |
| Hate | 0.91 | 0.79 | 0.91 | 0.75 | 0.91 | 0.76 | 0.91 |
| Davidson | 0.91 | 0.77 | 0.91 | 0.75 | 0.91 | 0.75 | 0.91 |
| Qian-Reddit | 0.91 | 0.88 | 0.92 | 0.89 | 0.91 | 0.88 | 0.92 |

**Table 3.** MTL (fixed parameter) RoBERTa token embeddings.

| Dataset | Accuracy | Precision Macro | Precision Weighted | Recall Macro | Recall Weighted | F1 Macro | F1 Weighted |
|---------|----------|-----------------|--------------------|--------------|------------------|----------|-------------|
| Xplain | 0.64 | 0.63 | 0.64 | 0.63 | 0.64 | 0.63 | 0.64 |
| Waseem | 0.84 | 0.81 | 0.84 | 0.78 | 0.84 | 0.78 | 0.84 |
| Kurrek | 0.84 | 0.84 | 0.84 | 0.84 | 0.84 | 0.84 | 0.84 |
| Gao–Huang | 0.75 | 0.70 | 0.75 | 0.70 | 0.75 | 0.69 | 0.75 |
| Hate | 0.90 | 0.75 | 0.89 | 0.72 | 0.9 | 0.73 | 0.89 |
| Davidson | 0.9 | 0.75 | 0.89 | 0.7 | 0.9 | 0.71 | 0.89 |
| Qian-Reddit | 0.91 | 0.88 | 0.91 | 0.88 | 0.91 | 0.88 | 0.91 |

**Table 4.** MTL (learned parameter) RoBERTa token embeddings.

| Dataset | Accuracy | Precision Macro | Precision Weighted | Recall Macro | Recall Weighted | F1 Macro | F1 Weighted |
|---------|----------|-----------------|--------------------|--------------|------------------|----------|-------------|
| Xplain | 0.65 | 0.64 | 0.65 | 0.64 | 0.65 | 0.63 | 0.64 |
| Waseem | 0.84 | 0.81 | 0.85 | 0.79 | 0.84 | 0.79 | 0.84 |
| Kurrek | 0.84 | 0.84 | 0.84 | 0.84 | 0.84 | 0.84 | 0.84 |
| Gao–Huang | 0.75 | 0.71 | 0.75 | 0.67 | 0.75 | 0.67 | 0.74 |
| Hate | 0.9 | 0.77 | 0.9 | 0.72 | 0.9 | 0.73 | 0.9 |
| Davidson | 0.9 | 0.76 | 0.89 | 0.70 | 0.9 | 0.71 | 0.89 |
| Qian-Reddit | 0.91 | 0.88 | 0.91 | 0.88 | 0.91 | 0.88 | 0.91 |

**Table 5.** MTL (hard) RoBERTa token embeddings.

| Dataset | Accuracy | Precision Macro | Precision Weighted | Recall Macro | Recall Weighted | F1 Macro | F1 Weighted |
|---------|----------|-----------------|--------------------|--------------|------------------|----------|-------------|
| Xplain | 0.65 | 0.64 | 0.65 | 0.64 | 0.65 | 0.64 | 0.65 |
| Waseem | 0.84 | 0.81 | 0.84 | 0.79 | 0.84 | 0.79 | 0.84 |
| Kurrek | 0.84 | 0.85 | 0.85 | 0.84 | 0.85 | 0.84 | 0.84 |
| Gao–Huang | 0.75 | 0.71 | 0.74 | 0.65 | 0.75 | 0.65 | 0.72 |
| Hate | 0.9 | 0.77 | 0.9 | 0.73 | 0.9 | 0.73 | 0.9 |
| Davidson | 0.9 | 0.76 | 0.89 | 0.69 | 0.9 | 0.72 | 0.89 |
| Qian-Reddit | 0.91 | 0.88 | 0.91 | 0.88 | 0.91 | 0.87 | 0.91 |

## 5. Conclusions and Future Work

With "Hate Speech" being the next term to be criminalized at the EU level and with growing activity on social media, automatic Hate Speech detection increasingly becomes a hot topic in the field of NLP. Despite a relatively large and recent amount of work surrounding this topic, we note the absence of a benchmarking system that could evaluate how different approaches compare against one another. In this context, the present paper intended to take a step forward towards the standardization of testing for Hate Speech detection. More precisely, our study intended to determine if sentiment analysis Datasets, which by far outweigh Hate Speech ones in terms of data availability, can help train a Hate Speech detection problem for which multi-task learning is used. Our aim was ultimately that of establishing a Dataset list with different features, available for testing and comparisons, since a standardization of the test Datasets used in Hate Speech detection is still lacking, making it difficult to compare the existing models. The secondary objective of the paper was to propose an intelligent baseline as part of this standardization, by testing multi-task learning, and to determine how it compares with single-task learning with modern transformer-based models in the case of the Hate Speech detection problem.

The results of all the performed experiments point to the fact that using transformer models yielded better accuracies overall than trying token embeddings. When speed is a concern, then using token embeddings is the preferred approach, as training them used less resources and yielded a comparable accuracy. Using auxiliary Datasets helped the models achieve higher accuracies only if the Datasets had the same range of classification (sentiment analysis or Offensive Language detection were complementary for Hate Speech), but also the same textual features (using tweet Datasets for longer text Datasets can be detrimental to its convergence).

Although the detection of Hate Speech has evolved over the last few years, with text classification evolving as well, there still are multiple improvement opportunities. A great advancement would be to train a transformer on a very large Hate Speech Dataset and then test the improvement on specific tasks. In addition to these, various other Dataset-related topics should be addressed, such as the connection between users or different hashtags and movement names and how these factor into detecting Hate Speech. That issue could be addressed by a combination between traditional approaches and graph neural networks. Furthermore, it would be interesting to receive a Dataset with all the indicators a social media platform has to offer.

One downside of current Datasets is the fact that, during our experiments, as well as during other experiments in similar works, non-derogatory, non-appropriative, as well as appropriative uses of Hate Speech words were very hard to classify, as they represent a very small portion of the annotated tweets. These kinds of usages should not be censored as they are impacting the targeted groups. Another example of Hate-Speech-related word usage, that is hard to classify, would be quoting a Hate Speech fragment of text with the intent to criticize it. Improvements in neural networks would have to be made in order to treat these kinds of usages.

As future work, we plan on expanding our testing on Datasets that subcategorize the detection of Hate Speech into different, fine-grained labels. One such Dataset that was used in this paper is the Waseem and Hovey Dataset [19]; another one should be SemEval-2019 Task 5 HatEval [40], which categorizes Hate Speech based on the target demographic. It would be interesting to observe how well features learned during a more general classification could be used to increase the classification accuracy of a finer-grained task. Moreover, another direction that this research could take is to expand the types of NLP applications for which the methods are tested. One such example would be handling Hate-Speech-related problems such as misogyny identification [41]. We hope the present study will stimulate and facilitate future research concerning this up-to-date topic, in all of these directions and in others, as well.

**Author Contributions:** Ş.D. and F.H. equally contributed to all aspects of the work. All authors have read and agreed to the published version of the manuscript.

**Funding:** This research received no external funding.

**Informed Consent Statement:** Not applicable.

**Data Availability Statement:** The datasets used in our experiments are available online at the following links: 1. https://github.com/zeeraktalat/hatespeech—Waseem Dataset; 2. https://github.com/t-davidson/hate-speech-and-offensive-language—Davidson Dataset; 3. https://github.com/sjtuprog/fox-news-comments—Gao&Huang Dataset; 4. https://github.com/hate-alert/HateXplain—Xplain Dataset; 5. https://github.com/networkdynamics/slur-corpus—Kurrek Dataset; 6. https://github.com/jing-qian/A-Benchmark-Dataset-for-Learning-to-Intervene-in-Online-Hate-Speech—Qian Dataset; 7. https://github.com/Vicomtech/hate-speech-dataset—Hate Dataset, all accessed on 28 January 2022.

**Acknowledgments:** We thank three anonymous reviewers for their comments and suggestions, which helped improve our paper.

**Conflicts of Interest:** The authors declare no conflict of interest.

## Appendix A

Detailed results obtained from evaluating different models on the benchmark Datasets are given here. All results feature accuracy, macro and weighted recall, precision, and F1-scores.

**Table A1.** Scores obtained on the benchmark Datasets using the K nearest neighbors algorithm.

| Dataset | Accuracy | Precision Macro | Recall Macro | F1 Macro |
|---|---|---|---|---|
| Xplain | 0.61 | 0.59 | 0.58 | 0.59 |
| Waseem | 0.78 | 0.63 | 0.55 | 0.59 |
| Kurrek | 0.68 | 0.68 | 0.67 | 0.67 |
| Gao–Huang | 0.72 | 0.51 | 0.51 | 0.51 |
| Hate | 0.87 | 0.70 | 0.65 | 0.67 |
| Davidson | 0.82 | 0.72 | 0.48 | 0.57 |
| Qian-Reddit | 0.82 | 0.77 | 0.77 | 0.77 |

**Table A2.** Scores obtained on the benchmark Datasets using the SVM algorithm.

| Dataset | Accuracy | Precision Macro | Recall Macro | F1 Macro |
|---|---|---|---|---|
| Xplain | 0.66 | 0.66 | 0.64 | 0.64 |
| Waseem | 0.80 | 0.78 | 0.73 | 0.76 |
| Kurrek | 0.80 | 0.80 | 0.80 | 0.80 |
| Gao–Huang | 0.74 | 0.50 | 0.54 | 0.52 |
| Hate | 0.89 | 0.51 | 0.52 | 0.52 |
| Davidson | 0.88 | 0.68 | 0.66 | 0.67 |
| Qian-Reddit | 0.85 | 0.83 | 0.81 | 0.83 |

**Table A3.** Scores obtained on the benchmark Datasets using the decision trees algorithm.

| Dataset | Accuracy | Precision Macro | Recall Macro | F1 Macro |
|---|---|---|---|---|
| Xplain | 0.67 | 0.66 | 0.65 | 0.64 |
| Waseem | 0.81 | 0.78 | 0.68 | 0.72 |
| Kurrek | 0.74 | 0.75 | 0.74 | 0.74 |
| Gao–Huang | 0.75 | 0.62 | 0.61 | 0.61 |
| Hate | 0.86 | 0.72 | 0.59 | 0.65 |
| Davidson | 0.87 | 0.65 | 0.67 | 0.66 |
| Qian-Reddit | 0.88 | 0.88 | 0.85 | 0.87 |

**Table A4.** Scores obtained on the benchmark Datasets using the random forest algorithm.

| Dataset | Accuracy | Precision Macro | Recall Macro | F1 Macro |
|---|---|---|---|---|
| Xplain | 0.62 | 0.62 | 0.59 | 0.61 |
| Waseem | 0.78 | 0.72 | 0.74 | 0.73 |
| Kurrek | 0.80 | 0.80 | 0.80 | 0.80 |
| Gao–Huang | 0.73 | 0.67 | 0.64 | 0.65 |
| Hate | 0.82 | 0.65 | 0.60 | 0.62 |
| Davidson | 0.87 | 0.67 | 0.62 | 0.64 |
| Qian-Reddit | 0.86 | 0.83 | 0.84 | 0.84 |

**Table A5.** Scores obtained on the benchmark Datasets using the GloVe embeddings with 2 LSTM layers and max pooling.

| Dataset | Accuracy | Precision Macro | Recall Macro | F1 Macro |
|---------|----------|-----------------|--------------|----------|
| Xplain | 0.65 | 0.65 | 0.65 | 0.65 |
| Waseem | 0.84 | 0.80 | 0.77 | 0.78 |
| Kurrek | 0.87 | 0.87 | 0.87 | 0.87 |
| Gao–Huang | 0.77 | 0.72 | 0.68 | 0.70 |
| Hate | 0.90 | 0.73 | 0.70 | 0.71 |
| Davidson | 0.91 | 0.74 | 0.72 | 0.78 |
| Qian-Reddit | 0.91 | 0.89 | 0.87 | 0.88 |

**Table A6.** Scores obtained on the benchmark Datasets using the convolutional neural network model. The embeddings were made with the help of GloVe vectors.

| Dataset | Accuracy | Precision Macro | Recall Macro | F1 Macro |
|---------|----------|-----------------|--------------|----------|
| Xplain | 0.55 | 0.54 | 0.54 | 0.54 |
| Waseem | 0.81 | 0.78 | 0.72 | 0.75 |
| Kurrek | 0.77 | 0.77 | 0.77 | 0.77 |
| Gao–Huang | 0.71 | 0.64 | 0.61 | 0.62 |
| Hate | 0.87 | 0.67 | 0.62 | 0.64 |
| Davidson | 0.87 | 0.71 | 0.64 | 0.67 |
| Qian-Reddit | 0.83 | 0.76 | 0.72 | 0.74 |

**Table A7.** Scores obtained on the benchmark Datasets using the bidirectional recurrent neural network layers. The embeddings were made with the help of GloVe vectors.

| Dataset | Accuracy | Precision Macro | Recall Macro | F1 Macro |
|---------|----------|-----------------|--------------|----------|
| Xplain | 0.65 | 0.65 | 0.66 | 0.65 |
| Waseem | 0.85 | 0.83 | 0.76 | 0.79 |
| Kurrek | 0.84 | 0.84 | 0.84 | 0.84 |
| Gao–Huang | 0.77 | 0.70 | 0.67 | 0.68 |
| Hate | 0.91 | 0.78 | 0.67 | 0.72 |
| Davidson | 0.91 | 0.74 | 0.73 | 0.73 |
| Qian-Reddit | 0.90 | 0.87 | 0.86 | 0.86 |

**Table A8.** Scores obtained on the benchmark Datasets using one-way interconnected recurrent layers. The embeddings were made with the help of GloVe vectors.

| Dataset | Accuracy | Precision Macro | Recall Macro | F1 Macro |
|---------|----------|-----------------|--------------|----------|
| Xplain | 0.64 | 0.64 | 0.64 | 0.64 |
| Waseem | 0.84 | 0.80 | 0.76 | 0.78 |
| Kurrek | 0.84 | 0.84 | 0.84 | 0.84 |
| Gao–Huang | 0.71 | 0.63 | 0.61 | 0.62 |
| Hate | 0.89 | 0.73 | 0.65 | 0.68 |
| Davidson | 0.91 | 0.77 | 0.72 | 0.74 |
| Qian-Reddit | 0.90 | 0.86 | 0.86 | 0.86 |

**Table A9.** Scores obtained on the benchmark Datasets using the CNN-GRU method. The embeddings were made with the help of GloVe vectors.

| Dataset | Accuracy | Precision Macro | Recall Macro | F1 Macro |
|---------|----------|-----------------|--------------|----------|
| Xplain | 0.65 | 0.64 | 0.64 | 0.64 |
| Waseem | 0.83 | 0.79 | 0.78 | 0.79 |
| Kurrek | 0.76 | 0.71 | 0.70 | 0.70 |
| Gao–Huang | 0.76 | 0.70 | 0.70 | 0.70 |
| Hate | 0.89 | 0.73 | 0.71 | 0.72 |
| Davidson | 0.89 | 0.73 | 0.72 | 0.72 |
| Qian-Reddit | 0.89 | 0.85 | 0.83 | 0.83 |

**Table A10.** Scores obtained on the benchmark Datasets using the learnable parameter encoding model. Embedding vectors were made with both ELMo and GloVe and then concatenated. The auxiliary Dataset is the SemEval 18 [27] Task1 Dataset.

| Dataset | Accuracy | Precision Macro | Recall Macro | F1 Macro |
|---------|----------|-----------------|--------------|----------|
| Xplain | 0.64 | 0.63 | 0.63 | 0.63 |
| Waseem | 0.81 | 0.80 | 0.81 | 0.80 |
| Kurrek | 0.88 | 0.87 | 0.87 | 0.87 |
| Gao–Huang | 0.78 | 0.73 | 0.70 | 0.71 |
| Hate | 0.91 | 0.77 | 0.71 | 0.74 |
| Davidson | 0.89 | 0.73 | 0.80 | 0.76 |
| Qian-Reddit | 0.89 | 0.85 | 0.87 | 0.86 |

**Table A11.** Scores obtained on the benchmark Datasets using the hard learning multi-task model. Embedding vectors were made with both ELMo and GloVe and then concatenated. The auxiliary Dataset is the SemEval 18 [27] Task1 Dataset.

| Dataset | Accuracy | Precision Macro | Recall Macro | F1 Macro |
|---------|----------|-----------------|--------------|----------|
| Xplain | 0.64 | 0.63 | 0.63 | 0.63 |
| Waseem | 0.79 | 0.81 | 0.75 | 0.78 |
| Kurrek | 0.88 | 0.87 | 0.87 | 0.87 |
| Gao–Huang | 0.78 | 0.73 | 0.72 | 0.72 |
| Hate | 0.91 | 0.78 | 0.72 | 0.75 |
| Davidson | 0.90 | 0.76 | 0.73 | 0.75 |
| Qian-Reddit | 0.87 | 0.87 | 0.87 | 0.87 |

**Table A12.** Scores obtained on the benchmark Datasets using the multi-task learning method in which only the last layers were separated. Embedding vectors were made with both GloVe and ELMo and then concatenated. The auxiliary Dataset is the SemEval 18 [27] Task1 Dataset.

| Dataset | Accuracy | Precision Macro | Recall Macro | F1 Macro |
|---------|----------|-----------------|--------------|----------|
| Xplain | 0.65 | 0.63 | 0.63 | 0.63 |
| Waseem | 0.83 | 0.80 | 0.80 | 0.80 |
| Kurrek | 0.87 | 0.87 | 0.87 | 0.87 |
| Gao–Huang | 0.79 | 0.73 | 0.73 | 0.73 |
| Hate | 0.90 | 0.80 | 0.70 | 0.74 |
| Davidson | 0.89 | 0.72 | 0.77 | 0.74 |
| Qian-Reddit | 0.90 | 0.88 | 0.89 | 0.89 |

**Table A13.** Scores obtained on the benchmark Datasets using 2 LSTM layers and embedding the words with both ELMo and GloVe embeddings.

| Dataset | Accuracy | Precision Macro | Recall Macro | F1 Macro |
|---------|----------|-----------------|--------------|----------|
| Xplain | 0.66 | 0.65 | 0.65 | 0.65 |
| Waseem | 0.81 | 0.79 | 0.78 | 0.79 |
| Kurrek | 0.85 | 0.82 | 0.84 | 0.83 |
| Gao–Huang | 0.79 | 0.74 | 0.72 | 0.73 |
| Hate | 0.91 | 0.78 | 0.74 | 0.76 |
| Davidson | 0.90 | 0.74 | 0.75 | 0.75 |
| Qian-Reddit | 0.90 | 0.86 | 0.89 | 0.87 |

## References

1. Framework Decision on Combating Certain Forms and Expressions of Racism and Xenophobia by Means of Criminal Law. 2008. Available online: https://eur-lex.europa.eu/legal-content/EN/TXT/?uri=LEGISSUM%3Al33178 (accessed on 25 January 2022).
2. United States Department of Justice—Learn about Hate Crimes. Available online: https://www.justice.gov/hatecrimes/learn-about-hate-crimes (accessed on 25 January 2022).
3. Council Framework Decision 2008/913/JHA of 28 November 2008 on Combating Certain Forms and Expressions of Racism and Xenophobia by Means of Criminal Law. Available online: https://ec.europa.eu/commission/presscorner/detail/en/IP_21_6561 (accessed on 25 January 2022).
4. Barron, J.A. Internet Access, Hate Speech and the First Amendment. *First Amend. L. Rev.* **2019**, *18*, 1. [CrossRef]
5. Facebook Reports Third Quarter 2021 Results. 2021. Available online: https://investor.fb.com/investor-news/press-release-details/2021/Facebook-Reports-Third-Quarter-2021-Results/default.aspx (accessed on 25 January 2022).

6. Twitter Reports Third Quarter 2021 Results. 2021. Available online: https://s22.q4cdn.com/826641620/files/doc_financials/20 21/q3/Final-Q3'21-earnings-release.pdf (accessed on 25 January 2022).
7. Xia, M.; Field, A.; Tsvetkov, Y. Demoting Racial Bias in Hate Speech Detection. In Proceedings of the Eighth International Workshop on Natural Language Processing for Social Media, Online, 10 July 2020; Association for Computational Linguistics: Stroudsburg, PA, USA, 2020; pp. 7–14. [CrossRef]
8. Rajput, G.; Punn, N.S.; Sonbhadra, S.K.; Agarwal, S. Hate Speech Detection Using Static BERT Embeddings. In Proceedings of the Big Data Analytics: 9th International Conference, BDA 2021, Virtual Event, 15–18 December 2021; Springer: Berlin/Heidelberg, Germany, 2021; pp. 67–77. [CrossRef]
9. Brown, A. What is Hate Speech? Part 1: The myth of hate. *Law Philos.* **2017**, *36*, 419–468. [CrossRef]
10. Kurrek, J.; Saleem, H.M.; Ruths, D. Towards a comprehensive taxonomy and large-scale annotated corpus for online slur usage. In Proceedings of the Fourth Workshop on Online Abuse and Harms, Online, 20 November 2020; Association for Computational Linguistics: Stroudsburg, PA, USA, 2020; pp. 138–149.
11. Mathew, B.; Saha, P.; Yimam, S.M.; Biemann, C.; Goyal, P.; Mukherjee, A. HateXplain: A Benchmark Dataset for Explainable Hate Speech Detection. *arXiv* **2021**, arXiv:2012.10289.
12. Davidson, T.; Warmsley, D.; Macy, M.; Weber, I. Automated Hate Speech detection and the problem of offensive language. In Proceedings of the 11th International AAAI Conference on Web and Social Media, Montreal, QC, Canada, 15–18 May 2017; Volume 11.
13. Nobata, C.; Tetreault, J.; Thomas, A.; Mehdad, Y.; Chang, Y. Abusive language detection in online user content. In Proceedings of the 25th International Conference on World Wide Web, Montreal, QC, Canada, 11–15 April 2016; pp. 145–153.
14. Plaza-Del-Arco, F.M.; Molina-González, M.D.; Ureña-López, L.A.; Martín-Valdivia, M.T. A Multi-Task Learning Approach to Hate Speech Detection Leveraging Sentiment Analysis. *IEEE Access* **2021**, *9*, 112478–112489. [CrossRef]
15. Awal, M.; Cao, R.; Lee, R.K.W.; Mitrović, S. AngryBERT: Joint Learning Target and Emotion for Hate Speech Detection. In *Advances in Knowledge Discovery and Data Mining, Proceedings of the 25th Pacific-Asia Conference, PAKDD 2021, Virtual Event, 11–14 May 2021*; Springer: Berlin/Heidelberg, Germany, 2021; pp. 701–713. [CrossRef]
16. Sarwar, S.M.; Murdock, V. Unsupervised Domain Adaptation for Hate Speech Detection Using a Data Augmentation Approach. *arXiv* **2021**, arXiv:2107.12866.
17. Rizoiu, M.A.; Wang, T.; Ferraro, G.; Suominen, H. Transfer Learning for Hate Speech Detection in Social Media. *arXiv* **2019**, arXiv:1906.03829.
18. Bokstaller, J.; Patoulidis, G.; Zagidullina, A. Model Bias in NLP–Application to Hate Speech Classification using transfer learning techniques. *arXiv* **2021**, arXiv:2109.09725.
19. Waseem, Z.; Hovy, D. Hateful symbols or hateful people? predictive features for hate speech detection on twitter. In Proceedings of the NAACL Student Research Workshop, San Diego, CA, USA, 12–17 June 2016; pp. 88–93.
20. Qian, J.; Bethke, A.; Liu, Y.; Belding-Royer, E.M.; Wang, W.Y. A Benchmark Dataset for Learning to Intervene in Online Hate Speech. In Proceedings of the 2019 Conference on Empirical Methods in Natural Language Processing and the 9th International Joint Conference on Natural Language Processing (EMNLP-IJCNLP), Hong Kong, China, 3–7 November 2019; Association for Computational Linguistics: Stroudsburg, PA, USA, 2019.
21. Rajamanickam, S.; Mishra, P.; Yannakoudakis, H.; Shutova, E. Joint Modelling of Emotion and Abusive Language Detection. In Proceedings of the 58th Annual Meeting of the Association for Computational Linguistics, Online, 5–10 July 2020; pp. 4270–4279. [CrossRef]
22. Hochreiter, S.; Schmidhuber, J. Long short-term memory. *Neural Comput.* **1997**, *9*, 1735–1780. [CrossRef] [PubMed]
23. Cho, K.; van Merriënboer, B.; Bahdanau, D.; Bengio, Y. On the Properties of Neural Machine Translation: Encoder–Decoder Approaches. In Proceedings of the SSST-8, Eighth Workshop on Syntax, Semantics and Structure in Statistical Translation, Doha, Qatar, 25 October 2014; Association for Computational Linguistics: Stroudsburg, PA, USA, 2014; pp. 103–111. [CrossRef]
24. Mollas, I.; Chrysopoulou, Z.; Karlos, S.; Tsoumakas, G. ETHOS: A multi-label Hate Speech detection Dataset. *Complex Intell. Syst.* **2022**. [CrossRef]
25. Devlin, J.; Chang, M.W.; Lee, K.; Toutanova, K. BERT: Pre-training of Deep Bidirectional Transformers for Language Understanding. In Proceedings of the 2019 Conference of the North American Chapter of the Association for Computational Linguistics: Human Language Technologies, Volume 1 (Long and Short Papers), Minneapolis, MN, USA, 2–7 June 2019; Association for Computational Linguistics: Stroudsburg, PA, USA, 2019; pp. 4171–4186. [CrossRef]
26. Ousidhoum, N.; Lin, Z.; Zhang, H.; Song, Y.; Yeung, D.Y. Multilingual and Multi-Aspect Hate Speech Analysis. In Proceedings of the 2019 Conference on Empirical Methods in Natural Language Processing and the 9th International Joint Conference on Natural Language Processing (EMNLP-IJCNLP), Hong Kong, China, 3–7 November 2019; Association for Computational Linguistics: Stroudsburg, PA, USA, 2019; pp. 4675–4684. [CrossRef]
27. Mohammad, S.M.; Bravo-Marquez, F.; Salameh, M.; Kiritchenko, S. SemEval-2018 Task 1: Affect in Tweets. In Proceedings of the International Workshop on Semantic Evaluation (SemEval-2018), New Orleans, LA, USA, 5–6 June 2018.
28. Gao, L.; Huang, R. Detecting Online Hate Speech Using Context Aware Models. In Proceedings of the International Conference Recent Advances in Natural Language Processing, RANLP 2017, Varna, Bulgaria, 2–8 September 2017; INCOMA Ltd.: Shoumen, Bulgaria, 2017; pp. 260–266. [CrossRef]

29.  De Gibert Bonet, O.; Perez Miguel, N.; García-Pablos, A.; Cuadros, M. Hate Speech Dataset from a White Supremacy Forum. In Proceedings of the 2nd Workshop on Abusive Language Online (ALW2), Brussels, Belgium, 31 October 2018; pp. 11–20. [CrossRef]
30.  Pedregosa, F.; Varoquaux, G.; Gramfort, A.; Michel, V.; Thirion, B.; Grisel, O.; Blondel, M.; Prettenhofer, P.; Weiss, R.; Dubourg, V.; et al. Scikit-learn: Machine learning in Python. *J. Mach. Learn. Res.* **2011**, *12*, 2825–2830.
31.  Mikolov, T.; Chen, K.; Corrado, G.; Dean, J. Efficient Estimation of Word Representations in Vector Space. *arXiv* **2013**, arXiv:1301.3781.
32.  Pennington, J.; Socher, R.; Manning, C.D. GloVe: Global vectors for word representation. In Proceedings of the 2014 Conference on Empirical Methods in Natural Language Processing (EMNLP), Doha, Qatar, 25–29 October 2014; pp. 1532–1543.
33.  Gardner, M.; Grus, J.; Neumann, M.; Tafjord, O.; Dasigi, P.; Liu, N.F.; Peters, M.; Schmitz, M.; Zettlemoyer, L. AllenNLP: A Deep Semantic Natural Language Processing Platform. In Proceedings of the Workshop for NLP Open Source Software (NLP-OSS), Melbourne, Australia, 20 July 2018; Association for Computational Linguistics: Stroudsburg, PA, USA, 2018; pp. 1–6. [CrossRef]
34.  Zhuang, L.; Wayne, L.; Ya, S.; Jun, Z. A Robustly Optimized BERT Pre-training Approach with Post-training. In Proceedings of the 20th Chinese National Conference on Computational Linguistics, Huhhot, China, 13–15 August 2021; Chinese Information Processing Society of China: Beijing, China, 2021; pp. 1218–1227.
35.  Peters, M.E.; Neumann, M.; Iyyer, M.; Gardner, M.; Clark, C.; Lee, K.; Zettlemoyer, L. Deep Contextualized Word Representations. In Proceedings of the 2018 Conference of the North American Chapter of the Association for Computational Linguistics: Human Language Technologies, Volume 1 (Long Papers), New Orleans, LA, USA, 1–6 June 2018; Association for Computational Linguistics: Stroudsburg, PA, USA, 2018; pp. 2227–2237. [CrossRef]
36.  Paszke, A.; Gross, S.; Massa, F.; Lerer, A.; Bradbury, J.; Chanan, G.; Killeen, T.; Lin, Z.; Gimelshein, N.; Antiga, L.; et al. PyTorch: An imperative style, high-performance deep learning library. *Adv. Neural Inf. Process. Syst.* **2019**, *32*, 8026–8037.
37.  Robbins, H.E. A Stochastic Approximation Method. *Ann. Math. Stat.* **2007**, *22*, 400–407. [CrossRef]
38.  Kingma, D.; Ba, J. Adam: A Method for Stochastic Optimization. In Proceedings of the International Conference on Learning Representations, Banff, AB, Canada, 14–16 April 2014.
39.  Lydia, A.; Francis, S. Adagrad—An Optimizer for Stochastic Gradient Descent. *Int. J. Inf. Comput.* **2019**, *6*, 566–568.
40.  Basile, V.; Bosco, C.; Fersini, E.; Nozza, D.; Patti, V.; Rangel Pardo, F.M.; Rosso, P.; Sanguinetti, M. SemEval-2019 Task 5: Multilingual Detection of Hate Speech Against Immigrants and Women in Twitter. In Proceedings of the 13th International Workshop on Semantic Evaluation, Minneapolis, MN, USA, 6–7 June 2019; Association for Computational Linguistics: Stroudsburg, PA, USA, 2019; pp. 54–63. [CrossRef]
41.  Fersini, E.; Rosso, P.; Anzovino, M.E. Overview of the Evalita 2018 Task on Automatic Misogyny Identification (AMI). In Proceedings of the Sixth Evaluation Campaign of Natural Language Processing and Speech Tools for Italian. Final Workshop (EVALITA 2018), Co-Located with the Fifth Italian Conference on Computational Linguistics (CLiC-it 2018), Turin, Italy, 12–13 December 2018; Volume 2263.

*Article*

# Intermediate-Task Transfer Learning with BERT for Sarcasm Detection

**Edoardo Savini and Cornelia Caragea ***

Department of Computer Science, University of Illinois at Chicago, Chicago, IL 60607, USA;
edoardosavini95@gmail.com
* Correspondence: cornelia@uic.edu

**Abstract:** Sarcasm detection plays an important role in natural language processing as it can impact the performance of many applications, including sentiment analysis, opinion mining, and stance detection. Despite substantial progress on sarcasm detection, the research results are scattered across datasets and studies. In this paper, we survey the current state-of-the-art and present strong baselines for sarcasm detection based on BERT pre-trained language models. We further improve our BERT models by fine-tuning them on related intermediate tasks before fine-tuning them on our target task. Specifically, relying on the correlation between sarcasm and (implied negative) sentiment and emotions, we explore a transfer learning framework that uses sentiment classification and emotion detection as individual intermediate tasks to infuse knowledge into the target task of sarcasm detection. Experimental results on three datasets that have different characteristics show that the BERT-based models outperform many previous models.

**Keywords:** sarcasm detection; intermediate-task transfer learning; emotion-enriched sarcasm detection

**MSC:** 68T50

**Citation:** Savini, E.; Caragea, C. Intermediate-Task Transfer Learning with BERT for Sarcasm Detection. *Mathematics* **2022**, *10*, 844. https://doi.org/10.3390/math10050844

Academic Editor: Victor Mitrana

Received: 1 February 2022
Accepted: 1 March 2022
Published: 7 March 2022

**Publisher's Note:** MDPI stays neutral with regard to jurisdictional claims in published maps and institutional affiliations.

## 1. Introduction

In recent years, the Internet has become the main source to communicate and share information. In particular, social media sites, microblogs, discussion forums, and online reviews have become more and more popular. They represent a way for people to express their own opinion with no inhibition and to search for some advice on various products or even vacation tips. Many companies take advantage of these sites' popularity to share their products and services, provide assistance, and understand costumer needs. For this reason, social media websites have developed into one of the main domains for the Natural Language Processing (NLP) research, especially in the areas of Sentiment Analysis and Opinion Mining. Analyzing people's sentiments and opinions could be useful to comprehend their behavior, monitor customer satisfaction, and increase sales revenue. However, these tasks appear to be very challenging [1,2] due to the dense presence of figurative languages in social media communities, such as Reddit or Twitter.

Our research focuses on a recurrent sophisticated linguistic phenomenon (and a form of speech act) that makes use of figurative language to implicitly convey contempt through the incongruity [3] between text and context: the sarcasm. Its highly figurative nature has caused sarcasm to be identified as one of the most challenging tasks in natural language processing [4], and has attracted significant attention in recent years along two lines of research: (1) understanding sarcasm from different online platforms by creating novel datasets [5–10]; and (2) designing approaches to effectively detect sarcasm from textual data. Although many previous works on this task focused on approaches based on feature engineering and standard classifiers such as Support Vector Machines to extract lexical cues recurrent in sarcasm [6,11,12], more recent works [13–15] have started to explore deep neural networks for sarcasm detection in order to capture the hidden intricacies from text.

Still, despite substantial progress on sarcasm detection, the research results are scattered across datasets and studies.

In this paper, we aim to further our understanding of what works best across several textual datasets for our target task: sarcasm detection. To this end, we present strong baselines based on BERT pre-trained language models [16]. We further propose to improve our BERT models by fine-tuning them on related intermediate tasks before fine-tuning them on our target task so that inductive bias is incorporated from related tasks [17]. We study the performance of our BERT models on three datasets of different sizes and characteristics, collected from the Internet Argument Corpus (IAC) [11], Reddit [18], and Twitter [7]. Table 1 shows examples of sarcastic comments from each of the three datasets. As we can see from the table, the dataset constructed by Oraby et al. [11] contains long comments, while the other two datasets have comments with fairly short lengths. Our purpose is to analyze the effectiveness of BERT and intermediate-task transfer learning with BERT on the sarcasm detection task and find a neural framework able to accurately predict sarcasm in many types of social platforms, from discussion forums to microblogs.

**Table 1.** Examples of sarcastic comments from our datasets.

| Oraby et al. [11]: | *"And, let's see, when did the job loss actually start?, Oh yes.. We can trace the troubles starting in 2007, with a big melt down in August/September of 2008. Let's see.. Obama must have been a terrible president to have caused that.. oh WAIT. That wasn't Obama, that was BUSH.. Excuse Me."* |
|---|---|
| Khodak et al. [18]: | *"Obama is in league with ISIS, he wins the shittiest terrorist fighter award."* |
| Mishra et al. [7]: | *"I can't even wait to go sit at this meeting at the highschool."* |

Our contributions are summarized as follows:

- We show that sarcasm detection results are scattered across multiple papers, which makes it difficult to assess the advancements and current state-of-the-art for this task.
- We establish strong baselines based on BERT pre-trained language models for this task. Our analysis is based on experimental results performed on three sarcasm datasets of different sizes (from small to large datasets) and covering different characteristics captured from various social platforms (from the Internet Argument Corpus to Reddit and Twitter).
- Inspired from existing research on sarcasm [6] which shows its correlation with sentiment and emotions, we find that the performance of BERT can be further improved by fine-tuning on data-rich intermediate tasks, before fine-tuning the BERT models on our sarcasm detection target task. We use diverse intermediate tasks (fine-grained emotion detection from general tweets, coarse-grained sentiment polarity by polarizing the emotions in the above dataset into positive and negative sentiment, and sentiment classification of movie reviews). We show that, depending on the characteristics of the target task data, different intermediate tasks are more useful than others. We make our code available to further research in this area (https://github.com/edosavini/TransferBertSarcasm, accessed on 23 March 2021).

## 2. Related Work

Experiments on automatic sarcasm detection represent a recent field of study. The first investigations made on text were focused on discovering lexical indicators and syntactic cues that could be used as features for sarcasm detection [6,11]. In fact, at the beginning, sarcasm recognition was considered as a simple text classification task. Many studies focused on recognizing interjections, punctuation symbols, intensifiers, hyperboles [19], emoticons [20], exclamations [21], and hashtags [22] in sarcastic comments. More recently, Wallace et al. [4] showed that many classifiers fail when dealing with sentences where context is needed. Therefore, newer works studied also parental comments or historical tweets of the writer [3,23,24].

In order to detect semantic and contextual information from a sarcastic statement, researchers started to explore deep learning techniques. The advantage of adopting neural networks is in their ability to induce features automatically, allowing them to capture long-range and subtle semantic characteristics that are hard to capture with manual feature engineering. For example, Joshi et al. [15] proposed different kinds of word embeddings (Word2Vec, GloVe, LSA), augmented with other features on word vector-based similarity, to apprehend context in phrases with no sentiment words. Poria et al. [25] developed a framework based on pre-trained CNNs to retrieve sentiment, emotion and personality features for sarcasm recognition. Zhang et al. [26] created a bi-directional gated recurrent neural network with a pooling mechanism to automatically detect content features from tweets and context information from history tweets. Ghosh and Veale [14] proposed a concatenation of 2-layer Convolutional Neural Networks with 2-layer Long-Short Term Memory Networks followed by a fully connected deep neural network and showed improved results over text based engineered features. Oprea and Magdy [9] studied intended vs. perceived sarcasm using CNN and RNN-based models.

Other authors leveraged user information in addition to the source text. For example, Amir et al. [13] used Convolutional Neural Networks (CNNs) to capture user embeddings and utterance-based features. They managed to discover homophily scanning a user's historical tweets. Hazarika et al. [27] proposed a framework able to detect contextual information with user embedding created through user profiling and discourse modeling from comments on Reddit. Their model achieves state-of-the-art results in one of the datasets (SARC) [8] we consider in our experiments.

Majumder et al. [28] used a Gated Recurrent Unit (GRU) with an attention mechanism within a multitask learning framework with sarcasm detection as the main task and sentiment classification as an auxiliary task and applied it on the dataset by Mishra et al. [7], which contains about a thousand tweets labeled with both sarcastic and sentiment labels. Their mechanism takes as input Glove word embeddings, shares the GRU model between the two tasks, and exploits a neural tensor network to fuse sarcasm and sentiment-specific word vectors. The authors were able to outperform the state-of-the-art previously obtained with a CNN model by Mishra et al. [29]. Plepi and Flek [30] used a graph attention network (GAT) over users and tweets from a conversation thread to detect sarcasm and used a BERT model as a baseline. Other works [31–33] focused on multi-modal sarcasm detection by analyzing the relationship between the text and images using models such as BERT [16], ResNet [34], or ViLBERT [35].

In contrast to the above works, we explore BERT pre-trained language models and intermediate-task transfer learning with BERT focusing solely on the text of each user post and establish strong baselines for sarcasm detection across several social platforms.

## 3. Baseline Modeling

### 3.1. BERT Pre-Trained Language Model

The BERT pre-trained language model [16] has pushed performance boundaries on many natural language understanding tasks. We fine-tune BERT `bert-base-uncased` from the HuggingFace Transformers library [36] on our target task, i.e., sarcasm detection, with an added single linear layer on top as a sentence classifier that uses the final hidden state corresponding to the [CLS] token.

### 3.2. Intermediate-Task Transfer Learning

Several works proposed to further improve pre-trained models by first fine-tuning a pre-trained model, e.g., BERT, on an intermediate task, before fine-tuning it again on the target task [17,37]. However, these works showed that this approach does not always boost the performance of a target task. Inspired by this idea and the progress on sarcasm detection, which showed a strong correlation between sarcasm and (implied negative) sentiment and emotions [6], we propose to explore transfer learning from the related intermediate tasks of sentiment classification and emotion detection, to understand if we can further improve the performance of our BERT models on the sarcasm detection target task. Figure 1 shows the steps taken in this transfer learning framework.

Next, we discuss our target task and the intermediate tasks used for transfer learning.

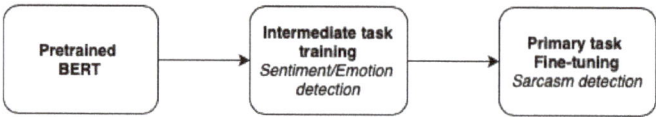

**Figure 1.** Our transfer learning framework.

### 3.2.1. Target Task

**Sarcasm Detection.** Our target task is sarcasm detection from textual inputs. Specifically, given a piece of text, e.g., a message, a tweet, a comment, or a sentence, the task is to predict if the text is sarcastic or not, *solely* from the text.

### 3.2.2. Intermediate Tasks

**Fine-Grained EmoNet.** EmoNet [38] is a Twitter dataset composed of tweets automatically annotated using distant supervision with the Plutchik-24 emotion set. Thus, by construction, the tweets in this dataset contain more explicit emotion-rich words. We obtained a smaller version of the dataset from the authors. This version contains about 50,000 tweets annotated with the Plutchik-8 emotion set (joy, surprise, trust, anticipation, sadness, fear, anger, disgust). We fine-tuned BERT on the EmoNet tweets in a supervised fashion before fine-tuning it on our sarcasm detection target task.

**Coarse-Grained EmoNet.** This dataset is the same as the EmoNet dataset above [38] except that we make the labels for each tweet more abstract according to the polarized emotions (positive and negative). We group all the emotion labels with negative insight (sadness, fear, anger, disgust) into a negative sentiment label (0) and group the remaining emotions (joy, surprise, trust, anticipation) into a positive class. We refer to this dataset as EmoNetSent. We fine-tuned BERT on EmoNetSent in a supervised fashion before fine-tuning it on our sarcasm detection target task.

**IMDB Movie Review.** The IMDB Movie Review dataset is a balanced sentiment dataset created by Maas et al. [39] for learning word vector representations to capture semantic information from text. It contains 50,000 polarized movie reviews labeled with binary sentiment classes (positive, negative). The authors avoided some preprocessing steps such as stemming and stop word removal in order to retain more indicative terms for sentiment. This dataset differs from the EmoNet dataset in terms of text (reviews) length and content. In fact, while EmoNet tweets contain short-length sentences explicitly dense of emotional charge, the IMDB dataset consists of very long phrases and sentences in which the sentiment (lexical) content appears more implicit and sparse along the sentences.

Table 2 shows examples from the datasets of our intermediate tasks, EmoNet and IMDB. We also give the number of examples in each of the intermediate tasks, EmoNet, EmoNetSent, and IMDB, in Tables 3, 4 and 5, respectively.

**Table 2.** Examples of sentences in the datasets of our intermediate tasks.

| EmoNet | *"It's just so great to have baseball back. #happy"* | joy (1) |
|--------|------------------------------------------------------|---------|
| IMDB | *"I rented this movie primarily because it had Meg Ryan in it, and I was disappointed to see that her role is really a mere supporting one. Not only is she not on screen much, but nothing her character does is essential to the plot. Her character could be written out of the story without changing it much."* | 0 |

**Table 3.** Number of tweets per emotion in the EmoNet dataset.

| Emotion | Dataset | Training | Dev | Test |
|---|---|---|---|---|
| Joy | 18,847 | 15,069 | 1884 | 1894 |
| Sadness | 9225 | 7400 | 932 | 893 |
| Fear | 6482 | 5198 | 643 | 641 |
| Anger | 3526 | 2795 | 346 | 385 |
| Surprise | 3451 | 2758 | 344 | 349 |
| Disgust | 2986 | 2362 | 309 | 315 |
| Trust | 2224 | 1779 | 233 | 212 |
| Anticipation | 1598 | 1312 | 142 | 144 |
| Total | 48,339 | 38,673 | 4833 | 4833 |

**Table 4.** Number of tweets per sentiment in the EmoNetSent dataset.

| Sentiment | Dataset | Training | Dev | Test |
|---|---|---|---|---|
| Negative | 22,219 | 17,755 | 2230 | 2234 |
| Positive | 26,120 | 20,918 | 2603 | 2599 |
| Total | 48,339 | 38,673 | 4833 | 4833 |

**Table 5.** Number of movie reviews per class in the IMDB dataset.

| Class | Training | Dev | Test |
|---|---|---|---|
| Positive | 20,000 | 2500 | 2500 |
| Negative | 20,000 | 2500 | 2500 |
| Total | 40,000 | 5000 | 5000 |

*3.3. Standard Neural Model*

**BiLSTM:** Since the Bidirectional Long Short Term Memory models perform generally well on text classification and exploit long term dependencies in text, we use these models as baselines for evaluation as well. A one-layer BiLSTM [40] with a hidden dimension of 100 is used to obtain features for each token, which are then mean pooled, followed by a fully connected layer and softmax.

**CNN:** Convolutional Neural Networks (CNNs) [41] also perform very well on many sentence classification tasks [41]. We note that CNN was generally used in prior works for our datasets. We used hyper-parameter settings from [41] when not available in prior work.

**4. Data**

To evaluate our models, we focus our attention on datasets with different characteristics, retrieved from different social media sites and having different sizes. Our first dataset is the Sarcasm V2 Corpus (https://nlds.soe.ucsc.edu/sarcasm2, accessed on 23 March 2021), created and made available by Oraby et al. [11]. Then, given the small size of this first dataset, we test our models also on a large-scale self-annotated corpus for sarcasm, SARC (http://nlp.cs.princeton.edu/SARC/, accessed on 23 March 2021), made available by Khodak et al. [18]. Last, in order to verify the efficacy of our transfer learning model on a dataset having a similar structure to the one used by our intermediate task, we selected also a dataset from Twitter (http://www.cfilt.iitb.ac.in/cognitive-nlp/, accessed on 29 March 2021), created by Mishra et al. [7]. The datasets are discussed below.

**Sarcasm V2 Corpus.** Sarcasm V2 is a dataset released by Oraby et al. [11]. It is a highly diverse corpus of sarcasm developed using syntactical cues and crowd-sourced annotation. It contains 4692 lines having both Quote and Response sentences from dialogue examples on political debates from the Internet Argument Corpus (IAC 2.0). The data is collected and divided into three categories: General Sarcasm (Gen, 3260 sarcastic comments and 3260 non-sarcastic comments), Rhetorical Questions (RQ, 851 rhetorical questions and 851 non-rhetorical questions) and Hyperbole (Hyp, 582 hyperboles and 582 non-hyperboles). We use the Gen Corpus for our experiments and select only the text of the Response sentence for our sarcasm detection task.

**SARC.** The Self-Annotated Reddit Corpus (SARC) was introduced by Khodak et al. [18]. It contains more than a million sarcastic and non-sarcastic statements retrieved from Reddit with some contextual information, such as author details, score, and parent comment. Reddit is a social media site in which users can communicate on topic-specific discussion forums called *subreddits*, each titled by a post called *submission*. People can vote and reply to the submissions or to their comments, creating a tree-like structure. This guarantees that every comment has its "parent". The main feature of the dataset is the fact that sarcastic sentences are directly annotated by the authors themselves, through the inclusion of the marker "/s" in their comments. This method provides reliable and trustful data. Another important aspect is that almost every comment is made of one sentence.

As the SARC dataset has many variants (Main Balanced, Main Unbalanced, and Pol), in order to make our analyses more consistent with the Sarcasm V2 Corpus, we run our experiments only on the first version of the Main Balanced dataset, composed of an equal distribution of both sarcastic (505,413) and non-sarcastic (505,413) statements (total train size: 1,010,826). The authors also provide a balanced test set of 251,608 comments, which we use for model evaluation.

**SARCTwitter.** To test our models on comments with a structure more similar to the EmoNet ones, we select the benchmark dataset used by Majumder et al. [28] and created by Mishra et al. [7]. The dataset consists of 994 tweets from Twitter, manually annotated by seven readers with both sarcastic and sentiment information, i.e., each tweet has two labels, one for sentiment and one for sarcasm. Out of 994 tweets, 383 are labeled as positive (sentiment) and the remaining 611 are labeled as negative (sentiment). Additionally, out of these 994 tweets, 350 are labeled as sarcastic and the remaining 644 are labeled as non-sarcastic. The dataset contains also eye-movement of the readers that we ignored for our experiment as our focus is to detect sarcasm *solely* from the text content. We refer to this dataset as SARCTwitter.

## 5. Experiments

### 5.1. Implementation Details

To obtain a reliable and well-performing model, we studied a supervised learning approach on the three sarcasm datasets. We implement our models using the AllenNLP library [42] and HuggingFace Transformers library [36]. To perform our experiments we use the AWS Platform, EC2 instances (Ubuntu Deep Learning AMI) with one GPU on a PyTorch environment.

Each input sentence is passed through our pre-trained Base Uncased BERT. We then utilize the semantic content in the first special token [CLS] and feed it into a linear layer. We then apply softmax [43] to compute the class probability and output the label with the highest probability.

We iterate over each dataset with a mini-batch of size 16. We use AdaGrad optimizer [44] having gradient clipping threshold set to 5.0. We tune hyper-parameters on the validation set of each dataset. For every epoch we compute F1-score and Accuracy. The training is stopped (for both target task and intermediate tasks) once the average F1 on the validation set ceases to grow after some consecutive epochs (the patience is set to 5).

Table 6 shows the performance of BERT with intermediate task fine-tuning on the validation set for each task. The corresponding BERT models were transferred and further fine-tuned on the target task.

**Table 6.** Results on the Intermediate Tasks.

| Intermediate Task | Avg_F1 | Accuracy |
|---|---|---|
| EmoNet | 49.11 | 60.65 |
| EmoNetSent | 84.64 | 84.69 |
| IMDB | 93.58 | 93.58 |

### 5.2. Experiments on Sarcasm V2 Corpus

Oraby et al. [11] performed supervised learning using SVM and, as the Sarcasm V2 dataset has a small size, they executed a 10-fold cross-validation on the data to obtain the state-of-the-art metrics shown in the results section. For our approach, we randomly divided the Gen Dataset into 90% training and 10% test set. Then, we split the temporary training set into 80% training and 20% validation set. We performed this procedure five times using a different random seed each time, obtaining five sets of data. Note that, as we can see from Table 7, all subsets were maintained balanced (i.e., with the same number of sarcastic and non-sarcastic data). We ran the same model over the five created splits and computed the mean values of the metrics that we obtained through the five executions.

**Table 7.** Sarcasm V2 dataset size.

| Set | Sarcastic | Not Sarcastic | Total |
|---|---|---|---|
| Training | 2348 | 2348 | 4696 |
| Validation | 586 | 586 | 1172 |
| Test | 326 | 326 | 652 |

### 5.3. Experiments on SARC

On the SARC dataset, as Khodak et al. [18] provided also a balanced test set for the training task, we only had to create our own validation set. We first removed some noise data from our training. Specifically, about 40 empty comments were found and deleted (which is equivalent to a really small percentage of the dataset–a negligible quantity that cannot affect our models' performance). We then divided our original training set into 80% training and 20% validation. Both collections have been shuffled and maintained balanced. We performed our evaluation with the same models used in the Sarcasm V2 experiments and compared our performance with previous works. Table 8 shows the size of each of the subsets used in our experiments.

**Table 8.** SARC Main Balanced dataset size.

| Set | Sarcastic | Non-Sarcastic | Total |
|---|---|---|---|
| Original Training | 505,390 | 505,390 | 1,010,780 |
| Training | 404,312 | 404,312 | 808,624 |
| Validation | 101,078 | 101,078 | 202,156 |
| Test | 125,804 | 125,804 | 251,608 |

### 5.4. Experiments on SARCTwitter

For the SARCTwitter dataset, we used an approach similar to the Sarcasm V2 Corpus. Unlike the above two datasets, the one by Mishra et al. [7] is not balanced, i.e., there are more non-sarcastic tweets than sarcastic ones. So, we decided to randomly split the dataset five times, keeping unchanged the ratio between the sarcastic and non-sarcastic tweets (as in the original set). Similarly to Sarcasm V2, we split the initial 994 tweets into 90% training and 10% test set. Then, we split again the obtained training set into 80% training and 20% validation, keeping always unchanged the ratio between the labels (see Table 9). We experimented with this dataset using all the baselines from the previous experiments.

**Table 9.** SARCTwitter dataset size.

| Set | Sarcastic | Not Sarcastic | Total |
|---|---|---|---|
| Training | 251 | 464 | 715 |
| Validation | 63 | 115 | 178 |
| Test | 35 | 63 | 98 |

## 6. Results

In this section, we discuss prior works for each dataset and present comparison results.

### 6.1. Results on Sarcasm V2 Corpus

#### 6.1.1. Prior Works

State-of-the-art on this dataset is obtained by Oraby et al. [11]. The authors run their experiment using the following models:

- SVM-W2V: An SVM classifier with Google News Word2Vec (W2V) [45] embeddings as features to capture semantic generalizations.
- SVM-N-grams: An SVM classifier with N-grams features, including unigrams, bigrams, and trigrams, sequences of punctuation and emoticons.

We show their state-of-the-art results in terms of F1-score computed on the Sarcastic label, on the last row of Table 10. To better underline the performance of BERT, we added also our own baseline models as terms of comparison, a simple BiLSTM and a CNN encoder, both fed with pre-trained contextualized ELMo embeddings trained on the 1 Billion Word Benchmark (https://www.statmt.org/lm-benchmark/, accessed on 19 March 2021) (approximately 800M tokens of news crawl data from WMT 2011 http://www.statmt.org/wmt11/translation-task.html, accessed on 19 March 2021).

#### 6.1.2. Analysis and Discussion on Sarcasm V2

The results in Table 10 reveal that all our experiments outperform the existing state-of-the-art for the Sarcasm V2 Corpus. Our BiLSTM and CNN baselines, that obtain similar performance with each other, exceed the previous state-of-the-art by 2% and they are outperformed by our simple BERT model by 4%. These results prove the efficacy of neural models with word embeddings over feature engineering methods with SVMs. The transfer models, except for TransferEmoNet, reach similar results. The lower performance of TransferEmoNet can be explained by the scarce emotion distribution in IAC. In fact, the Sarcasm V2 comments are mainly responses to debates, in which emotions such as fear and anticipation are very rare.

**Table 10.** Results on the Sarcasm V2 dataset. Bold font shows best performance overall.

| Model | F1-Score |
|---|---|
| BERT (no intermediate pre-training) | 80.59 |
| BERT + TransferEmoNet | 78.56 |
| BERT + TransferEmoNetSent | 80.58 |
| BERT + TransferIMDB | **80.85** |
| BiLSTM (ELMo) | 76.03 |
| CNN (ELMo) | 76.46 |
| SVM with N-Grams (Oraby et al. [11]) | 72.00 |
| SVM with W2V (Oraby et al. [11]) (SOTA) | 74.00 |

In this experiment, the model pre-trained on the IMDB dataset achieves state-of-the-art performance, outperforming the vanilla BERT model by 0.3%. The increase may be explained by the fact that the features of the Sarcasm V2 comments are more similar to the ones of movie reviews rather than tweets. That is, they are much longer in length than the tweets' lengths and this difference in lengths brings additional challenges to the models. The expressions of sentiment/emotions in EmoNet, i.e., lexical cues, are more obvious in EmoNet compared with IMDB. Thus, the model struggles more on the IMDB dataset, and hence, is able to learn better and more robust parameters since these examples are more challenging to the model, and therefore, more beneficial for learning. This also explains the lack of improvement for the TransferEmoNetSent model. However, the outcomes of this experiment underline that there is correlation between sarcasm and sentiment. BERT is able to outperform previous approaches on this dataset and acts as a strong baseline. Using BERT with intermediate task transfer learning can push the performance further.

### 6.2. Results on SARC

#### 6.2.1. Prior Works

We compared our best models with state-of-the-art networks and baselines examined by Hazarika et al. [27] on the Main Balanced version of SARC:

- Bag-of-words: A model that uses an SVM having a comment's word counts as features.
- CNN: A simple CNN that can only model the content of a comment.
- CNN-SVM: A model developed by Poria et al. [25] that exploits a CNN to model the content of the comments and other pre-trained CNNs to extract sentiment, emotion, and personality features from them. All these features are concatenated and passed to an SVM to perform classification.
- CUE-CNN: A method proposed by Amir et al. [13] that also models user embeddings combined with a CNN thus forming the CUE-CNN model.
- Bag-of-Bigrams: A previous state-of-the-art model for this dataset, by Khodak et al. [18], that uses the count of bigrams in a document as vector features.
- CASCADE (ContextuAl SarCAsm DEtector): A method proposed by Hazarika et al. [27] that uses user embeddings to model user personality and stylometric features, and combines them with a CNN to extract content features. We show the results from both versions, with and without personality features, in order to emphasize the efficacy of our model even in the absence of user personality feature.

#### 6.2.2. Analysis and Discussion on SARC

Table 11 shows the results of our models and of the described prior works in terms of F1-score. The table has been divided into two sections: the first section contains all the experiments that have been run on the sentences themselves without the use of any additional information, while the second part contains the performance of models that exploit personality features from the authors of the comments. Since all our models, including our BiLSTM baseline, do not use author information, they appear in the first section of the table.

We can notice that in the first section of the table, all our models outperform all the other prior works by at least 10% confirming the efficacy of capturing semantics through the pre-trained language models for the sarcasm prediction task. In addition, our simplest model trained with BERT Base outperforms all the previous works, including the previous state-of-the-art CASCADE, that makes use of personality features. Similar to the Sarcasm V2 experiments, here the transfer-learning improves the performance of BERT base model only slightly.

**Table 11.** Results on the SARC dataset. Bold font shows best performance overall.

| Models | F1-Score |
|---|---|
| No personality features | |
| BERT (no intermediate pre-training) | 77.49 |
| BERT + TransferEmoNet | 77.22 |
| BERT + TransferEmoNetSent | **77.53** |
| BERT + TransferIMDB | 77.48 |
| BiLSTM (ELMo) | 76.27 |
| Bag-of-words (Hazarika et al. [27]) | 64.00 |
| CNN (Hazarika et al. [27]) | 66.00 |
| CASCADE (Hazarika et al. [27]) (no personality features) | 66.00 |
| With personality features | |
| CNN-SVM (Poria et al. [25]) | 68.00 |
| CUE-CNN (Amir et al. [13]) | 69.00 |
| CASCADE (Hazarika et al. [27]) (with personality features) (SOTA) | 77.00 |

This behavior can be explained by the fact that comments from discussion forums, such as Reddit, are quite different in terms of content, expressiveness, and topic from the other social platforms of our intermediate tasks. For example, SARC comments' lengths can vary from 3/4 words to hundreds, while the IMDB movie reviews are generally much longer, composed of multiple sentences, whereas EmoNet tweets usually consist of just one or two sentences. In addition, on EmoNet the sentiment pattern is more pronounced as people are more prone to describe their emotional state on Twitter. In SARC, probably also because of the topics covered (e.g., politics, videogames), the emotion pattern is more implicit and harder to detect. In the movie reviews, on the other hand, the sentiment is quite explicit but the length of the sentences may cause a loss of information for the classifier and the sarcastic content is almost nonexistent. However, the sentiment information from EmoNet slightly improved the efficacy of the simple BERT classification, making our TransferEmoNetSent model the new state-of-the-art performance on the SARC dataset.

These results support the pattern discovered on the Sarcasm V2 dataset, highlighting BERT as the best-performing model and underlining the importance of sentiment in sarcasm classification. This statement will be confirmed by our last experiment.

### 6.3. Results on SARCTwitter

#### 6.3.1. Prior Works

We compared the BERT models with previous works provided by Mishra et al. [29]:

- CNN only text: A CNN-based framework that classifies tweets using only the information provided in their text.
- CNN gaze + text: An advanced framework developed by Mishra et al. [29] that adds cognitive features obtained from the eye-movement/gaze data of human readers to the previous CNN-based classifier in order to detect the sarcastic content of the tweets.
- GRU+MTL: The current state-of-the-art method by Majumder et al. [28] that uses multitask learning with sarcasm detection as the main task and sentiment classification as an auxiliary task. They used a GRU-based neural network with an attention mechanism.

#### 6.3.2. Analysis and Discussion on SARCTwitter

From Table 12, we can see that all our models outperform the previous state-of-the-art by at least 5%. The table underlines how our models are able to accurately detect sarcasm and proves the strength of large pre-trained language models for this task. In particular, even from this experiment, BERT is shown to be the most suitable model for sarcasm detection, outperforming the BiLSTM model by more than 1%.

**Table 12.** Results on SARCTwitter dataset. Bold font shows best performance overall.

| Model | F1-Score |
|---|---|
| BERT (no intermediate pre-training) | 96.34 |
| BERT + TransferEmoNet | 96.71 |
| BERT + TransferEmoNetSent | **97.43** |
| BERT + TransferIMDB | 95.96 |
| BiLSTM (ELMo) | 95.10 |
| CNN only text (Mishra et al. [29]) | 85.63 |
| CNN gaze + text (Mishra et al. [29]) | 86.97 |
| GRU+MTL (Majumder et al. [28]) (SOTA) | 90.67 |

Furthermore, unlike the previous experiments, where the addition of an intermediate task caused only slight improvements (no more than 0.3%) over the vanilla BERT model, here, the transfer learning models, especially on EmoNetSent, show improvement (~1% for EmoNetSent) over vanilla BERT. Indeed, the performance of vanilla BERT is close to that of BERT with intermediate task transfer learning on Sarcasm V2 and SARC, but we can see a larger improvement in performance between these two models on the SARCTwitter dataset (see Table 12). A potential reason for this is the size of these datasets. Both Sarcasm V2 and SARC are larger in size compared with SARCTwitter (e.g., SARC has 1M examples in the training set and the models are already well trained on this dataset and able to learn robust model parameters). The main purpose of intermediate task transfer learning is to use data-rich sources of relevant information (e.g., sentiment) when the dataset for the target task (i.e., sarcasm in our case) is small in size. Our results validate the fact that when the dataset size is small (e.g., as is the case with the SARCTwitter dataset) using BERT with intermediate task transfer learning achieves a substantially better performance compared with vanilla BERT. Interestingly, although the improvement of intermediate task transfer learning is very small on the SARC dataset, given the considerable size of SARC (i.e., 1M examples), in this SARC dataset even a small increase may be considered relevant.

Another potential reason for the increased performance of BERT with intermediate task transfer learning over vanilla BERT on SARCTwitter is that the EmoNet intermediate models are trained from the same social media domain and are rich in polarized emotions (positive/negative) that are useful for the detection of sarcasm. In fact, as this dataset structure is similar to the EmoNet one (i.e., short sentences from Twitter), both the emotion and sentiment information help improve the performance of the sarcasm classification task. On this dataset, our TransferEmoNetSent model reaches state-of-the-art performance, outperforming the previous state-of-the-art by almost 7% and boosting the simple BERT model's efficacy by more than 1%. In contrast, BERT + TransferIMDB performs worse than the vanilla BERT. We believe that this happens because of the domain (platform) mismatch (e.g., short text vs. longer text, more implicit vs. more explicit mentions of sarcasm or sentiment/polarized emotions).

These results confirm the pattern of the previous experiments, proving the correlation between sarcasm and sentiment, and also show that polarized emotional information can help the primary/target task with transfer from datasets where the emotional charge is more explicit, such as EmoNet which is annotated using distant supervision using lexical surface patterns [38].

## 7. Conclusions and Future Work

Sarcasm is a complex phenomenon which is often hard to understand, even for humans. In our work, we showed the effectiveness of using large pre-trained BERT language models to predict it accurately. We demonstrated how sarcastic statements themselves can be recognized automatically with a good performance without even having to further use contextual information, such as users' historical comments or parent comments. We also explored a transfer learning framework to exploit the correlation between sarcasm and the sentiment or emotions conveyed in the text, and found that an intermediate task training on a correlated task can improve the effectiveness of the base BERT models, with sentiment having a higher impact than emotions on the performance, especially on sarcasm detection datasets that are small in size. We thus established new state-of-the-art results on three datasets for sarcasm detection. Specifically, the improvement in performance of BERT-based models (with and without intermediate task transfer learning) compared with previous works on sarcasm detection is significant and is as high as 11.53%. We found that the BERT models that use only the message content perform better than models that leverage additional information from a writer's history encoded as personality features in prior work. We found this result to be remarkable. Moreover, if the dataset size for the target task—sarcasm detection—is small then intermediate task transfer learning (with sentiment as the intermediate task) can improve the performance further.

We believe that our models can be used as strong baselines for new research on this task and we expect that enhancing the models with contextual data, such as user embeddings, in future work, new state-of-the-art performance can be reached. Integrating multiple intermediate tasks at the same time could potentially improve the performance further, although caution should be taken to avoid the loss of knowledge from the general domain while learning from the intermediate tasks. We make our code available to further research in this area.

**Author Contributions:** All authors E.S. and C.C. contributed ideas and the overall conceptualization of the project. E.S. wrote the code/implementation of the project and provided an initial draft of the paper. All authors E.S. and C.C. worked on the writing and polishing of the paper and addressed reviewers' comments. All authors have read and agreed to the published version of the manuscript.

**Funding:** This research was funded by the National Science Foundation (NSF) and Amazon Web Services under grant number NSF-IIS: BIGDATA #1741353. Any opinions, findings, and conclusions expressed here are those of the authors and do not necessarily reflect the views of NSF.

**Institutional Review Board Statement:** Not applicable.

**Informed Consent Statement:** Not applicable.

**Data Availability Statement:** The dataset used in our experiments are available online at the following links: the Sarcasm V2 Corpus at https://nlds.soe.ucsc.edu/sarcasm2 (accessed on 23 March 2021), SARC at http://nlp.cs.princeton.edu/SARC/ (accessed on 23 March 2021), and SARCTwitter at http://www.cfilt.iitb.ac.in/cognitive-nlp/ (accessed on 29 March 2021).

**Acknowledgments:** We thank our anonymous reviewers for their constructive comments and feedback, which helped improve our paper. This research is supported in part by the National Science Foundation and Amazon Web Services (for computing resources).

**Conflicts of Interest:** The authors declare no conflict of interest.

## References

1. Maynard, D.; Greenwood, M. Who cares about Sarcastic Tweets? Investigating the Impact of Sarcasm on Sentiment Analysis. In Proceedings of the Ninth International Conference on Language Resources and Evaluation (LREC'14), Reykjavik, Iceland, 26–31 May 2014; pp. 4238–4243.
2. Sykora, M.; Elayan, S.; Jackson, T.W. A qualitative analysis of sarcasm, irony and related #hashtags on Twitter. *Big Data Soc.* **2020**, 7. [CrossRef]
3. Joshi, A.; Sharma, V.; Bhattacharyya, P. Harnessing context incongruity for sarcasm detection. In Proceedings of the 53rd Annual Meeting of the Association for Computational Linguistics and the 7th International Joint Conference on Natural Language Processing (Short Papers), Beijing, China, 26–31 July 2015; Volume 2.
4. Wallace, B.C.; Choe, D.K.; Kertz, L.; Charniak, E. Humans Require Context to Infer Ironic Intent (so Computers Probably do, too). In Proceedings of the 52nd Annual Meeting of the Association for Computational Linguistics (Short Papers), Baltimore, MD, USA, 22–27 June 2014; Volume 2, pp. 512–516. [CrossRef]

5.   Oraby, S.; El-Sonbaty, Y.; Abou El-Nasr, M. Exploring the Effects of Word Roots for Arabic Sentiment Analysis. In Proceedings of the Sixth International Joint Conference on Natural Language Processing, Nagoya, Japan, 14–19 October 2013; pp. 471–479.

6.   Riloff, E.; Qadir, A.; Surve, P.; De Silva, L.; Gilbert, N.; Huang, R. Sarcasm as Contrast between a Positive Sentiment and Negative Situation. In Proceedings of the 2013 Conference on Empirical Methods in Natural Language Processing, Seattle, WA, USA, 18–21 October 2013; pp. 704–714.

7.   Mishra, A.; Kanojia, D.; Bhattacharyya, P. Predicting readers' sarcasm understandability by modeling gaze behavior. In Proceedings of the AAAI Conference on Artificial Intelligence, Phoenix, AZ, USA, 12–16 February 2016.

8.   Khodak, M.; Risteski, A.; Fellbaum, C.; Arora, S. Automated WordNet Construction Using Word Embeddings. In Proceedings of the 1st Workshop on Sense, Concept and Entity Representations and Their Applications, Valencia, Spain, 4 April 2017; pp. 12–23. [CrossRef]

9.   Oprea, S.V.; Magdy, W. iSarcasm: A Dataset of Intended Sarcasm. In Proceedings of the 58th Annual Meeting of the Association for Computational Linguistics, Online, 5–10 July 2020; pp. 1279–1289. Available online: https://aclanthology.org/2020.acl-main.118/ (accessed on 12 February 2021).

10.  Chauhan, D.S.; Dhanush, S.R.; Ekbal, A.; Bhattacharyya, P. Sentiment and Emotion help Sarcasm? A Multi-task Learning Framework for Multi-Modal Sarcasm, Sentiment and Emotion Analysis. In Proceedings of the 58th Annual Meeting of the Association for Computational Linguistics, Online, 5–10 July 2020; pp. 4351–4360. [CrossRef]

11.  Oraby, S.; Harrison, V.; Reed, L.; Hernandez, E.; Riloff, E.; Walker, M. Creating and Characterizing a Diverse Corpus of Sarcasm in Dialogue. In Proceedings of the 17th Annual Meeting of the Special Interest Group on Discourse and Dialogue, Los Angeles, CA, USA, 13–15 September 2016; pp. 31–41.

12.  Liebrecht, C.; Kunneman, F.; van den Bosch, A. The perfect solution for detecting sarcasm in tweets #not. In Proceedings of the 4th Workshop on Computational Approaches to Subjectivity, Sentiment and Social Media Analysis, Atlanta, GA, USA, 14 June 2013; pp. 29–37.

13.  Amir, S.; Wallace, B.C.; Lyu, H.; Silva, P.C.M.J. Modelling context with user embeddings for sarcasm detection in social media. *arXiv* **2016**, arXiv:1607.00976.

14.  Ghosh, A.; Veale, T. Fracking sarcasm using neural network. In Proceddings of the Workshop on Computational Approaches to Subjectivity, Sentiment and Social Media Analysis, San Diego, CA, USA, 16 June 2016 .

15.  Joshi, A.; Tripathi, V.; Patel, K.; Bhattacharyya, P.; Carman, M. Are word embedding-based features useful for sarcasm detection? *arXiv* **2016**, arXiv:1610.00883.

16.  Devlin, J.; Chang, M.W.; Lee, K.; Toutanova, K. Bert: Pre-training of deep bidirectional transformers for language understanding. *arXiv* **2018**, arXiv:1810.04805.

17.  Pruksachatkun, Y.; Phang, J.; Liu, H.; Htut, P.M.; Zhang, X.; Pang, R.Y.; Vania, C.; Kann, K.; Bowman, S.R. Intermediate-Task Transfer Learning with Pretrained Models for Natural Language Understanding: When and Why Does It Work? *arXiv* **2020**, arXiv:2005.00628.

18.  Khodak, M.; Saunshi, N.; Vodrahalli, K. A Large Self-Annotated Corpus for Sarcasm. In Proceedings of the Eleventh International Conference on Language Resources and Evaluation (LREC 2018 ), Miyazaki, Japan, 7–12 May 2018.

19.  Kreuz, R.J.; Caucci, G.M. Lexical influences on the perception of sarcasm. In Proceedings of the Workshop on computational approaches to Figurative Language, Rochester, NY, USA, 26 April 2007; pp. 1–4.

20.  Carvalho, P.; Sarmento, L.; Silva, M.J.; De Oliveira, E. Clues for detecting irony in user-generated contents: Oh...!! it's so easy;-). In Proceedings of the 1st International CIKM Workshop on Topic-Sentiment Analysis for Mass Opinion, Hong Kong, China, 6 November 2009; pp. 53–56.

21.  Tsur, O.; Davidov, D.; Rappoport, A. ICWSM—A great catchy name: Semi-supervised recognition of sarcastic sentences in online product reviews. In Proceedings of the Fourth International AAAI Conference on Weblogs and Social Media, Washington, DC, USA, 23–26 May 2010.

22.  Davidov, D.; Tsur, O.; Rappoport, A. Semi-supervised recognition of sarcastic sentences in twitter and amazon. In Proceedings of the Fourteenth Conference on Computational Natural Language Learning, Uppsala, Sweden, 15–16 July 2010; pp. 107–116.

23.  Rajadesingan, A.; Zafarani, R.; Liu, H. Sarcasm detection on twitter: A behavioral modeling approach. In Proceedings of the Eighth ACM International Conference on Web Search and Data Mining, Shanghai, China, 2–6 February 2015; pp. 97–106.

24.  Bamman, D.; Smith, N.A. Contextualized sarcasm detection on twitter. In Proceedings of the Ninth International AAAI Conference on Web and Social Media, Oxford, UK, 26–29 May 2015.

25.  Poria, S.; Cambria, E.; Hazarika, D.; Vij, P. A deeper look into sarcastic tweets using deep convolutional neural networks. *arXiv* **2016**, arXiv:1610.08815.

26.  Zhang, M.; Zhang, Y.; Fu, G. Tweet sarcasm detection using deep neural network. In Proceedings of the COLING 2016, The 26th International Conference on Computational Linguistics, Osaka, Japan, 11–16 December 2016; pp. 2449–2460.

27.  Hazarika, D.; Poria, S.; Gorantla, S.; Cambria, E.; Zimmermann, R.; Mihalcea, R. CASCADE: Contextual Sarcasm Detection in Online Discussion Forums. In Proceedings of the 27th International Conference on Computational Linguistics, Santa Fe, NM, USA, 20–26 August 2018; pp. 1837–1848.

28.  Majumder, N.; Poria, S.; Peng, H.; Chhaya, N.; Cambria, E.; Gelbukh, A.F. Sentiment and Sarcasm Classification with Multitask Learning. *arXiv* **2019**, arXiv:1901.08014.

29. Mishra, A.; Dey, K.; Bhattacharyya, P. Learning cognitive features from gaze data for sentiment and sarcasm classification using convolutional neural network. In Proceedings of the 55th Annual Meeting of the Association for Computational Linguistics, Vancouver, BC, Canada, 30 July 2017–4 August 2017; pp. 377–387.

30. Plepi, J.; Flek, L. Perceived and Intended Sarcasm Detection with Graph Attention Networks. In *Findings of the Association for Computational Linguistics: EMNLP 2021*; Association for Computational Linguistics: Punta Cana, Dominican Republic, 2021; pp. 4746–4753. [CrossRef]

31. Cai, Y.; Cai, H.; Wan, X. Multi-Modal Sarcasm Detection in Twitter with Hierarchical Fusion Model. In Proceedings of the 57th Annual Meeting of the Association for Computational Linguistics, Florence, Italy, 28 July 2019–2 August 2019; pp. 2506–2515. [CrossRef]

32. Li, L.; Levi, O.; Hosseini, P.; Broniatowski, D. A Multi-Modal Method for Satire Detection using Textual and Visual Cues. In Proceedings of the 3rd NLP4IF Workshop on NLP for Internet Freedom: Censorship, Disinformation, and Propaganda, Barcelona, Spain, 20 December 2020; pp. 33–38.

33. Wang, X.; Sun, X.; Yang, T.; Wang, H. Building a Bridge: A Method for Image-Text Sarcasm Detection Without Pretraining on Image-Text Data. In Proceedings of the First International Workshop on Natural Language Processing Beyond Text, Online, 20 November 2020; pp. 19–29. [CrossRef]

34. He, K.; Zhang, X.; Ren, S.; Sun, J. Deep Residual Learning for Image Recognition. In Proceedings of the 2016 IEEE Conference on Computer Vision and Pattern Recognition (CVPR), Las Vegas, NV, USA, 27–30 June 2016; pp. 770–778. [CrossRef]

35. Lu, J.; Batra, D.; Parikh, D.; Lee, S. ViLBERT: Pretraining Task-Agnostic Visiolinguistic Representations for Vision-and-Language Tasks. In *Advances in Neural Information Processing Systems*; Wallach, H., Larochelle, H., Beygelzimer, A., d'Alché-Buc, F., Fox, E., Garnett, R., Eds.; Curran Associates, Inc.: Red Hook, NY, USA, 2019; Volume 32.

36. Wolf, T.; Debut, L.; Sanh, V.; Chaumond, J.; Delangue, C.; Moi, A.; Cistac, P.; Rault, T.; Louf, R.; Funtowicz, M.; et al. HuggingFace's Transformers: State-of-the-art Natural Language Processing. *arXiv* **2019**, arXiv:1910.03771.

37. Phang, J.; Févry, T.; Bowman, S.R. Sentence Encoders on STILTs: Supplementary Training on Intermediate Labeled-data Tasks. *arXiv* **2018**, arXiv:1811.01088.

38. Abdul-Mageed, M.; Ungar, L. EmoNet: Fine-Grained Emotion Detection with Gated Recurrent Neural Networks. In Proceedings of the 55th Annual Meeting of the Association for Computational Linguistics (Long Papers), Vancouver, BC, Canada, 30 July 2017–4 August 2017; Volume 1, pp. 718–728. [CrossRef]

39. Maas, A.L.; Daly, R.E.; Pham, P.T.; Huang, D.; Ng, A.Y.; Potts, C. Learning Word Vectors for Sentiment Analysis. In Proceedings of the 49th Annual Meeting of the Association for Computational Linguistics: Human Language Technologies, Portland, OR, USA, 19–24 June 2011; pp. 142–150.

40. Hochreiter, S.; Schmidhuber, J. Long short-term memory. *Neural Comput.* **1997**, *9*, 1735–1780. [CrossRef] [PubMed]

41. Kim, Y. Convolutional Neural Networks for Sentence Classification. In Proceedings of the 2014 Conference on Empirical Methods in Natural Language Processing (EMNLP), Doha, Qatar, 25–29 October 2014; pp. 1746–1751. [CrossRef]

42. Gardner, M.; Grus, J.; Neumann, M.; Tafjord, O.; Dasigi, P.; Liu, N.; Peters, M.; Schmitz, M.; Zettlemoyer, L. Allennlp: A deep semantic natural language processing platform. *arXiv* **2018**, arXiv:1803.07640

43. Bridle, J.S. Probabilistic interpretation of feedforward classification network outputs, with relationships to statistical pattern recognition. In *Neurocomputing*; Springer: Berlin/Heidelberg, Germany, 1990; pp. 227–236.

44. Duchi, J.; Hazan, E.; Singer, Y. Adaptive subgradient methods for online learning and stochastic optimization. *J. Mach. Learn. Res.* **2011**, *12*, 2121–2159.

45. Mikolov, T.; Chen, K.; Corrado, G.S.; Dean, J. Efficient Estimation of Word Representations in Vector Space. In Proceedings of the 1st International Conference on Learning Representations, ICLR 2013, Scottsdale, AZ, USA, 2–4 May 2013; Workshop Track Proceedings.

*Article*

# Parallel Stylometric Document Embeddings with Deep Learning Based Language Models in Literary Authorship Attribution

**Mihailo Škorić [1,\*], Ranka Stanković [1], Milica Ikonić Nešić [2], Joanna Byszuk [3] and Maciej Eder [3]**

[1] Faculty of Mining and Geology, University of Belgrade, Djusina 7, 11120 Belgrade, Serbia; ranka.stankovic@rgf.bg.ac.rs

[2] Faculty of Philology, University of Belgrade, Studentski Trg 3, 11000 Belgrade, Serbia; milica.ikonic.nesic@fil.bg.ac.rs

[3] Institute of Polish Language, Polish Academy of Sciences, al. Mickiewicza 31, 31-120 Kraków, Poland; joanna.byszuk@ijp.pan.pl (J.B.); maciej.eder@ijp.pan.pl (M.E.)

\* Correspondence: mihailo.skoric@rgf.bg.ac.rs

**Citation:** Škorić, M.; Stanković, R.; Ikonić Nešić, M.; Byszuk, J.; Eder, M. Parallel Stylometric Document Embeddings with Deep Learning Based Language Models in Literary Authorship Attribution. *Mathematics* 2022, 10, 838. https://doi.org/10.3390/math10050838

Academic Editors: Florentina Hristea and Cornelia Caragea

Received: 30 January 2022
Accepted: 28 February 2022
Published: 7 March 2022

**Abstract:** This paper explores the effectiveness of parallel stylometric document embeddings in solving the authorship attribution task by testing a novel approach on literary texts in 7 different languages, totaling in 7051 unique 10,000-token chunks from 700 PoS and lemma annotated documents. We used these documents to produce four document embedding models using Stylo R package (word-based, lemma-based, PoS-trigrams-based, and PoS-mask-based) and one document embedding model using mBERT for each of the seven languages. We created further derivations of these embeddings in the form of average, product, minimum, maximum, and $l^2$ norm of these document embedding matrices and tested them both including and excluding the mBERT-based document embeddings for each language. Finally, we trained several perceptrons on the portions of the dataset in order to procure adequate weights for a weighted combination approach. We tested standalone (two baselines) and composite embeddings for classification accuracy, precision, recall, weighted-average, and macro-averaged $F_1$-score, compared them with one another and have found that for each language most of our composition methods outperform the baselines (with a couple of methods outperforming all baselines for all languages), with or without mBERT inputs, which are found to have no significant positive impact on the results of our methods.

**Keywords:** document embeddings; authorship attribution; language modelling; parallel architectures; stylometry; language processing pipelines

**MSC:** 68T50

## 1. Introduction

Distant reading is a paradigm that involves the use of computational methods to analyze large collections of literary texts, aiming to complement the methods primarily used in the studies of theory and history of literature. The term was first mentioned by Moretti [1], when he proposed the use of quantitative text analysis methods in literary studies, pointing to their usefulness in the exploration of big text collections "at a distance" or looking at particular features within the texts. He argued this would help in the discovery of new information and patterns in corpora more objectively and enable scholars to learn more about the texts even without reading them in detail. The methodological novelty of his proposal lies in the use of text samples, statistics, metadata paratexts, and other features that were not commonly used in the study of literature until then.

Authorship analysis is a natural language processing (NLP) task that studies the characteristics of a text to extract information about its author. It is divided into three sub-tasks: author profiling, authorship verification, and authorship attribution. Author profiling is used to detect sociolinguistic attributes (e.g., gender or age), authorship verification is used to determine whether a certain person could have authored a given text, and authorship attribution assigns the text to the most likely author from a closed set of potential writers [2]. Authorship attribution (AA) is sometimes further divided into closed-set attribution, where the list of suspects necessarily includes the true author and open-set attribution, where the true author is not guaranteed to be represented in the list of suspects. AA methods are used in computational literary studies, resolving historical questions of unclear or disputed authorship [3], plagiarism detection (e.g., essays, research papers, and PhD thesis [4]), forensic investigations [5], and cyber-security (e.g., for author detection in case of threatening or harassing e-mails that were sent anonymously or under a pseudonym and social media analysis [6]).

Early methods drew primarily from linguistics and mathematics, with the earliest studies dating back to the 19th century and manual calculations of word frequencies, with one of the earliest works of the AA including successful authorship identification of particular works of Shakespeare [7] and of articles from the famous Federalist Papers set [8]. The field, however, started to develop rapidly with the introduction of computers and modern algorithms of machine learning. Up to date, the most extensive overview of the methods and their applications to specific problems is Stamatatos's 2009 survey [9] and the comparison of methods provided by Jockers and Witten [10].

As examples of quantitative text analysis, methods of AA are naturally in line with the distant reading paradigm. While contemporary research varies in the type of features and algorithms, all have roots in observation that grammatical words are strong predictors of style and author [8] especially those occupying the top of the frequency list (following Zipf's law). Another method that revolutionized the field was Burrows's Delta [11] (later perfected by Evert et al. [12,13]), which allowed for calculating differences between profiles of feature frequencies in a more balanced way than the one provided by Euclidean distances.

### 1.1. Stylometry

Both distant reading and AA belong to a broader theoretical framework of stylometry. Specifically, stylometry is a method of statistical analysis of texts, and it is applied, among other things, to distinguish between authorial literary styles. For each individual author, there is an assumption that he/she exhibits a distinct style of writing [14]. This fundamental notion makes it possible to use stylometric methodology to differentiate between documents written by different authors and solve the AA task [15].

Performance of particular stylometric methods strongly depends on the choice of language features as the relevant style-markers. The determination of which features are the best to use for particular tasks and how they should be ordered has been a subject of many debates over the years. The earliest approaches relied solely on words, and examined differences in their use for particular authors [7], or general differences using lists of most frequent words (MFW) [11]. Further studies experimented with various types of features, with discussions on whether words should be lemmatized [14,16,17].

Evert et al. [13] discussed AA based on distance measures, different performance of diverse distance measures, and normalization strategies, as well as specificity for language families. Instead of relying on a specified number of MFW, they identified a set of discriminant words by using the method of recursive feature elimination. By repeatedly training a support vector classifier and pruning the least important ones, they obtained a minimal set of features for optimal performance. The resulting set contained function words and not so common content words. Eder and Byszuk [18] also experimented with changing the order of MFW on the list of used features and its influence on the accuracy of classification, confirming that the most discriminative features do not necessarily overlap with the MFW. Among the non-word approaches, most attempts were made using chunks of subsequent letters (so called character n-grams) [19], or grammatical features.

Weerasinghe and Greenstadt [20] used the following textual features: character n-grams: (TF-IDF values for character n-grams, where $1 \leq n \leq 6$), PoS tag n-grams (TF-IDF value of PoS tag trigrams), special characters (TF-IDF values for 31 pre-defined special characters), frequencies of function words (179 NLTK stopwords), number of characters and tokens in the document, average number of characters per word, per document, distribution of word-lengths (1–10), vocabulary richness, PoS tag chunks, and noun and verb phrase construction. For each document pair, they extracted stylometric features from the documents and used the absolute difference between the feature vectors as input to the classifier. They built a logistic regression model trained on a small dataset, and a neural network based model trained on the large dataset.

One of the most interesting and recent proposals was made by Camps et al. [3], who attempted stylometric analysis of medieval vernacular texts, noting that the scribal variation and errors introduced over the centuries complicate the investigations. To counter this textual variance, they developed a workflow combining handwritten text recognition and stylometric analysis performed using a variety of lexical and grammatical features to the study of a corpus of hagiographic works, examining potential authorial groupings in a vastly anonymous corpus.

Despite the overall good performance of these various approaches, MFW still proved to be most effective in discrimination between authors. Popular tools for conducting stylometric analyses like Stylo R package [21] are still suggesting the use of word tokens, or word or character n-grams, while also supporting further deviations from classic MFW.

Apart from the above shallow text representations, often referred to as a bag-of-words models, recent studies in AA are also exploring context-aware representations, or features that take into account contextual information, usually extracted using neural networks.

Kocher and Savoy [22] proposed two new AA classifiers using distributed language representation, where the nearby context of each word in a document was used to create a vector-space representation for either authors or texts, and cosine similarities between these representations were used for authorship-based classification. The evaluations using the k-nearest neighbors (k-NNs) on four test collections indicated good performance of that method, which in some cases outperformed even the state-of-the-art methods. Salami and Momtazi [23] proposed a poetry AA model based on recurrent convolutions neural networks, which captured temporal and spatial features using either a poem or a single verse as an input. This model was shown to significantly outperform other state-of-the-art models.

Segarra et al. [24] used the normalized word adjacency networks as relational structures data between function words as stylometric information for AA. These networks express grammatical relationships between words but do not carry lexical meaning on their own. For long profiles with more than 60,000 words, they achieve high attribution accuracy even when distinguishing between a large number of authors, and also achieve reasonable rates for short texts (i.e., newspaper articles), if the number of possible authors is small. Similarly, Marinho et al. [25] presented another study that focuses on solving the AA task using complex networks, but by focusing on network subgraphs (motifs) as features to identify different authors.

Finally, state-of-the-art stylometry is also exploring a combination of several representations. Such a setup is usually referred to as parallel architecture. Arguably, the use of a heterogeneous classifier that combines independent classifiers with different approaches usually outperforms the ones obtained using a single classifier [26,27]. Segarra et al. [24] also showed that word adjacency networks and frequencies capture different stylometric aspects and that their combination can halve the error rate of existing methods.

### 1.2. Multilingual BERT in Authorship Attribution

Multilingual BERT (mBERT) is a 12 layer transformer (768 hidden units, 12 heads, and 110 million parameters), trained on the Wikipedia pages of 104 languages with a shared word piece vocabulary [28]. While corpora used varied in size between languages, up-sampling of words from low resource languages and down-sampling words from high resource languages was performed during the pre-training in order to equalize their representations, so no difference in results for different languages should be apparent when using the model.

Though it was shown that the information captured by this model can be used for various NLP tasks [29], few attempts were made to use it to tackle the problem of AA. Fabien et al. [30] present an approach based on the fine-tuning of this model for author classification. They evaluate the impact of adding stylometric and hybrid features in an ensemble approach and find improvement over state-of-the-art approaches on standardized tests. Iyer [29] focuses on training a random forest classifier on top of mBERT outputs to try and detect changes in style, without the additional fine-tuning of the model, and achieves good results on a short text AA task. These experiments were our motivation to use this model to create document embeddings for our research and combine them with other stylometric-based document embeddings in pursue of better results.

### 1.3. Research Questions, Aims, Means, and Novelty

Authorship attribution (as well as authorship verification) inevitably involves pairwise comparison of documents written by different authors, in order to determine the degree of similarity between them. A convenient way of presenting the final similarities is a symmetric matrix usually referred to as a distance matrix or a document embedding matrix. In the present study, document embedding matrices for each feature type and across each language collection will be used to perform classification benchmarks. Furthermore, our parallel architectures approach will rely on these embedding matrices, as they will be combined using different averaging strategies. This paper is focused on four research questions revolving around the efficiency of particular document embedding methods in solving the authorship attribution task:

RQ1 There is no single best document representation method suitable for the AA task across European languages;

RQ2 Several document embeddings can be combined in order to produce improved results for the said task;

RQ3 Adding weights to the inputs in a parallel architecture can induce further improvements of the results;

RQ4 Including deep learning-based transformations of the document in a parallel architecture can improve the results of the said architecture.

The general workflow used in this study involves the following steps:

1. Producing document embedding matrices for each standalone document representation and testing them against each other in AA for seven European languages. These representations include: the original document, a lemmatized document, a document where all tokens are substituted by their Universal PoS tags, and finally a document in which the words with most frequent PoS tags are masked by their respective tags;

2. Combining the standalone results document embedding matrices—on a matrix level into new composition-based embeddings, using five different methods, and testing them against one another in the same aforementioned test;

3. Creating perceptrons that use the said embeddings as inputs and training them for authorship verification on a chunk of our dataset in order to procure suitable weights for each representation in a composite architecture. The results are to be a set of weights for each language, and a set of weights trained without each language in order to avoid bias;

4. Test the acquired weights for mutual euclidean distances to find suitable language pairs and use transfer learning to generate and test weight-based embeddings for each of the seven languages;

5. Test the mBERT based-document embeddings as a standalone and include them in our new, composition-based embeddings using the aforementioned techniques. Compare the results of the embedding methods both with and without mBERT usage.

The main contributions of this paper are:

1. The introduction of new datasets. Four different document representations of 7051 10,000-token chunks from 700 novels written in 7 languages, as well as more then 130 different document embeddings of these chunks, which will be available as material for further research;

2. A novel approach to solve the AA task, combining document representations on embeddings level after the distance calculation for standalone methods, rather than the usual inline combination of features before distance calculation;

3. An architecture for training the weights for each document embeddings using a single perceptron with several document distances as inputs and a single distance as output;

4. Trained weights of different document representations for seven different languages as well as weights trained in a multilingual setting;

5. Evaluation of the proposed standalone and combination methods.

The second section of this paper will present the text collection that was used for this research and the main dataset preparation. The third section is related to the research workflow and describes the creation of all necessary document embeddings. The fourth section will describe the evaluation process and present the quantitative and qualitative results obtained, followed by the Discussion and Concluding remarks, together with plans for future research.

## 2. Dataset

The COST Action "Distant Reading for European Literary History" (https://www. distant-reading.net, accessed on 29 January 2022) coordinates the creation of a multilingual European Literary Text Collection (ELTeC) [31]. This resource will be used to establish best practices and develop innovative methods of Distant Reading for the multiple European literary traditions. Its core will contain at least 10 linguistically annotated 100 novels sub-collections comparable in their internal structure in at least 10 different European languages, totaling at least 1000 annotated full-text novels. The extended ELTeC will take the total number of full-text novels to at least 2500.

In order to create representative sub-collections for the corresponding languages, the novels were selected to evenly represent (1) novels of various sizes: short (10–50,000 words), medium (50–100,000 words), and long (more than 100,000 words); (2) four 20-year time periods T1 [1840–1859], T2 [1860–1879], T3 [1880–1899], T4 [1900–1920]; (3) the number of reprints, as a measure of canonicity (novels known to wider audience and completely forgotten), and (4) female and male authors [32].

This multiple encoding levels are provided in the ELTeC scheme: at level–0, only the bare minimum of markup is permitted, while at level–1 a slightly richer encoding is defined. At level–2, additional information is introduced to support various linguistic processing, with mandatory being part of speech (PoS) tags, named entities and lemmas.

In its current version, the ELTeC contains comparable corpora for 17 European languages, with each intended to be a balanced sample of 100 novels from the period 1840 to 1920. The current total number of novels is 1355 (104,084,631 words), with 10 languages reaching a collection of 100 encoded in level–1: Czech, German, English, French, Hungarian, Polish, Portuguese, Romanian, Slovenian, and Serbian. The current state in ELTeC corpus building can be seen in a github overview web page (https://distantreading.github.io/ELTeC, accessed on 29 January 2022). The action is set to finish by the end of April of 2022, so more novels are expected to be added. Each novel is supported by metadata concerning their production and reception, aiming to become a reliable basis for comparative work in data-driven textual analysis [31]. All novels and transformation scripts and available on GitHub for browse and download, and more curated versions are published periodically on Zenodo (https://zenodo.org/communities/eltec, accessed on 29 January 2022). ELTeC sub-collections and their derivations are already being used, for example in TXM (https://txm.gitpages.huma-num.fr/textometrie, accessed on 29 January 2022), SketchEngine [33,34], or for word embedding development.

The level–2 ELTeC collection currently contains 7 sub-collections of 100 novels for the following languages: German, English, French, Hungarian, Portuguese, Slovenian, and Serbian (as of December 2021). For the research in this paper, we used these 700 novels, since in this iteration each token is supplied with lemma and PoS tag as required for the experiment. The second column of Table 1 presents the number of words per language sub-collection, totaling in 58,061,996 for these 7 languages, while the third column contains the number of tokens, totaling in 73,692,461.

**Table 1.** Numerical data for seven language-specific text sub-collections.

| Language | Words | Tokens | Chunks per Derivation | Total Chunks | Number of Authors |
|---|---|---|---|---|---|
| German (*deu*) | 12,738,842 | 19,735,312 | 1934 | 7736 | 56 |
| English (*eng*) | 12,386,749 | 14,730,705 | 1431 | 5724 | 80 |
| French (*fra*) | 8,712,219 | 10,206,135 | 974 | 3896 | 74 |
| Hungarian (*hun*) | 6,948,590 | 8,250,330 | 772 | 3088 | 80 |
| Portuguese (*por*) | 6,799,385 | 8,007,906 | 754 | 3016 | 82 |
| Slovenian (*slv*) | 5,682,120 | 6,900,210 | 642 | 2568 | 47 |
| Serbian (*srp*) | 4,794,091 | 5,861,863 | 544 | 2176 | 66 |

For the purpose of this experiment, we produced four document representations for each novel, each in the form of vertical texts, consisting of: (1) words (as in vertical original text of the novel), (2) lemmas (as in vertical lemmatized text), (3) PoS tags (each token in verticalized text is replaced by its PoS tag) and (4) masked text, where tokens were substituted with PoS tag for following PoS tags: *ADJ, NOUNS, NPROP, ADV, VERB, AUX, NUM, SYM, X*, for PoS tags: *DET* and *PRON* tokens are substituted with lemma, while others: *ADP, CCONJ, INTJ, PART, PUNCT, SCONJ* remained unchanged, as inspired by [35].

Keeping in mind the remarkable variation in size of the novels within and across particular language collections, we applied chunking. Relaying on results presented in [36] and the well-known phenomenon: attribution effectiveness grows with the number of words analyzed, and at a certain point it tends to stabilize or slightly decrease [37]. After a few calibrating experiments with different sizes of chunks, we chose the 10,000 token sample size as the most representative. Each novel was split into chunks of exactly 10,000 tokens, with the last, shorter chunk, being excluded. This resulted in a dataset consisting of 28,204 chunks (documents)—7051 chunks per each of the 4 aforementioned document representations. Table 1 also presents the number of chunks for each language sub-collection. The produced dataset was used as the base for all further processing in this research, with each language collection considered separately.

## 3. Workflow

In this section we will explore the generation of all the 19 different word embedding types we envisioned. Firstly, we created five baseline, standalone embeddings: four based on stylometry, and one based on a deep-learning language model (Figure 1). Based on those, we derived 10 more using 5 simple combination techniques, and, finally, 4 more using weight-based linear combinations.

### 3.1. Stylo-Based Document Embeddings

When preparing document embeddings based on our document representations, we opted for the aforementioned Stylo R package in a manner depicted in the Figure 2. From a list of documents we produced a document embedding matrix containing stylometric distances between these documents grouped by the document representation from which they were derived. For calculating document similarities (distances), Stylo uses frequencies of $n$ most frequent words as features. Since our documents were already tokenized and divided into chunks of equal size, the remaining task was to calculate the specific frequencies. In order to produce a satisfying number of candidates for frequency tables, we used trigrams for chunks containing PoS tags and bigrams for chunks containing PoS-masked words. For these chunks we picked top 300 and 500 features, while for the original and lemmatized chunks we picked the 800 most frequent features.

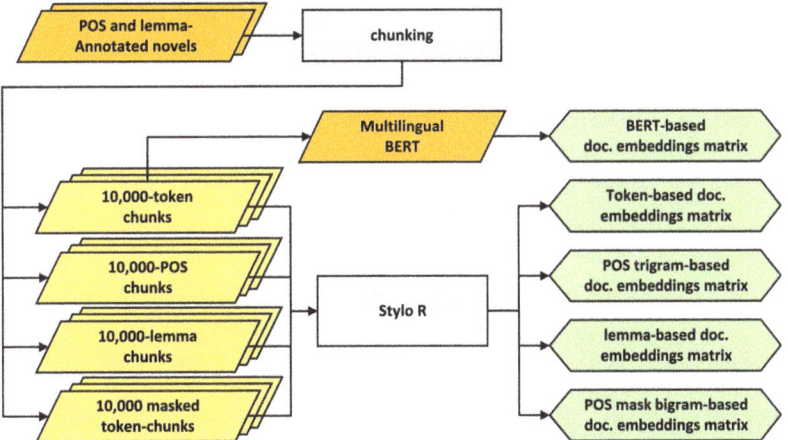

**Figure 1.** A flowchart depicting a path from the annotated novels to document embeddings using multilingual BERT and Stylo R package methods.

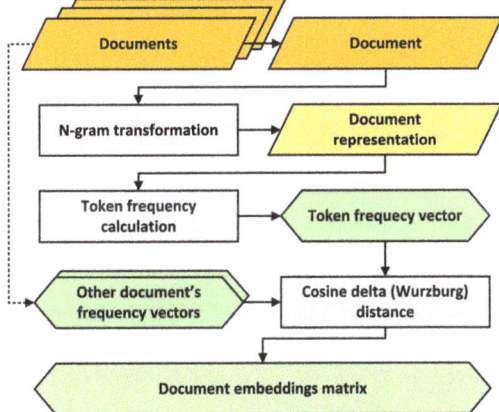

**Figure 2.** A flowchart describing a path from documents to document embeddings using Stylo R package, with N-gram transformation being applied only when generating non-unigram baseddocument representations.

For each representation, we calculated the cosine delta distance (also known as Würzburg distance) [12] between each two chunks regarding the previously obtained frequency tables. Distances were put together in symmetric, hollow matrices $D_t$, in which every cell $a_{i,j}$, $i,j \in \overline{\{1,k\}}$ represents distances between documents and $k$ is the number of documents for specific language. Thus,

$$
D_t = \begin{bmatrix} a_{1,1} & a_{1,2} & \cdots & a_{1,k} \\ a_{2,1} & a_{2,2} & \cdots & a_{2,k} \\ \vdots & \vdots & \ddots & \vdots \\ a_{k,1} & a_{k,2} & \cdots & a_{k,k} \end{bmatrix} = \begin{bmatrix} 0 & * & \cdots & * \\ * & 0 & \cdots & * \\ \vdots & \vdots & \ddots & \vdots \\ * & * & \cdots & 0 \end{bmatrix}, \tag{1}
$$

where $t \in \{word, pos, lemma, masked\}$ and $*$ denotes a numerical distance.

These four matrices, $D_{word}$, $D_{pos}$, $D_{lemma}$ and $D_{masked}$, produced for each of the seven languages, are used to convey document embeddings grouped by a document representation method. Each one contains mutual document distances for the same set of documents with distances differing between matrices as they were obtained using different representations of the same documents.

### 3.2. mBERT-Based Document Embeddings

As we were testing the use of mBERT embeddings without fine-tuning, like in the aforementioned paper [29], and since the source code of that solution is publicly available, we adapted it to fit the needs of this research. The complete process of generating a document embeddings matrix for each of the seven language using mBERT is shown in Figure 3, with a list of documents resulting in a matrix containing stylometric distances between them.

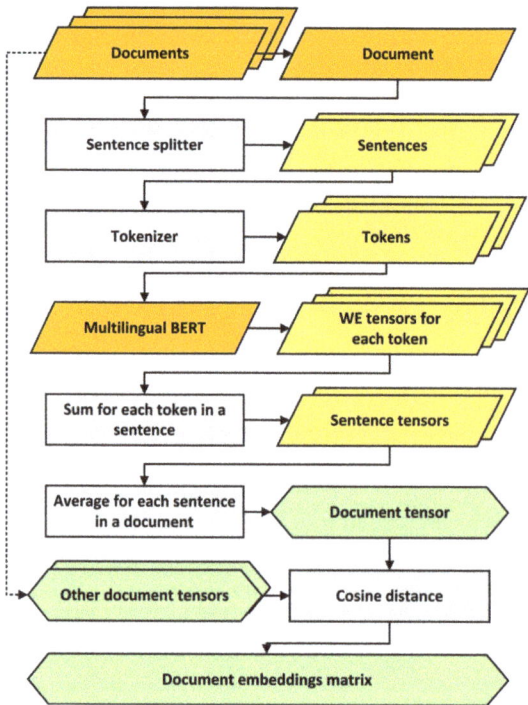

**Figure 3.** Flowchart describing the path from documents to document embeddings using mBERT.

In the first step, each document was split into sentences using several regular expressions. Since mBERT requires each sentence to have 512 tokens or less, longer sentences were trimmed. Sentences were tokenized using Google AI's BERT tokenizer [28] with 110k shared WordPiece vocabulary (provided by the mBERT authors). The model assigns each token in a sentence with a $768 \times 1$ word embedding. Those are then summed into sentence tensors of the same length. All sentence tensors in each document are averaged into a single $768 \times 1$ tensor, which is used as a document representation.

If there are $k$ documents, then there will be $k$ document tensors, $\vec{v}_1, \vec{v}_2, \ldots, \vec{v}_k$. Using cosine similarity $d_{i,j} = \frac{\langle \vec{v}_i, \vec{v}_j \rangle}{\|\vec{v}_i\| \cdot \|\vec{v}_j\|}$ between vector pairs we get distances between documents represented by those vectors $\vec{v}_i$, $\vec{v}_j$, $i, j \in \overline{\{1, k\}}$, with the final product being the document embedding matrix:

$$D_{bert} = \begin{bmatrix} a_{1,1} & a_{1,2} & \cdots & a_{1,k} \\ a_{2,1} & a_{2,2} & \cdots & a_{2,k} \\ \vdots & \vdots & \ddots & \vdots \\ a_{k,1} & a_{k,2} & \cdots & a_{k,k} \end{bmatrix}, \tag{2}$$

where $a_{i,j} = 1 - d_{i,j}$, $i, j \in \overline{\{1, k\}}$, $k \in \mathbb{N}$.

We produced one $D_{bert}$ document-embedding matrix for each language and added them to the ones previously obtained through Stylo R to be used as the main resource of this experiment.

### 3.3. Simple Composition-Based Document Embeddings

Each document embeddings matrix, $D_{word}$, $D_{pos}$, $D_{lemma}$, $D_{masked}$ and $D_{bert}$, was tested individually, but we also engaged in their simple composition in pursuit of better classification results. The goal was to create new, composed, document embeddings using the ones already available. Five methods were used to generate elements of composed embeddings matrices $D_m$. The motivation for the selection of these particular five methods was the choice of functions for which the domain is a vector space, and the co-domain is a set of real numbers, such as average, minimum, maximum, $l^2$ norm, or the product of coordinates of a vector. The goal was to produce a single scalar distance from an array of distances obtained for the same pair of documents, where each distance is obtained via a different method and is located in a separate document embedding matrix.

A matrix $D_m$ composed of particular document embeddings matrices is defined as follows. Assume there are $n$ matrices, $D_1, D_2, \ldots, D_n \in M_k(\mathbb{R})$, $n \in \{4, 5\}$, respectively,

$$\begin{bmatrix} a_{1,1}^{(1)} & a_{1,2}^{(1)} & \cdots & a_{1,k}^{(1)} \\ a_{2,1}^{(1)} & a_{2,2}^{(1)} & \cdots & a_{2,k}^{(1)} \\ \vdots & \vdots & \ddots & \vdots \\ a_{k,1}^{(1)} & a_{k,2}^{(1)} & \cdots & a_{k,k}^{(1)} \end{bmatrix}, \begin{bmatrix} a_{1,1}^{(2)} & a_{1,2}^{(2)} & \cdots & a_{1,k}^{(2)} \\ a_{2,1}^{(2)} & a_{2,2}^{(2)} & \cdots & a_{2,k}^{(2)} \\ \vdots & \vdots & \ddots & \vdots \\ a_{k,1}^{(2)} & a_{k,2}^{(2)} & \cdots & a_{k,k}^{(2)} \end{bmatrix}, \ldots, \begin{bmatrix} a_{1,1}^{(n)} & a_{1,2}^{(n)} & \cdots & a_{1,k}^{(n)} \\ a_{2,1}^{(n)} & a_{2,2}^{(n)} & \cdots & a_{2,k}^{(n)} \\ \vdots & \vdots & \ddots & \vdots \\ a_{k,1}^{(n)} & a_{k,2}^{(n)} & \cdots & a_{k,k}^{(n)} \end{bmatrix}. \tag{3}$$

Matrix $D_m$ is a composed matrix of matrices $D_1, D_2, \ldots, D_n$,

$$D_m = D_m(D_1, D_2, \ldots, D_n) = \begin{bmatrix} b_{1,1}^m & b_{1,2}^m & \cdots & b_{1,k}^m \\ b_{2,1}^m & b_{2,2}^m & \cdots & b_{2,k}^m \\ \vdots & \vdots & \ddots & \vdots \\ b_{k,1}^m & b_{k,2}^m & \cdots & b_{k,k}^m \end{bmatrix}, \tag{4}$$

where each element $b_{i,j}^m$, $i, j \in \overline{\{1, k\}}$, can be generated using a different method $m$ as:

$$b_{i,j}^m = \begin{cases} \frac{a_{i,j}^{(1)} + a_{i,j}^{(2)} + \ldots + a_{i,j}^{(n)}}{n}, & i, j \in \overline{\{1, k\}}, & m = mean \\ \min\{a_{i,j}^{(1)}, a_{i,j}^{(2)}, \ldots, a_{i,j}^{(n)}\}, & i, j \in \overline{\{1, k\}}, & m = min \\ \max\{a_{i,j}^{(1)}, a_{i,j}^{(2)}, \ldots, a_{i,j}^{(n)}\}, & i, j \in \overline{\{1, k\}}, & m = max \\ \sqrt{(a_{i,j}^{(1)})^2 + (a_{i,j}^{(2)})^2 + \ldots + (a_{i,j}^{(n)})^2}, & i, j \in \overline{\{1, k\}}, & m = l^2 \ norm \\ a_{i,j}^{(1)} \cdot a_{i,j}^{(2)} \cdot \ldots \cdot a_{i,j}^{(n)}, & i, j \in \overline{\{1, k\}}, & m = product \end{cases} \tag{5}$$

Since we wanted to test the effectiveness of inclusion of mBERT-based document embeddings into the composite environment, we generated two classes of composed-embeddings matrices. Using the procedure described above, they are

$$D_m = D_m(D_{word}, D_{pos}, D_{lemma}, D_{masked}), \tag{6}$$

$$D_{m\_b} = D_{m\_b}(D_{word}, D_{pos}, D_{lemma}, D_{masked}, D_{bert}), \tag{7}$$

where $m$ is one of methods described in Equation (5), and $m\_b$ represents inclusion of $D_{bert}$ matrix into the environment. Ultimately, one class of matrices ($D_{mean}$, $D_{min}$, $D_{max}$, $D_{l2norm}$ and $D_{product}$) is produced without mBERT embeddings using Equation (6), and the other ($D_{mean\_b}$, $D_{min\_b}$, $D_{max\_b}$, $D_{l2norm\_b}$ and $D_{product\_b}$) with mBERT embeddings using Equation (7), resulting in 10 new composite document embedding matrices for each language, all with the same shape and size as the previously cratered ones ($D_{word}$, $D_{pos}$, $D_{lemma}$, $D_{masked}$ and $D_{bert}$), only with possibly different distance values.

### 3.4. Weighted Composition-Based Document Embeddings

Apart from the above simple ways of combining the matrices $D_{word}$, $D_{pos}$, $D_{lemma}$, $D_{masked}$ and $D_{bert}$ into composition-based document embeddings, we also considered weighting the input matrices during the combination step, assuming that the weights are to be determined empirically. The motivation is, firstly, that particular features might influence parallel architectures to a different extent and, secondly, the importance of particular features might depend on the language. In our approach, a resulting composition-based matrix is a linear combination of the matrices $D_{word}$, $D_{pos}$, $D_{lemma}$ and $D_{masked}$ (and $D_{bert}$), each of them multiplied by a respective weight.

Let there be $n$ matrices as in Equation (3), and each is tied to a supposed specific weight $w^{(1)}, w^{(2)}, \ldots, w^{(n)} \in \mathbb{R}$. Then, each element (distance) of the weighted composed matrix $D_w$ can be generated by using a specific element of each of $n$ matrices separately and combining it with an appropriate weight using an expansion of the array's mean, namely the weighted arithmetic mean. Thus:

$$D_w = \begin{bmatrix} b_{1,1} & b_{1,2} & \cdots & b_{1,k} \\ b_{2,1} & b_{2,2} & \cdots & b_{2,k} \\ \vdots & \vdots & \ddots & \vdots \\ b_{k,1} & b_{k,2} & \cdots & b_{k,k} \end{bmatrix}, \tag{8}$$

where,

$$b_{i,j} = \frac{1}{C}\left(a_{i,j}^{(1)}w^{(1)} + a_{i,j}^{(2)}w^{(2)} + \ldots + a_{i,j}^{(n)}w^{(n)}\right), \; i,j \in \overline{\{1,k\}}, \tag{9}$$

$$C = w^{(1)} + w^{(2)} + \ldots + w^{(n)}. \tag{10}$$

In order to determine the appropriate weights for the matrices $D_{word}$, $D_{pos}$, $D_{lemma}$, $D_{masked}$ and $D_{bert}$, we opted to use a single perceptron artificial neural network with the number of inputs matching the number of matrices that we want to procure weights for (either 4 or 5 depending on whether mBERT input is used) and an output layer with a single node to ensure the number of weights trained matched the number of inputs.

Since a single output node was devised for the training, the perceptron was trained on authorship verification rather than attribution task, with a single output optimized to be closer to 1 if two documents are of the same author and closer to 0 if the two documents are of different authors (Figure 4). For the sake of training simplicity, and since we used cosine distances in our input document embedding matrices, all distances were converted to similarities, using Equation (11) before input, and reverted to distances afterwards using Equation (12) in order to match the other, previously created embeddings for easier evaluation,

$$S_s = 1 - D_s, \; s \in \{lemma, masked, pos, word, bert\}, \tag{11}$$

$$D_w = 1 - S_w. \tag{12}$$

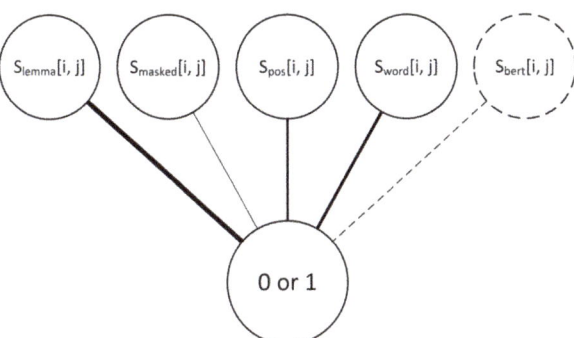

**Figure 4.** Visualisation of perceptron inputs and targeted outputs during the training phase—inputs for each iteration being distances between the same documents from four (or five) different embeddings and desired outputs of either 0 or 1.

Adam optimizer [38] with standard initial learning rate of 0.01 was used to train all of the perceptrons used in this research. The number of inputs with the desired output of 0 was truncated to the number of inputs with desired output of 1 in order to avoid author verification bias, and the distances between the documents that belong to the same novel were excluded from the training. The number of inputs for each training was afterwards truncated to 6384, which was the size of the available set for the smallest dataset, in order to avoid language bias in a multilingual setting. These inputs and outputs were split into training and validation sets in a 9:1 ratio, and the batch sizes were fixed at 64. The final epoch number was set to 356 according to other parameters and several training inspections. During these inspections what we were looking for specifically was the average number of epochs across languages before the validation error rate trend changes from descending to ascending, indicating over-fitting. Once the training of the perceptrons was completed, the model was used to predict the final weights as shown in Figure 5. The weights were then used to solve the Equation (9). It has to be emphasized that using the procured weights for any method satisfies $C = 1$ in the Equation (10), because the weights were normalized to sum up to 1. The normalized weights are presented in Table 2.

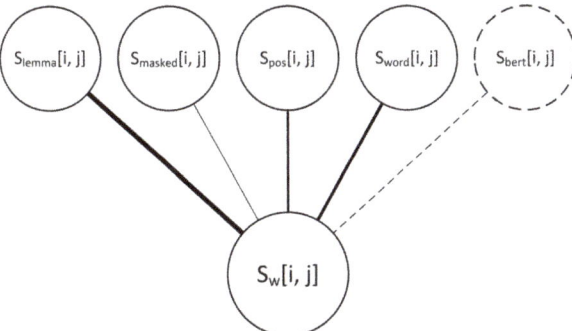

**Figure 5.** Visualisation of trained perceptron inputs and outputs—inputs being distances between the same documents from four (or five) different embeddings and the output being their new weighted-based scalar distance.

A total of 28 perceptrons were trained, 14 not using the mBERT (upper) and 14 using the mBERT inputs (bottom half of Table 2). Out of those 14, 7 were trained on inputs from each language respectively (labeled *lng* and *lng_b*, with *lng* being the acronym of the language used for the training) and 7 were trained on multilingual inputs, each excluding a different language (labeled *universal_excl_lng* and *universal_b_excl_lng* in Table 2, with *lng* being the acronym of the excluded language).

**Table 2.** Normalized weights acquired through training of 28 perceptrons.

| Trained on: | Words | Lemmas | PoS | Masked | mBERT |
|---|---|---|---|---|---|
| deu | 0.486 | 0.331 | 0.330 | −0.147 | |
| eng | 0.305 | 0.488 | 0.142 | 0.065 | |
| fra | 0.355 | 0.358 | 0.211 | 0.076 | |
| hun | 0.535 | 0.219 | 0.044 | 0.201 | |
| por | −0.128 | 0.686 | 0.063 | 0.379 | |
| slv | 0.298 | 0.476 | 0.154 | 0.072 | |
| srp | 0.397 | 0.223 | 0.226 | 0.155 | |
| universal_excl_deu | 0.321 | 0.472 | 0.132 | 0.074 | |
| universal_excl_eng | 0.354 | 0.407 | 0.210 | 0.029 | |
| universal_excl_fra | 0.255 | 0.498 | 0.160 | 0.087 | |
| universal_excl_hun | 0.303 | 0.511 | 0.176 | 0.010 | |
| universal_excl_por | 0.423 | 0.418 | 0.183 | −0.023 | |
| universal_excl_slv | 0.294 | 0.486 | 0.212 | 0.007 | |
| universal_excl_srp | 0.236 | 0.507 | 0.161 | 0.095 | |
| deu_b | 0.490 | 0.381 | 0.339 | −0.169 | −0.040 |
| eng_b | 0.373 | 0.558 | 0.076 | 0.021 | −0.028 |
| fra_b | 0.338 | 0.373 | 0.245 | 0.101 | −0.056 |
| hun_b | 0.508 | 0.243 | 0.086 | 0.241 | −0.078 |
| por_b | −0.118 | 0.776 | 0.078 | 0.310 | −0.047 |
| slv_b | 0.319 | 0.511 | 0.151 | 0.068 | −0.049 |
| srp_b | 0.466 | 0.208 | 0.225 | 0.149 | −0.048 |
| universal_b_excl_deu | 0.270 | 0.530 | 0.141 | 0.106 | −0.047 |
| universal_b_excl_eng | 0.272 | 0.532 | 0.176 | 0.068 | −0.048 |
| universal_b_excl_fra | 0.321 | 0.502 | 0.138 | 0.079 | −0.040 |
| universal_b_excl_hun | 0.340 | 0.495 | 0.178 | 0.028 | −0.041 |
| universal_b_excl_por | 0.467 | 0.379 | 0.217 | −0.019 | −0.043 |
| universal_b_excl_slv | 0.392 | 0.404 | 0.199 | 0.046 | −0.041 |
| universal_b_excl_srp | 0.326 | 0.516 | 0.150 | 0.052 | −0.044 |

Using the obtained weights and previously created document embedding matrices, we generated four new ones for each language using Equation (9). In order to avoid any bias problem, two strategies were employed. The first strategy was to, for each language, use universal weights where that language was excluded from their training e.g., applying *universal_excl_deu* weights on German (*deu*). Thus, from Equations (9) and (10) we derived:

$$D_{weights\_universal\_excl\_lng} = \sum_t \left( w_{universal\_excl\_lng\_t} D_t \right), \tag{13}$$

$$D_{weights\_universal\_b\_excl\_lng} = \sum_s \left( w_{universal\_b\_excl\_lng\_s} D_s \right), \tag{14}$$

for $t \in \{word, pos, lemma, masked\}$ and for $s \in \{word, pos, lemma, masked, bert\}$. We used these two formulas to generate two document embeddings based on universally trained weights, one without and one with the use of mBERT based embeddings.

Our second strategy was to involve direct transfer-learning and produce weight-based embeddings using the weights trained on a different language dataset, as another way to avoid the training-testing bias. Suitable weights to compute the document embedding matrix for a given language were selected through comparison of Euclidean distances of the trained weights for all languages. Results of these comparisons are presented in Table 3 (distances were calculated separately for perceptrons without and with mBERT input, presented in the upper and bottom half of the table, respectively).

**Table 3.** Euclidean distances between weights acquired through perceptron training, with bold indicating the shortest distances between different language weights.

|       | deu   | eng   | fra   | hun   | por   | slv   | srp   |
|-------|-------|-------|-------|-------|-------|-------|-------|
| deu   | 0.000 | 0.371 | **0.287** | 0.467 | 0.922 | 0.368 | 0.349 |
| eng   | 0.371 | 0.000 | 0.156 | 0.392 | 0.576 | **0.020** | 0.307 |
| fra   | 0.287 | 0.156 | 0.000 | 0.309 | 0.674 | **0.143** | 0.162 |
| hun   | 0.467 | 0.392 | 0.309 | 0.000 | 0.831 | 0.389 | **0.233** |
| por   | 0.922 | 0.576 | 0.674 | 0.831 | 0.000 | **0.573** | 0.753 |
| slv   | 0.368 | **0.020** | 0.143 | 0.389 | 0.573 | 0.000 | 0.293 |
| srp   | 0.349 | 0.307 | **0.162** | 0.233 | 0.753 | 0.293 | 0.000 |
|       | deu_b | eng_b | fra_b | hun_b | por_b | slv_b | srp_b |
| deu_b | 0.000 | 0.388 | **0.324** | 0.503 | 0.907 | 0.371 | 0.380 |
| eng_b | 0.388 | 0.000 | 0.267 | 0.410 | 0.610 | **0.116** | 0.412 |
| fra_b | 0.324 | 0.267 | 0.000 | 0.302 | 0.665 | **0.172** | 0.215 |
| hun_b | 0.503 | 0.410 | 0.302 | 0.000 | 0.825 | 0.378 | **0.178** |
| por_b | 0.907 | 0.610 | 0.665 | 0.825 | 0.000 | **0.570** | 0.843 |
| slv_b | 0.371 | **0.116** | 0.172 | 0.378 | 0.570 | 0.000 | 0.354 |
| srp_b | 0.380 | 0.412 | 0.215 | **0.178** | 0.843 | 0.354 | 0.000 |

Two new embeddings were generated for each language based on the nearest Euclidean neighbor in trained weights. For example, Serbian (*srp*) embeddings were calculated with French *fra*) weights (without mBERT) and with Hungarian (*hun*) weights (with mBERT) input, as shown via the bold values in Table 3 upper and lower part, respectively. Thus, based on Equations (9) and (10), we derived:

$$D_{weights\_transfer\_lng} = \sum_t \left( w_{xlng\_t} D_t \right), \tag{15}$$

$$D_{weights\_transfer\_b\_lng} = \sum_s \left( w_{xlng\_b\_s} D_s \right), \tag{16}$$

for $t \in \{word, pos, lemma, masked\}$ and for $s \in \{word, pos, lemma, masked, bert\}$ and *xlng* being the nearest Euclidean neighbor, minding distances of trained weights presented in Table 3.

## 4. Results

The results reported in this section rely on the following supervised classification setup. The evaluation was carried out for each of the 19 document embeddings (4 from Section 3.1, 1 from Section 3.2, 10 from Section 3.3, and 4 from Section 3.4) computed for each of the 7 languages, totaling in 133 evaluated document embeddings. Only the authors represented by at least two novels were chosen for the evaluation subset, in order to achieve a closed-set attribution scenario. All of their chunks (documents) were evaluated against all the other documents, excluding the ones originating from the same novel, in order to avoid easy hits.

Each resulting subset from the original document embeddings matrix contained pairwise comparisons (distances) between the selected documents and classification was thus performed by identifying the minimal distance for each document, which is equivalent to using the k-NN classifier with $k = 1$. If a document's nearest neighbour originates from another novel of the same author, it is considered a hit. In this section, we will report the overall performance for each document embeddings matrix via accuracy, precision, recall, weighted-average $F_1$-score, and macro-averaged $F_1$-score, as well as the statistical significance of the procured results. It should be noted that due to the nature of our test, where the domain of possible authors outnumbers the domain of expected authors, the macro-averaged $F_1$-score reflects the potential domain reduction, where the methods that predict fewer authors tend to have higher scores.

### 4.1. Baseline

As already mentioned, using the most frequent words as features has been the primary method of solving AA tasks for many decades. Therefore, we marked the word-based embeddings results as our primary baseline (*baseline 1*), while looking for improvements in accuracy and in weighted-averaged $F_1$-score across all the remaining embeddings.

Recently, however, for some highly-inflected languages, most frequent lemmas emerged as a better alternative to most frequent words [39]. The PoS tags and the document representation with masked words, where PoS labels are used to mask predefined set of PoS classes, also achieved good results for specific problems [35]. In evaluation of this experiment we used the following document representations: most frequent words, lemmas, PoS trigrams, and PoS-masked bigrams ($D_{word}$, $D_{lemma}$, $D_{pos}$ and $D_{masked}$), as the secondary baseline methods. Specifically, we used the best performing method (from the above list) for each language as a respective secondary baseline (*baseline 2*).

### 4.2. Quantitative Results

Obtained accuracy and weighted-average $F_1$ scores for each language inspected and each embedding produced, are shown in Tables 4 and 5, with the upper five embeddings representing the methods from which the baseline scores were derived. We looked at the correlation between these metrics (grouped by language) and calculated the average Pearson correlation coefficient of 0.9971 using Equation (17),

$$r = \frac{\sum_{i=1}^{n} \left( x_i - \overline{x} \right) \left( y_i - \overline{y} \right)}{\sqrt{\sum_{i=1}^{n} (x_i - \overline{x})^2 \sum_{i=1}^{n} (y_i - \overline{y})^2}}, \tag{17}$$

where $n$ is the sample size, $x_i$, $y_i$ are the individual data points indexed with $i$, $\overline{x} = \frac{1}{n}\sum_{i=1}^{n} x_i$ (the sample mean) and analogously for $\overline{y}$. Given a very high correlation between the two measures of performance, we decided to focus on one of these (i.e., accuracy) in the further presentation.

**Table 4.** Accuracy scores obtained in authorship attribution task evaluation, with italic indicating the baseline and bold indicating best performing methods for each language (baseline and overall).

| Embedding Base | deu | eng | fra | hun | por | slv | srp | avg |
|---|---|---|---|---|---|---|---|---|
| bert | 0.7129 | 0.5561 | 0.4444 | 0.6991 | 0.5925 | 0.5042 | 0.4918 | 0.5716 |
| word | 0.9203 | 0.8175 | **0.7561** | **0.9812** | 0.7245 | 0.7188 | **0.7279** | 0.8066 |
| pos | 0.8370 | 0.6632 | 0.6125 | 0.8088 | 0.7509 | 0.6958 | **0.7279** | 0.7280 |
| lemma | **0.9212** | **0.8351** | 0.7507 | 0.9781 | 0.8000 | **0.7729** | 0.7082 | **0.8237** |
| masked | 0.7346 | 0.6439 | 0.7046 | 0.9185 | **0.8113** | 0.7208 | 0.7016 | 0.7479 |
| *baseline 1* | *0.9203* | *0.8175* | *0.7561* | *0.9812* | *0.7245* | *0.7188* | *0.7279* | *0.8066* |
| *baseline 2* | *0.9212* | *0.8351* | *0.7561* | *0.9812* | *0.8113* | *0.7729* | *0.7279* | *0.8294* |
| mean | 0.9420 | 0.8158 | 0.8238 | 0.9937 | 0.8717 | 0.7646 | 0.7967 | 0.8583 |
| mean_b | 0.9420 | 0.8175 | 0.8238 | 0.9937 | 0.8717 | 0.7646 | **0.8000** | 0.8590 |
| max | 0.9257 | 0.8298 | 0.8049 | 0.9906 | 0.8226 | 0.7854 | 0.7541 | 0.8447 |
| max_b | 0.9257 | 0.8298 | 0.8049 | 0.9906 | 0.8226 | 0.7854 | 0.7541 | 0.8447 |
| min | 0.8433 | 0.6649 | 0.6341 | 0.8150 | 0.7547 | 0.6979 | 0.7344 | 0.7349 |
| min_b | 0.7129 | 0.5561 | 0.4444 | 0.6991 | 0.5925 | 0.5042 | 0.4918 | 0.5716 |
| product | 0.9375 | 0.8035 | 0.8157 | 0.9875 | **0.8792** | 0.7625 | **0.8000** | 0.8551 |
| product_b | 0.9058 | 0.7474 | 0.7453 | 0.9718 | 0.8189 | 0.7792 | 0.7836 | 0.8217 |
| l2-norm | 0.9466 | 0.8193 | 0.8293 | **0.9969** | 0.8717 | 0.7646 | 0.7869 | 0.8593 |
| l2-norm_b | 0.9466 | 0.8193 | 0.8293 | **0.9969** | 0.8717 | 0.7646 | 0.7869 | 0.8593 |
| weights_transfer | **0.9547** | **0.8421** | **0.8347** | **0.9969** | 0.8415 | 0.7854 | 0.796 | **0.8646** |
| weights_transfer_b | 0.9538 | 0.8404 | 0.8320 | **0.9969** | 0.8415 | **0.7917** | 0.7869 | 0.8633 |
| weights_universal | 0.9475 | 0.8316 | **0.8347** | 0.9906 | 0.8151 | 0.7812 | 0.7934 | 0.8563 |
| weights_universal_b | 0.9484 | 0.8386 | 0.8293 | 0.9906 | 0.8075 | 0.7771 | 0.7934 | 0.8550 |

**Table 5.** Weighted-average $F_1$-scores obtained through authorship attribution task evaluation, with italic indicating the baseline and bold indicating best performing methods for each language (baseline and overall).

| Embedding Base | deu | eng | fra | hun | por | slv | srp | avg |
|---|---|---|---|---|---|---|---|---|
| bert | 0.7423 | 0.5966 | 0.4912 | 0.7403 | 0.6510 | 0.5170 | 0.5226 | 0.6087 |
| word | 0.9387 | 0.8588 | **0.7992** | **0.9904** | 0.7742 | 0.7259 | **0.7518** | 0.8341 |
| pos | 0.8611 | 0.7200 | 0.6485 | 0.8675 | 0.8167 | 0.7181 | 0.7364 | 0.7669 |
| lemma | **0.9391** | **0.8753** | 0.7951 | 0.9840 | 0.8588 | **0.7860** | 0.7414 | **0.8542** |
| masked | 0.7822 | 0.7017 | 0.7718 | 0.9433 | **0.8705** | 0.7377 | 0.7140 | 0.7887 |
| *baseline 1* | *0.9387* | *0.8588* | *0.7992* | *0.9904* | *0.7742* | *0.7259* | *0.7518* | *0.8341* |
| *baseline 2* | *0.9391* | *0.8753* | *0.7992* | *0.9904* | *0.8705* | *0.7860* | *0.7518* | *0.8589* |
| mean | 0.9579 | 0.8484 | 0.8551 | 0.9968 | 0.9163 | 0.7771 | 0.8120 | 0.8805 |
| mean_b | 0.9579 | 0.8493 | 0.8551 | 0.9968 | 0.9163 | 0.7771 | 0.8174 | 0.8814 |
| max | 0.9436 | 0.8698 | 0.8412 | 0.9952 | 0.8790 | 0.7979 | 0.7740 | 0.8715 |
| max_b | 0.9436 | 0.8698 | 0.8412 | 0.9952 | 0.8790 | 0.7979 | 0.774 | 0.8715 |
| min | 0.8679 | 0.7199 | 0.6717 | 0.8741 | 0.8223 | 0.7212 | 0.7388 | 0.7737 |
| min_b | 0.7423 | 0.5966 | 0.4912 | 0.7403 | 0.6510 | 0.5170 | 0.5226 | 0.6087 |
| product | 0.9529 | 0.8364 | 0.8446 | 0.9933 | **0.9202** | 0.7775 | 0.8160 | 0.8773 |
| product_b | 0.9196 | 0.7734 | 0.7848 | 0.9789 | 0.8672 | 0.7947 | 0.8042 | 0.8461 |
| l2-norm | 0.9604 | 0.8509 | 0.8583 | **0.9984** | 0.9147 | 0.7777 | 0.8067 | 0.8810 |
| l2-norm_b | 0.9604 | 0.8509 | 0.8583 | **0.9984** | 0.9147 | 0.7777 | 0.8067 | 0.8810 |
| weights_transfer | **0.9660** | **0.8772** | **0.8644** | **0.9984** | 0.8866 | 0.7960 | **0.8220** | **0.8872** |
| weights_transfer_b | 0.9646 | 0.8770 | 0.8630 | **0.9984** | 0.8851 | **0.7988** | 0.8036 | 0.8844 |
| weights_universal | 0.9617 | 0.8658 | **0.8644** | 0.9937 | 0.8641 | 0.7934 | 0.8169 | 0.8800 |
| weights_universal_b | 0.9623 | 0.8735 | 0.8602 | 0.9952 | 0.8566 | 0.7878 | 0.8181 | 0.8791 |

The complete results for all metrics used in the evaluation (accuracy, precision, recall, weighted and macro-averaged $F_1$-score) for each language and embedding method are shown in the Appendix A Tables A1–A7.

The total improvement of each composite method over the primary and secondary baseline scores is shown in percentages in Table 6, followed by its visual representation in Figure 6, a heat map of the accuracy improvement of each composite methods over the primary (left) and the secondary (right) baseline, for each language inspected.

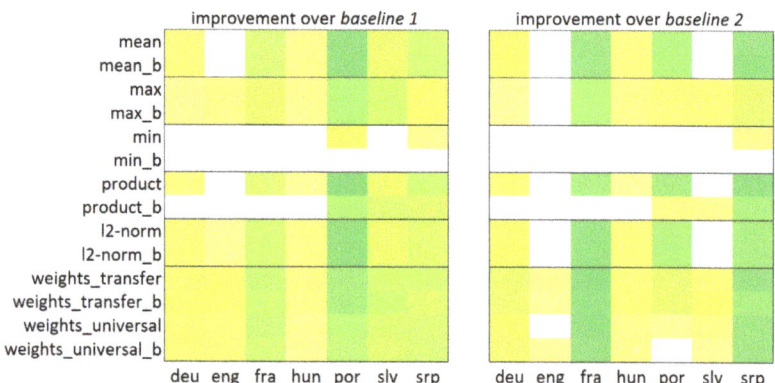

**Figure 6.** Heat map visualization representing the improvement of accuracy over primary (**left**) and secondary baseline (**right**) for each language, with yellow meaning low, green meaning high, and white meaning no improvement.

The effect of using mBERT embeddings in a composite environment is shown in Table 7, and it is calculated as a percentual difference of accuracy scores between the respective composition-based methods from the Table 4, with the results omitted from the table if equal to 0. Visual representation of the impact is depicted in the form of a heat map in Figure 7, grouped by composition method and language. The left side of the heat map visualizes data from Table 7 with yellow meaning low, green meaning high, and white meaning no improvement, and depicts cases in which the inclusion of mBERT improved the results. The right side of the heat map visualizes negated values from Table 7 with the same color codes, and depicts cases where the exclusion of mBERT improved the results.

**Table 6.** Accuracy scores with percentual increase/decrease between the primary (upper) and secondary (lower) baseline method and each composite method for each examined language, with the highest improvements for each language indicated in bold.

| Embedding Base | deu | eng | fra | hun | por | slv | srp |
|---|---|---|---|---|---|---|---|
| mean | 2.36% | −0.21% | 8.95% | 1.27% | 20.32% | 6.37% | 9.45% |
| mean_b | 2.36% | 0.00% | 8.95% | 1.27% | 20.32% | 6.37% | **9.91%** |
| max | 0.59% | 1.50% | 6.45% | 0.96% | 13.54% | 9.27% | 3.60% |
| max_b | 0.59% | 1.50% | 6.45% | 0.96% | 13.54% | 9.27% | 3.60% |
| min | −8.37% | −18.67% | −16.14% | −16.94% | 4.17% | −2.91% | 0.89% |
| min_b | −22.54% | −31.98% | −41.22% | −28.75% | −18.22% | −29.86% | −32.44% |
| product | 1.87% | −1.71% | 7.88% | 0.64% | **21.35%** | 6.08% | **9.91%** |
| product_b | −1.58% | −8.57% | −1.43% | −0.96% | 13.03% | 8.40% | 7.65% |
| l2-norm | 2.86% | 0.22% | 9.68% | **1.60%** | 20.32% | 6.37% | 8.11% |
| l2-norm_b | 2.86% | 0.22% | 9.68% | **1.60%** | 20.32% | 6.37% | 8.11% |
| w._transfer | **3.74%** | **3.01%** | **10.40%** | **1.60%** | 16.15% | 9.27% | 9.45% |
| w._transfer_b | 3.64% | 2.80% | 10.04% | **1.60%** | 16.15% | **10.14%** | 8.11% |
| w._universal | 2.96% | 1.72% | **10.40%** | 0.96% | 12.51% | 8.68% | 9.00% |
| w._universal_b | 3.05% | 2.58% | 9.68% | 0.96% | 11.46% | 8.11% | 9.00% |
| mean | 2.26% | −2.31% | 8.95% | 1.27% | 7.44% | −1.07% | 9.45% |
| mean_b | 2.26% | −2.11% | 8.95% | 1.27% | 7.44% | −1.07% | **9.91%** |
| max | 0.49% | −0.63% | 6.45% | 0.96% | 1.39% | 1.62% | 3.60% |
| max_b | 0.49% | −0.63% | 6.45% | 0.96% | 1.39% | 1.62% | 3.60% |
| min | −8.46% | −20.38% | −16.14% | −16.94% | −6.98% | −9.70% | 0.89% |
| min_b | −22.61% | −33.41% | −41.22% | −28.75% | −26.97% | −34.77% | −32.44% |
| product | 1.77% | −3.78% | 7.88% | 0.64% | **8.37%** | −1.35% | **9.91%** |
| product_b | −1.67% | −10.50% | −1.43% | −0.96% | 0.94% | 0.82% | 7.65% |
| l2-norm | 2.76% | −1.89% | 9.68% | **1.60%** | 7.44% | −1.07% | 8.11% |
| l2-norm_b | 2.76% | −1.89% | 9.68% | **1.60%** | 7.44% | −1.07% | 8.11% |
| w._transfer | **3.64%** | **0.84%** | **10.40%** | **1.60%** | 3.72% | 1.62% | 9.45% |
| w._transfer_b | 3.54% | 0.63% | 10.04% | **1.60%** | 3.72% | **2.43%** | 8.11% |
| w._universal | 2.85% | −0.42% | **10.40%** | 0.96% | 0.47% | 1.07% | 9.00% |
| w._universal_b | 2.95% | 0.42% | 9.68% | 0.96% | −0.47% | 0.54% | 9.00% |

**Table 7.** Percentual increase/decrease in accuracy when using the mBERT embeddings as composition input grouped by composition method and language, with results omitted if there is no change.

| embedding base | deu | eng | fra | hun | por | slv | srp |
|---|---|---|---|---|---|---|---|
| mean | | 0.21% | | | | | 0.41% |
| max | | | | | | | |
| min | −15.46% | −16.36% | −29.92% | −14.22% | −21.49% | −27.75% | −33.03% |
| product | −3.38% | −6.98% | −8.63% | −1.59% | −6.86% | 2.19% | −2.05% |
| l2-norm | | | | | | | |
| w._transfer | −0.09% | −0.20% | −0.32% | | | 0.80% | −1.23% |
| w._universal | 0.09% | 0.84% | −0.65% | | −0.93% | −0.52% | |

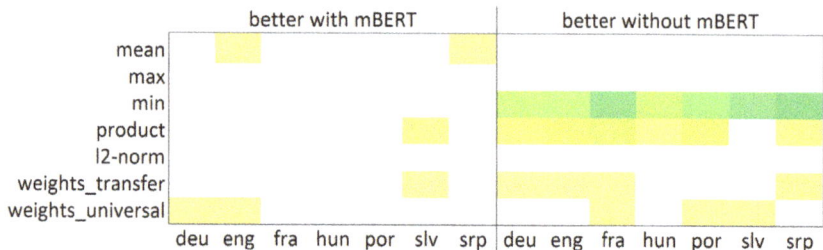

**Figure 7.** Heat map visualization representing the accuracy improvement in including mBERT inputs (**left**) and excluding them (**right**), with yellow meaning low, green meaning high, and white meaning no improvement.

*4.3. Qualitative Results*

The improvement of our composite method over the baseline for French (0.8347 vs. 0.7561) is remarkable and could not be due to mere chance. However, we cannot be equally sure in other cases. Even if the improvements are clearly noticeable, we cannot ascertain their statistical significance by simple eyeballing. In order to check the integrity of the quantitative results, then, we analyzed confusion matrices of the best performing (in terms of $f_1$-score and accuracy) baseline methods and best-performing overall methods for each of the seven languages. In each case, we used the Newcombe-Wilson continuity-corrected test [40], which is designed to test the significance between proportions of events.

Our comparisons show that the improvement over the primary baseline is statistically significant in the case of *deu* ($p = 0.001142$), *fra* ($p = 0.01062$), *por* ($p < 0.0001$), *slv* ($p = 0.01071$), and *srp* ($p = 0.04526$), at the conventional level of significance $\alpha = 0.05$. In the case of both *eng* and *hun*, the improvement over the baseline cannot be considered statistically significant. The explanation is rather straightforward for *hun*, since the baseline accuracy is already very high (0.9812), leaving little room for improvement. Chances are that the gain would have been more noticeable if our Hungarian dataset had contained novels more challenging for authorship discrimination. The behaviour of *eng* is more difficult to explain, but we assume it is related to its low-inflection, which diminishes the information gap between words and lemmas and its strict word-order, which diminishes the effect of the POS-based document representations.

If we apply the same testing procedure in relation to the secondary baseline—which records the most efficient standalone method for each language—a similar picture emerges. The improvement over such a more demanding baseline is statistically significant for *deu* ($p = 0.001494$), *fra* ($p = 0.01062$), *por* ($p = 0.01791$), and *srp* ($p = 0.04526$), at the level of significance $\alpha = 0.05$. As previously, *eng* ($p = 0.8092$) and *hun* ($p = 0.1285$) exhibited no significance. Additionally, the improvement against the secondary baseline in *slv* ($p = 0.5315$) cannot be considered significant anymore, and this is due to the very large divergence between the performance of words and the performance of lemmas in *slv* (0.7245 and 0.8113, respectively). Such a difference between two similar types of features has no simple explanation, but it inevitably made the winning type of features (i.e., the product of all the matrices) less impressive for *slo*.

**5. Discussion**

According to the accuracy scores presented in Table 4, the best scores for the baseline methods were divided mostly among word-based and lemma-based embeddings. Word-based embeddings performed best for *fra* (0.7561), *hun* (0.9812), and *srp* (0.7279), while lemma-based embeddings performed best for *deu* (0.9212), *eng* (0.8351) and *slv* (0.7729) for accuracy. PoS-mask-based embeddings were best-performing only for *por* (0.8113) and PoS-based embeddings matched the best accuracy score for *srp* (0.7279). These findings undoubtedly answer RQ1:

**RQ1**: *There is no single best document representation method suitable for the AA task across European languages.*

with all but mBERT-based embeddings marking the baseline for at least one language.

From the accuracy score improvement presented in the Table 6 (upper part) and its visualization in Figure 6, it can be observed that most of our composite embeddings (*min* being a clear outlier) outperform the primary baseline for most of the assessed languages, with four methods improving accuracy for all languages both with and without mBERT inputs. As for the more strict secondary baseline (represented by the best base method accuracy for each language), the improvements are presented in Table 6 (lower part). Our composition-based methods outperform this baseline by 10.4% for *fra*, 9.91% for *srp*, 8.37% for *por*, 3.64% for *deu*, 2.43% for *slv*, 1.6% for *hun*, and 0.84% for *eng* using the respective top-performing methods. Using the Newcombe-Wilson continuity-corrected test, we prove the statistical significance of these results for at least four languages (*fra*, *srp*, *por* and *deu*), while the improvements are present but debatable for the rest. In the case of *hun*, it should be noted that the baseline was already at 0.9812 and, considering this, our method actually reduced the error rate by 83% (from 0.0188 to 0.0031), which is an outstanding improvement. As for *slv*, the statistical significance of improvement was corroborated only against the primary baseline. With a definite improvement for at least four languages, these findings answer RQ2:

**RQ2**: *Several document embeddings can be combined in order to produce improved results for the said task.*

showing that they can indeed be used together in order to produce improved results for the said task, and that this method outperforms the established baseline for most languages. This is particularly significant given previous attempts at using lemmas and PoS as features, described in the Introduction, which presented them as worse classifiers than most frequent words.

The results of our weight-based combination methods, as presented in Table 6 and Figure 6, demonstrate that adding weights to the inputs in a parallel architecture can induce further improvements of the results.

The *weights–transfer* method, based on training weights on one and then applying them to distances from another language in a linear composition, was found to be the best performing solution for four out of seven languages (*deu*, *eng*, *fra*, and *slv*), and it matched the best solution for one language (*hun*). It was only outperformed by other compositions for two languages (*por* and *srp*), where the best performing method was found to be *product*-based simple composition. Note, however, that for *srp* the difference between the *product* method and the *weights–transfer* method was neglectable (0.8000 vs. 0.7967). With an average improvement of 4.47% across all languages (Figure 8), *weights–transfer* was found to be the best performing composition method, giving the answer to RQ3:

**RQ3**: *Adding weights to the inputs in a parallel architecture can induce further improvements of the results.*

Data from Table 7, as visualized in Figure 7, show that in a few cases the achievement was gained by including deep learning-based transformations of the document in a parallel architecture, with up to 2.19% for accuracy for *slv* in *product_b* over *product*. These results address RQ4,:

**RQ4**: *Including deep learning-based transformations of the document in a parallel architecture can improve the results of the said architecture.*

however, most of these improvements are statistically insignificant and it is apparent that for the majority of the methods there was no improvement in using mBERT. Moreover, the results deteriorate when mBERT's embeddings are composed with other methods, which is most likely due to the model not being trained nor fine-tuned on this task [41,42].

It should also be noted that distances between documents produced by calculating cosine similarity over mBERT outputs were by far lower (average of 0.0085) than the ones produced by Stylo R package (average of 0.9998). This resulted in them being completely ignored by the *max* composition method, and consequently made the results for *max* and *max_b* identical. For the same reasons, the distances produced by mBERT were picked for the *min* method every time, which resulted in *mean_b* being equal to *bert* (Table 4). Arguably, this explains why the *min* method never outperforms the baseline. A similar behaviour can be observed for the *l2-norm* method, where the final distance was squared. This leads to even smaller values and thus exponentially decreases the impact of mBERT on the final distance (resulting in equal results for *l2-norm* and *l2-norm_b*). The same remark applies to the *mean* method, except that here the impact decreases linearly rather than exponentially, which resulted in nearly identical results for *mean* and *mean_b*, as shown in Table 7 and Figure 7. With the exception of the *min* method, the only opportunity for the mBERT embeddings to actually influence the composite matrices were, firstly, the *product*-based simple composition, where the distance was multiplied by the product of all the other distances and, secondly, the weight-based methods, where the distance was multiplied by its optimized weight. In the case of the *product* method, it was shown that it negatively impacts the accuracy in six out of seven languages with a decrease of up to 8.63% (Table 7). As for the weight-based embeddings, the results are split, with some methods using the mBERT inputs outperforming the ones not using it. However, it must be noted that the weights of the mBERT inputs were set to low negative (gravitating around −0.045) during the training of all the 14 perceptrons using them, thus diminishing their impact on the final scores.

A summary of the improvements is presented in Figure 8, where the best performing composition methods were selected. The bar stands for the average percentual increase of accuracy scores of the six methods across all seven languages, while the points stand for the gain for each method and for each distinct language. It can be seen that the *l2-norm*, with an average improvement of 3.8%, is the best performing simple composition method. This is a valuable observation for AA tasks relying on limited resources, since the aggregation of simple features does not involve external language models (e.g., mBERT or trained weights), and requires less execution time. However, *weights_transfer* is the best performing method overall with 4.471% average improvement. This is also the only method achieving improvements for each of our scrutinized languages.

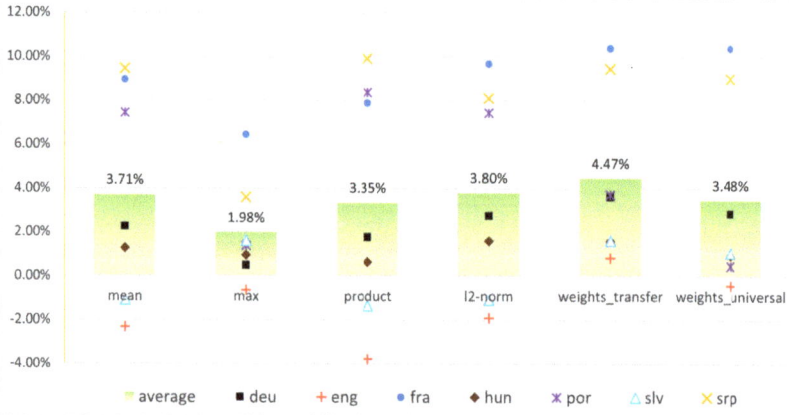

**Figure 8.** Average accuracy score gain over the best baseline method across seven languages for selected composition methods.

The benefits of this research mainly result from the use of a multilingual dataset, as this marks an effort to verify methods using multiple languages, including ones that are somewhat under-researched, particularly when it comes to stylometric applications (i.e., Hungarian, Serbian, Slovenian). Examining such a number of languages at a time provides us with a rare opportunity to generalize our findings. Using such diverse, yet similarly designed, corpora was possible thanks to the international COST Action, in which the authors actively participate, and which led to the creation of comparable representative corpora of European literature. This study further advances the Action's initiatives towards development of distant reading methods and tools, and towards analysis of European literature at the distance. The use of multilingual corpora allowed us to conduct transfer learning through document embeddings for one language, using the weights trained on other languages' datasets. The reasonable performance of the above method is in line with the findings of another outcome of the Action [43], which found that different types of information combined together improved the performance of BERT-based direct speech classifier. Secondly, the use of ELTeC level–2 corpora, which contain rich grammatical annotation that is encoded in a way that facilitates cross-language comparisons, allowed us to use information about lemmas and PoS. By examining them both on their own, and in combined embeddings, we were able to determine that combined lexical and grammatical information outperforms traditional word-based approaches. Finally, the paper also contributes to the efforts of making artificial intelligence and neural network based stylometric endeavors more transparent. While mBERT-based classifications are largely obtained in a black-box manner, the use of a shallow neural network in calculating weights produces clear and interpretable values.

This research also brought one unexpected result in discovering one unknown author. Namely, the author of the novel *Beogradske tajne* (Belgrade's secrets) in Serbian sub-collection has been unknown (according to the National and University libraries), but the computed distances suggested that the author is *Todorović Pera*. By further research, it was found that the same suspicion was raised by some historians.

Future research will, firstly, extend the application to other languages, as more text sub-collections are expected to be published within the same project. This would focus on the use of the best performing simple composition methods and the previously trained universal weights. Expanding the list of baseline methods with more different features (e.g., character n-grams, word length, punctuation frequency) and using them in further compositions, is also an obvious next step. We also expect that fine-tuning of mBERT for AA task should produce the expected results and allow for further investigations of RQ3, making it another area demanding further studies.

Another aspect we intend to test is the effect of document lengths on our proposed methods. Initial calibration tests, during which we settled with the fixed document length of 10,000 tokens, suggested an extended gap in accuracy scores of baseline and composition methods when dealing with shorter texts (2000 and 5000 tokens). We suspect that, since the baseline accuracy is lower when working with shorter texts, there is an increased possibility for improvement using the combination methods.

## 6. Conclusions

In this research, we tested standalone (word-based, lemma-based, PoS-based, and PoS mask-based) and composition-based embeddings (derived from the standalone ones using different methods of combining them on a matrix level, e.g., mean, product, $l^2$ norm of the matrices), compared them with one another, and found that for most of the examined languages most of our methods outperform the baseline. It is examined that our composition-based embeddings outperform the best baseline by a significant margin for four languages: German, French, Portuguese, and Serbian, and also bring a certain batch of improvements for Hungarian and Slovenian. Our transfer-learning-based method *weights_transfer* also outperformed the best baseline for every language, averaging in nearly 5% improvement. On the other hand, we found no statistically significant impact of the usage of out-of-the-box mBERT-based document representations on the performance of this composite models for this task. Based on all of the findings, we conclude that the combination of word, lemma, and PoS-based document representations can model the language to a greater extent than any of them alone, which is especially viable for languages where PoS-based embeddings carry enough information and for authorship attribution task.

Other benefits of our research include creating the multilingual document representations dataset (28,204 10,000-token documents), 133 literary document embeddings for 7 European languages and multilingually trained weights grouped by document representation and language, all of which can be used in future research in stylometry and natural language processing with an accent on the authorship attribution task.

**Author Contributions:** Conceptualization, M.Š. and R.S.; methodology, M.Š. and M.I.N.; software, M.Š.; validation, M.E., M.I.N. and M.Š.; formal analysis, M.Š.; investigation, J.B.; resources, R.S.; data curation, R.S.; writing—original draft preparation, M.Š.; writing—review and editing, all authors; visualization, M.Š.; supervision, R.S. and M.E.; project administration, J.B.; funding acquisition, J.B. All authors have read and agreed to the published version of the manuscript.

**Funding:** This research and work on the ELTeC corpora was performed in the framework of the project Distant Reading for European Literary History, COST (European Cooperation in Science and Technology) Action CA16204, with funding from the Horizon 2020 Framework Programme of the EU.

**Data Availability Statement:** All of the data produced by this experiment as well as the complete code, which can be used to reproduce the results of the study, is publicly available as a repository at https://github.com/procesaur/parallel-doc-embeds (accessed on 29 January 2022). Original document collections (ELTeC level–2) that were used to create datasets for this experiment are publicly available on GitHub for each language, respectively. https://github.com/COST-ELTeC/ELTeC-deu/tree/master/level2 (accessed on 29 January 2022); https://github.com/COST-ELTeC/ELTeC-eng/tree/master/level2 (accessed on 29 January 2022); https://github.com/COST-ELTeC/ELTeC-fra/tree/master/level2 (accessed on 29 January 2022); https://github.com/COST-ELTeC/ELTeC-hun/tree/master/level2 (accessed on 29 January 2022); https://github.com/COST-ELTeC/ELTeC-por/tree/master/level2 (accessed on 29 January 2022); https://github.com/COST-ELTeC/ELTeC-slv/tree/master/level2 (accessed on 29 January 2022); https://github.com/COST-ELTeC/ELTeC-srp/tree/master/level2 (accessed on 29 January 2022).

**Acknowledgments:** The authors thanks to numerous contributors to the ELTeC text collection, specially the members of the COST Action CA16204 Distant Reading for European Literary History: WG1 for preparing the text collections and WG2 for making the available annotated versions.

**Conflicts of Interest:** The authors declare no conflict of interest. The funders had no role in the design of the study; in the collection, analyses, or interpretation of data; in the writing of the manuscript, or in the decision to publish the results.

## Abbreviations

The following abbreviations are used in this manuscript:

| | |
|---|---|
| AA | Authorship Attribution |
| BERT | Bidirectional Encoder Representations from Transformers |
| CNN | Convolutional Neural Network |
| ELTeC | European Literary Text Collection |
| k-NN | k-Nearest Neighbors |
| mBERT | Multilingual BERT |
| NLP | Natural Language Processing |
| NLTK | Natural Language Toolkit |
| PoS | Part of Speech |
| TF-IDF | Term Frequency–Inverse Document Frequency |

## Appendix A

Complete evaluation results—accuracy, precision, recall, and weighted and macro-averaged $F_1$-scores for each language—are presented below (Tables A1–A7).

**Table A1.** Authorship attribution task evaluation metrics for German—*deu*.

| Embedding Base | Accuracy | Precision | Recall | Weighted $F_1$-Score | Macro $F_1$-Score |
|---|---|---|---|---|---|
| bert | 0.7129 | 0.8184 | 0.7129 | 0.7423 | 0.2582 |
| word | 0.9203 | 0.9790 | 0.9203 | 0.9387 | 0.4283 |
| pos | 0.8370 | 0.9154 | 0.8370 | 0.8611 | 0.3468 |
| lemma | 0.9212 | 0.9644 | 0.9212 | 0.9391 | 0.4815 |
| masked_2 | 0.7346 | 0.8949 | 0.7346 | 0.7822 | 0.2979 |
| mean | 0.9420 | 0.9863 | 0.9420 | 0.9579 | 0.4915 |
| mean_b | 0.9420 | 0.9863 | 0.9420 | 0.9579 | 0.4915 |
| max | 0.9257 | 0.9781 | 0.9257 | 0.9436 | 0.4623 |
| max_b | 0.9257 | 0.9781 | 0.9257 | 0.9436 | 0.4623 |
| min | 0.8433 | 0.9215 | 0.8433 | 0.8679 | 0.3714 |
| min_b | 0.7129 | 0.8184 | 0.7129 | 0.7423 | 0.2582 |
| product | 0.9375 | 0.9826 | 0.9375 | 0.9529 | 0.4773 |
| product_b | 0.9058 | 0.9556 | 0.9058 | 0.9196 | 0.4609 |
| l2-norm | 0.9466 | 0.9856 | 0.9466 | 0.9604 | 0.5053 |
| l2-norm_b | 0.9466 | 0.9856 | 0.9466 | 0.9604 | 0.5053 |
| weights_fra | 0.9547 | 0.9871 | 0.9547 | 0.9660 | 0.5403 |
| weights_fra_b | 0.9538 | 0.9854 | 0.9538 | 0.9646 | 0.5520 |
| weights_universal-deu | 0.9475 | 0.9861 | 0.9475 | 0.9617 | 0.5387 |
| weights_universal_b-deu | 0.9484 | 0.9861 | 0.9484 | 0.9623 | 0.5571 |

**Table A2.** Authorship attribution task evaluation metrics for English—*eng*.

| Embedding Base | Accuracy | Precision | Recall | Weighted $F_1$-Score | Macro $F_1$-Score |
|---|---|---|---|---|---|
| bert | 0.5561 | 0.6796 | 0.5561 | 0.5966 | 0.1134 |
| word | 0.8175 | 0.9482 | 0.8175 | 0.8588 | 0.2215 |
| pos | 0.6632 | 0.8415 | 0.6632 | 0.72 | 0.133 |
| lemma | 0.8351 | 0.9645 | 0.8351 | 0.8753 | 0.217 |
| masked_2 | 0.6439 | 0.8261 | 0.6439 | 0.7017 | 0.1329 |
| mean | 0.8158 | 0.9244 | 0.8158 | 0.8484 | 0.2052 |
| mean_b | 0.8175 | 0.9248 | 0.8175 | 0.8493 | 0.2166 |
| max | 0.8298 | 0.9523 | 0.8298 | 0.8698 | 0.2047 |
| max_b | 0.8298 | 0.9523 | 0.8298 | 0.8698 | 0.2047 |
| min | 0.6649 | 0.8385 | 0.6649 | 0.7199 | 0.1329 |
| min_b | 0.5561 | 0.6796 | 0.5561 | 0.5966 | 0.1134 |
| product | 0.8035 | 0.9223 | 0.8035 | 0.8364 | 0.2031 |
| product_b | 0.7474 | 0.8679 | 0.7474 | 0.7734 | 0.1717 |
| l2-norm | 0.8193 | 0.9236 | 0.8193 | 0.8509 | 0.2232 |
| l2-norm_b | 0.8193 | 0.9236 | 0.8193 | 0.8509 | 0.2232 |
| weights_slv | 0.8421 | 0.9487 | 0.8421 | 0.8772 | 0.2419 |
| weights_slv_b | 0.8404 | 0.9519 | 0.8404 | 0.877 | 0.235 |
| weights_universal-eng | 0.8316 | 0.9451 | 0.8316 | 0.8658 | 0.2292 |
| weights_universal_b-eng | 0.8386 | 0.9464 | 0.8386 | 0.8735 | 0.2405 |

Table A3. Authorship attribution task evaluation metrics for French—*fra*.

| Embedding Base | Accuracy | Precision | Recall | Weighted $F_1$-Score | Macro $F_1$-Score |
|---|---|---|---|---|---|
| bert | 0.4444 | 0.6286 | 0.4444 | 0.4912 | 0.1390 |
| word | 0.7561 | 0.8832 | 0.7561 | 0.7992 | 0.2927 |
| pos | 0.6125 | 0.7563 | 0.6125 | 0.6485 | 0.2210 |
| lemma | 0.7507 | 0.9025 | 0.7507 | 0.7951 | 0.2842 |
| masked_2 | 0.7046 | 0.8886 | 0.7046 | 0.7718 | 0.2539 |
| mean | 0.8238 | 0.9272 | 0.8238 | 0.8551 | 0.3757 |
| mean_b | 0.8238 | 0.9278 | 0.8238 | 0.8551 | 0.3755 |
| max | 0.8049 | 0.9298 | 0.8049 | 0.8412 | 0.2938 |
| max_b | 0.8049 | 0.9298 | 0.8049 | 0.8412 | 0.2938 |
| min | 0.6341 | 0.7625 | 0.6341 | 0.6717 | 0.2422 |
| min_b | 0.4444 | 0.6286 | 0.4444 | 0.4912 | 0.1390 |
| product | 0.8157 | 0.9164 | 0.8157 | 0.8446 | 0.3711 |
| product_b | 0.7453 | 0.8677 | 0.7453 | 0.7848 | 0.2987 |
| l2-norm | 0.8293 | 0.9276 | 0.8293 | 0.8583 | 0.3882 |
| l2-norm_b | 0.8293 | 0.9276 | 0.8293 | 0.8583 | 0.3882 |
| weights_slv | 0.8347 | 0.9295 | 0.8347 | 0.8644 | 0.3943 |
| weights_slv_b | 0.8320 | 0.9294 | 0.8320 | 0.8630 | 0.3710 |
| weights_universal-fra | 0.8347 | 0.9295 | 0.8347 | 0.8644 | 0.3827 |
| weights_universal_b-fra | 0.8293 | 0.9269 | 0.8293 | 0.8602 | 0.3699 |

Table A4. Authorship attribution task evaluation metrics for Hungarian—*hun*.

| Embedding Base | Accuracy | Precision | Recall | Weighted $F_1$-Score | Macro $F_1$-Score |
|---|---|---|---|---|---|
| bert | 0.6991 | 0.8204 | 0.6991 | 0.7403 | 0.2987 |
| word | 0.9812 | 1.0000 | 0.9812 | 0.9904 | 0.6423 |
| pos | 0.8088 | 0.9596 | 0.8088 | 0.8675 | 0.2905 |
| lemma | 0.9781 | 0.9909 | 0.9781 | 0.9840 | 0.7219 |
| masked_2 | 0.9185 | 0.9822 | 0.9185 | 0.9433 | 0.4289 |
| mean | 0.9937 | 1.0000 | 0.9937 | 0.9968 | 0.8433 |
| mean_b | 0.9937 | 1.0000 | 0.9937 | 0.9968 | 0.8433 |
| max | 0.9906 | 1.0000 | 0.9906 | 0.9952 | 0.7834 |
| max_b | 0.9906 | 1.0000 | 0.9906 | 0.9952 | 0.7834 |
| min | 0.8150 | 0.9661 | 0.8150 | 0.8741 | 0.2860 |
| min_b | 0.6991 | 0.8204 | 0.6991 | 0.7403 | 0.2987 |
| product | 0.9875 | 1.0000 | 0.9875 | 0.9933 | 0.7791 |
| product_b | 0.9718 | 0.9887 | 0.9718 | 0.9789 | 0.8254 |
| l2-norm | 0.9969 | 1.0000 | 0.9969 | 0.9984 | 0.9157 |
| l2-norm_b | 0.9969 | 1.0000 | 0.9969 | 0.9984 | 0.9157 |
| weights_srp | 0.9969 | 1.0000 | 0.9969 | 0.9984 | 0.9157 |
| weights_srp_b | 0.9969 | 1.0000 | 0.9969 | 0.9984 | 0.9157 |
| weights_universal-hun | 0.9906 | 0.9970 | 0.9906 | 0.9937 | 0.8412 |
| weights_universal_b-hun | 0.9906 | 1.0000 | 0.9906 | 0.9952 | 0.7826 |

**Table A5.** Authorship attribution task evaluation metrics for Portuguese—*por.*

| Embedding Base | Accuracy | Precision | Recall | Weighted $F_1$-Score | Macro $F_1$-Score |
|---|---|---|---|---|---|
| bert | 0.5925 | 0.8853 | 0.5925 | 0.6510 | 0.1152 |
| word | 0.7245 | 0.9051 | 0.7245 | 0.7742 | 0.2112 |
| pos | 0.7509 | 0.9646 | 0.7509 | 0.8167 | 0.1709 |
| lemma | 0.8000 | 0.9688 | 0.8000 | 0.8588 | 0.2826 |
| masked_2 | 0.8113 | 0.9752 | 0.8113 | 0.8705 | 0.2083 |
| mean | 0.8717 | 0.9861 | 0.8717 | 0.9163 | 0.3076 |
| mean_b | 0.8717 | 0.9861 | 0.8717 | 0.9163 | 0.3076 |
| max | 0.8226 | 0.9673 | 0.8226 | 0.8790 | 0.2778 |
| max_b | 0.8226 | 0.9673 | 0.8226 | 0.8790 | 0.2778 |
| min | 0.7547 | 0.9735 | 0.7547 | 0.8223 | 0.1724 |
| min_b | 0.5925 | 0.8853 | 0.5925 | 0.6510 | 0.1152 |
| product | 0.8792 | 0.9863 | 0.8792 | 0.9202 | 0.3333 |
| product_b | 0.8189 | 0.9572 | 0.8189 | 0.8672 | 0.2722 |
| l2-norm | 0.8717 | 0.9811 | 0.8717 | 0.9147 | 0.3493 |
| l2-norm_b | 0.8717 | 0.9811 | 0.8717 | 0.9147 | 0.3493 |
| weights_slv | 0.8415 | 0.9626 | 0.8415 | 0.8866 | 0.3250 |
| weights_slv_b | 0.8415 | 0.9593 | 0.8415 | 0.8851 | 0.3108 |
| weights_universal-por | 0.8151 | 0.9523 | 0.8151 | 0.8641 | 0.2920 |
| weights_universal_b-por | 0.8075 | 0.9473 | 0.8075 | 0.8566 | 0.2774 |

**Table A6.** Authorship attribution task evaluation metrics for Slovenian—*slv.*

| Embedding Base | Accuracy | Precision | Recall | Weighted $F_1$-Score | Macro $F_1$-Score |
|---|---|---|---|---|---|
| bert | 0.5042 | 0.5991 | 0.5042 | 0.5170 | 0.2819 |
| word | 0.7188 | 0.8148 | 0.7188 | 0.7259 | 0.4221 |
| pos | 0.6958 | 0.7906 | 0.6958 | 0.7181 | 0.4226 |
| lemma | 0.7729 | 0.8530 | 0.7729 | 0.7860 | 0.5034 |
| masked_2 | 0.7208 | 0.8093 | 0.7208 | 0.7377 | 0.4866 |
| mean | 0.7646 | 0.8603 | 0.7646 | 0.7771 | 0.5455 |
| mean_b | 0.7646 | 0.8603 | 0.7646 | 0.7771 | 0.5455 |
| max | 0.7854 | 0.8622 | 0.7854 | 0.7979 | 0.4819 |
| max_b | 0.7854 | 0.8622 | 0.7854 | 0.7979 | 0.4819 |
| min | 0.6979 | 0.7941 | 0.6979 | 0.7212 | 0.4363 |
| min_b | 0.5042 | 0.5991 | 0.5042 | 0.5170 | 0.2819 |
| product | 0.7625 | 0.8600 | 0.7625 | 0.7775 | 0.5482 |
| product_b | 0.7792 | 0.8657 | 0.7792 | 0.7947 | 0.4955 |
| l2-norm | 0.7646 | 0.8602 | 0.7646 | 0.7777 | 0.5455 |
| l2-norm_b | 0.7646 | 0.8602 | 0.7646 | 0.7777 | 0.5455 |
| weights_eng | 0.7854 | 0.8692 | 0.7854 | 0.7960 | 0.5411 |
| weights_eng_b | 0.7917 | 0.8600 | 0.7917 | 0.7988 | 0.4956 |
| weights_universal-slv | 0.7812 | 0.8743 | 0.7812 | 0.7934 | 0.5398 |
| weights_universal_b-slv | 0.7771 | 0.8668 | 0.7771 | 0.7878 | 0.5530 |

**Table A7.** Authorship attribution task evaluation metrics for Serbian—*spr*.

| Embedding Base | Accuracy | Precision | Recall | Weighted $F_1$-Score | Macro $F_1$-Score |
|---|---|---|---|---|---|
| bert | 0.4918 | 0.6537 | 0.4918 | 0.5226 | 0.2441 |
| word | 0.7279 | 0.8941 | 0.7279 | 0.7518 | 0.4200 |
| pos | 0.7279 | 0.8312 | 0.7279 | 0.7364 | 0.3765 |
| lemma | 0.7082 | 0.8973 | 0.7082 | 0.7414 | 0.3824 |
| masked_2 | 0.7016 | 0.7880 | 0.7016 | 0.7140 | 0.3676 |
| mean | 0.7967 | 0.9692 | 0.7967 | 0.8120 | 0.5383 |
| mean_b | 0.8000 | 0.9692 | 0.8000 | 0.8174 | 0.5404 |
| max | 0.7541 | 0.8896 | 0.7541 | 0.7740 | 0.4676 |
| max_b | 0.7541 | 0.8896 | 0.7541 | 0.7740 | 0.4676 |
| min | 0.7344 | 0.8360 | 0.7344 | 0.7388 | 0.3888 |
| min_b | 0.4918 | 0.6537 | 0.4918 | 0.5226 | 0.2441 |
| product | 0.8000 | 0.9668 | 0.8000 | 0.8160 | 0.5389 |
| product_b | 0.7836 | 0.9406 | 0.7836 | 0.8042 | 0.4453 |
| l2-norm | 0.7869 | 0.9622 | 0.7869 | 0.8067 | 0.5310 |
| l2-norm_b | 0.7869 | 0.9622 | 0.7869 | 0.8067 | 0.5310 |
| weights_fra | 0.7967 | 0.9709 | 0.7967 | 0.8220 | 0.5331 |
| weights_hun_b | 0.7869 | 0.9428 | 0.7869 | 0.8036 | 0.5098 |
| weights_universal-srp | 0.7934 | 0.9655 | 0.7934 | 0.8169 | 0.5464 |
| weights_universal_b-srp | 0.7934 | 0.9673 | 0.7934 | 0.8181 | 0.5325 |

## References

1. Moretti, F. Conjectures on World Literature. *New Left Rev.* **2000**, *1*, 54–68.
2. El, S.E.M.; Kassou, I. Authorship analysis studies: A survey. *Int. J. Comput. Appl.* **2014**, *86*, 22–29.
3. Camps, J.B.; Clérice, T.; Pinche, A. Stylometry for Noisy Medieval Data: Evaluating Paul Meyer's Hagiographic Hypothesis. *arXiv* **2020**, arXiv:2012.03845.
4. Stamatatos, E.; Koppel, M. Plagiarism and authorship analysis: Introduction to the special issue. *Lang. Resour. Eval.* **2011**, *45*, 1–4. [CrossRef]
5. Yang, M.; Chow, K.P. Authorship Attribution for Forensic Investigation with Thousands of Authors. In *Proceedings of the ICT Systems Security and Privacy Protection*; Cuppens-Boulahia, N., Cuppens, F., Jajodia, S., Abou El Kalam, A., Sans, T., Eds.; Springer: Berlin/Heidelberg, Germany, 2014; pp. 339–350.
6. Iqbal, F.; Binsalleeh, H.; Fung, B.C.; Debbabi, M. Mining writeprints from anonymous e-mails for forensic investigation. *Digit. Investig.* **2010**, *7*, 56–64. [CrossRef]
7. Mendenhall, T.C. The characteristic curves of composition. *Science* **1887**, *11*, 237–246. [CrossRef]
8. Mosteller, F.; Wallace, D.L. *Inference & Disputed Authorship: The Federalist*; CSLI Publications: Stanford, CA, USA, 1964.
9. Stamatatos, E. A survey of modern authorship attribution methods. *J. Am. Soc. Inf. Sci. Technol.* **2009**, *60*, 538–556. [CrossRef]
10. Jockers, M.L.; Witten, D.M. A comparative study of machine learning methods for authorship attribution. *Lit. Linguist. Comput.* **2010**, *25*, 215–223. [CrossRef]
11. Burrows, J. 'Delta': A Measure of Stylistic Difference and a Guide to Likely Authorship. *Lit. Linguist. Comput.* **2002**, *17*, 267–287. [CrossRef]
12. Evert, S.; Proisl, T.; Vitt, T.; Schöch, C.; Jannidis, F.; Pielström, S. Towards a better understanding of Burrows's Delta in literary authorship attribution. In Proceedings of the Fourth Workshop on Computational Linguistics for Literature, Denver, CO, USA, 4 June 2015; pp. 79–88.
13. Evert, S.; Proisl, T.; Schöch, C.; Jannidis, F.; Pielström, S.; Vitt, T. Explaining Delta, or: How do distance measures for authorship attribution work? Presented at Corpus Linguistics 2015, Lancaster, UK, 21–24 July 2015.
14. Kestemont, M. Function Words in Authorship Attribution. From Black Magic to Theory? In Proceedings of the 3rd Workshop on Computational Linguistics for Literature (CLfL@EACL), Gothenburg, Sweden, 27 April 2014; pp. 59–66.
15. R. Sarwar, Q. Li, T.R.; Nutanong, S. A scalable framework for cross-lingual authorship identification. *Inf. Sci.* **2018**, *465*, 323–339. [CrossRef]
16. Rybicki, J.; Eder, M. Deeper Delta across genres and languages: Do we really need the most frequent words? *Lit. Linguist. Comput.* **2011**, *26*, 315–321. [CrossRef]
17. Górski, R.; Eder, M.; Rybicki, J. Stylistic fingerprints, POS tags and inflected languages: A case study in Polish. In *Proceedings of the Qualico 2014: Book of Abstracts*; Palacky University: Olomouc, Czech Republic, 2014; pp. 51–53.

18. Eder, M.; Byszuk, J. Feature selection in authorship attribution: Ordering the wordlist. In *Digital Humanities 2019: Book of Abstracts*; Utrecht University: Utrecht, The Netherlands, 2019; Chapter 0930, p. 1.

19. Kestemont, M.; Luyckx, K.; Daelemans, W. Intrinsic Plagiarism Detection Using Character Trigram Distance Scores—Notebook for PAN at CLEF 2011. In Proceedings of the CLEF 2011 Labs and Workshop, Notebook Papers, Amsterdam, The Netherlands, 19–22 September 2011.

20. Weerasinghe, J.; Greenstadt, R. Feature Vector Difference based Neural Network and Logistic Regression Models for Authorship Verification. In Proceedings of the Notebook for PAN at CLEF 2020, Thessaloniki, Greece, 22–25 September 2020; Volume 2695.

21. Eder, M.; Rybicki, J.; Kestemont, M. Stylometry with R: A package for computational text analysis. *R J.* **2016**, *8*, 107–121. [CrossRef]

22. Kocher, M.; Savoy, J. Distributed language representation for authorship attribution. *Digit. Scholarsh. Humanit.* **2018**, *33*, 425–441. [CrossRef]

23. Salami, D.; Momtazi, S. Recurrent convolutional neural networks for poet identification. *Digit. Scholarsh. Humanit.* **2020**, *36*, 472–481. [CrossRef]

24. Segarra, S.; Eisen, M.; Ribeiro, A. Authorship Attribution Through Function Word Adjacency Networks. *Trans. Sig. Proc.* **2015**, *63*, 5464–5478. [CrossRef]

25. Marinho, V.Q.; Hirst, G.; Amancio, D.R. Authorship Attribution via Network Motifs Identification. In Proceedings of the 2016 5th Brazilian Conference on Intelligent Systems (BRACIS), Recife, Brazil, 9–12 October 2016; pp. 355–360.

26. Stamatatos, E.; Daelemans, W.; Verhoeven, B.; Juola, P.; López-López, A.; Potthast, M.; Stein, B. Overview of the Author Identification Task at PAN 2014. *CLEF (Work. Notes)* **2014**, *1180*, 877–897.

27. Akimushkin, C.; Amancio, D.R.; Oliveira, O.N. On the role of words in the network structure of texts: Application to authorship attribution. *Phys. A Stat. Mech. Its Appl.* **2018**, *495*, 49–58. [CrossRef]

28. Devlin, J.; Chang, M.; Lee, K.; Toutanova, K. BERT: Pre-training of Deep Bidirectional Transformers for Language Understanding. *arXiv* **2018**, arXiv:1810.04805.

29. Iyer, A.; Vosoughi, S. Style Change Detection Using BERT—Notebook for PAN at CLEF 2020. In Proceedings of the CLEF 2020 Labs and Workshops, Notebook Papers, Thessaloniki, Greece, 22–25 September 2020; Cappellato, L., Eickhoff, C., Ferro, N., Névéol, A., Eds.; CEUR-WS: Aachen, Germany, 2020.

30. Fabien, M.; Villatoro-Tello, E.; Motlicek, P.; Parida, S. BertAA: BERT fine-tuning for Authorship Attribution. In Proceedings of the 17th International Conference on Natural Language Processing (ICON), Patna, India, 18–21 December 2020; NLP Association of India (NLPAI): Indian Institute of Technology Patna: Patna, India, 2020; pp. 127–137.

31. Burnard, L.; Schöch, C.; Odebrecht, C. In search of comity: TEI for distant reading. *J. Text Encoding Initiat.* **2021**, *2021*, 1–21. [CrossRef]

32. Schöch, C.; Patras, R.; Erjavec, T.; Santos, D. Creating the European Literary Text Collection (ELTeC): Challenges and Perspectives. *Mod. Lang. Open* **2021**, *1*, 25. [CrossRef]

33. Kilgarriff, A.; Rychly, P.; Smrz, P.; Tugwell, D. The Sketch Engine. In Proceedings of the Eleventh EURALEX International Congress, Lorient, France, 6–10 July 2004; pp. 105–116.

34. Kilgarriff, A.; Baisa, V.; Bušta, J.; Jakubíček, M.; Kovář, V.; Michelfeit, J.; Rychlý, P.; Suchomel, V. The Sketch Engine: Ten years on. *Lexicography* **2014**, *1*, 7–36. [CrossRef]

35. Embarcadero-Ruiz, D.; Gómez-Adorno, H.; Embarcadero-Ruiz, A.; Sierra, G. Graph-Based Siamese Network for Authorship Verification. *Mathematics* **2022**, *10*, 277. [CrossRef]

36. Eder, M. Does Size Matter? Authorship Attribution, Small Samples, Big Problem. In *Digital Humanities 2010: Conference Abstracts*; King's College London: London, UK, 2010; pp. 132–134.

37. Eder, M. Style-markers in authorship attribution: A cross-language study of the authorial fingerprint. *Stud. Pol. Linguist.* **2011**, *6*, 99–114.

38. Kingma, D.P.; Ba, J. Adam: A Method for Stochastic Optimization. In Proceedings of the 3rd International Conference on Learning Representations, ICLR 2015, San Diego, CA, USA, 7–9 May 2015; Conference Track Proceedings; Bengio, Y., LeCun, Y., Eds.; International Conference on Representation Learning (ICLR): La Jolla, CA, USA, 2015; pp. 1–15.

39. Eder, M.; Piasecki, M.; Walkowiak, T. An open stylometric system based on multilevel text analysis. *Cogn. Stud. Études Cognitives* **2017**, *17*, 1–26. [CrossRef]

40. Newcombe, R.G. Estimation for the difference between independent proportions: comparison of eleven methods. *Stat. Med.* **1998**, *17*, 873–890. [CrossRef]

41. Ehrmanntraut, A.; Hagen, T.; Konle, L.; Jannidis, F. Type-and Token-based Word Embeddings in the Digital Humanities. In Proceedings of the Conference on Computational Humanities Research 2021, Amsterdam, The Netherlands, 17–19 November 2021; Volume 2989, pp. 16–38.

42. Brunner, A.; Tu, N.D.T.; Weimer, L.; Jannidis, F. To BERT or not to BERT-Comparing Contextual Embeddings in a Deep Learning Architecture for the Automatic Recognition of four Types of Speech, Thought and Writing Representation. In Proceedings of the 5th Swiss Text Analytics Conference (SwissText) and 16th Conference on Natural Language Processing (KONVENS), Zurich, Switzerland, 23–25 June 2020; pp. 1–11.

43. Byszuk, J.; Woźniak, M.; Kestemont, M.; Leśniak, A.; Łukasik, W.; Šeļa, A.; Eder, M. Detecting direct speech in multilingual collection of 19th-century novels. In Proceedings of the LT4HALA 2020-1st Workshop on Language Technologies for Historical and Ancient Languages, Marseille, France, 11–16 May 2020; pp. 100–104.

**mathematics**

MDPI

*Article*

# Unsupervised and Supervised Methods to Estimate Temporal-Aware Contradictions in Online Course Reviews

Ismail Badache, Adrian-Gabriel Chifu * and Sébastien Fournier

Department of Computer Science, Aix Marseille Université, CNRS, LIS, 13007 Marseille, France;
ismail.badache@univ-amu.fr (I.B.); sebastien.fournier@univ-amu.fr (S.F.)
* Correspondence: adrian.chifu@univ-amu.fr

**Citation:** Badache, I.; Chifu, A.-G.;
Fournier, S. Unsupervised and
Supervised Methods to Estimate
Temporal-Aware Contradictions in
Online Course Reviews. *Mathematics*
2022, *10*, 809. https://doi.org/
10.3390/math10050809

Academic Editors: Florentina Hristea,
Cornelia Caragea and Ioannis G.
Tsoulos

Received: 13 December 2021
Accepted: 25 February 2022
Published: 3 March 2022

**Publisher's Note:** MDPI stays neutral
with regard to jurisdictional claims in
published maps and institutional affiliations.

**Abstract:** The analysis of user-generated content on the Internet has become increasingly popular for
a wide variety of applications. One particular type of content is represented by the user reviews for
programs, multimedia, products, and so on. Investigating the opinion contained by reviews may
help in following the evolution of the reviewed items and thus in improving their quality. Detecting
contradictory opinions in reviews is crucial when evaluating the quality of the respective resource.
This article aims to estimate the contradiction intensity (strength) in the context of online courses
(MOOC). This estimation was based on review ratings and on sentiment polarity in the comments,
with respect to specific aspects, such as "lecturer", "presentation", etc. Between course sessions, users
stop reviewing, and also, the course contents may evolve. Thus, the reviews are time dependent,
and this is why they should be considered grouped by the course sessions. Having this in mind, the
contribution of this paper is threefold: (a) defining the notion of subjective contradiction around
specific aspects and then estimating its intensity based on sentiment polarity, review ratings, and
temporality; (b) developing a dataset to evaluate the contradiction intensity measure, which was
annotated based on a user study; (c) comparing our unsupervised method with supervised methods
with automatic feature selection, over the dataset. The dataset collected from *coursera.org* is in English.
It includes 2244 courses and 73,873 user-generated reviews of those courses. The results proved that
the standard deviation of the ratings, the standard deviation of the polarities, and the number of
reviews are suitable features for predicting the contradiction intensity classes. Among the supervised
methods, the J48 decision trees algorithm yielded the best performance, compared to the naive Bayes
model and the SVM model.

**Keywords:** sentiment analysis; aspect detection; temporality; rating; feature evaluation; contradiction
intensity

**MSC:** 68T50

## 1. Introduction

Since the evolution of the Internet, and more specifically of the Web 2.0, where users
also represent content producers, it has become essential to be able to analyze the associated
textual information in order to facilitate better navigation through it. In particular, Internet
users massively post comments about the content they watch or the products they buy.
However, it is often quite difficult to find one's way through these comments, partly because
of their quantity, but also because of the way they are written. It thus becomes essential to
carry out automatic processing [1–3].

It often happens for various aspects of a product or content to be discussed in the
comments, so in order to have a better idea of the product or content, it is necessary to
extract and compare the comments about these same aspects. Moreover, the very quantity
of comments concerning the same aspect is often important, and the opinions can be very
divergent. The idea of this article was to extract the opinions by aspect, to detect if there

was a contradiction among the opinions on the same aspect, and then to measure the intensity of this contradiction. This measure, then, allows the user reading the reviews to have a metric indicating if the reviews are all (or almost all) in the same direction, positive or negative, or if there is a large divergence of opinion on a specific aspect. The measure then indicates that it is difficult to tell if this aspect is rated positively or negatively. This measure enabled us to alert the user by indicating the points of disagreement present in the comments for particular aspects, thus highlighting the aspects for which the point of view is the most subjective to each person's appreciation. Table 1 shows an example of contradictory comments from an online course, concerning the "Lesson".

**Table 1.** Contradictory opinions example around the "Lesson" aspect, with polarities (Pol.) and ratings (Rat.).

| Source | Text on the Left | Aspect | Text on the Right | Pol. | Rat. |
|--------|------------------|--------|-------------------|------|------|
| Course | I thought the | Lesson | were really boring, never enjoyable | −0.9 | 2 |
| | I enjoyed very much the | Lesson | and I had a very good time | +0.9 | 5 |

In order to measure the intensity of the contradictions in the comments, it is first necessary to extract the aspects [4,5] from them and to measure the sentiments [6] expressed around these aspects. We therefore focused in this article only on the contradictions expressed through the subjectivity present in the comments. We did not deal with contradictions based on facts.

The contributions of this paper are the following:

- **(C1).** In this paper, we give the definition of the subjective contradiction occurring in reviews, around aspects. Four research questions were raised by this definition:

    - **RQ1:** How do we define the notion of subjective contradiction around an aspect? The definition of the notion of subjective contradiction is based on the notion of sentiment diversity with respect to aspects. We considered, in this article, the notion of diversity as the dispersion of sentiments (sentiment polarity);
    - **RQ2:** How can the strength (intensity) of a contradiction occurring in reviews be estimated? This was performed by computing the degree of dispersion of sentiment polarity around an aspect of a web resource;
    - **RQ3:** How do we balance the sentiment polarity around an aspect and the global rating of a review leading to the underlying question, when computing the intensity of a contradiction? What is the weight of the global rating of a review in the expression of feelings around an aspect?
    - **RQ4:** Freshness and temporality are essential in Web 2.0; it is therefore necessary to take into account the temporality of the reviews when computing contradiction intensity;

- **(C2).** We present the development of a data collection that allows the evaluation of the contradiction intensity estimation. The evaluation was based on a user study;
- **(C3).** We performed an experimental comparison, over our corpus, of the unsupervised method based on our definition of subjective contradiction with supervised methods with automatic feature selection.

To the best of our knowledge, no other model has tried to measure the contradiction's intensity for subjective elements. Thus, it was not possible for us to use specialized state-of-the-art models.

The paper is organized as follows. Section 2 of our paper presents the background and related work. The third section presents the learning model and the non-learning model that we used as a baseline. The fourth section presents our test dataset and the experiments and discussions around the results. The article ends with the conclusion Section.

## 2. Background and Related Work

The use of several state-of-the-art methods is necessary in order to establish a process as complex as contradiction detection. Moreover, very few—if any—studies deal with the detection and measurement of intensity in explicitly subjective sentences. This section presents some of the approaches needed for such detection and measurement, as well as related work such as fact-based contradiction detection, controversy detection, point-of-view detection, disagreement detection, and position detection.

### 2.1. Contradiction Detection Approaches

Our work was focused on detecting and assessing the level of subjective contradiction on a particular aspect in the comments. In the literature, some topics are related and relatively close to our work. Examples include work on fact contradiction, the detection and evaluation of controversies, disputes, scandals, the detection of viewpoints, and vandalized pages, mainly in Wikipedia.

One of the research interests that is closest to the present work is given by factual contradiction. The research of [7–10] is representative of this type of study. At present, there are two approaches that see contradictions as a type of textual inference (for instance, entailment identification) and whose analyses are based on the use of linguistic methods. In some works, such as those of Harabagiu et al. [7], the authors proposed to use linguistic features specific to this kind of problem, such as semantic information, for instance negations (for example: "I hate you"—"I don't hate you") or antonymy (i.e., words with opposite meanings—"light" vs. "dark" or "hot" vs. "cold"). Two mutually exclusive sentences, on the same topic, are then seen as a textual implication expressing a contradiction. In a similar way, in the work of [8], seven types of features (e.g., antonymy, negation, numeric mismatches) can be seen as contributing to a contradiction. These feature types can then lead to incorrect data ("The Eiffel Tower is 421 m high—The Eiffel Tower is 321 m high). The authors then define a contradiction as two sentences that cannot be true simultaneously. This definition cannot be applied to our case because we dealt with subjective expressions and not with factual data. A scalable and automatic solution to contradiction detection was also proposed by Tsytsarau et al. [9,10]. The solution considered by the authors was to aggregate the sentiment scores determined for the sentences and infer whether there is a contradiction or not. When the diversity in terms of sentiment is high, but the aggregation of the sentiment score tends towards zero, then there is a contradiction. However, the authors only sought to detect the presence or absence of a contradiction and not to evaluate its level. Fact contradictions may be studied with respect to a specific field, such as medicine [11]. In this paper, we focused on course reviews from an online platform. The contradiction we targeted concerns several reviews, for the same online course and for the same period (course session); thus, it may be characterized as extrinsic relative to one review in particular. Other research focused on intrinsic contradiction detection, for instance detecting self-contradicting articles from Wikipedia [12].

Our corpus is in English. However, there are works that have tackled contradictions in other languages, such as Spanish [13], Persian [14], or German [15]. The development of multilingual models can also be considered, as is already the case in the analysis of sentiments and emotions [16,17].

Another research topic, very close to ours, concerns controversy detection. The concepts of controversy and dispute are relatively similar, except that a controversy involves a large group of people who have strong disagreements about a particular issue. Indeed, the Merriam-Webster dictionary definition for controversy states: "argument that involves many people who strongly disagree about something, strong disagreement about something among a large group of people". A similar definition was given in [18,19], but with a temporal nuance: a controversy is usually defined as a discussion regarding a specific target entity, which provokes opposing opinions among people, for a finite duration of time. In the majority of works on controversies, the aim is to usually discover the subject of the controversy and not to quantify it or to find the level of virulence of the exchanges.

Discovering the subject of the controversy is then often seen as a problem of classification aiming to find out which documents, paragraphs, or sentences are controversial and which are not or to discover the subject itself. Balasubramanyan et al. [20] used a semi-supervised latent variable model to detect the topics and the degree of polarization these topics caused. Dori-Hacohen and Allan [21,22] treated the problem as a binary classification: whether the web page has a controversial topic or not. To perform this classification, the authors looked for Wikipedia pages that corresponded to the given web page, but displayed a degree of controversy. Garimella et al. [23] constructed a conversation graph on a topic, then partitioned the conversation graph to identify potential points of controversy, and measured the controversy's level based on the characteristics of the graph. Guerra et al. [24] constructed a metric based on the analysis of the boundary in a graph between two communities. The metric was applied to the analysis of communities on Twitter by constructing graphs from retweets. Jang and Allan [25] constructed a controversial language model based on DBpedia. Lin and Hauptmann [26] proposed to measure the proportion, if any, by which two collections of documents were different. In order to quantify this proportion, they used a measure based on statistical distribution divergence. Popescu and Pennacchiotti [19] proposed to detect controversies on Twitter. Three different models were suggested. They were all based on supervised learning using linear regression. Sriteja et al. [27] performed an analysis of the reaction of social media users to press articles dealing with controversial issues. In particular, they used sentiment analysis and word matching to accomplish this task. Other works sought to quantify controversies. For instance, Morales et al. [28] quantified polarity via the propagation of opinions of influential users on Twitter. Garimella et al. [29] proposed the use of a graph-based measure by measuring the level of separation of communities within the graph.

Quite close to our work is the concept of "point of view", also known in the literature as the notion of "collective opinions", where a collective opinion is the set of ideas shared by a group. There is also a proximity with the work on the notion of controversy, but with generally less opposition in the case of "points of view" than in that of "controversy". In a sense, the notion of points of view can also be seen as a controversy on a smaller scale. Among the significant works on the concept of "points of view" is [30], which used the multi-view Latent Dirichlet Allocation (LDA) model. In addition to topic modeling at the word level, as LDA performs, the model uses a variable that gives the point of view at the document level. This model was applied to the discovery of points of view in essays. Cohen and Ruths [31] developed a supervised-learning-based system for point of view detection in social media. The approach treats viewpoint detection as a classification problem. The model used to perform this task was an SVM. Similarly, Conover et al. [32] developed a system based on SVM and took into account social interactions in social networks in order to classify viewpoints. Paul and Girju [33] used the Topic-Aspect Model (TAM) by hijacking the model using aspects as viewpoints. The authors of [34] used an unsupervised approach inspired by LDA, based on Dirichlet distributions and discrete variables, to identify the users' point of view. Trabelsi and Zaïane [35] used the Joint Topic Viewpoint (JTV) model, which jointly models themes and viewpoints. JTV defines themes and viewpoint assignments at the word level and viewpoint distributions at the document level. JTV considers all words as opinion words, without distinguishing between opinion words and topic words. Thonet et al. [36] presented VODUM, an unsupervised topic model designed to jointly discover viewpoints, topics, and opinions in text.

A line of research that is also relatively similar to our work, even if it does not always involve the notion of subjectivity, is the problem of detecting expressions of restraint or the problem of detecting disagreement. This problem has been widely addressed in the literature. In particular, Galley et al. [37] used a maximum entropy classifier. They first identified adjacent pairs using a classification based on maximum entropy from a set of lexical, temporal, and structural characteristics. They then ranked these pairs as agreement or disagreement. Menini and Tonelli [38] used an SVM. They also used different characteristics based on the feelings expressed in the text (negative or positive). They also used semantic features (word embeddings, cosine similarity, and entailment). Mukherjee and Liu [39] adopted a semi-supervised approach to identify expressions of contention in discussion forums.

Another quite close research is the one concerning position detection. Position (stance) detection is a classification problem where the position of the author of the text is obtained in the form of a category label of this set: favorable, against, neither. Among the works on the notion of "stance", Mohammad et al. [40,41] used an SVM and relatively simple features based on N-grams of words and characters. In [42], the authors used a bi-Long Short-Term Memory (LSTM) in order to detect the position of the author of the text. The input of their model was a word embedding based on Word2Vec. Gottopati et al. [43] used an unsupervised approach to detect the position of an author. In order to perform this task, they used a template based on collapsed Gibbs sampling. Johnson and Goldwasser [44] used a weakly supervised method to extract the way questions are formulated and to extract the temporal activity patterns of politicians on Twitter. Their method was applied to the tweets of popular politicians and issues related to the 2016 election. Qiu et al. [34,45] used a regression-based latent factor model, which jointly models user arguments, interactions, and attributes. Somasundaran and Wiebe [46] used an SVM employing characteristics based on feelings and argumentation of opinions, as well as targets of feelings and argumentation. For more details on this topic, refer to [47].

Our work is relatively close to the detection and analysis of points of view, with however some differences. We focused on opposing points of view. Indeed, our subject of study relates to the subjective oppositions expressed by several individuals. It is this subjective opposition, with the formulation of an opinion using feelings, which we call "contradiction" within the article, that we tried to capture. Our work can also be considered close to the work on stance since we looked at oppositions. However, the observed oppositions were not the same since they were not favorable or unfavorable of an assertion, but rather positive or negative about an aspect. The main difference is yet again in the strong expression of subjectivity, which may be absent in the expression of stance. We did not consider our work as being exactly in the domain of controversies since there was no constructed argumentation. Indeed, we considered in our research reviews that were independent of each other, and we were not in the case of a discussion as in a forum, for example. Moreover, unlike most other authors, we did not only try to find out if there was a contradiction among several individuals. We **measured the strength** of this contradiction in order to obtain a level in the contradiction evaluation.

### 2.2. Methods for Aspect Detection

One of the first steps to be taken in order to detect and evaluate the intensity of a contradiction is to extract the necessary aspects. For this purpose, several methods are available. One of the first developed methods [48] used a frequent equational-sentences-based method, which represents a common information extraction technique. These approaches are relatively efficient and simple to implement, especially when the aspects are composed of a single word with a high frequency, but decrease in performance when the frequency of the aspects is relatively low. Other approaches, very widespread in the extraction of aspects, are, for example, the use of Conditional Random Fields (CRFs) or the use of Hidden Markov Models (HMMs) [49]. Other methods, unsupervised, are also often used in this task. For instance, Reference [50] developed a model based on the multi-grain topic model. In [4], the use of unsupervised Hierarchical Aspect Sentiment Models (HASMs) was proposed. This gives the possibility of discovering a hierarchical structure of the feelings integrating the aspects. The present work experimented on a corpus of online reviews. However, we want to stress that its goal was not to perform aspect extraction, but to detect and estimate the level of contradiction around aspects. Unlike recent work in this area [51], the present paper used a method that is simple to implement, which has been proven to work and which corresponds very well to our type of corpus: Poria et al. [5].

*2.3. Methods for Sentiment Analysis*

To detect and estimate subjective contradictions, it is essential to analyze the feelings around the aspects. Researchers have shown a great deal of interest with respect to the field of sentiment analysis. As for aspect extraction, there are supervised and unsupervised solutions, each with their own advantages and disadvantages. Thus, unsupervised methods are generally based on lexicons [52] or on corpus analysis [40]. Concerning supervised methods, sentiment analysis is mostly seen as a classification problem (neutral, positive, and negative classes). Thus, Pang et al. [53] proposed to treat this classification problem using classical methods, for instance SVM or Bayesian networks. More recently, with the advent of deep learning, methods based on Recursive Neural Networks (RNNs) have emerged, such as in [54]. Other works, also based on deep learning, are concerned with unsupervised methods, such as mLSTM [55]). In the work we present in this article, sentiment analysis was not the core of our research, but was part of the process of analyzing contradictions and estimating their intensity. This is why we took inspiration from two state-of-the-art works and compared them in order to choose the most efficient one. First, we were inspired by the work of [53] using a Bayesian classifier. Secondly, we were inspired by the work of [55] based on a neural network.

## 3. Time-Aware Contradiction Intensity

When considering contradictions, significant time lapses may occur between reviews. We therefore hypothesized that a contradiction occurs only if the comments are in the same time interval. This section presents our method for processing the reviews in order to detect contradictions and to measure their intensity by taking this temporal aspect into account. Figure 1 shows the entire process for detecting contradictions and measuring their intensity.

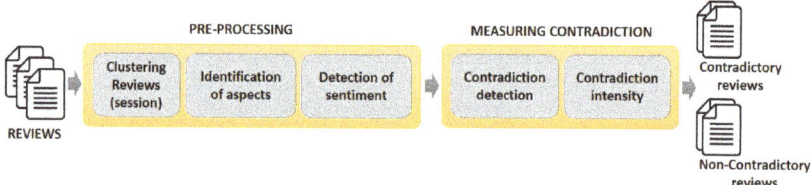

**Figure 1.** Temporal-sentiment-based contradiction intensity framework.

*3.1. Preprocessing*

Two dimensions were combined to measure the strength of the disagreement during a session: the polarity around the aspect and the rating linked with the review. Together, they define the so-called "review-aspect". We utilized a dispersion function based on these dimensions to measure the intensity of disagreement between opposing viewpoints.

### 3.1.1. Clustering Reviews Based on Sessions

The reviews represent online resources with a linear timeline, but "gaps" in this timeline can be observed in the case of some resources such as courses. These gaps symbolize the silence of the users writing the reviews (Figure 2). This happens frequently in the case of courses because they can take place on a specific date and are not continuous. The evolution of these discontinuities is therefore correlated with the evolution of the use of the resource. In the case of courses, these interruptions last on average 35 d. In order to better estimate the contradictions and to better analyze them, the reviews were grouped according to the sessions that were formed between two discontinuities. Thus, for a given aspect, only the contradictions of the same session were examined. The sessions were defined every X days or when there was a sufficiently dense sequence of reviews. In order to obtain these groupings of reviews, the following treatment was applied:

1. We computed a threshold that corresponds to the duration of the jump. This was performed on a per course basis and was based on the average time gaps between reviews (for instance, there was a gap of 35 d for the "Engagement and Nurture Marketing Strategies" lecture);
2. We grouped the reviews with respect to the above-mentioned threshold, on a per course basis;
3. We kept only the important sessions by suppressing the so-called "false sessions" (sessions that contained only a very low number of reviews).

Only the review clusters that had a significant number of reviews were considered for the evaluation. For instance, clusters resulting after the use of K-means [56] that contained only one or two reviews were discarded.

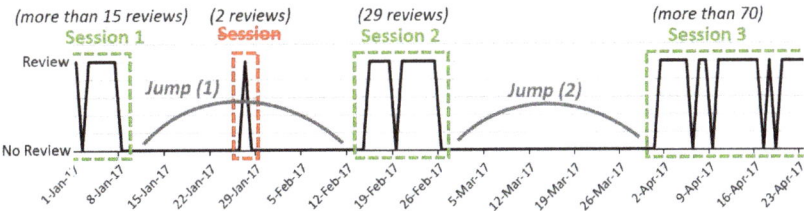

**Figure 2.** Review distribution with respect to the time dimension, for the lecture entitled "Engagement and Nurture Marketing Strategies".

Algorithm 1 describes the review groupings with respect to the course sessions. The next preprocessing step was the feature extraction for the review groups.

### 3.1.2. Aspect Extraction

In the context of our work, the aspect represents a frequently appearing noun that has emotion expressing terms around it. For instance, the term *speaker* is considered as an aspect. We based our aspect extraction on the research proposed in [5]. The method is well suited to the experiments conducted over our data. In addition, we applied the following processing steps:

1. The reviews corpus' term frequency was calculated;
2. The *Stanford Parser* https://nlp.stanford.edu:8080/parser/ (accessed on 5 January 2022) was used for the parts-of-speech labeling of reviews;
3. Nominal category (NN, NNS) https://cs.nyu.edu/grishman/jet/guide/PennPOS.html (accessed on 5 January 2022) terms were chosen;
4. Nouns having emotive terms in a five-term context window were considered (using the *SentiWordNet* https://sentiwordnet.isti.cnr.it/ (accessed on 5 January 2022) dictionary);
5. The extraction of the most common terms from the corpus was performed (the candidates for this step issued from the previous step). The aspects are represented by the before-mentioned terms.

**Example 1.** *Let D be a resource (document, e.g., course) and re its associated review. Table 2 illustrates the five steps for aspect extraction from a review.*

For example, re = *"Michael is a wonderful lecturer delivering the lessons in an easy to understand manner. The whole presentation was easy to follow. I don't recall any ambiguity in his teachings and his slide was clear. I also enjoy some of the assignments because I surprise myself by producing some great images. My main problem is the instructions of the assignments that causes a lot of students to be confused (there are many complaints expressed in the Discussion forum)."*

---

**Algorithm 1:** The reviews of a resource are grouped according to the time period (session) in which they were written.

---

**Input:** Days_Threshold (DsT), List_Reviews (LRs)
**Output:** Groups_of_Reviews (GRs)

1 GRs← ∅ ;    *// Creation and initialization of the output list of groups of reviews generated for a specific resource (in our case a "course")*

2 GRTemp ←— ∅ ;    *// Creation and initialization of the temporary list to save each group of reviews generated during a specific session (time period)*

3 List_GRTemp ←— ∅ ;    *// Creation and initialization of the temporary list to save the groups of reviews belonging to a session*

4 List_Number_Reviews_per_Session(LNRpS) ←— ∅ ;    *// Creation and initialization of the review number for each group per session*

5 K_Clusters = 2 ;    *// Specify the value of the K-means parameter to 2 types of clusters (sufficient/deficient reviews group)*

6 Target_Cluster ←— ∅ ;    *// Creation and initialization of the list to save only true reviews group identified by the K-means clustering algorithm*

   *// Forming reviews groups based on Days_Threshold (DsT) (session period)* **for** $i = 0$; $i<size(LRs) - 1$; $i++$ **do**
7   | **if** $|LRs(i).Date - LRs(i+1).Date| < DsT$ **then**
8   | | GRTemp.add(LRs(i));
9   | **else**
10  | | GRTemp.add(LRs(i)) ;
11  | | List_GRTemp.add(GRTemp);
12  | | Temp ←— ∅ ;
13  | **end**
14 **end**

   *// Counting the reviews in each review group stored in List_GRTemp*
15 **foreach** $gr \in List\_GRTemp$ **do**
16  | LNRpS.add(size(gr));
17 **end**

   *// Using K-means to distinguish the two types of reviews groups*
18 [C1, C2, Cluster1, Cluster2] = K-Means(K_Clusters, LNRpS) ;    *// K-Means algorithm*

   *// C1 and C2 are the centroids of each of the $k$ types of clusters (Cluster1 and Cluster2) i.e., sufficient/deficient reviews group*
19 **if** $C1>C2$ **then**
20  | Target_Cluster = Cluster1;
21 **else**
22  | Target_Cluster = Cluster2;
23 **end**

   *// Counting the reviews in each reviews group stored in List_GRTemp*
24 **foreach** $gr \in List\_GRTemp$ **do**
25  | **if** $size(gr) \in Target\_Cluster$ **then**
26  | | GRs.add(gr);
27  | **end**
28 **end**

---

Table 2 depicts the five steps. First, we computed the frequencies of the terms in the review set (as an example, the terms "course", "material", "assignment", "content", and "lecturer" occurred 44,219, 3286, 3118, 2947, and 2705 times, respectively). Secondly, we grammatically labeled each word ("NN" meaning singular noun and "NNS" meaning plural noun). Thirdly, only nominal category terms were selected. Fourthly, we retained only the nouns surrounded by terms belonging to the *SentiWordNet* dictionary ("Michael is a wonderful *lecturer* delivering the *lessons* in an easy to understand manner."). Finally, we considered as useful aspects only those nouns that were among the most frequent in the corpus of reviews (the useful aspects in these reviews were *lecturer, lesson, presentation, slide,* and *assignment*).

After constructing the aspect list characterizing the dataset, the sentiment polarity must be computed. The sentiment analysis method used for this is described in the following section.

**Table 2.** The aspect extraction steps for a review.

| Step Number | Step Detail |
|---|---|
| 1 | course: 44,219, material: 3,286, assignment: 3118, content: 2947,......, lecturer: 2705, lesson: 1251, presentation: 591, slide: 512, teaching: 119, image: 11, Michael: 2,......$term_i$ |
| 2 | $re = $ **Michael/NN** is/VBZ a/DT wonderful/JJ he/DT **lecturer/NN** delivering/VBG the/DT **lessons/NNS** in/IN an/DT easy/JJ to/TO understand/VB **manner/NN** ./.The/DT whole/JJ **presentation/NN** was/VBD easy/JJ to/TO follow/VB ./. I/PRP do/VBP n't/RB recall/VB any/DT **ambiguity/NN** in/IN his/PRP$ **teachings/NNS** and/CChis/PRP$ **slide/NN** was/VBD clear/JJ ./. I/PRP also/RB enjoy/VBP some/DT of/IN the/DT **assignments/NNS** because/IN I/PRP surprise/VB myself/PRP by/IN producing/VBG some/DT great/JJ **images/NNS** ./. My/PRP$ main/JJ **problem/NN** is/VBZ the/DT **instructions/NNS** of/IN the/DT **assignments/NNS** that/WDT causes/VBZ a/DT lot/NN of/IN **students/NNS** to/TO be/VB confused/JJ (/-LRB- there/EX are/VBP many/JJ **complaints/NNS** expressed/VBN in/IN the/DT **Discussion/NN forum/NN**)/-RRB- ./. |
| 3 | Michael, lecturer, job, lesson, manner, presentation, ambiguity, teachings, slide, assignments, images, problem, instructions, students, complaints, discussion, forum |
| 4 | Michael, lecturer, lesson, presentation, teachings, slide, assignments, images |
| 5 | lecturer, lesson, presentation, slide, assignments |

### 3.1.3. Sentiment Analysis

*SentiNeuron* https://github.com/openai/generating-reviews-discovering-sentiment (accessed on 5 January 2022), an unsupervised approach proposed in [55], was employed to detect sentiment polarity in the review-aspect. This model is based on the multiplicative Long Short-Term Memory (mLSTM), an artificial Recurrent Neural Network (RNN) architecture used in the field of deep learning. Radford et al. [55] discovered the mLSTM unit matching the output sentiment. The authors conducted a series of experiments on several test datasets, such as the review collections from Amazon [57] and IMDb https://www.cs.cornell.edu/people/pabo/movie-review-data/ (accessed on 5 January 2022). This approach provides an accuracy of 91.8% and significantly outperforms several state-of-the-art approaches such as those presented in [58]. *SentiNeuron* yields competitive performance, compared to several state-of-the-art models. In particular, this occurs when working on movie reviews (from IMDb) and also in our situation (*coursera.org* reviews). We note that the term polarity means sentiment, and it is a value between $-1$ and 1.

### 3.2. Contradiction Detection and Contradiction Intensity

In this section, we introduce a model without learning, allowing the detection of contradictions and the calculation of their intensities. We considered that subjective contradictions (e.g., based on subjective elements) are related to aspects, and these are surrounded by subjective terms. We then used pieces of text called review-aspects to study the contradiction between several of these review-aspects. This model was then used as a baseline. In this paper, we propose and then compared learning methods created to detect and to estimate the intensity of the contradiction.

**Definition 1.** *There is a contradiction between two portions of review-aspects $ra_1$ and $ra_2$ containing an aspect, where $ra_1$, $ra_2 \in D$ (document), when the opinions (polarities) around the aspect are opposite (i.e., $pol(ra_1) \times pol(ra_2) \leq 0$). We found that after several empirical experiments, the review-aspect $ra$ was defined by a five-word snippet before and after the aspect in review re.*

Contradiction intensity was estimated using two dimensions: polarity $pol_i$ and rating $rat_i$ of the review-aspect $ra_i$. Let each $ra_i$ be a point on the plane with coordinates $(pol_i, rat_i)$.

Our hypothesis was that the greater the distance (i.e., dispersion) between the values related to each review-aspect $ra_i$ of the same document $D$, the greater is the contradiction intensity. The dispersion indicator with respect to the centroid $ra_{centroid}$ with coordinates $(\overline{pol}, \overline{rat})$ is as follows:

$$Disp(ra_{rat_i}^{pol_i}, D) = \frac{1}{n} \sum_{i=1}^{n} Distance(pol_i, rat_i) \tag{1}$$

$$Distance(pol_i, rat_i) = \sqrt{(pol_i - \overline{pol})^2 + (rat_i - \overline{rat})^2} \tag{2}$$

$Distance(pol_i, rat_i)$ represents the distance between the point $ra_i$ of the scatter plot and the centroid $ra_{centroid}$ (see Figure 3), and $n$ is the number of $ra_i$. The two quantities $pol_i$ and $rat_i$ are represented on different scales; thus, their normalization becomes necessary. Since the polarity $pol_i$ is normalized by design, we only needed to normalize the rating values. We propose the following equation for normalization: $rat_i = \frac{rat_i - 3}{2}$ ($rat_i \in [-1, 1]$). In what follows, the divergence from the centroid of $ra_i$ is denoted by $Disp(ra_{rat_i}^{pol_i}, D)$. Its value varies according to the following:

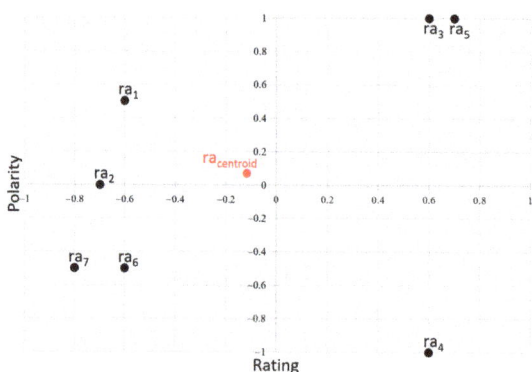

**Figure 3.** Dispersion of review-aspect $ra_i$.

- $Disp$ is positive or zero; if $Disp = 0$, there is no dispersion $ra_i = ra_{centroid}$;
- $Disp$ increases as $ra_i$ moves away from $ra_{centroid}$. (when there is increasing dispersion).

The coordinates $(\overline{pol}, \overline{rat})$ of the centroid $ra_{centroid}$ were computed in two possible ways, which are described below. A simple way is to compute the average of the $ra_i$ points; in this case, the centroid $ra_{centroid}$ corresponds to the average point of the coordinates $ra_i(pol_i, rat_i)$. Another, more refined, way is to weigh this average by the difference in absolute value between the two coordinate values (polarity and notation).

**(a) The average-based centroid.** In this scenario, the centroid's coordinates $ra_centroid$ were calculated as follows using the average of polarities and ratings:

$$\overline{pol} = \frac{pol_1 + pol_2 + ... + pol_n}{n}; \quad \overline{rat} = \frac{rat_1 + rat_2 + ... + rat_n}{n} \tag{3}$$

**(b) The weighted average-based centroid.** In this scenario, the centroid coordinates $ra_{centroid}$ were the weighted average of ratings and polarities:

$$\overline{pol} = \frac{c_1 \cdot pol_1 + c_2 \cdot pol_2 + ... + c_n \cdot pol_n}{n}$$
$$\overline{rat} = \frac{c_1 \cdot rat_1 + c_2 \cdot rat_2 + ... + c_n \cdot rat_n}{n} \tag{4}$$

where $n$ is the number of points $ra_i$. The coefficient $c_i$ was computed as follows:

$$c_i = \frac{|rat_i - pol_i|}{2n} \tag{5}$$

For a data point, if the values of the two dimensions were farther apart, our assumption was that such a point should be considered of high importance. **We hypothesized that a positive aspect in a low-rating review should have a higher weight, and vice versa.** Therefore, an importance coefficient was computed for each data point, based on the absolute value difference between the values over both dimensions. The division by $2n$ represents a normalization by the maximum value of the difference in absolute value ($max(|rat_i - pol_i|) = 2$) and $n$. For instance, for a polarity of $-1$ and a rating of 1, the coefficient is $1/n$ ($|-1-1|/2n = 2/2n = 1/n$), and for a polarity of 1 and a rating of 1, the coefficient is 0 ($|1-1|/2n = 0$).

### 3.3. Predicting Contradiction Intensity

Our model without learning has the advantage of being easy to implement and of not requiring a corpus. However, we had to tackle the issues of the selection of the most relevant and fruitful features for the measurement of the contradiction intensity. Indeed, as long as we did not try all the configurations of the features (rating, polarity), it was not possible to properly judge the efficiency of each of these features, nor to identify the best ones for this task. In addition, the previously presented computation method (Section 3.2) was simply based on a dispersion formula of the two scores associated with polarity and rating. In the present more in-depth study, we employed feature selection methods to determine the best-performing features (derived from the rating, polarity, and review) to consider in the contradiction intensity measurement task. The attribute selection methods aim to suppress the maximum amount of non-relevant and redundant information before the learning process [59]. They also automatically pick the subsets of features that produce the greatest results. This phase highlighted several sets of features. Thus, we evaluated the effectiveness of these sets by applying them to learning techniques in a specific context: the estimation of the intensity of contradiction in text (reviews left by users on MOOC resources). The learning techniques used are techniques that have proven successful in many tasks. We chose to use SVM, decision trees (J48), and naive Bayes for the first experiments. The results obtained based on feature selection were compared to those of our method without learning, in order to measure the potential gain brought in by such techniques.

## 4. Experimental Evaluation

This section presents the performed experiments and their results. After the introduction of our corpus and its study, the section presents and discusses the results obtained in the presence of our baseline. We then present the experiments that allowed us to select the features that gave the best results with the learning-based algorithms. The section ends with a presentation and comparison of the results obtained with the SVM, J48, and naive Bayes algorithms.

### 4.1. Description of the Test Dataset

This section presents in detail the corpus on which we based our experiments. It then presents how the corpus was obtained by means of a study of the annotations made for the qualification of the intensity of contradictions and for the analysis of feeling.

#### 4.1.1. Data

We are not aware of the existence of a standard dataset for evaluating the contradiction intensity (strength). Therefore, we built our own dataset by collecting 73,873 reviews and their ratings corresponding to 2244 English courses from *coursera.org* via its API https://building.coursera.org/app-platform/catalog (accessed on 5 January 2022) and web page *parsing*. This was performed during the time interval 10–14 October 2016. More detailed statistics on this Coursera dataset are depicted in Figure 4. Our entire test dataset, as well as its detailed statistics are publicly available https://pageperso.lis-lab.fr/ismail.ba dache/Reviews_ExtracTerms%20HTML/ (accessed on 5 January 2022).

| Field | | Total Number |
|---|---|---|
| Courses | | 2,244 |
| Courses Rated | | 1,115 |
| Reviews | | 73,873 |
| Reviews | ☆★★★★ | 1,705 |
| Reviews | ☆☆★★★ | 1,443 |
| Reviews | ☆☆☆★★ | 3,302 |
| Reviews | ☆☆☆☆★ | 12,202 |
| Reviews | ☆☆☆☆☆ | 55,221 |

**Figure 4.** Statistics on the Coursera dataset.

We were able to automatically capture 22 useful aspects from the set of reviews (see Figure 5). Figure 5 presents the statistics on the 22 detected aspects, for example for the *Slide* aspect, we recorded: 56 one-star ratings, 64 two-star ratings, 81 three-star ratings, 121 four-star ratings, 115 five-star ratings, 131 reviews with negative polarity, 102 reviews with positive polarity, as well as 192 reviews and 41 courses concerning this aspect.

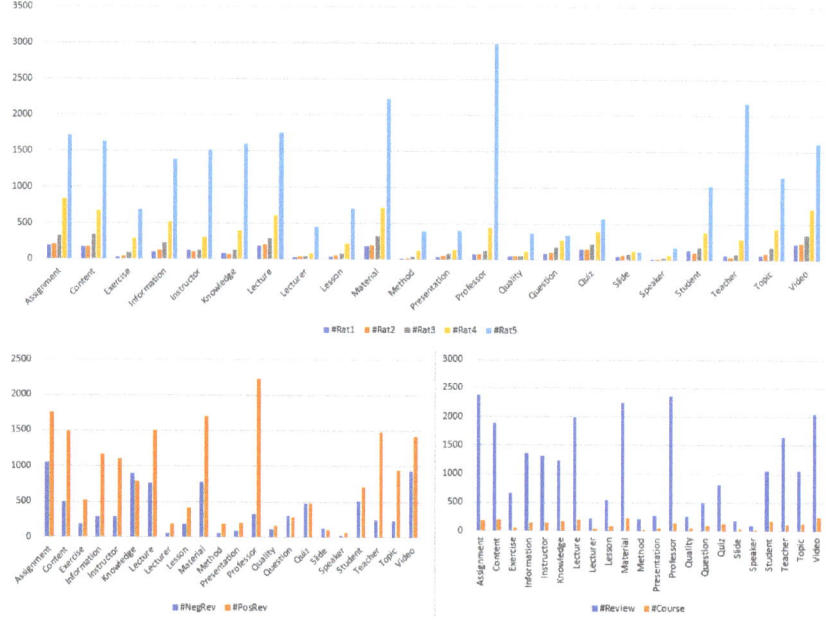

**Figure 5.** Different statistics about the extracted aspects.

### 4.1.2. User Study

For a given aspect, in order to obtain contradiction and sentiment judgments, we conducted a user study as follows:

1. The sentiment class for each review-aspect of 1100 courses was assessed by 3 users (assessors). Users must only judge the polarity of the involved sentiment class;
2. The degree of contradiction between these review-aspects (see Figure 6) was assessed by 3 new users.

Annotation corresponding to the above judgment was performed manually. For each aspect, on average, 22 review-aspects per course were judged (in total: 66,104 review-aspects of 1100 courses, i.e., 50 courses for each aspect). Exactly 3 users evaluated each aspect.

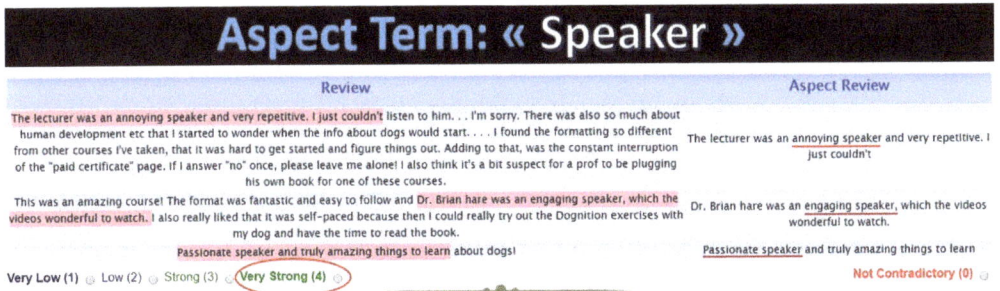

**Figure 6.** Evaluation system interface.

A 3-level assessment scale (*Negative, Neutral, Positive*) was employed for the sentiment evaluation in the review-aspects, in a per-course manner, and a 5-level assessment scale (*Very Low, Low, Strong, Very Strong,* and *Not Contradictory*) was employed for the contradiction evaluation, as depicted in Figure 6.

Using Cohen's Kappa coefficient $k$ [60], we estimated the agreement degree among the assessors for each aspect. In order to obtain a unique Kappa value, we calculated the pairwise Kappa of assessors, and then, we computed the average.

For each aspect from all the reviews, the distribution of the Kappa values is shown in Figure 7. The variation of the measure of agreement was between 0.60 and 0.91. Among the assessors, the average level of agreement was equal to 80%. Such a score corresponds to a strong agreement. Between the assessors who performed the sentiment annotation, the Kappa coefficient value was $k = 0.78$ (78% agreement), which also indicates a substantial agreement.

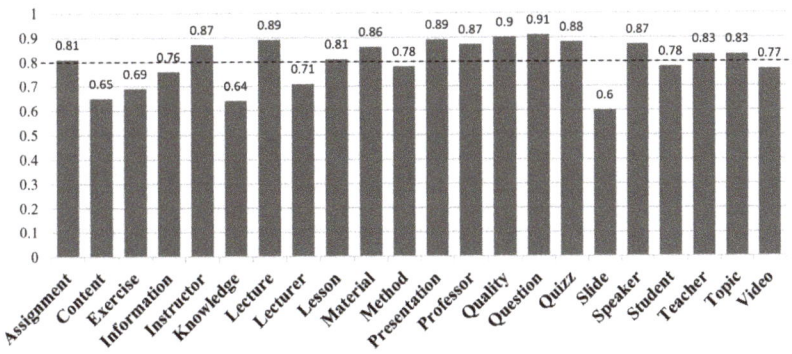

**Figure 7.** Distribution of the Kappa values $k$ per aspect. $<0$ poor agreement, 0.0–0.2 slight agreement, 0.21–0.4 fair agreement, 0.41–0.6 moderate agreement, 0.61–0.8 substantial agreement, and 0.81–1 perfect agreement.

## 4.2. Results and Discussion

This section presents the results obtained first using the learning-free model. We compared the results obtained with and without the use of review sessions and considering both the average-based centroid and the weighted average-based centroid scenarios (see Section 3.2) in turn. We studied the influence of the sentiment analysis algorithm on the results. We then compared the results obtained through the selection of features and the use of learning-based models such as SVM, decision trees, and naive Bayes.

### 4.2.1. Averaged and Weighted Centroid

In order to quantify the effectiveness of our proposal, we employed the same performance measure as for the SemEval competition https://alt.qcri.org/semeval2016/task7/ (accessed on 5 January 2022), that is to say, the correlation coefficient. We used Pearson's correlation coefficient, which considers our results against the annotator's judgments. The second performance measure was the precision (the number of correct estimations divided by the total number of estimations).

We must mention that:

- The training phase for the sentiment analysis was performed over 50 k reviews issued from the IMDb movie database https://ai.stanford.edu/~amaas/data/sentiment/ (the vocabulary used in the movie reviews is similar to the vocabulary used in our dataset);
- The accuracy of the sentiment analysis rose to 79%;
- The assessed sentiment judgments were considered as the ground truth, thus yielding 100% in terms of accuracy.

The results of our two centroid strategies—Config (1), *averaged centroid*—and Config (2), *weighted centroid*—are depicted in Table 3 and in Table 4, respectively. Both configurations have the variants *WITHOUT* review sessions (Table 3) and *WITH* review sessions (Table 4). In order to validate the statistical significance of the improvements (for both *WITH* and *WITHOUT*), compared with their respective baselines, we applied the paired Student's $t$-test. The statistical significance of the improvements, when $p$-value < 0.05 and $p$-value < 0.01, is represented in the tables by * and **, respectively. Next, we discuss the results.

**Table 3.** Correlation values with respect to the accuracy levels (WITHOUT considering review session). "*" represents significance with a $p$-value < 0.05 and "**" represents significance with a $p$-value < 0.01.

| Measure | Config (1): Averaged Centroid | Config (2): Weighted Centroid |
|---|---|---|
| **(Baseline) Sentiment analysis: 79% accuracy (naive Bayes)** | | |
| Pearson | 0.45 | 0.51 |
| Precision | 0.61 | 0.70 |
| **(a) Sentiment analysis: 93% accuracy (SentiNeuron)** | | |
| Pearson | 0.61* | 0.80 ** |
| Precision | 0.75 ** | 0.88 ** |
| **(b) Sentiment analysis: 100% accuracy (User judgments)** | | |
| Pearson | 0.68 ** | 0.87 ** |
| Precision | 0.82 ** | 0.91 ** |

**(a) WITHOUT review sessions.**

**Config (1): averaged centroid.** The averaged centroid dispersion measure yielded positive correlation values (moderate or even high) with respect to our annotator's judgments (Pearson: 0.45, 0.61, 0.68). The hypothesis was that having widely opposite review-aspect polarities would imply review-aspects divergent from the centroid, thus a highly intense dispersion. Moreover, when considering the users' sentiment judgments (Table 3 (b)), we obtained better results than when considering sentiment analysis models (Table 3, baseline and (a)). The improvements went from 35% for (baseline) (Pearson: 0.45, compared to 0.61) to 50% for (b) (Pearson: 0.45, compared to 0.68). The correlation coefficient conclusions stand for the precision as well. One may notice that a loss of 21% in terms of sentiment analysis accuracy (100–79%) led to a 34% loss in terms of precision.

**Config (2): weighted centroid.** This configuration yielded positive correlation values as well (0.51, 0.80, 0.87). One may note that the results when considering the weight of the centroids were better than when this particular weight was ignored. Compared to the averaged centroid (Config (1)), the improvements were 13% for naive Bayes, 31% for SentiNeuron, and 28% for the manual judgments, respectively. This trend was confirmed for the precision results as well. Thus, the sentiment analysis model significantly impacted the estimation quality of the studied contradictions.

**Table 4.** Correlation values with respect to accuracy levels (WITH considering review session). "*" represents significance with a $p$-value < 0.05 and "**" represents significance with a $p$-value < 0.01.

| Measure | Config (1): Averaged Centroid | Config (2): Weighted Centroid |
|---|---|---|
| **(Baseline) Sentiment analysis: 79% accuracy (naive Bayes)** | | |
| Pearson | 0.61 | 0.71 |
| Precision | 0.69 | 0.77 |
| **(a) Sentiment analysis: 93% accuracy (SentiNeuron)** | | |
| Pearson | 0.69 * | 0.82 * |
| Precision | 0.80 * | 0.87 * |
| **(b) Sentiment analysis: 100% accuracy (User judgments)** | | |
| Pearson | 0.73 ** | 0.91 ** |
| Precision | 0.83 ** | 0.92 ** |

**(b) WITH review sessions**

The correlation values remained positive when considering the review sessions, for both configurations (averaged and weighted centroids), as reflected in Table 4. This occurred for the two assumptions concerning sentiment analysis accuracy (i.e., 79% and 100%). This suggests that the impact of the sentiment analysis model was quite significant. In fact, the drop of 21% of sentiment accuracy implies an average drop of 23.5% in terms of contradiction detection performance. The performance was improved when considering the review sessions, compared to the results without the review sessions.

**Config (1): averaged centroid.** The results obtained with SentiNeuron (a) and with user judgments (b) (Table 4) were constantly better than in the case of the same scenarios without review sessions (Table 3). Thus, grouping the reviews by session was helpful for the contradiction intensity quantification (7% and 1.2% in terms of precision, for Scenarios (a) and (b), respectively). In addition, the contradiction intensity may be fairly estimated when considering only the reviews issued from one particular session.

**Config (2): weighted centroid.** This configuration was the best possible one. It had the strongest baseline, both in terms of Pearson's correlation coefficient and precision, and also the highest possible value, both in terms of precision (0.92) and correlation coefficient (0.91), amongst all configurations. Its strengths were represented by the weights assigned to the centroids and also by the grouping of the reviews according to their session (the time dimension).

To sum up, we noticed that the proposed approach performed well for every configuration that we considered. Config (2), coupled with the review sessions, yielded the best performance. The t-tests proved that the improvements were statistically significant with respect to the baselines. We hypothesized that the three-step preprocessing helped with the performance improvements, the clustering of reviews with respect to their course sessions being helpful in particular. When the sentiment analysis method performed well, the global results were also improved.

### 4.2.2. Best Feature Identification

In order to identify the most powerful features that estimated the contradiction intensity within our experiments, we considered several feature selection algorithms [59]. The aim of this type of algorithm is to filter out as much as possible the information redundancy in the dataset. In terms of framework, we employed the open-source tool called Weka https://www.cs.waikato.ac.nz/ml (accessed on 5 January 2022). This tool is written in Java, and it provides a wide spectrum of machine learning models and feature selection algorithms.

Figure 8 illustrates the 10 features we considered for the contradiction intensity prediction within the comments. The nature of the features $f_1$ to $f_8$ is given by a simple count, e.g., the polarity criteria $f_1$ and $f_2$ represent the number of negative and positive comments in the document, respectively. Criteria $f_4$, $f_5$, $f_6$, $f_7$, and $f_8$ are related to scoring. The rating may have values from one to five, where three means "average" and five means "excellent". Concerning the last two attributes, $f_9$ and $f_{10}$, they represent the variation in the ratings and polarities of the comments for a given aspect associated with a document (a course in our case). These two criteria were calculated based on the following standard deviation formula, proposed in [61]:

$$ s = \sqrt{\frac{\sum_{i=1}^{n}(x - \bar{x})^2}{n}} \tag{6} $$

where $x$ represents the feature value (ex.: scoring, polarity), $\bar{x}$ is the sample mean of the criterion concerned, and $n$ is the sample size.

| $f_i$ | Feature | Description |
|---|---|---|
| $f_1$ | #NegRev | Number of negative reviews on document |
| $f_2$ | #PosRev | Number of positive reviews on document |
| $f_3$ | #TotalRev | Total number of reviews on document |
| $f_4$ | #Rat1 | Number of reviews with rating ★★★★☆ |
| $f_5$ | #Rat2 | Number of reviews with rating ★★★★☆ |
| $f_6$ | #Rat3 | Number of reviews with rating ★★★★★ |
| $f_7$ | #Rat4 | Number of reviews with rating ★★★★☆ |
| $f_8$ | #Rat5 | Number of reviews with rating ★★★★☆ |
| $f_9$ | VarRat | Variation of ratings (using standard deviation) |
| $f_{10}$ | VarPol | Variation of polarities (using standard deviation) |

**Figure 8.** List of the exploited features.

For the experiments, 50 courses were randomly selected from the dataset, for each of the 22 aspects. Thus, we obtained a total of 1100 courses (instances). The intensity contradiction classes were then established, with respect to specific aspects. There were four classes: *Very Low* (230 courses), *Low* (264 courses), *Strong* (330 courses), and *Very Strong* (276 courses), with respect to the judgments provided by the annotators.

Since the distribution of the courses by class was not balanced and in order to avoid a possible model bias that would assign more observations than normal to the majority class, we applied a sub-sampling approach, and we obtained a balanced collection of 230 individuals by class, therefore a total of 920 courses.

After obtaining the balanced dataset, we applied the feature selection mechanisms on it. We performed five-fold cross-validation (a machine learning step widely employed for hyperparameter optimization).

The feature selection algorithms output feature significance scores for the four established classes. Their inner workings are different. They may be based on feature importance ranking (e.g., *FilteredAttributeEval*), or on the feature selection frequency during the cross-validation step (e.g., *FilteredSubsetEval*). We mention that we employed the default Weka parameter settings for these methods.

Since we applied five-fold cross-validation over the ten features, $n = 10$. The results concerning the selected features are summarized in Figure 9. There were two classes of selection algorithms:

- Based on ranking metrics to sort the features (marked by Rank in the figure);
- Based on the occurrence frequency during the cross-validation step (marked by #Folds in the figure).

One may note that a good feature has either a high rank or a high frequency.

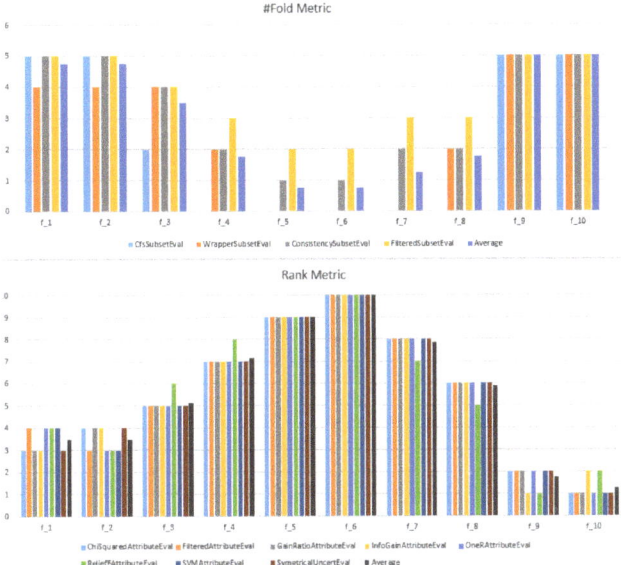

**Figure 9.** Features selected by the attribute selection algorithms.

The strongest features, by both the #Folds and the Rank metrics, were $f_{10}$: *VarPol*, $f_9$: *VarRat*, $f_1$: *#NegRev*, and $f_2$: *#PosRev*. The features with average importance were $f_3$: *#TotalRev*, $f_4$: *#Rat1*, and $f_8$: *#Rat5*, except for the case of *CfsSubsetEval*, for which the features $f_4$ and $f_8$ were not selected. The weakest features were $f_5$: *#Rat2*, $f_6$: *#Rat3*, and $f_7$: *#Rat4*.

### 4.2.3. Feature Learning Process for Contradiction Intensity Prediction

More tests were conducted, based on the proposed and discussed features. The instances (courses) corresponding to the 22 aspects were employed as the training data. Based on the confirmed effectiveness of the SVM [62], J48 (C4.5 implementation) [63], and naive Bayes [64] algorithms in the context of textual data analysis, we employed them in our study as well. The input is represented by a feature vector (please refer to Figure 8), with two possible scenarios: all the features together or the selected features as seen in the previous section. Then, the learning process estimates the corresponding contradiction class, that is to say *Very Low, Low, Strong,* or *Very Strong*. Five-fold cross-validation was applied for these experiments as well.

Figure 10 illustrates the learning process we put in place for the evaluation of the criteria. Let us recall that the feature selection step yielded the following feature sets (see Table 5):

1. For the *CfsSubsetEval* and the *WrapperSubsetEval* algorithms, the selected features were: $f_1$: *#NegRev*, $f_2$: *#PosRev*, $f_3$: *#TotalRev*, $f_9$: *VarRat*, and $f_{10}$: *VarPol*;
2. For *CfsSubsetEval*, the selected features were: $f_1$, $f_2$, $f_3$, $f_9$, and $f_{10}$;
3. For the *CfsSubsetEval* and the *WrapperSubsetEval* algorithms, the selected features were: $f_1$, $f_2$, $f_3$, $f_9$, and $f_{10}$;
4. For the other algorithms, all the features were selected: $f_1$: *#NegRev*, $f_2$: *#PosRev*, $f_3$: *#TotalRev*, $f_4$: *#Rat1*, $f_5$: *#Rat2*, $f_6$: *#Rat3*, $f_7$: *#Rat4*, $f_8$: *#Rat5*, $f_9$: *VarRat*, and $f_{10}$: *VarPol*.

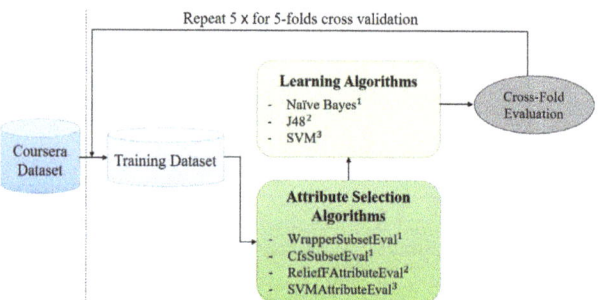

**Figure 10.** Learning process using the selection algorithms.

**Table 5.** Selected feature sets.

| Algorithm | Features |
| --- | --- |
| CfsSubsetEval | $f_1, f_2, f_3, f_9, f_{10}$ |
| WrapperSubsetEval | $f_1, f_2, f_3, f_4, f_8, f_9, f_{10}$ |
| Other algorithms | $f_1, f_2, f_3, f_4, f_5, f_6, f_7, f_8, f_9, f_{10}$ |

Regarding the input feature vector, we needed to decide how many features to consider, either all of them or only those proposed by feature selection. For the latter, we must decide what should be the machine learning algorithm to exploit them.

This type of discussion was conducted by Hall and Holmes [59]. They argued about the effectiveness of several feature selection methods by crossing them with several machine learning algorithms. They matched the best feature selection and machine learning techniques, since they noticed varying performance during the experiments. Inspired by their findings [59], we used the following couples of learning methods and feature selection algorithms:

- Feature selection: *CfsSubsetEval* (CFS) and *WrapperSubsetEval* (WRP); machine learning algorithm: naive Bayes;
- Feature selection: *ReliefFAttributeEval* (RLF); machine learning algorithm: J48 (the C4.5 implementation);
- Feature selection: *SVMAttributeEval* (SVM); machine learning algorithm: multi-class SVM (SMO function on Weka).

The naive Bayes algorithm represents the baseline, and statistical significance tests (paired *t*-test) were conducted to compare the performances. The results are shown in Table 6. Significance ($p$-value $< 0.05$) is marked by *, and strong significance ($p$-value $< 0.01$) is marked by **, in the table. We next discuss the obtained results.

**The results with the naive Bayes model:** This model yielded precision values of 0.72 and 0.68, corresponding to the WRP and the CFS feature selection algorithms, respectively. The feature selection algorithms overcame the performance obtained when considering all the features, which maxed out at 0.60, in terms of precision. Thus, the feature selection mechanisms helped the learning process of the machine learning algorithms. The classes for which the highest precision was obtained were *Very Low*, *Strong*, and *Very Strong*. The remaining class, *Low*, could not yield more than 0.46 in terms of precision, in the case of the WRP selection algorithm.

**Table 6.** Precision results for the machine learning techniques. Significance (*p*-value < 0.05) is marked by *, and strong significance (*p*-value < 0.01) is marked by **.

| Models | Intensity Class | Feature Selection Method | All the Features |
|---|---|---|---|
| Naive Bayes | Very Low | 0.81 (CFS) | 0.71 |
| | Low | 0.38 (CFS) | 0.34 |
| | Strong | 0.75 (CFS) | 0.66 |
| | Very Strong | 0.78 (CFS) | 0.69 |
| | Average | 0.68 (CFS) | 0.60 |
| | Very Low | 0.86 (WRP) | 0.72 |
| | Low | 0.46 (WRP) | 0.38 |
| | Strong | 0.76 (WRP) | 0.63 |
| | Very Strong | 0.80 (WRP) | 0.67 |
| | Average | 0.72 (WRP) | 0.60 |
| SVM | Very Low | 0.88 * (SVM) | 0.88 * |
| | Low | 0.72 ** (SVM) | 0.72 ** |
| | Strong | 0.78 * (SVM) | 0.78 * |
| | Very Strong | 0.90 ** (SVM) | 0.90 ** |
| | Average | 0.82 ** (SVM) | 0.82 ** |
| J48 | Very Low | 0.97 ** (RLF) | 0.97 ** |
| | Low | 0.92 ** (RLF) | 0.92 ** |
| | Strong | 0.97 ** (RLF) | 0.97 ** |
| | Very Strong | 0.98 ** (RLF) | 0.98 ** |
| | Average | 0.96 ** (RLF) | 0.96 ** |

**The results with the SVM model:** This model yielded better performance, compared to the naive Bayes classifier. The relative improvements of the SVM model, compared to naive Bayes, went from 14% in the case of WRP to 21% in the case of CFS. One should note that this model managed to yield better performance for the difficult class (*Low*). The feature selection algorithm *SVMAttributeEval* did not improve the performance, compared to considering all the features together. This behavior may occur because the performance was already quite high.

**The results with the J48 model:** This decision trees model yielded the best performance in terms of precision, when considering all the features. The relative improvements were 17%, with respect to the SVM model, 33% with respect to the naive Bayes model with the WRP selection algorithm, and finally, 41% with respect to the naive Bayes model with the CFS selection. The most difficult class for the other models, *Low*, obtained a performance of 92% in terms of precision, meaning relative improvements ranging from 28% to 142%, with respect to the other learning models. Moreover, the improvements were significant for all the involved classes. On the other hand, feature selection did not bring any improvement this time. As for the SVM model, this non-improvement must surely be due to the fact that the performance of the algorithm was already extremely high, and consequently, the impact of feature selection was very marginal.

In what follows, we compared the best results obtained by the two methods of contradiction intensity estimation. We refer to the unsupervised method, based on the review-aspect dispersion function taking into account the review sessions (as in Table 4), and to the supervised method, based on several features extracted by the selection algorithms within the learning process (see the average precision in Table 6). In terms of precision, naive Bayes used with the CFS feature selection algorithm registered the lowest precision result (68%), as can be seen in Tables 4 and 6. SVM performed relatively better than the unsupervised method with all of its configurations using an averaged centroid. Moreover, SVM even outperformed naive Bayes used with CFS and WRP with an improvement rate of 21% and 14%, respectively. However, the majority of the results obtained with the unsupervised method using the weighted centroid significantly outperformed those obtained using the averaged centroid or even those obtained by the supervised method using naive Bayes and SVM. In all these experiments, the best results were obtained by the J48 decision trees algorithm using the RLF selection algorithm. J48 recorded significant improvement rates over all other configurations, using both supervised and unsupervised methods: 17%, 33%, and 41%, over SVM, naive Bayes (WRP), and naive Bayes (CFS), respectively. Table 7 shows in detail the different improvement rates between J48 and the other configurations.

**Table 7.** Rates of improvement between the decision trees J48 and the various other configurations.

| Best Solution | The Different Configurations | Improvement Rate |
|---|---|---|
| | WITHOUT Considering Review Session | |
| | Sentiment Analysis: 79% accuracy (naive Bayes) | |
| | Averaged Centroid | 57% |
| | Weighted Centroid | 37% |
| | Sentiment Analysis: 93% accuracy (SentiNeuron) | |
| | Averaged Centroid | 28% |
| | Weighted Centroid | 9% |
| | Sentiment Analysis: 100% accuracy (user judgments) | |
| | Averaged Centroid | 17% |
| | Weighted Centroid | 5% |
| | WITH Considering Review Session | |
| | Sentiment Analysis: 79% accuracy (naive Bayes) | |
| | Averaged Centroid | 40% |
| | Weighted Centroid | 25% |
| | Sentiment Analysis: 93% accuracy (SentiNeuron) | |
| | Averaged Centroid | 20% |
| | Weighted Centroid | 10% |
| | Sentiment Analysis: 100% accuracy (user judgments) | |
| | Averaged Centroid | 15% |
| Decision trees J48 | Weighted Centroid | 4% |
| | Machine Learning Techniques | |
| Average Precision: 0.96 | Naive Bayes (CFS) | |
| | Very Low | 18.5% |
| | Low | 153% |
| | Strong | 28% |
| | Very Strong | 23% |
| | Average | 41% |
| | Naive Bayes (WRP) | |
| | Very Low | 12% |
| | Low | 109% |
| | Strong | 26% |
| | Very Strong | 20% |
| | Average | 33% |
| | SVM | |
| | Very Low | 9% |
| | Low | 33% |
| | Strong | 23% |
| | Very Strong | 7% |
| | Average | 17% |

To sum up, the results clearly showed that the contradiction intensity can be predicted by the J48 machine learning model, with good performance. The feature selection methods proved to be effective for one case out of three, with respect to the learning models (for naive Bayes). This similar performance between the versions with and without feature selection shows that, after a certain performance level yielded by the machine learning algorithm, the feature selection impact stayed quite limited. We conclude that the courses having highly divergent reviews were prone to containing contradictions with several intensity levels.

## 5. Conclusions

This research focused on the estimation of the contradiction intensity in texts, more in particular in MOOC course reviews. Unlike most other authors, we did not only try to find out if a contradiction occurred, but we were concerned with measuring its strength. The contradiction was identified around the aspects that generated the difference in opinions within the reviews. We hypothesized that the contradiction occurred when the sentiment polarities around these aspects were divergent. This paper's proposal to quantify the contradiction intensity was twofold, consisting of an unsupervised approach and a supervised one, respectively. Within the unsupervised approach, the review-aspects were represented as a function that estimated the dispersion (more intense contradictions occurred when the sentiment polarities and the ratings were dispersed in the bi-dimensional space characterized by sentiment polarity and ratings, respectively). The other idea was to group the reviews by sessions (the time dimension), allowing an effective treatment to avoid fake contradictions. The supervised approach considered several features and learned to predict the contradiction intensity. We hypothesized that the ratings and the sentiment polarities around an aspect may be useful as features to estimate the intensity of the contradictions. When the sentiment polarities and the ratings were diverse (in terms of the standard deviation), the chances of the contradictions being intense increased.

For the unsupervised approach, the weighted centroid configuration, coupled with the review sessions (considering the time dimension of the reviews), yielded the best performances.

For the supervised approach, the features *VarPol, VarRat, #PosRev, VarRat*, and *#NegRev* had the best chances to correctly predict the intensity classes for the contradictions. The feature selection study prove to be effective for one case out of three, with respect to the learning models (for naive Bayes). Thus, feature selection may be beneficial for the learning models that did not perform very well. The best performance was obtained by the J48 decision trees algorithm. This model was followed, in terms of precision, by the SVM model and, lastly, by the naive Bayes model.

The most important limitation of our proposal is that the models depend on the quality of the sentiment polarity estimation and of the aspect extraction method. That is why our future work will focus on finding ways of selecting methods for sentiment polarity estimation and aspect extraction that would be the most appropriate for this task.

Additionally, we aim to conduct larger-scale experiments, over various data types, since the so far, the promising results motivated us to investigate this topic even further.

**Author Contributions:** Conceptualization, A.-G.C. and S.F.; Data curation, I.B.; Formal analysis, I.B.; Supervision, S.F.; Validation, A.-G.C.; Writing (original draft), I.B., A.-G.C. and S.F.; Writing (review and editing), I.B., A.-G.C. and S.F. All authors have read and agreed to the published version of the manuscript.

**Funding:** This research received no external funding.

**Institutional Review Board Statement:** Not applicable.

**Informed Consent Statement:** Not applicable.

**Data Availability Statement:** Not applicable.

**Conflicts of Interest:** The authors declare no conflict of interest.

# References

1. Badache, I.; Boughanem, M. Harnessing Social Signals to Enhance a Search. *IEEE/WIC/ACM* **2014**, *1*, 303–309.
2. Badache, I.; Boughanem, M. Emotional social signals for search ranking. *SIGIR* **2017**, *3*, 1053–1056.
3. Badache, I.; Boughanem, M. Fresh and Diverse Social Signals: Any impacts on search? In Proceedings of the CHIIR '17: Proceedings of the 2017 Conference on Conference Human Information Interaction and Retrieval, Oslo, Norway, 7–11 March 2017; pp. 155–164.
4. Kim, S.; Zhang, J.; Chen, Z.; Oh, A.H.; Liu, S. A Hierarchical Aspect-Sentiment Model for Online Reviews. In Proceedings of the Twenty-Seventh AAAI Conference on Artificial Intelligence, Bellevue, WA, USA, 14–18 July 2013.
5. Poria, S.; Cambria, E.; Ku, L.; Gui, C.; Gelbukh, A.F. A Rule-Based Approach to Aspect Extraction from Product Reviews. In Proceedings of the Second Workshop on Natural Language Processing for Social Media, SocialNLP@COLING 2014, Dublin, Ireland, 24 August 2014; pp. 28–37. [CrossRef]
6. Wang, L.; Cardie, C. A Piece of My Mind: A Sentiment Analysis Approach for Online Dispute Detection. In Proceedings of the 52nd Annual Meeting of the Association for Computational Linguistics, ACL 2014, Baltimore, MD, USA, 22–27 June 2014; Short Papers; Volume 2, pp. 693–699.
7. Harabagiu, S.M.; Hickl, A.; Lacatusu, V.F. Negation, Contrast and Contradiction in Text Processing. In Proceedings of the Twenty-First National Conference on Artificial Intelligence and the Eighteenth Innovative Applications of Artificial Intelligence Conference, Boston, MA, USA, 16–20 July 2006; pp. 755–762.
8. de Marneffe, M.; Rafferty, A.N.; Manning, C.D. Finding Contradictions in Text. In Proceedings of the 46th Annual Meeting of the Association for Computational Linguistics, Columbus, OH, USA, 15–20 June 2008; pp. 1039–1047.
9. Tsytsarau, M.; Palpanas, T.; Denecke, K. Scalable discovery of contradictions on the web. In Proceedings of the 19th International Conference on World Wide Web, WWW 2010, Raleigh, NC, USA, 26–30 April 2010; pp. 1195–1196. [CrossRef]
10. Tsytsarau, M.; Palpanas, T.; Denecke, K. Scalable detection of sentiment-based contradictions. *DiversiWeb WWW* **2011**, *11*, 105–112.
11. Yazi, F.S.; Vong, W.T.; Raman, V.; Then, P.H.H.; Lunia, M.J. Towards Automated Detection of Contradictory Research Claims in Medical Literature Using Deep Learning Approach. In Proceedings of the 2021 Fifth International Conference on Information Retrieval and Knowledge Management (CAMP), Pahang, Malaysia, 15–16 June 2021; pp. 116–121. [CrossRef]
12. Hsu, C.; Li, C.; Sáez-Trumper, D.; Hsu, Y. WikiContradiction: Detecting Self-Contradiction Articles on Wikipedia. In Proceedings of the IEEE International Conference on Big Data (IEEE BigData 2021), Orlando, FL, USA, 15–18 December 2021.
13. Sepúlveda-Torres, R. Automatic Contradiction Detection in Spanish. In Proceedings of the Doctoral Symposium on Natural Language Processing from the PLN.net Network, Baeza, Spain, 19–20 October 2021.
14. Rahimi, Z.; Shamsfard, M. Contradiction Detection in Persian Text. *arXiv* **2021**, arXiv:2107.01987.
15. Pielka, M.; Sifa, R.; Hillebrand, L.P.; Biesner, D.; Ramamurthy, R.; Ladi, A.; Bauckhage, C. Tackling Contradiction Detection in German Using Machine Translation and End-to-End Recurrent Neural Networks. In Proceedings of the 2020 25th International Conference on Pattern Recognition (ICPR), Milan, Italy, 10–15 January 2021; pp. 6696–6701. [CrossRef]
16. Păvăloaia, V.D.; Teodor, E.M.; Fotache, D.; Danileţ, M. Opinion Mining on Social Media Data: Sentiment Analysis of User Preferences. *Sustainability* **2019**, *11*, 4459. [CrossRef]
17. Mohammad, S.M.; Turney, P.D. Crowdsourcing a word–Emotion association lexicon. *Comput. Intell.* **2013**, *29*, 436–465. [CrossRef]
18. Al-Ayyoub, M.; Rabab'ah, A.; Jararweh, Y.; Al-Kabi, M.N.; Gupta, B.B. Studying the controversy in online crowds' interactions. *Appl. Soft Comput.* **2018**, *66*, 557–563. [CrossRef]
19. Popescu, A.M.; Pennacchiotti, M. Detecting controversial events from twitter. In Proceedings of the 19th ACM International Conference on Information and Knowledge Management, Toronto, ON, Canada, 26–30 October 2010; pp. 1873–1876.
20. Balasubramanyan, R.; Cohen, W.W.; Pierce, D.; Redlawsk, D.P. Modeling polarizing topics: When do different political communities respond differently to the same news? In Proceedings of the Sixth International AAAI Conference on Weblogs and Social Media, Dublin, Ireland, 4–8 June 2012.
21. Dori-Hacohen, S.; Allan, J. Detecting controversy on the web. In Proceedings of the 22nd ACM international conference on Information & Knowledge Management, San Francisco, CA, USA, 27 October–1 November 2013; pp. 1845–1848.
22. Dori-Hacohen, S.; Allan, J. Automated Controversy Detection on the Web. In *Advances in Information Retrieval*; Hanbury, A., Kazai, G., Rauber, A., Fuhr, N., Eds.; Springer International Publishing: Cham, Germany, 2015; pp. 423–434.
23. Garimella, K.; Morales, G.D.F.; Gionis, A.; Mathioudakis, M. Quantifying Controversy in Social Media. In Proceedings of the Ninth ACM International Conference on Web Search and Data Mining, San Francisco, CA, USA, 22–25 February 2016; pp. 33–42. [CrossRef]
24. Guerra, P.C.; Meira, W., Jr.; Cardie, C.; Kleinberg, R. A measure of polarization on social media networks based on community boundaries. In Proceedings of the Seventh International AAAI Conference on Weblogs and Social Media, Cambridge, MA, USA, 8–11 July 2013.
25. Jang, M.; Allan, J. Improving Automated Controversy Detection on the Web. In Proceedings of the 39th International ACM SIGIR Conference on Research and Development in Information Retrieval, SIGIR 2016, Pisa, Italy, 17–21 July 2016; pp. 865–868. [CrossRef]

26. Lin, W.H.; Hauptmann, A. Are these documents written from different perspectives? A test of different perspectives based on statistical distribution divergence. In Proceedings of the 21st International Conference on Computational Linguistics and the 44th Annual Meeting of the Association for Computational Linguistics, Association for Computational Linguistics, Sydney, Australia, 6–8 July 2006; pp. 1057–1064.

27. Sriteja, A.; Pandey, P.; Pudi, V. Controversy Detection Using Reactions on Social Media. In Proceedings of the 2017 IEEE International Conference on Data Mining Workshops (ICDMW), New Orleans, LA, USA, 18–21 November 2017; pp. 884–889.

28. Morales, A.; Borondo, J.; Losada, J.C.; Benito, R.M. Measuring political polarization: Twitter shows the two sides of Venezuela. *Chaos Interdiscip. J. Nonlinear Sci.* **2015**, *25*, 033114. [CrossRef] [PubMed]

29. Garimella, K.; Morales, G.D.F.; Gionis, A.; Mathioudakis, M. Quantifying Controversy on Social Media. *Trans. Soc. Comput.* **2018**, *1*. [CrossRef]

30. Ahmed, A.; Xing, E.P. Staying informed: Supervised and semi-supervised multi-view topical analysis of ideological perspective. In Proceedings of the 2010 Conference on Empirical Methods in Natural Language Processing, Association for Computational Linguistics, Stroudsburg, PA, USA, 9–11 October 2010; pp. 1140–1150.

31. Cohen, R.; Ruths, D. Classifying political orientation on Twitter: It's not easy! In Proceedings of the Seventh International AAAI Conference on Weblogs and Social Media, Cambridge, MA, USA, 8–11 July 2013.

32. Conover, M.D.; Gonçalves, B.; Ratkiewicz, J.; Flammini, A.; Menczer, F. Predicting the political alignment of twitter users. In Proceedings of the 2011 IEEE Third International Conference on Privacy, Security, Risk and Trust and 2011 IEEE Third International Conference on Social Computing, Boston, MA, USA, 9–11 October 2011; pp. 192–199.

33. Paul, M.; Girju, R. A Two-Dimensional Topic-Aspect Model for Discovering Multi-Faceted Topics. In Proceedings of the AAAI'10: Twenty-Fourth AAAI Conference on Artificial Intelligence, Atlanta, GA, USA, 11–15 July 2010; AAAI Press: Atlanta, GA, USA, 2010; pp. 545–550.

34. Qiu, M.; Jiang, J. A Latent Variable Model for Viewpoint Discovery from Threaded Forum Posts. In Proceedings of the 2013 Conference of the North American Chapter of the Association for Computational Linguistics: Human Language Technologies, Atlanta, Georgia, 9–14 June 2013; Association for Computational Linguistics: Atlanta, GA, USA, 2013; pp. 1031–1040.

35. Trabelsi, A.; Zaiane, O.R. Mining contentious documents using an unsupervised topic model based approach. In Proceedings of the 2014 IEEE International Conference on Data Mining, Shenzhen, China, 14–17 December 2014; pp. 550–559.

36. Thonet, T.; Cabanac, G.; Boughanem, M.; Pinel-Sauvagnat, K. VODUM: A topic model unifying viewpoint, topic and opinion discovery. In *European Conference on Information Retrieval*; Spring: Berlin/Heidelberg, Germany, 2016; pp. 533–545.

37. Galley, M.; McKeown, K.; Hirschberg, J.; Shriberg, E. Identifying agreement and disagreement in conversational speech: Use of bayesian networks to model pragmatic dependencies. In Proceedings of the 42nd Annual Meeting on Association for Computational Linguistics, Stroudsburg, PA, USA, 21–26 July 2004; p. 669.

38. Menini, S.; Tonelli, S. Agreement and disagreement: Comparison of points of view in the political domain. In Proceedings of the COLING 2016, the 26th International Conference on Computational Linguistics, Technical Papers, Osaka, Japan, 11–16 December 2016; pp. 2461–2470.

39. Mukherjee, A.; Liu, B. Mining contentions from discussions and debates. In Proceedings of the 18th ACM SIGKDD International Conference on Knowledge Discovery and Data Mining, Beijing, China, 12–16 August 2012; pp. 841–849.

40. Mohammad, S.; Kiritchenko, S.; Zhu, X. NRC-Canada: Building the State-of-the-Art in Sentiment Analysis of Tweets. In Proceedings of the 7th International Workshop on Semantic Evaluation, SemEval@NAACL-HLT 2013, Atlanta, GA, USA, 14–15 June 2013; pp. 321–327.

41. Mohammad, S.; Kiritchenko, S.; Sobhani, P.; Zhu, X.; Cherry, C. SemEval-2016 Task 6: Detecting Stance in Tweets. In Proceedings of the 10th International Workshop on Semantic Evaluation (SemEval-2016), San Diego, CA, USA, 10–11 June 2016; Association for Computational Linguistics: San Diego, CA, USA; pp. 31–41. [CrossRef]

42. Augenstein, I.; Rocktäschel, T.; Vlachos, A.; Bontcheva, K. Stance detection with bidirectional conditional encoding. *arXiv* **2016**, arXiv:1606.05464.

43. Gottipati, S.; Qiu, M.; Sim, Y.; Jiang, J.; Smith, N. Learning topics and positions from debatepedia. In Proceedings of the 2013 Conference on Empirical Methods in Natural Language Processing, Seattle, WA, USA, 18–21 October 2013; pp. 1858–1868.

44. Johnson, K.; Goldwasser, D. "All I know about politics is what I read in Twitter": Weakly Supervised Models for Extracting Politicians' Stances From Twitter. In Proceedings of the COLING 2016, the 26th International Conference on Computational Linguistics, Technical Papers, Osaka, Japan, 11–16 December 2016; pp. 2966–2977.

45. Qiu, M.; Sim, Y.; Smith, N.A.; Jiang, J. Modeling user arguments, interactions, and attributes for stance prediction in online debate forums. In Proceedings of the 2015 SIAM International Conference on Data Mining, SIAM, Vancouver, BC, Canada, 30 April–2 May 2015; pp. 855–863.

46. Somasundaran, S.; Wiebe, J. Recognizing stances in ideological on-line debates. In Proceedings of the NAACL HLT 2010 Workshop on Computational Approaches to Analysis and Generation of Emotion in Text, Los Angeles, CA, USA, 10–12 June 2010; pp. 116–124.

47. Küçük, D.; Can, F. Stance detection: A survey. *ACM Comput. Surv. (CSUR)* **2020**, *53*, 1–37. [CrossRef]

48. Hu, M.; Liu, B. Mining and summarizing customer reviews. In Proceedings of the Tenth ACM SIGKDD International Conference on Knowledge Discovery and Data Mining, Seattle, WA, USA, 22–25 August 2004; pp. 168–177. [CrossRef]

49. Hamdan, H.; Bellot, P.; Béchet, F. Lsislif: CRF and Logistic Regression for Opinion Target Extraction and Sentiment Polarity Analysis. In Proceedings of the 9th International Workshop on Semantic Evaluation, SemEval@NAACL-HLT 2015, Denver, CO, USA, 4–5 June 2015; pp. 753–758.
50. Titov, I.; McDonald, R.T. Modeling online reviews with multi-grain topic models. In Proceedings of the 17th International Conference on World Wide Web, WWW 2008, Beijing, China, 21–25 April 2008; pp. 111–120. [CrossRef]
51. Tulkens, S.; van Cranenburgh, A. Embarrassingly Simple Unsupervised Aspect Extraction. In Proceedings of the 58th Annual Meeting of the Association for Computational Linguistics; Association for Computational Linguistics, Online, 5–10 July 2020; pp. 3182–3187. [CrossRef]
52. Turney, P.D. Thumbs Up or Thumbs Down? Semantic Orientation Applied to Unsupervised Classification of Reviews. In Proceedings of the 40th Annual Meeting of the Association for Computational Linguistics, Philadelphia, PA, USA, 6–12 July 2002; pp. 417–424.
53. Pang, B.; Lee, L.; Vaithyanathan, S. Thumbs up? Sentiment Classification using Machine Learning Techniques. In Proceedings of the 2002 Conference on Empirical Methods in Natural Language Processing, EMNLP 2002, Philadelphia, PA, USA, 6–7 July 2002.
54. Socher, R.; Perelygin, A.; Wu, J.; Chuang, J.; Manning, C.D.; Ng, A.Y.; Potts, C. Recursive Deep Models for Semantic Compositionality Over a Sentiment Treebank. In Proceedings of the 2013 Conference on Empirical Methods in Natural Language Processing, EMNLP 2013, Seattle, WA, USA, 18–21 October 2013; A Meeting of SIGDAT, a Special Interest Group of the ACL; Grand Hyatt Seattle: Seattle, WA, USA, 2013; pp. 1631–1642.
55. Radford, A.; Józefowicz, R.; Sutskever, I. Learning to Generate Reviews and Discovering Sentiment. *arXiv* **2017**, arXiv:1704.01444.
56. MacQueen, J. Some methods for classification and analysis of multivariate observations. In Proceedings of the fifth Berkeley symposium on mathematical statistics and probability, Berkeley, CA, USA, 21 June–18 July 1965.
57. McAuley, J.J.; Pandey, R.; Leskovec, J. Inferring Networks of Substitutable and Complementary Products. In Proceedings of the 21th ACM SIGKDD International Conference on Knowledge Discovery and Data Mining, Sydney, NSW, Australia, 10–13 August 2015; pp. 785–794. [CrossRef]
58. Looks, M.; Herreshoff, M.; Hutchins, D.; Norvig, P. Deep Learning with Dynamic Computation Graphs. In Proceedings of the 5th International Conference on Learning Representations, ICLR 2017, Toulon, France, 24–26 April 2017.
59. Hall, M.A.; Holmes, G. Benchmarking Attribute Selection Techniques for Discrete Class Data Mining. *IEEE Trans. Knowl. Data Eng.* **2003**, *15*, 1437–1447. [CrossRef]
60. Cohen, J. A coefficient of agreement for nominal scales. *Educ. Psychol. Meas.* **1960**, *20*, 37–46. [CrossRef]
61. Pearson, E.S.; Stephens, M.A. The Ratio of Range to Standard Deviation in the Same Normal Sample. *Biometrika* **1964**, *51*, 484–487. [CrossRef]
62. Vosecky, J.; Leung, K.W.; Ng, W. Searching for Quality Microblog Posts: Filtering and Ranking Based on Content Analysis and Implicit Links. In Proceedings of the Database Systems for Advanced Applications—17th International Conference, DASFAA 2012, Busan, Korea, 15–19 April 2012; pp. 397–413. [CrossRef]
63. Quinlan, J.R. *C4.5: Programs for Machine Learning*; Morgan Kaufmann: Burlington, MA, USA, 1993.
64. Yuan, Q.; Cong, G.; Magnenat-Thalmann, N. Enhancing naive bayes with various smoothing methods for short text classification. In Proceedings of the 21st World Wide Web Conference, WWW 2012, Lyon, France, 16–20 April 2012; pp. 645–646. [CrossRef]

## mathematics

MDPI

*Article*

# Cross-Lingual Transfer Learning for Arabic Task-Oriented Dialogue Systems Using Multilingual Transformer Model mT5

**Ahlam Fuad * and Maha Al-Yahya**

Department of Information Technology, College of Computer and Information Sciences, King Saud University, P.O. Box 145111, Riyadh 4545, Saudi Arabia; malyahya@ksu.edu.sa
* Correspondence: aabdulghni@ksu.edu.sa or 439204463@student.ksu.edu.sa

**Abstract:** Due to the promising performance of pre-trained language models for task-oriented dialogue systems (DS) in English, some efforts to provide multilingual models for task-oriented DS in low-resource languages have emerged. These efforts still face a long-standing challenge due to the lack of high-quality data for these languages, especially Arabic. To circumvent the cost and time-intensive data collection and annotation, cross-lingual transfer learning can be used when few training data are available in the low-resource target language. Therefore, this study aims to explore the effectiveness of cross-lingual transfer learning in building an end-to-end Arabic task-oriented DS using the mT5 transformer model. We use the Arabic task-oriented dialogue dataset (Arabic-TOD) in the training and testing of the model. We present the cross-lingual transfer learning deployed with three different approaches: mSeq2Seq, Cross-lingual Pre-training (CPT), and Mixed-Language Pre-training (MLT). We obtain good results for our model compared to the literature for Chinese language using the same settings. Furthermore, cross-lingual transfer learning deployed with the MLT approach outperform the other two approaches. Finally, we show that our results can be improved by increasing the training dataset size.

**Keywords:** cross-lingual transfer learning; task-oriented dialogue systems; Arabic language; mixed-language pre-training; multilingual transformer model; mT5; natural language processing

**MSC:** 68T50

**Citation:** Fuad, A.; Al-Yahya, M. Cross-Lingual Transfer Learning for Arabic Task-Oriented Dialogue Systems Using Multilingual Transformer Model mT5. *Mathematics* 2022, *10*, 746. https://doi.org/10.3390/math10050746

Academic Editors: Cornelia Caragea and Florentina Hristea

Received: 26 January 2022
Accepted: 24 February 2022
Published: 26 February 2022

**Publisher's Note:** MDPI stays neutral with regard to jurisdictional claims in published maps and institutional affiliations.

## 1. Introduction

Task-oriented dialogue systems (DS) are systems that help users to achieve a vast range of tasks using natural language conversations, such as restaurant reservations, flight bookings, and weather-forecast inquiries [1]. The demand on such systems has increased rapidly, due to the promising performance of English-based conversational DS [2–5]. However, most of these systems are unable to support various low-resource languages because of the lack of high quality annotated data for these languages. Arabic is one of the low-resource languages that is suffering from a lack of task-oriented dialogue datasets, and as such it is lagging behind DS development [6]. One of the common strategies to address this issue is to collect and annotate more data for every language, which is a cost-intensive process. Therefore, in order to address the lack of dialogue datasets, cross-lingual transfer learning is used. In this type of learning, knowledge of high-resource languages (such as English) is transferred into low-resource languages (such as Arabic) with few training data in the low-resource target language [7]. Cross-lingual transfer learning has shown good results for several tasks using pre-trained multilingual models [8,9].

In this work, we aimed to explore the effectiveness of cross-lingual transfer learning in building end-to-end Arabic task-oriented DS using the multilingual pre-trained language model mT5 [10]. These end-to-end systems must handle the tasks of tracking all entities in the dialogue, as well as generating suitable responses. To the best of our knowledge, this is the first work to examine the cross-lingual transfer ability of mT5 on Arabic task-oriented DS in few-shot scenarios. We aimed to answer two research questions:

- To what extent is cross-lingual transfer learning effective in end-to-end Arabic task-oriented DS using the mT5 model?
- To what extent does the size of the training dataset affect the quality of Arabic task-oriented DS in few-shot scenarios?

The rest of the paper is organized as follows: Related work in the area of task-oriented DS for multilingual models and cross-lingual transfer learning is explored in Section 2. Section 3 delineates the methodology of cross-lingual transfer learning used in this research. In Section 4, we present our experimental setup and the dataset used. The results and findings are discussed in Section 5. Finally, in Section 6, we summarize the research and highlight avenues for future research.

## 2. Related Works

In task-oriented DS, high-resource languages are those that have many dataset samples, whereas in low-resource languages there are few dataset samples. Therefore, it is important to provide datasets for these languages to advance research on end-to-end task-oriented DS. Cross-lingual transfer learning is a common and effective approach to build end-to-end task-oriented DS in low-resource languages [8,11,12]. Machine-translation and multilingual representations are the most used approaches in cross-lingual research. The authors of [8] introduced a multilingual dataset for task-oriented DS. It contained many annotated utterances in English, but few translated annotated English utterances to Spanish and Thai covering the weather, alarm, and reminder domains. They evaluated their approach using three cross-lingual transfer learning approaches: translating the training data, cross-lingual contextual word representations, and a multilingual machine-translation encoder. Their experiment showed that the latter two approaches outperformed the one in which the training data were translated. However, translating the training data achieves the best results in cases of zero-shot settings where there are no available target-language data. Moreover, they proved that joint training on both high-resource and low-resource target languages improved the performance on the target language.

In [11], Liu et al. proposed an attention-informed Mixed-Language Training (MLT) approach. This is a zero-shot adaptation approach for cross-lingual task-oriented DS. They used a code-switching approach, where code-switching sentences are generated from source-language sentences in English by replacing particular selected source words with their translations in German and Italian. They used task-related parallel word pairs in order to generate code-switching (mixed language) sentences. They obtained better generalization in the target language because of the inter-lingual semantics across languages. Their model achieved a significantly better performance with the zero-shot setting for both cross-lingual dialogue state tracking (DST) and natural language understanding (NLU) tasks than other approaches using a large amount of bilingual data.

Lin et al. [12] proposed a bilingual multidomain dataset for end-to-end task-oriented DS (BiToD). BiToD contains over 7000 multidomain dialogues for both English (EN) and Chinese (ZH), with a large bilingual knowledge base (KB). They trained their models using mT5 and mBART [13]. They evaluated their system in monolingual, bilingual, and cross-lingual settings. In the monolingual setting, they trained and tested the models on either English or Chinese dialogue data. In the bilingual setting, they trained the models on dialogue data in both languages. In the cross-lingual setting, they studied data in a specific language, and thus they used transfer learning to study the transferability of knowledge from a high-resource language to a low-resource language. For end-to-end task evaluation, they used: BLEU; Task Success Rate (TSR), to measure if the system provided the correct entity and answered all the requested information of a specific task; Dialogue Success Rate (DSR), to assess if the system completed all the tasks in the dialogue; and API Call Accuracy ($API_{Acc}$), to assess if the system generated a correct API call. In addition, they used the joint goal accuracy (JGA) metric to measure the performance of the DST. They suggested the possibility of improving system performance under low-resource conditions by leveraging the bilingual KB and cross-lingual transfer learning. In fact, BiToD achieved important progress in building a robust multilingual task-oriented DS.

Table 1 summarizes the performance of the most common state-of-the-art models in multilingual task-oriented DS using cross-lingual transfer learning. It is clear that there is a lack of standardized datasets in addition to a lack of fixed standards in using evaluation metrics [14].

**Table 1.** Performance comparison of the most common state-of-the-art multilingual models in task-oriented dialogue systems (DS) for cross-lingual settings.

| Study | Dataset | Dataset Size (Train/Validate/Test) | | Metrics |
|---|---|---|---|---|
| [8] Cross-lingual settings using cross-lingual pre-trained embeddings | Their own dataset across three domains: weather, alarm and reminder. | English (43k) 30,521/4181/8621 Spanish (8.6k) 3617/1983/3043 Thai (5k) 2156/1235/1692 | | — Exact match = 75.96, Domain accuracy (acc.) = 99.47, Intent acc. = 97.51, Slot F1 = 83.38 Exact match = 86.12, Domain acc. = 99.33, Intent acc. = 9.87, Slot F1 = 91.51 |
| [8] Cross-lingual settings using translating the training data | | English (43k) 30,521/4181/8621 Spanish (8.6k) 3617/1983/3043 Thai (5k) 2156/1235/1692 | | — Exact match = 72.49, Domain acc. = 99.65, Intent acc. = 98.47, Slot F1 = 80.60 Exact match = 73.37, Domain acc. = 99.37, Intent acc. = 97.41, Slot F1 = 80.38 |
| [11] Zero-shot setting using mBERT + transformer | Multilingual WOZ 2.0 | English (1k) 600/200/400 German (1k) 600/200/400 Italian (1k) 600/200/400 | | — Slot acc. = 70.77, JGA = 34.36, Request acc. = 86.97 Slot acc. = 71.45, JGA = 33.35, Request acc. = 84.96 |
| BiToD [12] cross-lingual | BiToD (cross-lingual) (ZH → EN) | English (EN) (3.6k) 2952/295/442 | mT5 | TSR = 6.78, DSR = 1.36, $API_{Acc}$ = 17.75, BLEU = 10.35, JGA = 19.86 |
| | | | mBART | TSR = 1.11, DSR = 0.23, $API_{Acc}$ = 0.60, BLEU = 3.17, JGA = 4.64 |
| | | | mT5 + CPT | TSR = 44.94, DSR = 24.66, $API_{Acc}$ = 47.60, BLEU = 29.53, JGA = 48.77 |
| | | | mBART + CPT | TSR = 36.19, DSR = 16.06, $API_{Acc}$ = 41.51, BLEU = 22.50, JGA = 42.84 |
| | | | mT5 + MLT | TSR = 56.78, DSR = 33.71, $API_{Acc}$ = 56.78, BLEU = 32.43, JGA = 58.3 |
| | | | mBART + MLT | TSR = 33.62, DSR = 11.99, $API_{Acc}$ = 41.08, BLEU = 20.01, JGA = 55.39 |
| | BiToD (EN → ZH) | Chinese (ZH) (3.5k) 2835/248/460 | mT5 | TSR = 4.16, DSR = 2.20, $API_{Acc}$ = 6.67, BLEU = 3.30, JGA = 12.63 |
| | | | mBART | TSR = 0.00, DSR = 0.00, $API_{Acc}$ = 0.00, BLEU = 0.01, JGA = 2.14 |
| | | | mT5 + CPT | TSR = 43.27, DSR = 23.70, $API_{Acc}$ = 49.70, BLEU = 13.89, JGA = 51.40 |
| | | | mBART + CPT | TSR = 24.64, DSR = 11.96, $API_{Acc}$ = 29.04, BLEU = 8.29, JGA = 28.57 |
| | | | mT5 + MLT | TSR = 49.20, DSR = 27.17, $API_{Acc}$ = 50.55, BLEU = 14.44, JGA = 55.05 |
| | | | mBART + MLT | TSR = 44.71, DSR = 21.96, $API_{Acc}$ = 54.87, BLEU = 14.19, JGA = 60.71 |

The symbol ($\rightarrow$) means that the model was built using cross-lingual transfer language approach by transfer the knowledge from the source language (on the left of the arrow) to the target language (on the right of the arrow).

In addition to the previous studies, Louvan et al. [15] suggested using a data augmentation approach to resolve the data scarcity in task-oriented DS. Data augmentation aims to produce extra training data, and it proved its success in different NLP tasks for English data [15]. As such, the authors studied its performance for task-oriented DS for non-English data. They evaluated their approach on five languages: Italian, Spanish, Hindi, Turkish, and Thai. They found that data augmentation improved the performance for all languages. Furthermore, data augmentation improved the performance of the mBERT model, especially for a slot-filling task.

To the best of our knowledge, the study of [12] is the most closely related work to ours. The authors leveraged mT5 and mBART to fine-tune a task-oriented dialogue task based on a new bilingual dialogue dataset. Although the performances of the pre-trained language models for task-oriented DS in English has encouraged the emergence of the multilingual models for task-oriented DS in low-resource languages, there is still a gap between the system performance of both low-resource and high-resource languages, due to the lack of high-quality data in the low-resource languages. To the best of our knowledge, no study exists for Arabic language task-oriented DS using multilingual models. Therefore, according to the current landscape of cross-lingual transfer learning in addition to the achieved performance of multilingual language models in task-oriented DS, we aimed to explore how far can mT5 be useful in building an Arabic end-to-end task-oriented DS using cross-lingual settings.

## 3. Methodology

The workflow of our task-oriented DS is based on a single Seq2Seq model using the pre-trained multilingual model mT5 [10]. D is the dialogue session that represents a sequence of user utterances ($U_t$) and system utterances ($S_t$) at turn t, where $D = \{U_1, S_1, \ldots, U_t, S_t\}$. The interaction between the user and system at turn t creates a dialogue history ($H_t$) that holds all the previous utterances of both the user and system determined by the context window size (w), where $H_t = \{U_{t-w}, S_{t-w}, \ldots, S_{t-1}; U_t\}$. Over the turn (t) of a dialogue session, the system tracks the dialogue state ($B_t$) and knowledge state ($K_t$), then generates the response (R). We first set the dialogue state and knowledge state to empty strings as $B_0$ and $K_0$, respectively. Then, the input at turn t was composed of the current dialogue history ($H_t$), previous dialogue state ($B_{t-1}$), and previous knowledge state ($K_{t-1}$). For each turn, the dialogue state updated from ($B_{t-1}$) to ($B_t$) and produced the Levenshtein Belief Spans at turn t ($Lev_t$), which holds the updated information. Finally, the system was queried with the determined constraint from the dialogue state in order to generate the API name, and then the system updated the knowledge state form ($K_{t-1}$) to ($K_t$). Both $K_t$ and the API name were used to generate the response, which was returned to the user.

### 3.1. Dataset

Arabic-TOD, a multidomain Arabic dataset, was used for training and evaluating end-to-end task-oriented DS. This dataset was created by manually translating the original English BiToD dataset into Arabic. Of 3689 English dialogues, the Arabic-TOD dataset contained 1500 dialogues with 30,000 utterances covering four domains (Hotels, Restaurants, Weather, and Attractions). The dataset comprised 14 intent types and 26 slot types. The Arabic-TOD dataset was preprocessed and prepared for the training step, then divided into 67%, 7%, and 26% for training, validation, and testing, respectively.

### 3.2. Evaluation Metrics

For DST evaluation, we used the JGA metric [16] to compare the predicted dialogue states to the ground truth for each dialogue turn. If all the predicted slot values exactly match the ground-truth values, the output of the model is correct.

For the end-to-end generation task, we employed the original evaluation metrics in [12]. The $API_{Acc}$ metric was used to measure if the system generated the correct API call. The TSR metric was used to measure whether the system had found the correct entity and answered all the task's requested information. The DSR metric was used to evaluate if the system completed all the dialogue tasks. Additionally, we computed the BLEU score [17] to measure the fluency of the generated response.

## 4. Experiments

We investigated the effectiveness of the powerful multilingual model mT5 for few-shot cross-lingual learning for end-to-end Arabic task-oriented DS. In the cross-lingual transfer learning, we transferred the knowledge from a high-resource language (English) to a low-resource language (Arabic). We used three approaches from the literature, [8,11,12]: mSeq2Seq, cross-lingual pre-training (CPT), and mixed-language pre-training (MLT).

*mSeq2Seq approach:* In this setting, we utilized the existing pre-trained mSeq2Seq model mT5, and directly fine-tuned these models on the Arabic dialogue data.

*Cross-lingual pre-training (CPT) approach:* In this setting, we pre-trained the mSeq2Seq model mT5 on English, and then fine-tuned the pre-trained models on the Arabic dialogue data.

*Mixed-language pre-training (MLT) approach:* In this setting, we used a KB (dictionary) that contained a mixed-lingual context (Arabic and English) for most of the entities. As such, we generated the mixed-language training data by replacing the most task-related keyword entities in English with corresponding keyword entities in Arabic from a parallel dictionary for both input and output sequences. The process of generating the mixed-language context is shown in Figure 1. In this setting, we initially pre-trained the mSeq2Seq model mT5 with the generated mixed language-training dialogue data, then fine-tuned the pre-trained models on the Arabic dialogue data. During the training, our model learned to capture the most task-related keywords in the mixed utterances, which helped the model capture the other unimportant task-related words that have similar semantics, e.g., days of the week—"السبت" (Saturday) and "الثلاثاء" (Tuesday).

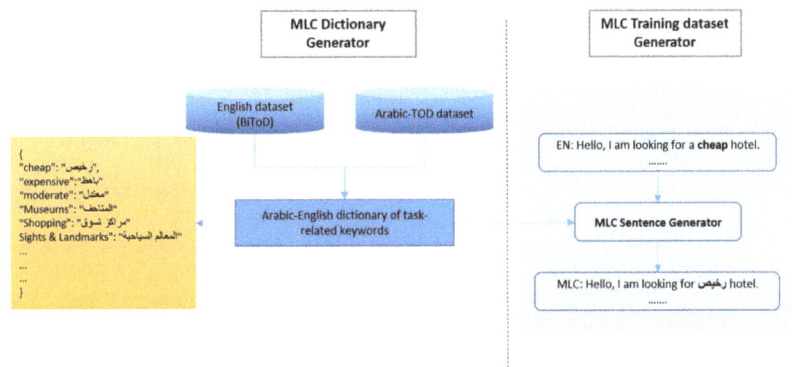

**Figure 1.** Mixed-language context (MLC) generation process.

In all these three approaches, we used the English BiToD dataset [12]. The Arabic-TOD dataset contained 10% of the English one. We intended to investigate if transferring the pre-trained multilingual language model mT5 to task-oriented DS could handle the paucity of the Arabic dialogue data.

*Experiment Setup*

We set up our experimental framework using the multilingual model mT5-small. We used the PyTorch framework [18] and the Transformers library [19]. We set the optimizer to AdamW [20] with a 0.0005 learning rate. We set the dialogue context window size at 2 and the batch size at 128, based on the best results in the existing literature. We first trained the models on English dialogues for 8 epochs, then fine-tuned the model on Arabic for 10 epochs. All the trainings took about 12 h using Google Colab.

**5. Results and Discussion**

Table 2 presents our findings compared to the previous experiments described in [12] on English and Chinese with the same settings in the three approaches: mSeq2Seq, CPT, and MLT. The results were calculated in terms of BLEU, API$_{ACC}$, TSR, DSR, and JGA. We compared our findings with those generated from [12], where in both works English represented the high-resource language used to transfer knowledge to the target language.

In [12], Chinese was considered as the low-resource target language, with 10% of the training dialogue, while in this work, Arabic was the low-resource target language, with 10% of the training dialogue.

**Table 2.** Cross-lingual experiment results of dialogue state tracking (DST) and end-to-end dialogue generation with 10% of Arabic-TOD dataset (AR) compared to 10% of Chinese dialogues in BiToD (ZH) [12]. Bold numbers indicate the best result according to the column's metric value.

| | mSeq2Seq Approach | | | | |
|---|---|---|---|---|---|
| | **TSR** | **DSR** | **API$_{Acc}$** | **BLEU** | **JGA** |
| AR | **18.63** | **3.72** | **15.26** | **9.55** | **17.67** |
| ZH [12] | 4.16 | 2.20 | 6.67 | 3.30 | 12.63 |
| | CPT Approach | | | | |
| AR | 42.16 | 14.18 | 46.63 | 23.09 | 32.71 |
| ZH [12] | **43.27** | **23.70** | **49.70** | 13.89 | **51.40** |
| | MLT Approach | | | | |
| AR | 42.16 | 14.49 | 46.77 | 23.98 | 32.75 |
| ZH [12] | **49.20** | **27.17** | **50.55** | 14.44 | **55.05** |

Our model outperformed the Chinese model using the cross-lingual model deployed by the mSeq2Seq approach, while the Chinese model outperformed ours on the other two approaches, except for BLEU. However, these poor results can be improved by increasing the Arabic-TOD dataset size under the few-shot learning scenarios. Due to the smallness of the Arabic-TOD dataset, we tried to re-implement the experiment utilizing all the data of the Arabic-TOD dataset, which comprised 27% of the size of the Chinese dataset in [12]. In so doing, we improved the results of the Arabic models, as shown in Table 3. We found a high improvement from the first approach, which still outperformed the Chinese model. Furthermore, Arabic obtained better results in terms of TSR, API$_{Acc}$, and BLEU than Chinese using the cross-lingual model deployed by the CPT approach. The cross-lingual model deployed by the MLT approach outperformed the Chinese model in terms of API$_{Acc}$ and BLEU.

**Table 3.** Three approaches in cross-lingual settings results of DST and end-to-end dialogue generation with all the Arabic-TOD dataset. Numbers in bold font indicate superior corresponding values to the Chinese model that were mentioned in Table 2.

| Evaluation Metrics<br>Approach | TSR | DSR | API$_{Acc}$ | BLEU | JGA |
|---|---|---|---|---|---|
| AR (mseq2seq) | **42.88** | **13.95** | **48.68** | **29.28** | **35.74** |
| AR<br>(CPT) | **47.18** | 18.14 | **52.10** | **31.16** | 36.32 |
| AR<br>(MLT) | 48.10 | 18.84 | **52.58** | **31.74** | 37.17 |

Overall, our findings indicate the excellent transferability of the cross-lingual multilingual language model mT5. Moreover, the MLT approach improved the performance of few-shot cross-lingual learning, which indicates that bilingual KB can facilitate the cross-lingual knowledge transfer in low-resource scenarios, such as in Arabic. In addition, the JGA values were relatively small for the Arabic models, due to the difficulty and multiplicity of tasks existing in Arabic-TOD datasets. As we mentioned earlier, we only translated the task-related keywords in the dialogues and did not translate names, locations, and addresses, which in return made parsing the Arabic utterances easier in a cross-lingual setting.

In summary, the cross-lingual setting is an effective approach for building an Arabic end-to-end task-oriented DS, in cases in which there is a scarcity of training data. Our results can be considered a baseline for the future of Arabic conversational systems.

*Impact of Arabic-TOD Dataset Size on Arabic Task-Oriented DS Performance*

We also investigated how our cross-lingual model deployed with MLT performed with different training dataset sizes in few-shot learning settings. We conducted further experiments with varying training data percentages on the Arabic-TOD dataset, ranging from 5% (50 examples) to 100% (1000 examples). We observed improvements when increasing the dataset size for cross-lingual training, as shown in Table 3. In this experiment, we focused on the cross-lingual model with the MLT approach, due to its previous performance. We fine-tuned the pre-trained models with the MLT approach on the few-shot Arabic dialogue data. To conclude, our results can be improved with dataset increases, as shown in Table 4. Although the dialogue dataset was small, it was sufficient to study the effectiveness of the cross-lingual model using the multilingual language model mT5 for Arabic end-to-end task-oriented DS.

**Table 4.** Few-shot learning results of cross-lingual model deployed with MTL approach on the Arabic-TOD dataset using training dataset of different sizes. Bold numbers indicate the best result according to the column's metric value.

| Dataset Size / Evaluation Metrics | TSR | DSR | $API_{Acc}$ | BLEU | JGA |
|---|---|---|---|---|---|
| 5% | 30.09 | 10.23 | 33.07 | 20.26 | 24.85 |
| 10% | 34.90 | 11.86 | 37.89 | 20.87 | 28.26 |
| 20% | 40.73 | 14.42 | 44.47 | 23.84 | 32.05 |
| 50% | 42.16 | 14.88 | 48.51 | 24.94 | 34.03 |
| 100% | **48.10** | **18.84** | **52.58** | **31.74** | **37.17** |

## 6. Conclusions and Future Work

In this work, we studied the effectiveness of cross-lingual transfer learning using the multilingual language model mT5 for Arabic end-to-end task-oriented DS. We used the Arabic-TOD dataset in training and testing the model. To address the problem of the small Arabic dialogue dataset, we presented cross-lingual transfer learning using three approaches. We obtained good results for our model compared to those in the literature for Chinese with the same settings. Therefore, cross-lingual transfer learning can improve the system performance of Arabic in cases of small datasets. Furthermore, we explored the impact of Arabic training dialogue data size on cross-lingual learning in few-shot scenarios and found improvements when increasing the training dataset size. Finally, the results obtained from our proposed model on the Arabic-TOD dataset can be considered a baseline for future researchers to build robust end-to-end Arabic task-oriented DS that tackle complex scenarios. In addition to the training dataset size, there are other factors that may influence the model's performance, such as the number of tasks and the number of turns (length) in the dialogue. Further experimentation to validate the influence of these factors will be addressed in future work.

**Author Contributions:** Conceptualization, A.F. and M.A.-Y.; methodology, A.F.; software, A.F.; validation, A.F.; formal analysis, A.F. and M.A.-Y.; investigation, A.F. and M.A.-Y.; resources, A.F. and M.A.-Y.; data curation, A.F.; writing—original draft preparation, A.F.; writing—review and editing, A.F. and M.A.-Y.; visualization, A.F. and M.A.-Y.; supervision, M.A.-Y.; project administration, M.A.-Y.; funding acquisition, M.A.-Y. All authors have read and agreed to the published version of the manuscript.

**Funding:** This research is supported by a grant from the Researchers Supporting Project No. RSP-2021/286, King Saud University, Riyadh, Saudi Arabia.

**Institutional Review Board Statement:** Not applicable.

**Informed Consent Statement:** Not applicable.

**Acknowledgments:** The authors extend their appreciation to the Researchers Supporting Project number RSP-2021/286, King Saud University, Riyadh, Saudi Arabia.

**Conflicts of Interest:** The authors declare no conflict of interest.

## References

1. McTear, M. *Conversational AI: Dialogue Systems, Conversational Agents, and Chatbots*; Morgan & Claypool Publishers LLC: San Rafael, CA, USA, 2020; Volume 13.
2. Wu, C.S.; Madotto, A.; Hosseini-Asl, E.; Xiong, C.; Socher, R.; Fung, P. Transferable multi-domain state generator for task-oriented dialogue systems. In Proceedings of the 57th Annual Meeting of the Association for Computational Linguistics, Florence, Italy, 28 July–2 August 2019; pp. 808–819. [CrossRef]
3. Peng, B.; Zhu, C.; Li, C.; Li, X.; Li, J.; Zeng, M.; Gao, J. Few-shot Natural Language Generation for Task-Oriented Dialog. *arXiv* **2020**, arXiv:2002.12328. [CrossRef]
4. Yang, Y.; Li, Y.; Quan, X. UBAR: Towards Fully End-to-End Task-Oriented Dialog Systems with GPT-2. *arXiv* **2020**, arXiv:2012.03539.
5. Hosseini-Asl, E.; McCann, B.; Wu, C.S.; Yavuz, S.; Socher, R. A simple language model for task-oriented dialogue. *Adv. Neural Inf. Process. Syst.* **2020**, *33*, 20179–20191.
6. AlHagbani, E.S.; Khan, M.B. Challenges facing the development of the Arabic chatbot. In Proceedings of the First International Workshop on Pattern Recognition 2016, Tokyo, Japan, 11–13 May 2016; Volume 10011, p. 7. [CrossRef]
7. Liu, Z.; Shin, J.; Xu, Y.; Winata, G.I.; Xu, P.; Madotto, A.; Fung, P. Zero-shot cross-lingual dialogue systems with transferable latent variables. In Proceedings of the 2019 Conference on Empirical Methods in Natural Language Processing and the 9th International Joint Conference on Natural Language Processing (EMNLP-IJCNLP), Hong Kong, China, 3–7 November 2019; pp. 1297–1303. [CrossRef]
8. Schuster, S.; Shah, R.; Gupta, S.; Lewis, M. Cross-lingual transfer learning for multilingual task oriented dialog. In Proceedings of the 2019 Conference of the North American Chapter of the Association for Computational Linguistics: Human Language Technologies, Minneapolis, MN, USA, 2–7 June 2019; Volume 1, pp. 3795–3805. [CrossRef]
9. Zhou, X.; Dong, D.; Wu, H.; Zhao, S.; Yu, D.; Tian, H.; Liu, X.; Yan, R. Multi-view response selection for human-computer conversation. In Proceedings of the EMNLP 2016—Conference on Empirical Methods in Natural Language Processing, Austin, TX, USA, 1–5 November 2016; pp. 372–381.
10. Xue, L.; Constant, N.; Roberts, A.; Kale, M.; Al-Rfou, R.; Siddhant, A.; Barua, A.; Raffel, C. mT5: A Massively Multilingual Pre-trained Text-to-Text Transformer. In Proceedings of the 2021 Conference of the North American Chapter of the Association for Computational Linguistics: Human Language Technologies, Online, 6–11 June 2020; pp. 483–498. [CrossRef]
11. Liu, Z.; Winata, G.I.; Lin, Z.; Xu, P.; Fung, P. Attention-informed mixed-language training for zero-shot cross-lingual task-oriented dialogue systems. In Proceedings of the AAAI 2020—34th Conference on Artificial Intelligence, New York, NY, USA, 7–12 February 2020; pp. 8433–8440. [CrossRef]
12. Lin, Z.; Madotto, A.; Winata, G.I.; Xu, P.; Jiang, F.; Hu, Y.; Shi, C.; Fung, P. BiToD: A Bilingual Multi-Domain Dataset For Task-Oriented Dialogue Modeling. *arXiv* **2021**, arXiv:2106.02787.
13. Liu, Y.; Gu, J.; Goyal, N.; Li, X.; Edunov, S.; Ghazvininejad, M.; Lewis, M.; Zettlemoyer, L. Multilingual denoising pre-training for neural machine translation. *Trans. Assoc. Comput. Linguist.* **2020**, *8*, 726–742. [CrossRef]
14. Sitaram, S.; Chandu, K.R.; Rallabandi, S.K.; Black, A.W. A Survey of Code-switched Speech and Language Processing. *arXiv* **2019**, arXiv:1904.00784.
15. Louvan, S.; Magnini, B. Simple data augmentation for multilingual NLU in task oriented dialogue systems. In Proceedings of the Seventh Italian Conference on Computational Linguistics CLIC-IT 2020, Bologna, Italy, 30 November–2 December 2020; Volume 2769. [CrossRef]
16. Henderson, M.; Thomson, B.; Williams, J. The second dialog state tracking challenge. In Proceedings of the 15th Annual Meeting of the Special Interest Group on Discourse and Dialogue (SIGDIAL), Philadelphia, PA, USA, 18–20 June 2014; pp. 263–272. [CrossRef]
17. Papineni, K.; Roukos, S.; Ward, T.; Zhu, W.-J. BLEU: A method for automatic evaluation of machine translation. In Proceedings of the 40th Annual Meeting on Association for Computational Linguistics, Philadelphia, PA, USA, 7–12 July 2001; pp. 311–318. [CrossRef]
18. PyTorch. Available online: https://pytorch.org/ (accessed on 17 November 2021).

19. Huggingface/Transformers: Transformers: State-of-the-Art Natural Language Processing for Pytorch, TensorFlow, and JAX. Available online: https://github.com/huggingface/transformers (accessed on 17 November 2021).
20. Loshchilov, I.; Hutter, F. Decoupled weight decay regularization. In Proceedings of the 7th International Conference on Learning Representations, New Orleans, LA, USA, 6–9 May 2017.

Article

# Improving Machine Reading Comprehension with Multi-Task Learning and Self-Training

**Jianquan Ouyang * and Mengen Fu**

College of Computer Cyberspace Security, Xiangtan University, Xiangtan 411105, China; ccdf.mengen@gmail.com
* Correspondence: oyjq@xtu.edu.cn

**Abstract:** Machine Reading Comprehension (MRC) is an AI challenge that requires machines to determine the correct answer to a question based on a given passage, in which extractive MRC requires extracting an answer span to a question from a given passage, such as the task of span extraction. In contrast, non-extractive MRC infers answers from the content of reference passages, including Yes/No question answering to unanswerable questions. Due to the specificity of the two types of MRC tasks, researchers usually work on one type of task separately, but real-life application situations often require models that can handle many different types of tasks in parallel. Therefore, to meet the comprehensive requirements in such application situations, we construct a multi-task fusion training reading comprehension model based on the BERT pre-training model. The model uses the BERT pre-training model to obtain contextual representations, which is then shared by three downstream sub-modules for span extraction, Yes/No question answering, and unanswerable questions, next we fuse the outputs of the three sub-modules into a new span extraction output and use the fused cross-entropy loss function for global training. In the training phase, since our model requires a large amount of labeled training data, which is often expensive to obtain or unavailable in many tasks, we additionally use self-training to generate pseudo-labeled training data to train our model to improve its accuracy and generalization performance. We evaluated the SQuAD2.0 and CAIL2019 datasets. The experiments show that our model can efficiently handle different tasks. We achieved 83.2EM and 86.7F1 scores on the SQuAD2.0 dataset and 73.0EM and 85.3F1 scores on the CAIL2019 dataset.

**Keywords:** machine reading comprehension; Natural Language Processing; multi-task learning; Self Training; pre-trained model

**Citation:** Ouyang, J.; Fu, M. Improving Machine Reading Comprehension with Multi-Task Learning and Self-Training. *Mathematics* **2022**, *10*, 310. https://doi.org/10.3390/math10030310

Academic Editors: Florentina Hristea and Cornelia Caragea

Received: 28 November 2021
Accepted: 16 January 2022
Published: 19 January 2022

**Publisher's Note:** MDPI stays neutral with regard to jurisdictional claims in published maps and institutional affiliations.

## 1. Introduction

Machine reading comprehension (MRC) aims to teach machines to answer questions after understanding a given passage [1,2], which can be broadly classified into two categories: Extractive MRC and Non-extractive MRC. Extractive MRC requires models to extract the answer span of a question from a reference text. For example, the tasks of close-test [3] and span extraction [4,5]. Figure 1 shows a span extraction sample in the SQuAD2.0 dataset [6]. In contrast, Non-extractive MRC infers answers to questions from the content of the referenced passage, including Yes/No question answering [7] and unanswerable question task [6]. Figure 2 shows an unanswerable question sample in the SQuAD2.0 dataset.

Due to the different task objectives, researchers usually research one type of task. However, realistic reading comprehension application scenarios usually require models that can handle many different types of tasks simultaneously. For example, the Chinese legal text dataset CAIL2019 reading comprehension dataset [8] consists of more than 39,000 sample data, which involve the content of civil and criminal first instance judgments. The dataset has three tasks: span extraction, yes/no questions answered, and unanswerable questions, where the span extraction task is the main task, accounting for 83% of total data.

Yes/no questions answering and unanswerable question task accounts for 14% and 3%, respectively. This requires multi-task learning.

Multi-task learning is a field of machine learning in which multiple tasks are learned in parallel while using a shared representation [9–11]. Compared with learning multiple tasks individually, this joint learning effectively increases the sample size for training the model, thus leading to performance improvement by increasing the generalization of the model [12]. To solve multi-tasking MRC is important, and some straightforward solutions have been proposed. Liu et al. [13] appended an empty word token to the context and added a simple classification layer for the MRC model. Hu et al. [14] used two auxiliary losses, independent span loss to predict plausible answers and independent no answer loss to determine the answerability of the question. Further, an extra verifier is used to determine whether the predicted answer is contained by the input snippets. Back et al. [15] developed an attention-based satisfaction score to compare question embeddings with candidate answer embeddings. Zhang et al. [16] proposed a verifier layer, which is a linear layer applied to context embeddings weighted by the start and end distributions over contextual word representations concatenated to [CLS] token representation for BERT. The above studies are based on the SQuAD2.0 dataset, but the SQuAD2.0 dataset only includes two different tasks. We want the model to be able to handle more tasks simultaneously, such as the CAIL2019 reading comprehension dataset, which contains three different tasks. Researchers usually set up three types of auxiliary losses to jointly train the model. We think that too much auxiliary loss may hurt the general model training, so we propose to fuse three different task outputs into a new span extraction output with only one loss function for global training.

Early neural reading models typically used various attention mechanisms to build interdependent representations of passages and questions, then predict answer boundaries in turn. A wide range of attention models have been employed, including Attention Sum Reader [17], Gated attention Reader [18], Self-matching Network [19], Attention over Attention Reader [20], and Bi-attention Network [21]. Recently, PrLMs have dominated the design of encoders for MRC with great success. These PrLMs include ELMo [22], GPT [23], BERT [24], XLNet [25], Roberta [26], ALBERT [27], and ELECTRA [28]. They bring impressive performance improvements for a wide range of NLP tasks for two main reasons: (1) language models are pre-trained on a large-scale text corpus, which allows the models to learn generic language features and serve as a knowledge base; (2) thanks to the Transformer architecture, language models enjoy a powerful feature representation learning capability to capture higher-order, long-range dependencies in text.

In the model training phase, since our model requires a large amount of labeled training data, which are often expensive to obtain or unavailable in many tasks, we additionally use self-training to generate pseudo-labeled training data to train our model to improve the accuracy and generalization performance of the model. Self-training [29,30] is a widely used semi-supervised learning method [31]. Most related studies follow the framework of traditional Self-Training and Co-Training and focus on designing better policies for selecting confident samples: trains the base model (student) on a small amount of labeled data, applies it to pseudo-labeled task-specific unlabeled data, uses pseudo-labels to augment the labeled data, and retrains the student model iteratively. Recently, self-training has been shown to obtain state-of-the-art performance in tasks such as image classification [32,33], few-shot text classification [34,35], and neural machine translation [36,37], and has shown complementary advantages to unsupervised pre-training [32].

In this paper, we propose a machine reading comprehension model based on multi-task fusion training, and we construct a multi-task fusion training reading comprehension model based on the BERT pre-training model. The model uses the BERT pre-training model to obtain contextual representations, which is shared by three downstream sub-modules of span extraction, yes/no question answering, and unanswerable questions. Next, we fuse the outputs of the three submodules into a new span extraction output, and we use a cross-entropy loss function for global training. We use a self-training method to generate pseudo-labeled data from unlabeled data to expand labeled data iteratively, thus improving the model performance and achieving better generalization. The experiments show that our model can efficiently handle different tasks. We achieved 83.2 EM and 86.7 F1 scores on the SQuAD2.0 dataset and 73.0 EM and 85.3 F1 scores on the CAIL2019 dataset.

| |
|---|
| **Passage:** The two halves of the city were actually founded and plotted as separate cities, but soon grew together. The north side is characterized by very diverse and fashionable urban neighborhoods near the city center and sprawling suburbs further north. South Oklahoma City is generally more blue collar working class and significantly more industrial, having grown up around the Stockyards and meat packing plants at the turn of the century, and is currently the center of the city's rapidly growing Latino community. |
| **Question:** Which side is more urban and fashionable? |
| **Gold Answer:** North Oklahoma City |

**Figure 1.** A extractive MRC example.

| |
|---|
| **Passage:** The plague struck various countries in the Middle East during the pandemic, leading to serious depopulation and permanent change in both economic and social structures. As it spread to western Europe, the disease entered the region from southern Russia also. By autumn 1347, the plague reached Alexandria in Egypt, probably through the port's trade with Constantinople, and ports on the Black Sea. During 1347, the disease travelled eastward to Gaza, and north along the eastern coast to cities in Lebanon, Syria and Palestine. |
| **Question:** What was one of the cities that had a port on the Black Sea? |
| **Gold Answer:** <no answer> |

**Figure 2.** A non-extractive MRC example.

## 2. Materials and Methods

### 2.1. Materials

Two publicly available datasets are used in this study including SQuAD2.0 [6] and CAIL2019 Reading comprehension dataset [8]. SQuAD 2.0 is a widely used MRC benchmark dataset, which combines the 100,000 questions from SQuAD 1.1 [4] with over 50,000 new, unanswerable questions that are the crowd adversarially written to look similar to the answerable questions. The training dataset contains 87,000 answerable questions and 43,000 unanswerable questions. The CAIL2019 reading comprehension dataset is primarily concerned with civil and criminal first-instance judgments. The training set includes more than 39,000 questions, mainly span extraction, containing more than 5000 YES/NO question answering and more than 1000 unanswerable questions.

### 2.2. Method

We focus on three reading comprehension tasks: span extraction, Yes/No question answering, and unanswerable questions. They all can be described as a triplet <P, Q, A>, where P is a passage and Q is a question for P. When question Q is a span extraction task, the correct answer A is a span text in P; when question Q is a Yes/No question answering, the correct answer A is the text "YES" or "NO"; when question Q is an unanswerable question, the correct answer A is the null string. We have conducted experiments on both SQUAD2.0 and CAIL2019 reading comprehension datasets, and our model should be able to predict the begin and end position in passage P and extract the span text as answer A for a question which is the span extraction task and return the text "YES" or "NO" for the question which is the Yes/No question answering. For the unanswerable question, the model can return a null string.

Our MRC model mainly includes two aspects of improvement: the multi-task fusion training model and the self-training method. The multi-task fusion training model mainly focuses on the fusion of multi-task outputs and training methods. Self-training mainly focuses on generating pseudo-labeled training data with high confidence from unlabeled data to expand the training data.

### 2.2.1. Embedding

We concatenate question and passage texts as the input, which is firstly represented as embedding vectors to feed an encoder layer. In detail, the input texts are first tokenized to word pieces(subword tokens). Let $T = \{t_1, t_2, ..., t_n\}$ denote as a sequence of subword tokens of length $N$. For each token, the embedding vector of the input text is the sum vector of its token embedding, position embedding, and token-type embedding.

We take $X = \{x_1, x_2, ..., x_n\}$ as the output of the encoding layer, which is an embedding feature vector of encoded sentence tokens of length $n$. Then, the embedded feature vector is fed to the interaction layer to obtain the contextual representation vector.

### 2.2.2. Interaction

Following Devlin at all. [24], the encoded sequence $X$ is processed using multiple layers of Transformers [38] to learn the context representation vector. In the next section, we use $H = \{h_1, h_2, ..., h_n\}$ to denote the last layer of hidden states of the input sequence. $H_c$ is denoted as the last layer of hidden states of the first token (classification token) in the sequence.

### 2.2.3. Multi-Tasking Fusion Training

As is shown Figure 3 depicts the whole architecture of our model. The unanswerable question task is to return an empty string as the answer after discriminating the question from the text, so we use a linear layer into which $H_c$ is fed as input to obtain the probability value $unk$ of the unanswerable question. The span extraction task is to find a span in the passage as an answer. We feed the last_layer hidden states $H$ into a linear layer with softmax operations to obtain two probability sequences $L_s$ and $L_e$. The Yes/No question answering task is to return the text "YES" or "NO" as the answer after understanding the question and the passage. We use sum-pooling to compress the hidden state H of the last layer into a vector as input to a linear layer to obtain predicted probability values $yes$ and $no$.

We use the predicted probability values of the three tasks $Ls$, $unk$, $yes$, and $no$ spliced together as the new start probability sequence $S$. In the same way, we can obtain the new end probability sequence $E$.

The training target for our model is defined as the cross-entropy loss of start $S$ and end $E$:

$$L = -\frac{1}{N} \sum_{i=0}^{N} \left[ log\left(p_{y_i^s}^s\right) + log\left(p_{y_i^e}^e\right) \right], \tag{1}$$

where $y_i^s$ and $y_i^e$ represent the true start and end positions of sample i respectively, and N is the number of samples.

For prediction, given output start and end probability sequences $S$ and $E$, we calculate the span score $score_{span}$, the unanswer score $score_{ua}$, the Yes-answer score $score_{yes}$ and the no-answer score $score_{no}$:

$$
\begin{aligned}
score_{span} &= max(S_k + E_l), 0 \leq k \leq l \leq n - 2, \\
score_{ua} &= S_0 + E_0, \\
score_{yes} &= S_{n-1} + E_{n-1}, \\
score_{no} &= S_n + E_n.
\end{aligned}
\tag{2}
$$

We get 4 answer scores, and we choose the answer with the largest score as the final answer by comparing them.

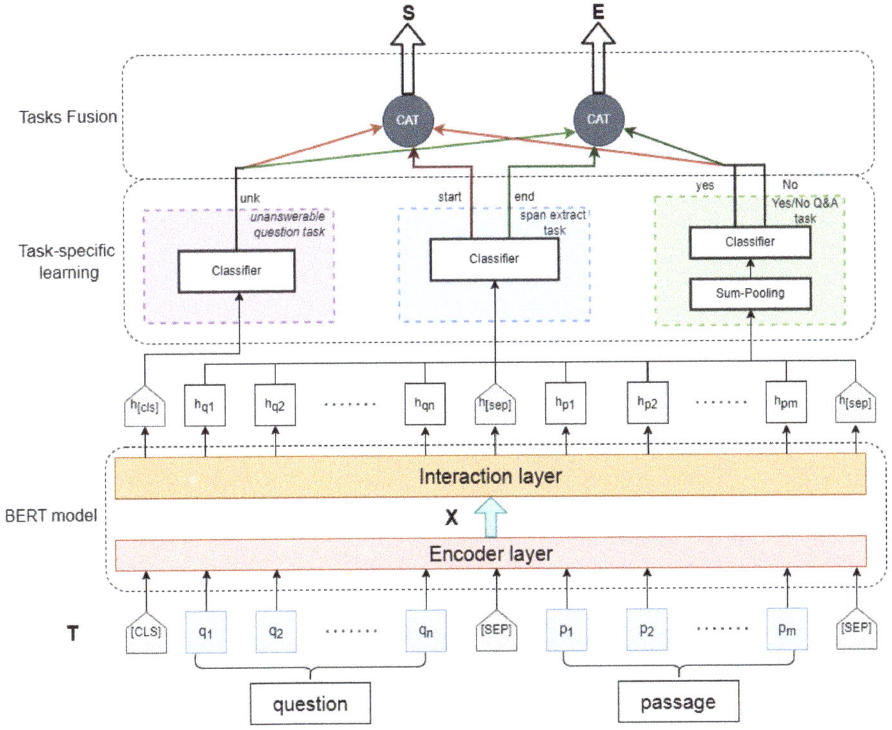

**Figure 3.** An overview of our base model. $T$ is the sequence of subword tokens after embedding, $X$ is the outputs of the encoder layer. Task-specific learning Module sets up three sub-modules to generate probability sequences or values of different answers for each sample. $CAT$ means concatenates the input sequence or value.

### 2.2.4. Self Training

The complete two-stage process is as specified in Algorithm 1. First, in the fine-tuning phase, the pre-trained MRC model is fine-tuned in a supervised manner on the labeled dataset $D_s$. The model is named $M_0$ and is then used as the starting point for the next phase. In the self-training phase, the training and labeling process is iterated several times. For each iteration $i$, we first generated pseudo-labels for the unlabeled dataset $D_t$ using the model $M_i$ and then trained $M_0$ on the unlabeled dataset using these labels.

---

**Algorithm 1** MRC self-training process

---

**Require:** Pre-trained MRC model, $M_p$; Labeled dataset, $D_s$; Unlabeled dataset, $D_t$; Number of self-training iterations, $N$; Threshold for filtering pseudo-labels, $\delta$

1: $M_0 \leftarrow train(M_p, D_s)$
2: $D_0 \leftarrow label(M_0, D_t, \delta)$
3: **for** $i \in [1, n]$ **do**
4:     $M_i \leftarrow train(M_{i-1}, D_{i-1})$
5:     $D_i \leftarrow label(M_i, D_t, \delta)$
6: **end for**
7: **return** $M_n$

---

The unlabeled dataset can be described as a tuple $< P_t, Q_t >$, where $P_t = \{p_1, p_2, ..., p_n\}$ is a passage, $Q_t = \{q_{11}, q_{12}, ..., q_{nm}\}$ is a question over $P_t$. To obtain pseudo-labels, we use the model running on the unlabeled dataset $D_t$, and Algorithm 2 explains the labeling process. For each unlabeled example $(c_i, q_i)$, the model gives $t$ predicted answers $A_{ij} = \{a_{ij1}, a_{ij2}, ..., a_{ijp}\}$ and the corresponding confidence $E_{ij} = \{e_{ij1}, e_{ij2}, ..., e_{ijp}\}$. Then we use a threshold to filter the data, only the examples with maximum confidence above the threshold are retained. For each question, the answer with the maximum confidence is used as a pseudo-label.

---

**Algorithm 2** Pseudo-label generation

---

**Require:** Model used in self-training process, $M$; Passages in unlabeled dataset, $C_t$; Questions in unlabeled dataset, $Q_t$; Unlabeled dataset, $D_t$; Threshold for filtering pseudo-labels, $\delta$

1: $D' \leftarrow \varnothing$
2: **for** $c_i \in C_t$ **do**
3:     **for** $q_{ij} \in Q_t$ **do**
4:         $A_{ij}, E_{ij} \in M(c_i, q_{ij})$
5:         **if** $max_\tau E_{ij} \geq \delta$ **then**
6:             $k \leftarrow argmax\ E_{ij}$
7:             $D' \leftarrow D' \cup (p_i, q_{ij}, a_{ijk})$
8:         **end if**
9:     **end for**
10: **end for**
11: **return** $D'$

---

In the span extraction task, the model answers questions by generating two probability distributions for contextual tokens. One is the start position and the other is the end position. The answer is then extracted by choosing the span between the start and end positions.

Here, we consider probability as a measure of confidence. More specifically, we take the distributions of the start and end tokens as input, then filter out unlikely candidates (for example, candidates whose end token precedes the start token) and perform a beam search with the sum of the start/end distributions as the confidence. The threshold was set to 0.95, which means that only those examples with the most confident answers scoring greater than 0.95 were used in the self-training phase.

### 3. Experiments and Results

#### 3.1. Experiments

##### 3.1.1. Evaluation

Metrics: Two official metrics are used to evaluate the performance of the model. Exact Match (EM) and a softer metric F1 score, which measures the average overlap between predicted and ground-truth answers at the token level.

Exact Match (EM): This metric measures the percentage of predictions that match any one of the ground truth answers exactly. For each question+answer pair, if the characters of the model's prediction exactly match the characters of (one of) the True Answer(s), EM = 1, otherwise EM = 0. This is a strict all-or-nothing metric; being off by a single character results in a score of 0. When assessing against a negative example, if the model predicts any text at all, it automatically receives a 0 for that example.

F1 Score: It is a common metric for classification problems, and is widely used in Question Answering. It is appropriate when we care equally about *precision* and *recall*. In this case, it's computed over the individual words in the prediction against those in the True Answer. The number of shared words between the prediction and the truth is the basis of the F1 score: *precision* is the ratio of the number of shared words to the total number of words in the prediction, and *recall* is the ratio of the number of shared words to the total number of words in the ground truth. The formula for the F1 score is the following:

$$F1\ score = 2 * \frac{precision * recall}{precision + recall} \tag{3}$$

### 3.1.2. Setup

We use the available pre-trained models as encoders to build the baseline MRC models: BERT, ALBERT, ELECTRA. Our implementations for BERT are based on Transformers' public Pytorch version of the scheme. We use pre-trained language model weights in the encoder module of the model, using all official hyperparameters. For fine-tuning in our task, we set the initial learning rate in $\{2 \times 10^{-5}, 3 \times 10^{-5}\}$ with a warmup rate of 0.1, and L2 weight decay of 0.01. Specifically, $2 \times 10^{-5}$ for BERT, $3 \times 10^{-5}$ for ALBERT and ELECTRA. For the batch size, BERT is set to 20, ALBERT and ELECTRA are set to 8. In all experiments, the maximum number of epochs was set to 3. Texts are tokenized using wordpieces [39], with a maximum length of 512. Hyperparameters were selected using the development set.

### 3.2. Results

Tables 1 and 2 compare our model with the current more advanced models on the SQuAD2.0 and CAIL2019 datasets. In the English dataset SQuAD2.0, our model improves compared to the NeurQuRI and BERT models but lags behind the ALBERT and ELECTRA models. This is because our model is constructed based on the pre-trained language model, and the ability of the pre-trained model to learn generic language representations is important for the overall model performance. Currently available pre-trained language models for machine-reading comprehension tasks include BERT, ALBERT, and ELECTRA. The ALBERT model as an improved model of the BERT model can effectively improve the downstream performance of multi-sentence coding tasks through three improvements: factorized embedding parameterization, cross-layer parameter sharing, and inter-sentence coherence loss. The ELECTRA model proposes a model training framework borrowed from the design of GAN networks and a new pre-training task of replaced token detection. These two improvements allow ELECTRA to learn more contextual representations than BERT. Theoretically, our model can be designed based on the ALBERT or ELECTRA pre-trained model. However, the problem is that the training time of the ALBERT or ELECTRA pre-trained model is much longer than that of the BERT model, and our self-training method requires iterative training of the model. As such, the time cost is unacceptable. In the Chinese reading comprehension dataset CAIL2019, we did not find an available Chinese ALBERT pre-training model, so we did not conduct a comparison experiment of ALBERT models. Our model improves compared to NeurQuRI, BERT, and ELECTRA models. Benefiting from our designed task-specific learning module, our model can identify different task samples and make correct answers better than other models.

**Table 1.** The results (%) for SQuAD2.0 dataset. Time means Training time of model, *ST* means our Self Training method (Section 2.2.4).

| Model | EM (%) | F1 (%) | Time (h) |
|---|---|---|---|
| NeurQuRI | 81.3 | 84.3 | 7 |
| BERT | 82.1 | 84.8 | 8.5 |
| ALBERT | 86.9 | 89.8 | 22.5 |
| ELECTRA | 87.0 | 89.9 | 20 |
| Our model | 82.9 | 86.4 | 8.5 |
| Our model + *ST* | 83.2 (+0.3) | 86.7 (+0.3) | 42.5 (5 iters) |

We fuse the outputs of different tasks into a new span extract output, train the model using a cross-entropy loss function. It can effectively prevent the imbalance from different task losses that confuse the whole model training. Our self-training method is also applied to the model successfully. The experiments show that the self-training method increases

0.3EM and 0.3F1 scores in the SQuAD2.0 dataset, and 0.9EM and 1.1F1 scores in the CAIL2019 reading comprehension dataset compared to our base model.

**Table 2.** The results (%) for CAIL2019 Reading comprehension dataset. Time means Training time of model, *ST* means our Self Training method (Section 2.2.4).

| Model | EM (%) | *F1* (%) | Time (h) |
|---|---|---|---|
| NeurQuRI | 67.2 | 79.8 | 5 |
| BERT | 69.5 | 81.7 | 6 |
| ELECTRA | 71.2 | 83.6 | 11 |
| Our model | 72.1 | 84.2 | 6 |
| Our model + *ST* | 73.0 (+0.9) | 85.3 (+1.1) | 30 (5 iters) |

## 4. Discussion

This paper compares the performance of three methods, including MLT with Fusion training, MLT with three auxiliary losses, and a pipeline approach. We implemented three comparative experiments in the CAIL2019 dataset. Based on the idea of Hu et al. [28], we adopt a BERT model to obtain context representation and use three auxiliary loss functions to process the output of different task modules. The training loss of the whole model is the weighted sum of the losses of the three modules. The pipeline approach uses a BERT model for training the extraction MRC task, turns non-extracted MRC tasks into a classification task, and learns the classification task directly for the sentences in each passage. Finally, the predicted results of the two models are combined and the scores are calculated.

The specific experimental comparison results are shown in Table 3. It can be seen that the performance of the pipeline approach is lower compared to the other two approaches. It may be the pipeline approach only optimizes the loss of one task and lacks the interaction of other tasks. However, the pipeline approach also has its advantages, such as better controllability of the results for each subtask and the convenience of manual observation for each subtask. In multi-task learning, the magnitude of task loss is considered a perceived similarity measure. Imbalanced tasks in this regard produce largely varied gradients which can confuse model training. MLT with three auxiliary losses uses a task weighting coefficient to help normalize the gradient magnitudes across the tasks. However, its specific implementation employing an average task loss weighting coefficient does not achieve the balance among tasks, which may lead to a bias of the model toward a particular task during training. Our research revealed that the outputs of the different MRC task modules can be fused into a sequence, and we put it into a loss function for training. The model can automatically learn the weight coefficient between different tasks during training and make reasonable judgments. Experiments show that our model, although lower than MLT with three auxiliary losses in the EM metric, exceeds it by 0.8% in the *F1* metric.

**Table 3.** Comparative experimental results of three multi-task learning methods.

| Training Method | EM | F1 |
|---|---|---|
| MLT with Fusion training | 72.1 | 84.2 |
| MLT with Three Auxiliary losses | 72.6 | 83.4 |
| Pipeline method | 70.6 | 81.0 |

It is well known that the size of the labeled dataset affects the performance of the pre-trained model for downstream task fine-tuning. After that, we apply self-training to the models trained above to investigate the effect of labeled datasets of different sizes on the effectiveness of the self-training method for the base model. We set the size of the unlabeled dataset used for the self-training approach to 100%. Figure 4 shows that the evaluation performance of base model fine-tuning is highly dependent on the size of the domain labeled data, and the self-training method always improves the evaluation performance of the base model. However, as the evaluation performance of the base model improves, the self-training method has less and less improvement on the effectiveness of the base model.

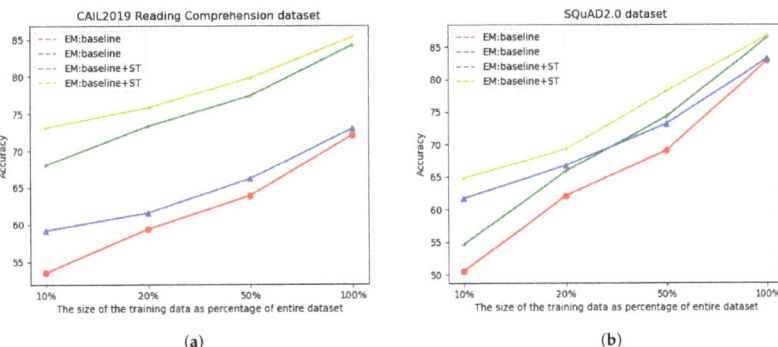

**Figure 4.** The results of different sized labeled datasets for self-training improvement. (**a**) SQuAD 2.0 dataset. (**b**) CAIL2019 Reading Comprehension dataset.

## 5. Conclusions

In this paper, we construct a multi-task fusion training reading comprehension model based on a BERT pre-training model. The model uses the BERT pre-training model to obtain contextual representations, which are then shared by three downstream sub-modules for span extraction, yes/no question answering and unanswerable questions, and we next fuse the outputs of the three sub-modules into a new span extraction output and use the fused cross-entropy loss function for global training. We use self-training to generate pseudo-labeled training data to train our model to improve its accuracy and generalization performance. However, our self-training approach requires iteratively training a model, which consumes a lot of time, and we consider it needs further optimization. Our model is designed for only three specific tasks and cannot be widely applied to more machine reading comprehension task scenarios. We hope to explore more effective multi-task methods for machine-reading comprehension in the future.

**Author Contributions:** Conceptualization J.O. and M.F.; methodology, J.O. and M.F.; software, M.F.; validation, J.O. and M.F.; formal analysis, J.O. and M.F.; investigation, J.O. and M.F.; resources, J.O.; data curation, J.O. and M.F.; writing—original draft preparation, M.F.; writing—review and editing, J.O. and M.F.; visualization, M.F.; supervision, J.O.; project administration, J.O. and M.F.; funding acquisition, J.O. and M.F. All authors have read and agreed to the published version of the manuscript.

**Funding:** This research has been supported by Key Projects of the Ministry of Science and Technology of the People Republic of China (2020YFC0832401).

**Institutional Review Board Statement:** Not applicable.

**Informed Consent Statement:** Not applicable.

**Data Availability Statement:** The CAIL2019 reading comprehension datasets used in our study are available at https://github.com/china-ai-law-challenge/CAIL2019. The SQuAD 2.0 datasets are available at https://rajpurkar.github.io/SQuAD-explorer.

**Conflicts of Interest:** The authors declare no conflict of interest.

## References

1. Hermann, K.M.; Kocisky, T.; Grefenstette, E.; Espeholt, L.; Kay, W.; Suleyman, M.; Blunsom, P. Teaching machines to read and comprehend. *Adv. Neural Inf. Process. Syst.* **2015**, *28*, 1693–1701.
2. Zhang, Z.; Yang, J.; Zhao, H. Retrospective Reader for Machine Reading Comprehension. In *Proceedings of the AAAI Conference on Artificial Intelligence, Virtual, 2–9 February 2021*; AAAI Press: Palo Alto, CA, USA, 2021; Volume 35, pp. 14506–14514.
3. Xie, Q.; Lai, G.; Dai, Z.; Hovy, E. Large-scale Cloze Test Dataset Created by Teachers. In Proceedings of the 2018 Conference on Empirical Methods in Natural Language Processing, Brussels, Belgium, 31 October–4 November 2018; pp. 2344–2356.
4. Rajpurkar, P.; Zhang, J.; Lopyrev, K.; Liang, P. SQuAD: 100,000+ Questions for Machine Comprehension of Text. In Proceedings of the 2016 Conference on Empirical Methods in Natural Language Processing, Austin, Texas, USA, 1–5 November 2016; pp. 2383–2392.
5. Inoue, N.; Stenetorp, P.; Inui, K. R4C: A Benchmark for Evaluating RC Systems to Get the Right Answer for the Right Reason. In Proceedings of the 58th Annual Meeting of the Association for Computational Linguistics, Stroudsburg, PA, USA, 6–8 July 2020; Association for Computational Linguistics: Stroudsburg, PA, USA, 2020; pp. 6740–6750.
6. Rajpurkar, P.; Jia, R.; Liang, P. Know what you don't know: Unanswerable questions for SQuAD. *arXiv* **2018**, arXiv:1806.03822.
7. Reddy, S.; Chen, D.; Manning, C.D. Coqa: A conversational question answering challenge. *Trans. Assoc. Comput. Linguist.* **2019**, *7*, 249–266. [CrossRef]
8. Xiao, C.; Zhong, H.; Guo, Z.; Tu, C.; Liu, Z.; Sun, M.; Xu, J. Cail2019-scm: A dataset of similar case matching in legal domain. *arXiv* **2019**, arXiv:1911.08962.
9. Jacob, I.J. Performance evaluation of caps-net based multitask learning architecture for text classification. *J. Artif. Intell.* **2020**, *2*, 1–10.
10. Peng, Y.; Chen, Q.; Lu, Z. An empirical study of multi-task learning on BERT for biomedical text mining. *arXiv* **2020**, arXiv:2005.02799.
11. Ruder, S.; Bingel, J.; Augenstein, I.; Søgaard, A. Latent multi-task architecture learning. In Proceedings of the AAAI Conference on Artificial Intelligence, Honolulu, HI, USA, 27 January 2019; AAAI: Honolulu, HI, USA, 2019; Volume 33, pp. 4822–4829.
12. Zhang, Y.; Yang, Q. A survey on multi-task learning. *IEEE Trans. Knowl. Data Eng.* **2021**, *2*, 1–10. [CrossRef]
13. Liu, X.; Li, W.; Fang, Y.; Kim, A.; Duh, K.; Gao, J. Stochastic answer networks for squad 2.0. *arXiv* **2018**, arXiv:1809.09194.
14. Hu, M.; Wei, F.; Peng, Y.; Huang, Z.; Yang, N.; Li, D. Read+ verify: Machine reading comprehension with unanswerable questions. In Proceedings of the AAAI Conference on Artificial Intelligence, Palo Alto, CA, USA, 2–9 February 2019; Volume 33, pp. 6529–6537.
15. Back, S.; Chinthakindi, S.C.; Kedia, A.; Lee, H.; Choo, J. NeurQuRI: Neural question requirement inspector for answerability prediction in machine reading comprehension. In Proceedings of the International Conference on Learning Representations, New Orleans, LA, USA, 6–9 May 2019.
16. Zhang, Z.; Wu, Y.; Zhou, J.; Duan, S.; Zhao, H.; Wang, R. SG-Net: Syntax-guided machine reading comprehension. In Proceedings of the AAAI Conference on Artificial Intelligence, New York, NY, USA, 7–12 February 2020; Volume 34, pp. 9636–9643.
17. Kadlec, R.; Schmid, M.; Bajgar, O.; Kleindienst, J. Text Understanding with the Attention Sum Reader Network. In Proceedings of the 54th Annual Meeting of the Association for Computational Linguistics (Volume 1: Long Papers), Berlin, Germany, 7–12 August 2016; pp. 908–918.
18. Dhingra, B.; Liu, H.; Yang, Z.; Cohen, W.W.; Salakhutdinov, R. Gated-Attention Readers for Text Comprehension. In Proceedings of the 55th Annual Meeting of the Association for Computational Linguistics (Volume 1: Long Papers), Vancouver, BC, Canada, 30 July–4 August 2017; pp. 1832–1846.
19. Park, C.; Song, H.; Lee, C. S3-NET: SRU-based sentence and self-matching networks for machine reading comprehension. *ACM Trans. Asian -Low-Resour. Lang. Inf. Process. (TALLIP)* **2020**, *19*, 1–14. [CrossRef]
20. Cui, Y.; Chen, Z.; Wei, S.; Wang, S.; Liu, T.; Hu, G. Attention-over-Attention Neural Networks for Reading Comprehension. In Proceedings of the 55th Annual Meeting of the Association for Computational Linguistics (Volume 1: Long Papers), Vancouver, BC, Canada, 30 July–4 August 2017; pp. 593–602.
21. Kim, J.H.; Jun, J.; Zhang, B.T. Bilinear attention networks. *arXiv* **2018**, arXiv:1805.07932.
22. Sarzynska-Wawer, J.; Wawer, A.; Pawlak, A.; Szymanowska, J.; Stefaniak, I.; Jarkiewicz, M.; Okruszek, L. Detecting formal thought disorder by deep contextualized word representations. *Psychiatry Res.* **2021**, *304*, 114135. [CrossRef] [PubMed]
23. Brown, T.B.; Mann, B.; Ryder, N.; Subbiah, M.; Kaplan, J.; Dhariwal, P.; Amodei, D. Language models are few-shot learners. *arXiv* **2020**, arXiv:2005.14165.
24. Devlin, J.; Chang, M.W.; Lee, K.; Toutanova, K. Bert: Pre-training of deep bidirectional transformers for language understanding. *arXiv* **2018**, arXiv:1810.04805.
25. Yang, Z.; Dai, Z.; Yang, Y.; Carbonell, J.; Salakhutdinov, R.R.; Le, Q.V. Xlnet: Generalized autoregressive pretraining for language understanding. *Adv. Neural Inf. Process. Syst.* **2019**, *32*, 5753–5763.
26. Liu, Y.; Ott, M.; Goyal, N.; Du, J.; Joshi, M.; Chen, D.; Stoyanov, V. Roberta: A robustly optimized bert pretraining approach. *arXiv* **2019**, arXiv:1907.11692.
27. Lan, Z.; Chen, M.; Goodman, S.; Gimpel, K.; Sharma, P.; Soricut, R. Albert: A lite bert for self-supervised learning of language representations. *arXiv* **2019**, arXiv:1909.11942.

28. Clark, K.; Luong, M.T.; Le, Q.V.; Manning, C.D. Electra: Pre-training text encoders as discriminators rather than generators. *arXiv* **2020**, arXiv:2003.10555.
29. Lee, D.H. Pseudo-label: The simple and efficient semi-supervised learning method for deep neural networks. In *Workshop on Challenges in Representation Learning*; ICML: Atlanta, GA, USA, 2013; Volume 3, p. 896.
30. Yarowsky, D. Unsupervised word sense disambiguation rivaling supervised methods. In Proceedings of the 33rd Annual Meeting of the Association for Computational Linguistics, Cambridge, MA, USA, 26–30 June 1995; pp. 189–196.
31. Zhu, X.; Goldberg, A.B. Introduction to semi-supervised learning. *Synth. Lect. Artif. Intell. Mach. Learn.* **2009**, *3*, 1–130. [CrossRef]
32. Zoph, B.; Ghiasi, G.; Lin, T.Y.; Cui, Y.; Liu, H.; Cubuk, E.D.; Le, Q.V. Rethinking pre-training and self-training. *arXiv* **2020**, arXiv:2006.06882.
33. Zhao, R.; Liu, T.; Xiao, J.; Lun, D.P.; Lam, K.M. Deep multi-task learning for facial expression recognition and synthesis based on selective feature sharing. In Proceedings of the 2020 25th International Conference on Pattern Recognition (ICPR), Milan, Italy, 10–15 January 2021; IEEE: Piscataway, NJ, USA, 2021; pp. 4412–4419.
34. Wang, Y.; Mukherjee, S.; Chu, H.; Tu, Y.; Wu, M.; Gao, J.; Awadallah, A.H. Adaptive self-training for few-shot neural sequence labeling. *arXiv* **2020**, arXiv:2010.03680.
35. Li, C.; Li, X.; Ouyang, J. Semi-Supervised Text Classification with Balanced Deep Representation Distributions. In Proceedings of the 59th Annual Meeting of the Association for Computational Linguistics and the 11th International Joint Conference on Natural Language Processing, Bangkok, Thailand, 1–6 August 2021; pp. 5044–5053.
36. He, J.; Gu, J.; Shen, J.; Ranzato, M.A. Revisiting self-training for neural sequence generation. *arXiv* **2019**, arXiv:1909.13788.
37. Jiao, W.; Wang, X.; Tu, Z.; Shi, S.; Lyu, M.R.; King, I. Self-Training Sampling with Monolingual Data Uncertainty for Neural Machine Translation. *arXiv* **2021**, arXiv:2106.00941.
38. Vaswani, A.; Shazeer, N.; Parmar, N.; Uszkoreit, J.; Jones, L.; Gomez, A.N.; Polosukhin, I. Attention is all you need. In *Advances in Neural Information Processing Systems*; NeurIPS Proceedings: Long Beach, CA, USA, 2017; pp. 5998–6008.
39. Wu, Y.; Schuster, M.; Chen, Z.; Le, Q.V.; Norouzi, M.; Macherey, W.; Dean, J. Google's neural machine translation system: Bridging the gap between human and machine translation. *arXiv* **2016**, arXiv:1609.08144.

## mathematics

### Article

# Evaluating Research Trends from Journal Paper Metadata, Considering the Research Publication Latency

**Christian-Daniel Curiac [1], Ovidiu Banias [2,\* and Mihai Micea [1]**

[1] Computer and Information Technology Department, Politehnica University of Timisoara, V. Parvan 2, 300223 Timisoara, Romania; christian.curiac@cs.upt.ro (C.-D.C.); mihai.micea@cs.upt.ro (M.M.)

[2] Automation and Applied Informatics Department, Politehnica University of Timisoara, V. Parvan 2, 300223 Timisoara, Romania

\* Correspondence: ovidiu.banias@aut.upt.ro

**Abstract:** Investigating the research trends within a scientific domain by analyzing semantic information extracted from scientific journals has been a topic of interest in the natural language processing (NLP) field. A research trend evaluation is generally based on the time evolution of the term occurrence or the term topic, but it neglects an important aspect—research publication latency. The average time lag between the research and its publication may vary from one month to more than one year, and it is a characteristic that may have significant impact when assessing research trends, mainly for rapidly evolving scientific areas. To cope with this problem, the present paper is the first work that explicitly considers research publication latency as a parameter in the trend evaluation process. Consequently, we provide a new trend detection methodology that mixes auto-ARIMA prediction with Mann–Kendall trend evaluations. The experimental results in an electronic design automation case study prove the viability of our approach.

**Keywords:** Mann–Kendall test; Sen's slope; auto-ARIMA method; paper metadata; research trend

---

**Citation:** Curiac, C.-D.; Banias, O.; Micea, M. Evaluating Research Trends from Journal Paper Metadata, Considering the Research Publication Latency. *Mathematics* **2022**, *10*, 233. https://doi.org/10.3390/math10020233

Academic Editors: Florentina Hristea and Cornelia Caragea

Received: 12 November 2021
Accepted: 9 January 2022
Published: 13 January 2022

**Publisher's Note:** MDPI stays neutral with regard to jurisdictional claims in published maps and institutional affiliations.

## 1. Introduction

For many scientific, industrial, and economic activities, collecting observations over time is a common procedure. Such data are generally formalized as discrete time-series, defined as sequences of observations $X_t$ taken at successive points in time $t$. The analysis of time-series employs carefully selected mathematical models for a two-fold purpose: (i) to understand the underlying mechanism that produces the observed data sequence and (ii) to predict future values of a given series based on its past values. This analysis often focuses on identifying past (or forecasting future) trends within the series of observations that may efficiently and synthetically characterize the time evolution of the variable under investigation.

In the natural language processing (NLP) field, trend analysis plays an important role, a relevant example in this respect being the evaluation of research trends using key term occurrences in scientific literature [1]. Due to their reduced sensitivities to outliers [2], the lack of assumptions concerning the data sample distribution [3] or homoscedasticity [4], non-parametric trend tests tend to be favored by researchers over parametric methods. In particular, the Mann–Kendall (MK) test statistic being a robust trend indicator when dealing with censored data, arbitrary non-Gaussian data distributions or time series with missing observations [5] have become almost standard methods for NLP applications [1,6–12].

To evaluate topic trends and identify "hot" research topics in two academic fields (i.e., information sciences and accounting) using paper titles and abstracts, Marrone [1] employed the Mann–Kendall test with Sen's slope analysis. In medicine-related NLP applications, Marchini et al. [6] used the same method to analyze the urologic research trends described by 12 key terms, Chakravorti et al. [13] employed the MK trend evaluation method to detect and characterize mental health trends in online discussions, while Modave et al. [14] evaluated perception and attitude trends in breast cancer twitter messages.

Moreover, Sharma et al. [7] used the Mann–Kendall test to understand machine learning research topic trends using metadata from journal papers. In [8], Zou analyzed the journal titles and abstracts to explore the temporal popularity of 50 drug safety research trends over time using the MK test, while Neresini et al. [15] used the Hamed and Rao [2] MK variant to extract trends from correlated time series. All of these papers assess actual research trends by applying trend evaluation methods directly to key term occurrences in metadata from published papers without explicitly considering the publication latency.

In our perspective, in evaluating the research trends using information extracted from published journal articles, an important issue has to be considered: there is a time lag that may range up to one year or even more from the end of the research work until the journal paper is published. This delay obviously has an important impact mainly for fast developing domains [16,17], where the trends abruptly change, driven by rapid theory or technology advancements. To cover the identified gap, we propose a novel trend, computing methodology, backed on a new method: n-steps-ahead Mann–Kendall test (nsaMK). This method is based on auto-ARIMA forecasting, which is coupled with the Yue-Wang variant of the Mann–Kendall (MK) test. To the best of our knowledge, our method is the first that incorporates the effects of research publication latency on research trends evaluations.

The main contributions of this paper are summarized below:

- A novel methodology that includes the new nsaMK method to identify term trends from metadata from journal paper, when considering the inherent time lag between the research completion and paper publication date;
- A definition of the research publication latency and an empirical formula to derive the number of prediction steps considered by the proposed method to countermeasure the effect of the journal review and publication process upon the research trend evaluation;
- An evaluation of the new nsaMK method in an electronic design automation case study by comparing it with the classical MK trend test. The superiority of nsaMK is confirmed by a 45% reduction of the mean square error of Sen's slope evaluations and by an increase of correct term trend indications with 66%.

The rest of the paper is organized as follows. Section 2 describes the two algorithms that represent the pillars on which our strategy is built: auto-ARIMA prediction and the Mann–Kendall trend test with Sen's slope estimator. Section 3 presents the proposed methodology and the new method for term trend evaluation. Section 4 presents an illustrative example of using the nsaMK trend test by comparing it with classical MK, while Section 5 concludes the paper.

## 2. Preliminaries

This section briefly presents the two algorithms (i.e., auto-ARIMA, MK with Sen's slope) that constitute the foundation upon which the proposed nsaMK method is built.

### 2.1. Time-Series ARIMA Model Prediction. Auto-ARIMA Method

To accomplish the primary goal of time series prediction, to estimate future values based on past and current data samples, diverse mathematical models can be used. In the case of a non-seasonal time-series, a widely used class of models is the AutoRegressive Integrated Moving Average (ARIMA) proposed by Box and Jenkins back in 1970, to extend the statistical and predictive performances of AutoRegressive Moving Average (ARMA) models for a non-stationary time-series [18,19].

The ARMA family of models [20], denoted $ARMA(p, q)$, describes stationary stochastic processes using two polynomials, one for the autoregressive part $AR(p)$ and one for the moving-average part $MA(q)$:

$$X_t = \sum_{i=1}^{p} \varphi_i X_{t-1} + \sum_{j=1}^{q} \theta_i \varepsilon_{t-1} + \varepsilon_t + c, \tag{1}$$

where $p$ is the autoregressive order, $q$ is the moving average order, $\varphi_i$ and $\theta_j$ are the model's coefficients, $c$ is a constant, and $\varepsilon_t$ is a white noise random variable.

The $ARMA(p,q)$ model from (1) can be rewritten in a compact form using the backward shift operator $B$ ($BX_t = X_{t-1}$) as:

$$\varphi(B)X_t = \theta(B)\varepsilon_t + c, \tag{2}$$

where the two polynomials in $B$ are:

$$\varphi(B) = 1 - \varphi_1 B - \varphi_2 B^2 - \cdots - \varphi_p B^p \tag{3}$$

and

$$\theta(B) = 1 + \theta_1 B + \theta_2 B^2 + \cdots + \theta_q B^q. \tag{4}$$

In practice, the use of ARMA models is restrained to stationary time-series (i.e., time-series for which the statistical properties do not change over time) [19]. To address this issue, Box and Jenkins [18] applied a differencing procedure for transforming non-stationary time-series into stationary ones.

The first difference of a given time-series $X_t$ is a new time-series $Y_t$ where each observation is replaced by the change from the last encountered value:

$$Y_t = X_t - X_{t-1} = (1-B)X_t. \tag{5}$$

Generalizing, the $d$th differences may be formalized as:

$$Y_t = (1-B)^d X_t. \tag{6}$$

By applying the generalized differencing process (6) to the ARMA model described by (2), a general $ARIMA(p,d,q)$ model is obtained in the form [19]:

$$\varphi(B)(1-B)^d X_t = \theta(B)\varepsilon_t + c, \tag{7}$$

where $d$ is the differencing order needed to make the original time-series stationary.

For a specified triplet $(p,d,q)$, the coefficients $\varphi_i$ and $\theta_j$ are generally obtained using the maximum likelihood parameter estimation method [21], while the most suitable values for the orders $p$, $d$, and $q$ can be derived using the auto-ARIMA method [22]. The auto-ARIMA method varies the $p$, $d$, and $q$ parameters in given intervals and evaluates a chosen goodness-of-fit indicator to select the best fitting $ARIMA(p,d,q)$ model. In our implementation, we employed Akaike information criterion ($AIC$) that can be computed by:

$$AIC = -2log(L) + 2k, \tag{8}$$

where $L$ is the maximum value of the likelihood function for the model, and $k$ is the number of estimated parameters of the model, in our case $k = p + q + 2$ if $c \neq 0$ and $k = p + q + 1$ if $c = 0$ [22]. When $AIC$ has a minimal value, the best trade-off between the model's goodness of fit and its simplicity is achieved.

### 2.2. Mann–Kendall Trend Test with Sen's Slope Estimator

Mann–Kendall (MK) [23] is a non-parametric test, which is widely used to detect monotonic trends in a time-series. Its robustness against censored and non-Gaussian distributed data o time series with missing or noisy observations [5] that are frequently encountered in a term occurrence time series makes MK an almost standard trend test method in NLP [1,6–12]. A brief description of the MK method is provided below.

Let us consider a time-series chunk of length $n$, denoted by $x_i$ with $i = 1, 2, \ldots, n$. The MK trend test analyzes changes in signs for the differences between successive points by computing the MK statistic $S$:

$$S = \sum_{k=1}^{n-1} \sum_{j=k+1}^{n} sgn(x_j - x_k),$$ (9)

where $sgn(x)$ is the signum function

$$sgn(x_j - x_k) = \begin{cases} 1 & if(x_j - x_k) > 0 \\ 0 & if(x_j - x_k) = 0 \\ -1 & if(x_j - x_k) < 0 \end{cases}$$ (10)

For a sufficiently large $n$ (e.g., $n \leq 10$), $S$ has approximately a normal distribution of zero mean and variance $V(S)$ given by:

$$V(S) = \frac{1}{18}\left[n(n-1)(2n+5) - \sum_{p=1}^{m} r_p(r_p - 1)(2r_p + 5)\right],$$ (11)

where $m$ represents the number of tied groups (i.e., successive observations having the same value) and $r_p$ is the rank of the $p$th tied group.

The standardized form of the MK z-statistic ($Z_{MK}$), having a zero mean and unit variance, is given by:

$$Z_{MK} = \begin{cases} \frac{S-1}{\sqrt{V(S)}} & for\ S > 0 \\ 0 & for\ S = 0, \\ \frac{S+1}{\sqrt{V(S)}} & for\ S < 0 \end{cases}$$ (12)

a positive value indicates an upward trend, while a negative one describes a downward trend.

The original version of MK test provides poor results in the case of correlated time-series. In order to solve this issue, Yue and Wang [24], proposed the replacement of the variance $V(S)$ in Equation (12) with a value that considers the effective sample size $n^*$:

$$V^*(S) = \frac{n}{n^*}V(S) = \left[1 + 2\sum_{s=1}^{n-1}(1 - \frac{s}{n})\rho_s\right]V(S),$$ (13)

where $\rho_s$ represents the lag-s serial correlation coefficient for the $x_i$ time-series and can be computed using the following equation:

$$\rho_s = \frac{\frac{1}{n-s}\sum_{v=1}^{n-s}[x_v - E(x_i)][x_{v+s} - E(x_i)]}{\frac{1}{n}\sum_{v=1}^{n}[x_v - E(x_i)]^2}.$$ (14)

In practice, to evaluate if the z-statistic computed by Equation (12) is reliable, the two-sided $p$-value is calculated using the exact algorithm given in [25]. This $p$-value expresses the plausibility of the null hypothesis $H_0$ (i.e., no trend in the time series) to be true [26]. The lesser the $p$-value, the higher significance level of the z-statistic. Thus, if the two-sided $p$-value of the MK test is below a given threshold (e.g., $p$-value < 0.01), then a statistically significant trend is present in the data series.

Since the z-statistic coupled with the $p$-value of the MK test can reveal a trend in the data series, the magnitude of the trend is generally evaluated using Sen's slope $\beta$, which is computed as the average of the slopes corresponding to all lines defined by pairs of time series observations [27]:

$$\beta = median\left(\frac{x_j - x_i}{j - i}\right), \ j > i$$ (15)

where $\beta < 0$ indicates a downward trend and $\beta > 0$ an upward time series trend.

## 3. Proposed Research Term Trend Evaluation

This section provides our proposed methodology to identify research term trends using journal paper metadata and its subsequent method (i.e., nsaMK).

### 3.1. Proposed Methodology

A paper may be first published in two different forms: (i) as an electronic paper version published in advance of its print edition (i.e., "online first" or "article in press"); or, (ii) directly as the final version of the paper included in journal or conference volumes. In both cases, the time lag between research completion and corresponding paper publication becomes an important issue when forecasting research trends based on already published papers. Obviously, in the second case, the time to access the enclosed research may be considerably increased to one year or even more, making the need for an n-steps-ahead research trend forecasting even more evident.

**Definition 1.** *publication latency* $(t_{PL})$ *is the average time lag from the date a manuscript is submitted to the date when the resulting paper is first published. The publication latency is specific to the journal where the paper is published.*

The publication latency is practically the mean time to review, revise, and first publish scientific papers in a specified publication. It can be obtained by averaging the time needed for individual papers to be published. Since this type of information is generally not included in paper metadata records, it needs to be manually extracted from the final versions of the papers.

**Definition 2.** *research publication latency* $(t_{RPL})$ *is the average time lag from the moment a research is completed to the date when the resulting paper is first published.*

In order to compute the research publication latency for a given research $t_{RPL}$, beside the publication latency $t_{PL}$ induced by the journal, we have to consider the mean time for paper writing $t_{PW}$:

$$t_{RPL} = t_{PL} + t_{PW} \qquad \text{[years]}, \qquad (16)$$

The mean time for paper writing $t_{PW}$ is a positive value that can be taken in the interval between one and eight weeks depending on the type of publication (e.g., for a paper published as a short communication $t_{PW}$ has lower values, while for long papers, the values may be considerably higher). For our evaluations, we considered $t_{PW} = 0.1$ years.

Our methodology to evaluate research term trends based on information contained in journal paper metadata consists of three phases:

- Phase I: identify the number of steps N to be predicted. This number depends on the research publication latency and on the moment in time for which the research trends are computed and can be obtained using the following formula:

$$N = \lfloor t_{RPL} + \tau \rceil \qquad \text{[years]}, \qquad (17)$$

where $\lfloor . \rceil$ is the rounding (nearest integer) function, and $\tau$ is the time deviation from the moment in time the last value in the annual time series was recorded to the date for which the research trends are computed. Since the published papers within a year are grouped in journal issues that are generally uniformly distributed during that year, we may consider that the recording day for each year is the middle of that year. Thus, if we want to calculate the research trends on 1 January, 2021, when having the last time series observation recorded for 2020, $\tau = 0.5$ years, while if we calculate the research trends for 2 July, 2021, $\tau = 1$ year.

- Phase II: form the annual time series for a specified key term by computing the number of its occurrences in paper metadata (i.e., title, keywords and abstract) during each year. For this, the following procedure can be used: each paper's metadata are automatically or manually collected; the titles, keywords, and abstracts are concatenated into a text document, which is fed into an entity-linking procedure (e.g., TagMe [28], AIDA [29], Wikipedia Miner [30]), to obtain the list of terms that characterizes the paper; and, count the number of papers per each year where the key term occurs.
- Phase III: apply the proposed n-steps-ahead Mann–Kendall procedure for the annual time series containing the occurrences of the specified key term.

The proposed nsaMK method is described in the next paragraph.

### 3.2. N-Steps-Ahead Mann–Kendall Method

In order to evaluate the term trend from the term occurrence time series, we propose a two-step approach: (i) to the original time-series $x_i$ with $i = 1, 2, \ldots, k$, we add $N$ predicted values $x_{k+1}, x_{k+2}, \ldots, x_{k+N}$ using the auto-ARIMA method presented in Section 2.1; and then, (ii) apply the Yue and Wang [24] variant of MK test with the Sen's slope estimation described in Section 2.2, to the concatenated time-series $x_i$ with $i = 1, 2, \ldots, k + N$. We term the resulting trend evaluation method as n-steps-ahead Mann–Kendall (nsaMK).

It is noteworthy to mention that, at the end of first step, all negative predictions provided by the auto-ARIMA method need to be set to zero since the term occurrences cannot take negative values.

We use the auto-ARIMA method, considering its efficiency in forecasting large categories of time-series [18,19,22]. Since this method adds upon the existing serial correlation of time-series observations, we need to employ an MK test variant that can cope with serial correlation, namely the variant proposed by Yue and Wang [24]. Using this MK variant, the statistically significant trends are identified based on z-statistic and two-sided $p$-value, while the trend magnitudes are evaluated using Sen's slope.

## 4. Experimental Results

We tested our research trend evaluation methodology against the standard Mann–Kendall test with Sen's slope method (Yue and Wang variant), using journal paper metadata from 2010 to 2019, with the observations from 2020 as ground truth. We evaluated the trends of the main key terms that characterized the highly dynamic research domain of electronic design automation (EDA) using paper metadata extracted from the IEEE Transactions on Computer-Aided Design of Integrated Circuits and Systems (TCAD). For this particular journal, the publication latency, evaluated for the papers published in the first quarter of 2020, is $t_{PL} = 0.55$ years. By selecting a time deviation $\tau = 0.5$ years that corresponds to research trend evaluation for 1 January 2021, the number of steps $N$ to be predicted is equal to one, according to Equation (17).

### 4.1. Data Acquisition and Preprocessing

For each TCAD paper published in the interval 2010–2020, we extracted the paper metadata that included titles, abstracts, keywords, authors, digital object identifiers, and publication year fields, using the IEEEXplore API.

Attempting to summarize, as accurately as possible, the content of each journal paper, we built a compound abstract by concatenating the title, the keywords, and the abstract of the given paper. We chose to process each of these compound abstracts using the TagMe [28] entity linking procedure, with the link-probability parameter set to 0.1, in order to build a processed abstract, containing a list of encountered key terms.

The main terms that characterize the EDA domain have been identified by evaluating the normalized document frequency $(ndf)$ [31] for all terms found in the processed abstracts belonging to journal papers published in 2020, by computing:

$$ndf(\mathcal{T}, C) = \frac{df(\mathcal{T}, C)}{\mathcal{N}} \tag{18}$$

where $df(\mathcal{T}, C)$ is the document frequency of term $\mathcal{T}$ in the collection of documents $C$, while $\mathcal{N}$ is the total number of documents from the corpus $C$. After sorting the terms in descending order of their $ndf$ scores, we retain the first 300 EDA terms, considering that this number arguably reflects the current status of a domain. Table 1 presents the top 24 terms in EDA based on their normalized document frequency score for 2020.

**Table 1.** Top 24 EDA terms in 2020 and their normalized document frequency score.

| Rank | Term | *ndf* | Rank | Term | *ndf* |
|------|------|-------|------|------|-------|
| 1. | integrated circuit | 0.211 | 13. | neural network | 0.064 |
| 2. | optimization | 0.163 | 14. | low power | 0.059 |
| 3. | computer architecture | 0.136 | 15. | hybrid | 0.055 |
| 4. | algorithm | 0.130 | 16. | system on chip | 0.055 |
| 5. | logic gates | 0.125 | 17. | mathematical model | 0.053 |
| 6. | computational modeling | 0.121 | 18. | power | 0.044 |
| 7. | latency | 0.094 | 19. | convolutional neural network | 0.044 |
| 8. | fpga | 0.090 | 20. | logic | 0.044 |
| 9. | task analysis | 0.084 | 21. | memory management | 0.044 |
| 10. | energy efficiency | 0.073 | 22. | real time systems | 0.042 |
| 11. | machine learning | 0.071 | 23. | cmos | 0.042 |
| 12. | ram | 0.067 | 24. | nonvolatile memory | 0.041 |

### 4.2. nsaMK Method Evaluation

In order to compare our nsaMK method with the traditional MK method, we compute $z$-score, $p$-value, and Sen's slope for each of the three hundred EDA terms, considering the corresponding $ndf$ values for ten consecutive years, in three cases:

- Using the Yue and Wang variant of MK test for journal papers published between 2011 and 2020 (MK2020). The results of the MK2020 are considered as ground-truth.
- Using our nsaMK method when considering journal papers published between 2010 and 2019 and the predicted values for 2020 (nsaMK2020).
- Using the Yue and Wang variant of MK test for journal papers published between 2010 and 2019 (MK2019).

By this, the results provided by the new method (nsaMK2020) are compared with the ones offered by MK2019, MK2020 being considered as ground truth.

The parameters for the auto-ARIMA procedure were chosen as follows: the autoregressive order $p \in \{1, 2, 3\}$, the moving average order $q \in \{0, 1, 2\}$, and the differencing order $d \in \{0, 1, 2\}$, while the best ARIMA predictor was automatically selected using the Akaike information criterion described by Equation (8). Since the autoregressive order $p$ cannot be equal to zero, the use of the Yue and Wang variant of the MK test is reasonable.

The obtained results for the top 24 terms in EDA are presented in Table 2, where, in the last column, we use check marks to label all key terms for which our method achieves superior performance (i.e., the Sen's slopes offered by nsaMK2020 are closer to the ground truth than the ones provided by MK2019). We may notice that within the top 24 EDA terms in 75% of the cases our method is superior, while on the entire 300 term set this percentage is 66%. Moreover, for the entire set of 300 terms, the mean square error of the Sen's slopes for our method is 45% better than the one provided by the classic MK method ($5.045 \times 10^{-7}$ vs. $9.041 \times 10^{-6}$), while for the 24 best ranked EDA terms presented in Table 2, the mean square error is 48% less for our method ($2.559 \times 10^{-6}$ vs. $5.282 \times 10^{-6}$). When considering only the relevant trends according to $p$-values (i.e., $p$-value $< 0.01$), the results are almost similar: in the 300 terms set, there are 130 terms with identified trends, and for 87 of them (66.9%), our method yields better performance.

In Figures 1 and 2, we present two representative examples, namely for the 'algorithm' and 'logic gates' key terms. The light blue observations (i.e., for 2010–2019) are used to compute the slope marked with black solid line by MK2019, the last nine light blue observations, together with the pink-marked auto-ARIMA prediction are used by nsaMK2020 to evaluate the slope presented with red dotted line, and the last nine light blue observations together with the dark blue observation for 2020 are used by MK2020 to reveal the real trend depicted with a blue dashed line (ground truth).

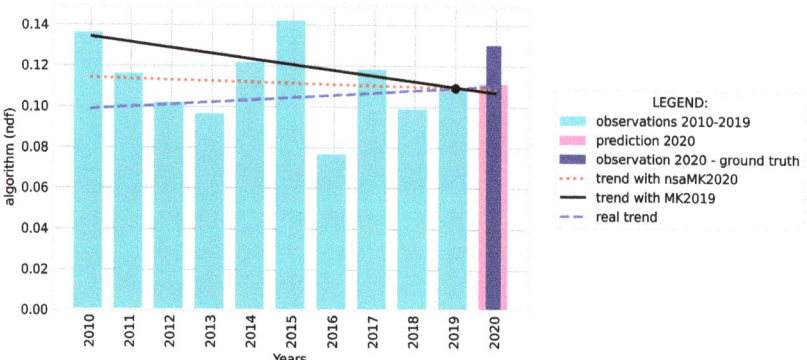

**Figure 1.** Trend evaluation comparison for the key term 'algorithm'.

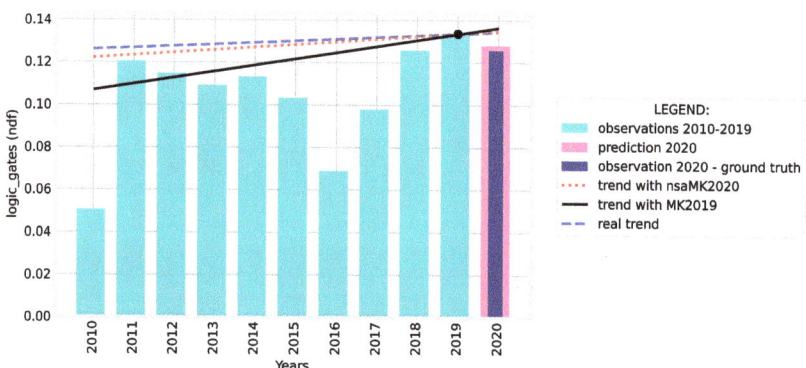

**Figure 2.** Trend evaluation comparison for the key term 'logic gate'.

**Table 2.** Comparison results of nsaMK and MK methods for the top 24 terms in EDA.

| | Term | nsaMK2020 | | | MK2019 | | | MK2020—Ground Truth | | | |
|---|---|---|---|---|---|---|---|---|---|---|---|
| | | z | p-Value | Slope | z | p-Value | Slope | z | p-Value | Slope | |
| 1 | integrated circuit | $-5.057$ | $4.2 \times 10^{-7}$ | $-0.008$ | $-2.715$ | $0.00662$ | $-0.005$ | $-4.809$ | $1.5 \times 10^{-6}$ | $-0.008$ | ✓ |
| 2 | optimization | $8.494$ | $0$ | $0.005$ | $5.964$ | $2.4 \times 10^{-9}$ | $0.005$ | $10.738$ | $0$ | $0.006$ | ✓ |
| 3 | computer architecture | $4.856$ | $1.2 \times 10^{-6}$ | $0.009$ | $4.059$ | $4.9 \times 10^{-5}$ | $0.009$ | $6.828$ | $8.6 \times 10^{-12}$ | $0.012$ | ✓ |
| 4 | algorithm | $0$ | $1$ | $-0.000$ | $-2.047$ | $0.04060$ | $-0.002$ | $1.061$ | $0.28868$ | $0.001$ | ✓ |
| 5 | logic gates | $0.597$ | $0.54995$ | $0.001$ | $1.257$ | $0.20871$ | $0.002$ | $0.300$ | $0.76357$ | $0.000$ | ✓ |
| 6 | computational modeling | $0.590$ | $0.55509$ | $-0.000$ | $-0.522$ | $0.60141$ | $-0.000$ | $1.714$ | $0.08649$ | $0.001$ | ✓ |
| 7 | latency | $1.459$ | $0.14438$ | $0.001$ | $2.027$ | $0.04261$ | $0.001$ | $4.459$ | $8.2 \times 10^{-6}$ | $0.004$ | ✓ |
| 8 | fpga | $3.910$ | $9.2 \times 10^{-5}$ | $0.006$ | $1.842$ | $0.06533$ | $0.003$ | $3.571$ | $0.00035$ | $0.008$ | ✓ |
| 9 | task analysis | $1.862$ | $0.06250$ | $0$ | $1.816$ | $0.06932$ | $0$ | $2.031$ | $0.04216$ | $0.001$ | |
| 10 | energy efficiency | $5.235$ | $1.6 \times 10^{-7}$ | $0.007$ | $4.005$ | $6.1 \times 10^{-5}$ | $0.004$ | $4.894$ | $9.8 \times 10^{-7}$ | $0.007$ | ✓ |
| 11 | machine learning | $5.856$ | $4.7 \times 10^{-9}$ | $0.003$ | $4.512$ | $6.3 \times 10^{-6}$ | $0.003$ | $5.025$ | $5.0 \times 10^{-7}$ | $0.005$ | ✓ |
| 12 | ram | $4.346$ | $1.3 \times 10^{-5}$ | $0.002$ | $4.232$ | $2.3 \times 10^{-5}$ | $0.003$ | $5.118$ | $3.0 \times 10^{-7}$ | $0.004$ | |
| 13 | neural network | $1.938$ | $0.05250$ | $0.002$ | $0.907$ | $0.36428$ | $0$ | $2.892$ | $0.00382$ | $0.004$ | ✓ |
| 14 | low power | $0$ | $1$ | $0.000$ | $1.712$ | $0.08684$ | $0.001$ | $1.910$ | $0.05607$ | $0.001$ | |
| 15 | hybrid | $3.298$ | $0.00097$ | $0.003$ | $2.580$ | $0.00987$ | $0.002$ | $4.213$ | $2.5 \times 10^{-5}$ | $0.004$ | ✓ |
| 16 | system on chip | $3.637$ | $0.00027$ | $0.003$ | $6.111$ | $9.8 \times 10^{-10}$ | $0.004$ | $3.694$ | $0.00022$ | $0.003$ | ✓ |
| 17 | mathematical model | $-5.016$ | $5.2 \times 10^{-7}$ | $-0.005$ | $-0.924$ | $0.35519$ | $-0.004$ | $-3.686$ | $0.00022$ | $-0.004$ | |
| 18 | power | $-4.734$ | $2.1 \times 10^{-6}$ | $-0.002$ | $-3.678$ | $0.00023$ | $-0.001$ | $-2.532$ | $0.01133$ | $-0.001$ | |
| 19 | convolutional neural network | $3.842$ | $0.00012$ | $0.001$ | $3.275$ | $0.00105$ | $0.001$ | $3.361$ | $0.00077$ | $0.002$ | ✓ |
| 20 | logic | $0.497$ | $0.61901$ | $0.000$ | $-0.685$ | $0.49291$ | $-0.001$ | $2.419$ | $0.01553$ | $0.001$ | ✓ |
| 21 | memory management | $5.262$ | $1.4 \times 10^{-7}$ | $0.003$ | $5.672$ | $1.4 \times 10^{-8}$ | $0.003$ | $9.513$ | $0$ | $0.004$ | ✓ |
| 22 | real time systems | $0$ | $1$ | $0$ | $2.307$ | $0.02102$ | $0.002$ | $1.859$ | $0.06289$ | $0.003$ | |
| 23 | cmos | $7.518$ | $5.5 \times 10^{-14}$ | $0.003$ | $7.646$ | $2.0 \times 10^{-14}$ | $0.004$ | $6.133$ | $8.6 \times 10^{-10}$ | $0.002$ | ✓ |
| 24 | nonvolatile memory | $2.058$ | $0.03958$ | $0.001$ | $2.701$ | $0.00690$ | $0.002$ | $5.340$ | $9.2 \times 10^{-8}$ | $0.003$ | |

For Figure 1, the best auto-ARIMA prediction for 2020 was obtained when $p = 1$, $d = 0$, and $q = 1$, with an AIC score of $-38.633$. We may observe that the trend changes from "decreasing" when considering 2010–2019 to "increasing" (ground-truth) and our method nsaMK offers a more appropriate result than MK2019. In the case depicted in Figure 2 the auto-ARIMA obtained the best results when $p = 1$, $d = 0$, and $q = 0$, where the AIC score was $-35.658$. We may observe that the trend provided with our nsaMK method offers a more suitable result than MK2019.

All methods and experiments were implemented in python 3.8 based on the Mann–Kendall trend test function *yue_wang_modification_test()* from pyMannKendall 1.4.2 package [32], ARIMA prediction function derived from *tsa.statespace.SARIMAX()* included in statsmodels 0.13.0 package [33], and *CountVectorizer()* from scikit-learn 1.0.1 library.

It is worth mentioning that the efficiency of using the nsaMK method strongly depends on the prediction accuracy provided by ARIMA models. In future work, we intend to analyze how the trend evaluation performances change when replacing the ARIMA method in our methodology with exponential smoothing or neural network forecasting. Other limitations of our method are induced by the use of the Mann–Kendall trend test, which has poor results when the time series includes periodicities and tends to provide inconclusive results for short datasets.

## 5. Conclusions

This paper introduces research publication latency as a new parameter that needs to be considered when evaluating research trends from journal paper metadata, mainly within rapidly evolving scientific fields. The proposed method comprises two steps: (i) a prediction step performed using the auto-ARIMA method to estimate the most recent research evolution that is not yet available in publications; and, (ii) a trend evaluation step using a suitable variant of the Mann–Kendall test with Sen's slope evaluation. Our simulations, using paper metadata collected from IEEE Transactions on Computer-Aided Design of Integrated Circuits and System, provide convincing results.

**Author Contributions:** Conceptualization, C.-D.C.; methodology, C.-D.C., O.B. and M.M.; software, C.-D.C., O.B. and M.M.; validation, C.-D.C., O.B. and M.M.; formal analysis, C.-D.C., O.B. and M.M.; investigation, C.-D.C., O.B. and M.M.; resources, O.B. and M.M.; data curation, C.-D.C., O.B. and M.M.; writing—original draft preparation, C.-D.C. and O.B.; writing—review and editing, C.-D.C., O.B. and M.M.; supervision, O.B. and M.M. All authors have read and agreed to the published version of the manuscript.

**Funding:** This research received no external funding.

**Institutional Review Board Statement:** Not applicable.

**Informed Consent Statement:** Not applicable.

**Data Availability Statement:** Not applicable.

**Conflicts of Interest:** The authors declare no conflict of interest.

## References

1. Marrone, M. Application of entity linking to identify research fronts and trends. *Scientometrics* **2020**, *122*, 357–379. [CrossRef]
2. Hamed, K.H. Trend detection in hydrologic data: The Mann–Kendall trend test under the scaling hypothesis. *J. Hydrol.* **2008**, *349*, 350–363. [CrossRef]
3. Önöz, B.; Bayazit, M. The power of statistical tests for trend detection. *Turk. J. Eng. Environ. Sci.* **2003**, *27*, 247–251.
4. Wang, F.; Shao, W.; Yu, H.; Kan, G.; He, X.; Zhang, D.; Ren, M.; Wang, G. Re-evaluation of the power of the mann-kendall test for detecting monotonic trends in hydrometeorological time series. *Front. Earth Sci.* **2020**, *8*, 14. [CrossRef]
5. Hirsch, R.M.; Slack, J.R. A nonparametric trend test for seasonal data with serial dependence. *Water Resour. Res.* **1984**, *20*, 727–732. [CrossRef]
6. Marchini, G.S.; Faria, K.V.; Neto, F.L.; Torricelli, F.C.M.; Danilovic, A.; Vicentini, F.C.; Batagello, C.A.; Srougi, M.; Nahas, W.C.; Mazzucchi, E. Understanding urologic scientific publication patterns and general public interests on stone disease: Lessons learned from big data platforms. *World J. Urol.* **2021**, *39*, 2767–2773. [CrossRef]

7. Sharma, D.; Kumar, B.; Chand, S. A trend analysis of machine learning research with topic models and mann-kendall test. *Int. J. Intell. Syst. Appl.* **2019**, *11*, 70–82. [CrossRef]

8. Zou, C. Analyzing research trends on drug safety using topic modeling. *Expert Opin. Drug Saf.* **2018**, *17*, 629–636. [CrossRef]

9. Merz, A.A.; Gutiérrez-Sacristán, A.; Bartz, D.; Williams, N.E.; Ojo, A.; Schaefer, K.M.; Huang, M.; Li, C.Y.; Sandoval, R.S.; Ye, S.; et al. Population attitudes toward contraceptive methods over time on a social media platform. *Am. J. Obstet. Gynecol.* **2021**, *224*, 597.e1–597.e4. [CrossRef] [PubMed]

10. Chen, X.; Xie, H. A structural topic modeling-based bibliometric study of sentiment analysis literature. *Cogn. Comput.* **2020**, *12*, 1097–1129. [CrossRef]

11. Chen, X.; Xie, H.; Cheng, G.; Li, Z. A Decade of Sentic Computing: Topic Modeling and Bibliometric Analysis. *Cogn. Comput.* **2021**, 1–24. [CrossRef]

12. Zhang, T.; Huang, X. Viral marketing: Influencer marketing pivots in tourism–a case study of meme influencer instigated travel interest surge. *Curr. Issues Tour.* **2021**, 1–8. [CrossRef]

13. Chakravorti, D.; Law, K.; Gemmell, J.; Raicu, D. Detecting and characterizing trends in online mental health discussions. In Proceedings of the 2018 IEEE International Conference on Data Mining Workshops (ICDMW), Singapore, 17–20 November 2018; pp. 697–706.

14. Modave, F.; Zhao, Y.; Krieger, J.; He, Z.; Guo, Y.; Huo, J.; Prosperi, M.; Bian, J. Understanding perceptions and attitudes in breast cancer discussions on twitter. *Stud. Health Technol. Inform.* **2019**, *264*, 1293. [PubMed]

15. Neresini, F.; Crabu, S.; Di Buccio, E. Tracking biomedicalization in the media: Public discourses on health and medicine in the UK and Italy, 1984–2017. *Soc. Sci. Med.* **2019**, *243*, 112621. [CrossRef]

16. King, A.L.O.; Mirza, F.N.; Mirza, H.N.; Yumeen, N.; Lee, V.; Yumeen, S. Factors associated with the American Academy of Dermatology abstract publication: A multivariate analysis. *J. Am. Acad. Dermatol.* **2021**. [CrossRef] [PubMed]

17. Andrew, R.M. Towards near real-time, monthly fossil $CO_2$ emissions estimates for the European Union with current-year projections. *Atmos. Pollut. Res.* **2021**, *12*, 101229. [CrossRef]

18. Box, G.; Jenkins, G.; Reinsel, G. *Time-Series Analysis: Forecasting and Control*; Holden-Day Inc.: San Francisco, CA, USA, 1970; pp. 575–577.

19. Chatfield, C. *Time-Series Forecasting*; CRC Press: Boca Raton, FL, USA, 2000.

20. Whittle, P. *Hypothesis Testing in Time-Series Analysis*; Almquist and Wiksell: Uppsalla, Sweden, 1951.

21. Cryer, J.; Chan, K. *Time-Series Analysis with Applications in R*; Springer Science & Business Media: New York, NY, USA, 2008.

22. Hyndman, R.; Athanasopoulos, G. *Forecasting: Principles and Practice*; OTexts: Melbourne, Australia, 2018.

23. Şen, Z. *Innovative Trend Methodologies in Science and Engineering*; Springer: New York, NY, USA, 2017.

24. Yue, S.; Wang, C. The Mann–Kendall test modified by effective sample size to detect trend in serially correlated hydrological series. *Springer Water Resour. Manag.* **2004**, *18*, 201–218.:WARM.0000043140.61082.60. [CrossRef]

25. Best, D.; Gipps, P. Algorithm AS 71: The upper tail probabilities of Kendall's Tau. *J. R. Stat. Society. Ser. C (Appl. Stat.)* **1974**, *23*, 98–100. [CrossRef]

26. Helsel, D.; Hirsch, R.; Ryberg, K.; Archfield, S.; Gilroy, E. *Statistical Methods in Water Resources*; Technical Report; US Geological Survey Techniques and Methods, Book 4, Chapter A3; Elsevier: Amsterdam, The Netherlands, 2020; 458p.

27. Sen, P.K. Estimates of the regression coefficient based on Kendall's tau. *J. Am. Stat. Assoc.* **1968**, *63*, 1379–1389. [CrossRef]

28. Ferragina, P.; Scaiella, U. TagMe: On-the-fly annotation of short text fragments (by Wikipedia entities). In *International Conference on Information and Knowledge Management*; ACM: Toronto, ON, Canada, 2010; pp. 1625–1628.

29. Yosef, M.A.; Hoffart, J.; Bordino, I.; Spaniol, M.; Weikum, G. Aida: An online tool for accurate disambiguation of named entities in text and tables. *Proc. VLDB Endow.* **2011**, *4*, 1450–1453. [CrossRef]

30. Milne, D.; Witten, I.H. Learning to link with wikipedia. In Proceedings of the 17th ACM conference on Information and knowledge management, Napa Valley, CA, USA, 26–30 October 2008; pp. 509–518.

31. Happel, H.J.; Stojanovic, L. Analyzing organizational information gaps. In Proceedings of the 8th Int. Conference on Knowledge Management, Graz, Austria, 3–5 September 2008; pp. 28–36.

32. Hussain, M.; Mahmud, I. PyMannKendall: A python package for non parametric Mann–Kendall family of trend tests. *J. Open Source Softw.* **2019**, *4*, 1556. [CrossRef]

33. Seabold, S.; Perktold, J. Statsmodels: Econometric and statistical modeling with python. In Proceedings of the 9th Python in Science Conference, Austin, TX, USA, 28 June–3 July 2010; pp. 92–96.

*Article*

# Identifying the Structure of CSCL Conversations Using String Kernels

Mihai Masala [1,2,*], Stefan Ruseti [1], Traian Rebedea [1], Mihai Dascalu [1,3], Gabriel Gutu-Robu [1] and Stefan Trausan-Matu [1,3]

[1] Computer Science and Engineering Department, University Politehnica of Bucharest, 313 Splaiul Independentei, 060042 Bucharest, Romania; stefan.ruseti@upb.ro (S.R.); traian.rebedea@upb.ro (T.R.); mihai.dascalu@upb.ro (M.D.); gabriel.gutu@upb.ro (G.G.-R.); stefan.trausan@upb.ro (S.T.-M.)
[2] 'Simion Stoilow' Institute of Mathematics of the Romanian Academy, 21 Calea Grivitei, 010702 Bucharest, Romania
[3] Academy of Romanian Scientists, Str. Ilfov, Nr. 3, 050044 Bucharest, Romania
* Correspondence: mihai_dan.masala@upb.ro

**Abstract:** Computer-Supported Collaborative Learning tools are exhibiting an increased popularity in education, as they allow multiple participants to easily communicate, share knowledge, solve problems collaboratively, or seek advice. Nevertheless, multi-participant conversation logs are often hard to follow by teachers due to the mixture of multiple and many times concurrent discussion threads, with different interaction patterns between participants. Automated guidance can be provided with the help of Natural Language Processing techniques that target the identification of topic mixtures and of semantic links between utterances in order to adequately observe the debate and continuation of ideas. This paper introduces a method for discovering such semantic links embedded within chat conversations using string kernels, word embeddings, and neural networks. Our approach was validated on two datasets and obtained state-of-the-art results on both. Trained on a relatively small set of conversations, our models relying on string kernels are very effective for detecting such semantic links with a matching accuracy larger than 50% and represent a better alternative to complex deep neural networks, frequently employed in various Natural Language Processing tasks where large datasets are available.

**Keywords:** Natural Language Processing; educational technology; neural networks; CSCL conversations; string kernels

**Citation:** Masala, M.; Ruseti, S.; Rebedea, T.; Dascalu, M.; Gutu-Robu, G.; Trausan-Matu, S. Identifying the Structure of CSCL Conversations Using String Kernels. *Mathematics* **2021**, *9*, 3330. https://doi.org/10.3390/math9243330

Academic Editors: Florentina Hristea and Cornelia Caragea

Received: 10 November 2021
Accepted: 17 December 2021
Published: 20 December 2021

**Publisher's Note:** MDPI stays neutral with regard to jurisdictional claims in published maps and institutional affiliations.

## 1. Introduction

With an increased prevalence of online presence, accelerated by the current COVID-19 pandemic [1], online messaging applications are gaining an increased popularity. Online social networks make a significant percentage of these platforms, but standalone chat applications are also widely adopted. These platforms are not used only for entertainment purposes, but their applications cover various activities, including and even promoting collaborative learning and creative thinking [2].

Artificial Intelligence techniques have been widely employed in various educational settings [3,4], ranging from classifying learning styles [5,6], to finding active collaborators within a group [7], to providing personalized feedback [8,9], and even customizing curriculum content [10]. Student learning styles (Diverger, Assimilator, Converger or Accommodator using Kolb's Learning Style Inventory [11]) can be precisely classified based on learner's EEG waves and further correlated with IQ and stress levels [5,6]. In collaborative learning settings, automated systems classify students based on their implication and collaboration activity, and provide information to support and enhance students' involvement in key moments [7]. Moreover, online interaction patterns changed in the current pandemic context, both in online learning environments [12] and in general, with an increased online participation, whose traces can be effectively used to create even more advanced predictive models.

Education leans on online communication to enhance the learning process by integrating facilities, such as discussion forums or chat conversations, to stimulate collaboration among peers and with course tutors [13]. Nevertheless, group size has a major impact on delivery time, level of satisfaction, and overall quality of the result [14]. Usually, these conversations occur between more than two participants, which leads to numerous context changes and development of multiple discussion threads within the same conversation [15,16]. As the number of participants increases, the conversation may become harder to follow, as the mix of different discussion threads becomes more frequent. Moreover, divergences and convergences appear between these threads, which may be compared to dissonances and consonances among counterpointed voices in polyphonic music, which have a major role in knowledge construction [15,16].

Focusing on multi-participant chat conversations in particular, ambiguities derived from the inner structure of a conversation are frequent due to the mixture of topics and of messages on multiple discussion threads, that may overlap in short time spans. As such, establishing links between utterances greatly facilitates the understanding of the conversation and improves its readability, while also ensuring coherence per discussion thread. Applications that allow users to manually annotate the utterances they are referring to, when writing their reply, have long existed [17], whereas popular conversation applications (e.g., WhatsApp) successfully integrated such functionalities. Although users are allowed to explicitly add references to previous utterances when issuing a reply, they do not always annotate their utterances, as this process feels tedious and interrupts the flow of the conversation.

Our research objective is to automatically discover semantic links between utterances from multi-participant chat conversations using a supervised approach that integrates neural networks and string kernels [18]. In terms of theoretical grounding, we establish an analogy to the sentence selection task for automated question answering—in a nutshell, detecting semantic links in chat conversations is similar, but more complex. In question answering, most approaches [19–22] consider that the candidate sentence most similar to the question is selected as the suitable answer. In our approach, the user reply is semantically compared to the previous utterances in the conversation, and the most similar contribution is selected while considering a sliding window of previous utterances (i.e., a predefined time-frame or using a preset number of prior utterances). It is worth noting that we simplified the problem of identifying links between two utterances by reducing the context of the conversation to a window of adjacent utterances. Nevertheless, we emphasize the huge discrepancy in terms of dataset sizes between the question answering task and the small collections of conversations currently available for our task.

We summarize our core contributions as follows:

- Employing a method grounded in string kernels used in conjunction with state of the art NLP features to detect semantic links in conversations; in contrast to previous studies [23,24], we also impose a threshold for practical usage scenarios, thus ensuring the ease of integration of our model within chat environments;

- Providing extensive quantitative and qualitative results to validate that the lexical information provided by string kernels is highly relevant for detecting semantic links across multiple datasets and multiple learning frameworks (i.e., classification and regression tasks);

- Obtaining state of the art results on two different datasets by relying on string kernels and handcrafted conversation-specific features. Our method surpasses the results of Gutu et al. [25,26] obtained using statistical semantic similarity models and semantic distances extracted from the WordNet [27] ontology. In addition, our experimental results argue that simpler supervised models, fine-tuned on relatively small datasets, such as those used in Computer-Supported Collaborative Learning (CSCL) research, may perform better on specific tasks than more complex deep learning approaches frequently employed on large datasets.

In the following subsections we present state-of-the-art methods for computing text similarity and for detecting semantic links.

### 1.1. Lexical and Semantic Models for Text Similarity

Early models to compute semantic similarity consider semantic distances (e.g., path length, Wu-Palmer [28], or Leackock-Chodorow [29]) in lexicalized ontologies, namely WordNet [27], as well as Latent Semantic Analysis (LSA) [30]. LSA uses a term-document matrix which stores the number of occurrences of each term in every document. Singular Value Decomposition followed by a projection on the most representative dimensions is then performed to transform the matrix into a latent semantic space. Semantic similarity scores between words are calculated using cosine similarity scores within this semantic vector space.

#### 1.1.1. Word Embeddings

Word embeddings represent words in a vector space using their context of occurrence within a corpus. Among existing models, word2vec is one of the most frequently used embeddings methods. Word2vec uses distributed word embeddings computed using a simple neural network that considers the context of words as n-gram co-occurrences [31]; the similarity between two texts is determined using cosine similarity. Word2vec, in the skip-gram framework, is in fact a generative neural model [32] trained to predict the words that appear in the context of a given word. Another popular model, Glove [33], computes word embeddings using an approach based on a count-based approach, using the number of occurrences of any two words within a text. Both models rely on word level representations for texts. Another approach is offered by FastText [34] which uses character n-grams as an extension of word2vec and thus is able to compute character n-grams embeddings. This method is very useful for determining embeddings for out-of-vocabulary words, e.g., words that do not appear or are not very frequent in the corpora used for training the embeddings space.

#### 1.1.2. String Kernels

String kernels [35] are functions used at the character level. The underlying assumption is that a satisfactory similarity measure between two documents can be associated with the number of shared sub-strings of a predefined size. Instead of representing texts in this sub-string induced space, string kernels use a function which replicates the dot-product of two texts in this high-dimensional space. The higher the value of the kernel function, the more similar the texts are.

Variations in the size of n-grams (commonly between 2 and 10 characters) enable the generation of different string kernels. String kernels also vary depending on the function used for computing the overlap between two texts. The most common string kernels are spectrum, intersection, and presence [36]. Spectrum is calculated as the dot-product between the frequencies of n-grams (Equation (1)). Intersection kernel relies on the minimum of the two frequencies (Equation (2)). The presence kernel encodes whether an n-gram is present or not in a string by using presence bits (Equation (3)). In our experiments, normalized versions of these kernels were used.

$$k_p^s(a,b) = \sum_{v \in \Sigma^p} num_v(a) \cdot num_v(b) \tag{1}$$

$$k_p^{\cap}(a,b) = \sum_{v \in \Sigma^p} min\{num_v(a), num_v(b)\} \tag{2}$$

$$k_p^{0/1}(a,b) = \sum_{v \in \Sigma^p} in_v(a) \cdot in_v(b) \tag{3}$$

where:

- $\Sigma^p$ = all $p$-grams of a given size $p$,
- $num_v(s)$ = number of occurrences of string ($n$-gram) $v$ in document $s$,
- $in_v(s)$ = 1 if string ($n$-gram) $v$ occurs in document $s$, 0 otherwise.

String kernels can also be used as features for different classifiers to solve tasks such as native language identification [37], protein fold prediction, or digit recognition [38]. Beck and Cohn [39] use the Gaussian Process framework on string kernels with the goal of optimizing the weights related to each n-gram size, as well as decay parameters responsible for gaps and matches. Their results show that such a model outperforms linear baselines on the task of sentiment analysis. Another important result is that, while string kernels are better than other linear baselines, non-linear methods outperform string kernels; thus, non-linearly combining string kernels may further improve their performance. One such extension was proposed by Masala et al. [18] for the task of question answering. The authors show that a shallow neural network based on string kernels and word embeddings yielded good results, comparable to the ones obtained by much more complex neural networks. The main advantage of the approach is that a small number of parameters needs to be learned, which allows the model to be also trained and used on small datasets, while concurrently ensuring a very fast training process. We rely on a similar approach for detecting semantic links in chat conversations, a task with significantly smaller datasets than question answering.

### 1.1.3. Neural Models for Text Similarity

Neural-based models have been widely used for computing similarity between paragraphs for question answering tasks [21,40,41]. Given a question and a list of candidate answers, the task of selecting the most reasonable answer is also known as answer selection (a sub-task of question answering). The general approach for computing the similarity between two text sequences is the following: compute an inner representation for both text segments using a neural network and then apply a similarity function (which, in turn, can be modelled with a neural network). Common neural models used for answer selection include Bidirectional Long Short-Term Memory (Bi-LSTM) [42] or Convolutional Neural Networks (CNN) [43]. Because there is no restriction on the length of the analyzed sentences, the dynamic number of outputs of the Bi-LSTM must be converted into a fixed-length representation. This transformation can be performed by simple average or max pooling, concatenation of the first and the last output, or by more complex methods such as applying another CNN layer on top of these inner representations [41].

In addition, attention mechanisms are frequently employed in neural network models as they enable long-range dependencies between parts of the input [44,45]. In the context of question answering, the attention mechanism allows the model to also take into account the question, when computing the representation of a candidate answer. Intuitively, attention allows the model to peek at the question when computing the representation of the answer, thus providing the ability to better focus on the relevant parts of the answer (with regards to the question). Dos Santos et al. [21] proposed the usage of an attention mechanism that allows both the question and the answer to influence each others' representation. After computing the inner representations of the question and answer using either a Bi-LSTM or a CNN, the authors combined the representations into a single fixed-size matrix from which attention weights are extracted, and afterwards used to compute the final representations of the question and answer.

Bachrach et al. [40] proposed the usage of a global view of the question together with its inner representation, when computing the attention weights. One way of obtaining such global information from the question is to use a multi-layer perceptron (MLP) on the bag-of-words representation of the question. Wang et al. [46] explored the use of comparison functions (e.g., element-wise subtraction and multiplication, a simple MLP) for combining the attention-weighted representation of the question with the representation of the answer, followed by a CNN for the final classification step.

Transformer-based architectures [47] have become popular in the NLP domain because of their state-of-the-art performance on a wide range of tasks [48–53]. The idea behind the Transformer architecture was to replace the classical models used for processing sequences (e.g., RNNs or CNNs) with self-attention mechanisms that allow global and complex interactions between any two words in the input sequence. For example, BERT [48] used multiple layers of Transformers trained in a semi-supervised manner. The training of BERT is based on two tasks: Masked LM (MLM)—in which a random token (word) is masked and the model is asked to predict the correct word—and Next Sentence Prediction (NSP)—in which the model is given two sentences A and B and is trained to predict whether sentence B follows sentence A. In our experiments, we consider the NSP pretrained classifier.

### 1.2. Detection of Semantic Links

The manual annotation of semantic links is a time consuming and difficult task. Although many chat applications provide the possibility to explicitly introduce such links, participants frequently forget or do not think it is necessary to add links to the referred contribution, as the process breaks the conversation flow. Techniques for automated annotation of such links were previously developed and were referred to as *implicit links detection* [54] or *chat disentanglement* [55–58].

#### 1.2.1. Semantic Distances and Semantic Models

Previous experiments by Gutu et al. [25,26] considered semantic distances between utterances in a floating window and statistical semantic similarity models trained on large corpora of documents. The authors explored the optimal window sizes in terms of the distance (expressed as count of intermediary utterances) and time spent between two utterances in order to search for semantic links. For a given reply, the contribution with the highest semantic score from the window was chosen as the referred utterance. The performance of this approach in detecting semantic links was evaluated based on the explicitly referred links added by participants from a conversation [25]. A corpus of 55 CSCL chats with multiple participants was used for this experiment. The same corpus was used in the current study and is detailed later on in Section 2.1.1.

#### 1.2.2. Neural Networks

Long Short-Term Memory (LSTM) [59] networks have been used to capture the message-level and context-level semantics of chat utterances with the end goal of disentanglement [57]. Jiang et al. [56] proposed a two stage method with a NN backbone for chat disentanglement. In the first stage, a Siamese Hierarchical Convolutional Neural Network (SHCNN) is used for estimating the similarity of two utterances that was further used to establish the disentangled conversations. Li et al. [58] used Transformer-based architectures [47] to detect semantic links. Their model considered Bidirectional LSTM networks on top of a BERT model to capture the intricate interactions between multiple utterances and, finally, to identify pairs of related utterances. We emphasize that, especially in the case of state-of-the art NLP architectures, a significant amount of data is required to properly train the aforementioned models.

Besides the textual content of a contribution, previous experiments by Masala et al. [23,24] used additional meta-information to discover semantic links using NN classifiers. Such conversation-specific meta information included the time spent between two utterances, the distance between them, or whether the two utterances belonged to the same author [23,24]. Mehri et al. [60] also employed Recurrent Neural Networks (RNNs) for modelling semantic relationships between chat utterances. Semantic information was used together with meta-information (such as distance between utterances) for thread partitioning and the detection of direct replies in conversations.

### 1.2.3. Other Computational Approaches

Previous work by Trausan-Matu and Rebedea [54] considered speech acts [61] for identifying continuations or question answering patterns between utterances. Moldovan et al. [62] argued that speech acts can be determined with a high accuracy by only using the first few words in the contribution. Moreover, the dialogue between participants can highlight patterns that may be automatically identified. In an educational context [63], student profiles were created by analyzing the interactions between the teacher and the student, as well as the posts in the discussion forums.

## 2. Method

### 2.1. Datasets

### 2.1.1. Corpus of CSCL Chat Conversations

Our experiments were performed on a collection of 55 chat conversations (ChatLinks dataset, available online at https://huggingface.co/datasets/readerbench/ChatLinks, accessed on 10 November 2021) held by Computer Science undergraduate students [15,25]. Participants had to discuss on software technologies that support collaborative work in a business environment (e.g., blog, forum, chat, wiki). Each student had to uphold one preferred technology in the first part of the conversation, introducing benefits or disadvantages for each CSCL technology, followed by a joint effort to define a custom solution most suitable for their virtual company in the second part of the chat. The discussions were conducted using ConcertChat [17], a software application which allows participants to annotate the utterance they refer to, when writing a reply. The vision behind these interactions was grounded in Stahl's vision of group cognition [64] in which difficult problems can be solved easier by multiple participants using a collaborative learning environment.

Two evaluations were considered. The first one relies on the *exact matching* between two utterances, which checks whether the links are identical with the references manually added by participants while discussing. The second approach considers *in-turn matching* which checks whether the detected links belong to the same block of continuous utterances written by the same participant, as defined in the manually annotated references. The automated approach computes similarity scores between each given contribution and multiple previous utterances, within a pre-imposed window size. The highest matching score is used to establish the semantic link. A conversation excerpt depicting an exact matching between the reference and semantic link is shown in Table 1. An in-turn matching example is shown in Table 2. In both cases, the emphasized text shows the utterance which denotes the semantic link. The Ref ID column shows the explicit manual annotations added by the participants.

**Table 1.** Fragments extracted from conversations showing exact matching (Semantic link is highlighted in bold).

| Utt. ID | Ref. ID | Speaker | Content |
|---------|---------|---------|---------|
| **257** | | **Razvan** | **High-activity forum threads can be automatically taken to chat if sufficient users are online** |
| 258 | | Bogdan | I think it's a good ideea let the user post their pictures, their favorite books, movies |
| 259 | 257 | Andreea | and if the time between posts is very short |
| **260** | **258** | **Andreea** | **a user profile, of course** |
| 261 | | Bogdan | that way big communities will be created |
| **262** | **258** | **Razvan** | **personal, social blogs, chatrooms and forums besides educational ones** |

**Table 1.** *Cont.*

| Utt. ID | Ref. ID | Speaker | Content |
|---|---|---|---|
| **177** | | **Oana** | **i belive that on forums, you can also show that "human" part :)** |
| 178 | 177 | Tibi | yes ...but you cannot build a relationship |
| 179 | | Tibi | a long term relationship |
| **180** | | **Oana** | **With who?** |
| 181 | | Oana | With other people? |
| 182 | | Oana | Why's that? |
| 183 | | Oana | You can interact with anybody. |
| 184 | | Oana | You post a message, about a topic |
| 185 | | Oana | Furthermore, other people can answer to that message or say an opinion... |
| 186 | 180 | Tibi | as i said before...people became attached of your writing...they want to descover more of you... |
| 187 | | Oana | It's a kind of conversation |
| **188** | | **Oana** | **Furthermore, any conversation can lead to a relation** |
| **189** | **188** | **Tibi** | **yes...but on a certain topic only...** |
| 190 | | Oana | Yes, well, I have my own kind of writting :) |
| 191 | 189 | Oana | yes, but if you want, you can go and change that topic |

**Table 2.** Fragments extracted from conversations showing in-turn matching (Semantic link is highlighted in bold).

| Utt. ID | Ref. ID | Speaker | Content |
|---|---|---|---|
| 107 | | Lucian | They do not require any complicate client application, central mediation |
| **108** | | **Lucian** | **Actually, all this arguments are pure technical** |
| 109 | | Lucian | The single and best reason for which chats are the best way of communication in this age of technology is that |
| 110 | | Lucian | Chat emulate the natural way in which people interact. By talking, be argumenting ideas, by shares by natural speech |
| 111 | | Lucian | Hence,chat is the best way to transform this habit in a digital era. |
| 112 | | Lucian | We can start debating now? :D |
| 113 | 111 | Florin | I would like to contradict you on some aspects |
| 379 | | Alina | No, curs.cs is an implementation of moodle |
| 380 | | Alina | Moodle is jus a platform |
| 381 | | Alina | You install it on a servere |
| **382** | | **Alina** | **and use it** |
| 383 | | Alina | Furthermore, populate it wih information. |
| 384 | | Andreea | and students are envolved too in development of moodle? |
| 385 | | Alina | It has the possibility of wikis, forums, blogs. I'm not sure with the chat, though. |
| 386 | 379 | Stefan | Yes that is right |

The manually added links were subsequently used for determining accuracy scores for different similarity metrics, using the previous strategies (e.g., exact and in-turn matching). The 55 conversations from the corpus made up to 17,600 utterances, while 4500 reference links were added by participants (e.g., about 29% of utterances had a corresponding reference link). Out of the 55 total conversations, 11 of them were set aside and used as a test set.

A previous study by Gutu et al. [25] showed that 82% of explicit links in the dataset were covered by a distance window of 5 utterances; 95% of annotations were covered by enlarging the window to 10 utterances, while a window of 20 utterances covered more than 98% of annotated links, while considering time-frames, a 1 min window contained only 61% of annotations, compared to the 2 min window which contains about 77% of all annotated links. A wider time-frame of 3 min included about 93% of all links, while a

5 min window covered more than 97% of them. As our aim was to keep the majority of links and to remove outliers, a 95% coverage was considered ideal. Smaller coverages were included in our comparative experiments. Thus, distances of 5 and 10 utterances were considered, while time-frames of 1, 2, and 3 min were used in the current experiments.

### 2.1.2. Linux IRC Reply Dataset

Besides the previous collection of chat conversations, we also used the chat conversations dataset proposed by Mehri et al. [60] for classifying pairs of utterances. This dataset was specifically built to capture direct reply relationships between utterances. The data consists of a subset of '#Linux IRC log data' [55], manually annotated with direct reply relationships. Volunteers, familiar with Linux, were instructed to go through the chat messages and select the immediate parents for every message. A message might have no parents (e.g., when starting a new conversation thread) or it might have multiple parents (e.g., an answer to a multi-participant thread). On average, a message had 1.22 direct parents and 1.70 direct children in this dataset, while this dataset is not related to formal education, it is a great example of using chats in communities of practice in the real world (e.g., specialists working on Linux).

### 2.2. Neural Model for Semantic Links Detection

One of our key insights is that answers connect to questions in a similar manner to how semantic links connect utterances, in the sense of information flow or continuation of ideas. Therefore, we theorize that answer selection methods can be effective in detecting semantic links. We adapt the model introduced by Masala et al. [18] for answer selection to our task. Figure 1 presents the processing flow. The goal of our model is to combine lexical features (in the form of string kernels) with semantic and conversation-specific information to better capture semantic links between utterances.

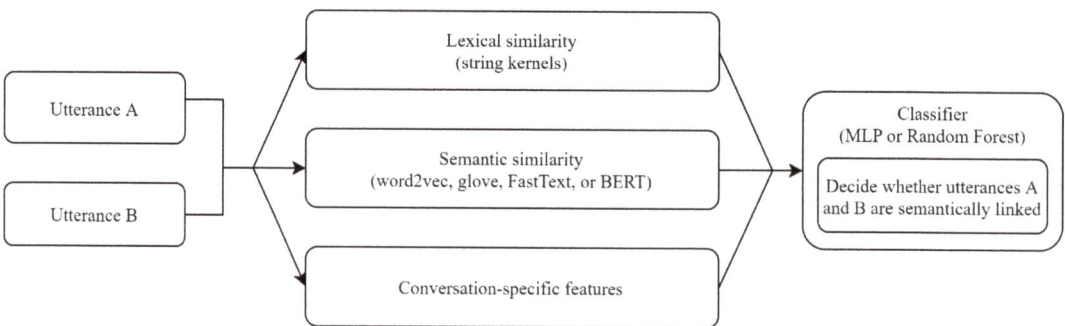

**Figure 1.** Conceptual diagram of our approach.

Moreover, we establish strong supervised and unsupervised baselines for evaluating our approach, namely:

- Path Length [25]: Previous best results for detecting semantic links were achieved on the same dataset in an unsupervised manner by using WordNet Path Length as similarity distance. Path Length is based on the shortest length path between two concepts in the WordNet ontology.
- String Kernels: We use string kernels as a measure of similarity; we experiment with intersection, presence and spectrum kernels [36], on a 3–7 g range .
- AP-BiLSTM [21]: A supervised method which achieves top results on the answer selection task. Both utterances are passed through a Bidirectional LSTM network. Attention vectors are extracted from the hidden states (at each time step), leading to

attention-based representations for both utterances. Cosine similarity is then used on the attention-weighted utterances for computing the similarity between them.

- BERT [48]: We use a pretrained BERT-base model to compute the probability that two utterances follow one another, as a continuation of ideas. For this task, we fine-tune BERT, following the approach proposed by Devlin et al. [48]. Therefore we optimize the binary cross-entropy loss with Adam optimizer [65] with a learning rate of $1 \times 10^{-5}$, using batches of size 32 for 7 epochs. All hyperparameters were selected using 10-fold cross-validation.

Three different types of string kernels (spectrum, presence and intersection) were considered in the proposed supervised neural model, each with five character n-gram ranges: 1–2, 3–4, 5–6, 7–8, and 9–10. Hence, we compute 15 similarity scores for each pair of utterances, and we combine the above-mentioned features using a simple feed-forward multilayer perceptron (MLP) with one hidden layer. The MLP computes a single number for each pair of utterances, namely a similarity score. The hidden layer size was set to 8 for all follow-up experiments, while the batch size was fixed at 100. Hinge loss (Equation (4)) was used as objective function, similar to the loss proposed by Hu and Lu [66] for finding similarities between two sentences. The margin M was set to 0.1 and minimized using the Adam optimizer [65]. The previous utterance most similar to the current one is selected as the semantic link by our model, as well as for the baselines.

$$e(u_r, u^+, u^-) = max(0, M + sim(u_r, u^-) - sim(u_r, u^+)) \qquad (4)$$

where:

- $u_r$ refers to the utterance for which the link is computed,
- $u^+$ refers to the manually annotated utterance,
- $u^-$ is an incorrect utterance contained within the current window,
- $sim(u_r, u)$ refers to the semantic similarity score calculated by the MLP between the two utterances representations,
- $M$ is the desired margin among positive and negative samples.

Furthermore, we enhance the lexical information with conversation-specific information, including details regarding the chat structure, as well as semantic information. The conversation-specific features are computed for each candidate contribution (for a link) as follows: we check whether the contribution contains a question, or the candidate and the link share the same author, while referring to the chat structure, we use the number of in-between utterances and the time between any two given utterances. Two methods for computing semantic information were considered. Given two utterances, the first method computes the embedding of each utterance as the average over the embeddings (e.g., pretrained word2vec, FastText and GloVe models) of all words from the given utterance, followed by cosine similarity. The second method relies on BERT, namely the Next Sentence Prediction classifier, which is used to compute the probability that the two utterances follow one another.

### 2.3. Detecting Direct Replies in Linux IRC Chats

To further validate the effectiveness of string kernels in modeling chat conversations, we investigate the use of string kernels as a feature extraction method on a different dataset and on a slightly different task. Instead of framing the explicit link detection problem as regression (e.g., given an utterance, find its semantic link by computing a score), we treat it as a classification (e.g., a binary classification to establish whether two utterances are connected or not). Starting from the approach proposed by Mehri et al. [60], we train a classifier which outputs, for two given utterances, the probability of the first one being a reply to the second message. Features extracted from string kernels are also considered, resulting in three categories of features (see Table 3): conversation-specific features, semantic information, and lexical information. We further note that for this task, we aim to replicate as accurately as possible the Mehri's et al. [60] approach by using the same model architecture, features, and training methods, the only difference being that we investigate the usage of string kernels and BERT-based features.

**Table 3.** Features used in the reply classifier.

|  |  |  |
|---|---|---|
| Conversation | Time | Time difference between the two utterances (in seconds) |
| | Distance | The number of messages between the two utterances |
| | Same author | Whether two utterances have the same author |
| | Mention child | Whether the parent message mentions the author of the child message |
| | Mention parent | Whether the child message mentions the author of the parent message |
| Semantic | RNN output | Probability outputted by the RNN |
| | BERT | Probability outputted by BERT NSP |
| Lexical | String Kernels | Similarities given by string kernels |

We consider two approaches for capturing semantic information. The first model considers an RNN trained on the Ubuntu Dialogue Corpus, as proposed by Lowe et al. [67]. The purpose of this network is to model semantic relationships between utterances and it is trained on a large dataset of chat conversations. We use a siamese Long Short-Term Memory (LSTM) [59] network to model the probability of a message following a given context. Both the context and the utterance are processed first using a word embedding layer with pre-trained GloVe [33] embeddings, which are further fine-tuned. After the embedding layer, the representations of context and utterance are processed by the LSTM network. Let $c$ and $r$ be the final hidden representation of the context and of the utterance, respectively. These representations, alongside a learned matrix $M$, are used to compute the probability of a reply (see Equation (5)).

$$P(reply|context) = \sigma(c^T M r) \tag{5}$$

The same training procedure introduced by Lowe et al. [67] is applied, namely minimizing the cross-entropy of all labeled (context, contribution) pairs by considering a hidden layer size of 300, an Adam optimizer with gradients clipped to 10, and a 1:1 ratio between positive examples and negative examples (that are randomly sampled from the dataset). In our implementation, a dropout layer was also added after the embedding layer and after the LSTM layer for fine-tuning the embeddings, with the probability of dropping inputs set to 0.2.

The second method is more straightforward and it is based on BERT [48]. We use a pretrained BERT-base model and we query the model for whether two utterances are connected, using the Next Sentence Prediction classifier.

Furthermore, we employ string kernels as a feature extraction method for lexical information. Given a pair of utterances, we compute their lexical similarity with three string kernels (spectrum, presence and intersection) at different granularity (n-gram ranges): 1–2, 3–4, 5–6, 7–8 and 9–10. Thus, a lexical feature vector $v \in \mathcal{R}^{15}$ is computed for each pair of messages.

Mehri's et al. [60] training methodology was used, namely the Linux IRC reply dataset was split into a set of positive examples (annotated replies) and a set of negative examples (the complement of the annotated replies). This leads to a very imbalanced dataset, with most pairs being non-replies. One method to alleviate this problem is to only consider pairs of message within a time frame of 129 s [60] one from another. Different classifiers relying on the features described in Table 3 were trained using 10-fold cross-validation. Decision trees, a simple Multi-Layer Perceptron (MLP) with a hidden size of 20, and random forest [68] were considered in our experiments, each with their benefits and drawbacks.

## 3. Results

The following subsections provide the results on the two tasks, namely semantic links and direct reply detection, arguing their strong resemblance in terms of both models and features. Subsequently, we present a qualitative interpretation of the results.

### 3.1. Semantic Links Detection in the CSCL Chat Conversations

We first evaluate our approach on the CSCL chats dataset described in Section 2.1.1. Our supervised neural network is compared with state-of-the-art methods for answer selection and semantic links detection. We also compare our model with an unsupervised method based only on string kernels. For this baseline, the considered n-gram range (3–7) was selected to maximize the accuracy on a small evaluation set. All supervised methods are trained and evaluated using 10-fold cross-validation. Note that results are reported on the test set.

The following pretrained embeddings were used in our experiments: word2vec, FastText, and GloVe. The word2vec [32] embeddings were pretrained on the Google News Dataset. The FastText embeddings [34] were pretrained on Wikipedia, whereas the GloVe embeddings [33] were pretrained on a Wikipedia 2014 dump and Gigaword 5 (https://catalog.ldc.upenn.edu/LDC2011T07 accessed on 10 November 2021). All these pretrained models are publicly available and widely used in NLP research.

Results are presented in Table 4. The first part includes the accuracy obtained by the baseline methods, while the AP-BiLSTM is a top performing model in the task of answer selection, it performs about the same as the unsupervised path length method for our specialized task of detecting semantic links. AP-BiLSTM obtains even worse performance on the in-turn metric. This is due to the small size of the training dataset compared to the large number of parameters of the model. The BERT-based method outperforms other baselines by a significant margin on every window-time frame, but its performance degrades with larger windows. One possible reason is that the BERT model is pretrained on English Wikipedia and BookCorpus which contain longer sentences, especially when compared to the utterances from the first dataset, while we fine-tune the entire model, its small number of samples cannot alleviate this problem.

**Table 4.** Results for semantic links detection (Exact matching accuracy (%)/In-turn matching accuracy (%)).

| Window (Utterances) | 5 | | | 10 | | |
|---|---|---|---|---|---|---|
| Time (mins) | 1 | 2 | 3 | 1 | 2 | 3 |
| Path Length [25] | 32.44/41.49 | 32.44/41.49 | not reported | 31.88/40.78 | 31.88/40.78 | not reported |
| AP-BiLSTM [21] | 32.95/34.53 | 32.39/35.89 | 33.97/37.58 | 33.86/35.10 | 28.89/31.82 | 24.49/28.32 |
| Intersection kernel | 31.40/34.59 | 33.87/39.58 | 33.58/40.01 | 31.71/34.78 | 32.24/37.66 | 29.47/35.24 |
| Presence kernel | 31.84/34.94 | 33.97/39.81 | 33.58/40.01 | 31.80/34.89 | 32.33/37.71 | 29.67/35.41 |
| Spectrum kernel | 31.21/34.34 | 33.45/39.12 | 33.17/39.49 | 31.39/34.46 | 31.56/36.72 | 28.75/34.26 |
| BERT | 40.07/41.99 | 43.45/47.07 | 44.47/48.42 | 40.41/42.33 | 41.53/45.15 | 38.15/38.60 |
| NN using sk | 35.21/36.90 | 35.55/39.39 | 35.77/39.95 | 35.55/37.02 | 34.08/37.47 | 30.24/33.74 |
| NN using sk + conv | 37.92/39.39 | 45.48/49.66 | 47.06/51.80 | 38.14/39.50 | 46.27/50.79 | **47.85/52.93** |
| NN using sk+sem | 36.45/38.14 | 36.90/40.47 | 36.00/40.29 | 36.68/38.14 | 35.10/38.26 | 31.26/34.76 |
| NN using sk + sem + conv | 37.02/38.60 | 46.38/50.00 | 48.08/52.25 | 37.24/38.71 | 47.29/51.46 | **49.09/53.83** |
| NN using sk + BERT | 37.35/38.71 | 39.16/42.21 | 39.61/43.00 | 37.24/38.60 | 37.13/40.18 | 33.52/36.90 |
| NN using sk + BERT + conv | 40.40/42.21 | 46.72/49.88 | 48.08/51.91 | 40.63/42.43 | 46.95/50.33 | 48.08/52.37 |

Note: sk—string kernels; conv—conversation-specific features, namely window and time (window—# of in-between utterances; time—elapsed time between utterances); question and author (question—whether the utterance contains a question; author—if the utterance shares the same author as the utterance containing the link); sem—semantic information. **Bolded** values represent the best results with and without semantic information.

Unsupervised string kernels by themselves provide inconclusive results as they are not always better than previous methods, but they do seem to work better especially for larger windows. Moreover, we find that there is no convincing difference between any of three types of string kernel functions.

The results obtained using the neural model are presented in the middle part of Table 4. We performed multiple experiments by introducing conversation-specific and semantic features independently (second and third row), and together (fourth row). Word2vec, FastText, and Glove (embedding size 100 and 300) are used for extracting semantic information, with no significant difference in results. Conversation-specific features provide a significant accuracy increase for the task of detecting semantic links. Previous studies found a similar conclusion, as the path length method uses the distance between two utterances as a weighting factor [25], while semantic information improves performance, we cannot consider that the gain is impressive.

In the last part of Table 4, we present the results obtained when extracting semantic information with the method based on BERT. However, despite BERT's Transformer model complexity, the results are similar with the word embeddings semantic encoding. Additional discussions of the results in Table 4 are presented in Section 4.

### 3.2. Imposing a Threshold for Practical Usage Scenarios

In order to make our system ready for use in practice, we propose a threshold in the following manner: (a) run our model for each utterance in the conversation, (b) pick the utterance with the highest similarity score, and (c) if this score is higher (or equal) than the threshold, recommend adding the semantic link in the conversation. If the similarity score is lower than the threshold, we consider that the given utterances are not linked to any previous utterance. Setting the threshold is of utmost importance: a too high value will likely generate a high number of false negatives, while a too low value would yield more false positives. All of the following experiments and results refer only to the exact match metric.

Overall, the absolute value of the similarity score obtained on a pair of utterances is not very relevant per se due to the minimization of the hinge loss. The similarity scores become relevant in context, when compared with each other (in a given window). For this reason, we cannot simply look at the absolute values generated by the model, we need to look at the relation between scores obtained by utterances in the same window. Therefore, we compute, for each of the 10 folds, the mean and standard deviation values across all predictions. Next, for each fold, we search for the threshold value that maximizes the F1 score. For each threshold value, we compute how far this value (in terms of standard deviation) is from the mean prediction value. This distance is computed independently for each fold (as the model is trained for each fold). The mean value of those distances is used for computing the threshold, then a model is trained on the entire training set and the following formula is used for establishing the final threshold (Equation (6)):

$$threshold = mean_p + mean_d * std_p \tag{6}$$

where:

- $mean_p$ is the mean of the predictions on the training set,
- $std_p$ is the standard deviation of the predictions on the training set,
- $mean_d$ is the mean of the distances between the mean prediction and the best threshold found for each fold.

The final values are the following: $mean_p = 0.478$, $std_p = 0.14$, $mean_d = 1.32$, which lead to a $threshold = 0.66$. We evaluate our approach on the test set with the threshold set to 0.66 and obtain an F1 Score of 0.31 (for the positive class) and a 51.67% accuracy. In a practical scenario, if the semantic link suggestion is incorrect, the user might just ignore the predicted link.

### 3.3. Detecting Direct Replies

As previously mentioned in Section 2.3, we first train a siamese-LSTM on the large Ubuntu Dialogue Corpus [67] to predict whether an utterance follows a sequence of utterances. Our implementation slightly outperforms the results reported in [67], using as metric the 1 in 10 next utterance recall: 95.2% versus 92.6% for R@5, 80.0% versus 74.5% for R@5, and 65.4% versus 60.4% for R@1. For all following experiments, we consider our implementation of siamese-LSTM.

In Table 5, we present the results of the proposed methods on the Linux IRC reply dataset. To better understand how informative are string kernels, we made three sets of experiments for each classifier: (a) one set using conversation-specific and semantic features as proposed in [60] (with the addition of semantic information obtained by using pretrained BERT; see the first two columns in Table 5), (b) a second set of experiments including lexical features (presented in the middle half of Table 5), and (c) the last set where semantic information is replaced with the features extracted with string kernels (in the last column of Table 5. We used 250 trees for the random forest classifier and we adjusted the class weights to penalize false positive to better handle the imbalanced dataset. Specifically, the class weight of the positive class was 1, whereas the weight of the negative class was set to *#non_replies/#replies*.

We can observe in Table 5 that lexical information provided by string kernels can be combined with more complex features (such as semantic features obtained by siamese-LSTM) to improve performance. Out of all the classifiers, the random forest model performed the best (0.65 F1 score; 0.75 precision and 0.57 recall for the reply class).

**Table 5.** F1 scores (positive class) for reply detection on Linux IRC reply dataset. **C** denotes Conversation features, **S** denotes semantic information while **L** stands for lexical information. More details about used features can be found in Table 3.

| Method | C + S(RNN) | C + S(BERT) | C + S(RNN) + L | C + S(BERT) + L | C + L |
|---|---|---|---|---|---|
| Decision Tree | 0.53 | 0.54 | 0.54 | 0.56 | 0.55 |
| MLP | 0.60 | 0.60 | 0.62 | 0.61 | 0.60 |
| Random Forest | 0.59 | 0.62 | 0.63 | **0.65** | 0.63 |

In addition, we identify which features were the most important for the random forest model by considering Gini feature importance [68]. For the case in which we do not use lexical information, the semantic information is the most important feature (Gini value of 0.40), followed by time difference (Gini value of 0.27), and space difference (Gini value of 0.14); see Figure 2.

**Figure 2.** Gini feature importance for random forest without string kernels.

When adding string kernels, the semantic information is still the most important feature (Gini value of 0.16), followed by time and distance conversation features (Gini value of 0.15 and 0.12, respectively), and by string kernels on ngrams of size 1–2 (Gini value of 0.11); see Figure 3.

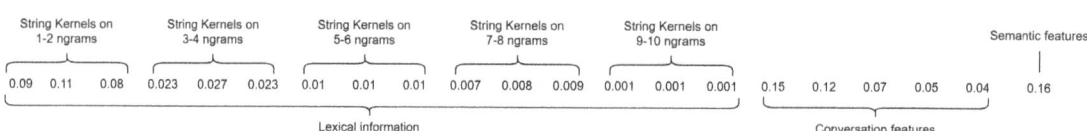

**Figure 3.** Gini feature importance for random forest with string kernels.

If the semantic information is replaced with lexical information, the conversation features become more important, but still the lexical features are the most informative; see Figure 4. In all cases relying on lexical information (see Figures 3 and 4), the features extracted by using string kernels are, as a whole, the most informative features with Gini values of 0.41 and 0.49, respectively. More discussions of the results in Table 5 can be found in the last part of Section 4.

Finally, we note that the rather low F1 scores for the task of detecting semantic links (especially compared to other NLP tasks) are mainly due to the intricate nature of the task. Solving the task of detecting semantic links in chats implies properly disentangling discourse structure, both at individual level and when multiple participants are involved throughout an evolving conversation.

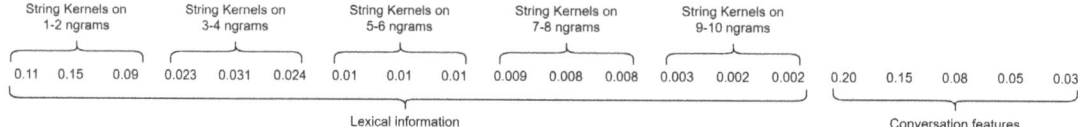

**Figure 4.** Gini feature importance for random forest with string kernels replacing semantic information.

### 3.4. Qualitative Interpretation of the Results

In this section, we provide a qualitative interpretation of the results obtained by the proposed neural model using string kernels. In the top half of Table 6 we present two simple examples of semantic links, one as direct answer to a previously stated question, and a second one as an addition to a previous idea. The proposed model is capable of detecting when an author continues their idea in a new utterance (see lower part of Table 6).

**Table 6.** Example of correct semantic link prediction (**explicit link**/*predicted link*).

| Utt. ID | Ref. ID | Speaker | Content |
|---------|---------|---------|---------|
| *120* | | *Adrian* | *so tell me why the chat could provide collaborative learning?* |
| 121 | 120 | Maria | for example if we have to work on a project and everybody has a part to do we can discuss it in a conference |
| *122* | | *Adrian* | *you can discuss the premises but not the whole project* |
| 123 | 120 | Andreea | well, you can have a certain amount of info changed |
| 124 | 122 | Maria | you can discuss the main ideas and if someone encounters problems he can ask for help and the team will try to help him |
| *216* | | *Dan* | *are there private wikis?* |
| 217 | | Ana | yes...there are wikis that need authentication... |
| 218 | 216 | Dan | by private i understand that only certain users can modify their content |

Our model also detects distant semantic links (see Table 7) and interleaved semantic links (see Table 8). Table 9 presents two examples of complex interactions in which our system correctly detects semantic links.

**Table 7.** Example of correct semantic link prediction (**explicit link**/*predicted link*).

| Utt. ID | Ref. ID | Speaker | Content |
|---|---|---|---|
| *139* | | *Lucian* | *To CHAT with a teacher and with our colleagues which have knowledge and share it with us.* |
| 140 | | Florin | yes, but I do not agree that chat's are the best way to do that |
| 141 | | Lucian | For example, we could read a book about NLP but we could learn much more by CHATTING with a teacher of NLP |
| 142 | | Claudia | but that chat is based on some info that we have previously read |
| ... | | ... | ... |
| 145 | 139 | Sebi | yes but the best way to share your knowledge is to make publicly with other people who wants to learn something. In chats you can do this just with the people who are online, in forums everybody can share it |
| *62* | | *Alexandru* | *the blog supports itself on something our firm calls a "centeredcommunity"...the owner of the blog is the center...interacting with thecenter (artist, engineer, etc. ) is something very rewarding* |
| 63 | | Alexandru | and i would like to underline once again the artistic side of the blog |
| 64 | | Alexandru | blog is ART |
| 65 | | Raluca | you can also share files in a chat conference, in realtime |
| 66 | 62 | Radu | you're right... blogs have their place in community interaction |

**Table 8.** Example of correct semantic link prediction (**explicit link**/*predicted link*).

| Utt. ID | Ref. ID | Speaker | Content |
|---|---|---|---|
| *173* | | *Ionut* | *as the wiki grow the maintenance becomes very hard, and it consumes a lot of human resources* |
| *174* | | *Bogdan* | *many users manage that information, so the chores are distributed* |
| 175 | 174 | Ionut | this would be a pro for wikis |
| 176 | 173 | Bogdan | yes, but the wiki grows along with the users that manage that wiki |
| *186* | | *Costin* | *I mean can an admin take the rights to another admin even if the firstone became admin after the second one?* |
| 187 | | Ionut | who can also have the right to give admin permissions |
| *188* | | *Tatar* | *wikis are good for documentation but is not a communication tool* |
| 189 | 188 | Ionut | so "Thumbs up!" for chat here! |
| 190 | 186 | Bogdan | I think if some admin does not do their job, he could lose the status |

**Table 9.** Example of correct semantic link prediction (**explicit link**/*predicted link*).

| Utt. ID | Ref. ID | Speaker | Content |
|---|---|---|---|
| *168* | | *Octavian* | *it s meant to improve the quality of a web site* |
| 169 | | Oana | So it;s just to inform you... |
| 170 | | Octavian | yes |
| 171 | 168 | Tibit | there isan advantage in owning a blog...by having a somehow informal kind ofrelationship...you can get people attached to your writing... |
| 172 | | Tibit | you can let them kow a part of you that cannot be shown on forums and wikis |
| 173 | | Tibit | you humanise the content |
| *174* | | *Octavian* | *yes, i agree with you* |
| 175 | 174 | Oana | I don;t |
| 176 | | Tibit | why so? |
| *177* | | *Oana* | *i belive that on forums, you can also show that "human" part :)* |
| 178 | 177 | Tibit | yes ...but you cannot build a relationship |
| *188* | | *Luis* | *Let ustake the socket example. Using blog the information will be posted andthe users can asks questions and receive extra information* |
| *189* | *188* | *Cristi* | *this is a dynamic advantage of the blog* |
| 190 | | Cristi | but what if there was a little error in the example? |
| *191* | | *Alex* | *how are they able ask questions if they can modify the page?* |
| 192 | 189 | Luis | in general blog ideal for presenting products, implementation ideas , for advertising |
| 193 | 191 | Luis | you jst put a comment |

However, the model is not perfect—in about half of the cases, it is unable to detect the correct semantic link (e.g., the best accuracy is 49.09%). Nevertheless, we must consider that the detection of correct links is a difficult task even for human readers due to complex interactions between utterances (see examples in Table 10).

**Table 10.** First example of **wrong** semantic link prediction (**explicit link**/*predicted link*).

| Utt. ID | Ref. ID | Speaker | Content |
|---|---|---|---|
| **156** | | **Delia** | **It can also make it easier to communicate with larger groups** |
| 157 | | Delia | where will be having this conversation if the chat would not exist?:P |
| *158* | | *Cristian* | *it's the easiest way to solve a problem indeed, but only if the person is available* |
| 159 | | Delia | the availability is prerequisitive |
| 160 | | Delia | yup |
| 161 | | Delia | but who is not online ourdays?:) |
| 162 | 156 | Marian | yes but what about when you have a problem none of your friends know how to solve |
| **288** | | **Andreea** | **if kids get used to it at an early age, they would have an easier time later** |
| 289 | | Razvan | blog posts, chatting, video conferences are ok |
| 290 | | Razvan | I thinks it's dirrect enough |
| *291* | | *Andreea* | *maybe the teacher and the students could do something fun together, like a trip :)* |
| 292 | 288 | Mihai | yes,this is a very important thing, every teacher should promote elearning |

In some cases, the model fails to capture semantic relationships due to the simplistic way of extracting the semantic information. This shortcoming can be observed in the first example of Table 11, as the model fails to capture the relatedness of the verbs "moderate" and "administarte", although in this case it can be attributed to the misspelling of the verb *administrate*. Our model also fails to reason—the model selects as the semantic link in the example presented in the bottom half of Table 11) an utterance by the same participant who refers to herself as "you".

**Table 11.** Second example of **wrong** semantic link prediction (**explicit link**/*predicted link*).

| Utt. ID | Ref. ID | Speaker | Content |
|---|---|---|---|
| *242* | | *Alex* | *whenyou need to have a discution between multiple people and you need itstored so other people would be able to read it, you should definetlyuse a forum* |
| **243** | | **Luis** | **We need someone to administarte that forum. so it will waste their time** |
| 244 | | Alex | what other solution you have? |
| 245 | 243 | Cristi | exacly, someone has to moderate the discussions |
| *51* | | *Alexandru* | *and sometimes you do :)* |
| **52** | | **Raluca** | **you save a text file when you only chat or save a video file if you really need it** |
| 53 | | Radu | Theidea of community is the fact that most of the members should know whatis going on. If you do not want others (ousiders) to see the inside messages, than you can create a private forum and never give it's IPaddress or DNS name to anyone :) |
| 54 | 51 | Raluca | i agree with you here |

In other cases, utterances simply do not provide enough information (see Table 12). More complex features might help overcome these limitations. Nevertheless, some limitations are also due to the way the problem was formulated, as each utterance is analysed independently.

**Table 12.** Third example of **wrong** semantic link prediction (**explicit link**/*predicted link*).

| Utt. ID | Ref. ID | Speaker | Content |
|---|---|---|---|
| *400* | | *Bogdan* | *let us suppose that we use these technics in a serial mode:...so, every method corresponds to a step in clasification...* |
| 401 | | Mihai | yes, we can combine the powers of every techniques and come out with a very versatile machine learning software |
| **402** | | **Bogdan** | **and each step can get a result...** |
| 403 | 402 | Mihai | or we can choose a method depending on the nature of the problem, taking into consideration that each one fits best on a few type of problems |

## 4. Discussion

Answer selection techniques, in conjunction with string kernels, were evaluated as a method for detecting semantic links in chat conversations. We used two datasets with related tasks (i.e., detection of semantic links as a classification task or as a regression task) to validate our approach.

The proposed neural model greatly improves upon the previous state-of-the-art for semantic link detection, boosting the exact match accuracy from 32.44% (window/time frame: 5 utterances/1 min) to 47.85% (window/time frame: 10 utterances/3 min). The neural network model outperforms previous methods for all combinations of considered frames. It is important to note that the neural network models generalize very well—e.g., performance is better for larger windows. This was not the case with any other methods presented in the first part of Table 4, where we included several strong baselines from previous works.

The addition of semantic information to our model increased its performance, but not by a large margin, especially when compared to the performance gained by adding conversation features. This highlights that an answer selection framework imposed upon the semantic link detection task has some limitations. The largest observed gain for semantic information was achieved on longer frames (e.g., window/time frame: 10 utterances/3 min, improvement from 47.85% to 49.09%), which means that semantic information becomes more helpful when discriminating between a larger number of candidates (larger window).

An interesting observation is that using BERT for extracting semantic information (last part of Table 4) does not bring significant improvements. We believe this is the case because the BERT pretrained model is trained on much longer and structurally different sentences (e.g., Wikipedia texts versus chat messages).

The results on the Linux IRC reply dataset (Table 5) are compelling. The first important observation is that the usage of string kernels improves the performance for all combinations of features (see the first two columns of Table 5 with any of the last three columns of Table 5). Similar to the first set of experiments (on the CSCL chat corpus; see Table 4), semantic information helps the model better capture direct links, but it is not critical. Using string kernels to replace semantic information (see last column of Table 5) proves to be very effective, obtaining better performance than the model without string kernels, but with semantic information (first two columns of Table 5).

Based on two different datasets, two slightly different tasks (regression and classification), and two different models, we observe the same patterns: string kernels are very effective at utterance level, while state-of-the-art semantic similarity models under-perform when used for utterance similarity. Besides higher accuracy, string kernels are also a lot faster and, if used in conjunction with a neural network on top of them, achieve state of the art results with a small number of parameters. This allows the model to be trained very fast, even on a CPU.

## 5. Conclusions

Computer-Supported Collaborative Learning environments have shown an increased usage, especially when it comes to problem-solving tasks, being very useful in the context of online activities imposed by the COVID-19 pandemic. For such purposes, chat environments are usually seen as a suitable technology. In addition, chats can sometimes incorporate a facility that allows participants to explicitly mark the utterance they are referring to, when writing a reply. In conversations with a higher number of participants, several discussion topics emerge and continue in parallel, which makes the conversation hard to follow.

This paper proposes a supervised approach inspired by answer selection techniques to solve the problem of detecting semantic links in chat conversations. A supervised neural model integrating string kernels, semantic and conversation-specific features was presented as an alternative to complex deep learning models, especially when smaller datasets are available for training. The neural network learnt to combine the lexical and semantic features together with other conversation-specific characteristics, like the distance and time spent between two utterances. Results were compared to findings in the question answering field and validated the proposed solution as suitable for detecting semantic links in a small dataset, such as the collection of CSCL conversations. Our best model achieves 49.09% accuracy for exact match and 53.58% for in-turn metric. String kernels were successfully combined with semantic and conversation-specific information using neural networks, as well as other classifiers such as decision trees and random forests. State-of-the-art results (0.65 F1 score on the reply class) were also obtained using string kernels for reply detection on the Linux IRC reply dataset.

String kernels provide a fast, versatile, and easy approach for analyzing chat conversations, and should be considered as a central component to any automated analysis method that involves chat conversations, while the neural network provided relevant results for the explicit links detection task, the semantic information did not bring important additional information to the network. The experiments on the reply detection task lead to very similar results. Nonetheless, an inherent limitation of our model is generated by the answer selection framework imposed on the semantic link detection task (i.e., not considering the flow of conversation and addressing utterances independently).

The proposed method allows participants to more easily follow the flow of a discussion thread within a conversation by allowing the disambiguation of the conversation threads. As such, we provide guidance while reading entangled discussion with multiple inter-twined discussion threads. This is of great support for both educational and business-related tasks. Moreover, chat participants can obtain an overview of their involvement by having access to the inter-dependencies between their utterances and the corresponding discussion threads. Another facility might aim at limiting the mixture of too many discussion topics by providing guidance to focus only on the topics of interest. With accuracy scores slightly over 50%, the proposed method may still require human confirmation or adjustment, if the detected link is not suitable. Finally, the automated detection of semantic links can be used to model the flow of the conversation by using a graph-based approach, further supporting the understanding and analysis of the conversation's rhetorical structure.

Our method does not take into account the context in which the replies occur, which might prove to be important for detecting semantic links. Further experiments target gathering an extended corpora of conversations to further advance the chat understanding subdomain.

**Author Contributions:** Conceptualization, T.R., M.D. and S.T.-M.; Data curation, M.M. and G.G.-R.; Formal analysis, M.M.; Funding acquisition, T.R. and M.D.; Investigation, M.M.; Methodology, M.M., S.R. and G.G.-R.; Project administration, T.R. and M.D.; Resources, G.G.-R. and S.T.-M.; Software, M.M.; Supervision, T.R., M.D. and S.T.-M.; Validation, M.M., S.R. and G.G.-R.; Visualization, M.M.; Writing—original draft, M.M.; Writing—review & editing, S.R., T.R., M.D. and S.T.-M. All authors have read and agreed to the published version of the manuscript.

**Funding:** This research was supported by a grant of the Romanian National Authority for Scientific Research and Innovation, CNCS—UEFISCDI, project number TE 70 PN-III-P1-1.1-TE-2019-2209, "ATES—Automated Text Evaluation and Simplification" and POC-2015 P39-287 IAVPLN.

**Institutional Review Board Statement:** The study was conducted according to the guidelines of the Declaration of Helsinki. Both datasets (ChatLinks and Reply Annotations) used in this work are from external sources and are available freely online.

**Informed Consent Statement:** Informed consent was obtained from all subjects involved in the study.

**Data Availability Statement:** In this work, we use two public corpora available at: https://huggingface.co/datasets/readerbench/ChatLinks (accessed on 10 November 2021) and http://shikib.com/td_annotations (accessed on 10 November 2021).

**Conflicts of Interest:** The authors declare no conflict of interest. The funders had no role in the design of the study; in the collection, analyses, or interpretation of data; in the writing of the manuscript, or in the decision to publish the results.

## References

1. Cinelli, M.; Quattrociocchi, W.; Galeazzi, A.; Valensise, C.M.; Brugnoli, E.; Schmidt, A.L.; Zola, P.; Zollo, F.; Scala, A. The COVID-19 social media infodemic. *Sci. Rep.* **2020**, *10*, 16598.
2. Alalwan, N.; Al-Rahmi, W.M.; Alfarraj, O.; Alzahrani, A.; Yahaya, N.; Al-Rahmi, A.M. Integrated three theories to develop a model of factors affecting students' academic performance in higher education. *IEEE Access* **2019**, *7*, 98725–98742. [CrossRef]
3. Dutt, A.; Ismail, M.A.; Herawan, T. A systematic review on educational data mining. *IEEE Access* **2017**, *5*, 15991–16005. [CrossRef]
4. Chen, L.; Chen, P.; Lin, Z. Artificial intelligence in education: A review. *IEEE Access* **2020**, *8*, 75264–75278. [CrossRef]
5. Rashid, N.A.; Nasir, T.M.; Lias, S.; Sulaiman, N.; Murat, Z.H.; Abdul Kadir, R.S.S. Learners' Learning Style classification related to IQ and Stress based on EEG. *Procedia Soc. Behav. Sci.* **2011**, *29*, 1061–1070. [CrossRef]
6. Rashid, N.A.; Taib, M.N.; Lias, S.; Bin Sulaiman, N.; Murat, Z.H.; Abdul Kadir, R.S.S. EEG theta and alpha asymmetry analysis of neuroticism-bound learning style. In Proceedings of the 2011 3rd International Congress on Engineering Education: Rethinking Engineering Education, The Way Forward, ICEED 2011, Kuala Lumpur, Malaysia, 7–8 December 2011; pp. 71–75. [CrossRef]
7. Anaya, A.R.; Boticario, J.G. Clustering learners according to their collaboration. In Proceedings of the 2009 13th International Conference on Computer Supported Cooperative Work in Design, CSCWD 2009, Santiago, Chile, 22–24 April 2009; pp. 540–545. [CrossRef]
8. Rus, V.; D'Mello, S.; Hu, X.; Graesser, A.C. Recent advances in conversational intelligent tutoring systems. *AI Mag.* **2013**, *34*, 42–54. [CrossRef]
9. Zhang, H.; Magooda, A.; Litman, D.; Correnti, R.; Wang, E.; Matsmura, L.C.; Howe, E.; Quintana, R. eRevise: Using natural language processing to provide formative feedback on text evidence usage in student writing. In Proceedings of the AAAI Conference on Artificial Intelligence, Honolulu, HI, USA, 27 January–1 February 2019; Volume 33, pp. 9619–9625.
10. Hamdi, M.S. MASACAD: A multi-agent approach to information customization for the purpose of academic advising of students. *Appl. Soft Comput. J.* **2007**, *7*, 746–771. [CrossRef]
11. Kolb, D.A. *Experiential Learning: Experience as the Source of Learning and Development*; Prentice Hall: Englewood Cliffs, NJ, USA, 1984.
12. Dascalu, M.D.; Ruseti, S.; Dascalu, M.; McNamara, D.S.; Carabas, M.; Rebedea, T.; Trausan-Matu, S. Before and during COVID-19: A Cohesion Network Analysis of Students' Online Participation in Moodle Courses. *Comput. Hum. Behav.* **2021**, *121*, 106780. [CrossRef]
13. Stahl, G. *Group Cognition. Computer Support for Building Collaborative Knowledge*; MIT Press: Cambridge, MA, USA, 2006.
14. Blanco, M.; Gonzalez, C.; Sanchez-Lite, A.; Sebastian, M.A. A practical evaluation of a collaborative learning method for engineering project subjects. *IEEE Access* **2017**, *5*, 19363–19372. [CrossRef]
15. Trausan-Matu, S. Computer support for creativity in small groups using chats. *Ann. Acad. Rom. Sci. Ser. Sci. Technol. Inf.* **2010**, *3*, 81–90.
16. Trausan-Matu, S. The polyphonic model of collaborative learning. In *The Routledge International Handbook of Research on Dialogic Education*; Mercer, N., Wegerif, R., Major, L., Eds.; Routledge: London, UK, 2019; pp. 454–468.
17. Holmer, T.; Kienle, A.; Wessner, M. Explicit referencing in learning chats: Needs and acceptance. *Innov. Approaches Learn. Knowl. Shar. Proc.* **2006**, *4227*, 170–184. [CrossRef]
18. Masala, M.; Ruseti, S.; Rebedea, T. Sentence selection with neural networks using string kernels. *Procedia Comput. Sci.* **2017**, *112*, 1774–1782. [CrossRef]
19. Rajpurkar, P.; Zhang, J.; Lopyrev, K.; Liang, P. SQuAD: 100,000+ Questions for Machine Comprehension of Text. In Proceedings of the 2016 Conference on Empirical Methods in Natural Language Processing, Austin, TX, USA, 1–5 November 2016; pp. 2383–2392.
20. Shen, G.; Yang, Y.; Deng, Z.H. Inter-Weighted Alignment Network for Sentence Pair Modeling. In Proceedings of the 2017 Conference on Empirical Methods in Natural Language Processing, Copenhagen, Denmark, 9–11 September 2017; pp. 1179–1189.
21. dos Santos, C.; Tan, M.; Xiang, B.; Zhou, B. Attentive Pooling Networks. *CoRR* **2016**, *2*, 4.
22. Yu, L.; Hermann, K.M.; Blunsom, P.; Pulman, S. Deep learning for answer sentence selection. *arXiv* **2014**, arXiv:1412.1632.
23. Masala, M.; Ruseti, S.; Gutu-Robu, G.; Rebedea, T.; Dascalu, M.; Trausan-Matu, S. Help Me Understand This Conversation: Methods of Identifying Implicit Links Between CSCL Contributions. In Proceedings of the European Conference on Technology Enhanced Learning, Leeds, UK, 3–6 September 2018; Springer: Cham, Switzerland, 2018; pp. 482–496. [CrossRef]
24. Masala, M.; Ruseti, S.; Gutu-Robu, G.; Rebedea, T.; Dascalu, M.; Trausan-Matu, S. Identifying implicit links in CSCL chats using string kernels and neural networks. In Proceedings of the International Conference on Artificial Intelligence in Education, London, UK, 27–30 June 2018; Springer: Cham, Switzerland, 2018; pp. 204–208. [CrossRef]
25. Gutu, G.; Dascalu, M.; Rebedea, T.; Trausan-Matu, S. Time and Semantic Similarity—What is the Best Alternative to Capture Implicit Links in CSCL Conversations? In Proceedings of the 12th International Conference on Computer Supported Collaborative Learning (CSCL), Philadelphia, PA, USA, 18–22 June 2017; pp. 223–230.
26. Gutu, G.; Dascalu, M.; Ruseti, S.; Rebedea, T.; Trausan-Matu, S. Unlocking the Power of Word2Vec for Identifying Implicit Links. In Proceedings of the IEEE 17th International Conference on Advanced Learning Technologies, ICALT 2017, Timisoara, Romania, 3–7 July 2017; pp. 199–200. [CrossRef]
27. Miller, G.A. WordNet: A lexical database for English. *Commun. ACM* **1995**, *38*, 39–41. [CrossRef]
28. Wu, Z.; Palmer, M. Verb Semantics and Lexical Selection. In Proceedings of the 32nd Annual Meeting on Association for Computational Linguistics, Las Cruces, NM, USA, 27–30 June 1994; pp. 133–138. [CrossRef]

29. Leacock, C.; Chodorow, M. Combining Local Context and WordNet Similarity for Word Sense Identification. In *WordNet: An Electronic Lexical Database*; Fellbaum, C., Ed.; MIT Press: Cambridge MA, USA, 1998; pp. 265–283.

30. Landauer, T.K.; Dumais, S.T. A solution to Plato's problem: The Latent Semantic Analysis Theory of Acquisition, Induction, and Representation of Knowledge. *Psychol. Rev.* **1997**, *104*, 211–240. [CrossRef]

31. Mikolov, T.; Chen, K.; Corrado, G.; Dean, J. Efficient Estimation of Word Representation in Vector Space. In Proceedings of the Workshop at ICLR, Scottsdale, AZ, USA, 2–4 May 2013.

32. Mikolov, T.; Chen, K.; Corrado, G.; Dean, J. Distributed Representations of Words and Phrases and their Compositionality. In *Advances in Neural Information Processing Systems*; Curran Associates Inc.: Red Hook, NY, USA, 2013; pp. 1–9.

33. Pennington, J.; Socher, R.; Manning, C.D. GloVe: Global Vectors for Word Representation. In Proceedings of the 2014 Conference on Empirical Methods in Natural Language Processing, Doha, Qatar, 25–29 October 2014; pp. 1532–1543. [CrossRef]

34. Bojanowski, P.; Grave, E.; Joulin, A.; Mikolov, T. Enriching word vectors with subword information. *Trans. Assoc. Comput. Linguist.* **2017**, *5*, 135–146. [CrossRef]

35. Lodhi, H.; Saunders, C.; Shawe-Taylor, J.; Cristianini, N.; Watkins, C. Text Classification using String Kernels. *J. Mach. Learn. Res.* **2002**, *2*, 419–444. [CrossRef]

36. Ionescu, R.T.; Popescu, M.; Cahill, A. Can characters reveal your native language? A language-independent approach to native language identification. In Proceedings of the 2014 Conference on Empirical Methods in Natural Language Processing (EMNLP), Doha, Qatar, 25–29 October 2014; pp. 1363–1373.

37. Ionescu, R.T.; Popescu, M.; Cahill, A. String Kernels for Native Language Identification: Insights from Behind the Curtains. *Comput. Linguist.* **2016**, *42*, 491–525.

38. Gönen, M.; Alpaydın, E. Multiple Kernel Learning Algorithms. *J. Mach. Learn. Res.* **2011**, *12*, 2211–2268.

39. Beck, D.; Cohn, T. Learning Kernels over Strings using Gaussian Processes. In Proceedings of the Eighth International Joint Conference on Natural Language Processing, Taipei, Taiwan, 27 November–1 December 2017; Volume 2, pp. 67–73.

40. Bachrach, Y.; Zukov-Gregoric, A.; Coope, S.; Tovell, E.; Maksak, B.; Rodriguez, J.; McMurtie, C. An Attention Mechanism for Answer Selection Using a Combined Global and Local View. *arXiv* **2017**, arXiv:1707.01378.

41. Tan, M.; dos Santos, C.; Xiang, B.; Zhou, B. Improved Representation Learning for Question Answer Matching. In Proceedings of the 54th Annual Meeting of the Association for Computational Linguistics, Berlin, Germany, 7–12 August 2016; pp. 464–473.

42. Graves, A.; Schmidhuber, J. Framewise Phoneme Classification with Bidirectional LSTM and Other Neural Network Architectures. *Neural Netw.* **2005**, *18*, 602–610. [CrossRef] [PubMed]

43. Kim, Y. Convolutional Neural Networks for Sentence Classification. In Proceedings of the 2014 Conference on Empirical Methods in Natural Language Processing (EMNLP 2014), Doha, Qatar, 25–29 October 2014; pp. 1746–1751.

44. Luong, M.T.; Pham, H.; Manning, C.D. Effective approaches to attention-based neural machine translation. In Proceedings of the Conference on Empirical Methods in Natural Language Processing, Lisbon, Portugal, 17–21 September 2015; pp. 1412–1421.

45. Bahdanau, D.; Cho, K.; Bengio, Y. Neural Machine Translation by Jointly Learning to Align and Translate. In Proceedings of the 3rd International Conference on Learning Representations, ICLR 2015, San Diego, CA, USA, 7–9 May 2015.

46. Wang, S.; Jiang, J. A Compare-Aggregate Model for Matching Text Sequences. *arXiv* **2016**, arXiv:1611.01747.

47. Vaswani, A.; Shazeer, N.; Parmar, N.; Uszkoreit, J.; Jones, L.; Gomez, A.N.; Kaiser, L.; Polosukhin, I. Attention Is All You Need. In *Advances in Neural Information Processing Systems*; Curran Associates Inc.: Red Hook, NY, USA, 2017; pp. 5998–6008. [CrossRef]

48. Devlin, J.; Chang, M.W.; Lee, K.; Toutanova, K. BERT: Pre-training of Deep Bidirectional Transformers for Language Understanding. In Proceedings of the 2019 Conference of the North American Chapter of the Association for Computational Linguistics: Human Language Technologies, NAACL-HLT 2019, Minneapolis, MN, USA, 2–7 June 2019; pp. 4171–4186.

49. Radford, A.; Narasimhan, K.; Salimans, T.; Sutskever, I. *Improving Language Understanding by Generative Pre-Training*; Technical Report; OpenAI: San Francisco, CA, USA, 2018.

50. Radford, A.; Wu, J.; Child, R.; Luan, D.; Amodei, D.; Sutskever, I. *Language Models Are Unsupervised Multitask Learners*; Technical Report; OpenAI: San Francisco, CA, USA, 2019.

51. Liu, Y.; Ott, M.; Goyal, N.; Du, J.; Joshi, M.; Chen, D.; Levy, O.; Lewis, M.; Zettlemoyer, L.; Stoyanov, V. RoBERTa: A Robustly Optimized BERT Pretraining Approach. *arXiv* **2019**, arXiv:1907.11692.

52. Yang, Z.; Dai, Z.; Yang, Y.; Carbonell, J.; Salakhutdinov, R.; Le, Q.V. XLNet: Generalized Autoregressive Pretraining for Language Understanding. In Proceedings of the Advances in Neural Information Processing Systems 32: Annual Conference on Neural Information Processing Systems, NeurIPS 2019, Vancouver, BC, Canada, 8–14 December 2019; pp. 5754–5764.

53. Lan, Z.; Chen, M.; Goodman, S.; Gimpel, K.; Sharma, P.; Soricut, R. ALBERT: A Lite BERT for Self-supervised Learning of Language Representations. In Proceedings of the 8th International Conference on Learning Representations, ICLR 2020, Addis Ababa, Ethiopia, 26–30 April 2020.

54. Trausan-Matu, S.; Rebedea, T. A polyphonic model and system for inter-animation analysis in chat conversations with multiple participants. In Proceedings of the International Conference on Intelligent Text Processing and Computational Linguistics, Iasi, Romania, 21–27 March 2010; Springer: Berlin/Heidelberg, Germany, 2010; Volume 6008, pp. 354–363. [CrossRef]

55. Elsner, M.; Charniak, E. Disentangling chat. *Comput. Linguist.* **2010**, *36*, 389–409. [CrossRef]

56. Jiang, J.Y.; Chen, F.; Chen, Y.Y.; Wang, W. Learning to disentangle interleaved conversational threads with a siamese hierarchical network and similarity ranking. In Proceedings of the 2018 Conference of the North American Chapter of the Association for Computational Linguistics: Human Language Technologies, Volume 1 (Long Papers), New Orleans, LA, USA, 1–6 June 2018; pp. 1812–1822.

57. Liu, H.; Shi, Z.; Gu, J.C.; Liu, Q.; Wei, S.; Zhu, X. End-to-End Transition-Based Online Dialogue Disentanglement. In Proceedings of the Twenty-Ninth International Joint Conference on Artificial Intelligence, IJCAI-20, Yokohama, Japan, 7–15 January 2020; pp. 3868–3874.

58. Li, T.; Gu, J.C.; Zhu, X.; Liu, Q.; Ling, Z.H.; Su, Z.; Wei, S. DialBERT: A Hierarchical Pre-Trained Model for Conversation Disentanglement. *arXiv* **2020**, arXiv:2004.03760.

59. Hochreiter, S.; Schmidhuber, J. Long Short-Term Memory. *Neural Comput.* **1997**, *9*, 1735–1780. [CrossRef]

60. Mehri, S.; Carenini, G. Chat Disentanglement: Identifying Semantic Reply Relationships with Random Forests and Recurrent Neural Networks. In Proceedings of the International Joint Conference on Natural Language Processing (IJCNLP2017), Taipei, Taiwan, 27 November–1 December 2017; pp. 615–623.

61. Searle, J.R. *Speech Acts*; Cambridge University Press: Cambridge, UK, 1969. [CrossRef]

62. Moldovan, C.; Rus, V.; Graesser, A.C. Automated Speech Act Classification for Online Chat. *MAICS* **2011**, *710*, 23–29.

63. Rus, V.; Maharjan, N.; Tamang, L.J.; Yudelson, M.; Berman, S.R.; Fancsali, S.E.; Ritter, S. An Analysis of Human Tutors' Actions in Tutorial Dialogues. In Proceedings of the International Florida Artificial Intelligence Research Society Conference (FLAIRS 2017), Marco Island, FL, USA, 22–24 May 2017; pp. 122–127.

64. Stahl, G. *Studying Virtual Math Teams*; Springer Science & Business Media: New York, NY, USA, 2009.

65. Kingma, D.; Ba, J. Adam: A method for stochastic optimization. In Proceedings of the 3rd International Conference for Learning Representations, San Diego, CA, USA, 7–9 May 2015. [CrossRef]

66. Hu, B.; Lu, Z. Convolutional Neural Network Architectures for Matching Natural Language Sentences. In *Advances in Neural Information Processing Systems*; MIT Press: Cambridge, MA, USA, 2014; pp. 1–9.

67. Lowe, R.; Pow, N.; Serban, I.; Pineau, J. The ubuntu dialogue corpus: A large dataset for research in unstructured multi-turn dialogue systems. *arXiv* **2015**, arXiv:1506.08909.

68. Breiman, L. Random Forests. *Mach. Learn.* **2001**, *45*, 5–32. [CrossRef]

 *mathematics*

MDPI

*Article*

# Definition Extraction from Generic and Mathematical Domains with Deep Ensemble Learning

Natalia Vanetik *,† and Marina Litvak *,†

Software Engineering Department, Shamoon College of Engineering, Bialik 56, Beer Sheva 8434231, Israel
* Correspondence: natalyav@sce.ac.il (N.V.); marinal@ac.sce.ac.il (M.L.)
† These authors contributed equally to this work.

**Abstract:** Definitions are extremely important for efficient learning of new materials. In particular, mathematical definitions are necessary for understanding mathematics-related areas. Automated extraction of definitions could be very useful for automated indexing educational materials, building taxonomies of relevant concepts, and more. For definitions that are contained within a single sentence, this problem can be viewed as a binary classification of sentences into definitions and non-definitions. In this paper, we focus on automatic detection of one-sentence definitions in mathematical and general texts. We experiment with different classification models arranged in an ensemble and applied to a sentence representation containing syntactic and semantic information, to classify sentences. Our ensemble model is applied to the data adjusted with oversampling. Our experiments demonstrate the superiority of our approach over state-of-the-art methods in both general and mathematical domains.

**Keywords:** definition extraction; deep learning; ensemble; mathematical domain

**Citation:** Vanetik, N.; Litvak, M. Definition Extraction from Generic and Mathematical Domains with Deep Ensemble Learning. *Mathematics* **2021**, *9*, 2502. https://doi.org/10.3390/math9192502

Academic Editors: Cornelia Caragea and Florentina Hristea

Received: 1 September 2021
Accepted: 1 October 2021
Published: 6 October 2021

**Publisher's Note:** MDPI stays neutral with regard to jurisdictional claims in published maps and institutional affiliations.

## 1. Introduction

Definitions play a very important role in scientific and educational literature because they define the major concepts that are operated inside the text. Despite mathematical and generic definitions being pretty similar in their linguistic style (see the example of two definitions below: the first, defining ASCII, is general, while the second defines mathematical object), supervised identification of mathematical definitions benefits from a training on a mathematical domain, as we previously showed in [1].

**Definition 1.** *American Standard Code for Information Interchange, also called ASCII, is a character encoding based on English alphabet.*

**Definition 2.** *The magnitude of a number, also called its absolute value, is its distance from zero.*

Naturally, we expect to find mathematical definitions in mathematical articles, which frequently use formulas and notations in both definitions and surrounding text. The number of words in mathematical text is smaller than in standard text due to the formulas that are used to express the former. The mere presence of formulas is not a good indicator of a definition sentence because the surrounding sentences may also use notations and formulas. As an example of such text, Definition 3, below, contains a definition from Wolfram MathWorld. Only the first sentence in this text is considered a definition sentence, even though other sentences also contain mathematical notations.

**Definition 3.** *A finite field is a field with a finite field order (i.e., number of elements), also called a Galois field. The order of a finite field is always a prime or a power of a prime. For each prime power, there exists exactly one (with the usual caveat that "exactly one" means "exactly one up to an isomorphism") finite field $GF(p^n)$, often written as $\mathbb{F}_{p^n}$ in current usage.*

Definition extraction (DE) is a challenging and popular task today, as shown by a recent research call at SemEval-2020 shows (https://competitions.codalab.org/competitions/20900, accessed on 1 September 2021).

Multiple current methods for automatic DE view it as a binary classification task, where a sentence is classified as a definition or a non-definition. A supervised learning process is usually applied for this task, employing feature engineering for sentence representation. However, all recently published works study generic definitions, without evaluation of their methods on mathematical texts.

In this paper, we describe a supervised learning method for automatic DE from both generic and mathematical texts. Our method applies ensemble learning to adjusted-by-oversampling data, where 12 deep neural network-based models are trained on a dataset with labeled definitions and then applied on test sentences. The final label of a sentence is decided by the ensemble voting.

Our method is evaluated on four different corpora; three for generic DE and one is an annotated corpus of mathematical definitions.

The main contributions of this paper are (1) the introduction of a new corpus of mathematical texts with annotated sentences and (2) an evaluation of an ensemble learning model for the DE task, (3) an evaluation of the introduced ensemble learning model on a general and mathematical domains, including (4) cross-domain experiments. We performed extensive experiments with different ensemble models on four datasets, including the introduced one. Our experiments demonstrate the superiority of our model for the three out of four datasets, belonging to two different domains. The paper is organized as follows. Section 2 contains a survey of up-to-date related work. Section 3 describes our approach. Section 4 provides the evaluation results and their analysis. Finally, Section 5 contains our conclusions.

## 2. Related Work

Definition extraction has been a popular topic in NLP research for more than a decade [2], and it remains a challenging and popular task today as a recent research call at SemEval-2020 show. Prior work in the field of DE can be divided into three main categories: (1) rule-based methods, (2) machine-learning methods relying on manual feature engineering, and (3) methods that use deep learning techniques.

Early works about DE from text documents belong to the first category. These works rely mainly on manually crafted rules based on linguistic parameters. Klavans and Muresan [3] presented the DEFINDER, a rule-based system that mines consumer-oriented full text articles to extract definitions and the terms they define; the system is evaluated on definitions from on-line dictionaries such as the UMLS Metathesaurus [4]. Xu et al. [2] used various linguistic tools to extract kernel facts for the definitional question-answering task in Text REtrieval Conference (TREC) 2003. Malaise et al. [5] used semantic relations to mine defining expressions in domain-specific corpora, thus detecting semantic relations between the main terms in definitions. This work is evaluated on corpora from fields of anthropology and dietetics. Saggion and Gaizauskas [6], Saggion [7] employed analysis of on-line sources to find lists of relevant secondary terms that frequently occur together with the definiendum in definition-bearing passages. Storrer and Wellinghoff [8] proposed a system that automatically detects and annotates definitions for technical terms in German text corpora. Their approach focuses on verbs that typically appear in definitions by specifying search patterns based on the valency frames of definitor verbs. Borg et al. [9] extracted definitions from nontechnical texts using genetic programming to learn the typical linguistic forms of definitions and then using a genetic algorithm to learn the relative importance of these forms. Most of these methods suffer from both low recall and precision (below 70%), because definition sentences occur in highly variable and noisy syntactic structures.

The second category of DE algorithms relies on semi-supervised and supervised machine learning that use semantic and other features to extract definitions. This approach generates DE rules automatically but relies on feature engineering to do so. Fahmi and Bouma [10] presented an approach to learning concept definitions from fully parsed text with a maximum entropy classifier incorporating various syntactic features; they tested this approach on a subcorpus of the Dutch version of Wikipedia. In [11], a pattern-based glossary candidate detector, which is capable of extracting definitions in eight languages, was presented. Westerhout [12] described a combined approach that first filters corpus with a definition-oriented grammar, and then applies machine learning to improve the results obtained with the grammar. The proposed algorithm was evaluated on a collection of Dutch texts about computing and e-learning. Navigli and Velardi [13] used Word-Class Lattices (WCLs), a generalization of word lattices, to model textual definitions. The authors introduced a new dataset called WCL that was used for the experiments. They achieved a 75.23% F1 score on this dataset. Reiplinger et al. [14] compared lexico-syntactic pattern bootstrapping and deep analysis. The manual rating experiment suggested that the concept of definition quality in a specialized domain is largely subjective, with a 0.65 agreement score between raters. The DefMiner system, proposed in [15], used Conditional Random Fields (CRF) to predict the function of a word and to determine whether this word is a part of a definition. The system was evaluated on a W00 dataset [15], which is a manually annotated subset of ACL Anthology Reference Corpus (ACL ARC) ontology. Boella and Di Caro [16] proposed a technique that only uses syntactic dependencies between terms extracted with a syntactic parser and then transforms syntactic contexts to abstract representations to use a Support Vector Machine (SVM). Anke et al. [17] proposed a weakly supervised bootstrapping approach for identifying textual definitions with higher linguistic variability. Anke and Saggion [18] presented a supervised approach to DE in which only syntactic features derived from dependency relations are used.

Algorithms in the third category use Deep Learning (DL) techniques for DE, often incorporating syntactic features into the network structure. Li et al. [19] used Long Short-Term Memory (LSTM) and word vectors to identify definitions and then tested this approach on the English and Chinese texts. Their method achieved a 91.2% F-measure on the WCL dataset. Anke and Schockaert [20] combined Convolutional Neural Network (CNN) and LSTM, based on syntactic features and word vector representation of sentences. Their experiments showed the best F1 score (94.2%) on the WCL dataset for CNN and the best F1 score (57.4%) on the W00 dataset for the CNN and Bidirectional LSTM (BLSTM) combination, both with syntactically enriched sentence representation. Word embedding, when used as the input representation, have been shown to boost the performance in many NLP tasks, due to its ability to encode semantics. We believe that a choice to use word vectors as input representation in many DE works was motivated by its success in NLP-related classification tasks.

We use the approach of [20] as a starting point and as a baseline for our method. We further extend this work by (1) additional syntactic knowledge in a sentence representation model, (2) testing additional network architectures, (3) combining 12 configurations (that were the result of different input representations and architectures) in a joint ensemble model, and (4) evaluation of the proposed methodology on a new dataset of mathematical texts. As previously shown in our and others' works [1,20], dependency parsing can add valuable features to the sentence representation in the DE task, including mathematical DE. The same works showed that a standard convolutional layer can be sufficiently applied to automatically extract the most significant features from the extended representation model, which improves accuracy for the classification task. Word embedding matrices enhanced with dependency information naturally call for CNN due to their size and CNN's ability to decrease dimensionality swiftly. On the other hand, sentences are sequences for which LSTM is naturally suitable. In [1], we explored how the order of the CNN and LSTM layers and the input representation affect the results. To do that, we evaluated and compared between 12 configurations (see Section 3.3). As result, we obtained a conclusion that CNN and its combination with LSTM, applied on a syntactically enriched input representation, outperform other configurations. However, as we show in our experimental evaluation (see Section 4), all the models individually are inferior to the ensemble approach.

Following recent research demonstrating the superiority of pretrained language models on many NLP tasks, including DE [21,22], we apply fine-tuned BERT [23,24] on our data and compare its results with the results of the proposed method.

### 3. Method

This section describes out method, including representation of input sentences, individual composition models, and their combination through ensemble learning.

### 3.1. Sentence Representation

First, we generate a sentence matrix from word vectors of its words as follows. Every word $w$ is represented by its $k = 300$-dimensional word vector $\vec{w}$ [25], and all sentences are assumed as having the same length $n$, using zero padding where necessary; as a result, we obtain a sentence matrix denoted by $S_{n \times k}$.

Then, we generate the following three syntactically enriched representations:

1. **(m)**—an extension of matrix $S_{n \times k}$ with the dependency information, where a dependency is represented by the average of word vectors of the two words participating in it as:

$$m = S_{n \times k} \circ [\vec{r_{ij}}^{avg}]_{ij}$$

2. **(ml)**—an extension of (m) with one-hot encoding of dependency labels between pairs of words [20]; formally, it includes the average of word vectors of dependency words, and dependency label representations as follows:

$$ml = S_{n \times k} \circ [\vec{r_{ij}}^{avg} \circ dep_{ij}]_{ij}$$

3. **(mld)**—it is composed of the full dependency information, including concatenation of word vectors for dependency words, dependency label, and dependency depth. In contrast to the first two representations, (mld) does not contain the matrix $S_{n \times k}$ itself, but only the dependency information as follows:

$$mld = [\vec{w_i} \circ \vec{w_j} \circ dep_{ij} \circ depth_{ij}]_{ij}$$

The dependency representations in the input configurations described above, are depicted in Figure 1. All input vectors are zero-pad to compensate for vector size differences. In all representations we use fastText vectors pretrained on English webcrawl and Wikipedia [26], based on our observation in [1] about superiority of fastText vectors over other pretrained word vectors.

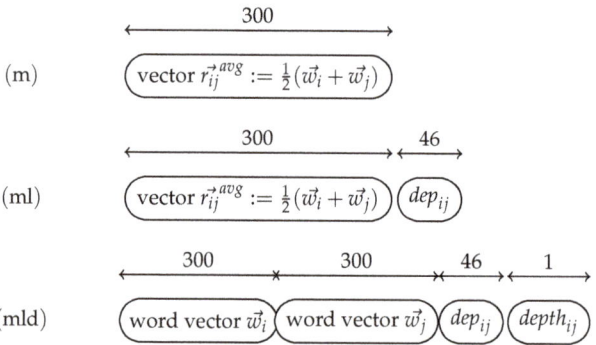

**Figure 1.** Dependency representation for input configurations (m), (ml) and (mld).

### 3.2. Composition NN Models

We use the approach of Anke and Schockaert [20] as a starting point and as a baseline for our method. We further extend this work by additional syntactic knowledge in a sentence representation model, and by additional changes in network architectures, based on [1]. We experiment with two layers: convolutional layer which can help to automatically extract the most significant features before performing the classification task (given big matrices representing sentences with word vectors and syntax features) and Bidirectional LSTM layer which is very suitable for sentences as sequences. We use four neural models:

1.  Pure 2-dimensional CNN model,
2.  Pure Bidirectional LSTM model,
3.  Mixed model with a CNN layer followed by a Bidirectional LSTM layer, denoted by CNN_LSTM (see Figure 2),
4.  Mixed model with a Bidirectional LSTM layer followed by a CNN layer, denoted by LSTM_CNN (see Figure 3).

Every one of those models is used in conjunction with the three sentence representations described in Section 3.1, giving us total of 12 models.

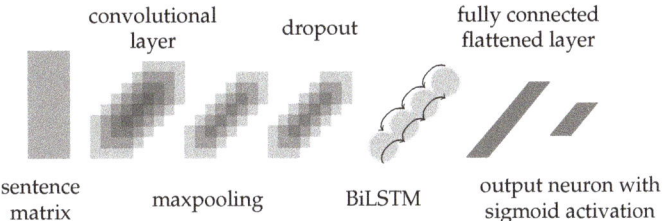

**Figure 2.** CNN_LSTM network architecture.

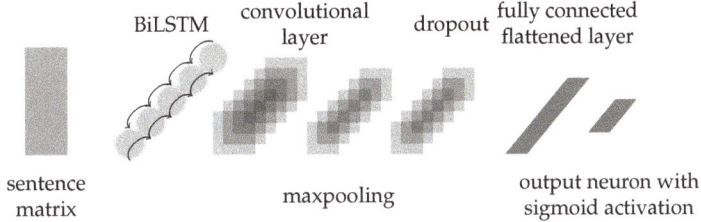

**Figure 3.** LSTM_CNN network architecture.

The intuition behind using mixed models is supported by known benefits of their composition layers—CNN can automatically extract features, while LSTM is a classification model that is context-aware. The experiment, performed in [1], was aimed to examine which order of layers is beneficial for the DE task—first to extract features from the original input and then feed them to the context-aware classifier, or first to calculate hidden states with context-aware LSTM gates and then feed them into CNN classifier for feature extraction before the classification layer. The results demonstrated the superiority of models with a CNN layer, which can be explained by the ability of CNN to learn features and reduce the number of free parameters in a high-dimensional sentence representation, allowing the network to be more accurate with fewer parameters. Due to a high-dimensional input in our task (also in context-aware representation, produced by LSTM gates), this characteristic of CNN appears to be very helpful.

### 3.3. Ensemble Pipeline

Given two basic models, two different combinations of CNN and LSTM layers, and three variations of the sentence representation, we finally obtain 12 different models which are trained and then applied separately on the test sentences. We have applied oversampling with a 'minority' setting to a dataset (It is worth noting that a general practice of changing class weights in all the models did not result in accuracy improvement in our experiments.). To produce a final label for each test sentence, ensemble voting was applied. Figure 4 depicts the pipeline of our approach. We tried different supervised models for ensemble voting, which we describe in the Experiments section. The dataset (denoted as data X in Figure 4) was split in the following manner: 70% and 5% of the dataset was used for training and validation of the individual models, respectively. Then, the trained individual models were applied on 25% of the X data (denoted as Y in Figure 4), while the entire Y data were further split as follows: 5% of the X data (or 20% of Y) were used as a training set and 20% of X (equals to 80% of Y) as a test set for the ensemble model.

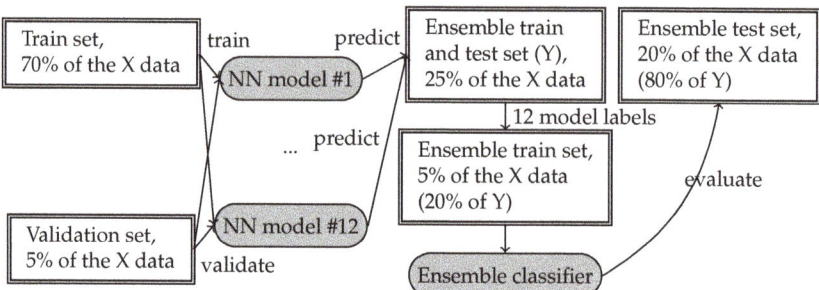

**Figure 4.** Pipeline of our approach for ensemble learning.

To see the advantage of our ensemble approach, we also evaluated every one of the 12 neural models individually on the data after oversampling. The pipeline of individual model evaluation is depicted in Figure 5.

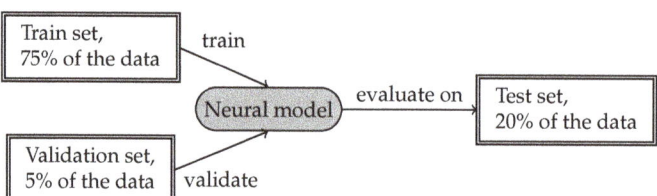

**Figure 5.** Evaluation pipeline for individual NN models.

### 4. Experiments

Our experiments aim at testing our hypothesis about superiority of the ensemble of all 12 composition models over single models and SOTA baselines.

Based on the feature analysis described in Section 4.8, we decided to employ all 12 configurations as composition models and, based on the observations from our previous work [1], we use pretrained fastText (further denoted by FT) word embedding in all of them.

Tests were performed on a cloud server with 32 GB of RAM, 150 GB of PAGE memory, an Intel Core I7-7500U 2.70 GHz CPU, and two NVIDIA GK210GL GPUs.

### 4.1. Tools

The models were implemented with help of the following tools: (1) Stanford CoreNLP wrapper [27] for Python (tokenization, sentence boundary detection, and dependency parsing), (2) Keras [28] with Tensorflow [29] as a back-end (NN models), (3) fastText vectors pretrained on English webcrawl and Wikipedia [26], (4) Scikit-Learn [30] (evaluation with F1, recall, and precision metrics), (5) fine-tunable BERT python package [24] available at https://github.com/strongio/keras-elmo (accessed on 1 September 2021), and (6) WEKA software [31]. All neural models were trained with batch size 32 and 10 epochs.

### 4.2. Datasets

In our work we use the following four datasets–DEFT, W00, WCL, and WFMALL–that are described below. The dataset domain, number of sentences for each class, majority vote values, total number of words, and number of words with non-zero fastText (denoted by FT) word vectors are given in Table 1.

**Table 1.** Dataset statistics.

| Dataset | Domain | Definitions | Non-Definitions | Majority | Words | Covered by FT |
|---------|--------|-------------|-----------------|----------|-------|---------------|
| WCL | General | 1871 | 2847 | 0.603 | 21,297 | 16,645 |
| DEFT | General | 562 | 1156 | 0.673 | 7644 | 7350 |
| W00 | General | 731 | 1454 | 0.665 | 8261 | 7003 |
| WFMALL | Math | 1934 | 4206 | 0.685 | 13,138 | 8238 |

#### 4.2.1. The WCL Dataset

The World-Class Lattices (WCL) dataset [32] was introduced in [33]. It is constructed from manually annotated Wikipedia articles in English. We used the WCL v1.2 version that contains 4719 annotated sentences, 1871 of which are proper definitions and 2847 are *distractor* sentences that have similar structures with proper definitions, but are not actually definitions. This dataset focuses on generic definitions in various areas. A sample definition sentence from this dataset is

*American Standard Code for Information Interchange (TARGET) is a character encoding based on English alphabet.*

and a sample distractor is

*The premise of the program revolves around TARGET, Parker an 18-year-old country girl who moves back and forth between her country family, who lives on a bayou houseboat, and the wealthy Brents, who own a plantation and pancake business.*

WCL contains the following annotations: (1) the DEFINIENDUM field (DF), referring to the word being defined and its modifiers, (2) the DEFINITOR field (VF), referring to the verb phrase used to introduce a definition, (3) the DEFINIENS field (GF) which includes the genus phrase, and (4) the REST field (RF), which indicates all additional sentence parts. According to the dataset description, existence of the first three fields indicates that a sentence is a definition.

#### 4.2.2. The DEFT Dataset

The DEFT corpus, proposed in [34], consists of annotated content from two different data sources: various 2017 SEC contract filings from the publicly available US Securities and Exchange Commission EDGAR (SEC) database, and sentences from the https://cnx.org/ open source textbooks (accessed on 1 September 2021). The partial corpus is available for download from GitHub at https://github.com/adobe-research/deft_corpus (accessed on 1 September 2021). We have used this part of the DEFT corpus in our experiments; it contains 562 definition sentences and 1156 non-definition sentences. A sample definition sentence from this dataset is

*A hallucination is a perceptual experience that occurs in the absence of external stimulation.*

and a sample non-definition sentence is

*In monocots, petals usually number three or multiples of three; in dicots, the number of petals is four or five, or multiples of four and five.*

### 4.2.3. The W00 Dataset

The W00 dataset [35], introduced in [15], was compiled from ACL ARC ontology [36] and contains 2185 manually annotated sentences, with 731 definitions and 1454 non-definitions; the style of the distractors is different from the one used in the WCL dataset. A sample definition sentence from this dataset is

*Our system, SNS (pronounced "essence"), retrieves documents to an unrestricted user query and summarizes a subset of them as selected by the user.*

and a sample distractor is

*The senses with the highest confidence scores are the senses that contribute the most to the function for the set.*

Annotation of the W00 dataset is token-based, with each token in a sentence identified by a single label that indicates whether a token is a part of a term ($T$), a definition ($D$), or neither ($O$). According to the original annotation, a sentence is considered not to be a definition if all its tokens are marked as $O$. Sentence that contains tokens marked as $T$ or $D$ is considered to be a definition.

### 4.2.4. The WFMALL Dataset

The WFMALL dataset is an extension of the WFM dataset [37], introduced by us in [1]. It was created by us after collecting and processing all 2352 articles from Wolfram Mathworld [38]. The final dataset contains 6140 sentences, of which 1934 are definitions and 4206 are non-definitions. Sentences were extracted automatically and then manually separated into two categories: definitions and statements (non-definitions). All annotators (five in total) have at least BSc degree and learned academic mathematical courses (research group members, including three research students). The data were semi-automatically segmented to sentences with Stanford CoreNLP package and then manually assessed. All malformed sentences (as result of wrong segmentation) were fixed, 116 very short sentences (with less than 3 words) were removed. All sentences related to Wolfram Language ( https://en.wikipedia.org/wiki/Wolfram_Language, accessed on 1 September 2021) were removed because they relate to a programming language and describe how mathematical objects are expressed in this language, and not how they are defined. Sentences with formulas only, without text, were also removed. The final dataset was split to nine portions, saved as Unicode text files. Three annotators worked on each portion. First, two annotators labeled sentences independently. Then, all sentences that were given different labels were finally annotated by the third annotator (controller) (We decided that a label with majority vote will be selected. Therefore, the third annotator (controller) labeled only the sentences with contradict labels.). The final label was set by majority vote. The Kappa agreement between annotators was 0.651, which is considered substantial agreement.

This dataset is freely available for download from GitHub (https://drive.google.com/drive/folders/1052akYuxgc2kbHH8tkMw4ikBFafIW0tK?usp=sharing, accessed on 1 September 2021). A sample definition sentence from this dataset is

*The $(7, 3, 2)$-von Dyck group, also sometimes termed the $(2, 3, 7)$-von Dyck group, is defined as the von Dyck group with parameters $(7, 3, 2)$.*

and a sample non-definition is

*Any 2-Engel group must be a group of nilpotency class 3.*

### 4.3. Evaluation Setup

Datasets were oversampled with the 'minority' setting, and split to the NN training set (70%), the NN validation set (5%), and the NN test set (25%). Then the labels of all 12 models on the NN test set were used to form the ensemble dataset, which was further split into the ensemble training set (5% of the original data size) and the ensemble test set

(20% of the original data size). In this setting, we have a test set size identical to those of baselines that used 75% training, 5% validation, and 20% test set split.

For the consistency of the experiment, it was important to us to keep the same training and validation sets for individual models, whether as stand-alone or as composition models in an ensemble. Additionally, all evaluated and compared models, including ensemble, were evaluated on the same test set. Because ensemble models were trained using traditional machine-learning algorithms, no validation set was needed for them.

### 4.4. Text Preprocessing

Regarding all four datasets described above, we applied the same text preprocessing steps in the following manner:

- Sentence splitting was derived explicitly from the datasets, without applying any additional procedure, in the following manner: DEFT, WCL, and W00 datasets came pre-split, and sentence splitting for the new WFMALL dataset was performed semi-automatically by our team (using Stanford CoreNLP SBD, followed by manual correction, due to many formulas in the text).
- Tokenization and dependency parsing were performed on all sentences with the help of the Stanford CoreNLP package [39].
- For the W00 datasets used in [20] for DE, we replaced parsing by SpaCy [40] with the Stanford CoreNLP parser.
- We applied fastText [41] vectors pretrained on English webcrawl and Wikipedia (available at [26]).

### 4.5. Baselines

We compared our results with five baselines:

- DefMiner [15], which uses Conditional Random Fields to detect definition words;
- BERT [23],[24], fine-tuned on the training subset of every dataset for the task of sentence classification;
- CNN_LSTM$_{ml}$, proposed in [20];
- CNN_LSTM$_m$, which is the top-ranked composition model on the adjusted WFMALL dataset.
- CNN_LSTM$_{mld}$, which is the top-ranked composition model on the adjusted W00 dataset.

We applied two supervised models for the ensemble voting: Linear Regression (LR) and Random Forest (RF). The results reported here are the average over 10 runs, with random reshuffling applied to the dataset each time (We did not apply a standard 10-fold cross validation due to a non-standard proportion between a training and a test dataset. Additionally, 10-fold cross validation was not applied on individual models, as it is not a standard evaluation technique for deep NNs.). We also applied the majority voting, denoted as Ensemble majority (Our code will be released once the paper is accepted).

### 4.6. Results for the Mathematical Domain

Table 2 contains the evaluation results (accuracy) for all systems on the WFMALL dataset, with bold font indicating the best scores. It can be seen that (1) oversampling improves performance of NN baselines and (2) all ensemble models outperform the baseline systems and all the individual NN models.

**Table 2.** Final results for the WFMALL dataset.

| Baseline | Oversample | Accuracy |
|---|---|---|
| Fine-tuned BERT | no | 0.760 |
| Fine-tuned BERT | yes | 0.750 |
| CNN_LSTM$_m$ | no | 0.860 |
| CNN_LSTM$_{ml}$ | no | 0.864 |
| CNN_LSTM$_{mld}$ | no | 0.867 |
| DefMiner | N\A | 0.704 |
| **Model** | **Oversample** | **Accuracy** |
| CNN$_m$ | yes | 0.909 |
| CNN$_{ml}$ | yes | 0.913 |
| CNN$_{mld}$ | yes | 0.884 |
| CNN_LSTM$_m$ | yes | **0.922** |
| CNN_LSTM$_{ml}$ | yes | 0.917 |
| CNN_LSTM$_{mld}$ | yes | **0.922** |
| LSTM$_m$ | yes | 0.884 |
| LSTM$_{ml}$ | yes | 0.906 |
| LSTM$_{mld}$ | yes | 0.916 |
| LSTM_CNN$_m$ | yes | 0.901 |
| LSTM_CNN$_{ml}$ | yes | 0.891 |
| LSTM_CNN$_{mld}$ | yes | 0.909 |
| Ensemble majority | yes | 0.925 |
| Ensemble LR | yes | 0.937 |
| Ensemble RF | yes | **0.943** |

*4.7. Results for the General Domain*

To see that our approach may be used for general definitions as well, we have chosen the WCL dataset [15], the W00 dataset [15] and the DEFT dataset [34]. The DefMiner system (used here as one of the baselines) is the system that was first applied to W00, and to this day it produced the best results on it; several systems that were suggested in the literature [1,20,42], were unable to outperform the DefMiner system on W00.

Tables 3–5 contain the evaluation results (accuracy) for all systems on the W00, the DEFT, and the WCL datasets, respectively; the best results are marked in bold. The tables show that (1) oversampling significantly improves performance of NN baselines, resulting in superiority over DefMiner on W00, and (2) the ensemble models (at least one of them) significantly outperform all individual neural models and baselines, including DefMiner and fine-tuned BERT.

The WCL dataset is considered to be an 'easy' dataset with several proposed systems [20,34] reporting accuracy of over 0.98 on this dataset; however, none of the methods suggested in these works achieve similar results on more challenging datasets such as DEFT and W00.

**Table 3.** Final results for the W00 dataset.

| Baseline | Oversample | Accuracy |
|---|---|---|
| Fine-tuned BERT | no | 0.670 |
| Fine-tuned BERT | yes | 0.620 |
| CNN_LSTM$_m$ | no | 0.709 |
| CNN_LSTM$_{ml}$ | no | 0.716 |
| CNN_LSTM$_{mld}$ | no | 0.705 |
| DefMiner | N\A | 0.819 |

**Table 3.** *Cont.*

| Model | Oversample | Accuracy |
|---|---|---|
| $CNN_m$ | yes | 0.828 |
| $CNN_{ml}$ | yes | 0.825 |
| $CNN_{mld}$ | yes | 0.825 |
| $CNN\_LSTM_m$ | yes | 0.817 |
| $CNN\_LSTM_{ml}$ | yes | 0.799 |
| $CNN\_LSTM_{mld}$ | yes | 0.839 |
| $LSTM_m$ | yes | 0.785 |
| $LSTM_{ml}$ | yes | 0.783 |
| $LSTM_{mld}$ | yes | 0.812 |
| $LSTM\_CNN_m$ | yes | 0.772 |
| $LSTM\_CNN_{ml}$ | yes | 0.791 |
| $LSTM\_CNN_{mld}$ | yes | 0.783 |
| Ensemble majority | yes | **0.879** |
| Ensemble LR | yes | 0.850 |
| Ensemble RF | yes | 0.854 |

**Table 4.** Final results for the DEFT dataset.

| Baseline | Oversample | Accuracy |
|---|---|---|
| Fine-tuned BERT | no | 0.670 |
| Fine-tuned BERT | yes | 0.670 |
| $CNN\_LSTM_m$ | no | 0.719 |
| $CNN\_LSTM_{ml}$ | no | 0.732 |
| $CNN\_LSTM_{mld}$ | no | 0.717 |
| DefMiner | N\A | 0.710 |

| Model | Oversample | Accuracy |
|---|---|---|
| $CNN_m$ | yes | 0.826 |
| $CNN_{ml}$ | yes | 0.819 |
| $CNN_{mld}$ | yes | 0.853 |
| $CNN\_LSTM_m$ | yes | 0.850 |
| $CNN\_LSTM_{ml}$ | yes | 0.839 |
| $CNN\_LSTM_{mld}$ | yes | 0.832 |
| $LSTM_m$ | yes | 0.801 |
| $LSTM_{ml}$ | yes | 0.786 |
| $LSTM_{mld}$ | yes | 0.824 |
| $LSTM\_CNN_m$ | yes | 0.789 |
| $LSTM\_CNN_{ml}$ | yes | 0.824 |
| $LSTM\_CNN_{mld}$ | yes | 0.822 |
| Ensemble majority | yes | **0.867** |
| Ensemble LR | yes | 0.850 |
| Ensemble RF | yes | 0.846 |

**Table 5.** Final results for the WCL dataset.

| Baseline | Oversample | Accuracy |
|---|---|---|
| Fine-tuned BERT | no | 0.94 |
| Fine-tuned BERT | yes | 0.95 |
| $CNN\_LSTM_m$ | no | 0.948 |
| $CNN\_LSTM_{ml}$ | no | 0.947 |
| $CNN\_LSTM_{mld}$ | no | 0.945 |
| DefMiner | N\A | 0.797 |

**Table 5.** *Cont.*

| Model | Oversample | Accuracy |
|---|---|---|
| $CNN_m$ | yes | 0.955 |
| $CNN_{ml}$ | yes | 0.965 |
| $CNN_{mld}$ | yes | 0.958 |
| $CNN\_LSTM_m$ | yes | 0.964 |
| $CNN\_LSTM_{ml}$ | yes | 0.965 |
| $CNN\_LSTM_{mld}$ | yes | 0.956 |
| $LSTM_m$ | yes | 0.950 |
| $LSTM_{ml}$ | yes | 0.950 |
| $LSTM_{mld}$ | yes | 0.959 |
| $LSTM\_CNN_m$ | yes | 0.953 |
| $LSTM\_CNN_{ml}$ | yes | 0.950 |
| $LSTM\_CNN_{mld}$ | yes | 0.957 |
| Ensemble majority | yes | **0.972** |
| Ensemble LR | yes | 0.963 |
| Ensemble RF | yes | **0.972** |

### 4.8. Cross-Domain Results

We also conducted a cross-domain analysis using the best individual neural models and ensemble models for every dataset in the mathematical and the general domains (Table 6); the best scores are marked in bold.

The individual models were trained on data set X and tested on dataset Y, with X coming from one domain and Y from another, as depicted in Figure 6. In this case, we selected the individual neural model that was the most successful for the training dataset.

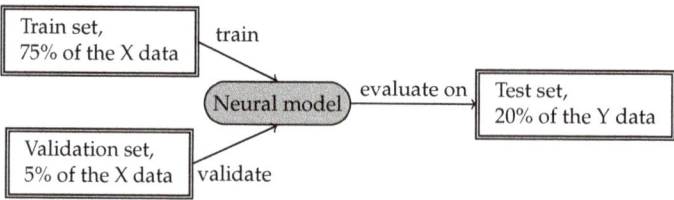

**Figure 6.** Pipeline of cross-domain evaluation of individual NN models for X (training) → Y (test) datasets.

For the ensemble evaluation, we trained all 12 models and the ensemble classifier using the same pipeline as in Section 3.3 on the training set (denoted as Dataset X in Figure 7). Then, these 12 models produce the labels for both 5% of the Dataset X (20% from its test set that is used for training ensemble weights) and 20% of the Dataset Y (its entire test set). The ensemble model is trained on 5% of the Dataset X and applied on 20% of the Dataset Y, using labels produced by 12 trained individual models.

To make this process fully compatible to an in-domain testing procedure (depicted in Figures 4 and 5), we used the same dataset splits both for evaluation of individual models (see Figure 6) and for evaluation of ensemble models (see Figure 7).

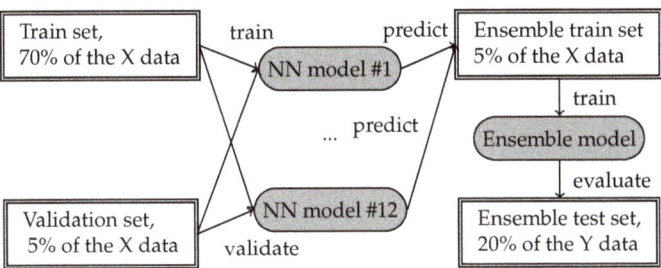

**Figure 7.** Pipeline of ensemble cross-domain evaluation for X (training) → Y (test) datasets.

**Table 6.** Cross-domain tests.

| Training→Test | Model | Resampling | Accuracy |
|---|---|---|---|
| WCL→WFMALL | CNN_LSTM$_{ml}$ | yes | **0.754** |
| | Ensemble LR | yes | 0.633 |
| | Ensemble RF | yes | 0.661 |
| | Ensemble majority | yes | 0.656 |
| W00→WFMALL | CNN_LSTM$_{mld}$ | yes | 0.575 |
| | Ensemble LR | yes | 0.638 |
| | Ensemble RF | yes | 0.651 |
| | Ensemble majority | yes | **0.664** |
| DEFT→WFMALL | CNN$_{ml}$ | yes | **0.761** |
| | Ensemble LR | yes | 0.581 |
| | Ensemble RF | yes | 0.592 |
| | Ensemble majority | yes | 0.620 |
| WFMALL→WCL | CNN_LSTM$_m$ | yes | **0.832** |
| | Ensemble LR | yes | 0.608 |
| | Ensemble RF | yes | 0.590 |
| | Ensemble majority | yes | 0.601 |
| WFMALL→W00 | CNN_LSTM$_m$ | yes | 0.700 |
| | Ensemble LR | yes | 0.666 |
| | Ensemble RF | yes | 0.691 |
| | Ensemble majority | yes | **0.709** |
| WFMALL→DEFT | CNN_LSTM$_m$ | yes | **0.738** |
| | Ensemble LR | yes | 0.605 |
| | Ensemble RF | yes | 0.634 |
| | Ensemble majority | yes | 0.659 |

As we can see from Table 6, all cases where the training set comes from one domain and the test set is from another domain produce the significantly lower accuracy than that reported in Tables 2–5. This is a testament to the fact that general definition domain and mathematical domain are quite different.

### 4.9. Parameter Selection and Evaluation

Our work aimed to evaluate the effect of syntactic information for the task of definition extraction. The prior work [20] in this field has demonstrated that relying on the word information alone (such as word embedding) does not produce good results. Furthermore, classification accuracy depends heavily on the dataset—higher accuracy scores are achieved on the WCL dataset [32] by methods in [20] and [1] because both the word embeddings used for the task and the data originate in Wikipedia. On other datasets such as DEFT, W00, and our WFMALL accuracy scores of individual models (see Tables 2–5) are significantly lower.

To combat this situation, we experimented with different neural models and their parameters, such as the number of layers, type of layers, learning rate, and so on. However, the classification accuracy was only slightly affected by the change in these parameters—for instance, increasing the number of training epochs above 15 did not improve the scores at all. The final parameters we used for our neural models appear in Table 7.

**Table 7.** NN parameters for the individual models.

| Parameter | Value (s) |
|---|---|
| learning rate | 0.01 (default) |
| number of layers and neurons | one convolutional layer for the CNN and CNN_LSTM, one bidirectional LSTM layer for LSTM and LSTM_CNN |
| activation | sigmoid for the last layer, ReLU for the other layers |
| loss | binary_crossentropy |
| regularization | 0.01 for all regularization parameters |
| optimizer | Adam |
| dropout | 0.5 |

Furthermore, we incorporated syntactic information into our models using input representations depicted in Figure 1. However, we observed that individual models rank differently on different datasets, and there is no clear advantage in using one specific syntactic representation because such a selection does not translate well across datasets. Therefore, we decided to use the ensemble model to compensate for variation in the data, and to use resampling to balance the data.

To analyze the importance and necessity of composition models in our ensemble, we performed feature selection by evaluating the information gain of labels produced by each model. The results are shown in Table 8 for the four datasets; the highest ranking attributes are shown in bold. As can be seen, with one exception per dataset, all models with the first or only CNN layer are ranked higher than other models. As such, we can conclude that models that use CNN as their first layer are more successful and have higher influence on the ensemble scores, but their exact influence also depends on a dataset. However, feature backward elimination showed that all 12 models are necessary and produce the best accuracy in ensemble. Eliminating individual models one by one from the ensemble produced less accurate ensemble models.

**Table 8.** Information gain rankings for individual models within the ensemble model.

| Model | WFMALL | W00 | DEFT | WCL |
|---|---|---|---|---|
| $CNN_m$ | 0.585 | 0.349 | 0.349 | 0.735 |
| $CNN_{ml}$ | 0.594 | 0.341 | 0.341 | 0.781 |
| $CNN_{mld}$ | 0.529 | **0.423** | **0.423** | 0.748 |
| $CNN\_LSTM_m$ | **0.625** | 0.393 | 0.393 | 0.780 |
| $CNN\_LSTM_{ml}$ | 0.606 | 0.368 | 0.368 | **0.782** |
| $CNN\_LSTM_{mld}$ | 0.609 | 0.362 | 0.362 | 0.741 |
| $LSTM_m$ | 0.507 | 0.296 | 0.269 | 0.714 |
| $LSTM_{ml}$ | 0.557 | 0.269 | 0.296 | 0.718 |
| $LSTM_{mld}$ | 0.584 | 0.328 | 0.328 | 0.755 |
| $LSTM\_CNN_m$ | 0.549 | 0.285 | 0.285 | 0.726 |
| $LSTM\_CNN_{ml}$ | 0.538 | 0.346 | 0.346 | 0.715 |
| $LSTM\_CNN_{mld}$ | 0.576 | 0.338 | 0.338 | 0.746 |

*4.10. Error Analysis*

We tried to understand which sentences represented difficult cases for our models. During annotation process, we found that multiple sentences were assigned different labels by different annotators. Finally, the label for such sentences was decided by majority voting, but all annotators agreed that the decision was not unambiguous. Based on our observation and manual analysis, we believe that most of the false positive and false negative cases were created by such sentences. We categorized these sentences to the following cases:

1.   Sentences describing properties of a mathematical object. Example (annotated (gold standard label = "definition") as *definition*):

*An extremum may be local ( a.k.a. a relative extremum); an extremum in a given region which is not the overall maximum or minimum ) or global.*

We did not instruct our annotators regarding labeling this sentence type and let them make decisions based on their knowledge and intuition. As result, this sentence type received different labels from different annotators.

2. Sentences providing alternative naming of a known (and previously defined) mathematical object. Example (annotated as *non-definition*):

   *Exponential growth is common in physical processes such as population growth in the absence of predators or resource restrictions (where a slightly more general form is known as the law of growth).*

We received the same decisions and the same outcomes in our dataset with this sentence type as with type (1).

3. Formulations—sentences that define some mathematical object by a formula (in contrast to a verbal definition, that explains the object's meaning). Example (annotated as *non-definition*):

   l *Formulas expressing trigonometric functions of an angle 2x in terms of functions of an angle x, sin(2x) = [FORMULA].*

If both definition and formulation sentences for the same object were provided, our annotators usually assigned them different labels. However, rarely a mathematical object can be only defined by a formula. Additionally, sometimes it can be defined by both, but the verbal definition is not provided in an analyzed article. In such cases, annotators assigned the "definition" label to the formulation sentence.

4. Sentences that are parts of a multi-sentence definition. Example (annotated as *non-definition*):

   *This polyhedron is known as the dual, or reciprocal.*

We instructed our annotators not to assign "definition" label to sentences that do not contain comprehensive information about a defined object. However, some sentences were still annotated as "definition", especially when they appear in a sequence.

5. Descriptions—sentences that describe mathematical objects but do not define them unequivocally. Example (annotated as *non-definition*):

   *A dragon curve is a recursive non-intersecting curve whose name derives from its resemblance to a certain mythical creature.*

Although this sentence resembles a legitimate definition (grammatically), it was labeled as non-definition because its claim does not hold in both directions (not every recursive non-intersecting curve is a dragon curve). Because none of our annotators was expert in all mathematical domains, it was difficult for them to assign the correct label in all similar cases.

As result of subjective annotation (which occurs frequently in all IR-related areas), none of the ML models trained on our training data were very precise with the ambiguous cases such as those described above. Below are several examples of sentences misclassified as definitions (false positives (with gold standard label "non-definition" but classified as "definition")), from each type described in the list above:

1. Property description:

   *Every pentagonal number is 1/3 of a triangular number.*

2. Alternative naming:

   *However, being in "one-to-one correspondence" is synonymous with being a bijection.*

3. Formulations and notations:

   *The binomial distribution is therefore given by $P_p(n|N) = [FORMULA]$.*
   *For a binary relation R, one often writes aRb to mean that $(a, b)$ is in $R \times R$.*

4. Partial definition:

> *A center X is the triangle centroid of its own pedal triangle iff it is the symmedian point.*

This sentence was annotated as non-definition, because it does not define the symmedian point.

5. Description:

> *The cyclide is a quartic surface, and the lines of curvature on a cyclide are all straight lines or circular arcs.*

Most misclassified definitions (false negatives) can be described by an atypical grammatical structure. Examples of such sentences can be seen below:

> *Once one countable set S is given, any other set which can be put into a one-to-one correspondence with S is also countable.*
> *The word cissoid means "ivy-shaped".*
> *A bijective map between two metric spaces that preserves distances,*
> *i.e., d(f(x), f(y)) = d(x, y), where f is the map and d(a, b) is the distance function.*

We propose to deal with some of the identified error sources as follows. Partial definitions can probably be discarded by applying part-of-speech tagging and pronouns detection. Coreference resolution (CR) can be used for identification of the referred mathematical entity in a text. Additionally, the partial definitions problem should be resolved by reduction of the DE task to multi-sentence DE. Formulations and notations can probably be discarded by measuring the ratio between mathematical symbolism and regular text in a sentence. Sentences providing alternative naming for mathematical objects can be discarded if we are able to detect the truth definition and then select it from multiple candidates. It can also be probably resolved with the help of such types of CR as split antecedents and coreferring noun phrases.

### 4.11. Discussion

As can be seen from all four experiments, ensemble outperforms individual models, despite latter being trained on more data. This outcome definitely supports the superiority of the ensemble approach for both domains.

It is worth noting that BERT did not perform well on our task. We explain it by the difference between the general domain of its training and our application domain of definitions and the lack of syntactic information in its input representation.

The scores of individual models approve again that syntactic information embedded into a sentence representation usually delivers better performance in both domains.

As our cross-domain evaluation results show, general definition domain and mathematical domain are quite different and, therefore, transfer cross-domain learning performs significantly worse than traditional single-domain learning.

### 5. Conclusions

In this paper, we introduce a new approach for DE, using ensemble from deep neural networks. Because it is a supervised approach, we adjust the class distribution of our datasets with oversampling. We evaluate this approach on datasets from general and mathematical domains. Our experiments on four datasets demonstrate superiority of ensemble voting over multiple state-of-the-art methods.

In the future, we intend to adapt our methodology for multi-sentence definition extraction.

**Author Contributions:** Conceptualization, N.V. and M.L.; methodology, N.V. and M.L.; software, N.V.; validation, N.V. and M.L.; formal analysis, investigation, resources, N.V. and M.L.; writing—original draft preparation, N.V. and M.L.; writing—review and editing, N.V. and M.L. All authors have read and agreed to the published version of the manuscript.

**Funding:** This research received no external funding.

**Data Availability Statement:** The WFMALL dataset is freely available for download from https://github.com/NataliaVanetik1/wfmall, accessed on 1 September 2021.

**Acknowledgments:** The authors express their deep gratitude to Guy Shilon and Lior Reznik for their help with server configuration.

**Conflicts of Interest:** The authors declare no conflict of interest.

## Abbreviations

The following abbreviations are used in this manuscript, in the order of their appearance:

| | |
|---|---|
| DE | Definition Extraction |
| NLP | Natural Language Processing |
| WCL | World-Class Lattice |
| DL | Deep Learning |
| CRF | Conditional Random Fields |
| CNN | Convolutional Neural Network |
| LSTM | Long Short-Term memory |
| BLSTM | Bidirectional LSTM |
| SOTA | State of the Art |
| NN | Neural Network |
| FT | fastText word vectors |
| LR | Logistic Regression |
| RF | Random Forest |

## References

1. Vanetik, N.; Litvak, M.; Shevchuk, S.; Reznik, L. Automated discovery of mathematical definitions in text. In Proceedings of the 12th Language Resources and Evaluation Conference, Marseille, France, 13–15 May 2020; pp. 2086–2094.
2. Xu, J.; Licuanan, A.; Weischedel, R.M. *TREC 2003 QA at BBN: Answering Definitional Questions*; TREC: Gaithersburg, MD, USA, 2003; pp. 98–106.
3. Klavans, J.L.; Muresan, S. Evaluation of the DEFINDER system for fully automatic glossary construction. In Proceedings of the AMIA Symposium, American Medical Informatics Association, Washington, DC, USA, 3–7 November 2001; p. 324.
4. Schuyler, P.L.; Hole, W.T.; Tuttle, M.S.; Sherertz, D.D. The UMLS Metathesaurus: Representing different views of biomedical concepts. *Bull. Med. Libr. Assoc.* **1993**, *81*, 217. [PubMed]
5. Malaisé, V.; Zweigenbaum, P.; Bachimont, B. Detecting semantic relations between terms in definitions. In Proceedings of CompuTerm 2004: 3rd International Workshop on Computational Terminology, Geneva, Switzerland, 29 August 2004.
6. Saggion, H.; Gaizauskas, R.J. Mining On-line Sources for Definition Knowledge. In Proceedings of the International FLAIRS Conference, Miami Beach, FL, USA, 12–14 May 2004; pp. 61–66.
7. Saggion, H. Identifying Definitions in Text Collections for Question Answering. In Proceedings of the International Conference on Language Resources and Evaluation, LREC, Lisbon, Portugal, 26–28 May 2004.
8. Storrer, A.; Wellinghoff, S. Automated detection and annotation of term definitions in German text corpora. In Proceedings of the International Conference on Language Resources and Evaluation, LREC, Genoa, Italy, 24–26 May 2006; Volume 2006.
9. Borg, C.; Rosner, M.; Pace, G. Evolutionary algorithms for definition extraction. In Proceedings of the 1st Workshop on Definition Extraction. Association for Computational Linguistics, Borovets, Bulgaria, 18 September 2009; pp. 26–32.
10. Fahmi, I.; Bouma, G. Learning to identify definitions using syntactic features. In Proceedings of the Workshop on Learning Structured Information in Natural Language Applications, Trento, Italy, 3 April 2006.
11. Westerhout, E.; Monachesi, P.; Westerhout, E. Combining pattern-based and machine learning methods to detect definitions for elearning purposes. In Proceedings of the RANLP 2007 Workshop "Natural Language Processing and Knowledge Representation for eLearning Environments", Borovets, Bulgaria, 27–29 September 2007.
12. Westerhout, E. Definition extraction using linguistic and structural features. In Proceedings of the 1st Workshop on Definition Extraction. Association for Computational Linguistics, Borovets, Bulgaria, 18 September 2009; pp. 61–67.
13. Navigli, R.; Velardi, P. Learning word-class lattices for definition and hypernym extraction. In Proceedings of the 48th Annual Meeting of the Association for Computational Linguistics. Association for Computational Linguistics, Uppsala, Sweden, 11–16 July 2010; pp. 1318–1327.
14. Reiplinger, M.; Schäfer, U.; Wolska, M. Extracting glossary sentences from scholarly articles: A comparative evaluation of pattern bootstrapping and deep analysis. In Proceedings of the ACL-2012 Special Workshop on Rediscovering 50 Years of Discoveries. Association for Computational Linguistics, Jeju Island, Korea, 10 July 2012; pp. 55–65.
15. Jin, Y.; Kan, M.Y.; Ng, J.P.; He, X. Mining scientific terms and their definitions: A study of the ACL anthology. In Proceedings of the 2013 Conference on Empirical Methods in Natural Language Processing, Seattle, WA, USA, 18–21 October 2013; pp. 780–790.
16. Boella, G.; Di Caro, L. Extracting definitions and hypernym relations relying on syntactic dependencies and support vector machines. In Proceedings of the 51st Annual Meeting of the Association for Computational Linguistics (Volume 2: Short Papers), Sofia, Bulgaria, 4–9 August 2013; Volume 2, pp. 532–537.

17. Anke, L.E.; Saggion, H.; Ronzano, F. Weakly supervised definition extraction. In Proceedings of the International Conference Recent Advances in Natural Language Processing, Hissar, Bulgaria, 5–11 September 2015; pp. 176–185.
18. Anke, L.E.; Saggion, H. Applying dependency relations to definition extraction. In Proceedings of the International Conference on Applications of Natural Language to Data Bases/Information Systems, Montpellier, France, 18–20 June 2014; Springer: Berlin/Heidelberg, Germany, 2014; pp. 63–74.
19. Li, S.; Xu, B.; Chung, T.L. Definition Extraction with LSTM Recurrent Neural Networks. In *Chinese Computational Linguistics and Natural Language Processing Based on Naturally Annotated Big Data*; Springer: Berlin/Heidelberg, Germany, 2016; pp. 177–189.
20. Anke, L.E.; Schockaert, S. Syntactically Aware Neural Architectures for Definition Extraction. In Proceedings of the 2018 Conference of the North American Chapter of the Association for Computational Linguistics: Human Language Technologies, Volume 2 (Short Papers), New Orleans, LA, USA, 2–4 June 2018; Volume 2, pp. 378–385.
21. Avram, A.M.; Cercel, D.C.; Chiru, C. UPB at SemEval-2020 Task 6: Pretrained Language Models for Definition Extraction. In Proceedings of the Fourteenth Workshop on Semantic Evaluation, Barcelona, Spain, 12–13 December 2020; pp. 737–745.
22. Xie, S.; Ma, J.; Yang, H.; Lianxin, J.; Yang, M.; Shen, J. UNIXLONG at SemEval-2020 Task 6: A Joint Model for Definition Extraction. In Proceedings of the Fourteenth Workshop on Semantic Evaluation, Barcelona, Spain, 12–13 December 2020; pp. 730–736.
23. Devlin, J.; Chang, M.W.; Lee, K.; Toutanova, K. Bert: Pre-training of deep bidirectional transformers for language understanding. In Proceedings of the NAACL-HLT 2019, Minneapolis, MN, USA, 2–7 June 2019; pp. 4171–4186.
24. Peters, M.E.; Neumann, M.; Iyyer, M.; Gardner, M.; Clark, C.; Lee, K.; Zettlemoyer, L. Deep contextualized word representations. In Proceedings of the NAACL, New Orleans, LA, USA, 1–6 June 2018.
25. Mikolov, T.; Sutskever, I.; Chen, K.; Corrado, G.S.; Dean, J. Distributed representations of words and phrases and their compositionality. In Proceedings of the Advances in Neural Information Processing Systems, Harrahs and Harveys, Lake Tahoe, CA, USA, 5–10 December 2013; pp. 3111–3119.
26. Grave, E.; Bojanowski, P.; Gupta, P.; Joulin, A.; Mikolov, T. FastText Word Vectors. Available online: https://fasttext.cc/docs/en/crawl-vectors.html (accessed on 1 January 2018).
27. Manning, C.; Surdeanu, M.; Bauer, J.; Finkel, J.; Bethard, S.; McClosky, D. Python Interface to CoreNLP Using a Bidirectional Server-Client Interface. Available online: https://github.com/stanfordnlp/python-stanford-corenlp (accessed on 1 January 2019).
28. Chollet, F. Keras. Available online: https://keras.io (accessed on 1 January 2015).
29. Abadi, M.; Agarwal, A.; Barham, P.; Brevdo, E.; Chen, Z.; Citro, C.; Corrado, G.S.; Davis, A.; Dean, J.; Devin, M.; et al. TensorFlow: Large-Scale Machine Learning on Heterogeneous Systems. 2015. Available online: tensorflow.org. (accessed on 1 January 2015).
30. Pedregosa, F.; Varoquaux, G.; Gramfort, A.; Michel, V.; Thirion, B.; Grisel, O.; Blondel, M.; Prettenhofer, P.; Weiss, R.; Dubourg, V.; et al. Scikit-learn: Machine Learning in Python. *J. Mach. Learn. Res.* **2011**, *12*, 2825–2830.
31. Hall, M.; Frank, E.; Holmes, G.; Pfahringer, B.; Reutemann, P.; Witten, I.H. The WEKA data mining software: An update. *ACM Sigkdd Explor. Newsl.* **2009**, *11*, 10–18. [CrossRef]
32. Navigli, R.; Velardi, P.; Ruiz-Martínez, J.M. WCL Definitions Dataset. Available online: http://lcl.uniroma1.it/wcl/ (accessed on 1 September 2020).
33. Navigli, R.; Velardi, P.; Ruiz-Martínez, J.M. An Annotated Dataset for Extracting Definitions and Hypernyms from the Web. In Proceedings of the International Conference on Language Resources and Evaluation, LREC, Valetta, Malta, 19–21 May 2010.
34. Spala, S.; Miller, N.A.; Yang, Y.; Dernoncourt, F.; Dockhorn, C. DEFT: A corpus for definition extraction in free-and semi-structured text. In Proceedings of the 13th Linguistic Annotation Workshop, Florence, Italy, 1 August 2019; pp. 124–131.
35. Jin, Y.; Kan, M.Y.; Ng, J.P.; He, X. W00 Definitions Dataset. Available online: https://bitbucket.org/luisespinosa/neural_de/src/afedc29cea14241fdc2fa3094b08d0d1b4c71cb5/data/W00_dataset/?at=master (accessed on 1 January 2013).
36. Bird, S.; Dale, R.; Dorr, B.J.; Gibson, B.R.; Joseph, M.T.; Kan, M.; Lee, D.; Powley, B.; Radev, D.R.; Tan, Y.F. The ACL Anthology Reference Corpus: A Reference Dataset for Bibliographic Research in Computational Linguistics. In Proceedings of the International Conference on Language Resources and Evaluation, LREC, Marrakech, Morocco, 26 May–1 June 2008.
37. Vanetik, N.; Litvak, M.; Shevchuk, S.; Reznik, L. WFM Dataset of Mathematical Definitions. Available online: https://github.com/uplink007/FinalProject/tree/master/data/wolfram (accessed on 1 January 2019).
38. Weisstein, E. *Wolfram Mathworld*. Available online: https://www.wolframalpha.com/ (accessed on 1 January 2019).
39. Manning, C.; Surdeanu, M.; Bauer, J.; Finkel, J.; Bethard, S.; McClosky, D. The Stanford CoreNLP natural language processing toolkit. In Proceedings of the 52nd Annual Meeting of the Association for Computational Linguistics: System Demonstrations, Baltimore, MD, USA, 23–25 June 2014; pp. 55–60.
40. Honnibal, M.; Johnson, M. An Improved Non-monotonic Transition System for Dependency Parsing. In Proceedings of the 2015 Conference on Empirical Methods in Natural Language Processing; Association for Computational Linguistics, Lisbon, Portugal, 17–21 September 2015; pp. 1373–1378.
41. Grave, E.; Bojanowski, P.; Gupta, P.; Joulin, A.; Mikolov, T. Learning Word Vectors for 157 Languages. In Proceedings of the International Conference on Language Resources and Evaluation LREC, Miyazaki, Japan, 7–12 May 2018.
42. Veyseh, A.; Dernoncourt, F.; Dou, D.; Nguyen, T. A joint model for definition extraction with syntactic connection and semantic consistency. In Proceedings of the AAAI Conference on Artificial Intelligence, New York, NY, USA, 7–12 February 2020; Volume 34, pp. 9098–9105.

*Article*

# To Batch or Not to Batch? Comparing Batching and Curriculum Learning Strategies across Tasks and Datasets

**Laura Burdick** \*,†, **Jonathan K. Kummerfeld and Rada Mihalcea**

Computer Science and Engineering, University of Michigan, Ann Arbor, MI 48109, USA;
jkummerf@umich.edu (J.K.K.); mihalcea@umich.edu (R.M.)
\* Correspondence: lburdick@umich.edu
† Current address: 2260 Hayward Street, Ann Arbor, MI 48109, USA.

**Abstract:** Many natural language processing architectures are greatly affected by seemingly small design decisions, such as batching and curriculum learning (how the training data are ordered during training). In order to better understand the impact of these decisions, we present a systematic analysis of different curriculum learning strategies and different batching strategies. We consider multiple datasets for three tasks: text classification, sentence and phrase similarity, and part-of-speech tagging. Our experiments demonstrate that certain curriculum learning and batching decisions do increase performance substantially for some tasks.

**Keywords:** natural language processing; word embeddings; batching; word2vec; curriculum learning; text classification; phrase similarity; part-of-speech tagging

**Citation:** Burdick, L.; Kummerfeld, J.K.; Mihalcea, R. To Batch or Not to Batch? Comparing Batching and Curriculum Learning Strategies across Tasks and Datasets. *Mathematics* **2021**, *9*, 2234. https://doi.org/10.3390/math9182234

Academic Editors: Florentina Hristea, Cornelia Caragea and David Pugalee

Received: 28 June 2021
Accepted: 4 September 2021
Published: 11 September 2021

## 1. Introduction

When designing architectures for tasks in natural language processing (NLP), relatively small methodological details can have a huge impact on the performance of the system. In this paper, we consider several methodological decisions that impact NLP systems that are based on word embeddings. Word embeddings are low-dimensional, dense vector representations that capture semantic and syntactic properties of words. They are often used in larger systems to accomplish downstream tasks.

We analyze two methodological decisions involved in creating word embeddings: batching and curriculum learning. For batching, we consider what batching method to use, and what batch size to use. We consider two batching methods, which we denote as *basic batching* and *cumulative batching*. Curriculum learning is the process of ordering the data during training. We consider three curriculum learning strategies: *ascending curriculum*, *descending curriculum*, and *default curriculum*.

Our batching and curriculum learning choices are evaluated using three downstream tasks: text classification, sentence and phrase similarity, and part-of-speech tagging. We consider a variety of datasets of different sizes in order to understand how these strategies work across diverse tasks and data.

We show that for some tasks, batching and curriculum learning decisions do not have a significant impact, but for other tasks, such as text classification on small datasets, these decisions are important considerations. This paper is an empirical study, and while we make observations about different batching and curriculum learning decisions, we do not explore the theoretical reasons for these observations.

To begin, we survey related work before introducing the methodology that we use to create the word embeddings and apply batching and curriculum learning. Next, we define architectures for our three downstream tasks. Finally, we present our results, and discuss future work and conclusions.

## 2. Related Work

Our work builds off previous work on word embeddings, batching, and curriculum learning.

### 2.1. Word Embeddings

Throughout this paper, we use a common word embedding algorithm, word2vec [1,2], which uses a shallow neural network to learn embeddings by predicting context words. We use the skip-gram word2vec model, a one-layer feed-forward neural network which tries to optimize the log probability of a target word, given its context words.

In many cases, word embeddings are used as features in a larger system architecture. The work of Collobert et al. [3] was an early paper that took this approach, incorporating word embeddings as inputs to a neural network that performed part-of-speech tagging, chunking, named entity recognition, and semantic role labeling. This line of work has been expanded to include many other tasks, including text similarity [4], sentiment analysis [5], and machine translation [6]. In this paper, we use word embeddings in systems for text classification, sentence and phrase similarity, and part-of-speech tagging.

We explore two methodological decisions in creating word embeddings: batching and curriculum learning.

### 2.2. Batching

We use two batching approaches (denoted as *basic batching* and *cumulative batching*). Basic batching was first introduced in Bengio et al. [7], and cumulative batching was first introduced in Spitkovsky et al. [8]. These approaches are described in more detail in Section 3.2.

While we use the batching approaches described in these papers, we analyze their performance on different tasks and datasets. Basic batching was originally proposed for synthetic vision and word representation learning tasks, while cumulative batching was applied to unsupervised dependency parsing. We use these batching techniques on NLP architectures built with word embeddings for the tasks of text classification, sentence and phrase similarity, and part-of-speech tagging.

In addition to using two batching techniques, we vary the number of the batches that we use. This was studied previously; Smith et al. [9] showed that choosing a good batch size can decrease the number of parameter updates to a network.

### 2.3. Curriculum Learning

This work also explores curriculum learning applied to word embeddings. Curriculum refers to the order that the data are presented to the embedding algorithm. Previous work has shown that the curriculum of the training data has some effect on the performance of the created embeddings [10]. Curriculum learning has also been explored for other tasks in NLP, including natural language understanding [11] and domain adaptation [12].

## 3. Materials and Methods

In order to evaluate the effectiveness of different batching and curriculum learning techniques, we choose a diverse set of tasks and architectures to explore. Specifically, we consider the downstream tasks of text classification, sentence and phrase similarity, and part-of-speech (POS) tagging. These were chosen because they have varying degrees of complexity. Sentence and phrase similarity, where word embeddings are compared using cosine similarity, has a very simple architecture, while part-of-speech tagging uses a more complex LSTM architecture. Text classification uses a linear classifier, which is more complex than a simple cosine similarity, but less complex than a neural network.

Figure 1 shows the experimental setup for these three tasks. For each task, we begin by training word2vec word embeddings, using Wikipedia training data. We apply batching and curriculum learning to the process of training word embeddings. These embeddings are then passed to a task-specific architecture.

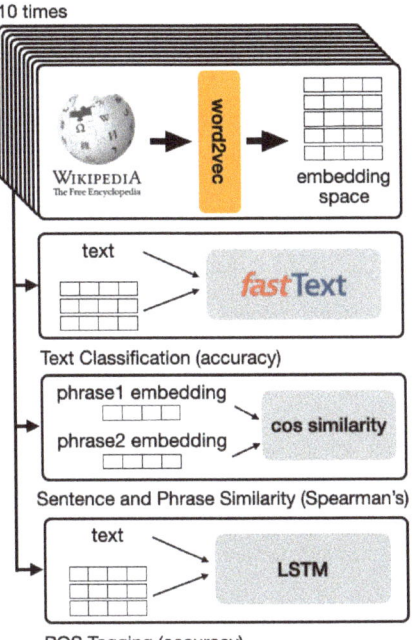

**Figure 1.** Experimental setup for text classification, sentence and phrase similarity, and POS tagging.

*3.1. Initial Embedding Spaces*

To obtain word embeddings, we begin with a dataset of sentences from Wikipedia (5,269,686 sentences; 100,003,406 words; 894,044 tokens) and create word2vec skip-gram embeddings [1]. We use 300 dimensions and a context window size of 5.

Because the word2vec embedding algorithm uses a shallow neural network, there is randomness inherent to it. This algorithmic randomness can cause variation in the word embeddings created [13,14]. In order to account for variability in embeddings, we train 10 embedding spaces with different random initializations for word2vec. (We randomize the algorithm by changing the random seed. We use the following ten random seeds: 2518, 2548, 2590, 29, 401, 481, 485, 533, 725, 777.) We use these 10 spaces to calculate the average performance and standard deviation, which allows us to characterize the variation that we see within the algorithm.

During the process of creating word embeddings, we use different batching and curriculum learning strategies.

*3.2. Batching*

We apply batching to the Wikipedia dataset input to the word embedding algorithm. We batch words (and their contexts) using two strategies: basic batching and cumulative batching, visualized in Figure 2. For each batching strategy, we consider different numbers of batches, ranging exponentially between 2 and 200.

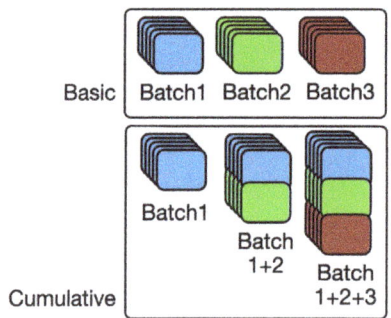

**Figure 2.** Basic vs. cumulative batching. Rectangles represent chunks of the training data, with different colors representing different sections of the data.

### 3.2.1. Basic Batching

As described in Bengio et al. [7], we split the data up into $X$ disjoint batches. Each batch is processed sequentially, and each batch is run for $n$ epochs (Batch 1 runs for $n$ epochs, then Batch 2 runs for $n$ epochs, etc.). Once a batch is finished processing, it is discarded and never returned to. Both $X$ and $n$ are hyperparameters. We try different values of $X$ between 2 and 200; we set $n = 5$ for all experiments.

### 3.2.2. Cumulative Batching

Our second batching strategy [8] begins in the same way, with the data split up into $X$ disjoint batches. In this strategy, the batches are processed cumulatively (Batch 1 is run for $n$ epochs, then Batches 1 and 2 combined are run for $n$ epochs, etc.). We try different values of $X$ between 2 and 200; we set $n = 5$ for all experiments.

### 3.3. Curriculum Learning

In addition to batching, we apply different curriculum learning strategies to the Wikipedia dataset input to the word embedding algorithm.

We consider three different curricula for the data: the *default* order of Wikipedia sentences, *descending* order by sentence length (longest to shortest), and *ascending* order by sentence length (shortest to longest). Note that curriculum learning only applies to the Wikipedia dataset used to create the word embeddings, rather than the task-specific datasets used for training.

Qualitatively looking at Wikipedia sentences ordered by length, both the shortest and the longest sentences tend to be unnatural sounding. The shortest sentences are only a single token, such as a single word or a single punctuation mark. Some of these are most likely the result of incorrect sentence tokenization. The longest sentences tend to be either run-on sentences, or lists of a large number of items. For instance, the longest sentence is 725 tokens long, and it lists numerical statistics for different countries. This unnaturalness may adversely affect the embedding algorithm when using either the ascending or descending curriculum. It is possible that a more complex ordering of the data would achieve better performance; we leave this exploration to future work.

When evaluating curriculum learning and batching strategies, our baseline strategy is a default curriculum with basic batching.

Once we have created word embeddings using a specific batching and curriculum learning strategy, the embeddings are input into task-specific architectures for each of our three downstream tasks.

### 3.4. Task 1: Text Classification

The first task we consider is text classification—deciding what category a particular document falls into. We evaluate 11 datasets, shown in Table 1. (For all tasks, sentences are tokenized using NLTK's Tokenizer.) These datasets span a wide range of sizes (from 96 sentences to 3.6 million training sentences), as well as number of classes to be categorized (from 2 to 14).

**Table 1.** Data statistics (number of training sentences, number of test sentences, number of classes) for text classification. The first eight datasets are from Zhang et al. [15]. Two datasets have both a polarity (pol.) version with two classes and a full version with more classes.

| Dataset | # Sent. (Train) | # Sent. (Test) | # Classes |
|---|---|---|---|
| Amazon Review (pol.) | $3.6e6$ | $4e5$ | 2 |
| Amazon Review (full) | $3e6$ | $6.5e5$ | 5 |
| Yahoo! Answers | $1.4e6$ | $6e4$ | 10 |
| Yelp Review (full) | $6.5e5$ | $5e4$ | 5 |
| Yelp Review (pol.) | $5.6e5$ | $3.8e4$ | 2 |
| DBPedia | $5.6e5$ | $7e4$ | 14 |
| Sogou News | $4.5e5$ | $6e4$ | 5 |
| AG News | $1.2e5$ | 7600 | 4 |
| Open Domain Deception | 5733 | 1435 | 2 |
| Personal Email | 260 | 89 | 2 |
| Real Life Deception | 96 | 25 | 2 |

Of particular note are three datasets that are at least an order of magnitude smaller than the other datasets. These are the Open Domain Deception Dataset [16] and the Real Life Deception Dataset [17], both of which classify statements as truthful or deceptive, as well as the Personal Email Dataset [18], which classifies e-mail messages as personal or non-personal.

After creating embedding spaces, we use fastText [19] for text classification. (Available online at https://fasttext.cc/. (accessed on 7 September 2021.) FastText represents sentences as a bag of words and trains a linear classifier to classify the sentences. The performance is measured using accuracy.

*3.5. Task 2: Sentence and Phrase Similarity*

The second task that we consider is sentence and phrase similarity: determining how similar two sentences or phrases are. We consider three evaluation datasets, shown in Table 2. The Human Activity Dataset [20] consists of pairs of human activities with four annotated relations each (similarity, relatedness, motivational alignment [MA], and perceived actor congruence [PAC]). The STS Benchmark [21] has pairs of sentences with semantic similarity scores, and the SICK dataset [22] has pairs of sentences with relatedness scores.

**Table 2.** Data statistics for sentence and phrase similarity.

| Dataset | # Pairs (Train) | # Pairs (Test) | # Tokens (Train) |
|---|---|---|---|
| Human Activity | 1373 | 1000 | 1446 |
| STS Benchmark | 5749 | 1379 | 14,546 |
| SICK | 4439 | 4906 | 2251 |

For each pair of phrases or sentences in our evaluation set, we average the embeddings for each word, and take the cosine similarity between the averaged word vectors from both phrases or sentences. We compare this with the ground truth using Spearman's correlation [23]. Spearman's correlation is a measure of rank correlation. The values of two variables are ranked in order, and then Pearson's correlation [24] (a measure of linear correlation) is taken between the ranked values. Spearman's correlation assesses monotonic relationships (are values strictly not decreasing, or strictly not increasing?), while Pearson's correlation assesses linear relationships.

### 3.6. Task 3: Part-of-Speech Tagging

Our final task is part-of-speech (POS) tagging—determining the correct part-of-speech for a given word in a sentence. For evaluation, we use two datasets: the email and answers datasets from the English Universal Dependencies Corpus (UD) [25], shown in Table 3.

**Table 3.** Data statistics for POS tagging.

| Dataset | # Sentences (Train) | # Sentences (Test) |
|---|---|---|
| UD Answers | 2631 | 438 |
| UD Email | 3770 | 606 |

After creating embedding spaces, we use a bi-directional LSTM implemented using DyNet [26] to perform POS tagging. An LSTM is a type of recurrent neural network that is able to process sequential data [27]. This is an appropriate architecture for part-of-speech tagging because we want to process words sequentially, in the order that they appear in the sentence. Our LSTM has 1 layer with a hidden dimension size of 50, and a multi-layer perceptron on the output. Performance is measured using accuracy.

## 4. Results

We apply the different curriculum learning and batching strategies to each task, and we consider the results to determine which strategies are most effective.

### 4.1. Task 1: Text Classification

For the larger text classification datasets (>120,000 training sentences), there are no substantial differences between different curriculum and batching strategies. However, we do see differences for the three smallest datasets, shown in Figure 3. To compare across datasets of different sizes, we show the number of sentences per batch, rather than the number of batches. Because these graphs show many combinations of curriculum and batching strategies, we report numbers on each dataset's dev set.

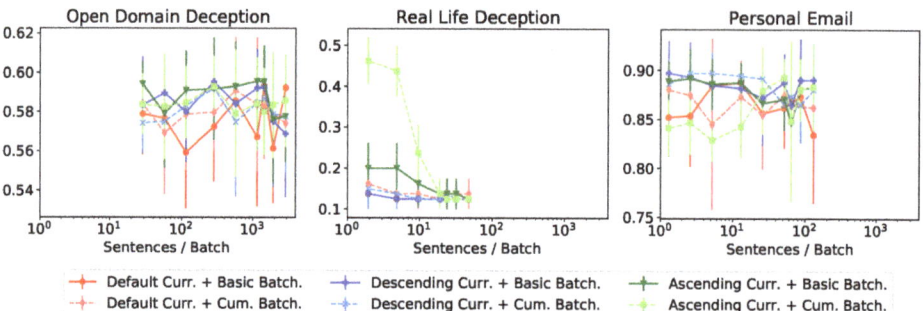

**Figure 3.** Accuracy scores on the development set for three text classification datasets. Different lines indicate models trained with different curriculum and batching strategies (basic, cumulative). Datasets span different ranges of the x-axis because they are different sizes. Error bars show the standard deviation over ten word2vec embedding spaces, trained using different random seeds.

On the smallest dataset, Real Life Deception (96 training sentences), we see that above approximately ten batches, ascending curriculum with cumulative batching outperforms the other methods. On the test set, we compare our best strategy (ascending curriculum with cumulative batching) with the baseline setting (default curriculum with basic batching), both with 100 batches, and we see no significant difference. This is most likely because the test set is so small (25 sentences).

### 4.2. Task 2: Sentence and Phrase Similarity

Next, we consider results from the sentence and phrase similarity task, shown in Figure 4. Because these graphs show many combinations of curriculum and batching strategies, we report numbers on each dataset's train set (we use the train sets rather than the dev sets because there is no training or hyperparemeter tuning).

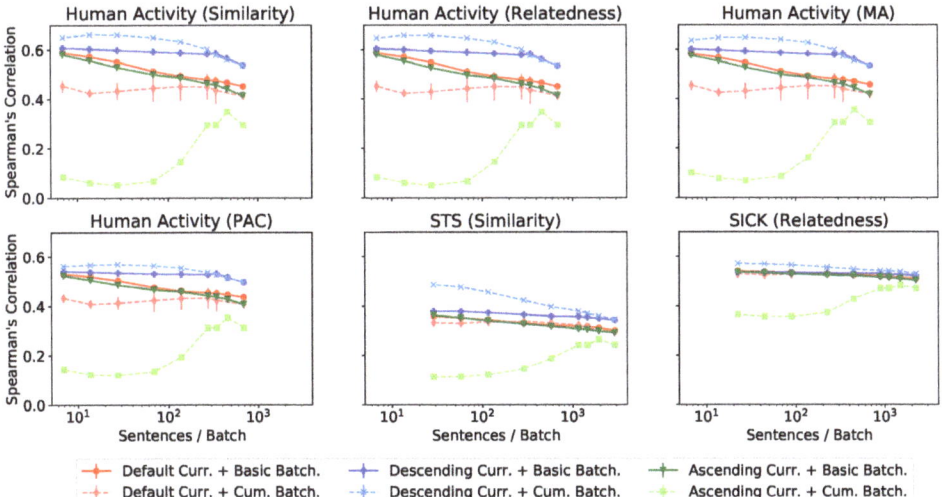

**Figure 4.** Spearman's correlation scores on the train set for sentence and phrase similarity tasks. Different lines indicate models trained with different curriculum and batching strategies (basic, cumulative). Datasets span different ranges of the x-axis because they are different sizes. Error bars show the standard deviation over ten word2vec embedding spaces trained using different random seeds.

First, we note that the relative performance of different strategies remains consistent across all three datasets and across all six measures of similarity. An ascending curriculum with cumulative batching performs the worst by a substantial amount, while a descending curriculum with cumulative batching performs the best by a small amount. As the number of sentences per batch increases, the margin between the different strategies decreases. On the test set, we compare our best strategy (descending curriculum with cumulative batching) with the baseline setting (default curriculum with basic batching), and we see in Table 4 that the best strategy significantly outperforms the baseline with five batches.

**Table 4.** Spearman's correlation on the test set for similarity tasks (all have a standard deviation of 0.0).

| Dataset | Human Activity | | | | | |
| | Sim. | Rel. | MA | PAC | STS | SICK |
|---|---|---|---|---|---|---|
| Baseline | 0.36 | 0.33 | 0.33 | 0.22 | 0.27 | 0.51 |
| Best | 0.43 | 0.41 | 0.41 | 0.29 | 0.32 | 0.53 |

For all six measures, we observe a time vs. performance trade-off: the fewer sentences are in a batch, the better the performance is, but the more computational power and time it takes to run.

### 4.3. Task 3: Part-of-Speech Tagging

Finally, there are no significant differences in POS tagging between batching and curriculum learning strategies. For the previous two tasks, we have seen the largest changes in performance on the smallest dataset. Both of the datasets that we use to evaluate POS tagging are relatively large (>2500 sentences in the training data), which may explain why we do not see significant performance differences here.

## 5. Conclusions

One strategy does not perform equally well on all tasks. On some tasks, such as POS tagging, the curriculum and batching strategies that we tried have no effect at all. Simpler tasks that rely most heavily on word embeddings, such as sentence and phrase similarity and text classification with very small datasets, benefit the most from fine-tuned curriculum learning and batching. We have shown that making relatively small changes to curriculum learning and batching can have an impact on the results; this may be true in other tasks with small data as well.

In general, cumulative batching outperforms basic batching. This is intuitive because cumulative batching sees the same training example more times than basic batching, and overall sees the training data more times. As the number of sentences per batch increases, the differences between cumulative and basic batching shrink. Even though cumulative batching has higher performance, it takes more computational time and power than basic batching. We see a trade-off here between computational resources and performance.

It is inconclusive what the best curriculum is. For text classification, the ascending curriculum works best, while for sentence and phrase similarity, the descending curriculum works best. One hypothesis for why we see this is that for text classification, the individual words are more important than the overall structure of the sentence. The individual words are able to determine which class the sentence is a part of. Therefore, the algorithm does better when it looks at smaller sentences first, before building to larger sentences (an ascending curriculum). With the smaller sentences, the algorithm can focus more on the words and less on the overall structure. For sentence and phrase similarity, it is possible that the overall structure of the sentence is more important than the individual words because the algorithm is looking for overall similarity between two phrases. Thus, a descending curriculum, where an algorithm is exposed to longer sentences first, works better for this task.

We have explored different combinations of curriculum learning and batching strategies across three different downstream tasks. We have shown that for different tasks, different strategies are appropriate, but that overall, cumulative batching performs better than basic batching.

Since our experiments demonstrate that certain curriculum learning and batching decisions do increase the performance substantially for some tasks, for future experiments, we recommend that practitioners experiment with different strategies, particularly when the task at hand relies heavily on word embeddings.

## 6. Future Work

There are many tasks and NLP architectures that we have not explored in this work, and our direct results are limited to the tasks and datasets presented here. However, our work implies that curriculum learning and batching may have similar effects on other tasks and architectures. Future work is needed here.

Additionally, the three curricula that we experimented with in this paper (default, ascending, and descending) are relatively simple ways to order data; future work is needed to investigate more complex orderings. Taking into account such properties as the readability of a sentence, the difficulty level of words, and the frequency of certain part-of-speech combinations could create a better curriculum that consistently works well on a large variety of tasks. Additionally, artificially simplifying sentences (e.g., substituting simpler words or removing unnecessary clauses) at the beginning of the curriculum, and then gradually increasing the difficulty of the sentences could be helpful for "teaching" the embedding algorithm to recognize increasingly complex sentences.

There are many other word embedding algorithms (e.g., BERT [28], GloVe [29]); batching and curriculum learning may affect these algorithms differently than they affect word2vec. Different embedding dimensions and context window sizes may also make a difference. More work is needed to explore this.

Finally, our paper is an empirical study, with our observations indicating that the observed batching variation is something that researchers should consider, even though we do not explore the theoretical reasons for this.

The code used in the experiments is publicly available at https://lit.eecs.umich.edu/downloads.html (accessed on 7 September 2021).

**Author Contributions:** Conceptualization, L.B., J.K.K. and R.M.; methodology, L.B., J.K.K. and R.M.; software, L.B. and J.K.K.; investigation, L.B. and J.K.K.; writing—original draft preparation, L.B.; writing—review and editing, L.B., J.K.K. and R.M.; supervision, J.K.K. and R.M.; project administration, R.M.; funding acquisition, R.M. All authors have read and agreed to the published version of the manuscript.

**Funding:** This material is based in part upon work supported by the National Science Foundation (NSF #1344257), the Defense Advanced Research Projects Agency (DARPA) AIDA program under grant #FA8750-18-2-0019, and the Michigan Institute for Data Science (MIDAS). Any opinions, findings, and conclusions or recommendations expressed in this material are those of the authors and do not necessarily reflect the views of the NSF, DARPA, or MIDAS.

**Institutional Review Board Statement:** Not applicable.

**Informed Consent Statement:** Not applicable.

**Data Availability Statement:** *Wikipedia:* The Wikipedia dataset used to create the initial embedding spaces was used in Tsvetkov et al. [10] and is available by contacting the authors of that paper. *Text classification:* Amazon Review (pol.), Amazon Review (full), Yahoo! Answers, Yelp Review (full), Yelp Review (pol.), DBPedia, Sogou News, and AG News are available at https://course.fast.ai/datasets#nlp. (accessed on 7 September 2021). The Open Domain Deception Dataset is available at https://lit.eecs.umich.edu/downloads.html. (accessed on 7 September 2021) under "Open-Domain Deception." The Real Life Deception Dataset is available at https://lit.eecs.umich.edu/downloads.html (accessed on 7 September 2021) under "Real-life Deception". The Personal Email Dataset is available at https://lit.eecs.umich.edu/downloads.html (accessed on 7 September 2021) under "Summarization and Keyword Extraction from Emails". *Sentence and phrase similarity:* The Human Activity Dataset is available at https://lit.eecs.umich.edu/downloads.html (accessed on 7 September 2021) under "Human Activity Phrase Data". The STS Benchmark is available at https://ixa2.si.ehu.es/stswiki/index.php/STSbenchmark (accessed on 7 September 2021). The SICK dataset is available at https://wiki.cimec.unitn.it/tiki-index.php?page=CLIC (accessed on 7 September 2021). *Part-of-speech tagging:* The English Universal Dependencies Corpus is available at https://universaldependencies.org/ (accessed on 7 September 2021).

**Conflicts of Interest:** The authors declare no conflict of interest.

# References

1. Mikolov, T.; Sutskever, I.; Chen, K.; Corrado, G.S.; Dean, J. Distributed representations of words and phrases and their compositionality. In Proceedings of the Advances in Neural Information Processing Systems, Lake Tahoe, NA, USA, 5–10 December 2013; pp. 3111–3119.
2. Mikolov, T.; Chen, K.; Corrado, G.; Dean, J. Efficient estimation of word representations in vector space. *arXiv* **2013**, arXiv:1301.3781.
3. Collobert, R.; Weston, J.; Bottou, L.; Karlen, M.; Kavukcuoglu, K.; Kuksa, P. Natural language processing (almost) from scratch. *J. Mach. Learn. Res.* **2011**, *12*, 2493–2537.
4. Kenter, T.; de Rijke, M. Short Text Similarity with Word Embeddings. In Proceedings of the 24th ACM International on Conference on Information and Knowledge Management, Melbourne, Australia, 19–23 October 2015; Association for Computing Machinery: New York, NY, USA, 2015; CIKM '15; pp. 1411–1420. [CrossRef]
5. Faruqui, M.; Dodge, J.; Jauhar, S.K.; Dyer, C.; Hovy, E.; Smith, N.A. Retrofitting Word Vectors to Semantic Lexicons. In Proceedings of the 2015 Conference of the North American Chapter of the Association for Computational Linguistics: Human Language Technologies, Denver, CO, USA, 31 May–5 June 2015; Association for Computational Linguistics: Stroudsburg, PA, USA, 2019; pp. 1606–1615. [CrossRef]

6. Mikolov, T.; Le, Q.V.; Sutskever, I. Exploiting similarities among languages for machine translation. *arXiv* **2013**, arXiv:1309.4168.
7. Bengio, Y.; Louradour, J.; Collobert, R.; Weston, J. Curriculum learning. In Proceedings of the International Conference on Machine Learning, Montreal, QC, Canada, 14–18 June 2009; pp. 41–48.
8. Spitkovsky, V.I.; Alshawi, H.; Jurafsky, D. From Baby Steps to Leapfrog: How "Less is More" in Unsupervised Dependency Parsing. In Proceedings of the Human Language Technologies: The 2010 Annual Conference of the North American Chapter of the Association for Computational Linguistics, Los Angeles, CA, USA, 2–4 June 2010; Association for Computational Linguistics: Stroudsburg, PA, USA, 2019; pp. 751–759.
9. Smith, S.L.; Kindermans, P.J.; Ying, C.; Le, Q.V. Don't decay the learning rate, increase the batch size. In Proceedings of the International Conference on Learning Representations, Vancouver, BC, Canada, 30 April–3 May 2018.
10. Tsvetkov, Y.; Faruqui, M.; Ling, W.; MacWhinney, B.; Dyer, C. Learning the Curriculum with Bayesian Optimization for Task-Specific Word Representation Learning. In Proceedings of the 54th Annual Meeting of the Association for Computational Linguistics (Volume 1: Long Papers), Berlin, Germany, 7–12 August 2016; pp. 130–139.
11. Xu, B.; Zhang, L.; Mao, Z.; Wang, Q.; Xie, H.; Zhang, Y. Curriculum Learning for Natural Language Understanding. In Proceedings of the 58th Annual Meeting of the Association for Computational Linguistics; Association for Computational Linguistics, Online, 5–10 July 2020; pp. 6095–6104. [CrossRef]
12. Zhang, X.; Shapiro, P.; Kumar, G.; McNamee, P.; Carpuat, M.; Duh, K. Curriculum Learning for Domain Adaptation in Neural Machine Translation. In Proceedings of the 2019 Conference of the North American Chapter of the Association for Computational Linguistics: Human Language Technologies, Minneapolis, MN, USA, 2–9 June 2019; Association for Computational Linguistics: Stroudsburg, PA, USA, 2019; pp. 1903–1915. [CrossRef]
13. Antoniak, M.; Mimno, D. Evaluating the Stability of Embedding-based Word Similarities. *Tran. Assoc. Comput. Linguist.* **2018**, *6*, 107–119. [CrossRef]
14. Wendlandt, L.; Kummerfeld, J.K.; Mihalcea, R. Factors Influencing the Surprising Instability of Word Embeddings. In Proceedings of the 2018 Conference of the North American Chapter of the Association for Computational Linguistics: Human Language Technologies, New Orleans, LA, USA, 1–6 June 2018; Assocation for Computational Linguistics: Stroudsburg, PA, USA, 2019; pp. 2092–2102. [CrossRef]
15. Zhang, X.; Zhao, J.; LeCun, Y. Character-level convolutional networks for text classification. In Proceedings of the Advances in Neural Information Processing Systems, Montreal, QC, Canada, 7–12 December 2015; pp. 649–657.
16. Pérez-Rosas, V.; Abouelenien, M.; Mihalcea, R.; Burzo, M. Deception detection using real-life trial data. In Proceedings of the 2015 ACM on International Conference on Multimodal Interaction, Seattle, WA, USA, 9–13 November 2015; ACM: Seattle, WA, USA, 2015; pp. 59–66.
17. Pérez-Rosas, V.; Mihalcea, R. Experiments in open domain deception detection. In Proceedings of the 2015 Conference on Empirical Methods in Natural Language Processing, Lisbon, Portugal, 17–21 September 2015; pp. 1120–1125.
18. Loza, V.; Lahiri, S.; Mihalcea, R.; Lai, P.H. Building a Dataset for Summarization and Keyword Extraction from Emails. In Proceedings of the Ninth International Conference on Language Resources and Evaluation, Reykjavik, Iceland, 26–31 May 2014; European Languages Resources Association: Paris, France, 2014; pp. 2441–2446.
19. Joulin, A.; Grave, E.; Bojanowski, P.; Mikolov, T. Bag of Tricks for Efficient Text Classification. In Proceedings of the 15th Conference of the European Chapter of the Association for Computational Linguistics, Valencia, Spain, 3–7 April 2017; Association for Computational Linguistics: Stroudsburg, PA, USA, 2017; pp. 427–431.
20. Wilson, S.; Mihalcea, R. Measuring Semantic Relations between Human Activities. In Proceedings of the Eighth International Joint Conference on Natural Language Processing (Volume 1: Long Papers), Asian Federation of Natural Language Processing, Taipei, Taiwan, 27 November–1 December 2017; pp. 664–673.
21. Cer, D.; Diab, M.; Agirre, E.; Lopez-Gazpio, I.; Specia, L. SemEval-2017 Task 1: Semantic Textual Similarity Multilingual and Crosslingual Focused Evaluation. In Proceedings of the 11th International Workshop on Semantic Evaluation, Vancouver, BC, Canada, 3–4 August 2017; Association for Computational Linguistics: Stroudsburg, PA, USA, 2017; pp. 1–14. [CrossRef]
22. Bentivogli, L.; Bernardi, R.; Marelli, M.; Menini, S.; Baroni, M.; Zamparelli, R. SICK through the SemEval glasses. Lesson learned from the evaluation of compositional distributional semantic models on full sentences through semantic relatedness and textual entailment. *Lang. Resour. Eval.* **2016**, *50*, 95–124. [CrossRef]
23. Spearman, C. Correlation calculated from faulty data. *Br. J. Psychol. 1904–1920* **1910**, *3*, 271–295. [CrossRef]
24. Sedgwick, P. Pearson's correlation coefficient. *Bmj* **2012**, *345*, e4483 . [CrossRef]
25. Nivre, J.; de Marneffe, M.C.; Ginter, F.; Goldberg, Y.; Hajič, J.; Manning, C.D.; McDonald, R.; Petrov, S.; Pyysalo, S.; Silveira, N.; et al. Universal Dependencies v1: A Multilingual Treebank Collection, Language Resources and Evaluation. In Proceedings of the Tenth International Conference on Language Resources and Evaluation, Portorož, Slovenia, 23–28 May 2016; European Languages Resources Association: Paris, France, 2016; pp. 1659–1666.
26. Neubig, G.; Dyer, C.; Goldberg, Y.; Matthews, A.; Ammar, W.; Anastasopoulos, A.; Ballesteros, M.; Chiang, D.; Clothiaux, D.; Cohn, T.; et al. DyNet: The Dynamic Neural Network Toolkit. *arXiv* **2017**, arXiv:1701.03980.
27. Hochreiter, S.; Schmidhuber, J. Long Short-Term Memory. *Neural Comput.* **1997**, *9*, 1735–1780. [CrossRef] [PubMed]

28. Devlin, J.; Chang, M.W.; Lee, K.; Toutanova, K. BERT: Pre-training of Deep Bidirectional Transformers for Language Understanding. In Proceedings of the 2019 Conference of the North American Chapter of the Association for Computational Linguistics: Human Language Technologies, Minneapolis, MN, USA, 2–9 June 2019; Association for Computational Linguistics: Stroudsburg, PA, USA, 2019; pp. 4171–4186.

29. Pennington, J.; Socher, R.; Manning, C. GloVe: Global Vectors for Word Representation. In Proceedings of the 2014 Conference on Empirical Methods in Natural Language Processing, Association for Computational Linguistics, Doha, Qatar, 25–29 October 2014; pp. 1532–1543. [CrossRef]

MDPI

St. Alban-Anlage 66

4052 Basel

Switzerland

Tel. +41 61 683 77 34

Fax +41 61 302 89 18

www.mdpi.com

*Mathematics* Editorial Office

E-mail: mathematics@mdpi.com

www.mdpi.com/journal/mathematics